JONES & BARTLETT LEARNING INFORMATION SYSTEMS SECURITY & ASSURANCE SERIES

Security Strategies in Linux Platforms and Applications

MICHAEL JANG

JONES & BARTLETT
LEARNING

World Headquarters
Jones & Bartlett Learning
40 Tall Pine Drive
Sudbury, MA 01776
978-443-5000
info@jblearning.com
www.jblearning.com

Jones & Bartlett Learning Canada
6339 Ormindale Way
Mississauga, Ontario L5V 1J2
Canada

Jones & Bartlett Learning
 International
Barb House, Barb Mews
London W6 7PA
United Kingdom

Jones & Bartlett Learning books and products are available through most bookstores and online booksellers. To contact Jones & Bartlett Learning directly, call 800-832-0034, fax 978-443-8000, or visit our website, www.jblearning.com.

This publication is designed to provide accurate and authoritative information in regard to the subject matter covered. It is sold with the understanding that the publisher is not engaged in rendering legal, accounting, or other professional service. If legal advice or other expert assistance is required, the service of a competent professional person should be sought.

Production Credits
Chief Executive Officer: Ty Field
President: James Homer
SVP, Chief Operating Officer: Don Jones, Jr.
SVP, Chief Technology Officer: Dean Fossella
SVP, Chief Marketing Officer: Alison M. Pendergast
SVP, Chief Financial Officer: Ruth Siporin
SVP, Business Development: Christopher Will
VP, Design and Production: Anne Spencer
VP, Manufacturing and Inventory Control: Therese Connell
Editorial Management: High Stakes Writing, LLC, Editor and Publisher: Lawrence J. Goodrich
Reprints and Special Projects Manager: Susan Schultz
Associate Production Editor: Tina Chen
Director of Marketing: Alisha Weisman
Associate Marketing Manager: Meagan Norlund
Cover Design: Anne Spencer
Composition: Mia Saunders Design
Cover Image: © ErickN/ShutterStock, Inc.
Chapter Opener Image: © Rodolfo Clix/Dreamstime.com
Printing and Binding: Malloy, Inc.
Cover Printing: Malloy, Inc.

ISBN: 978-0-7637-9189-6

6048
Printed in the United States of America
14 13 12 11 10   10 9 8 7 6 5 4 3 2 1

Contents

To my beautiful wife, Donna,
who has made life worth living again

Preface

Purpose of This Book

This book is part of the Information Systems Security & Assurance Series from Jones & Bartlett Learning (*www.jblearning.com*). Designed for courses and curriculums in IT Security, Cybersecurity, Information Assurance, and Information Systems Security, this series features a comprehensive, consistent treatment of the most current thinking and trends in this critical subject area. These titles deliver fundamental information-security principles packed with real-world applications and examples. Reviewed by Certified Information Systems Security Professionals (CISSPs), they deliver comprehensive information on all aspects of information security. Reviewed word for word by leading technical experts in the field, these books are not just current, but forward-thinking—putting you in the position to solve the cybersecurity challenges not just of today, but of tomorrow, as well.

Security Strategies in Linux Platforms and Applications covers every major aspect of security on a Linux system. The first part of this book describes the risks, threats, and vulnerabilities associated with Linux as an operating system. As Linux is the standard platform behind Apache, the most prominent Web server on the Internet, the focus is on Linux as a server operating system. To that end, this book uses examples from two of the major distributions built for the server, Red Hat Enterprise Linux and Ubuntu (Server Edition).

With Linux, security is much more than just firewalls and permissions. Part 2 of the book shows you how to take advantage of the layers of security available to Linux—user and group options, filesystems, and security options for important services, as well as the security modules associated with AppArmor and SELinux. It also covers encryption options where available.

The final part of this book explores the use of both open source and proprietary tools when building a layered security strategy for your Linux operating system environments. With these tools, you can define a system baseline, audit the system state, monitor system performance, test network vulnerabilities, detect security breaches, and more. You will also learn basic practices associated with security alerts and updates, which are just as important.

Just as Linux is built from the ground up as a network operating system, Linux is built to be secure in networks. Security works well in an open source ecosystem, but the paradigms are different. The open source community has its own security organization, its own certifications, and a wealth of freely available tools. Amazingly, the U.S. National

Security Agency has even lent its expertise to the Linux community in its efforts to create a more secure computing infrastructure. They have freely released their contributions under open source licenses.

When you are done with this book, you will understand the importance of custom firewalls, restrictions on key services, golden baseline systems, and custom local repositories. You will even understand how to customize and recompile the Linux kernel. You will be able to use open source and commercial tools to test the integrity of various systems on the network. The data you get from such tools will identify weaknesses and help you create more secure systems.

Learning Features

The writing style of this book is practical and conversational. Each chapter begins with a statement of learning objectives. Step-by-step examples of information security concepts and procedures are presented throughout the text. Illustrations are used both to clarify the material and to vary the presentation. The text is sprinkled with Notes, Tips, FYIs, Warnings, and sidebars to alert the reader to additional helpful information related to the subject under discussion. Chapter Assessments appear at the end of each chapter, with solutions provided in the back of the book.

Throughout this book are references to commands and directives. They may be included in the body of a paragraph, in a monospaced font like this: `apt-get update`. Other commands or directives may be indented between paragraphs, like the directive shown here:

```
deb http://us.archive.ubuntu.com/ubuntu/ lucid main restricted
```

When a command is indented between paragraphs, it's meant to include a Linux command line prompt. You will note two different prompts in the book. The first prompt is represented with a $. As shown here, it represents the command line prompt from a regular user account:

```
$ ls -ltr > list_of_files
```

The second prompt is represented by a #. As shown here, it represents the command line prompt from a root administrative account:

```
# /usr/sbin/apachectl restart
```

Sometimes, the command or directive is so long, it has to be broken into two different lines due to the formatting requirements of this book. Line wraps are indicated by a curved arrow, as is shown at the start of what looks like the second line of the `iptables` command. It is just a continuation arrow, which would be typed as a continuous command on the command line or an appropriate configuration file.

```
iptables -A RH-Firewall-1-INPUT -i eth0 -s 10.0.0.0/8
↪-j LOG --log-prefix "Dropped private class A addresses".
```

Chapter summaries are included in the text to provide a rapid review or preview of the material and to help students understand the relative importance of the concepts presented.

Audience

The material is suitable for undergraduate or graduate computer science majors or information science majors, students at a two-year technical college or community college who have a basic technical background, or readers who have a basic understanding of IT security and want to expand their knowledge. It assumes basic knowledge of Linux administration at the command line interface.

Acknowledgments

I would like to thank Jones & Bartlett Learning and and David Kim of Security Evolutions for the opportunity to write this book and be a part of the Information Systems Security & Assurance Series project. This book required a more substantial team effort than ordinary book projects. I would also like to thank the amazing project manager, Kim Lindros; the top-notch technical reviewer, Mike Chapple; the sharp copyeditor, Kate Shoup; the marvelous compositor, Mia Saunders; the eagle-eyed proofreader, Ruth Walker; and Larry Goodrich along with Angela Silvia of High Stakes Writing for facilitating the entire process.

In addition, I acknowledge the gracious help of Billy Austin of the SAINT corporation, along with Mike Johnson of AccessData with respect to their products. The author also acknowledges the fortitude of Linux security professionals everywhere, white-hat hackers at heart who have to deal with cultural biases from the mainstream security community along with the legitimate fears of the open source community.

Most importantly, I could not do what I do without the help and support of my wife, Donna. She makes everything possible for me.

About the Author

MICHAEL JANG is currently a full-time writer, specializing in Linux and related certifications. His experience with computers dates back to the days of badly shuffled punch cards. He has written books such as *RHCE Red Hat Certified Engineer Study Guide*, *LPIC-1 In Depth*, *Ubuntu Server Administration*, and *Linux Annoyances for Geeks*. He is also the author of numerous video courses, and teaches preparation courses on Red Hat certification.

PART ONE

Is Linux Really Secure?

Security Threats to Linux

P EOPLE WHO BELIEVE IN LINUX want to believe that their operating system is inherently more secure. Linux does have advantages because fewer viruses, worms, and other malware are written for Linux. But there are some juicy targets installed on many Linux systems. For example, Linux is a common platform for relatively insecure file-sharing servers such as the **Network File System (NFS)** and **Samba**. In addition, many Linux users still prefer connecting to remote systems with clear-text protocols such as **Telnet**.

The fact is, risks abound with Linux:

- It's easy to boot fully functional Linux operating systems from a CD drive or a universal serial bus (USB) key, bypassing the access control settings of the operating system installed on the system.
- The standard installation routine of some popular Linux distributions activates potentially vulnerable services.
- Because Linux volumes are not encrypted by default, it's easy to read data from media taken from a physical Linux system.
- Users on Linux systems may make the same security mistakes as users on other systems. Unless prompted, they may never change their passwords. And they're subject to the same "social engineering" issues as people who use other operating systems.

A skilled Linux user with malicious intent may pose a more serious threat to your networks than you imagine.

Most Linux software is released under open source licenses. In other words, the source code is publicly available to all. While some say this provides an advantage to users who want to break into a system, open source advocates believe in the power of collaborative development. Even the U.S. National Security Agency (NSA) has contributed a significant amount of code to Linux. To paraphrase the original developer of the Linux kernel, "Many eyes make all security issues shallow."

The mechanics of information security (IS) on Linux are somewhat different from the mechanics of IS with other operating systems. The principles, however, are the same. In this chapter, you'll examine several models for measuring security, review some attacks on open source software, and learn about different factors that affect security.

Chapter 1 Topics

This chapter covers the following topics and concepts:

- The fundamentals of Linux information security
- How security works as a process in the open source world
- What basic policy and regulatory requirements apply in information security
- What the basic concepts used to measure information security are
- The open source security testing methodology manual
- How Linux fits in the seven domains of IT infrastructure
- What kinds of attacks happen on open source software
- How security differs in an open source world
- The costs and benefits of security measures on Linux

Chapter 1 Goals

When you complete this chapter, you will be able to:

- Understand standard and open source criteria for measuring information security
- Describe the basics of security in an open source world
- Explain various roles of Linux systems in the IT architecture

The Fundamentals of Linux Information Security

The most secure systems are never connected to a network. Such systems are kept in secure facilities, with access limited to qualified personnel who are up to date with the latest security developments. Their ethical standards have been verified with background checks rivaling those performed by national intelligence agencies. They're well paid. They're immune to temptations put forth by competitors and enemies. They are not prone to sloppy administration. And curiosity does not motivate them to seek out data to which they should not have access.

Of course, such standards do not reflect reality. Users need network and Internet connections. True physical security can be expensive. Overworked administrators do not always keep up to speed with the latest in software and security issues. High-level background checks may prevent security professionals from starting work for months. Humans may be enticed by temptations put forth by competitors and even enemies. And the same curiosity that makes for good systems administrators may tempt these professionals to see they can crack a system.

While this book does not address how administrators are motivated, it does describe tools that can help the responsible administrator maximize the security of Linux platforms and applications.

To some extent, information security on Linux systems is no different from information security on Microsoft or Apple systems. As an administrator, you'll take many of the same steps as you would to secure Windows and Macintosh platforms. You'll create firewalls, set up bastions, manage users, encrypt filesystems, configure servers, customize applications, and work with intrusion prevention and detection systems. The Linux paradigm is different in some ways, however. With Linux, you get to customize a kernel. In addition, there is frequently no one choice for certain security controls. For example, if you want to set up **mandatory access control**, you have to choose between Security Enhanced Linux (SELinux) and Application Armor (AppArmor).

> **NOTE**
>
> While the terms "file system" and "filesystem" are used interchangeably in Linux, this book uses the term "filesystem."

The basic procedures of server security should already be familiar to you; servers in locked rooms, password security with **Basic Input/Output System (BIOS)** and **Unified Extensible Firmware Interface (UEFI)** menus, network security for the Intelligent Platform Management Interface (IPMI), physical access limited to authorized users, and so on. However, server security is especially important in the Linux context. One reason is that it is trivial to boot a fully functional version of Linux from CD/DVD or USB media with full administrative privileges to a system.

Hackers, Crackers, White Hats, and Black Hats

The open source and Microsoft-security communities diverge when talking about **hackers** and **crackers**. The Microsoft-focused security community accepts and uses the public definition of "hacker" as someone who wants to break into computers. In contrast, valued members of the Linux and open source communities think of themselves positively as "hackers"—people who just want to create better software. These communities define people who are threats to IS as "crackers"—people who want to crack into their networks, decrypt their communications, and so on. If you're talking to an open source audience, be aware of the distinction. Many open source professionals take personal offense at anyone who refers to a hacker in a negative light.

The organizations that promote Linux security refer to hackers as people who want to create better software. In fact, the main organization associated with open source security, **Institute for Security and Open Methodologies (ISECOM)**, refers to hackers in a positive light. It asserts, "The principles of hacking should be taught in schools." In fact, several of its officials support the Hacker Highschool project (*http://hackerhighschool.org*). And a number of ISECOM officials are authors of *Hacking Linux Exposed*, published by McGraw-Hill, 2008, an excellent book designed to enhance security on Linux systems.

As this book is intended in part for use by Microsoft-focused security professionals who work on Linux, it intends to respect the differences between the two security communities. To that end, the term **white-hat hacker** will be used to refer to authorized users and developers who want to do good things with software. In contrast, the term **black-hat hacker** will be used to refer to users and developers who want to crack software and break into networks.

Security As a Process in the Open Source World

Many organizations treat security as a reactive process, but networks are more secure when you're proactive about security. To be sure, unanticipated security issues do appear. However, the best IS processes anticipate problems before they arise. Such processes define the functionality in the seven domains of IT (discussed later in the chapter) as they apply to your users and networks.

In this chapter, you'll look at four models for configuring security as a process. In the open source community, there is the **Open Source Security Testing Methodology Manual (OSSTMM)**. In other circles, there is the **CIA triad** of confidentiality, integrity, and availability. There is the **Parkerian hexad**, which adds three more concepts to the CIA triad. In addition, there are the seven domains of a typical IT infrastructure. Although you'll see all four models in this chapter, because Linux is an open source system, this chapter focuses most on the OSSTMM. A standard OSSTMM audit reviews security as a process. The audit should find any gaps in the process that affect security and recommend appropriate changes.

Laws and Regulatory Requirements in Information Security

As an IS professional, you need to understand the effects of certain laws and regulatory requirements. Of course, the details should be left to legal professionals. These same laws and regulations affect all operating systems and services. As such, laws and regulations vary by country—and sometimes even by province or state—and the requirements can be complex. Briefly, most laws and regulatory requirements that affect IS relate to privacy, disclosure, and computer crimes. Shortly, you'll read about *OSSTMM 3.0 Lite*, a simplified version of the latest OSSTMM procedures. It is available as a manual in PDF format. As such, it provides a starting point for laws that may apply in a number of different countries. Such laws are just a starting point, but they form the basis of more detailed regulations.

The SCO Sideshow

Because this chapter addresses Linux-related legal and regulatory requirements, it would not be complete without a discussion of the legal action associated with the SCO Group. In its previous incarnations as Caldera Systems, it developed a fairly popular Linux distribution.

In March of 2003, the SCO Group filed suit against IBM, eventually for $5 billion. In brief, SCO alleges that IBM took UNIX source code and released it in Linux under open source licenses without authorization. That lawsuit is still ongoing, but as of this writing, most of SCO's evidence against IBM has been disallowed.

SCO also wanted Linux users to purchase licenses if they continued to use that operating system. To that end, SCO sued a couple of corporate Linux users, AutoZone and the company then known as Daimler-Chrysler, claiming their use of Linux violated SCO's copyrights in UNIX. Although the lawsuit against AutoZone is still ongoing, AutoZone's stock is near its all-time high.

As of this writing, Novell claims that it owns the noted copyrights in UNIX and has sued SCO because of its allegations against IBM. Although Novell 's stock is not doing as well, its Linux business is reportedly doing quite well.

Based on the evidence as published, the markets have made their judgment. SCO was delisted from NASDAQ in 2007 and is currently in Chapter 11 bankruptcy protection. In contrast, IBM is near a 10-year high, and Red Hat was recently added to the New York Stock Exchange.

An excellent source for the latest information on these legal actions is *Groklaw.net*, run by Pamela Jones.

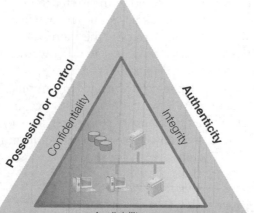

FIGURE 1-1

The CIA triad and the Parkerian hexad.

Measuring Information Security

Information security predates computers. Indeed, early principles of information security are based on the aforementioned CIA triad. Some professionals go further with the concept of the Parkerian hexad, which add the concepts of possession or control, authenticity, and utility. These concepts can help you as a security professional formulate a more complete IS plan for your networks.

In this section, you'll examine how each of these concepts applies, in general terms, to Linux platforms and applications and how the Parkerian hexad interacts with the CIA triad. Specifically, the CIA concept of confidentiality may extend to the Parkerian concept of possession or control. The CIA concept of integrity may extend to the Parkerian concept of authenticity. Finally, the CIA concept of availability may extend to the Parkerian concept of utility (see Figure 1-1).

While some security professionals swear by the Parkerian hexad, others dispute its usefulness. What concepts you and your colleagues choose to secure your systems and networks is up to you and your team.

Confidentiality

Confidentiality is a CIA triad concept that relates to preventing the unauthorized disclosure of private information, such as usernames, passwords, and salary data. Confidentiality is often a legal requirement, based on laws such as the following:

- The **Health Insurance Portability and Accountability Act (HIPAA)**, which regulates security for personal health data
- The **Sarbanes-Oxley (SOX) Act**, which specifies financial-disclosure requirements as they relate to the stocks of publicly traded companies
- The **Gramm-Leach-Bliley Act (GLBA)**, which protects personal financial information

Those are just some of the laws that apply within the United States.

These and other laws may specify how data is protected, which may affect other elements of the CIA triad and Parkerian hexad. Furthermore, these laws may specify financial and other penalties for security violations. In other words, these legal requirements may drive how you secure your systems and networks.

Confidentiality on a Linux platform may be protected in a number of ways. Passwords are used to protect the confidentiality of more than just user accounts. File-system encryption can help protect the confidentiality of storage media, even if they fall into the wrong hands. Bastionized servers may help protect the confidentiality of information and services installed on those systems.

Possession or Control

Possession or control is a Parkerian hexad concept closely related to confidentiality. Data isn't really secure unless you have possession or control of associated media. One risk is that confidential data is frequently stored on easily transportable devices. The loss of a laptop, the theft of a portable drive, or even a few seconds of copying to a USB key or Secure Digital card can mean a loss of control of data.

Rogue administrators or thieves can slip a hard drive out of a RAID array for maintenance or later analysis. Even permanently attached internal hard drives on many servers can be removed in a matter of seconds. While such data can be encrypted in a number of ways, encrypted data can be deciphered with enough time and patience. And that is a loss of possession and control.

Such a loss of control can be expensive. Some companies have had to supply current and former employees with years of credit reports after a corporate laptop or drive with confidential data was lost or stolen.

Integrity

Integrity is a CIA concept that means you can trust the data. In this context, integrity means only authorized users can change data such as grades, salaries, bills, votes, and more.

Developers can help administrators verify the integrity of downloaded files with **GNU Privacy Guard (GPG)** keys, which are the open source implementation of **Pretty Good Privacy (PGP)** keys. Administrators can help preserve the integrity of data on their servers with appropriate ownership and permissions on files and directories. They can further protect the integrity of key filesystems with read-only access.

Linux systems make it relatively easy to verify the integrity of downloaded packages. With the right GPG keys, you can be relatively sure that the kernel update package downloaded from that normally reliable mirror site hasn't been infected or replaced by a Trojan package.

Authenticity

Authenticity is a Parkerian hexad concept. It relates to the CIA concept of integrity. Authenticity can help users and administrators verify that communication, data, payments, and so on are genuine. Authenticity goes both ways. The use of secure passwords can help businesses verify the identity of customers. At the same time, the use of images and **passphrases** can help customers verify that they're actually communicating with a financial institution and are not sending financial data to scammers.

Options for verifying authenticity on a Linux system include passphrases for secure access, integrity scanners such as Tripwire, and GPG keys to verify the integrity of everything from e-mail to downloaded packages.

Availability

The CIA concept of **availability** is important to users. Availability means users have access to their data when they want it. If data is not available, users complain. Problems with availability can fall into three areas:

- **Denial of service issues**—Attacks such as the so-called "**ping of death**" can prevent connections from legitimate users. Linux firewalls make it easy to minimize the effect of such attacks without completely blocking that useful `ping` command.
- **Overloaded networks**—Poorly designed networks may have bottlenecks that slow data transmission. Although bottlenecks are not by themselves a security issue, slower networks may motivate users to bypass standard security requirements.
- **Overzealous administrators**—Security that discourages users can reduce their productivity in the workplace. Security that is too complex may lead users to unsafe practices such as writing passwords on their desks. Linux makes it easy customize requirements for password changes and complexity.

Utility

Utility is a Parkerian hexad concept. It is closely related to the CIA concept of availability. For example, to decrypt some partitions or volumes in Linux, a password may be required during the boot process. Such encryption can help protect data in case the hard drive is stolen.

There are records of Linux systems that have run continuously for years. A password that may be required during the boot process could have been lost during that time. If that password is lost, an attempted reboot of an encrypted root directory filesystem may fail. In that case, the data is no longer useful. Of course, while there are ways to automatically enter the password during the boot process, the use of such methods would cancel out the benefits of encrypting the volume.

In a similar fashion, an e-mail encrypted with a GPG private key may be authentic, confidential, controlled, available, and have integrity. Without the corresponding public key, however, the recipients won't be able to read the e-mail, rendering that information useless.

The Open Source Security Testing Methodology Manual

While security professionals may use some variation of the triad or hexad to make sure they've covered all elements of IS, open source security professionals use a different system, based on the OSSTMM. The OSSTMM is a peer-reviewed manual developed through ISECOM. The information described here is based on *OSSTMM 3.0 Lite*, developed by Peter Herzog.

The OSSTMM uses a number of paradigms that may differ from those described by the **International Information Systems Security Certification Consortium (ISC)²**. For example, OSSTMM professionals refer to IS as a form of protection from risk. As cited in *Hacking Linux Exposed*:

> "Security is the separation of an asset from a threat. Protection can take two forms: protect the asset or destroy the threat."

Although the focus of this book is protecting the asset, IS goes beyond this. The OSSTMM model also considers legislation, regulation, and corporate policy. OSSTMM audits are performed in 17 categories. To qualify IS personnel, OSSTMM offers professional certifications in three areas.

Measures of OSSTMM Compliance

Compliance is a measure of how fully you meet a requirement. The plan that you use to comply with requirements should include design parameters for networks, provide measurable goals for secure systems, and drive the development of security solutions. OSSTMM security professionals perform audits designed to measure compliance in three areas:

- **Legislation**—OSSTMM professionals can create customized audits based on applicable legal requirements, such as HIPAA.
- **Regulation**—OSSTMM professionals can measure compliance to regulations from private industry groups or governmental agencies, such as the Payment Card Industry Data Security Standard (PCI DSS).
- **Policy**—OSSTMM auditors can measure compliance to specified policies of the business or organization in question.

OSSTMM Channels

ISECOM is constantly updating its requirements. As of this writing, OSSTMM version 3.0 was under intensive development. One major change of OSSTMM 3.0 is that security audits are now divided into three channels, specified by their acronyms:

- **COMSEC—Communications security (COMSEC)** is associated with networks in two areas. Data networks include network communication over physical cables. Telecommunication networks include both digital and analog lines from public telephone networks.

- **SPECSEC**—**Spectrum security (SPECSEC)** includes electronic communications over the electromagnetic spectrum, including wireless networks.
- **PHYSSEC**—**Physical security (PHYSSEC)** is divided into two subcategories: the human element and nonelectronic physical factors.

OSSTMM Test Methodologies

Security professionals may perform OSSTMM audits for each of the three OSSTMM channels. As shown in Figure 1-2, OSSTMM audit includes 17 test modules in five phases:

- **Regulatory**—Three audits: posture review, logistics, and active detection verification.
- **Definitions**—Four audits: visibility, access verification, trust verification, and controls verification.
- **Information**—Six audits: process verification, configuration verification, property validation, segregation review, exposure verification, and competitive intelligence scouting.
- **Interactive controls**—Three audits: quarantine verification, privileges audit, and survivability validation.
- **Alert and log review**—One audit: alert and log review. You'll read about the modules that fall into each phase in the following subsections.

These test modules provide a systematic method for assessing the current security status of a system in the COMSEC, SPECSEC, and PHYSSEC channels.

Regulatory Phase

With the Posture Review module, the regulatory phase is based on the legal and regulatory requirements. Related policy reviews include available contracts and service level agreements. Data is collected on system age and potential points of failure. Furthermore, the Posture Review examines organizational culture and norms.

Success in the Logistics module can prevent false positives and negatives. This module specifies the limitations of the audit, split into three areas:

- **Framework**—Framework parameters include physical security, domain names, Internet service providers (ISPs), Domain Name Service (DNS) information, and more.
- **Network quality**—These parameters can help measure the speed and packet-loss rates for a network.
- **Time**—Time parameters are broad. They include local, supplier, and customer holidays; time-to-live (TTL) information for transmitted data; and time-server synchronization.

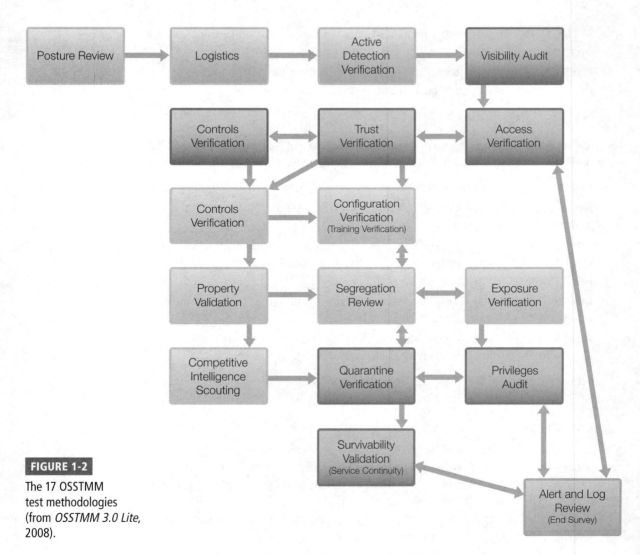

FIGURE 1-2

The 17 OSSTMM
test methodologies
(from *OSSTMM 3.0 Lite*,
2008).

The Active Detection Verification module can help define interactive tests. With
appropriate limits, this module covers the right range of events, response criteria,
and responses. This module is split into two areas:

- **Filtering**—Filtering defines whether incoming and outgoing requests,
  such as access to Web sites, are inspected for inappropriate information.

- **Active detection**—This defines responses to probes and penetration testing.
  Furthermore, this part of the module maps applications, systems, and networks
  that produce logs and alarms.

Definitions Phase

The definitions phase starts with a Visibility Audit module. This module is focused on clients, servers, routers, and more. It specifies the systems to be tested. This module is split into three areas:

- **Network surveying**—This defines the perimeter of the network, checks DNS databases, and reviews broadcasts, routing protocols, **Internet Control Message Protocol (ICMP)** routing and responses, Simple Network Management Protocol (SNMP) names, certain ports of the Transmission Control Protocol/Internet Protocol (TCP/IP) suite, and more.

- **Enumeration**—Enumeration examines Web links, e-mail headers, network responses, and more to measure how the network is seen internally and externally.

- **Identification**—This matches the characteristics of a network with responses from system and service identification tools.

The Access Verification module includes the full range of access requests, from user logins to packet-service banners to responses to known Trojan services. This module is divided into three areas:

- **Access**—Access audits relate to connection protocols, **Internet Protocol Security (IPSec)**, along with attempted connections through the **Transmission Control Protocol (TCP)**, **User Datagram Protocol (UDP)**, and ICMP protocols.

- **Services**—Services audits relate to open TCP/IP ports, virtual Web site configuration, **Voice over IP (VoIP)** communication, and more.

- **Authentication**—These audits list all methods that provide some level of access, including potentially cracked services that may not be locked down.

The Trust Verification module relates to services or systems that allow any form of user access without credentials. This module is divided into three areas:

- **Spoofing**—These audits check whether a network is susceptible to spoofed addresses, such as those from within a local network. It also checks for possible DNS cache poisoning.

- **Phishing**—These audits look for external copies of your Web site, reviews domain records for similar names, and verifies control of mail targets.

- **Resource abuse**—These audits review how far a cracker can get into your system, including any variances between multiple servers with the same functionality.

The Controls Verification module is designed to measure whether your security efforts make a difference. This module is divided into four areas:

- **Nonrepudiation**—In this context, nonrepudiation is a measure of integrity for issues such as login access or system verification.

- **Confidentiality**—In this context, confidentiality reviews options for secure encrypted communication. Related audits may verify the extent and availability of protected communication.

- **Privacy**—A privacy audit in this context specifies secure services, along with the security required based on levels of clearance such as secret and top secret. It may also extend to the use of nonstandard port numbers.
- **Integrity**—This uses procedures such as checksums that allow all authorized parties to verify that a message or file is as intended.

Information Phase

The information phase starts with a Process Verification module to verify existing security procedures along with related real-world practices. This information phase module is divided into four areas:

- **Maintenance**—A maintenance audit examines current the timeliness, access, notification, and responsiveness with current security procedures.
- **Misinformation**—Misinformation in this context measures whether crackers can create false alarms or otherwise misdirect security professionals.
- **Due diligence**—Due diligence measures gaps between rules and real-world practices.
- **Indemnification**—Indemnification documents insurance, legal disclaimers, and support contracts available for your network.

The Configuration Verification module can help you gather technical and nontechnical information. It may include tests that attempt to bypass security measures. In addition, it verifies the default conditions of the network. This module is divided into four areas:

- **Configuration controls**—A configuration-controls audit measures the baseline configuration for the operating system, installed applications, physical and virtual equipment, and more.
- **Common configuration errors**—This section reviews services for redundancy, hidden administrative accounts, and any additional administrative access.
- **Awareness mapping**—Awareness mapping measures gaps between established procedures and what users believe these procedures really mean.
- **Awareness hijacking**—Awareness hijacking reviews the robustness of the security configuration. It may test whether a cracker can convince users to ignore security procedures.

The Property Validation module covers intellectual property and software licensing. While licensing does not apply to open source software, it may apply indirectly based on support contracts. The Property Validation module is divided into three areas:

- **Sharing**—A sharing audit verifies whether non-free software, non–open source software, or other intellectual property has been copied or reproduced without appropriate documentation.

- **Black market**—An audit of black-market intellectual property reviews unauthorized sales of non-free or non–open source software.
- **Sales channels**—A sales-channels audit reviews public information for nonlicensed or black-market information in the same areas.

The Segregation Review module is similar to a privacy review. It determines whether personal or private information is separate from business or organizational data. The Segregation Review module is divided into four areas:

- **Privacy containment mapping**—This defines what, where, and how private information is stored, as well as how it may be shared with authorized personnel.
- **Disclosure**—A disclosure audit verifies procedures for releasing private information along with the security of intellectual property such as service contracts and software keys.
- **Limitations**—An audit on limitations reviews alternatives for users covered by the Americans with Disabilities Act (ADA). It also audits information collection from underage users.
- **Discrimination**—A discrimination audit in this area relates to how your system may treat users from underrepresented and underage groups.

The Exposure Verification module reviews publicly available information for data that may help a cracker or other malicious user break into your systems. A related audit will list information that should be kept private, such as organizational charts, resumes, and login information.

The Competitive Intelligence Scouting module reviews published data for information that may help competitors, crackers, or malicious users. This module is divided into four categories:

- **Business grinding**—Business grinding specifies access points to your property and network. A business-grinding audit defines how, what, and where key information is stored.
- **Profiling**—A profiling audit defines the skill levels of internal and external personnel. It also checks for a picture of skills within the organization, based on public job descriptions.
- **Business environment**—A business-environment audit, in this context, checks for confidential information related to external business relationships. It also measures the Web presence of the organization based on third-party links.
- **Organizational environment**—An audit of the organizational environment examines the internal corporate situation from information gatekeepers to turnover to social factors.

Interactive Controls Phase

The interactive controls phase starts with the Quarantine Verification module, including black-and-white lists. A related audit tests the system for containment of potentially aggressive or malicious contacts in two areas:

- **Containment process identification**—This limits information available to outside users such as competitive sales personnel, journalists, and job seekers.
- **Containment levels**—An audit of containment levels verifies appropriate limits on outside users while allowing access based on legal and regulatory requirements.

The Privileges Audit module measures the consequences of unauthorized access to regular accounts when combined with limited or full administrative permissions. Audit tasks in this module test the system in three areas:

- **Identification**—An identification audit measures how user credentials may be checked through legitimate or fraudulent means.
- **Authorization**—An authorization audit examines how users may gain access through fraud, malicious use of default accounts, and password cracking.
- **Escalation**—An escalation audit may investigate trusted users. It also looks at what happens if physical access media such as smart cards fall into the wrong hands. In addition, it reviews escalation channels for possible breaches.

The Survivability Validation module measures the resilience of an IS system after some number of security breaches based on single points of failure. This module is divided into three categories:

- **Resilience**—A resilience audit defines those single points of failure for a service or system, along with the impact of the compromised service.
- **Continuity**—Continuity specifies backup systems and alternate channels in the context of access delays and response times.
- **Safety**—Safety concerns are related to any IS-based dangers to people or property.

Alert and Log Review Phase

The final module, Alert and Log Review, reviews the other audit modules with respect to depth, utility, and reliability. This module is divided in two areas:

- **Alarm**—A good alarm provides a local or system-wide warning that may be elevated to appropriate management for review.
- **Storage/retrieval**—A storage and retrieval audit verifies tracking of unprivileged access along with the quality of that access.

OSSTMM Certifications

Qualified OSSTMM security professionals should perform regular audits of open source software. If you're interested in becoming an open source security professional, consider one or more of the following OSSTMM certifications from ISECOM:

FYI

The contrasting certifications from (ISC)² are the **Systems Security Certified Practitioner (SSCP)** and the **Certified Information Systems Security Professional (CISSP)**. As of February of 2010, per (ISC)², "the SSCP is ideal for those working towards positions such as Network Security Engineers, Security Systems Analysts, or Security Administrators." They also suggest that the SSCP is suitable for personnel who "do not have information security as a primary part of their job description."

The CISSP certification is more comprehensive, requiring a level of professional experience in multiple security domains.

- **Security Analyst**—An **OSSTMM Professional Security Analyst (OSPA)** can assess legal requirements, design security tests, and measure controls in the context of the scientific method. OSPAs are qualified to create an official OSSTMM audit report.
- **Security Expert**—The **OSSTMM Professional Security Expert (OSPE)** certification is designed for professionals with "little networking and security experience."
- **Security Tester**—An **OSSTMM Professional Security Tester (OSPT)** is qualified to use various security programs on Linux. The OSPT exam combines paper questions with real-time tests of an appropriate network.
- **Wireless Security Expert**—The **OSSTMM Professional Wireless Security Expert (OWSE)** exam is based on an audit of an operational wireless infrastructure.

Linux and the Seven Domains of a Typical IT Infrastructure

Linux advocates believe that users would be best served if Linux were installed on all computers, especially in the enterprise. But that is not realistic. Linux is typically installed on networks as servers, most commonly as file and print servers. Linux workstations are highly prized, however, by scientists and graphic artists. Indeed, many major motion pictures have been finished on Linux workstations.

Linux brings important benefits to the IT enterprise. By and large, Linux is immune to malware written for Microsoft operating systems. Furthermore, multiple operating systems on a network are more resistant to single points of failure.

> **NOTE**
> Linux is a clone of the UNIX operating system. Current versions of the Macintosh operating systems are also based on a clone of UNIX. So some malware may affect both Linux and Macintosh operating systems.

Several books in this series refer to the seven domains of a typical IT infrastructure. As shown in Figure 1-3, they include all users and systems in a typical enterprise network. The following sections describe how these seven domains fit in the context of Linux security. To describe these mappings, it's helpful to review a bit about the history of Linux.

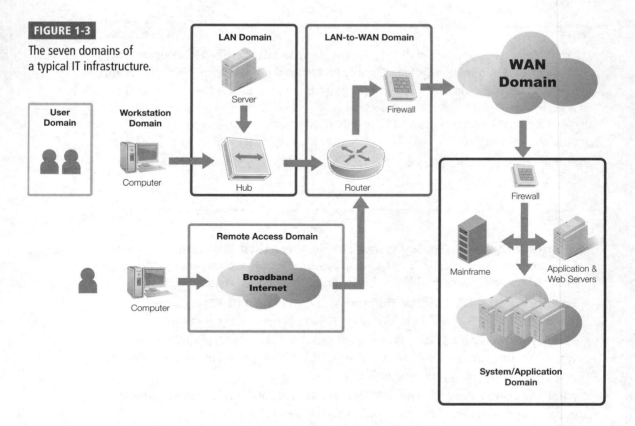

FIGURE 1-3

The seven domains of a typical IT infrastructure.

A Short History of Linux

To understand the value of Linux in the IT architecture, it's important to understand its history. The original Linux kernel was developed in 1991 by Linus Torvalds. Strictly speaking, the Linux kernel is the essence of that operating system. But the kernel is not enough. To make the Linux kernel useful, you need the system tools and libraries from the GNU project. As a combined effort, the operating system known as Linux is more formally known as GNU/Linux.

The GNU project developed its tools and libraries as clones of corresponding UNIX tools and libraries. In other words, while these clones work in the same way, they are built from different source code. Thus, Linux includes the advantages of UNIX as an enterprise-ready operating system without the limitations of UNIX licensing. It also includes the networking advantages of UNIX, dating back to its development at the universities that were integral in the network that would become the Internet.

The Linux development model is based on a number of open source licenses, including the **GNU General Public License (GPL)**. In essence, open source licenses allow anyone to use, modify, and improve the source code. Anyone can release improvements to open source software as long as they also release the source code for such improvements under the same open source licenses.

Several organizations have built the kernel, tools, and libraries—with applications—into a coherent group of packages known as a distribution. This book focuses on Red Hat Enterprise Linux and Ubuntu Server Edition, two of the most popular distributions for the enterprise. Readers should not interpret this book's focus on these distributions as a lack of respect for the excellent work of the dozens of other companies and organizations that release their own Linux distributions.

The source code for Red Hat Enterprise Linux is released under open source licenses. However, the compiled code, also known as binaries, is the intellectual property of Red Hat. Under open source licenses, anyone has the right to compile the source code released by Red Hat into their own binaries. Several third-party organizations have done so for years, taking care to omit Red Hat trademarks and any other Red Hat intellectual property. Two examples of such releases are the Community Enterprise distribution, known as CentOS, and Scientific Linux, from developers at CERN and Fermilab.

In contrast, **Canonical**, the private company behind the Ubuntu distribution, releases the source code and binaries under open source licenses.

Both Canonical and Red Hat make money on their expertise. They offer paid support for their distributions. While Canonical as a private company does not release its financial information, Red Hat has been so successful, it joined the New York Stock Exchange during the latest economic downturn.

Red Hat and Canonical (Ubuntu) release robust, "enterprise-ready" distributions. Novell also has a robust enterprise-ready distribution: SUSE Linux. But as of this writing, Red Hat has more of a presence in the Linux marketplace. SUSE Linux also uses the Red Hat Package Manager. In contrast, the Ubuntu distribution uses packages built with the Debian Package Manager. If you're familiar with the prerequisites for this book, you should already be familiar with the `rpm` and `dpkg` commands along with their package-management companions, the `yum` and `apt-*` commands.

Most Linux distributions include all the tools, services, applications and packages associated with a variety of workstations and servers. But servers don't require a GUI, and workstations don't require most server services. Such extra services present additional security hazards.

Linux in the User Domain

The User Domain includes actual people who are users on your network. In Linux, users have login names, passwords, home directories, default shells, and more. Users may be members of one or more groups as well as part of the User Domain. Linux user (and group) security is based first on authentication limits specified in the shadow password suite. Users may be configured with different levels of administrative privileges.

In Linux, many services have their own special accounts. These services should not have a password or a login shell. Nevertheless, such accounts are still part of the shadow password suite. You should already be familiar with the basics of the shadow password suite. While the concepts are covered in elementary Linux books, the details are very important to Linux security. For this reason, you'll get a chance to review how Linux works in the User Domain in Chapter 4.

Linux in the Workstation Domain

Many scientists and engineers prefer Linux. Likewise, many graphics designers prefer Linux. And of course, many home hobbyists prefer Linux. While a number of these users may enjoy tinkering with their systems, the default installations of many systems include services and applications that aren't really necessary. If unmaintained, these services and applications may present security risks. In a worst-case scenario, they may even provide footholds for crackers/black-hat hackers. Such users could then use these compromised workstations to break into more valuable parts of your networks.

A number of major movie studios develop their movies on Linux. While the graphics capabilities of Linux workstations are important, the networking features of Linux graphical software may present risks not only to workstations but also to your network.

If you're responsible for the security of Linux workstations, you'll be working with perhaps the most knowledgeable users in computing. Not only will you need to apply the lessons throughout this book on various Linux systems, you'll also have to explain them to your users.

Linux in the LAN Domain

As a clone of UNIX, Linux shares its heritage as an operating system built for networking. With a few commands and configuration files, it's easy to configure Linux on any **Internet Protocol version 4 (IPv4)** or **Internet Protocol version 6 (IPv6)** local area network (LAN). To that end, Linux works well in the LAN Domain. Linux supports most network cards through 10G Ethernet. It's just as easy to customize hardware addresses as it is to customize static IP addresses.

It's a straightforward process to customize firewalls, access controls, and more on any Linux system in the LAN Domain. As security risks exist inside a network, you may want to activate firewalls and access controls on every Linux workstation in the LAN Domain.

Linux in the LAN-to-WAN Domain

Linux excels as a gateway system—the transition between a LAN and a wide area network (WAN) such as the Internet. It's a straightforward process to configure Linux as a firewall.

A Linux gateway can help other systems hide from the WAN through **masquerading**. With the right firewall configuration, it can help protect a LAN from threats transmitted over the WAN.

With a little planning, Linux can be configured as a bastion host—a system designed with a single function, such as a Web server. Such bastions are often configured in the LAN-to-WAN Domain. All other services are uninstalled or inactivated on the bastion. The only open communication ports on that system are those needed for its function (for example, to act as a Web server) and possibly a port for remote administration.

Because they are hardened against attacks, bastion hosts are often configured outside a main firewall, accessible to the general Internet. You'll read more about how to set up Linux as a bastion host in Chapter 6.

Linux in the System/Application Domain

Linux works well as a server operating system. The default installation of many Linux distributions includes a number of server services that work "out of the box." Linux systems are so reliable, many go for months at a time without being rebooted. Every service is a potential risk, however. If a cracker breaks into any system through a flaw in one service, all other services on that system may be at risk. The default configuration of many Linux systems includes active versions of a number of services, many of which are never used on most workstations. In Chapter 6, you'll learn to manage those risks.

In addition, a number of Linux security updates involve the installation of a new kernel, which requires a reboot. A reboot with a new kernel may be risky. New kernels may not work because of the way many administrators customize their Linux systems. You'll learn about some of these issues in Chapter 10.

Linux in the Remote Access Domain

The Remote Access Domain includes access from remote workstations. By definition, such workstations are not always connected to your LAN. Users in this domain may use anything from traditional telephone modems to fiber-optic connections to connect to a network. One of the risks is the easy availability of clear text remote access services such as Telnet.

Linux excels as a remote access server. You can configure it as a Secure Shell (SSH) server for encrypted connections—even over the Internet. You can configure it as a Remote Authentication Dial In User Service (RADIUS) for authentication. The open source version is known as FreeRADIUS. If you're willing to accept the security risks, you can even configure it for remote access to user home directories via the File Transfer Protocol (FTP).

Ideally, all remote access should be encrypted for security. In Chapter 8, you'll read about SSH and options for tunneling, such as IPSec.

Linux in the WAN Domain

By definition, a WAN includes connections between LANs from different geographical areas. While a network that connects LANs in a single urban area is known as a metropolitan area network (MAN), it is also part of the WAN Domain.

While the biggest WAN is the Internet, many enterprises maintain their own WANs. To connect different LANs in a WAN, enterprises configure connectivity through routers and gateways. Most WANs include connections through the public Internet, which presents its own risks.

Linux is an excellent tool in the WAN Domain. You can configure Linux as gateways, filtering and forwarding network packets between desired LANs.

Attacks on Open Source Software

As the popularity and importance of open source software grow, malicious attacks on Linux and related applications will also grow. For now, the number of attacks is relatively small. Linux security professionals can stay up to date with the latest security advisories by monitoring Web sites such as *http://linuxsecurity.com* along with the security mailing list for your Linux distribution.

Some companies, including Red Hat and Canonical (Ubuntu), go further. They support the applications included with their distributions even though they're developed by third parties. To that end, Red Hat and Canonical include security reports with issues related to those third-party applications. There may be a time lag between security reports from the developers of a key service and the corresponding security report from the company behind a distribution, however. If services such as **Apache** and **Squid** are mission critical, you may want to monitor the appropriate mailing lists from their developers.

Security vulnerabilities in open source software are sometimes critical. One example from 2008 affected SSH, the encrypted remote access service used by many open source administrators to manage their systems. As described by the United States Computer Emergency Readiness Team (US-CERT), Technical Cyber Security Alert TA08-137A noted a weakness in the random number generator. In other words, SSH encryption keys weren't as random as they should have been. That made systems based on the Debian distribution (including Ubuntu) vulnerable to a brute-force attack. The open source community responded quickly; in fact, a fix was available before the US-CERT alert was even issued.

Security in an Open Source World

Open source advocates suggest that the companies behind proprietary operating systems don't publicize security issues until they have solutions ready for their users. It often takes time to develop security patches. During that time period, users of such operating systems may be vulnerable. And when a new security issue receives no publicity, even the most vigilant security professionals may be caught off guard.

In contrast, security issues on open source systems are publicized as soon as they're known. If you know about a security issue with an open source application, you can isolate or deactivate that application until a solution is available.

If the application is popular, many open source developers start working on the problem almost immediately. Although few of these developers are paid for this work, the popularity of many open source applications often means faster responses to security issues.

Of course, if you're using a less-popular open source application, the response to security issues may be slower. But for the great majority of services, there are open source alternatives.

Because professionals in the open source world generally report all problems, comparing security between open source and proprietary operating systems is like comparing apples and oranges. In other words, the problems listed from sources such as US-CERT may overstate the number of security issues associated with open source software.

> **NOTE**
>
> While most open source developers are volunteers, the reputations they develop due to their efforts frequently help them get work in their professions. While companies like Red Hat and Canonical are not paid for the source code they develop, many organizations are willing to pay for the support services of their developers through subscriptions.

A critical advantage of Linux security updates relates to the kernel. As of this writing, Microsoft just released an update for Windows XP that (when combined with some third-party software) made some systems unbootable. Recovery from such updates is often difficult. While it's possible that a Linux kernel update might not work on some systems, a standard Linux kernel update makes it easy to access to the former working kernel.

If more serious errors appear in a Linux system, many distributions include bootable rescue media. In addition, many Linux distributions are available in a "live CD" format. Both are excellent ways to recover from problems that make the operating system unbootable.

Costs and Benefits of Linux Security Measures

What you do in IS depends on costs and benefits. In other words, you need to balance the costs of additional security versus the benefits of additional security, such as not having to pay legal penalties associated with security breaches.

Ideally, every networked host is hardened as a bastion host, with a single purpose in mind. Until recent developments in virtualization, costs forced many administrators to put servers to multiple uses. A security breach in one service is a potential risk to all other services on that server.

The Costs of Security

For most organizations, security is an expense. The work of security professionals can be expensive. Secure systems often require additional hardware and software. When you plan a security strategy, you need to be aware of these costs.

For those who won't trust their security systems management to just anyone, many excellent proprietary security-management programs are available. These include the following:

- **System management tools**—Red Hat, Canonical, and Novell all offer commercial system-management tools that can help you manage large groups of systems from a single interface. For more information on the capabilities of the Red Hat Network and Canonical's Landscape, see Chapter 11.

- **Security-testing tools**—Companies such as Tripwire and Cimcor offer commercial tools that can help detect unauthorized changes to key systems. For more information, see Chapter 13.

If you're working with Linux administrators, you know that they'll look to open source solutions before trying commercial security programs. Yes, you avoid licensing costs with open source software. But the use of open source software may increase costs in other areas. These costs include the time required for administrators to learn and use these systems as well as the additional hardware that may be needed to securely create, test, and maintain these programs.

The Benefits of Security

A good IS system can help you avoid a number of costs. Many laws and regulations specify financial penalties for security breaches. Customers who learn about security problems with your systems may take their business elsewhere. Security issues may lead you to take down critical systems, which can affect the productivity of others in the organization.

The Effects of Virtualization

In an ideal IS world, every system would be self-contained. Access would be limited to those users who could physically get to the system. Network connections would not be required. That's not realistic, however.

The next best choice is to set up every system as a bastion host: configured for one purpose and isolated as much as possible from other systems. That, however, could mean dozens—perhaps hundreds (or more)—servers in every enterprise. With virtualization, it's possible to configure dozens of servers on just a few physical systems. The savings in hardware and power are well known. The savings in terms of more secure servers may be just as important.

A virtualized system configured as a bastion host is used for one purpose. By definition, security breaches on that system don't affect anything else on that system. Administrators can respond to a security breach by identifying the problem, isolating that system, or even replacing that system with a backup. Backups of virtual machines are easy to create because virtual hard drives are just large files.

The frontiers of virtualization are advancing. Some organizations are already configuring individual desktop applications in their own virtual machines. Security breaches in one desktop application, when virtualized and isolated from others, are less likely to affect other applications.

Such advances in virtualization may pose a challenge, however. Administration in an enterprise with possibly dozens of virtual machines on each workstation will require automation.

CHAPTER SUMMARY

Linux includes a number of different paradigms with respect to security. Kernels can be customized; access controls can keep a system locked down. For many, information security goes beyond the CIA triad concepts of confidentiality, integrity, and availability to the Parkerian hexad concepts of possession or control, authenticity, and utility.

While most IS books are focused on (ISC)^2 paradigms, open source security is based on the OSSTMM. That open source manual starts with current legislation, regulation, and policy; it uses COMSEC, SPECSEC, and PHYSSEC channels; it analyzes the current IS structure with 17 test methodologies. These methodologies provide perspective on the seven domains of a typical IT infrastructure in the context of Linux.

While crackers attack Microsoft software more frequently, they also attack open source software. Fortunately, the efforts of the open source community makes short work of most security issues. While the work you put into security should be quantified in costs and benefits, details are beyond the scope of this book. Fortunately, virtualization has changed the basic cost/benefit equation, making it possible to configure many more bastion hosts on the same physical hardware.

KEY CONCEPTS AND TERMS

Apache
Authenticity
Availability
Basic Input/Output System (BIOS)
Black-hat hacker
Canonical
Certified Information Systems Security Professional (CISSP)
CIA triad
Communications Security (COMSEC)
Confidentiality
Cracker
GNU General Public License (GPL)

GNU Privacy Guard (GPG)
GNU's Not UNIX (GNU)
Gramm-Leach-Bliley Act (GLBA)
Hacker
Health Insurance Portability and Accountability Act (HIPAA)
Institute for Security and Open Methodologies (ISECOM)
Integrity
International Information Systems Security Certification Consortium (ISC)^2
Internet Control Message Protocol (ICMP)
Internet Protocol Security (IPSec)

Internet Protocol version 4 (IPv4)
Internet Protocol version 6 (IPv6)
Mandatory access control
Masquerading
Network File System (NFS)
Open Source Security Testing Methodology Manual (OSSTMM)
OSSTMM Professional Security Analyst (OSPA)
OSSTMM Professional Security Expert (OSPE)
OSSTMM Professional Security Tester (OSPT)

continued

> **KEY CONCEPTS AND TERMS,**
> *continued*
>
> **OSSTMM Professional Wireless
>   Security Expert (OWSE)**
> **Parkerian hexad**
> **Passphrase**
> **Phishing**
> **Physical Security (PHYSSEC)**
> **Ping of death**
>
> **Possession or control**
> **Pretty Good Privacy (PGP)**
> **Samba**
> **Sarbanes-Oxley (SOX) Act**
> **Spectrum Security (SPECSEC)**
> **Spoofing**
> **Squid**
> **Systems Security Certified
>   Practitioner (SSCP)**
>
> **Telnet**
> **Transmission Control Protocol
>   (TCP)**
> **Unified Extensible Firmware
>   Interface (UEFI)**
> **User Datagram Protocol
>   (UDP)**
> **Utility**
> **Voice over IP (VoIP)**
> **White-hat hacker**

CHAPTER 1 ASSESSMENT

1. Which of the following terms is associated with malicious users in the open source community?

A. Hackers
B. Crackers
C. Techies
D. Nerds

2. Which of the following concepts is *not* part of the CIA triad?

A. Authority
B. Access
C. Authenticity
D. Availability

3. Which of the following security certifications is associated with open source software?

A. SSCP
B. CISSP
C. RHCE
D. OSPA

4. Which of the following OSSTMM channels is associated with wireless security?

A. COMSEC
B. SPECSEC
C. PHYSSEC
D. WIRESEC

5. Which of the following is *not* an OSSTMM audit phase?

A. Licensing
B. Regulatory
C. Definitions
D. Information

6. Which of the following components makes up the core of the Linux operating system?

A. Cloned software from UNIX
B. The kernel
C. Linux libraries
D. Linux services

7. Which of the following is an open source license?

A. Freeware
B. Public domain
C. GNU GPL
D. Any Microsoft license

8. From the following options, name the component that is *not* part of a Linux User Domain.

A. Regular users
B. Regular groups
C. Service users
D. Computer users

9. From the following options, select a security advantage of open source software.

A. The efforts of the open source community

B. Secrecy in the source code

C. No information is released before a solution is available

D. None of the above

10. Which of the following methods can be used to recover from an unbootable situation in Linux, minimizing any risk of lost data? (Select two.)

A. Recovery mode

B. Live CD

C. Reinstalling Linux

D. UEFI modification

11. From the following list, which is a system management tool for Linux?

A. Red Hat Zenworks

B. The Ubuntu network

C. Landscape

D. Systems management server

12. Which of the following is a positive effect of virtualization on security?

A. Many virtual machines will confuse malicious users

B. Virtual machines can be configured with many services

C. Virtual machines can be configured as firewalls

D. Additional virtual machines make it possible to configure more bastion hosts

13. A developer who just wants to create better software in the open source world is known as a _____.

14. The open source license associated with the GNU project is _____.

Basic Components
of Linux Security

THIS CHAPTER COVERS BASIC COMPONENTS of Linux security. It also gives you an overall view of how this book discusses Linux security. As such, it paves the way for future chapters, which contain details that you can implement on your networks.

The essence of Linux is the **kernel**, the most important component in Linux security. The starting point for any operating system is the boot process. This chapter examines security in both areas. It moves beyond the basic operating system with an overview of security risks associated with Linux applications. Linux security also depends on the authentication databases that apply to users and groups. User security forms the foundation for file ownership and access controls.

In addition, Linux security depends on networks and service access, which can be protected with firewalls and mandatory access control systems. Of course, network communication is important, and can be protected with encryption.

As security threats continue, it's important to keep up to speed with the latest Linux security updates. Updates can be a challenge if you administer a large number of systems, especially if they're virtual machines. Finally, if you administer systems based on different Linux distributions, you need to be aware of the differences between the major **Linux distributions**.

Chapter 2 Topics

This chapter covers the following topics and concepts:

- How Linux security starts with the kernel
- How you can better secure a system during the boot process
- Linux security issues that exist beyond the operating system
- Which user authentication databases are available for Linux
- How files can be protected with ownership, permissions, and access controls
- How to use firewalls and mandatory access controls in a layered defense
- How to use encrypted communications to protect Linux networks
- How you can track the latest Linux security updates
- The effect of virtualization on security
- How distributions vary

Chapter 2 Goals

When you complete this chapter, you will be able to:

- Describe security features, starting with the boot process
- Understand basic security options for users, groups, and files
- Work with basic security features for networks
- Review appropriate resources for the latest security updates

Linux Security Starts with the Kernel

This section reviews the basic philosophy behind the **Linux kernel** along with the types of kernels that are available. To that end, you'll learn about the differences between the stock kernels released by Linux developers, along with how developers of a distribution modify them.

Frequently, the solution to a security issue is the installation of a new kernel. Although the differences between kernels are often minor, the work required to install a kernel is the same. If you choose to use a custom kernel, it may better serve your needs. However, it takes a lot more work to customize and compile a kernel. Furthermore, when a security issue requires a kernel **patch**, you'll have to repeat the process of customizing and recompiling a kernel.

> **NOTE**
>
> This section serves as a preview of Chapter 10, where you'll examine the costs and benefits of different kinds of kernels. It should give you a better feel for when to use kernels that are already customized for a distribution or when to compile a custom kernel.

> **FYI**
>
> The choice of a **monolithic kernel** or a **modular kernel** is a matter of debate. If you combined all kernel modules into a monolithic kernel, it would load more quickly, without fragmentation. On the other hand, operating-system monolithic kernels may be huge, as they include drivers for every conceivable kind of hardware and lots of additional software. Linux developers generally prefer modular kernels for most systems, with the possible exception of specialty hardware such as cell phones and point-of-sale terminals.

The Basic Linux Kernel Philosophy

The Linux kernel is robust. In other words, the operating system continues to run even when many parts of the Linux kernel aren't working.

One reason the Linux kernel is robust is its structure. It includes a monolithic core and modular components. The monolithic part of the kernel contains those drivers and options essential to the kernel boot process. The modular part of the kernel adds everything else needed for smooth operation, including many drivers that enable communication with installed hardware.

For example, most Linux sound cards are connected with drivers that are loaded with kernel modules if and as needed. If that kernel module fails, it does not affect other parts of the Linux operating system. You may just have to live without sound until you can load or reload a working driver. In contrast, the kernels associated with Microsoft Windows (through XP/2003) are monolithic; the failure of any driver within the Microsoft kernel is more likely to lead to a fatal error in that operating system.

Basic Linux Kernels

Most Linux kernel developers are volunteers. Only a few are affiliated with a specific distribution such as Red Hat or Ubuntu. They follow **open source** principles. They are open about their development work. They share their progress online. Through the **Linux Kernel Organization** at *http://kernel.org*, they release production and developmental kernels. Their stock production kernels are used for the core of every Linux distribution.

If you want to create a custom kernel, one place to start is the stock Linux kernel. You can customize that kernel using some of the changes made by the developers of a Linux distribution, without the need to appeal to a wide audience.

When security issues appear, Linux developers release changes to the kernel in the form of a patch. You can download that patch, apply it to the existing **source code**, compile the combined source code, and then update your system.

While the developers behind various Linux distributions use the same patches, they test their changes on all their target systems. There's often a lag between the release of a security patch and the release of an updated kernel customized for a distribution. On the other hand, developers compile the resulting kernel for you. All you need to do is install it on your system.

Distribution-Specific Linux Kernels

For most users, it's best to stick with the **binary kernel** released for a Linux distribution. That distribution-specific kernel has been compiled and built with the intended hardware in mind, and in many cases has been labeled as such. For example, the standard kernel for Ubuntu's Server Edition has a file name with a `-server` extension, such as `vmlinuz-2.6.31-14-server`. Even if the kernel is not so labeled, it may be optimized for certain purposes—for example, high availability or database support.

When security issues appear with a Linux kernel, most popular Linux distributions release updates fairly quickly. They've done the work to compile the kernel for you. Their compiled kernel packages will even automatically update standard Linux boot loaders. All you need to do is download and install the updated kernel.

Custom Linux Kernels

If you choose to customize a Linux kernel, you'll need to get into its nuts and bolts. In Chapter 10, you'll discover that the Linux kernel is quite customizable. A recent check of a standard Red Hat Enterprise Linux kernel includes about 3,000 different kernel options. If you want to preview some of these options, look for a `config-*` file in the `/boot` directory of a Linux system. It's a text file. These options are divided in a number of categories. One standard customization menu with some of these categories is shown in Figure 2-1.

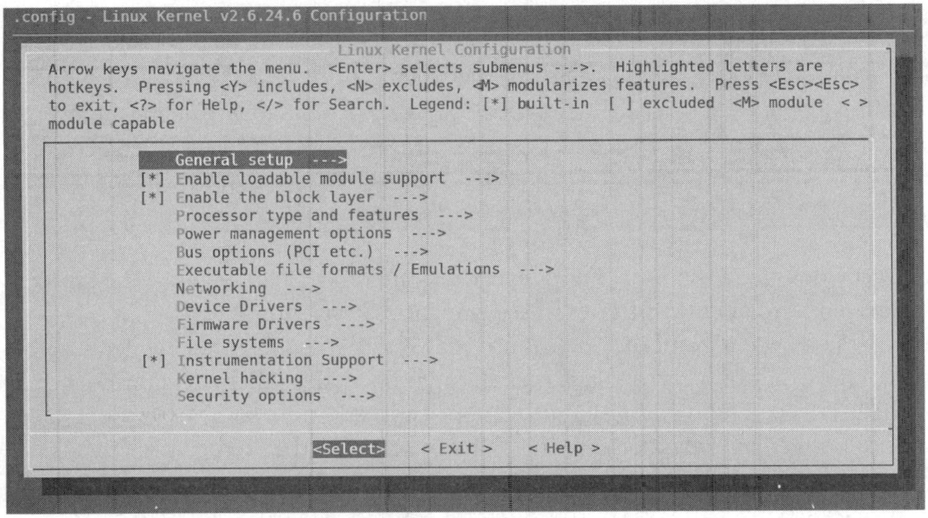

2

Basic Components of Linux Security

FIGURE 2-1

A Linux kernel configuration menu.

TABLE 2-1 Basic configuration categories for the Linux kernel.

CATEGORY	DESCRIPTION
General setup	Includes a variety of basic kernel settings
Loadable module support	Sets conditions for how modules are loaded for a modular kernel
Block layer	Defines how block devices can be loaded
Processor type and features	Configures support for a variety of processor types and memory levels
Power management options	Defines available power-management features
Bus options	Specifies support for hardware cards
Executable file formats/ emulations	Associated with executable and linkable format binaries
Networking	Includes network drivers, protocols, and more
Device drivers	Support for a wide variety of hardware
Firmware drivers	Supports nonvolatile systems such as the Basic Input/Output System (BIOS) and the Unified Extensible Firmware Interface (UEFI)
Filesystems	Includes various filesystem formats
Instrumentation support	Adds options for performance modules
Kernel hacking	Designed for kernel debugging
Security options	Includes options such as Security Enhanced Linux (SELinux) and Application Armor (AppArmor)
Cryptographic API	Defines supported encryption algorithms for application programming interfaces (APIs)
Virtualization	Adds code for hardware-based virtual machines
Library routines	Includes modules for cyclic redundancy checks

Table 2-1 provides an overview of the categories of options associated with the Linux kernel. As kernel development continues, these categories may change.

Take some time to understand the options associated with the Linux kernel. It's worth the trouble. Even if you never recompile a kernel, that knowledge will help you understand how the kernel can help maintain Linux security. In addition, some of those options can be changed in real time, with the help of options in the /proc/ directory.

If you choose to recompile a kernel, you'll need to download the source code. In general, it's best to start from one of two different source-code trees. You can start with the stock kernel source code released by the developers of the Linux kernel. Alternatively, you can start with the source code released by a distribution. As the source code for all Linux kernels are freely available under open source licenses, the choice is yours.

In Chapter 10, you'll learn how to customize and compile the Linux kernel. Linux administrators who want the most secure kernel will remove or disable many features. If used by a black-hat hacker, some of these features may lead to security risks. But take care. Test any changes that you make. With thousands of options, some changes could make that kernel unusable.

> ⚠ **WARNING**
>
> The programming libraries required to compile the Linux kernel can present security risks. If a black-hat hacker breaks into that system, that person can run those compilers to build more dangerous malware. If you choose to compile a custom kernel, you need to either compile that kernel on a system isolated for that purpose or remember to uninstall those libraries.

Linux Kernel Security Options

Linux kernel security options range far and wide. Direct options may enable features such as AppArmor, SELinux, and **iptables**-based firewalls. Indirect options may make it easier for malicious users to break into your systems. Three basic kernel security options, as listed in the Linux Security HOWTO, include the following:

- `CONFIG_FIREWALL` for network firewalls
- `CONFIG_IP_MASQUERADE` for IP address masquerading to help protect systems on a LAN
- `IP_FORWARDING` to set up a system as a gateway

These are just a few of the options described in Chapter 10.

Security in the Boot Process

In Chapter 3, you'll read about security challenges associated with the boot process, starting with the security in the server room. These challenges include the ways a malicious user can boot a fully functional version of Linux on your servers from a **live CD**—with full root administrative access. Even without a live CD, some distributions allow a user to boot Linux with full administrative privileges—without a password.

For the purposes of this chapter, the boot process ends once the Linux kernel is loaded on the system. As you'll see in the next major section, the startup process continues by loading preconfigured services.

Physical Security

Physical security goes beyond locks in the server room. It also involves security for CD/DVD drives and universal serial bus (USB) ports. While a live CD may in some cases be an excellent way to recover from problems on a server or workstation, access to such systems should be limited. Live CDs provide password-free access to the administrative account. Therefore, a malicious user with a live CD may be able to do anything that an administrator can do to your system.

The Threat of the Live CD

It's not enough to set up secure usernames and passwords on your systems. A black-hat hacker with physical access may be able to boot a live CD Linux distribution such as **Knoppix**, Ubuntu, or even **CentOS** directly on your servers. It doesn't matter if the Linux distribution on the live CD differs from that on the hard drive. It also doesn't matter if the Linux kernel on the live CD has a different version number. Many live CDs even provide a graphical user interface (GUI), making it relatively easy for less-experienced black-hat hackers to break into your system.

All that's needed is boot access from a CD/DVD drive or a USB port. Once booted, a live CD provides password-free administrative access to any system. At that point, it's easy to access hard drives on the local system.

Boot Process Security

Anyone with physical access to your systems may be able to access boot menus, such as those available through a BIOS or a UEFI menu. Such menus should be password-protected. Network access to the UEFI menu should be disabled. If possible, these menus should be used to exclude all options but the hard drive with the operating system from the boot process.

Boot process security extends to the boot menu for the operating system. Linux includes two options for boot loaders: the **Grand Unified Bootloader (GRUB)** and the **Linux Loader (LILO)**. Both boot loaders include their own boot menus. Both boot menus can be used to start other operating systems, such as other versions of Linux or even Microsoft Windows. Both boot loaders also include a number of security risks.

In fact, unless password protected, both boot loaders can be used to boot a system into single-user mode, with full administrative privileges. On most Linux distributions, an administrative password isn't required to access this mode.

Other boot loaders can be installed on most systems, including Microsoft options such as NTLDR and bootmgr, as well as third-party options such as Bootit and Partition Magic. Each of these boot loaders can be used to start a Linux operating system. Because this is a book on securing Linux platforms and applications, Chapter 3 will focus on securing the Linux options.

More Boot Process Issues

The Transmission Control Protocol/Internet Protocol (TCP/IP) suite includes default port numbers for hundreds of services, such as 22 for SSH and 23 for Telnet. Some security professionals prefer to use nonstandard port numbers for key services. That obscurity can slow the efforts of black-hat hackers who want to break into a system.

Some services require network access during the boot process. For example, if you keep servers synchronized with the **Network Time Protocol (NTP)**, those servers access external NTP servers during the boot process. The standard NTP port is 123. If you want to block that port after the boot process is complete, you need to make sure the associated firewall rule isn't run until after the NTP client is synchronized.

Virtual Physical Security

Virtual machines add another dimension to the challenges of physical security. Standard Linux user and group options add security to virtual machines. However, anyone who gains access to a virtual machine can more easily change virtual physical components. For example, a black-hat hacker who adds a live CD file to a virtual CD drive would arouse less suspicion than a black-hat hacker who unlocks a CD/DVD drive on an actual physical system.

> **NOTE**
>
> It's easier to modify virtual physical hardware. Although it takes some time to lock out or remove CD/DVD drives from physical systems, it's relatively easy to remove a CD/DVD drive from a virtual system. Although it is easier to install Linux from a CD/DVD drive, there is little need for that drive after installation is complete.

Linux Security Issues Beyond the Basic Operating System

While most Linux distributions include a substantial number of applications and services, the essence of the Linux operating system is the kernel. Many security risks exist in applications and services beyond the kernel, however.

One of the main advantages of Linux is its structure as a multi-user operating system. When properly configured, Linux services run on nonprivileged accounts. If a black-hat hacker breaks into one service, that user may gain access to the corresponding nonprivileged account. However, that user won't have access to other accounts.

A GUI is also beyond the basic Linux operating system. If included, a GUI introduces a whole raft of additional security risks, discussed shortly.

Service Process Security

For the purposes of this chapter, the boot process ends when the Linux kernel is loaded. The startup process then begins automatically, loading and starting a series of services configured in the **default runlevel**. A **runlevel** defines the services to be run. The default runlevel defines the services to be run after a system is booted up. You'll read about runlevel and service management in Chapter 6.

TABLE 2-2 Typical default active services.

SERVICE	DESCRIPTION
cups	Common UNIX Printing System (CUPS) service
isdn	Integrated Services Digital Network (ISDN) services
microcode_ctl	Microcode utility for Intel 32-bit processors
ntpd	Network Time Protocol (NTP) daemon
pcscd	PC smart card daemon
portmap	Remote procedure call (RPC) port-number mapper
sshd	Secure Shell (SSH) service
syslog	System log message service
xientd	The extended internet super server

Red Hat Enterprise Linux includes a number of services that are active by default. Most users do not need many of these services. Table 2-2 lists services that were active after installation of a fairly minimal 64-bit server system. The services in Table 2-2 are listed in lowercase because that's how they appear in the /etc/init.d/ directory.

If any service is not maintained, related security flaws may not get fixed. And yes, black-hat hackers monitor security bulletins. If they learn about a security problem before you do, they'll have the advantage. If you aren't paying attention to a security issue, a black-hat hacker can use information from security bulletins to help break into your system. In Chapter 6, you'll learn about the risks associated with these services, along with how to keep these services to a minimum. This process can help you create bastion hosts where you need them most.

The extended internet super server may be especially troublesome. First, for the editors in the audience, the term "internet" is lowercase because it refers only to a group of interconnected networks, not the Internet. Second, it governs a number of network services configured in separate files in the /etc/xinetd.d/ directory.

> **NOTE**
>
> The "very secure FTP server" is a GPL version 2-licensed **File Transfer Protocol (FTP)** server for UNIX and Linux. You'll learn about it in depth in Chapter 9.

Other services that may be active on default Linux installations include the Apache Web server, the Samba file server, the Network File System service, the **sendmail** e-mail service, and the very secure FTP server. Because security issues on some of these services are relatively common, administrators should disable these services if they're not being used.

Security Issues with the GUI

Applications that require a GUI are common security risks. Although malware written for Windows GUI applications may not affect Linux GUI applications, similar risks do apply. Furthermore, the GUI itself is a security risk. On Linux, the GUI is a networkable client-server system. Users can log into a GUI remotely. Users can also run GUI clients over a network. In fact, administrators can configure a system to display GUI clients on a remote terminal. So malware on one Linux GUI application can be spread across a network to other GUI systems.

For these reasons, Linux security experts encourage administrators to avoid installing the GUI unless absolutely necessary. In the Linux world, a system without a GUI is no handicap. Linux administrators are accustomed to configuring services from the command-line interface. As strange as it sounds, you don't even need a GUI to test the proper operation of a number of "graphical" services such as Apache and sendmail.

> **NOTE**
>
> One Linux server access control program, xhost, supports clear-text authentication. Like Telnet, xhost makes it easy for black-hat hackers to read any information sent over that connection, including usernames and passwords. The SSH service can solve both problems, as it supports encrypted logins as well as networking of individual GUI clients.

The User Authentication Databases

There are four major user authentication databases available for Linux. The local Linux authentication database is known as the shadow password suite. The files of the shadow password suite are /etc/passwd, /etc/group, /etc/shadow, and /etc/gshadow. These files include encrypted passwords, user and group accounts, home directories, and login shells. As you'll see in Chapter 4, these files also include special users configured for services and administrators.

The other three user authentication databases are designed as a central authentication database for multiple systems on a network. When properly configured, a user can log into any connected workstation. That workstation checks login credentials from that central database. Two of these databases are native to Linux: the Network Information Service (NIS) and the Lightweight Directory Access Protocol (LDAP). With the help of the **Winbind** service, Linux can also serve as the domain controller repository for some authentication databases commonly used on Microsoft-based networks.

> **NOTE**
>
> Incidentally, you can configure Windows NT–style authentication databases on Linux servers. When Samba version 4 is released—expected sometime in 2010—you'll be able to configure Linux as a domain controller for Microsoft networks instead of a Windows 2003/2008 server.

In all these cases, the user and the group get both a user ID and a group ID number. With those ID numbers, each user (and group) can own files on the local Linux system. Each networked user can be configured as a member of other special groups with administrative privileges, just like any other Linux user.

The advantage of NIS is that it can start with the files of the shadow password suite. NIS has two disadvantages, however: It is relatively insecure and does not support authentication of Microsoft users or groups. In contrast, while LDAP is a more complex authentication scheme, it does support authentication of both Linux/UNIX and Microsoft users and groups.

In a Linux authentication database, a user is typically configured as a member of a group with the same name. For example, if a Linux system has a user named mike, that user is a member of a group named mike. That Linux user mike may be a member of other groups. For example, one group may have print-administration privileges; another group may have access to telephone modems.

To help manage this variety of authentication databases, Linux uses the /etc/nsswitch.conf file, also known as the name service switch file. That file lists databases associated with a number of different configuration files in the /etc/ directory, in some specific order. That order determines where the local system looks first to verify a username and password. Red Hat includes a descriptive configuration tool for all these databases and more, shown in Figure 2-2.

Linux supplements authentication databases with a system known as **pluggable authentication modules (PAM)**. The rules associated with PAM files in the /etc/pam.d/ directory can further specify local access limits for different administrative tools and commands.

Some Linux appliances, such as home routers, include default usernames and password. It is important to configure such appliances with nondefault usernames and strong passwords. One recently discovered botnet, named for Chuck Norris, can infect and take over such Linux appliances if their administrators retain standard or weak usernames and passwords. The botnet was discovered by Masaryk University researchers in the Czech Republic with the help of a **honeypot**, which tempts black-hat hackers with seemingly valuable data.

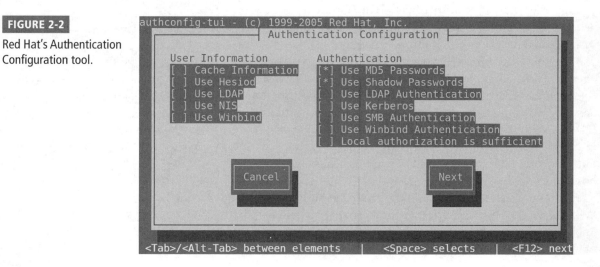

FIGURE 2-2

Red Hat's Authentication Configuration tool.

So Many Access Controls

In Linux, there are several different systems known as access controls. Even if you've studied them in other Linux books, it may be difficult to keep them straight. So here's a short primer of various access controls in Linux.

Discretionary access controls are read, write, and execute permissions that can be given to users and groups. Linux includes two types of discretionary access controls: standard octal read, write, and execute permissions; and **access control lists (ACLs)**.

ACLs provide a second layer of discretionary access control. Specifically, they support read, write, and execute permissions that may supersede other discretionary access controls. But ACLs require additional configuration, as described in Chapter 5.

Mandatory access controls are systems like SELinux and AppArmor. You'll have to choose one or the other, as these systems are not compatible. While SELinux is the default for Red Hat distributions, AppArmor is the default for many other Linux distributions, including Ubuntu and SUSE.

When used together, discretionary and mandatory access controls provide multiple layers of protection. These controls are usually also coupled with the firewall protection associated with the `iptables` command. Most `iptables` rules also control access to systems and protocols, making them another layer of access control.

File Ownership, Permissions, and Access Controls

Everything on Linux is represented by a file. A directory is a special kind of file, which should be executable for users who are allowed to list files on that directory. Other special kinds of files include devices, commonly used to represent and communicate with certain hardware components, character devices such as sound cards, block devices such as drives and partitions, and soft links, which can connect files across different partitions or volumes.

Every file and directory on a Linux system is owned by a specific user and group. With discretionary access controls, the user owner can set different read, write, and executable permissions for the user owner, the group owner, and all other users.

While a lot can be done with read, write, and execute permissions for a file, such permissions may not provide enough control. For an additional layer of permissions, Linux can work with access control lists. To make that happen, the target Linux filesystem(s) must be configured and mounted with the access control list option. Once mounted, you can configure access control masks that supersede regular file permissions. For more details on access control lists and standard file permissions, see Chapter 5.

Current Linux distributions may include one or two levels of administrative access control. The standard configuration file for custom administrative permissions is /etc/sudoers. Later distributions support fine-grained access to hardware components through the **PolicyKit**.

Firewalls and Mandatory Access Controls

Firewalls and mandatory access controls may seem to be unrelated. However, it's common to use them together in a layered defense for Linux systems. The layers go deeper, however. Several layers of firewalls are available on modern Linux systems. Since the advent of kernel version 2.6, the foundation of the Linux firewall has been the iptables command. Other firewalls are available for services that depend on the Transmission Control Protocol (TCP) Wrappers libraries, such as libwrap.so.0.

It's common practice on Linux to supplement these firewalls with mandatory access control systems such as SELinux and AppArmor. SELinux has received quite a bit of acclaim because it was developed by—and still receives code contributions from—the U.S. National Security Agency (NSA). But the configuration of SELinux is somewhat challenging.

Because firewalls and mandatory access controls can be configured differently on every system, you can set up different levels of protection in a trusted network and in areas such as a demilitarized zone (DMZ) to serve certain kinds of traffic from the general Internet.

Firewall Support Options

Of course, you can create a firewall at the command-line interface with the iptables command. But that command can be tricky. It can block access by port, by IP address, by protocol type, and more.

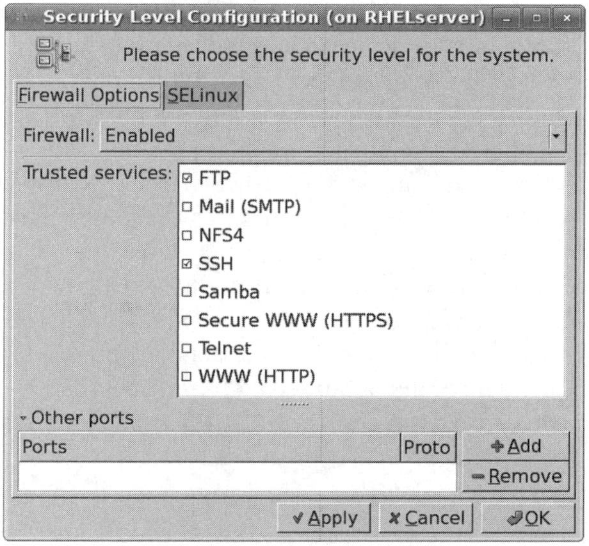

FIGURE 2-3

The Security Level Configuration tool for firewalls.

Custom firewalls can include dozens of `iptables` commands. Some Linux distributions make it easier to configure a firewall with tools like the `ufw` Firewall Configuration tool found on Ubuntu systems and the Security Level Configuration tool found on Red Hat systems. Figure 2-3 illustrates some of the capabilities of the Security Level Configuration tool.

You can configure a second layer of firewalls for services that use TCP Wrappers libraries. Specifically, if you use a service that depends on the library known as `libwrap`, you can protect that service with directives in the `/etc/hosts.allow` and `/etc/hosts.deny` configuration files. It can even block access by user and IP address. For more information on `iptables` and TCP Wrapper firewalls, see Chapter 7.

Some services allow you to configure a third layer of firewalls. For example, the Samba service can be configured to limit access to servers to certain users on specific networks. The SSH service can be set to accept connections only on nonstandard TCP/IP ports. The Apache service can limit access to certain users—and prohibit connections from groups of IP addresses. Many of these services can block access by user and IP address. Firewalls for individual services are described in Chapter 9.

You can configure a fourth layer of firewalls for services associated with the `/etc/xinetd.conf` configuration file, also known as the extended internet super server. Those services have configuration files in the `/etc/xinetd.d/` directory. You can control access by host name or IP address. For more on protecting these services, see Chapter 6.

Mandatory Access Control Support

To paraphrase a famous philosopher, networks cannot be protected by firewalls alone. The mandatory access controls associated with SELinux and AppArmor provide another layer of security. When properly configured, these controls can check access to services and commands to make sure they're run only by intended users, in properly labeled directories.

> **TIP**
>
> You can't use both SELinux and AppArmor on the same system.

Proper mandatory access controls make a system more robust. Compromised users, even service users with some level of administrative privileges, can't use other services.

However, the configuration of a mandatory access control system requires discipline. For example, you can't just add a new directory to help organize FTP server files. With a mandatory access control system like SELinux, you must make sure those directories are labeled and configured for their intended purposes.

It's normally best to administer a system from the command-line interface. However, some of these tools are tricky. Some GUI tools can help less-familiar administrators understand more about the service. To that end, Red Hat's SELinux Administration tool, shown in Figure 2-4, is excellent.

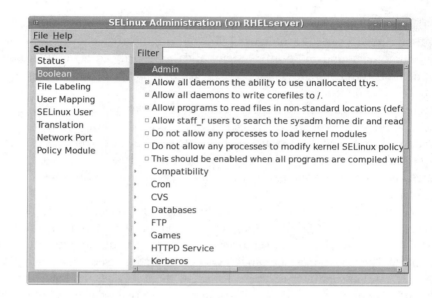

FIGURE 2-4

The SELinux Administration tool.

In a similar fashion, AppArmor includes profiles for specific commands. You can add profiles for additional commands as you learn more about mandatory access control. In contrast, SELinux is an all-or-nothing security tool, with restrictions for just about everything.

Both AppArmor and SELinux include a trial mode, where violations are logged without preventing access. On AppArmor, this is known as complain mode; on SELinux, this is known as permissive mode. The resulting log files can help you better customize either of these mandatory access control systems.

Many administrators complain that SELinux is too difficult to administer, violating the Parkerian hexad concept of utility. On the other hand, you need to add profiles for AppArmor one at a time. In other words, without some additional work, AppArmor's level of protection is somewhat limited. Read more about both options in Chapter 7; the choice is yours.

Networks and Encrypted Communication

In the current security environment, you might be surprised by the number of users who still use clear-text communication protocols. Telnet is still a popular way to log into remote systems. Unencrypted protocols are still frequently used for other functions such as file transfers, e-mails, and backups.

Clear-text communication dates back to the early days of UNIX, which was used primarily at universities where colleagues were more likely to trust each other. As enterprises move from UNIX to Linux, a few older users may retain their preference for applications that use clear-text networking. Given Linux's status as a clone of UNIX, the easy availability of clear text and unencrypted services has not discouraged such users.

In Chapters 8 and 9, you'll learn about insecure protocols still in common use and what you can do about them.

With the ready availability of secure connection protocols, there is no reason to use clear-text connection tools such as Telnet. With the `ssh` command, you can connect to remote systems with the SSH server. The communication—and just as important, the password—are encrypted by default. You can even set up passphrases using private and public keys of 1,024 bits (or more). Passphrases are more secure than passwords. Given the private- and public-key combination, the passphrase is never transmitted over the network.

> **NOTE**
>
> Telnet is still a useful tool. It can help you verify that a service is accessible. You can use the `telnet` command both locally and over a network to verify the availability of a service over any TCP/IP port. You'll see how that works in Chapter 13.

SSH can be used for more than just shell connections. It can be used to securely transmit backups and more. It can even used to connect securely to a remote GUI client. While it's possible to tunnel many different connections over SSH, standard SSH packages include an FTP client for encrypted connections.

The Latest Linux Security Updates

For many regular users, it's good enough to download and install updates provided by a distribution when they become available. But Linux is used by a range of users, from home hobbyists to engineers and scientists who know a lot about Linux, to administrators like you, and more. The response of each of these groups to a security update may vary. You'll read about update options in detail in Chapter 11.

The developers behind most Linux distributions do an excellent job with security updates. They monitor security issues in real time. They monitor the work of the open source community as security issues are addressed.

Linux Security Updates for Regular Users

Generally, the package updates released for a distribution have been tested with standard configurations. Linux users who don't have a lot of time to maintain their systems may choose to set up automatic updates. That works if the user trusts the company and the open source community behind a distribution. Alternatively, you can read every security bulletin to see if and how the problem affects the systems on your networks.

In general, it's not too difficult to back out of a security update. In the worst case, configuration files can be saved. Updates can be uninstalled. Older versions of updated packages can be installed again.

Linux distributions are designed to retain at least one older kernel when a new kernel is installed. So, if a new kernel makes system unbootable, a user can still boot a system into the older kernel.

Linux Security Updates for Home Hobbyists

Some people think of Linux users as tinkerers, people who like to experiment with their computers. Home hobbyists like to work with the latest in hardware. Some hardware manufacturers develop drivers for Microsoft operating systems first. Even then, not all hardware manufacturers release their drivers under an open source license. Linux developers frequently have to compile their own code to work with the latest hardware. The first versions of compiled code may be tied to a specific kernel release.

Some specialty software may also be tied to a specific version of a kernel. Examples include some VMware and Virtualbox virtual machine systems. If you install a new kernel, you'll need to reinstall and/or recompile the code for that software. If you install a kernel security update, you're installing a different kernel release. That may mean that you have to recompile the code associated with certain drivers or software. That may be a lot of work. So even for kernel security updates, the home hobbyist may want to read the notes associated with the new kernel. If, for example, the security update fixes problems associated with packet forwarding, a home hobbyist does not need to install that new kernel on a regular workstation.

Linux Security Updates for Power Users

Users who run Linux at home are more likely to be happy to run Linux in the enterprise. However, these users may want to install software that requires additional work to compile. Such software is often tied to a specific version of a kernel. An administrator who pushes the installation of a different kernel on that workstation may cause additional work for that power user. That power user may be unhappy.

It may be best to give power users as little administrative control as possible. In other words, you may want to keep power users from installing special software or kernel-version-specific hardware drivers. Otherwise, the power user may blame you for the decision to install security updates, even when the issue is severe. Power users may believe they can defend their systems better than you can.

Placing limitations on administrative control—at least for power-user workstations— is not always possible. Developers need ready access to administrative tools such as compilers. Because black-hat hackers may use these tools, such workstations should be more carefully isolated from the network.

Security Updates for Linux Administrators

As a Linux security professional, you read all security bulletins related to software on your systems. You consider the effects of updates before deciding whether they should be installed.

If you determine that the security bulletin does not apply to the systems on your network, don't install that update. Unless some changes are made, that update will still be there. Depending on several factors, the updated software may be in a distribution-specific repository or a download from a public server maintained by the developers of the software in question. For more information, see Chapter 11.

To deviate from updates provided for a distribution, you can create a local update repository, loaded with packages customized for local systems. You then configure the systems on the local network to take their updates from that local repository. Yes, that may involve some extra additional work, but a local update repository can also save bandwidth on a network's connection to the Internet.

In other words, every Linux workstation and server normally gets its updates from remote repositories somewhere on the Internet. All packages downloaded for a specific distribution are the same. Linux workstations may require periodic updates of huge packages, such as for the OpenOffice.org suite. If you create a local update repository, these packages are downloaded from the Internet only once. The updates can then be sent over the local network to each system.

Linux Security Update Administration

If you administer just a few Linux systems, you can manage their updates directly. As the administrator, you may be able to administer those systems with a tool such as SSH. You can then run needed update commands on those systems.

If you administer a substantial number of Linux systems, consider the centralized management tools available for several Linux distributions. Tools such as the Red Hat Network, Canonical's Landscape, and Novell's Zenworks support the administration of groups of computers from a centralized interface. While these tools require subscription fees, they do save time.

With these tools, you can set up a single command or a script to be run on a group of computers. For example, you might set up different update commands for servers, engineering workstations, and data-entry systems.

Continuity and Resiliency with Virtualization

Virtualization makes it easy to start with a very secure baseline system. Because virtual-machine hard disks reside on only a few very large files, it takes just a few commands to create new virtual machines. In other words, you can start with an ultra-secure bastion system and add a single service, blocking packets to all unused ports, and securing every other account and directory with appropriate mandatory access controls.

Because virtualization is a fact of life in the enterprise (and even on smaller networks), this book also examines the impact of virtual machines on security. It looks at how you can use virtual machines to your advantage. Finally, it examines how you can deal with the resulting proliferation of virtual systems. A virtual machine that is forgotten is not updated. And a system that is not updated is an open invitation to an black-hat hacker to break into your system. If that system remains forgotten, it can serve as a foothold— a way for that black-hat hacker to break into more important parts of your network.

While virtualization has roots in the time sharing found on mainframe systems, it has taken a number of new turns for modern computers. To that end, this book classifies virtualization in five different categories:

- **Applications**—While a number of companies are developing virtual machines that encapsulate single applications, Linux already has an application-level virtualization tool known as Wine Is Not an Emulator (WINE).
- **Platform-level virtual machines**—The first virtual machines were applications installed in operating systems. Examples of virtual machines installed as applications include VMware Player, VMware Workstation, Virtualbox (open source edition), and Parallels desktop.
- **Paravirtualization**—A software interface for virtual machines with limited resources. Paravirtualized virtual machines can be configured on older CPUs. Paravirtualization is probably the model closest to that offered by older mainframe systems.
- **Hardware-assisted virtualization**—A hardware interface where a virtual machine has access to specialized CPUs.
- **Bare metal virtualization**—A few specialized systems can be installed directly on servers. For example, VMware's ESX and Citrix's XenServer products are installed directly on a server, providing a kernel customized for direct installation of virtual machines. Bare metal virtualization works on a limited number of specialized servers.

To confirm that a system can handle hardware virtualization, examine the `/proc/cpuinfo` file. If it is an Intel CPU, it should include the `vmx` flag. If it is a CPU from Advanced Micro Devices (AMD), it should include the `svm` flag.

Variations Between Distributions

One of the hallmarks of open source software is diversity. For example, you can select from at least four different Simple Mail Transfer Protocol (SMTP) servers to manage e-mail on a network. While some distributions focus on system administration, others focus on consumer applications such as multimedia. There are even live CD Linux distributions with security tools. You'll read about some of them in Chapter 13.

Despite the diversity in standard services, you can generally install (or remove) the software, services, and applications of your choice on any Linux system. For example, while Ubuntu developers include **Postfix** as the default SMTP server, you can install other SMTP servers, including sendmail, **Exim**, and **Qmail**, directly from Ubuntu repositories.

A Basic Comparison: Red Hat and Ubuntu

This book focuses on two Linux distributions: Red Hat Enterprise Linux and Ubuntu Server Edition. The developers behind these distributions have made different choices. Although the Red Hat and Ubuntu distributions occupy a large share of the Linux marketplace, there may be another distribution that better fits your needs. Understanding the differences between these distributions can help you make a better choice.

The biggest difference may be the package-management system. Not surprisingly, Red Hat uses the Red Hat Package Manager to build packages from source code and install them on the Red Hat distribution. Because Ubuntu built its distribution from Debian Linux, it uses the Debian Package Manager to build and install its packages.

There are also similarities between these distributions. For example, Red Hat and Canonical (Ubuntu) both release distributions with long-term support. Red Hat supports its Enterprise Linux releases for seven years. Although Red Hat has declared that it would release its Enterprise Linux distribution every 18 to 24 months, it has now been more than three years since the release of Red Hat Enterprise Linux 5. Because of the delay, Red Hat has extended support for this release beyond seven years.

Ubuntu releases distributions every six months, and releases more robust distributions every two years. These releases are noted as long-term support (LTS) releases. The server edition of every Ubuntu LTS release is supported for five years.

Along with long-term support, Red Hat and Canonical have made a number of other similar decisions. Both companies offer subscriptions to a Web-based support tool that allows authorized users to administer groups of Linux systems remotely.

Both Red Hat and Canonical have made similar choices for some default services. For example, both use Apache as the default Web server, the **very secure File Transfer Protocol daemon (vsftpd)** service as the default FTP server, and the **Common UNIX Printing System (CUPS)** as the default print server. Incidentally, both Red Hat and Canonical use the GNU Network Object Model Environment (GNOME) as the default graphical desktop.

There are differences that go beyond the package-management system, however. For example, Ubuntu includes a minimal installation option with its server release, well suited for bastions on virtual machines. That installation includes a kernel optimized to work as part of a virtual guest.

Red Hat and Ubuntu have also made different choices in terms of default applications. Of course, you can override these with the applications of your choice. In many cases, Red Hat and Ubuntu also support these alternatives.

Sometimes, Red Hat and Ubuntu learn from each other. Given their releases under open source licenses, they can take the source code from a competitive distribution and use it themselves. Ubuntu uses a number of GUI administrative tools originally built for Red Hat. Red Hat is in transition from **Xen** to the **Kernel-based Virtual Machine (KVM)** as its native virtualization platform, already in use on Ubuntu systems.

More Diversity in Services

Linux includes a diverse range of services. If a security issue arises with one service, it's normally best to install the update or patch to address the security issue. Sometimes, however, that update might cause more severe problems.

In that case, you may want to consider a different service. Table 2-3 lists a number of alternatives for different services. It is not by any means a complete list. However, it does describe alternatives if one service option has a fatal security flaw. It also gives you an idea of how many services could be installed on a single server.

Not all of these services are released under open source licenses. For example, Sendmail, in upper case, is a commercial release; sendmail, in lower case, is an open source release.

TABLE 2-3   Alternatives for different services.

FUNCTION	SERVICE OPTIONS
Domain Name System (DNS)	**Berkeley Internet Name Domain (BIND), Daniel J. Bernstein's DNS (djbdns)**
FTP	Professional FTP Daemon (ProFTPD), Troll FTP, vsFTP, **Trivial FTP**
Graphical desktop environment	GNOME, K Desktop Environment (KDE), Xfce, Lightweight X11 Desktop Environment (LXDE)
Graphical user interface	X.org, **XFree86**
Graphical login manager	**GNOME Display Manager (GDM), KDE Display Manager (KDM), X Display Manager (XDM)**
Incoming mail services	**Cyrus, Dovecot**
Printing	CUPS, System V, **Line Printer next generation (LPRng)**
Remote connections	Secure Shell (SSH), Remote Shell (RSH), Telnet, **Kerberos Telnet**
SMTP mail services	Postfix, sendmail, **Sendmail**, Exim, Qmail
Structured Query Language databases	**MySQL, PostgreSQL**, proprietary options from Sybase, Oracle
Web server	Apache, Boa, Caudium, lighthttpd, Roxen, Sun Java, Zeus

CHAPTER SUMMARY

Linux security starts with the kernel. The modularity of the Linux kernel means that it is more robust. Many modular options affect security. To that end, you need to choose whether to accept the kernel as customized for your distribution or whether to customize and compile the kernel yourself. Linux security continues with the boot process. Good security prevents unauthorized users from booting from a live CD and selecting administrative options from the GRUB or LILO boot loaders. Beyond the basic operating system, you should keep active services to a minimum. If possible, don't install the GUI.

Linux security is enhanced by local and network authentication databases. File ownership and permissions start with discretionary access controls, enhanced by access control lists. Administrative permissions can be configured in the `/etc/sudoers` file and through the PolicyKit. Firewalls start with the `iptables` net filter command. Firewalls can be enhanced on TCP Wrapper services, configured through extended internet super server services, and through options on many other services. Mandatory access control systems such as SELinux and AppArmor add another layer of control, protecting your system even if there is a security breach. With the availability of SSH, there is no reason to use clear-text protocols such as Telnet.

With respect to security, you may need to pick and choose whether to download a security update. Some security updates may not apply to all configurations. Chapter 11 discusses various factors with respect to security. Virtualization adds another dimension to security. It makes it more cost effective to set up bastion hosts. Finally, if you understand the differences between Linux distributions, you can make better decisions when it comes to choosing security options for the network.

KEY CONCEPTS AND TERMS

iptables
portmap
sshd
syslog
Access control lists (ACLs)
Binary kernel
Berkeley Internet Name
  Domain (BIND)
CentOS
Common UNIX Printing
  System (CUPS)
Cyrus
Default runlevel
Discretionary access control
Daniel J Bernstein's DNS (djbdns)
Domain Name System (DNS)
Dovecot
Exim
File Transfer Protocol (FTP)
GNOME Display Manager (GDM)

Grand Unified Bootloader
  (GRUB)
Graphical desktop environment
Graphical login manager
Honeypot
KDE Display Manager (KDM)
Kerberos Telnet
Kernel
Kernel-based Virtual Machine
  (KVM)
Knoppix
Linux distribution
Linux kernel
Linux Kernel Organization
Linux Loader (LILO)
Live CD
Modular kernel
Monolithic kernel
MySQL
Network Time Protocol (NTP)

Open source
Patch
Pluggable authentication
  modules (PAM)
PolicyKit
Postfix
PostgreSQL
Qmail
Runlevel
sendmail
Sendmail
Source code
Trivial File Transfer Protocol
  (TFTP)
very secure File Transfer
  Protocol daemon (vsftpd)
Winbind
X Display Manager (XDM)
XFree86
Xen

CHAPTER 2 ASSESSMENT

1. Which of the following statements best describes the structure of the Linux kernel?

A. A single monolithic kernel

B. A completely modular kernel

C. A modular core with monolithic components

D. A monolithic core with modular components

2. The Web site associated with the Linux Kernel Organization is _____.

3. Which of the following statements is *not* true about a live CD distribution? Assume your system can boot from appropriate locations.

A. It can be booted from a DVD drive.

B. It can be booted from a USB port.

C. It automatically installs that Linux distribution on your system.

D. It provides administrative control of your system without a password.

4. Which of the following is a security risk associated with the LILO boot loader?

A. Changes to LILO can be password protected.

B. It supports password-free access to the administrative account.

C. It allows a user to boot Microsoft Windows.

D. It supports the booting of a monolithic Linux kernel.

5. Which of the following services should *not* be disabled on a bastion host used as an FTP server? Assume that the host is administered remotely, over an encrypted connection.

A. SSH

B. Telnet

C. CUPS

D. iptables

6. Which of the following is *not* a potential security issue with respect to the Linux GUI?

A. The Linux GUI is a client-server system.

B. Linux GUI applications can be networked.

C. Linux GUI applications can be accessed over an SSH connection.

D. Users can log into the Linux GUI remotely.

7. Which of the following authentication tools work locally?

A. NIS

B. PAM

C. LDAP

D. Winbind

8. Which of the following is an example of discretionary access controls?

A. SELinux

B. AppArmor

C. PolicyKit

D. User-defined read, write, and execute permissions

9. Which of the following options is *not* used to block access from certain IP addresses?

A. `iptables`

B. SELinux

C. TCP Wrappers

D. Extended internet super server

10. Which of the following statements best describes the role of mandatory access controls?

A. They protect other services after a security breach in an account.

B. They protect a system from black-hat hacker access through firewalls.

C. They disable clear-text services such as Telnet.

D. They provide specific requirements for access to critical services.

11. Packages associated with SSH include a client for which of the following protocols?

A. Samba

B. FTP

C. Telnet

D. SMTP

12. Under normal circumstances, what happens when a system can't be booted with a newly installed Linux kernel?

A. You need to install the old kernel.

B. The system can't be booted. You need to reinstall that Linux distribution.

C. The system can't be booted. You need to recover the old Linux kernel with the help of a recovery or rescue mode for that distribution.

D. The old kernel is still available through the boot loader.

13. What is the best course of action if you want to take control of those packages that are updated on your distribution?

A. Create your own update repository.

B. Deselect the packages that should not be updated.

C. Change to a different distribution.

D. Use the update repositories from a different distribution.

14. Which of the following is *not* a standard open source option for SMTP e-mail services?

A. sendmail

B. Postfix

C. Dovecot

D. Exim

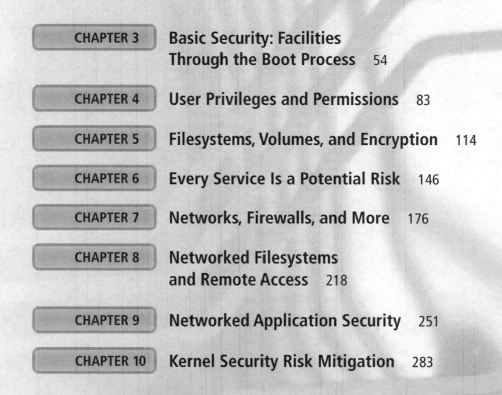

PART TWO

Layered Security and Linux

Basic Security: Facilities Through the Boot Process

ASIC ELEMENTS OF COMPUTER SECURITY begin in the server room. What you do there defines the additional steps required to secure servers, workstations, and more. Security is enhanced with developments in Trusted Computing Modules on motherboards. Such modules are compatible with open source principles. Physical security issues take another dimension on virtual machines.

Security issues continue with the boot process, as a black-hat hacker can use poorly configured boot systems and boot loaders to gain administrative access to your systems. Security issues continue with the kernel, as the developers behind Linux distributions include settings for a wide audience. Obscurity can help, as it can increase the challenges to a black-hat hacker. Properly configured, obscurity does not have to limit access to authorized users. To help you make sure everything is covered, ISECOM includes the five process controls of nonrepudiation, confidentiality, privacy, integrity, and alarm as a guide.

Chapter 3 Topics

This chapter covers the following topics and concepts:

- Why physical security in the server room is essential
- How Trusted Computing works in the context of open source
- What security concepts on virtual hosts and guests are
- How to lock down boot hardware
- How Linux boot loaders can be made more secure
- What risks are associated with a standard supported kernel
- How obscurity can help security
- How the five process controls can protect assets
- What best practices for basic security are

Security in the Server Room and the Physical Server

The starting point for any security infrastructure is physical. If a black-hat hacker can steal a physical system, he can take the time he needs to break locks. With physical access, the black-hat hacker can identify usernames and passwords, gain administrative access, decrypt encrypted drives, and more. Even when a computer is kept secure, it's important to understand the physical risks associated with a computer. Addressing those risks can help you understand why it's important to lock down boot hardware, boot loaders, kernels, and more.

Security can be expensive, however. In addition, the most extensive security measures may be unrealistic in some organizations where people and even customers need access to rooms with servers, workstations, and other network hardware.

Physical and Environmental Security Factors

If possible, it's best to keep servers in secure facilities. Servers contain data critical to the organization. Ideally, secure facilities include locks, with access limited to authorized personnel. **Biometric controls** such as fingerprint readers and retinal scanners provide more security than key cards. Secure facilities generally include closed-circuit cameras in case of a break-in. Redundant sources of power can help keep such security systems running.

The physical environment around a computer is also important. Computers produce heat. Computers have trouble with humidity. Fans and other cooling devices inside computer power systems are frequently not enough. Computers in server rooms frequently need specialized cooling systems. Systems shut down when they get too hot. Systems can short out if water gets into a system. If you don't have a lot of space in a server room or if you have to store servers in a small closet, the environmental challenges may be greater.

A lot of this is expensive. Funds even in the richest corporations are limited. Organizations can afford this kind of security have more to protect. The amount of money your organization should spend on security depends in part on the value of data on your systems.

Security and Form Factors

To understand a server's security requirements, you need a basic understanding of available form factors. For traditional servers, three form factors are most common:

- **Tower**—The tower is the typical server form factor. They appear superficially similar to the traditional desktop system. Tower servers generally include space and slots for expansion and additional features.
- **Blade**—Relative to a tower, the blade includes a physically stripped-down physical form. Its design minimizes the use of space, power supplies, and so on. Some blade servers may be configured without individual power supplies.
- **Rack**—As suggested by its name, rack servers are normally mounted in racks. In addition, rack servers often have their own power supplies.

Each of these options may use common storage systems, connected with high-speed external interfaces such as FireWire, Internet Small Computer System Interface (iSCSI), Fibre Channel, and more.

Groups of blade and rack servers are frequently stored in racks. Both types of servers are thin and designed to be stored in small spaces. They can be secured in racks, consolidating data storage in a fairly small area. Such servers are often screwed into place, making it more difficult for a black-hat hacker to remove a system in order to crack it in private. However, blade and rack servers can be expensive, and are unfamiliar to many.

Tower servers may be less secure. Once removed from cables, tower servers can be carried to other rooms. Tower servers are designed for easy access and maintenance. Unless tower server cases are locked, however, that easy access means a black-hat hacker can disconnect and remove a hard drive from that server in a matter of seconds.

In part to enhance security, many servers don't have CD/DVD or floppy drives and have fewer universal serial bus (USB) ports. That reduces the risks associated with booting other media such as live CDs. Many Linux distributions can be installed over a network, using the **Pre-boot eXecution Environment (PXE)** to connect to a remote installation server. Many (if not most) systems include a PXE-enabled network card. CD/DVD drives aren't even necessary to install the operating system.

Physical Access Ports

Some of the physical access ports related to the boot process are discussed later in this chapter. You need to be concerned about more than the boot process, however. Other physical access ports matter for security. Serial ports on servers are designed for administrative access. A black-hat hacker with a roll-up USB keyboard and access to a monitor port can send commands directly to that system.

Security Beyond the Server

Open, insecure, physically accessible ports on a hub, switch, or router are an open invitation to a black-hat hacker to listen in on a network. With standard Ethernet networks, all systems listen to all messages transmitted on the network. That means a black-hat hacker with a **protocol analyzer** (known colloquially as a sniffer) can listen in and record data transmitted on a network.

Linux includes a number of excellent tools for listening in on network communications. When done ethically, a white-hat hacker can use a tool such as **Wireshark** to make sure users aren't connecting over a network via clear-text services such as Telnet. In contrast, a black-hat hacker can use Wireshark to read the password of someone who has just logged into a different system using Telnet.

Open Source Trusted Platform Modules and Open Trusted Computing

The current version of the **Trusted Platform Module (TPM)** is not open source. It is designed to verify the authenticity of users. With TPM, organizations supposedly can verify your identity in financial and other secure transactions. TPM chips may be installed on connected hardware boards or directly on the motherboard. According to IBM, TPM chips can be used in four areas:

- Password protection
- Software license protection
- Digital rights management (DRM)
- Disk encryption

An industry consortium known as the **Trusted Computing Group (TCG)** established the specifications behind TPM. According to their Web site (*http://www.trustedcomputing group.org*) as of February 2010, TCG standards are defined in eight areas:

- Infrastructure (network)
- Mobile devices
- PC clients
- Servers
- Software stack (to provide standard application programming interfaces to use the TPM)
- Storage (for dedicated storage systems)
- Trusted network connect (for endpoint integrity after a network connection is made)
- Trusted Platform Module (specifications for the TPM architecture)

The TPM specifications apply only to the PC client and server areas. Other areas use different chips, such as the Mobile Trusted Module (MTM) chip for mobile devices.

The success of such provisions is uncertain. For example, some have reported that Apple Computer has installed TPM chips on its Intel-based systems. Nevertheless, the so-called Hackintosh version of the latest Apple OSX operating system is readily available for non-Apple hardware.

Disk encryption is designed to protect data on hard drives, even if they're stolen and separated from the TPM chip on the motherboard. In February 2010, a former U.S. Army security specialist demonstrated how to break the encryption scheme associated with the TPM chip. With that knowledge, a black-hat hacker could decrypt hard disks protected with a TPM algorithm.

As of this writing, Linux disk-encryption systems do not use the TPM chip. For more information on encrypting Linux volumes, see Chapter 5.

A number of open source luminaries have objected to the use of TPM, primarily citing privacy concerns. However, open source security professionals from the Institute for Security and Open Methodologies (ISECOM) have worked to address these objections, primarily through the **Open Trusted Computing (OpenTC)** consortium, sponsored by the European Union.

The Basics of Trusted Computing

Because the TPM chip has caused controversy in the open source community, it's important to understand its principles in some detail. Remember, because it is endorsed by ISECOM, TPM is now acceptable to many open source professionals. Trusted computing, as defined in *Hacking Linux Exposed*, relies on three elements:

- Measurements
- Roots of trust
- Chain of trust

> **NOTE**
>
> Don't confuse hash functions such as SHA-1 and SHA-3 with checksums. A **hash function** is a procedure or function that converts a large amount of data to a single (long) number. In contrast, a checksum is that number.

Measurements

In Trusted Computing, a measurement is an integrity check. It's a means to reliably identify a piece of software. As of this writing, it depends on a **Secure Hash Algorithm 1 (SHA-1)** hash that configures a 160-bit hash identifier for a program. Because of known weaknesses in that algorithm, a **Secure Hash Algorithm 3 (SHA-3)** hash is under development, with a hoped-for release date of 2012. Spurring the development of SHA-3 is a competition sponsored by the National Institute of Standards and Technology (NIST). The NIST Web site is at *http://www.nist.gov*.

Roots of Trust

A root of trust is based on a small program, something that can be easily analyzed. To that end, the TCG defines three roots of trust:

- The **Root Trust for Measurement (RTM)** is used to verify the integrity of a program. The core RTM often resides in the first boot program, the Basic Input/Output System (BIOS), or the Unified Extensible Firmware Interface (UEFI).

- The **Root Trust for Storage (RTS)** uses an endorsement key created by the TPM chip to store data that is then implicitly trusted by the operating system.

- The **Root Trust for Reporting (RTR)** reports on the integrity of a software component, using the aforementioned SHA-1 keys.

When the roots of trust are verified, TPM can proceed.

Chain of Trust

The **chain of trust** is associated with a sequence of programs. One example is the boot process for a Linux system. On a server, it would verify the UEFI, any secondary read-only memory (ROM) peripheral software, the master boot record (MBR) on the target hard drive, the boot loader, and the operating-system loader for the kernel.

On a Linux system, a TPM-compatible boot loader is derived from the Linux Grand Unified Bootloader (GRUB), a program known as **TrustedGRUB**. That boot loader includes two stages. The first stage boots the basic system, and the second stage boots the actual operating system. You'll read about securing GRUB and configuring TrustedGRUB later in this chapter.

Objections to TPM

In the open source community, objections to TPM are crystallized in the position of **Richard Stallman**, president of the **Free Software Foundation (FSF)**. In a letter that dates back to the development of Trusted Computing, entitled "Can You Trust Your Computer," Stallman notes that the TPM chip "is designed to make sure your computer will systematically disobey you," with digital signature keys outside user control. In essence, Stallman believes that Trusted Computing and the TPM chip will allow governments and big businesses a back door to control your computer systems. Despite work done by ISECOM to accommodate the needs of open source in TPM chip specifications, Stallman was holding fast to his position as of January 2010.

FYI

While there is a lot of disdain for Stallman and his politics, he has an influential place in the open source community. The FSF is the organization behind the GNU's Not UNIX (GNU) project, the group of developers who cloned the UNIX commands and libraries that are packaged with the Linux kernel. It is also the organization behind the signature open source license, the General Public License (GPL). In other words, Linux may not have become viable without the work of the FSF. If you encounter objections from open source colleagues to Trusted Computing, be prepared to discuss the work done by ISECOM to make Trusted Computing work with the principles of open source.

NOTE

The Electronic Frontier
Foundation (EFF) is a self-
described "donor-funded
nonprofit" created to
protect the digital rights
of consumers.

TPM in an Open Source World

Despite the objections of some open source advocates, many open
source developers work with industry groups to implement TPM
in Linux. The **Electronic Frontier Foundation (EFF)** has been working
with the TCG but as of this writing has not been able to get its proposal
for an **owner override** into the TPM specification.

On the other hand, you do not have to activate the TPM chip—
and if you do activate the TPM chip, you can clear the TPM ownership.
However, there is no way to take fine-grained control of the use of TPM.
That leads to an all-or-nothing scenario in which the system either has the protection
and privacy issues of the TPM or it doesn't. A reboot is required between changes. Some
documentation suggests that a cold restart is required on some systems. To be effective,
an owner override would have to be selective. The owner could use the TPM chip, say,
in banking transactions, but override it when making a backup of a software CD
(assuming that backup is allowed by the copyright owner).

Stallman's FSF is the group behind GRUB. But because the software has been released
under the GPL, an open source license, developers have altered the GRUB source code
to comply with TCG standards. These versions of GRUB have been released at **SourceForge**,
the self-described "largest open source software development Web site." SourceForge
is at *http://sourceforge.net*.

In addition, open source developers have configured a **TCG Software Stack**, available
as a package known as **trousers**. Xen is an open source virtualization solution
that includes support for TPM on the **virtual host**. It's an open question whether the
OpenTC consortium will be able to protect open source and privacy interests in future
TPM specifications.

NOTE

Most commands in this book require
administrative privileges. The commands
described in this chapter assume you're
in an account with administrative
privileges. Best practices in Linux suggest
that administrators should not log in as
the root user unless absolutely necessary.
For more information on how to run
administrative commands without
logging in as root, see Chapter 4.

As of this writing, among Linux native virtualization
solutions, Xen supports TPM and the Kernel-based
Virtual Machine (KVM) does not. As Red Hat Enterprise
Linux is moving from Xen to KVM, TPM implementation
will be more difficult on Linux systems—at least until
KVM developers implement TPM on their systems.

TPM Packages

Both Red Hat Enterprise Linux and Ubuntu
Server include TPM-related open source packages.
They include **trousers**, the package with the
TCG software stack; and **tpm-tools**, the package
with management tools for TPM hardware.

If you have and choose to use a TPM chip on a Linux system, you'll first need to enable TPM in the UEFI or BIOS menus. Once enabled, the next boot of Linux should create a /dev/tpm0 device file. At that point, you'll be able to install the noted packages. On Red Hat, the service script in the /etc/init.d/ directory is named tcsd; on Ubuntu, the script in that directory is named trousers. For example, to activate TPM software on a Red Hat system, you'd run the following command:

```
# /etc/init.d/tcsd start
```

To make sure TPM support survives a reboot, you also have to make sure the service starts in appropriate runlevels. On a Red Hat system, you can run the following command to make sure tcsd is active in runlevels 2, 3, 4, and 5:

```
# chkconfig tcsd on
```

On an Ubuntu system, the installation of the trousers package activates the service by default in the standard Ubuntu runlevel 2. If you want to deactivate that package, the most secure option is to uninstall it with the apt-get remove trousers command.

Configure TPM on a Linux System

You've confirmed there's a TPM chip on the local system, activated it in the UEFI/BIOS, and installed the trousers and tpm-tools packages. You've rebooted the system and activated the tscd service. At this point, you're ready to take control of the local TPM chip.

If the TPM chip is accessible to the Linux system, you'll see it in the output to the tpm_version command. The output should show a chip version number and more.

Now you're ready to take ownership of the TPM system with the tpm_takeownership command. Be careful. You're prompted for two passwords: the owner password and the **Storage Root Key (SRK)** password. Those passwords can differ. The SRK is an RTS key, used to encrypt keys stored outside the TPM chip.

In some cases, if you make a mistake, you can take ownership again—but the process is a bit intricate. The following are basic steps:

1. Reboot and disable the TPM in the UEFI/BIOS menu.
2. Boot Linux.
3. To make sure TPM is disabled, run the tpm_version command.
   If that leads to an error, you'll know that TPM has been properly disabled.
4. Power down the system. A reboot is not sufficient in this case.
5. Access the UEFI/BIOS menu and re-enable the TPM chip.
6. You should see TPM-related modules in the list of loaded modules.
   For details, run the lsmod | grep tpm command.

Once complete, you can run other tpm_* commands. Table 3-1 describes some of these commands.

TABLE 3-1 Important TPM control commands.

TPM COMMAND	DESCRIPTION
tpm_clear	Returns TPM data to the original un-owned state; requires a reboot
tpm_getpubek	Lists the public portion of the TPM endorsement key
tpm_restrictpubek	Limits access to the public portion of the TPM endorsement key
tpm_selftest	Checks the status of the TPM chip
tpm_setactive	Reports the active state of the TPM; may also activate or deactivate the TPM software, subject to a reboot
tpm_setownable	Manages the ownership status on the TPM chip
tpm_setpresence	Manages or changes TPM lock and enable commands
tpm_takeownership	Configures an owner for the TPM chip
tpm_version	Reports the version and manufacturer number for the TPM chip

Security on Virtual Hosts and Guests

Security on a virtual host depends on the virtual machine software in use. As described in Chapter 2, virtual machine software is available in five levels: applications, platform virtual machines, paravirtualization, hardware-assisted virtualization, and bare metal virtualization. Of course, this does not include applications such as Parallels Workstation and VMware Player, which create virtual machines that appear as another application on the virtual host. The operating system or application that runs in the virtual machine software is the **virtual guest**.

Security on Virtual Hosts

In Linux, security on virtual hosts varies by virtual machine software. That software may be a tempting target to many black-hat hackers. If breached, a black-hat hacker could conceivably use virtual host software to penetrate both the host and the guest operating systems.

Security with Virtual Applications

The standard open source Linux native application-level virtual host is known as Wine Is Not an Emulator (WINE). It implements the Microsoft Windows Application Programming Interface (API) in user space. In other words, it does not require Linux kernel modules or special kernel settings. Because it implements some basic functionality found on Microsoft operating systems, it is also susceptible to some malware found on Microsoft systems.

Because WINE is normally run from regular user accounts, however, any problems should remain isolated and not migrate to any other part of the Linux system. Nevertheless, WINE is certainly another means by which a black-hat hacker can attack a Linux system.

Security with Platform Virtual Machines

Several platform virtual machines are available for Linux. Examples include VMware Server, Parallels Workstation, and Virtualbox, Open Source Edition. Because these platforms are generally run by regular users, any risk from these virtual hosts should also be limited. Of course, security updates for these virtual machines depend on their corporate sponsors.

Security with Paravirtualization

Because paravirtualization uses a simplified interface, it works on older CPUs. It uses abstractions to simplify the interface to virtual host hardware. But because it requires a specially customized virtual guest, the security implications are there.

Security with Hardware Virtual Machines

The two most popular Linux native hardware virtual machine systems are Xen and KVM.

Hardware virtual machines require certain CPU features. Intel has accommodated these features as Virtualization Technology (VT). AMD has accommodated these features as Secure Virtual Machine (SVM). CPUs with these features are often installed on systems with TPM chips. When KVM implements TPM, its hardware virtual machines will have the same assurance in the boot process as previously described.

Security with Bare Metal Virtualization

Of course, if you're using bare metal virtualization, the virtual machine software is itself the host. Additionally, the security on that system is vendor specific. For example, VMware's ESX product runs on a custom microkernel.

Security on Virtual Guests

One of the advantages of virtual machines is that a problem that affects one virtual guest does not necessarily affect another virtual guest, even when configured on the same virtual host. However, these virtual guests are networked. They receive their updates from the same (or similar) sources. Problems that affect one virtual guest can easily affect another.

Each platform virtual machine may have different options for networking. They may be configured on different subnets or on the same network as other systems on the LAN. In some cases, a virtual guest may be allowed to communicate only with/through the virtual host. Naturally, the choice in this area can affect the security of the virtual host.

Locking Down Boot Hardware

The risks associated with physical access ports fall into two categories. First, there are the physical access ports on a server. As previously noted, a black-hat hacker with access to a CD/DVD drive or USB port and a live CD/DVD can gain administrative access to a system. This applies to servers, workstations, and desktops. But there's more. To enhance physical security on a server system, consider the following measures:

- Make sure cases on tower servers are locked. A black-hat hacker who disconnects a BIOS battery could reset any configured passwords.
- Secure the installation of blade and rack servers with nonstandard tools such as Allen nuts.
- Remove any CD/DVD drives. If you use a CD/DVD to start the installation of an operating system, that should be all that's needed. Other CD/DVD-based Linux software can be installed from mounting their .iso files as virtual CD/DVDs.
- Secure any unused external ports. Black-hat hackers with access to a USB port— or any other bootable port—could boot the operating system of their choice on your system.

Similar issues apply to virtual hosts. Of course, it's not possible to physically lock down a virtual server. "Physical security" on a virtual host depends on the permissions that apply to associated files. It is easier to install or remove noted virtual components, including CD/DVD drives and USB ports.

Beyond boot hardware, open ports on networking equipment are an open invitation to malicious users.

Locking Down Boot Loaders

> **NOTE**
>
> The terms "bootloader" and "boot loader" are synonymous and are used interchangeably. This book will use "boot loader" unless the proper name of a program specifies "bootloader" as one word.

While there are many excellent non-Linux boot loaders, this is a book on securing Linux platforms and applications. To that end, this chapter will cover two basic boot loaders: the Linux Loader (LILO) and the Grand Unified Bootloader (GRUB). Although LILO is no longer included with many Linux distributions, including Red Hat, it is still used surprisingly often on Linux systems.

There are several versions of GRUB in common use today. Version 1 (shown as version 0.97) is still the default for Red Hat, Fedora, and SUSE distributions. Upcoming sections in this chapter refer to it as "traditional GRUB." Version 2 is the default for the latest Ubuntu releases. In addition, for those who use the TPM chip described earlier in this chapter, there is a trusted version of GRUB known as TrustedGRUB.

Hard-Drive Device Files

Various Linux hardware components, including hard drives, are associated with device files. Traditionally, they've fallen into two categories. On slightly older distribution releases (including Red Hat Enterprise Linux 5), Parallel Attached Technology Attachment (PATA) hard drives were classified by their attachment location. For example, the first hard drive attached to the master connection on the primary controller was assigned the /dev/hda file name. Small Computer System Interface (SCSI) and Serial Advanced Technology Attachment (SATA) hard drives aren't normally installed on the same system; they're named sequentially starting with /dev/sda.

If you have PATA drives and are not sure of their associated device files, run the fdisk -l command as the root user. The output of that command lists all detected drives and configured partitions, with their device file names.

With the latest Linux distribution releases, there is no longer a difference in device files. PATA, SATA, and SCSI hard drives are given sequential device file names starting with /dev/sda. To reduce confusion, it's normally best to avoid mixing drive types on a single system.

KVM has introduced another hard-drive option known as a **virtio block device**. It is a paravirtualized device that works in a hardware-virtualized machine. Because paravirtualization is essentially a shortcut, it makes for a faster virtual hard drive. Related hard drives may have device files such as /dev/vda1.

Partitions take the hard-drive device file one step further. The first partition on the first drive on the latest Linux system is given the file name /dev/sda1.

When locking down a boot loader, be aware. Some options in the boot loader are designed to help the forgetful administrator reset a lost root password. Those same options make it possible to log in as the administrative user without a password. In this section, you'll learn how to make it more difficult to access the root account in this manner— at least from the LILO and GRUB boot menus. The forgetful administrator can still reinstall a CD/DVD drive and boot a live CD to recover a lost root password.

Back Up the Current Boot Loader

The following sections specify changes to a system's boot loader. If you're just trying to learn about boot loader options, be careful. It's best to back up the current boot loader on a system before making any changes. If something goes wrong, you'll be able to use the rescue media available for the distribution to recover the boot loader.

If the system includes a floppy drive, GRUB and LILO can both be set up on that drive. The commands vary depending on your configuration. If it is properly configured, you'll be able to boot the current system from that specially configured floppy drive. While you may also be able to set up the same backup boot loader on a USB drive, not all systems can boot from that drive.

But not all systems have floppy drives. Alternatively, you could simply back up key files associated with the current boot loader. If something goes wrong, you can use the rescue mode associated with the local distribution or a live CD to boot the system, access the local drives, and restore the boot loader from backup. Don't forget to use the appropriate command (`grub-install` or `lilo`) to write appropriate information to the MBR of the correct local hard drive.

Securing LILO

LILO is rarely available in the standard packages for many Linux distributions. In fact, it has not been maintained since 2007. But LILO still has a following among many longtime Linux users. Because it is still in relatively common use, the **Linux Professional Institute (LPI)** decided in 2009 to retain LILO in the objectives for both its Level 1 and Level 2 exams. Therefore, it is appropriate to cover it here.

Because the latest Linux documentation rarely covers LILO, this section provides instructions on how to install LILO. Because the `lilo` package is available from Ubuntu repositories, these instructions are based on Ubuntu 9.10. As tested, the steps on other versions of Ubuntu aren't significantly different. These steps also assume that Debian-based packages prompt for configuration options during the installation process. You won't see such prompts on Red Hat systems.

1. Run the `apt-get install lilo` command to install the package with any dependencies.
2. You'll be prompted with the LILO configuration menu during the installation process, with some notes. Accept the only option given.
3. Create an **/etc/lilo.conf** configuration file. A model is available in the `conf.sample` file in the `/usr/share/doc/lilo/examples/` directory. Read the rest of this section to learn how to customize the file for this system.
4. After saving changes to `/etc/lilo.conf`, run the `lilo -v` command. The `-v` is for verbose mode; while the `-v` isn't required, verbose mode can help verify appropriate installation.
5. If there's more than one hard drive on the local system, you may have to specify the associated device file. For example, the `lilo /dev/hda` command installs the LILO configuration file on the MBR of the first PATA hard drive.

Now examine the code shown in Figure 3-1. Table 3-2 describes the directives shown.

If you want to minimize the risk that a black-hat hacker even sees the LILO menu during the boot process, consider changing the `delay` directive to some minimum amount. If you delete the `delay` and `prompt` directives, the system automatically boots

```
# /etc/lilo.conf: Sample LILO boot loader configuration.

boot=/dev/sda
prompt

install=menu
map=/boot/map
vga=normal

default=Linux
delay=100
image=/vmlinuz
        password=option1password
        root=/dev/sda1
        initrd=/initrd.img
        label=Linux
        read-only
other=/dev/sdb1
        password=option2password
        label=Windows
        table=/dev/sdb
```

FIGURE 3-1

A Linux loader configuration file.

without a delay. When coupled with appropriate directives in the UEFI and/or BIOS menus, this could almost automatically boot the default system. Of course, that means you have to use a rescue or live CD to boot in a different manner.

By default, LILO does include the noted `prompt` directive, which allows administrators to boot a system into single-user mode. Also known as runlevel 1, single-user mode automatically boots a system into the root administrative account. The user is not prompted for the root password.

Most LILO configuration files do not include `password` directives. Those directives can prompt the user for the noted password before booting into the associated stanza. As you can see in Figure 3-1, however, the password is shown in clear text. As such, access to the LILO configuration file should be limited to the root user. The standard is 600 permissions, which is read-write access limited to the user owner. For more information on discretionary permissions, see Chapter 4.

In this configuration, the `image` and `initrd` directives point to soft links from the top-level root directory to the actual locations of the Linux kernel and initial RAM disk files. It's equally valid to point these directives to the full path to the actual files.

Other versions of LILO are available; the version created for HP Itanium 64-bit systems is designed for Extensible Firmware Interface (EFI)-based hardware. However, the last version of LILO for standard PCs and servers was released in 2007. Most work from Linux developers on the boot loader now focuses on GRUB.

> **NOTE**
>
> Generally, if you choose LILO, it should be installed on the MBR of one of the first two hard drives on a system. If you've configured a different boot loader on the MBR, however, you can set up LILO on the partition with the `/boot` directory. If it's the first partition of the first SATA drive, the associated command is `lilo /dev/sda1`.

TABLE 3-2 LILO directives from Figure 3-1.

DIRECTIVE	DESCRIPTION
boot=/dev/sda	Boots from the first available hard drive
prompt	Adds a prompt to the boot loader menu
install=menu	Installs a standard LILO menu
map=/boot/map	Specifies the location of the map file; on pre-1998 systems, had to be on the first 1,024 cylinders of the drive
vga=normal	Configures a low-level Video Graphics Array (VGA) mode for the menu
password=	Sets a password either for menu selection or a specific menu option, depending on location
default=Linux	Specifies the default stanza, based on the label directive in each stanza
delay=100	Sets a delay in tenths of a second; delay=100 is a 10-second delay before booting the default stanza
image=/vmlinuz	Specifies the location of the Linux kernel; it may be a soft link to the actual kernel file
root=/dev/sda1	Notes the first partition of the first drive as the location of the top-level root directory
initrd=/initrd.img	Specifies the location of the initial RAM disk
read-only	Boots the kernel in read-only mode, which is standard until filesystems are mounted
other=/dev/sdb1	Specifies the location for a non-Linux operating system
table=/dev/sdb	Notes the location for the other noted operating system; functionally equivalent to the GRUB chainloader command

Security and Traditional GRUB

This section defines the standard GRUB boot loader installed on Red Hat Enterprise Linux, version 0.97. The same version of GRUB is also installed on the latest version of OpenSUSE Linux. The details of the GRUB boot loader are well covered in more introductory Linux texts. In this section, you'll look at how to make this GRUB configuration more secure.

```
# grub.conf generated by anaconda
#
# Note that you do not have to rerun grub after making changes to this
file
# NOTICE:  You have a /boot partition.  This means that
#          all kernel and initrd paths are relative to /boot/, eg.
#          root (hd0,0)
#          kernel /vmlinuz-version ro root=/dev/VolGroup00/LogVol00
#          initrd /initrd-version.img
#boot=/dev/hda
default=0
timeout=5
splashimage=(hd0,0)/grub/splash.xpm.gz
hiddenmenu
title Red Hat Enterprise Linux Server (2.6.18-164.el5)
       root (hd0,0)
       kernel /vmlinuz-2.6.18-164.el5 ro root=/dev/VolGroup00/LogVol00
       initrd /initrd-2.6.18-164.el5.img
~
"/etc/grub.conf" 17L, 619C
```

FIGURE 3-2

A traditional GRUB configuration file.

First, examine the standard version of the GRUB configuration file, shown in Figure 3-2. As noted in the comments, /dev/hda is the hard drive to be booted.

You can make a couple of changes to help secure this configuration file. First, the timeout=5 directive gives a black-hat hacker five seconds to open the local GRUB menu. During this time, the screen message shown here is an open invitation:

"Press any key to enter the menu"

If you were to change timeout=5 to timeout=0, that would make it much more difficult for a black-hat hacker to know what boot loader is configured, much less access the GRUB menu. But it's still possible, so you need to consider the following options shown in the standard GRUB menu:

"Press enter to boot the selected OS, 'e' to edit the commands before booting, 'a' to modify the kernel arguments before booting, or 'c' for a command line"

Anyone who can modify kernel arguments can easily boot into single-user mode, with root administrative access. Yes, there are some distributions that make password-free administrative access a bit more difficult. However, anyone who can get to the kernel command line can bypass the root password requirement.

All a black-hat hacker needs to do is add an init=/bin/sh or init=/bin/bash directive to the end of the kernel command line. Figure 3-3 includes changes made to secure the system. An additional password-protected stanza has been added for administrative purposes.

FIGURE 3-3

A protected GRUB
configuration file.

```
# grub.conf generated by anaconda
#
# Note that you do not have to rerun grub after making changes to this file
# NOTICE:  You have a /boot partition.  This means that
#          all kernel and initrd paths are relative to /boot/, eg.
#          root (hd0,0)
#          kernel /vmlinuz-version ro root=/dev/VolGroup00/LogVol00
#          initrd /initrd-version.img
#boot=/dev/hda
default=0
timeout=1
splashimage=(hd0,0)/grub/splash.xpm.gz
hiddenmenu
password --md5 $1$gPzaS/$GQ76C6BM0eURPsMdGSSyk1
title Red Hat Enterprise Linux Server (2.6.18-164.el5)
        root (hd0,0)
        kernel /vmlinuz-2.6.18-164.el5 ro root=/dev/VolGroup00/LogVol00
        initrd /initrd-2.6.18-164.el5.img
title Red Hat Enterprise Linux Server Reccovery (2.6.18-164.el5)
        password --md5 $1$HyzaS/$JAwLr0CIDnMEE6B2A6cGP0
        root (hd0,0)
        kernel /vmlinuz-2.6.18-164.el5 ro root=/dev/VolGroup00/LogVol00 single
        initrd /initrd-2.6.18-164.el5.img
"/etc/grub.conf" 23L, 909C written
```

The password shown is encrypted with the **Message Digest 5 (MD5)** algorithm hash. The grub-md5-crypt command is available for that purpose. That command adds a salt— that is, some random characters—to make decryption more difficult. The two encrypted hashes shown are based on the same password, but appear different because of the salt.

One second is left in the timeout to give responsible administrators a chance to open the menu. The first password protects access to the GRUB commands, kernel arguments, and GRUB command line.

Note the new stanza, which supports access to single-user mode. While it's password protected, it's certainly a risk to have it in the GRUB menu. Nevertheless, it is a feature found in the GRUB menu configured on Ubuntu systems.

As GRUB relies on a pointer from the MBR, all you need to do is save the configuration file. If GRUB is already the system boot loader, you don't need to reload it. Of course, if you're converting from another boot loader, you'll have to install GRUB. For example, to configure GRUB on the first SATA drive, you'd run the following command:

```
# grub-install /dev/sda
```

Yes, these changes make it more difficult for an administrator to, say, boot into an older Linux kernel. If that administrator can't access the GRUB menu, he still has the option to use the rescue or recovery mode associated with the installation CD/DVDs for many Linux distributions.

Security and GRUB 2.0

Developers are working furiously on **GRUB 2.0**. It has the potential to be a more secure boot loader than any previous open source system. However, as of this writing, developers have recently implemented the ability to protect options with passwords. GRUB 2.0 has not been implemented in Red Hat Enterprise Linux 5 or even the allied Fedora 12 release.

In traditional GRUB, an entry such as `root (hd0,0)` points to the first hard drive and the first partition on that drive. If it's a SATA drive, it suggests that `/boot` directory files are mounted on the `/dev/sda1` partition. In GRUB 2.0, the corresponding command for `/dev/sda1` would be `set root=(hd0,1)`. In other words, while the number for sequential drives still starts with 0, the number for sequential partitions for GRUB 2.0 starts with 1.

Until encrypted password protection is fully tested by regular users on GRUB 2.0, its security may not be as reliable as that of traditional GRUB.

As of this writing, GRUB 2.0 configuration files start with settings in the `/etc/default/grub` configuration file. If GRUB 2.0 is implemented on Red Hat systems, expect to find the associated GRUB 2.0 configuration file in the `/etc/sysconfig/` directory. Even without passwords, several GRUB 2.0 directives are of interest, as described in Table 3-3.

GRUB 2.0 configuration files include incremental files in the `/etc/grub.d/` directory. The standard scripts in this directory load settings from `/etc/default/grub`, set the theme for the GRUB menu, locate kernels, and probe disks for other operating systems. There's a special file (`40_custom`) for administrator-defined input.

Whenever you make changes to any GRUB 2.0 configuration file, make sure to run the `update-grub` command. It's a simple script that uses the `grub-mkconfig` command to collect data from the aforementioned configuration files and write changes to the `/boot/grub/grub.cfg` file.

TABLE 3-3 Security-related GRUB 2.0 directives.

DIRECTIVE	DESCRIPTION
GRUB_TIMEOUT	The number of seconds before the default option is booted. Don't set to –1, as that disables the timeout and displays the menu.
GRUB_HIDDEN_TIMEOUT	The number of seconds with a blank screen is displayed. Pressing the Shift key during this time reveals the GRUB menu.
GRUB_HIDDEN_TIMEOUT_QUIET	Determines whether the GRUB_HIDDEN_TIMEOUT countdown is displayed.
GRUB_DISABLE_LINUX_RECOVERY	Determines whether the standard recovery mode option, which supports password-free root access, is shown in the menu.

Configure TrustedGRUB

If you want to configure a boot loader that takes advantage of a TPM chip on the local system, consider TrustedGRUB. Properly configured, it can become a part of the so-called chain of trust that verifies important parts of the boot process. TrustedGRUB isn't yet available as a regular package for Red Hat Enterprise Linux 5 or Ubuntu Server Edition.

However, as of early 2010, TrustedGRUB is available directly from its developers at *http://sourceforge.net/projects/trustedgrub/*. IBM documents an installation process using this software at *http://publib.boulder.ibm.com/infocenter/lnxinfo/v3r0m0/index.jsp*. Before you make any changes, be sure to back up the current boot loader as suggested earlier.

The following steps implement TrustedGRUB on a server system with Red Hat Enterprise Linux 5. Some of the associated packages to compile this package should be removed later to prevent their use by black-hat hackers. Some of the scripts and compilation commands shown can take a few minutes (or more). Similar steps should work on other Linux distributions:

1. Download the latest available version of TrustedGRUB from its SourceForge project area at the aforementioned *http://sourceforge.net* Web site. The following assumes that the package has a `tar.gz` extension. Such packages are colloquially known as a tarballs.

2. Unpack and uncompress the noted package. For example, in this case, the `tar xzf TrustedGRUB-1.1.4.tar.gz` command will unpack and uncompress the noted archive. The files are loaded into a directory of the same name.

3. Run the `build_tgrub.sh` script in the unpacked subdirectory. If you see an error message related to automake and autoconf, install the `automake`, `autoconf`, `imake`, and `gcc` packages, along with dependencies. (If you're installing these packages on a bastion host, you'll want to remove them later, as they could help a black-hat hacker create more dangerous malware.)

4. Navigate to a second-level TrustedGRUB subdirectory. If you downloaded the noted tarball in the root user's home directory, that'll be the `/root/TrustedGRUB-1.1.4/TrustedGRUB-1.1.4/` directory. Review the `INSTALL` text file in that directory. Any instructions you see there supersede any directions that follow here.

5. Run the `./configure` command to set up the code that has been unpacked. Run the `make` and `make install` commands to compile and install that code.

6. Now you're ready to replace key files in the legacy GRUB boot loader. Assuming your backup is in order, this should not intimidate you. In the `/boot/grub/` directory, delete the `stage1`, `stage2`, and `*.1_5` files in that directory.

7. Navigate back to the second level TrustedGRUB subdirectory. Use the following commands to replace the boot loader files that were just deleted:

```
# cp stage1/stage1 /boot/grub/

# cp stage2/stage2 /boot/grub/
```

8. To implement these changes, run commands at the GRUB command prompt. The commands that follow assume that the /boot directory is mounted on the first hard drive, on the first partition:

```
# grub

grub> root (hd0,0)
grub> setup (hd0)

grub> quit
```

You should see messages associated with the stage 1 and stage 2 boot loaders. Do not be concerned about messages related to the stage 1.5 boot loader, as that's not required in TrustedGRUB. Also, if the /boot directory were mounted on the second hard drive, on the third partition, the commands at the grub> prompt would be root (hd1,2) and setup (hd1).

9. The system should now be ready for a reboot. Have your backups in order and a rescue/recovery disk or a live CD ready in case things don't work.

At some point in the future, it should be easier to make TrustedGRUB part of the chain of trust verified by a TPM chip on the system motherboard. At that time, the right packages should be available in open source repositories, ready for standard installation on enterprise distributions such as those released by Red Hat and Ubuntu.

The menu should not look much different from a regular traditional GRUB menu. It also retains options from the traditional GRUB configuration file, **/boot/grub/grub.conf**. But with TrustedGRUB and a TPM chip, you'll have one more check on the integrity of the operating system that is booted.

Challenges with a Standard Supported Kernel

If you're running Linux on the desktop, a standard kernel may include a number of server-related features that you don't need and may never use. In the same fashion, if you're running Linux on the server, a standard kernel may include a number of desktop-related features that you don't need and may never use. For these reasons, Red Hat, Ubuntu, and a number of other Linux distributions include somewhat customized kernels.

Questions with Standard Kernels

The key questions in this section are multifold:

- What kernels can be installed on your system?
- What kernel is best for your needs?
- When do you consider a different kernel?

Chapter 10 addresses these questions in more detail. It also includes a number of follow-up questions, such as when to install a newer kernel for more security, when to use the stock kernel, and when to build your own secure kernel.

One common requirement is different kernels for different architectures. In other words, if a Linux distribution supports a CPU, it should have built a kernel customized for that CPU. So generally, the developers of a distribution will build different kernels at least for regular Intel/AMD 32-bit and 64-bit systems. While the kernel file names for these generic CPUs may seem specific to Intel or AMD, they generally can be used on CPUs from either company. For example, administrators who prefer Ubuntu and have an Intel 64-bit system may install a kernel such as `linux-server_2.6.31.14.27_amd64.deb` on that system.

> **NOTE**
>
> Red Hat has decided that it will not support Itanium 64-bit systems starting with its Red Hat Enterprise Linux 6 release.

This interchangeability may go further. For example, some multi-core systems can work well with both 32-bit and 64-bit kernels. However, this interchangeability may break down with other CPUs. For example, kernels designed for Intel Itanium 64-bit systems can only work on those systems. If you're looking for a generic kernel, consider the standard 32-bit Linux kernel. It's designed to work with more architectures than any other kernel.

Standard Virtual Machine Kernels

Some special configurations may require different kernels. For example, the Xen virtual machine monitor requires a special Linux kernel. That kernel is installed on both the host and the guest virtual machine.

Perhaps the biggest advance is the kernel customized to work as a virtual machine guest. Because it takes work to simulate different hardware components, fewer options are configured for virtual machines. That makes it possible to remove or disable modules for a great majority of existing hardware. For example, Ubuntu has created a Just Enough Operating System (JeOS) kernel optimized for VMware and KVM-based virtual machines. Such kernels can work with a relatively small footprint; Ubuntu virtual machine kernels have a documented minimum RAM requirement of 128 MB.

Limits on Standard Kernels

Although there are standard kernels built for different architectures and functions, standard kernels released for a distribution still have to work with a wide variety of hardware and software. Sure, server kernels do not need to be optimized for the GUI. Likewise, desktop kernels generally do not need to be optimized for databases or file servers.

Security is another limitation on standard kernels. For example, the installation of a server-optimized kernel on a desktop system can increase security risks. A black-hat hacker could use features in the server kernel to attack other systems. While installing a desktop-optimized kernel on a server system may be less of a risk, it still doesn't work as well. For example, the server kernel for one distribution is designed to address 64 GB of RAM—a lot more than the desktop version of the kernel, which is designed to address 4 GB of RAM.

The Costs and Benefits of Obscurity

In some ways, obscurity is the antithesis of open source. Obscurity may be as simple as a label, such as the labeling of an Apache server as a Microsoft Web server. Obscurity can also be more complex—something that requires special configuration options for both client and server systems on a network. The belief is that obscurity can help in a "defense in depth" scheme, which can make it more difficult for a black-hat hacker to gather information about your system. In many cases, however, obscurity doesn't provide much of an obstacle. The question is whether the configuration required to put obscurity into practice is worth the trouble. In fact, most security professionals now use the term "security through obscurity" as a derogatory phrase for systems or practices that depend upon the obscurity of their mechanism for their security.

Now for more specifics. You'll look at obscurity in four areas. First, there's the boot hardware. The hardware doesn't have to be "real"; on virtual machines, the boot hardware is virtual. Also, boot hardware varies widely. Obscurity continues with the boot process, with the messages that are transmitted to or hidden from the screen. Obscurity goes further in key-configuration files, as options in some key boot files do make it more difficult for a black-hat hacker to understand the configuration of a system. Finally, administrators can make life more difficult for black-hat hackers by using obscure nonstandard ports for network services.

Obscurity in the Boot Menus

Just as security starts with the boot process, so too does obscurity. Many modern systems are configured to zip by the BIOS/UEFI menus as quickly as possible. Unless you know the magic key to press, you can't display these menus. Basic options with these menus that enhance security include the following:

- Hiding or blanking out boot screens
- Password-protecting BIOS/UEFI menus
- Changing the boot order to avoid automatic booting from floppy, CD/DVD, USB, and other ports or disabling booting from such ports if possible
- Disabling external connection ports, such as USB and serial ports

Of course, these options may not be available in all BIOS/UEFI boot menus. Some of these options may be relatively simple to bypass. Nevertheless, every obstacle presented to a black-hat hacker will slow that person down. Every obstacle buys time, which may make the black-hat hacker look for an easier mark, which may allow other physical-security options such as cameras to alert appropriate personnel.

Obscurity in the boot process does make things more difficult for administrators who need access to such menus. If appropriate, you can use a system like the **baseboard management controller (BMC)** to access and administer the boot menus from remote locations. While it's certainly more convenient to access such systems remotely, it's also a security risk. And because it is not a Linux tool, it won't be addressed further here. Special passwords in the boot menus should be kept secure.

Obscurity in the Linux Boot Loader

Obscurity on a Linux system goes a bit further. As described earlier in this chapter, the menu associated with the GRUB or LILO boot loaders can be hidden. Furthermore, details within boot loader configuration files can also hide important details such as the volume with the top-level root directory. For example, the following entry from an older GRUB configuration file clearly identifies the volume with the top-level root directory:

```
kernel /vmlinuz-2.6.24-24-generic.x86_64 root=/dev/sda2
↪ ro quiet splash
```

In contrast, the following alternatives from two different GRUB configuration files obscure the location of the top-level root directory.

```
kernel /vmlinuz-2.6.24-24-generic.x86_64 root
↪=UUID=d7b8f43a-4409-8ffaaabb86db ro quiet splash
```

```
kernel /vmlinuz-2.6.18-53.1.4.el5 ro root=LABEL=/ rhgb quiet
```

> **NOTE**
>
> As described in the preface, line wraps are indicated by a curved arrow [↪] for layout purposes. It is just a continuation arrow, which means you type the command as one continuous line rather than two or more lines as shown.

In both cases, the volume with the top-level root directory is obscured. The Universally Unique Identifier (UUID) number in the first line was created with the uuidgen command. The LABEL in the second line was created with the e2label command. The LABEL or UUID is connected to the filesystem information for the volume device file. You can check that information for a volume device file such as /dev/sda2 with the dumpe2fs /dev/sda2 command.

Older Linux distributions displayed boot messages that described the process of an installation. Those boot messages include services that are started with the operating system. Every active network service on a system is a potential avenue of attack. Standard boot options on current Linux distributions hide or otherwise obscure those boot messages with the quiet directive shown with each of the displayed kernel commands.

Obscurity in the Linux part of the boot process means administrators need to know more. The process for accessing the boot menu needs to be well documented. How many people know to press the shift key to access the GRUB 2.0 menu? But overall, the costs of obscurity in the boot loader are small.

Obscurity in Other Linux Boot Configuration Files

Other Linux configuration files matter in the boot process. Perhaps the most important of these is **/etc/fstab**, which specifies how volumes such as partitions, redundant array of independent disks (RAID) arrays, or logical volumes are to be mounted. Figure 3-4 shows an Ubuntu installation with UUIDs. In the /etc/fstab file shown, UUIDs are used to identify the volumes associated with certain directories. But comments

```
# /etc/fstab: static file system information.
#
# Use 'blkid -o value -s UUID' to print the universally unique identifier
# for a device; this may be used with UUID= as a more robust way to name
# devices that works even if disks are added and removed. See fstab(5).
#
# <file system> <mount point>    <type>  <options>        <dump>  <pass>
proc           /proc            proc    defaults          0       0
# / was on /dev/vda3 during installation
UUID=61368ff5-37c3-4132-800c-da389a8abf5a /             ext4    errors=remount-ro
 0        1
# /boot was on /dev/vda1 during installation
UUID=9197a8e4-db42-4802-ab0f-99e803ea2752 /boot         ext2    defaults          0
      2
# swap was on /dev/vda5 during installation
#UUID=476467ff-9ac3-4bac-9840-3cc5b1ef206f none          swap    sw
0       0
/dev/mapper/cryptswap1 none swap sw 0 0
~
```

FIGURE 3-4

The /etc/fstab file can use more obscurity.

are also included to identify the original volume device files. The default permissions for /etc/fstab make it "world-readable." Any black-hat hacker can read this file and get too much information about what directories are mounted on what volumes.

Comments in /etc/fstab are not necessary for mounting configured directories. You can safely delete them without affecting the boot process.

Obscurity in Services

Linux services themselves can't be easily hidden within a system. Many configuration files and scripts are tied to standard file names. If you change a file name or directory, chances are good that you'll also need to change some software code. The level of effort required to make such changes is rather high.

Obscurity in services normally relates to the network port on which that service communicates. Standard ports for many services are shown in the **/etc/services** file. While it's not difficult to change the communications port for many services, you'd also need to change the communications ports on firewalls, clients, and more.

For more information on service-related security, read Chapters 6 and 7. After reading those chapters, you may decide that obscurity in services is not worth the effort required to configure it.

Besides, with tools such as the nmap command, it's not very difficult for a black-hat hacker to identify nonstandard ports for network services. And those nonstandard ports may confuse your users, violating the principles of availability and utility in the CIA triad and Parkerian hexad.

Basic Security and the Five Process Controls

Interactive controls relate to protecting assets within and at the edge of a network. Those controls are well addressed with the security features described throughout this book. One possible exception is indemnification, which is based on legal requirements beyond the scope of this book.

This section is focused on the five process controls. These controls can help protect data assets beyond secure networks. These controls are nonrepudiation, confidentiality, privacy, integrity, and alarm.

These process controls were briefly described in Chapter 1 in the context of an Open Source Security Testing Methodology Manual (OSSTMM) audit.

Nonrepudiation

Nonrepudiation controls prevent an individual who has taken an action from later denying that action. Black-hat hackers want to stay anonymous. Networks with nonrepudiation controls make it more difficult for a black-hat hacker to hide.

Several examples of nonrepudiation include the following:

* The use of digital signatures to assure a recipient of a message sender's identity
* Tests of the integrity of logs with respect to access
* Documentation of the depth of interaction between the user and the service
* Verification of user identities for all interactions
* Methods that prevent the use of false identities

Good logs, such as those that can be configured for the Apache Web server, can identify the Internet Protocol (IP) address, time zone, browser, and operating system of each user. While this data is better if each user is required to log into the system, such data by itself does not itself ensure nonrepudiation.

Confidentiality

Confidentiality ensures the secure private transmission of data between two users. Sure, black-hat hackers can try to get in the middle of that transmission. They can try to mimic or spoof the identity of one of the two parties. Encryption makes that process more difficult. This is an area where open source can help. It's easier to verify encryption with open source methods. The open review of open source software can give users confidence that their identities and data can be protected.

Privacy

In this context, privacy specifies those methods that protect user data. One way to ensure privacy is to change the connection method every time. Privacy as a process control assumes that some black-hat hacker may always be listening. If so, that user will know the technique used to make a connection. Some connections are initiated by port knocking, where connection attempts are made to a sequence of known closed ports.

Port knocking is private only if the connections are made through a secure tunnel, such as IP packets that are encapsulated. Another example of privacy is the use of one-time passwords. The password on the client and server should match. The passwords change in the same way on both client and server every time because both are configured with the same algorithm.

Integrity

The integrity of information is important. If information has integrity, you know it hasn't been changed. If a black-hat hacker can intercept a secret message such as the balance of a bank account and change it, only the black-hat hacker is served.

Integrity as a process requires options such as digital signatures. As a process control, integrity depends on tools such as a TPM chip or a GNU Privacy Guard (GPG) key. That tool verifies the digital signature, ensuring the integrity of the data between the source and the destination.

IBM is taking this concept one step further with the **Integrity Measurement Architecture (IMA)**. The IMA is a Linux security module that uses the TPM to check the executable files associated with Linux before it is loaded during the boot process. IBM has stated explicitly that IMA is not related to DRM.

Alarm

An alarm, such as one of those available from log files, is an important tool to the security professional. A good alarm is based on sufficient cause, such as suspicious activity from what should be an inactive account.

A black-hat hacker has a couple of options with respect to alarms. He could try to replace alarm-related commands with Trojans. In this case, such Trojans would be nonfunctional commands or scripts with appropriate file names. He could also try to delete the associated log files. The resulting lack of an alarm is one possible cause of false negatives. He could try to set off additional alarms, so administrators start to ignore them. There are so many logs that an administrator has to deal with, such false positives could cause a security professional to stop trusting the alarm.

Best Practices: Basic Security

The "best practices" section in this and upcoming chapters is designed as a "lessons learned" review of the chapter. If you already know the basics of a particular topic, the notes from this section may be all that you need.

First, some security is required wherever the server is stored. It takes mere seconds for someone to remove an unsecured server. It takes just a few more seconds for someone to remove a hard drive from an unsecured server. Anyone with access to a bootable device such as a CD/DVD drive or USB port can boot his own system on your servers. Anyone with access to an open network port can watch your traffic with a protocol analyzer. Anything you can do to secure these systems will help.

The TPM chip has caused controversy within the open source community. Primary objections come from the FSF and the EFF. ISECOM is working to address open source concerns with this chip through the OpenTC consortium. Some Linux developers are using the measurement, roots of trust, and chain of trust features of Trusted Computing to develop the TCG Software Stack. TrustedGRUB can help ensure the integrity of the boot process. The status of TPM support on virtual machines varies.

Virtual machine security depends on the status of virtual hosts and virtual guests. Virtual machine software is available in five levels: applications, platform virtual machines, paravirtualization, hardware-assisted virtualization, and bare metal virtualization.

It's also important to lock down boot hardware—and not just with servers. It's just as important to lock down UEFI/BIOS boot menus, along with boot loaders. If unsecured, boot loaders allow anyone to start the installed Linux system with root administrative privileges. With certain changes, the root password isn't even required. It's important to protect at least those options with passwords. Options are also available to hide and/or minimize how long boot loader menus appear or are accessible. If a TPM chip is available on a system, you may consider installing TrustedGRUB to take advantage of its support.

The developers behind many distributions make a number of standard supported kernels available. Such kernels may be customized for servers, desktops, or even virtual guests. It's best to avoid mixing kernels on different systems. For example, the use of a server kernel on a desktop system may introduce server-related security risks on that system.

In some areas, obscurity can help enhance security. Obscurity goes beyond the use of nonstandard ports for network services. Most systems allow you to blank out a boot screen. Linux boot loaders can be hidden. Settings in Linux boot loaders can minimize the boot messages seen by a user. Settings in Linux initial configuration files such as /etc/fstab can make it more difficult to identify important partitions and volumes.

Security in this area also relates to the five process controls defined by the OSSTMM. These controls are nonrepudiation, confidentiality, privacy, integrity, and alarm. These controls can be related to the security settings in basic facilities through the boot process.

CHAPTER SUMMARY

The focus of this chapter is on the boot process—from the moment a system is powered up to the time you can log into a Linux system. It covered basic security issues related to physical and virtual servers. To that end, it described how you can lock down boot hardware. It provided details on how you can lock down Linux boot loaders. This chapter also covered how obscurity can help, from the BIOS/UEFI menu through options with four different boot loader menus. It also covered basic security in the context of the five process controls as defined by the OSSTMM.

KEY CONCEPTS AND TERMS

`/boot/grub/grub.conf`
`/etc/fstab`
`/etc/lilo.conf`
`/etc/services`
`tpm-tools`
`trousers`
Baseboard management controller (BMC)
Biometric controls
Chain of trust
Electronic Frontier Foundation (EFF)
Free Software Foundation (FSF)
GRUB 2.0
Hash function

Integrity Measurement Architecture (IMA)
Linux Professional Institute (LPI)
Message Digest 5 (MD5)
Open Trusted Computing (OpenTC)
Owner override
Pre-boot eXecution Environment (PXE)
Protocol analyzer
Root Trust for Measurement (RTM)
Root Trust for Reporting (RTR)
Root Trust for Storage (RTS)
Secure Hash Algorithm 1 (SHA-1)

Secure Hash Algorithm 3 (SHA-3)
SourceForge
Stallman, Richard
Storage Root Key (SRK)
TCG Software Stack
Trusted Computing Group (TCG)
Trusted Platform Module (TPM)
TrustedGRUB
Virtio block device
Virtual guest
Virtual host
Wireshark

CHAPTER 3 ASSESSMENT

1. Which of the following hardware components is *not* used to boot a Linux system?

    A. A PXE-enabled network card
    B. A USB port
    C. A CD drive
    D. An Ethernet port

2. From the following answers, what is *not* addressed by a TPM chip?

    A. DRM
    B. Disk encryption
    C. KVM virtual machines
    D. Chain of trust

3. Which of the following roots of trust is associated with the BIOS/UEFI?

    A. The Root Trust for Reporting
    B. The Root Trust for Storage
    C. The Root Trust for Management
    D. The Root Trust for Networking

4. Which of the following packages implements TPM support on Linux? (Select two.)

    A. `tpm-tools`
    B. `tpm-drm`
    C. `trousers`
    D. `tcg`

5. Name the Linux service associated with virtual application support.

    A. KVM
    B. WINE
    C. VMware Player
    D. Xen

6. Which of the following directives in a LILO configuration file specifies the time before the default operating system is booted?

    A. delay
    B. timeout
    C. default
    D. period

7. The command that can be used to set up an encrypted password for a traditional GRUB configuration file is _____ .

8. From the following commands, which one updates the GRUB 2.0 configuration file read by the boot loader?

    A. `grub-setup`
    B. `grub-mkconfig`
    C. `grub-install`
    D. `grub-set-default`

9. In a TrustedGRUB configuration file, which of the following directives refers to the first partition on the second hard drive?

    A. `root (hd1,2)`
    B. `root (hd2,1)`
    C. `root (hd1,1)`
    D. `root (hd0,2)`

10. Which of the following kernel types is most likely to address the most RAM?

    A. Desktop
    B. Server
    C. Virtual machine
    D. Generic

11. Which of the following kernel types is most likely to work with the smallest amount of RAM?

    A. Desktop
    B. Server
    C. Virtual machine
    D. Generic

12. The GRUB 2.0 menu is hidden during the boot process. Which of the following keys, when pressed at the appropriate time, reveals the menu?

    A. Alt
    B. Shift
    C. Del
    D. Ctrl

13. Which of the following options can be substituted for a partition device in the `/etc/fstab` configuration file? (Select two.)

    A. `sysfs`
    B. LABEL
    C. `/proc`
    D. UUID

14. Which of the following concepts is *not* one of the five OSSTMM process controls?

    A. Privacy
    B. Alarm
    C. Authenticity
    D. Integrity

User Privileges and Permissions

T MAY SEEM LIKE A CLICHÉ, but security starts with you. That's also an appropriate slogan for your users. Linux privileges and permissions for users start with the **shadow password suite**. The privileges available to a Linux user may seem like high school in a way, as they depend on the groups to which users belong. In this chapter, you'll see how to set up Linux users with a variety of permissions and privileges. You'll also see how users with a common interest can be set up in their own special group.

Of course, some users are more trusted than others. Those users may be given a variety of administrative privileges. Linux logs allow you to track who logs in—and who tries and fails to log in—to monitored systems. Other Linux authentication schemes include Pluggable Authentication Modules (PAM) and the PolicyKit. Of course, user privileges and permissions may apply over a network. Two options for implementing these include the **Network Information Service (NIS)** and the **Lightweight Directory Access Protocol (LDAP)**.

Chapter 4 Topics

This chapter covers the following topics and concepts:

- What the shadow password suite is
- Which user privileges are available
- How to secure groups of users
- How to configure the hierarchy of administrative privileges
- What regular and special permissions are
- How authorized and unauthorized access can be tracked through logs
- What the essentials of Pluggable Authentication Modules (PAM) are
- How the PolicyKit can authorize access
- Which tools you have for network authentication
- What best practices are for user privileges and permissions

Chapter 4 Goals

When you complete this chapter, you will be able to:

- Configure regular and special user privileges and permissions
- Set up users with varying levels of administrative rights
- Use fine-grained administrative controls including PAM and the PolicyKit
- Understand options for network authentication

The Shadow Password Suite

The configuration of users and groups on a Linux system used to be a simple matter. Users were configured in /etc/passwd and groups were configured in /etc/group. As users on Linux systems could be trusted, it didn't matter that those files were readable by any user.

Such a configuration is not realistic with the current state of computer security. Even when encrypted, it's not a good practice to store passwords in a world-readable file. Additional restrictions on passwords can also enhance security. Those are some of the reasons for the development of the shadow password suite, which add the /etc/shadow and /etc/gshadow files to the database.

The files of the shadow password suite are fundamental to Linux. You may have read about them before in other texts. Because those files are the foundation of Linux user and group security, you'll read about them again here. Before you can understand the basics of network authentication schemes such as NIS and LDAP, you need to understand these files. It's even possible to use these files from one system as the starting point for these network authentication databases.

/etc/passwd

The /etc/passwd file contains basic information for each user account. It defines the users configured on the local system. It may seem a bit misnamed, however. As you can see from most current versions of this file, it no longer contains even a salted hashed version of the actual password. Even so, it is the starting point for individual user accounts.

Each /etc/passwd file contains seven columns of information, delineated by colons. Table 4-1 describes these columns from left to right.

Many accounts in the user-authentication database include a standard login shell in the last column, such as /bin/bash or /bin/sh. A black-hat hacker who somehow gets access to that account would get access to a regular shell equipped with a full array of commands.

Changing the default shell for these nonstandard users can enhance security. Two fake shells available for this purpose are /bin/false and /sbin/nologin. In some distributions, the nologin shell is found in the /usr/sbin/ directory.

TABLE 4-1 Data in /etc/passwd, by column.

COLUMN	DESCRIPTION
Username	Login name
Password	May be set to x or *. An x in a standard password column refers to /etc/shadow for the actual password. An * is shown if the account is disabled.
User ID	A numeric identifier for the user
Group ID	A numeric identifier for the primary group of the user
User information	Comments for the user; sometimes known as the GECOS field, based on its development as the General Electric Comprehensive Operating System
Home directory	The directory accessed when logging into the given account
Login shell	The start shell for the user

TABLE 4-2	Data in /etc/group, by column.
COLUMN	**DESCRIPTION**
Groupname	Most Linux systems are configured with users as members of their own group. Other groups may be administrative and more.
Password	Normally set to x, which refers to /etc/shadow for any password.
Group ID	A numeric identifier for the group.
Group members	A comma-delineated list of users who are members of the group.

/etc/group

The /etc/group file contains basic information for each group account. It defines the groups configured on the local system. It's a simple file that includes user members of each group. Users who are members of certain groups may have special privileges, or may be part of a common project. They may have privileges to certain hardware components. They may have some level of administrative privileges. Several of these groups are described later in this chapter. Each /etc/group file contains four columns of information, delineated by colons. Table 4-2 describes these columns from left to right.

/etc/shadow

User access to the /etc/shadow file is limited to the root administrative user. Even then, default access to the administrative user is limited to read-only. In some cases, access may be allowed to users who are members of the shadow group. It adds detailed password information to users defined in the /etc/passwd file. Per the shadow password suite, that password is modified by a salted hash, normally using the Message Digest 5 (MD5) algorithm. An /etc/shadow file contains eight columns of information, delineated by colons. Table 4-3 describes these columns from left to right.

The password-related options in /etc/shadow are especially important. If a black-hat hacker breaks into a system and manages to get a copy of /etc/shadow, it'll take a little time for the hacker to decipher those salted hashed passwords. If you change passwords before the black-hat hacker has time to use a rainbow table, your systems will be that much more secure.

/etc/gshadow

User access to the /etc/gshadow file is limited to the root administrative user. On some distributions, access may be allowed to users who are members of the shadow group. The /etc/gshadow file is analogous to the /etc/shadow file, except it's for groups. Group administrators and an associated salted hashed password may be added to this file. The difference with /etc/shadow is that passwords are rarely configured; when they are, /etc/gshadow doesn't specify password lifetime parameters. Each /etc/gshadow file contains four columns of information, delineated by colons. Table 4-4 describes these columns from left to right.

Passwords in /etc/gshadow can be set with the gpasswd command. A group administrator is not required. For example, the following command allows you to set the password for the project group, which can be used to authenticate the newgrp or **sg** commands:

```
# gpasswd project
```

TABLE 4-3 Data in /etc/shadow, by column.

COLUMN	DESCRIPTION
Username	Login name
Password	A password that has normally been changed to a salted hash; if it starts with 1, it's been modified with the MD5 algorithm
Date of last password change	Date of last password change, in number of days after January 1, 1970
Minimum password life	Number of days a password must be retained
Maximum password life	Number of days the same password can be retained
Password warning period	Number of days before password expiration when a warning is given
Inactive period	Number of days after password expiration when an account is made inactive
Disabled period	Number of days after password expiration when an account is disabled

TABLE 4-4   Data in `/etc/gshadow`, by column.

COLUMN	DESCRIPTION
Groupname	Most Linux systems are configured with users as members of their own group. Other groups may be administrative and more.
Password	Normally set to ! if there's no password.
Group administrator	A user who is authorized to add users to the group.
Group members	A comma-delineated list of users who are members of the group.

TABLE 4-5   `/etc/login.defs` security-related directives for new users and groups.

DIRECTIVE	DESCRIPTION
FAILLOG_ENAB	Failed login attempts are collected in the binary `/var/log/faillog` file, unless `pam_tally` is configured in PAM (described later in this chapter)
LOG_OK_LOGINS	Successful logins are collected in a log file defined by `/etc/syslog.conf`
SYSLOG_SU_ENAB	Uses of the `su` command are logged
SYSLOG_SG_ENAB	Uses of the `sg` command are logged
FTMP_FILE	Login failures collected in an associated file
PASS_MAX_DAYS	Maximum number of days a password can be used
PASS_MIN_DAYS	Minimum number of days a password must be retained
PASS_MIN_LENGTH	Minimum password length
LOGIN_TIMEOUT	Maximum time for a console login

Defaults for the Shadow Password Suite

When you create new users and groups, the settings are based on defaults configured in the /etc/login.defs file. If you're interested in more rigorous security, you may consider setting or changing the configuration directives shown in Table 4-5.

A number of directives associated with PAM , described later in this chapter, have superseded a number of directives traditionally used in /etc/login.defs. For newly created users, the contents of the /etc/skel/ directory are copied to that user's home directory with appropriate permissions.

Privileged and Unprivileged User and Group ID Numbers

Every user and group has a **user ID (UID)** and **group ID (GID)** number. With the release of Linux kernel 2.6 in 2003, the number of available UIDs and GIDs was raised from a 16-bit number to a 32-bit number. In other words, the highest legal UID and GID numbers are somewhere over 4 billion. That should be more UID and GID numbers than are needed in any modern enterprise. UIDs and GIDs are further limited, however. The /etc/login.defs file defines standards for those numbers with the UID_MIN and GID_MIN directives. Depending on the distribution, the minimum UID and GID number for a regular user or group may be 100, 500, 1000, or some other relatively low number. UIDs and GIDs below that minimum are reserved for administrative, service, and other privileged accounts.

You'll also find maximum UIDs and GIDs defined in /etc/login.defs. These are arbitrary numbers. UIDs and GIDs above that number are often used by other authentication systems such as NIS, LDAP, and Microsoft authentication through Samba.

Some special high UID numbers are associated with fewer privileges than a regular user has. Two prime examples are the users nobody and nfsnobody. They may be assigned the second-to-last possible 16- or 32-bit UID. For example, the nobody account on an Ubuntu system may be assigned a UID number of 65534, the second-to-last possible 16-bit UID. In contrast, the nfsnobody account on a Red Hat system may have a UID number of 4294967294, the second-to-last possible 32-bit UID. These accounts have matching GID numbers.

While accounts with such UID and GID numbers are supposed to have fewer privileges than regular users, that's documented only in the information in the user-authentication database.

TABLE 4-6   Standard user- and group-management commands.

COMMAND	DESCRIPTION
useradd	Adds users to the shadow password suite based on defaults in /etc/login.defs, except when modified by useradd command options
usermod	Modifies user settings in the shadow password suite
userdel	Deletes users; by itself, the command retains the user home directory
groupadd	Creates a new group
groupmod	Modifies group information
groupdel	Deletes an existing group
groups	Lists group membership of the current user
chage	Revises aging information for a user's password

Shadow Password Suite Commands

A variety of commands and tools are available to create, modify, and delete users and groups. Generally, the commands shown in Table 4-6 are well covered in more elementary Linux texts. As a security administrator, be prepared to use these commands frequently to make sure users and groups are created with appropriate levels of security.

Although many excellent GUI user- and group-management tools are available, as a Linux administrator, you need to be prepared to administer users and groups from the command line. Besides, the GUI is itself a security risk, as discussed in Chapter 6.

A Variety of Choices with User Privileges

While the privileges discussed in this section are partially administrative in nature, they relate to privileges that users may want on regular workstations. The permissions in question support access to hardware such as modems, sound cards, printers, and scanners.

On Ubuntu distributions, user privileges to special hardware are implemented through group memberships. While those groups are listed in /etc/groups, a clearer description is available in the Ubuntu Users Settings tool, accessible in the GUI with the users-admin command. Depending on the release, you'll click Properties or Advanced Settings, and then select the User Privileges tab. The window that appears is shown in Figure 4-1. You'll see a description of some of the groups associated with special user privileges.

If you select one of the options shown in Figure 4-1, the Users Settings tool applies the **usermod** command to make the subject user a member of the noted group. Of course, as a Linux administrator, you may choose to apply the usermod command more directly. Alternatively, you can add desired users to the noted groups even more directly by editing the /etc/group and /etc/gshadow files. After all, these are text files and can be modified in any text editor.

Table 4-7 may help you identify groups associated with the descriptions shown in Figure 4-1. The groups in the table are the group names found in the /etc/group and /etc/gshadow files. Some of the descriptions in the User Settings window may be less than perfect. For example, "ethernet" should not be lowercase, and sharing files with the local network should not be limited to Samba. As development proceeds, the descriptions in the User Settings window shown in Figure 4-1 may change.

> **▶ TIP**
>
> Don't modify a text configuration file with a binary editor such as OpenOffice.org Writer. Changes written to those files are likely to render them unusable. Changes to key configuration files may even lead to unbootable systems. If you want to edit the files of the shadow password suite, use the vipw and vigr commands. These commands override the read-only permissions of the /etc/shadow and /etc/gshadow files.

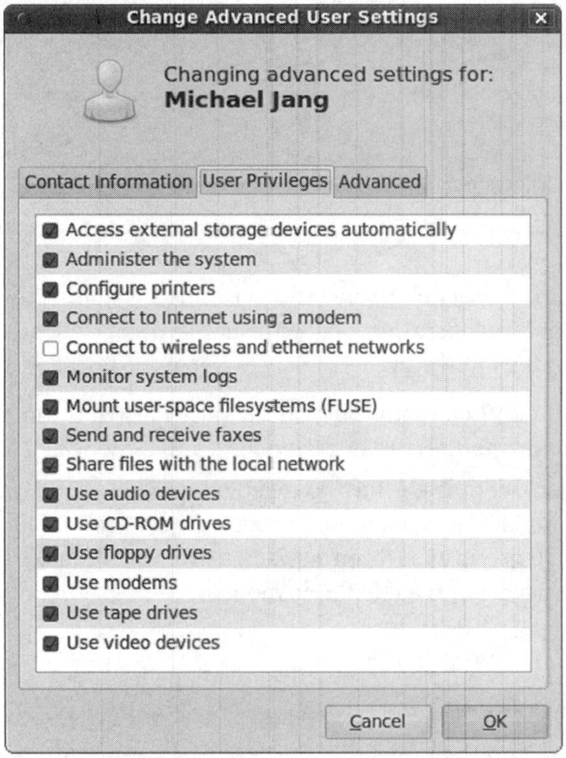

FIGURE 4-1

User privileges
as a member
of special groups.

TABLE 4-7 Groups with special permissions for users.

DESCRIPTION	GROUP NAME
Access external storage devices automatically	`plugdev`
Administer the system	`admin`
Configure printers	`lpadmin`
Connect to the Internet using a modem	`dip`
Connect to wireless and ethernet networks	`netdev`
Monitor system logs	`adm`
Mount user-space filesystems (FUSE)*	`fuse`
Send and receive faxes	`fax`
Share files with the local network	`sambashare`
Use audio devices	`audio`
Use CD-ROM drives	`cdrom`
Use floppy drives	`floppy`
Use modems	`dialout`
Use tape drives	`tape`
Use video devices	`video`

* FUSE is an acronym for Filesystems in USErspace.

The groups described in this section apply only to Ubuntu systems. It's certainly possible to configure other Linux distributions with such group privileges, however. To do so, you'll need to do the following:

- If the specified groups don't already exist on the target distribution, in both the `/etc/group` and `/etc/shadow` configuration files, you may need to create them.
- On an Ubuntu system, identify the files owned by the noted group. One method is with the `find` command. For example, the following command identifies those files owned by the `dip` group. On Ubuntu systems, user members of that group are allowed to dial out through a telephone modem.

  `# find / -group dip`

- Check the octal permissions associated with the noted files. For more information on octal permissions, see Chapter 5.
- If those same files exist on the target distribution, use commands like `chgrp` and `chmod` to modify ownership and octal permissions accordingly. In some cases, you may need to create the target files.

Securing Groups of Users

Administrators need to be able to set up users in special groups, with dedicated directories.
Administrators can give those users rights and privileges on dedicated directories. The
noted directories can be shared by groups of workers. Before configuring such groups,
you need to understand how the **user private group scheme** works in Linux.

User Private Group Scheme

Linux users are typically assigned to at least one group, which is based on that user's
account. For example, most current Linux systems with user kim also have a group
named kim. Of course, user kim may be a member of other groups with access to
hardware, administrative privileges, and more.

Every user has a primary group. To identify that group, review the third and fourth
fields in the /etc/passwd file. For most user accounts, the numbers in these fields are the
same. To verify the group name associated with each number, check the /etc/group file.

Linux distributions that don't implement the user private group scheme may assign
all users to the same group. That group is typically named users, with a GID of 100.

Create a Special Group

If you're creating a group for a special set of users, you'll probably want to set up a
directory for their exclusive use. The following instructions describe how you can set up
a /home/special directory for some series of users in a group named project. Assume
the user members of that group are users larry, kim, kate, mike1, and mike2. Assume
those user accounts have already been created. Further assume there is a user nobody
with a nonprivileged UID.

1. Run a command like mkdir /home/special to create the directory
   for the special group.

2. Create the group named project. Make sure to assign that group a GID that can't
   otherwise be assigned. To be sure, check the /etc/login.defs file and make
   sure the GID number is greater than the GID_MAX setting. If the local system uses
   network authentication, make sure the GID number isn't assignable in any of
   those systems.

3. For example, to create a group named project with a GID of 100000, run the
   following command:

   ```
   # groupadd -g 100000 project
   ```

4. Assign the noted users to that project group. While you can do so with the
   usermod command, one user at a time, you can also directly edit the /etc/group
   and /etc/gshadow files to add the noted users. Given a GID of 100000, the
   applicable lines in these files would be as follows:

   ```
   project:x:100000:larry,kim,kate,mike1,mike2
   project:!::larry,kim,kate,mike1,mike2
   ```

5. Set up appropriate ownership in the newly created directory. The following command ensures that nobody can change permissions in the /home/special directory:

```
# chown nobody.project /home/special
```

Alternatively, if you wanted to give user larry ownership of the directory, you could run the following command:

```
# chown larry.project /home/special
```

6. Finally, the following command sets up special octal permissions on the directory.

```
# chmod 2770 /home/special
```

As described later in this chapter, the 2 in the noted chmod command assigns the so-called **Set Group ID (SGID) bit** to the directory. Alternatively, if you just wanted to set the SGID bit, run the chmod g+s /home/special command.

Once configured, all members of the project group will be able to copy files to the /home/special directory. The SGID bit in that directory assigns group ownership to any files copied to that directory. Thus, all users who are members of that project group will have group-ownership access rights to files in that directory.

If you run these steps from a GUI command-line console, you'll have to log completely out of the GUI and log back in again before the noted ownership and permissions take effect.

A Hierarchy of Administrative Privileges

You could always run administrative commands as the root user. That can be dangerous, however, because the actions required to undelete a file are complex. While it's common to delete groups of directories and subdirectories, that's a risky business. Say, for example, you wanted to delete the hypothetical /usr/src/someone-source/ directory along with its files and subdirectories. You could run the following command as the root administrative user:

```
# rm -rf /usr/src/someone-source
```

That is a risky command.

An accidental space added in the wrong place in that command would delete every file on the local system. That's one reason why most Linux administrators prefer to log in and even administer a system from a regular account.

This section explains how that's possible—how regular accounts can be configured as administrators for certain servers. It explains the use of the **su** and sg commands with super-user and super-group privileges. It further explains how to run fine-grained rights to administrative tools through the **sudo** command, authorized through the /etc/sudoers file.

Administrative Privileges in Services

Some services support the configuration of administrative privileges. Perhaps the prime example is the Common UNIX Printing System (CUPS). In its main configuration file, /etc/cups/cupsd.conf, you may find a SystemGroup directive. That directive can be configured to assign a group such as lpadmin or sys as a print administrator group. Users who are members of that group will have print administrative rights to CUPS. When CUPS prompts for an administrative user and password, that print administrator can enter his or her regular username and password.

Administrative privileges to other services are more subtle, based on group ownership of special files. For example, Ubuntu systems authorize access to many log files for users who are members of the adm group. One way to verify the files owned by the adm group is with the following command:

```
# find / -group adm
```

Assuming that the group owner of such files has at least read privileges, users who are members of the adm group will be able to read those files.

The su and sg Commands

The su and sg commands allow users to take the identity of others. You can set it up for one command or you can assume the identity of another user or group until you log out of that new user or group. You can use the su command by itself to log in from a regular account into the root administrative account. That action prompts for the root password.

Since logging in as the root administrative user is dangerous, the right way to use the su command is with the -c switch. This applies administrative privileges for that one command. For example, the following command opens the noted /dev/sda drive in the fdisk utility.

```
$ su -c '/sbin/fdisk /dev/sda'
```

Before the command is executed, you're prompted for the root administrative password. Once changes are complete, the su command returns the shell to your regular account.

You can also use the su command to log into a different account. For example, if you have the password of the user named humu, you can log into his or her account with the following command:

```
$ su - humu
```

The sg command allows a user to join a group on a temporary basis. It works only if there's a group password in the /etc/gshadow file. For example, if you have a regular account named humu, and have the group password for the project group described earlier in this chapter, you can use the sg command to access that directory. The following command would copy the noted file from user humu's home directory:

```
$ sg project -c 'cp /home/humu/mycontribution.doc /home/project'
```

Just remember, the use of such passwords can be a security risk. Because the root administrative password is all-powerful for a system, it should be shared with as few people as possible. In addition, if you send an administrative password over a network, that's a risk, even over an encrypted connection. That's one reason for the sudo command, configured in the /etc/sudoers file.

Options with sudo and /etc/sudoers

The Linux way to configure limited administrative permissions is based on the sudo command, configured in the /etc/sudoers configuration file. With sudo, authorized users need only enter their own regular passwords to run configured administrative commands. In the following sections, you'll look at basic options in /etc/sudoers, take a more extensive view of the commands that can be delegated through /etc/sudoers, and see how the sudo command works with this file.

> **NOTE**
>
> It is possible to log into the root account in Ubuntu. You can boot a system into the recovery mode option normally configured in the Grand Unified Bootloader (GRUB) menu described in Chapter 3. Alternatively, if your account is configured with appropriate privileges, you can run the sudo su command. Once in the root account, you can activate logins to that account by creating a password. The passwd command in the root account makes it easy.

The sudo command is so important in the Ubuntu distribution that you won't even find a root administrative password on Ubuntu releases. Ubuntu disables logins to the root account. The first user on an Ubuntu system is given membership in the admin group. A regular user who is a member of the admin group can run administrative commands with full privileges (if that group is appropriately configured in /etc/sudoers). As described later, all that user needs to do is to enter his or her own password when prompted.

Basic Options in /etc/sudoers

The standard /etc/sudoers file contains the following entry, which gives the root administrative user full privileges through sudo:

    root ALL=(ALL) ALL

The format of this line is as follows (if run_as_username is not included, it's assumed that the command that follows is run as root):

    user system=run_as_username command

The user can be any regular user account in /etc/passwd. Alternatively, a name with a % in front specifies a group. So the following entry configures full administrative privileges for members of the admin group:

    %admin ALL=(ALL) ALL

If your account is listed as a member of the admin group in /etc/group, you can run any administrative command. From your regular account, the following command would open the /dev/sda hard drive in the fdisk utility. The sudo command prompts for your user password, not the root administrative password:

```
$ sudo /sbin/fdisk /dev/sda
```

Of course, any black-hat hacker who finds the username and password of someone in the admin group would have full administrative privileges. Fortunately, though, because the username is something other than root, the black-hat hacker might not know what he or she has.

Nevertheless, that's one reason why you as a security administrator can configure /etc/sudoers with more fine-grained administrative privileges. It's a file worth protecting. By default, it's accessible only to the root administrative user and is configured with read-only privileges. As such, you can't edit it in just any text editor. To edit it, you need to run the visudo command as the root user. As the name implies, it opens /etc/sudoers in the vi editor, requiring some knowledge of that editor. Many (if not most) entry-level Linux texts describe the use of the vi editor in detail.

The Red Hat Enterprise Linux 5 version of this file is especially instructive. First, examine the last lines of the file, which are normally commented out. This line allows members of the users group, from all systems, to run the commands shown. Note how the full path to each command is required. This is a generic line, however; the mount and umount commands aren't even located in the /sbin directory.

```
%users  ALL=/sbin/mount /mnt/cdrom, /sbin/umount /mnt/cdrom
```

If you're testing on a Red Hat system, try changing the default option shown above to include some relevant commands. For example, the following replacement code allows members of the users group to use fdisk on the /dev/sda drive (and only that drive) and to use the yum command to update and install packages:

```
%users  ALL=/sbin/fdisk /dev/sda, /usr/bin/yum
```

More Detailed Options with /etc/sudoers

The power of /etc/sudoers comes earlier in the Red Hat version of this file, with the aliases. You can set up aliases for a group of users, systems, and administrative commands. Here's just one example: Say you want to set up an administrator with the right to reprioritize or kill a process. The following command alias directive assigns appropriate administrative tools to the PSMGMT alias:

```
Cmnd_Alias PSMGMT= /bin/nice,
↪ /bin/kill, /usr/bin/kill, /usr/bin/killall
```

You can then assign that to a group of users with the authority to use these commands on all systems with the following directive:

```
%psusers ALL = PSMGMT
```

TABLE 4-8   Groups of commands in /etc/sudoers.

VARIABLE	COMMANDS
NETWORKING	route, ifconfig, ping, dhclient, net, iptables, rfcomm, wvdial, iwconfig, mii-tool
SOFTWARE	rpm, up2date, yum
SERVICES	service, chkconfig
LOCATE	updated
STORAGE	fdisk, sfdisk, parted, partprobe, mount, umount
DELEGATING	sudo, chown, chmod, chgrp
PROCESSES	nice, kill, killall
DRIVERS	modprobe

The standard Red Hat version of /etc/sudoers includes a more extensive example of administrative tools assigned to command aliases here:

```
# %sys ALL = NETWORKING, SOFTWARE, SERVICES, STORAGE, DELEGATING,
PROCESSES, LOCATE, DRIVERS
```

If activated, this line would enable privileges to an extensive series of administrative commands. Table 4-8 lists the commands associated with each variable. It should also give you a good idea of what basic administrative commands are really important in Linux.

If you know Linux in detail, you may realize this list is not complete. For example, you could set up commands like iwconfig, iwlist, and iwspy in their own wireless networking group. You may want to add commands like insmod and rmmod to the DRIVERS group.

Use the sudo Command

Regular users may be configured with permissions in the /etc/sudoers file. Members of the aforementioned admin group can run administrative commands from regular accounts. For example, if your account is a member of the admin group, you could open the second SATA drive on the local system for editing with the following command:

```
$ sudo /sbin/fdisk /dev/sdb
```

The first time such a trusted user prefaces an administrative command with the sudo command, he or she will see the following response:

```
We trust you have received the usual lecture from the local System
  Administrator. It usually boils down to these three things:

#1) Respect the privacy of others.
#2) Think before you type.
#3) With great power comes great responsibility.

Password:
```

When you see this message, enter the regular password for your account. The root administrative password, if it exists, should not work here. If that root password does work, then your regular and root passwords are identical, and that's a different security risk.

If your user account is not authorized through /etc/sudoers, you'll see the following message:

```
blackhat is not in the sudoers file. This incident will be reported.
```

The incident is reported in the appropriate log file, based on the logging service described later in this chapter.

Regular and Special Permissions

This section will be relatively short, because Chapter 5 covers permissions in detail. Linux files and directories have a user and a group owner. Permissions are split into three groups: the user who owns the file, the users in the group that owns the file, and all other users.

Regular permissions are read, write, and execute. Special permissions go beyond execute bits and can extend the executable permissions. In general, these special permissions, especially the **Set User ID (SUID) bit,** may be a security risk. If there's a binary that's vulnerable to the ptrace system call, however, the SUID or Set Group ID (SGID) bit may stop that system call in its tracks, preventing a black-hat hacker from taking control of the process.

Chapter 5 explains the chmod command described in this section in more detail.

The Set User ID Bit

Special permissions for the user are known as the SUID bit. A file with the SUID bit allows other users to run that command, with the permissions assigned to that user owner. One command with the SUID bit is /usr/bin/passwd. When you apply the ls -l command to this file, you'll see the following output:

```
-rwsr-xr-x 1 root root 27768 Jul 17  2006 /usr/bin/passwd
```

The s in the fourth alphanumeric character position is the SUID bit. As a result, the /usr/bin/passwd command is accessible to all users. That's limited by its PAM configuration, however, as described later in this chapter.

There are two methods to set the SUID bit on an executable file. The following command just sets the SUID bit on the `/home/michael/filename` file:

```
# chmod u+s /home/michael/filename
```

Alternatively, the following command sets the SUID bit with read and write permissions for the user and group owners of the file:

```
# chmod 4660 /home/michael/filename
```

> **NOTE**
>
> The `ping -f` command can flood a system with Internet Control Message Protocol (ICMP) packets. Hypothetically, without an interval, the `ping -f` command would send 100 packets per second to the given IP address. Because that can overwhelm a system, that ability is limited to the root administrative user.

The SUID bit can be a security issue. A black-hat hacker may be able to use it from any account. While the `/usr/bin/passwd` command is carefully protected in a PAM configuration file, other SUID files may not be so well protected. One way to identify files on the local system with the SUID bit is with the following command:

```
# find / -perm +4000
```

One standard executable command with the SUID bit is `/bin/ping`. If you believe regular users should not be given access to the `ping` command or are paranoid about users starting a **ping storm**, you should unset the SUID bit on this file. To do so, run the following command:

```
# chmod u-s /bin/ping
```

The Set Group ID Bit

As described earlier in this chapter, one use for the SGID bit is for shared directories. In that example, the SGID bit was set on the `/home/special` directory. Ownership of files written by user members of that `project` group was modified. The SGID bit makes the `project` group the owner of all such files written to the `/home/special` directory. One way to identify files on the local system with the SGID bit is with the following command:

```
# find / -perm +2000
```

The SGID bit is also frequently found on executable files intended to be run by groups. However, it's a way to protect certain binaries from attacks using the `ptrace` system call. One file protected by the SGID bit is the `ssh-agent` command. Without the SGID bit, a `ptrace` system call could bypass a passphrase-based Secure Shell (SSH) connection to a remote system.

The Sticky Bit

Like the SGID bit, the **sticky bit** is also normally applied to a shared directory. It allows any user to add files to and delete files from that directory. Unlike the SGID bit, the sticky bit doesn't change the ownership of any files added to that directory. Perhaps the most common use for the sticky bit is the `/tmp` directory. Users who are logging into the GUI require the ability to write to that directory. However, users do not have the ability to overwrite or delete files written there by other users.

While other users may be able to read what is written to /tmp, they won't be able to delete or overwrite those files. If you want to set the sticky bit on a different directory, the chmod command can help. The following command sets just the sticky bit on the /newtmp directory:

```
# chmod o+t /newtmp
```

Alternatively, the following command sets the sticky bit with read, write, and execute permissions for all users on the /newtmp directory:

```
# chmod 1777 /newtmp
```

Tracking Access Through Logs

Linux supports logging for services and the kernel. Until recently, this was configured in two different service daemons, syslogd and klogd, in the /sbin/ directory. The latest versions of Linux include a successor, the /sbin/rsyslogd daemon. The functionality has not changed. The system and kernel logs are so intertwined, they're usually part of the same package, rsyslog or sysklogd. In either case, Ubuntu and Red Hat take different approaches to logging configurations from this file.

This section focuses on tracking access—that is, finding those log files that record login attempts and especially login failures. These services classify log messages in a number of areas. The relevant categories are **auth** and authpriv. In the language of the log-service configuration files, auth and authpriv are known as "facilities." While both transmit the same messages, the authpriv facility is normally associated with a more secure file.

This section addresses the basics of tracking access through logs. If you're an administrator for multiple systems, however, you may prefer a system that sends you an alert when something goes wrong. That's a log-monitoring system. One option for such monitoring is the logwatch log analyzer service, described in Chapter 12.

Authorization Log Options

Many Linux distributions are in transition from the sysklogd to the rsyslog package. The main sysklogd configuration file is /etc/syslog.conf. The main configuration file from the rsyslog package is /etc/rsyslog.conf. On Ubuntu systems, it refers to the 50-default.conf file in the /etc/rsyslog.d/ directory.

Despite the changes to the names and locations of the configuration files, the basic directives haven't changed. Specifically, for Debian-based systems such as Ubuntu, the following directive sends information on login attempts to the /var/log/auth.log file:

```
auth,authpriv.*   /var/log/auth.log
```

For Red Hat-based systems, the following directive sends information on login attempts to the /var/log/secure file:

```
authpriv*  /var/log/secure
```

4

**User Privileges
and Permissions**

FIGURE 4-2

Failed remote login
attempts.

```
Feb 21 10:49:28 RHELserver sshd[27551]: Invalid user test from 60.217.234.134
Feb 21 10:49:28 RHELserver sshd[27552]: input_userauth_request: invalid user tes
t
Feb 21 10:49:28 RHELserver sshd[27551]: pam_unix(sshd:auth): check pass; user un
known
Feb 21 10:49:28 RHELserver sshd[27551]: pam_unix(sshd:auth): authentication fail
ure; logname= uid=0 euid=0 tty=ssh ruser= rhost=60.217.234.134
Feb 21 10:49:28 RHELserver sshd[27551]: pam_succeed_if(sshd:auth): error retriev
ing information about user test
Feb 21 10:49:30 RHELserver sshd[27551]: Failed password for invalid user test fr
om 60.217.234.134 port 41495 ssh2
Feb 21 10:49:30 RHELserver sshd[27552]: Received disconnect from 60.217.234.134:
 11: Bye Bye
Feb 21 10:49:32 RHELserver sshd[27553]: Invalid user test1 from 60.217.234.134
Feb 21 10:49:32 RHELserver sshd[27554]: input_userauth_request: invalid user tes
t1
Feb 21 10:49:32 RHELserver sshd[27553]: pam_unix(sshd:auth): check pass; user un
known
Feb 21 10:49:32 RHELserver sshd[27553]: pam_unix(sshd:auth): authentication fail
ure; logname= uid=0 euid=0 tty=ssh ruser= rhost=60.217.234.134
Feb 21 10:49:32 RHELserver sshd[27553]: pam_succeed_if(sshd:auth): error retriev
ing information about user test1
/var/log/secure.1
```

Authorization Log Files

The aforementioned log files are important tools in the battle to keep a system secure.
Courtesy of the `/etc/logroate.conf` file and a regular **cron** script, logs are rotated
on a weekly basis. Linux systems configured in this way typically include several weeks
of logs. Logs from previous weeks have a `.?` extension, where the ? is a number. (The ?
is a standard Linux single alphanumeric character wildcard.)

The size of these log files may be important. A big jump in the size of any log file
indicates increased activity. While this increased activity may just be a result of user-based
cron jobs that are run more frequently, it may also reflect a large number of external login
attempts. Look at the `/var/log/secure.1` file in Figure 4-2.

The log file excerpt in Figure 4-2 displays messages associated with an attempt to
log into a system named RHELserver, first as user `test` and then as user `test1`. It also
provides information on the protocol, the IP address of the attacker, and the result.

Pluggable Authentication Modules

PAM is used primarily to regulate access to administrative tools and commands. It works
as an additional layer of security for users. A substantial number of services and systems
are PAM-aware. In other words, with the right modules, access to those services and
systems can be regulated by rules defined in PAM configuration files in the `/etc/pam.d/`
directory.

To review available PAM modules for your distribution, search the applicable archives.
On a Red Hat–based system, you can search with the `yum search pam` command. On an
Ubuntu system, you can search with the `apt-cache search libpam` command. Just the
titles in the output shown in Figure 4-3 provide a feel for the full capabilities of PAM.

```
michael@LucidServerVM:~$ apt-cache search libpam
libpam-ck-connector - ConsoleKit PAM module
libpam-cracklib - PAM module to enable cracklib support
libpam-doc - Documentation of PAM
libpam-gnome-keyring - PAM module to unlock the GNOME keyring upon login
libpam-krb5 - PAM module for MIT Kerberos
libpam-ldap - Pluggable Authentication Module for LDAP
libpam-modules - Pluggable Authentication Modules for PAM
libpam-mount - PAM module that can mount volumes for a user session
libpam-opie - Use OTPs for PAM authentication
libpam-p11 - PAM module for using PKCS#11 smart cards
libpam-radius-auth - The PAM RADIUS authentication module
libpam-runtime - Runtime support for the PAM library
libpam-smbpass - pluggable authentication module for Samba
libpam0g - Pluggable Authentication Modules library
libpam0g-dev - Development files for PAM
opie-server - OPIE programs for maintaining an OTP key file
update-motd - superceded by pam_motd in libpam-modules
ldapscripts - Add and remove user and groups (stored in a LDAP directory)
libpam-afs-session - PAM module to set up a PAG and obtain AFS tokens
libpam-alreadyloggedin - PAM module to skip password authentication for logged u
sers
libpam-apparmor - changehat AppArmor library as a PAM module
libpam-blue - PAM module for local authenticaction with bluetooth devices
```

FIGURE 4-3

PAM-related packages on Ubuntu.

PAM is configured in specific files in the /etc/pam.d/ directory. Those files, such as passwd and sshd, accurately depict the command or service that is regulated.

The Structure of a PAM Configuration File

The structure of a PAM configuration file is based on its modules, available from the /lib/security/ directory. If you don't find a desired module here, you may need to install another PAM-related package. Each line in a PAM configuration file is set up in the following format:

```
module_type control_flag module_file (arguments)
```

Older versions of PAM required the full path to the module. Current versions assume the module is in the /lib/security/ directory. If installed, more information on a module_file, such as the arguments used for a module, may be available from a man page. That leaves the module_type and control_flag options. First, there are four different module types available:

- **auth**—Authenticates users by verifying passwords, group memberships, and even Kerberos tickets. Also known as authentication management.
- **account**—Checks the validity of the account based on expiration dates, time limits, or configuration files with restricted users. Also known as account management.
- **password**—Controls changes to user passwords. May also control the number of login attempts. Also known as password management.
- **session**—Makes the connection work; it may mount appropriate directories and send information to system logs. Also known as session management.

There is an implicit fifth module type, include, which incorporates the configuration directives from another file.

4

User Privileges and Permissions

Next, there are four different control flags available. Success or failure in the flag determines the next step for the configuration file:

- **required**—The module in the current line must work before PAM proceeds to the next line in the file. Alternatively, if the module doesn't work, the authentication attempt fails. However, PAM proceeds to test the lines that follow.
- **requisite**—The module in the current line must work before PAM proceeds to the next line in the file. If the module doesn't work, then the authentication attempt fails and PAM does not proceed to the lines that follow.
- **sufficient**—Assuming no previous `required` or `requisite` control flag has failed, success in this flag means the request for access is approved.
- **optional**—This flag is normally ignored unless no other control flags have returned success or failure.

With that information in hand, look at some directives in files in the `/etc/pam.d/` directory. A couple of important password `module_type` directives from Red Hat's `system-auth` file are shown here:

```
password    requisite    pam_cracklib.so try_first_pass retry=3
```

The first command uses the `pam_cracklib` module. When a new password is entered, that module checks the new password against dictionary words. The `try_first_pass` argument looks for and uses any password that was previously entered. The `retry=3` argument allows a user to try to enter the password three times.

```
password sufficient pam_unix.so md5 shadow nullok
↪try_first_pass use_authtok
```

This next command uses Message Digest 5 (MD5) hashes for passwords, in the context of the shadow password suite. The `nullok` option allows null passwords, which is sometimes required for accounts that run PAM-protected services.

PAM Configuration for Users

You can further configure a PAM configuration file to limit access to certain services or commands to specified users. That's made possible by the `pam_listfile` module. One example that puts that module into effect is the Red Hat version of the very secure FTP daemon, `vsftpd`. Access to this service is limited in the `/etc/pam.d/vsfptd` configuration file, courtesy of the following directive:

```
auth required pam_listfile.so item=user sense=deny
↪file=/etc/vsftpd/ftpusers onerr=succeed
```

This line relates to authentication management. The `required` means any access attempt must pass this test, based on the `pam_listfile` module. The `sense=deny` option denies access to users listed in the noted file, `/etc/vsftpd/ftpusers`. If that file doesn't exist, the `onerr=succeed` option means any limitations are ignored.

FYI

The leading developers of the PolicyKit are affiliated with freedesktop.org. The freedesktop.org group was created to manage interoperability projects on different Linux X Window System desktop environments. That group is loosely associated with the Free Standards Group at the Linux Foundation, which also happens to be the current sponsor of the work of Linus Torvalds on the Linux kernel.

After some attempts to integrate their work, the developers of the K Desktop Environment (KDE) no longer are working on PolicyKit development. As an alternative, KDE developers are working on KAuth as a substitute authentication framework. This book does not cover KAuth because the default GUI desktop environment for the covered distributions is GNOME. Besides, the intent of this book is to encourage administration from the command line interface.

Authorizing Access with the PolicyKit

The PolicyKit is another method for customizing access for regular users, focused on GUI tools. It can help customize access to administrative tools in a more fine-grained way relative to the /etc/sudoers file. While Red Hat is working on the PolicyKit through its Fedora releases, it likely won't be implemented in the official Red Hat release until Red Hat Enterprise Linux 6. Nevertheless, they've taken a leading role in PolicyKit development through the related Fedora project.

As of this writing, Red Hat's work on the PolicyKit is not complete. So this section will summarize some of its capabilities and configuration directories. When work is complete, you'll be able to assign access to many individual administrative tools not only by user but also by the terminal location of the user. In other words, administrators who connect remotely may be required to provide additional verification.

The configuration files for the PolicyKit have changed significantly over the past couple of years. Because they may continue to change, this section will focus on basic concepts.

How the PolicyKit Works

When a user in the admin group opens an administrative tool, that user doesn't get immediate access. Instead, the user needs to click an Unlock button and then enter his or her regular password. At least, that's based on default PolicyKit settings.

The PolicyKit can be configured in a number of different ways. With implicit authorizations, you can leave the access rules to admin users in /etc/sudoers. And you can go further. Such access can be limited to the local console.

NOTE

Earlier versions of the PolicyKit were so restrictive, they did not allow access by the `root` user to GUI administrative tools unless root was made a part of the `admin` group. That restriction has been since lifted.

Furthermore, with explicit authorizations, you can regulate the access to administrative tools by user. That access can last for a single local section or may be set permanently, even after a reboot. Needless to say, such a policy would make the associated account a more appealing target to a black-hat hacker.

PolicyKit Concepts

The PolicyKit assumes privileged tools are associated with two distinct processes: policies and mechanisms. In this context, a policy defines rules for executing an administrative tool. A mechanism runs in privileged mode.

The mechanism includes three parts: the subject, the object, and the action. The subject is the administrative tool in question. The object is the device or file to be modified. That object may be a device or a configuration file. The action specifies how the device or configuration file is to be modified. For example, a PolicyKit action may format a USB key through its object configuration file, using a formatting administrative tool.

Because the PolicyKit is relatively new, it's a work in progress. Early versions of the PolicyKit were configured in part in the `/etc/PolicyKit/` directory. The PolicyKit also includes rules on subject administrative tools in the `/etc/dbus-1/system.d/` directory. Once processed, you'll find rules in the `/var/lib/PolicyKit/` (or `/var/lib/polkit-1/`) directory.

Later versions of the PolicyKit replace the `PolicyKit/` subdirectory with the `polkit-1/` subdirectory.

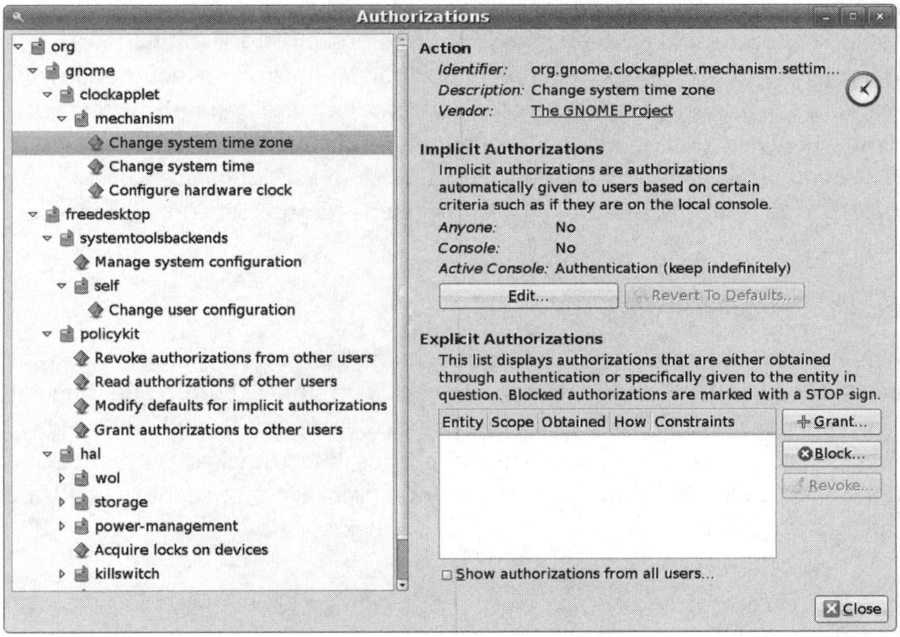

FIGURE 4-4

The PolicyKit Authorizations tool.

TABLE 4-9 PolicyKit subject identifiers.

POLICYKIT SUBJECT	DESCRIPTION	CONFIGURATION FILE
Clock management	System and hardware time management	`org.gnome.ClockApplet.Mechanism.conf`
Manage system configuration	Access to the PolicyKit	`system-tools-backends.conf`
Hardware	Wake on LAN, storage, power management	`hal.conf`
Avahi	Zero-configuration networking	`avahi-dbus.conf`
Bluetooth	Bluetooth hardware	`bluetooth.conf`
User monitoring	User tracking	`ConsoleKit.conf`
Printing	Spooler access	`cups.conf`
Dbus	Interface to DHCP	`dhcdbd.conf`
NetworkManager	Network configuration	`NetworkManager.conf, nm-applet.conf`
PolicyKit management	Access to PolicyKit tools	`org.freedesktop.PolicyKit.conf`

While both Red Hat and Ubuntu are moving away from the PolicyKit GUI configuration tool, it's still instructive for those who might be more familiar with GUI tools. It's available on slightly older releases such as Ubuntu Hardy Heron and Fedora 11. An example is shown in Figure 4-4.

You can configure PolicyKit options to regulate access from regular users to a number of systems, as described in Table 4-9. You can find the associated configuration file in the `/etc/dbus-1/system.d/` directory. These files regulate the interface between the **dbus** system and the PolicyKit.

The list of PolicyKit subjects is evolving, so what you see in Table 4-9 is just a partial list.

More on the PolicyKit Configuration

The actual PolicyKit configuration directives, once processed from their locations in the `/etc/` directory, can be found in the `/var/lib/polkit-1/` (or `/var/lib/PolicyKit/`) subdirectories. Perhaps the most interesting related work can be found on the Fedora project.

Once a regular or an administrative user is properly authenticated, future PolicyKit configuration files likely mean that a regular user won't have to constantly enter a password for regular desktop tasks such as changing the time zone on the local clock.

Furthermore, it appears that administrators won't have to constantly enter passwords for access to administrative tools.

The PolicyKit and Local Authority

With local authority features, the PolicyKit can provide one more layer of protection in case a black-hat hacker is able to connect to your system remotely. You can configure policies to require local access. Actual physical local access may be difficult for servers in racks and in remote locations, however.

The relevant commands are part of a console kit package; the name may vary by distribution. Three key commands include `ck-history`, `ck-list-sessions`, and `ck-launch-session`. These commands are of interest by themselves because they can help identify logged-in users in detail. If you see information about a session that you don't recognize, these commands may be able to help you identify the user and source.

With respect to the PolicyKit, these commands can help identify the user and type of session. The PolicyKit can use that information to determine whether to accept authentication from that user for the configured administrative tool.

The `ck-history` Command

The `ck-history` command can provide extended information about recent users—not only regular users, but also GUI access with the GNOME Display Manager (GDM). Useful options include the following:

- `--frequent`—Lists users by the frequency of their recent logins.
- `--last`—Lists last-logged-in users, by user, session, seat, and time. The `--last-compat` switch may provide a more readable format.

While you can review available options with the `ck-history -h` command, it's still a work in progress. As of this writing, several of the options shown in the output are not yet active. If you run the `ck-history` command by itself, you may not get any output, as there is no default option for the command.

The `ck-list-sessions` Command

The `ck-list-sessions` command can provide extended information about current login sessions. When run on a remote system, it would display a login at the console, in the GUI, and from a remote location as three different sessions. The command includes details such as the time when the session was started, the remote host, the UID, and even the GUI display device if applicable.

The `ck-launch-session` Command

The `ck-launch-session` command is useful for remote administrators. The PolicyKit can be used to limit access to specified administrative tools based on whether the console is local or remote. The `ck-launch-session` command can start a local session from a remote connection.

Network User Verification Tools

It's all fine and good to know how to authenticate users on a local system. But networks don't work very well unless users can log into not just a single system but an entire network. Linux includes two basic options for network-based authentication: NIS and LDAP. These are known as directory services.

Of course, you may not want to enable root administrative authentication to all systems with one network login. Even the relatively insecure NIS system makes it difficult to set up a single root administrative account for a network.

Users on Linux systems can also be configured on Microsoft-based authentication systems. Their usernames and passwords can be translated to Linux usernames and passwords with the right plug-in. If you're working with a Microsoft LDAP database, the associated Samba server plug-in is `idmap_ldap`.

As of this writing, on Microsoft Active Directory networks, Linux can be configured only as a member server of an Active Directory domain. Preliminary versions of Samba 4.0 suggests that when this version is finally released, you'll be able to configure Linux as a fully functional Active Directory domain controller, with a full database of usernames and passwords.

Alternatively, you can configure Linux with Samba as an old-style Microsoft Primary Domain Controller (PDC), based on the authentication database first created for the Windows NT 4 server operating system. While Microsoft no longer supports Windows NT 4 with security updates, Samba developers will continue to support PDC features for the foreseeable future.

NIS If You Must

If you want to set up a network-authentication scheme and already understand the shadow password suite, NIS is a relatively simple option. It allows you to use the standard shadow password suite files as the authentication database for the local network. Configuration is a straightforward process. Once the NIS server is configured, all you need to do is point NIS clients to the server for authentication in `/etc/yp.conf` and `/etc/nsswitch.conf`.

NIS is not secure. It transmits data, including password hashes, over the network without encryption. Any black-hat hacker who gets hold of these password hashes can eventually decrypt such passwords. So this book recommends that you avoid NIS. But if you run NIS, be sure to configure behind a secure network firewall. Even then, the security of your passwords will depend on the integrity of every one of your users. In addition, if any system on the local network is ever taken over by a black-hat hacker, you should assume that account passwords would be compromised.

One step you can take is to enable the `/var/yp/securenets` file. Unfortunately, this file can limit access only by IP address. Another step you can take is to secure the `portmap` service using the TCP Wrapper control files discussed in Chapter 7. If the `portmap` package is version 5 or above, it is known as a secure portmapper, and cannot be used in concert with `/var/yp/securenets`.

TABLE 4-10	Suggested standard port numbers for NIS services.		
SERVICE	**DESCRIPTION**	**SUGGESTED PORT**	**COMMAND**
ypserv	NIS server	834	YPSERVARGS="-p 834"
ypbind	Binder between NIS server/client	835	YPBINDARGS="-p 835"
yppasswd	Password management	836	YPPASSWDDARGS="-p 836"
ypxfrd	Map transfer server	837	YPXFRDARGS="-p 837"

Of course, you can further secure a system for NIS. If you have firewalls on the NIS server, review the output to the `rpcinfo -p` command. It'll provide information on the Transmission Control Protocol/Internet Procotol (TCP/IP) ports used by NIS, along with the protocol.

Not all NIS ports are automatically static. Fortunately, they can be fixed with options in the `/etc/default/nis` or `/etc/sysconfig/network` configuration files. Table 4-10 includes suggested port options for various NIS services. The noted port numbers are not currently assigned.

LDAP Shares Authentication

If you're configuring authentication on a network, LDAP may be the more secure choice. Because it can also be used to authenticate users on Microsoft and Apple operating systems, it may be a better choice for a network with multiple operating systems. It supports encryption using both the Secure Sockets Layer (SSL) and its successor, Transport Layer Security (TLS).

Such encryption requires a digital certificate. Without an encryption certificate, LDAP would also transmit passwords over a network in clear text. You can always purchase a digital certificate from an official authority such as VeriSign, Comodo, or GoDaddy. Alternatively, you can create an unofficial digital certificate with the `openssl` command. This is sometimes known as a self-signed certificate.

If you're looking to install LDAP on a local network, the Linux implementation is known as OpenLDAP. Most of the client and server packages start with `openldap`. In addition, you may want additional tools to connect the LDAP database with PAM and the name server switch configuration file in `/etc/nsswitch.conf`. Typical names for such packages include `libpam_ldap` and `nss_ldap`.

While the format of a user account in LDAP differs from that of the files of the shadow password suite, that shouldn't be a handicap. If the migration tools aren't already included in your Open LDAP server package, look for a `migrationtools` package for your distribution.

LDAP doesn't have the same network port issues as NIS, as it normally uses port number 3306 for its communication.

Best Practices: User Privileges and Permissions

The "best practices" section in this and upcoming chapters is designed as a "lessons learned" review of the chapter. If you already know the basics of a particular topic, the notes from this section may be all that you need.

First, it's important to protect the files of the shadow password suite. Because the `/etc/passwd` and `/etc/group` files are world-readable, `/etc/shadow` and `/etc/gshadow` should be readable only by the root administrative user. As a Linux administrator, you need to know how to create, delete, and otherwise manage user accounts from the command line.

You can give users two kinds of special privileges. There are the standard privileges associated with hardware components such as CDs, telephone modems, and audio devices. In addition, there are the administrative privileges associated with system configuration, file sharing, and print management.

With the Linux user private group scheme, users are members of their own special group. As an administrator, you can create a special group of users. With the help of the SGID bit, that directory can be shared by those users, secure from perusal by others. The SUID, SGID, and sticky bits are special permissions that support different kinds of access by regular users.

Linux provides a hierarchy of administrative privileges. Access to such privileges is available with the `su`, `sg`, and `sudo` commands. Some administrative privileges are tied to membership in certain Linux groups. The `sudo` command is especially important because it supports special privileges for regular users as configured in `/etc/suoders`.

Linux logs are system and kernel logs. Loggable authentication events are based on the `auth` and `authpriv` options in related configuration files. Such logs are stored in the `/var/log/` directory and are rotated on a weekly basis. Attempts by black-hat hackers to log into your systems may be found in files such as `auth.log` and `secure` in the noted directory.

PAM modules are used to further regulate access to administrative commands. PAM configuration files can be found in the `/etc/pam.d/` directory, using modules stored in the `/lib/security/` directory. The four different module types are `auth`, `account`, `password`, and `session`. The success or failure of the PAM module depends on the control flag that applies, which may be `required`, `requisite`, `sufficient`, and `optional`.

For GUI tools, the PolicyKit goes further. It regulates access between the `dbus` system and components that you may want to control in the GUI. It can regulate access to a variety of tools by user. It can regulate access by whether the user is local or remote. Just as the PolicyKit is in development for GNOME, KAuth is in development for the KDE.

If you have a network-authentication database, security issues are there as well. The two Linux-based authentication databases are NIS and LDAP. NIS is easier to set up because it can almost directly use the files of the shadow password suite. In their default configuration, both services send passwords in clear text. LDAP can be protected with a certificate authority from a third party such as VeriSign or GoDaddy, or a self-signed certificate created with the `openssl` command. NIS has no such option for encryption.

CHAPTER SUMMARY

The focus of this chapter was user security. It started with the files of the shadow password suite. Within that structure, Linux administrators can assign standard and administrative privileges based on group memberships. You can further customize administrative privileges in the /etc/sudoers file. The SUID, SGID, and sticky bits may be used to set up specialized privileges for executable files and shared directories.

Login access can be tracked through logs collected in the /var/log/ directory. PAM modules can further customize user access to key administrative tools. The PolicyKit can go even further to customize user access within the GNOME desktop environment. Two Linux-based options are available for network-based authentication: NIS and LDAP.

KEY CONCEPTS AND TERMS

account	required	Group ID (GID)
auth	requisite	Lightweight Directory Access
chage	session	Protocol (LDAP)
dbus	sg	Network Information Service
--frequent	su	(NIS)
groupadd	sudo	Ping storm
groupdel	sufficient	Set Group ID (SGID) bit
groupmod	useradd	Set User ID (SUID) bit
--last	userdel	Shadow password suite
optional	usermod	Sticky bit
password		User ID (UID)
		User private group scheme

CHAPTER 4 ASSESSMENT

1. Which of the following files is *not* normally readable by all users?

A. /etc/passwd
B. /etc/shadow
C. /etc/group
D. /etc/login.defs

2. Which of the following files contains information about time limits on a password?

A. /etc/passwd
B. /etc/shadow
C. /etc/group
D. /etc/gshadow

3. Which of the following commands can be used to revise expiration information on a user password?

A. useradd
B. passwd
C. groupmod
D. chage

4. The _____ command searches for all files owned by the group named audio. Assume you're logged into the root administrative account.

5. Which of the following statements is true with the user private group scheme?

A. There are no private groups in Linux.
B. User information in the group is private.
C. The primary UID for the user is the same as the primary GID for the user.
D. Users are members of the same private group.

6. Members of which of the following groups are frequently set up as printer administrators? (Select two.)

A. admin
B. adm
C. lpadmin
D. sys

7. Which of the following commands only requires the password of a configured standard user?

A. sudoers
B. sudo
C. su
D. sg

8. Enter the _____ command to open and edit the /etc/sudoers file in a command-line console.

9. Which of the following special permissions is associated with a shared directory? That directory is *not* accessible to others who are *not* members of the group owner of that directory.

A. SUID
B. SGID
C. Sticky bit
D. Executable bit

10. Which of the following options in a log configuration file collects information on login attempts and failures?

A. auth
B. sys
C. log
D. user

11. Which of the following PAM modules is least related to login information?

A. auth
B. account
C. password
D. session

12. Enter the _____ directory for PAM modules.

13. Which of the following PolicyKit concepts is associated with configuring access rules to special desktop tools by user?

A. Implicit authorizations
B. Explicit authorizations
C. Administrative authorizations
D. PolicyKit authorizations

14. Which of the following PolicyKit commands can be used to identify user logins by session? (Select two.)

A. ck-history
B. ck-list-sessions
C. ck-launch-session
D. ck-logins

15. Which of the following commands can help identify network ports used by NIS through the portmapper?

A. nismap -p
B. ypbind -p
C. rpcinfo -p
D. portmap -p

Filesystems, Volumes, and Encryption

A S A LINUX EXPERT, you already know how to set up partitions, logical volumes, and redundant array of independent disks (RAID) systems. You know how to configure those systems on selected directories. You know how to format those **filesystems**. But there are choices that can enhance security or at least limit the risk to important data. These choices relate to how such volumes are organized, how they're mounted, and how they're formatted. Of course, encryption of such filesystems can also enhance security.

While file and folder permissions are basic to Linux, they are the starting point for security on Linux. You'll examine those permissions when they're local and when they're mounted from remote systems. With the right settings, selected filesystems can be configured and mounted with quotas and access control lists. This chapter examines those topics in detail.

Chapter 5 Topics

This chapter covers the following topics and concepts:

- How to organize filesystems
- What options for journals, formats, and file size affect security
- How to use encryption
- What basic concepts for file and folder permissions are
- What basic concepts for networked file and folder permissions are
- How to configure and implement quotas on a filesystem
- How to configure and implement access control lists on a filesystem
- What best practices are for filesystems, volumes, and encryption

Filesystem Organization

In Linux, all data is stored as files. A filesystem specifies how those files are stored, marked, and retrieved. As you'll see in this chapter, filesystems can be local or remote. In this section, you'll review some basics of a filesystem, the **filesystem hierarchy standard (FHS)**, how filesystems can be organized, and when it is practical to configure a Linux filesystem in read-only mode.

Filesystem Basics

At its core, a filesystem is a database. Filesystems are configured to store data. In Linux, filesystems are associated with a particular device filename. That device might be named /dev/sda1, which is a standard device file for the first partition on a standard first hard drive. Or that file might be set to something like /dev/md0, which is a standard device file for the first configured local **software RAID** array. Alternatively, that device could be /dev/VolGroup00/LogVol00, which is a standard device file for a logical volume.

FYI

Software RAID on Linux is slightly misnamed, as it is based on an array of partitions, not disks. But software RAID is more flexible. While it's most efficient to set up software RAID arrays based on partitions of equal sizes, that's not required. Of course, to take advantage of the redundancy associated with RAID, you need to make sure the partitions that make up the RAID array are from different physical hard drives. Otherwise, the failure of a single physical disk could lead to the loss of multiple elements of the RAID array, potentially leading to the loss of all data on the array.

5

Filesystems, Volumes, and Encryption

Files on a device are accessible only when they're mounted on a Linux directory. The way filesystems are mounted on different Linux directories is documented in the /etc/fstab configuration file. In the next section, you'll review the filesystem hierarchy standard (FHS). You can mount a filesystem on just about any of those directories (or subdirectories). But beware: It's not appropriate to mount a separate filesystem on every directory.

The word "filesystem" has several different meanings in Linux. These include the following:

- A construct of space on a hard drive such as a partition, RAID array, or logical volume
- The device files associated with a partition, RAID array, or logical volume, such as /dev/sda1, /dev/md0, or /dev/VolGroup00/LogVol00
- The format method associated with a partition, RAID array, or logical volume, such as ext3 or vfat
- A mounted directory, such as the /boot/ directory filesystem

Incidentally, "filesystem" is sometimes also written as two words: file system.

The Filesystem Hierarchy Standard (FHS)

The FHS is the way files and directories are organized on a Linux system. Because the current version of the FHS was defined back in 2004, most Linux distributions include their own variations. These directories may be dedicated to different functions such as the boot process, user files, logs, command utilities, and more. Table 5-1 defines the major directories of the FHS. It includes only first-level subdirectories; in other words, it does not describe second-level subdirectories such as /etc/X11/. It includes notes on those directories that are practical to mount separately, along with directories that you could choose to mount in read-only mode.

As shown in Table 5-1, some directories just belong with the top-level root directory. They include /bin/, /dev/, /etc/, /lib/, and /sbin/. If they're mounted on different filesystems and there's a problem with the different filesystem such as corruption, that could keep a system from booting.

Some of you may see additional subdirectories such as /proc/, /selinux/, /sys/, /net/, /smb/, and /tftpboot/. The first three are virtual filesystems, created during the boot process in local memory. The /net/ and /smb/ directories are standard mount points for networked filesystems using the automounter. The /tftpboot/ directory is a common location for Trivial File Transfer Protocol (TFTP) server files, which may include terminal-based systems such as those associated with the Linux Terminal Server Project (LTSP).

TABLE 5-1   Important filesystem hierarchy standard directories.

DIRECTORY	DESCRIPTION
/	Top-level root directory, always mounted separately
/bin/	Basic command-line utilities, should always be a part of /
/boot/	Linux kernel, initial RAM disk, bootloader files; frequently mounted separately
/dev/	Device files for hardware and software, should always be part of /
/etc/	Configuration files, should always be part of /
/home/	Home directories for every regular user; frequently mounted separately
/lib/	Program libraries; should always be part of / (/lib64/ may exist on 64-bit systems)
/media/	Standard mount point for removable media such as CD/DVD drives and universal serial bus (USB) keys; may also be used for other volumes such as a directory formatted to a Microsoft file system
/mnt/	Common legacy mount point for removable media and temporary filesystems
/opt/	Common location for some third-party applications; may be empty and can be mounted separately
/root/	The home directory for the root administrative user; should always be part of /
/sbin/	Primarily for administrative commands; should always be part of /
/srv/	Directory commonly used for network services such as those that share using FTP and HTTP; may be helpful to mount separately
/tmp/	Common location for temporary files; if the /tmp/ filesystem is full, users would not be able to log into the GUI
/usr/	Small programs generally accessible to all users; could be mounted separately and read-only
/var/	Log files, print spools; some distributions use it for network service files; may be helpful to mount separately

FYI

Linux uses the word **root** in several contexts. By itself, root is the name of the standard Linux administrative user. The top-level root directory is symbolized by the forward slash (/). In contrast, the home directory of the root user is /root, which is a subdirectory of the top-level root directory (/). And in the configuration file for the Grand Unified Bootloader (GRUB), the root (hd0,0) directive specifies the partition with the files normally mounted on the /boot directory.

Good Volume Organization Can Help Secure a System

Generally, if you have more space available on a local system, you'll be able to configure additional directories on different filesystems. If you're configuring a bastion host with a small amount of space, it's often best to configure a single partition for the entire system. But if the system has a little bit of extra space, it's often best to isolate some filesystems. In some cases, an isolated filesystem may minimize damage of extra large files that would otherwise overload the capabilities of the system. In other cases, an isolated filesystem includes the most variable files and is easier to back up.

NOTE

The sections that follow describe first-level directories configured as separate filesystems. Directories at lower levels, such as /var/ftp/ or /home/michael/ can also be configured as separate filesystems.

The following sections specify different directories that you may set up on different filesystems and the reasons why this is practical. Other directories either just belong with the top-level root directory (/) or are designed for mounting with removable media.

The /boot/ Filesystem

By default, Red Hat–based distributions set up the /boot/ directory on a separate filesystem, always on a separate partition. It's not realistic to set up the /boot/ directory as a logical volume, as it contains the Linux kernel and initial RAM disk files needed before Linux can read a logical volume. While it is possible to set up /boot/ on a RAID array, a /boot/ filesystem is typically pretty small at 100 to 500 MB, is infrequently changed, and is therefore easier to back up.

The 100 or 500 MB that Red Hat configures for /boot/ is typically plenty of space for four or five versions of the Linux kernel and associated initial RAM disks. Older versions of the Linux kernel can typically be deleted. Generally, only developers have a need for more versions of the Linux kernel on any single system.

The /home/ Filesystem

You'll probably have more reasons to set up the /home/ directory as a separate filesystem. It's easier back up user files configured in that way. It'll be easier to upgrade a distribution to a later release with much less risk to user files. Given the importance of user files, it may be helpful to set up the /home/ directory on a RAID array. If your system includes a growing number of users, it may be helpful to set up the /home/ directory on a logical volume. Of course, with some extra work, you can set up a RAID array from two (or more) logical volumes.

The /opt/ Filesystem

While /opt/ is not frequently used, it is a standard location for third-party applications. While those applications may take advantage of standard Linux configuration files in /etc/ and libraries in /lib/, the applications in /opt/ are generally not important in the actual Linux boot process. Examples of Linux applications that use this filesystem include the following:

* Adobe Acrobat
* Cross-over Office
* OpenOffice.org Suite (when installed directly from a downloaded package from *openoffice.org*)
* RealPlayer for Linux

Because the /opt/ directory is not often checked, it may be helpful to set it up as a separate filesystem. In fact, it's an excellent candidate for a logical volume. If the number of third-party applications on the local system grows, a configuration as a logical volume makes it easier to expand the space allocated to the /opt/ directory.

The /srv/ Filesystem

The /srv/ filesystem is designed to contain files associated with some FTP and HTTP services. Some distributions set up the same services in subdirectories of the /var/ directory. The same issues that apply to /srv/ also apply to those /var/ subdirectories.

As uploads can and often are enabled especially to FTP services, it can be helpful to set up the /srv/ directory in a separate filesystem. If someone chooses to upload a library of multi-gigabyte movie files to your FTP server, a separate filesystem would act as a barrier, keeping that upload from affecting any other filesystem.

The /tmp/ Filesystem

The /tmp/ directory is a common location for temporary files such as shared downloads. It's also a location for files associated with logins to the GUI. If the /tmp/ filesystem is full, users who try to log into the GUI are "stuck" with the command line.

So if your systems use the /tmp/ directory for shared downloads, it may be helpful to set it up on a separate filesystem for that directory, so users who download too much do not overload the local system.

The /var/ Filesystem

Files in the /var/ directory can easily grow quite large. Some distributions use subdirectories of /var/ to contain files associated with some servers. Uploads to such servers, if limits can be breached, could quickly overload the space available on just about any system.

In addition, the /var/ directory contains log files. The logs for enterprise-level Web sites can easily grow to several gigabytes every day. If such a directory of logs is not maintained, this array of large files could quickly overload just about any system.

The configuration of the /var/ directory on a separate filesystem can limit such risks.

Read-Only Filesystems

It is often possible and even desirable to set up a few filesystems in "read-only" mode. When configured correctly, such filesystems can make it just a bit more difficult for black-hat hackers to do real damage to your systems. Three filesystem candidates for mounting in read-only mode are /boot/, /opt/, and /usr/. Of course, if you were to update a kernel or install a new package, you'd have to remount the filesystem in read-write mode so the kernel or package files could be written to the appropriate directories.

The following is a possible read-only configuration directive for the /boot/ directory in the /etc/fstab configuration file:

```
/dev/sda1  /boot  ext2   ro,exec,auto,nouser,async 1 2
```

If you're familiar with the format of the /etc/fstab file, you should already know that an option like defaults would mount the noted filesystem in read-write mode. Of course, since you'll also have to mount that filesystem in read-write mode when updating related components such as the Linux kernel, it may be helpful to have the read-write configuration line in comments in the same file. That means that /etc/fstab file might also include the following line for the /boot/ directory filesystem:

```
# /dev/sda1  /bootext2   defaults 1 2
```

Not all filesystems should be mounted in read-only mode. Users who log into the GUI need write access to the filesystem with the /tmp/ directory. Log information is not available unless the system can write to the filesystem with the /var/ directory. New packages can't be installed unless the system has write access to the filesystems associated with the /etc/, /usr/, and /lib/ directories. Of course, you could remount a filesystem in read-write mode when installing or updating software.

Closely related to the concept of a read-only filesystem is the use of a live CD/DVD-based distribution. While users can write to filesystems configured from most live CD/DVDs, files are written only in the RAM memory configured as a virtual drive. Such changes are lost as soon as the system is shut down. And by definition, anything written to that system is not written to the live CD/DVD. So if there is a security breach, the information on the CD/DVD media is not affected.

```
 1  FAT12             24  NEC DOS          81  Minix / old Lin  bf  Solaris
 2  XENIX root        39  Plan 9           82  Linux swap / So  c1  DRDOS/sec (FAT-
 3  XENIX usr         3c  PartitionMagic   83  Linux            c4  DRDOS/sec (FAT-
 4  FAT16 <32M        40  Venix 80286      84  OS/2 hidden C:   c6  DRDOS/sec (FAT-
 5  Extended          41  PPC PReP Boot    85  Linux extended   c7  Syrinx
 6  FAT16             42  SFS              86  NTFS volume set  da  Non-FS data
 7  HPFS/NTFS         4d  QNX4.x           87  NTFS volume set  db  CP/M / CTOS / .
 8  AIX               4e  QNX4.x 2nd part  88  Linux plaintext  de  Dell Utility
 9  AIX bootable      4f  QNX4.x 3rd part  8e  Linux LVM        df  BootIt
 a  OS/2 Boot Manag   50  OnTrack DM       93  Amoeba           e1  DOS access
 b  W95 FAT32         51  OnTrack DM6 Aux  94  Amoeba BBT       e3  DOS R/O
 c  W95 FAT32 (LBA)   52  CP/M             9f  BSD/OS           e4  SpeedStor
 e  W95 FAT16 (LBA)   53  OnTrack DM6 Aux  a0  IBM Thinkpad hi  eb  BeOS fs
 f  W95 Ext'd (LBA)   54  OnTrackDM6       a5  FreeBSD          ee  EFI GPT
10  OPUS              55  EZ-Drive         a6  OpenBSD          ef  EFI (FAT-12/16/
11  Hidden FAT12      56  Golden Bow       a7  NeXTSTEP         f0  Linux/PA-RISC b
12  Compaq diagnost   5c  Priam Edisk      a8  Darwin UFS       f1  SpeedStor
14  Hidden FAT16 <3   61  SpeedStor        a9  NetBSD           f4  SpeedStor
16  Hidden FAT16      63  GNU HURD or Sys  ab  Darwin boot      f2  DOS secondary
17  Hidden HPFS/NTF   64  Novell Netware   b7  BSDI fs          fd  Linux raid auto
18  AST SmartSleep    65  Novell Netware   b8  BSDI swap        fe  LANstep
1b  Hidden W95 FAT3   70  DiskSecure Mult  bb  Boot Wizard hid  ff  BBT
1c  Hidden W95 FAT3   75  PC/IX

Command (m for help):
```

FIGURE 5-1

Linux partition type identifiers.

Journals, Formats, and File Sizes

As odd as it sounds, the choices made with respect to journals, formats, and file sizes can affect security with respect to availability, as defined in Chapter 1. To that end, the selection of a filesystem can affect how well it resists an attack. A journal in a filesystem is a list of changes to be written. Therefore, the data on a **journaled filesystem** is more likely to survive a power surge. But only certain types of Linux filesystems are journaled—and the journaling format you select relates in part to the size of most files found on that filesystem.

Linux can handle an impressive array of filesystem formats. If you have any doubts, take a look at the Linux version of the `fdisk` drive-management tool. Figure 5-1 shows a list of available filesystem partition type identifiers (IDs).

If you're reading carefully, you may already realize that a filesystem partition identifier and a filesystem format is not the same thing. When `fdisk` creates a partition, it assumes you're using the standard Linux partition ID of 83. If you're setting up a different kind of partition, you'll need to know different partition types.

> ▶ **TIP**
>
> It is possible to use Linux's `fdisk` to create partitions suited to a wide variety of operating systems. But if you want to create a partition associated with a different operating system, it's generally best to do so with tools native to that operating system.

Partition Types

The focus of this section is on current Linux partition types. It does not address partitions normally associated with any other operating system. In most cases, the partitions on your Linux systems will be one of five different partition types, as follows:

- **82**—Linux `swap` is used for partitions dedicated to swap space.
- **83**—Linux is used for standard partitions with data.
- **85**—Linux `extended` is the label for the partition that can contain logical partitions.
- **8e**—Linux `LVM` configures a partition that can be used as a component of a logical volume.
- **fd**—Linux `raid auto` specifies partitions that can be used as components of a RAID array.

Most Linux partitions with data are of type 83. If you want to format a partition to the `ext2`, `ext3`, `ext4`, `reiserfs`, or `xfs` filesystems, you'll want to configure a partition of that type.

The Right Format Choice

Linux format commands apply to a partition, a logical volume, or a RAID array. For example, once you run a command such as the following on an associated device file, the partition, logical volume, or RAID array identified by the `/dev/sda`1 device file is formatted and ready for use:

```
# mkfs.ext3 /dev/sda1
```

But what format should you select for a filesystem? Well, it depends. Start with the standard Linux filesystem formats: `ext2`, `ext3`, and `ext4`. These represent the second, third, and fourth extended filesystems. (The original Linux extended filesystem, `ext`, is obsolete.)

- **ext2**—The second extended filesystem does not include journaling. If there are problems, Linux has to check every block for unwritten data. But journaling requires additional space. Because the partition associated with the `/boot/` directory can be small, it may be well suited to the `ext2` filesystem. Writes to that partition are infrequent.
- **ext3**—The third extended filesystem writes data to a journal before writing it to the actual filesystem. Because the system writes to file twice, performance is slower.
- **ext4**—The fourth extended filesystem is suited for filesystems with some large files. It includes a defragmentation tool.

Other major Linux filesystems include variations on journaling. The **xfs** filesystem developed by the company originally known as Silicon Graphics is suited for systems that require the transfer of larger files. The `ext4` filesystem is fairly new and also supports larger files. The **reiserfs** filesystem is a common option on the SUSE distribution. Based on the concept of balanced trees, it's suited for filesystems with a few large and many very small files.

Available Format Tools

It's easy to find the format commands available on a local system. Just about all of them are variations on the **mkfs** command. If command-completion features are active on your shell, all you need to do is type mkfs and press the Tab key twice. With the right packages, the mkfs command can be used to format all the filesystems just described. It also can be used to format Microsoft VFAT and NTFS filesystems.

You can use these commands to format the partition, logical volume, or RAID array of your choice. For example, the following commands are two different ways to format the /dev/md0 RAID array:

```
# mkfs.ext3 /dev/md0
# mkfs -t ext3 /dev/md0
```

A slight variation on the mkfs command is designed to format swap partitions; that's the mkswap command.

Using Encryption

Linux supports a number of different options for encrypting files, directories, and volumes. In this section, you'll look at the wide variety of encryption tools available for Linux. But this section is just a snapshot; it's not meant to be a comprehensive list. You'll also see an example of how each of these data types can be encrypted. The tool selected is based on the default tool used for Ubuntu and Red Hat distributions.

Generally, you don't need to encrypt everything. The files of an open source operating system are well known. However, user files are often sensitive and are therefore excellent candidates for encryption. To that end, perhaps the prime candidate for encryption is any partition, volume, or RAID array associated with the /home/ directory. Alternatively, you might just encrypt the home directory of a specific user or just a few selected files.

Encryption Tools

Linux supports a wide variety of encryption tools. Such tools can be split into two categories: **kernel-space** and **user-space**. Kernel-space tools depend primarily on modules that can be loaded with the Linux kernel. User-space tools can more easily utilize the libraries loaded in the /lib/ directory. In general, while kernel-space encryption is faster, user-space encryption is easier to implement.

Most Linux kernels support a wide variety of encryption options. To get a sense of what's included, run the following command, which returns all lines with the term CRYPT in the configuration of the currently loaded kernel.

```
# grep CRYPT /boot/config-`uname -r`
```

Options for encryption tools are described in the sections that follow. Some tools listed in one category may be used to encrypt data in two or all three categories.

TABLE 5-2	Linux file-encryption commands.
COMMAND	**DESCRIPTION**
`bcrypt`	Uses the blowfish encryption algorithm, based on a passphrase
`ccrypt`	Uses the U.S. Advanced Encryption Standard (AES), uses passphrases
`gpg`	Users may select from different encryption algorithms; may use passphrases or public and private key pairs
`ncrypt`	Users may select from different encryption algorithms; passphrases are hashed
`pad`	Uses "one time pad" encryption

Encrypted Files

Perhaps the most common standard for file encryption on Linux is based on the GNU Privacy Guard (GPG) command, gpg, a user-space tool. But that's just one of many Linux tools available for file encryption. Several other Linux tools are shown in Table 5-2.

Now look at two ways that the **gpg** command can be used. By default, it uses the CAST-128 block cipher encryption algorithm.

Encryption With a Passphrase

With the -c switch, you can encrypt any file with a passphrase. The first time the gpg command is run, it'll create a standard public key in the user's home directory, in the .gnupg/ subdirectory. But that public key isn't used in this case. The user is prompted for a passphrase.

The selected file is saved in encrypted format, with the .gpg extension. Of course, if you're concerned about someone reading files in the local directory, you should delete the original unencrypted file. You can then send the encrypted file to others as desired.

Users can then decrypt the file with the gpg command. The user who runs that command is prompted for the original passphrase.

Encryption with a Public/Private Key Pair

Before you can protect a file with a GPG-based public/private key pair, you need to create those keys. To do so, run the gpg --gen-key command. You're prompted to choose from three different options:

- **Elgamal**—A probabilistic encryption scheme developed by Taher Elgamal. When running the gpg command, this scheme is paired with DSA for digital signatures.
- **DSA**—Digital Signature Algorithm, used by the U.S. government for digital signatures.
- **RSA**—A public-key algorithm, named for its developers, Rivest, Shamir, and Adelman.

Despite the available options, the documentation from the developers of GPG suggests that you should choose the first option because the other options simply provide digital signatures. The latest version of Ubuntu includes a fourth option, which includes RSA-based encryption and digital signatures. If this is the first time you've used the gpg --gen-key command, you'll see the following messages:

```
gpg: directory `/home/michael/.gnupg' created

gpg: new configuration file `/home/michael/.gnupg/gpg.conf' created

gpg: WARNING: options in `/home/michael/.gnupg/gpg.conf'
↳ are not yet active during this run

gpg: keyring `/home/michael/.gnupg/secring.gpg' created

gpg: keyring `/home/michael/.gnupg/pubring.gpg' created
```

After selecting a key, be prepared to select the following:

- An encryption-key size of between 1,024 and 4,096 bits
- A key lifetime in days, weeks, months, or years; alternatively, choose the default setting of 0, which means the key does not expire
- A name, e-mail address, and comment
- A passphrase

The key depends in part on a random number generator. If you get a "not enough random bytes available" message, you'll need to run a command that reads or writes a lot. One simple method is to open up a second terminal and run the following command a few times:

```
$ cat /boot/initrd* > /dev/null
```

When successful, you'll see messages similar to the following:

```
gpg: /home/michael/.gnupg/trustdb.gpg: trustdb created

gpg: key CA58E7F6 marked as ultimately trusted

public and secret key created and signed.
```

To confirm the creation of a private and public key pair, run the gpg --list-keys command. This assumes you've set up the gpg command on both local and remote systems. The first two steps export and copy public-private key pair on system A. The user on system B can encrypt a file and then send it to user A. Finally, user A can use his or her private key to decrypt the file.

1. On system A, export the public key with the following command. The name you use should reflect the name shown in the output from the gpg --list-keys command. The gpg.pub filename is arbitrary; you can use the filename of your choice. Quotes are not required around the name.

   ```
   $ gpg --export Michael Jang > gpg.pub
   ```

2. Copy the public key file (gpg.pub in this example) to system B. It may be sent by e-mail, or it could be copied by other means such as the scp command described in Chapter 8.

3. On system B, import the public key with the following command:

   ```
   $ gpg --import gpg.pub
   ```

   If successful, you'll see messages similar to the following:

   ```
   gpg: key CA58E7F6: public key "Michael Jang (This is
   ↪ an encryption test)
   <michael@example.org>" imported
   gpg: Total number processed: 1
   gpg:     imported: 1  (RSA: 1)
   ```

4. On system B, verify the import with the gpg --list-keys command. The last key shown should reflect the information from the same command run on system A.

5. On system B, encrypt the file of your choice. Quotes around the name, taken from the gpg --list-keys command, are required. This command encrypts the wagthedog.odt file in the file named wagthedog.enc.

   ```
   $ gpg --out wagthedog.enc --recipient "Michael Jang"
   ↪ --encrypt wagthedog.odt
   ```

6. Copy the encrypted file to system A.

7. On system A, run the following command to decrypt the noted file:

   ```
   $ gpg --out wagthedog.odt --decrypt wagthedog.enc
   ```

8. Still on system A, you'll be prompted for the passphrase created earlier in this section with messages similar to those shown here. The correct passphrase decrypts the noted file, with information on the encryption key.

   ```
   You need a passphrase to unlock the secret key for
   user: "Michael Jang (This is an encryption test)
   <michael@example.org>" 1024-bit RSA key,
   ID 33A09C78, created 2010-03-21 (main key
   ID CA58E7F6)
   Enter passphrase:
   ```

Encrypted Directories

Ubuntu has recently made it easy to set up an encrypted directory for a single user during the installation process. It makes sense to encrypt the directory of that first user, especially since that user has implicit administrative privileges defined through the /etc/sudoers configuration file, as described in Chapter 4. While the standard Ubuntu method is with the **enterprise cryptographic filesystem (eCryptfs)**, other options are available. One alternative uses loopback encrypted filesystems based on the pluggable authentication modules (PAM) mount module. The eCryptfs system includes both kernel-space and user-space components.

One advantage of the Ubuntu system is that the password for the user's account is also used as a passphrase for that user's encrypted directory. So unlike with many encrypted partitions, you don't have to enter a passphrase during the boot process.

If you've chosen to encrypt a home directory during the Ubuntu installation process, you'll see the hidden .ecryptfs/ and .Private/ subdirectories in that home directory. You'll also see something similar to the following output from the mount command, which suggests that the encrypted files are actually in the .Private/ subdirectory.

```
/home/michael/.Private on /home/michael type ecryptfs
```

Those files are decrypted when they're mounted on the user's home directory using the **ecryptfs** option. One relatively simple way to set up the same type of encryption for user directories is with the ecrypt-setup-private command. Try this command on a system where a home directory is not encrypted. You don't even need (or want) root administrative access in this case, as the encrypted directory is presumably owned by the user in question. When the encrypt-setup-private command is entered, the user is prompted for two things:

- The login passphrase, which is really that user's login password
- A mount passphrase, which can be used to manually remount the directory from a rescue system

If successful, you'll see the hidden directories just described in the noted user's home directory. If there are errors, they may be related to the encryption modules that are or are not loaded. For example, the lsmod command run on an Ubuntu system where directory encryption is enabled includes the following output:

```
Module          Size    Used by
sha256_generic  11191   2
aes_i586         7268   6
aes_generic     26863   1 aes_i586
dm_crypt        11131   1
```

The loaded modules related to encryption include the following:

- **Secure hash algorithm (SHA)** with 256 bits (sha256_generic)
- **Advanced encryption standard (AES)** for x86 CPUs (aes_i586)
- **Disk encryption subsystem** (dm_crypt)

One command that may load all these modules simultaneously is the following:

```
# modprobe dm_crypt
```

Encrypted Partitions and Volumes

While the latest encryption schemes are often associated with more recent kernels, that is not always the case. Red Hat has enabled filesystem encryption during the installation process starting with the release of Red Hat Enterprise Linux version 5.3. Since the previous section focused on an Ubuntu method for encryption, this section focuses on the Red Hat method for encryption, with guidance from the *Red Hat Enterprise Linux 5 Installation Guide*. To that end, Red Hat uses the **Linux unified key setup (LUKS)** disk-encryption specification. It'll work if the dm_crypt module is loaded, which can be verified in the output from the lsmod command. LUKS is also a user-space tool.

The basic steps are as follows:

1. Create the desired partition, logical volume, or RAID array to be used as an encrypted partition or volume.

2. Based on the device file to be used, fill the device with random data. The /dev/urandom device is a Linux-based random number generator. For example, if the partition device is /dev/vda1, you'd run the following command:

   ```
   # dd if=/dev/urandom of=/dev/vda1
   ```

   This command may take some time; one test suggests 10 minutes per gigabyte of space being randomized.

3. Format the device with the **cryptsetup** command, using the noted LUKS extension.

   ```
   # cryptsetup luksFormat /dev/vda1
   ```

   If you see an error message related to the VIA padlock, the dm_crypt and related cryptographic modules may not be loaded.

4. To verify detailed encryption information for the noted device, run the following command:

   ```
   # cryptsetup luksDump /dev/vda1
   ```

5. The noted partition or volume should now be encrypted. The next step is to set up a device name to be used when the volume is decrypted during the boot process, which you can do with the following command (substitute as desired for /dev/vda1 and secret):

   ```
   # cryptsetup luksOpen /dev/vda1 secret
   ```

      If desired, you can use the `cryptsetup luksUUID /dev/vda1` command to set up a universally unique identifier (UUID) for the encrypted volume.

6. You should now be able to find more information on the noted volume with the `dmestup /dev/mapper/secret` command.

7. Format the device as desired; the following example formats the noted device to the `ext3` filesystem format:

```
# mkfs -t ext3 /dev/mapper/secret
```

8. You're now ready to mount the noted `/dev/mapper/secret` device on the directory of your choice. Two more steps are required to make the mount survive a reboot. For the purpose of this exercise, create a directory named `/encrypted`.

9. Create or add information from the partition or volume to the `/etc/crypttab` configuration file. For the parameters given, you'd add the following line to that file:

```
secret /dev/vda1 none
```

If a UUID is used, you can substitute that for the `/dev/vda1` device file. Use the UUID=*uuidnumber* format, where *uuidnumber* is the UUID number created with the `cryptsetup luksUUID /dev/vda1` command.

10. Implement the result in the `/etc/fstab` configuration file. In this case, you can use the `/dev/mapper/secret` or the `/dev/mapper/luks-`*uuidnumber* device filenames.

Local File and Folder Permissions

While the concepts of file ownership and permissions are basic to Linux, these concepts make up the standard discretionary access control system. So while this section should be review for most, file permissions are an elementary part of security on Linux. If you're already familiar with file permissions, this section should be a simple review.

Strictly speaking, there are no separate folders in Linux. Everything in Linux is a file. Folders that might exist in file browsers such as Nautilus and Konqueror are based on Linux directories. And directories are just a special kind of file. There are other special kinds of Linux files.

To summarize, just about all you need to know with respect to file and folder permissions is shown in the output from the `ls -l` command. The first letter or dash in each line of output indicates the type of file. For our purposes, you need be aware of three types of files. A dash (`-`) indicates a regular file; a d indicates a directory, and an l indicates a soft-linked file.

These basic file and folder permissions are known as one method of discretionary access control. In this case, file and folder permissions meet discretionary access control requirements as access is regulated by file and the identity of users. A second level of discretionary access control is based on access control lists (ACLs) discussed later in this chapter.

Basic File Ownership Concepts

Every file has two owners: a user and a group. In many cases, those owners look like the same user. Based on the user private group scheme discussed in Chapter 4, every user is a member of a group of the same name. But any other user can be a member of any group. Just to be clear, take a look at this output from the `ls -l /var/log/cups/access_log` command:

```
-rw------- 1 root lp 10387 Mar 10 14:46 access_log
```

The user owner of this file is `root`, and the group owner of this file is `lp`.

File ownership in Linux can be modified with the **chown** and **chgrp** commands. These commands are straightforward; the `chown` command changes the identity of the user who owns a file. The `chgrp` command changes the identity of the group that owns a file. The `chown` command is a bit more capable, as it can change both the user and group owner of a file simultaneously. For example, the following command assigns the user named `donna` and the group named `users` as the owners of the noted file:

```
# chown donna.users somefile
```

For both commands, the `-R` switch changes ownership recursively. For example, if you have to set up user `temp1` as a replacement for user `worker`, you can change the name and ownership of all files in user `worker`'s directory with the following commands:

```
# mv /home/worker /home/temp1
# chown -R temp1.temp1 /home/temp1
```

Basic File-Permission Concepts

Standard Linux file permissions can be assigned in three categories: for the user owner, the group owner, and all other users on the local system. In short, these categories are known as user, group, and others. More Linux permissions are associated with access control lists, described later in this chapter.

Each file may be configured with read, write, and execute permissions for the user owner, the group owner, and every other user. Examine the output from an `ls -l /home` command on a hypothetical directory:

```
drwxr-xr-- 1 root project 100387 Mar 10 12:43 project
```

The first d confirms this is a directory. The nine characters that follow specify the permissions for the user, group, and others.

The first trio of characters is `rwx`, which specifies that the user owner, the root administrative user, has read, write, and execute permissions on the /home/`project`/ directory.

The second trio of characters is `r-x`, which specifies that the group owner, the `project` group, has read and execute permissions on that directory. The permissions assigned to the group apply to members of that group. Therefore, every user who is a member of the `project` group has those same read and execute permissions on the /home/`project`/ directory.

Finally, the last trio of characters is r - -, which is supposed to provide read permissions to all other users on that directory. But that's not too helpful to those other users. If your account is not root or a member of the project group and you tried to run the ls -l /home/project/ command, all you'd see are filenames with question marks where you might expect to see information on owners and permissions.

If you set this up on your system, try the **chmod** 751 /home/project/ command. Now log in as a regular user who is not a member of the project group. You should now be able to read the files in the /home/project/ directory with just those executable permissions.

In other words, if you're going to allow anyone but the root administrative user to read a directory, you'll need to make sure the executable bit is set. You'll review how the chmod command can be used to modify permissions shortly.

But first, look at the output from the ls -l /etc/grub.conf file on a Red Hat system:

```
lrwxrwxrwx 1 root root 22 Feb  1 10:44 /etc/grub.conf ->
↪ ../boot/grub/grub.conf
```

The first letter in the output confirms this file is a soft link. That's further confirmed by the end of the output, where the /etc/grub.conf file actually is redirected to the actual file, /boot/grub/grub.conf.

The permissions may appear too generous. You don't want everyone to be able to modify or even see the contents of the local GRUB configuration file.

Fortunately, that's not the case. The actual permissions are based on those set on the actual file, /boot/grub/grub.conf. On Red Hat systems, permissions are read-write just for the user owner of the file.

Changing File Permissions

The focus of this section is the chmod command. The most efficient way to use chmod is based on an octal representation of the permissions of the user owner, group owner, and other users. Each type may or may not have read, write, and execute permissions. That's three bits. In a binary system, $2^3 = 8$, which is why such permissions can be represented octally, as described in Table 5-3.

For example, a file with read, write, and execute permissions is given a value of 7, obtained by simply adding together the numerical representations of the desired permissions ($4 + 2 + 1 = 7$).

TABLE 5-3 Permissions represented in octal format.

PERMISSION	NUMERICAL REPRESENTATION
r	4
w	2
x	1

The user owner of a file has the right to use the `chmod` command to change permissions on a file. So to change the permissions for the user, group, and others in a file, you need three numbers. For example, look at the following command, where `localfile` is some arbitrary file in the local directory:

```
$ chmod 754 localfile
```

The first 7 represents read, write, and execute permissions for the user owner of the file. The 5 that follows represents read and execute permissions for the group owner of the file. The final 4 represents just read permissions for all other users.

The `chmod` command can do more. It can also represent and change the set user ID (SUID), set group ID (SGID), and sticky-bit permissions described in Chapter 4. These special bits are also represented numerically, in octal format, as shown in Table 5-4.

So if you're working in octal format, the `chmod` command can be used not only to set permissions for all users, but also to set special permissions for all users. These special permissions become the first number in a `chmod` command. So hypothetically, if you were to run the following command:

```
$ chmod 5764 testfile
```

That would set the SUID and sticky bit on the `testfile`. It would assign read, write, and execute permissions to the user owner. It would assign read and write permissions to the group owner. Finally, it would assign read-only permissions to all other users.

If you just want to change permissions for a single user or group, or just for other users, a different format of `chmod` switches can help. As this is just another way to set permissions, here are a couple of examples:

```
# chmod u+wx filename
```

The noted command adds write and executable permissions to the noted `filename`.

```
# chmod o+t newdirectory
```

The noted command adds the sticky bit to the directory named `newdirectory`.

TABLE 5-4	Special permissions represented in octal format.
SPECIAL PERMISSION	**NUMERICAL REPRESENTATION**
SUID	4
SGID	2
Sticky bit	1

technical TIP

Default permissions depend on the current value of the umask, available in the output from the umask command. For example, the default value of umask for regular Ubuntu users is 0022. Despite the description of the chmod command and special permissions, the first number is ignored. The second number applies to the regular user owner, and presumably masks nothing.

With this umask, user owners of a new directory get full read, write, and execute permissions. However, user owners of new files get only read and write permissions. Execute permissions on new regular files are disabled by default.

Networked File and Folder Permissions

Whatever permissions exist on the local and client systems, the actual permissions that are transmitted and available are based on those configured in the server configuration file. In Linux, three major services that network files and folders (which are really directories) are the Network File System (NFS), Samba, and the File Transfer Protocol (FTP). In fact, the file and directory permissions that you see from shared directories may be overridden by those file and directory permissions configured in those services.

NFS Issues

While three major versions of NFS are still in common use, two are inherently insecure. NFS versions 2 and 3 do not require any sort of user authentication when a client connects to a shared directory. In other words, the only access controls for NFS versions 2 and 3 services are based on domain names and/or IP addresses. All a black-hat hacker has to do is find an open port on a hub, switch, or router, connect his or her laptop, find an appropriate IP address, and connect to your NFS shared directory.

Basic NFS Security Issues

By default, all current versions of NFS prevent some security issues, such as root administrative access to files and directories. However, that is not assured, if the wrong options are set in the /etc/exports configuration file.

Some special configuration may be required to minimize risks. For example, while unknown users (and the local root administrative user) are supposed to be redirected to an account like **nobody** or **nfsnobody**, the UID associated with that "safe" account may vary by distribution. In some cases, that UID may be 65534; in other cases, that UID may be 4294967294.

In either case, you should check that account in the files of the password authentication database. For example, this excerpt from one version of /etc/passwd may be a risk, as a black-hat hacker who gains access to the nfsnobody account will see a shell if a login is allowed.

```
nfsnobody:x:4294967294:4294967294:
➥ Anonymous NFS User:/var/lib/nfs:/bin/sh
```

Additional problems relate to different user-authentication databases. For example, while the first user on an Ubuntu system has a UID of 1000, the first user on a Red Hat system has a UID of 500. So even if those users have identical names and passwords, the user on one client won't be able to access his or her files on a shared directory from a second client.

NFS Permissions and Authentication

All versions of NFS set up shares with read-only or read-write access. Whatever access is allowed in the NFS /etc/exports configuration file supersedes any access of actual files. In fact, when you run the ls -l command on an NFS-mounted directory, the permissions you see don't have to match the permissions configured in the /etc/exports file.

NFS version 4 (NFSv4) systems, when properly configured, are somewhat more secure. They can be used with a Kerberos ticket server to authenticate users.

NFSv4 also supports ACLs. As with regular ACLs on Linux, NFS-based ACLs can override standard read, write, and executable permissions for files on shared directories.

Samba/CIFS Network Permissions

Samba is the Linux implementation of Microsoft networking. As Microsoft has added to its systems with the Common Internet File System (CIFS), Samba developers have kept pace. As a result, current Linux systems can share directories and printers on a Microsoft-based network. It's even possible to have a Samba-based network of nothing but Linux computers. The focus of this section is the main Samba configuration file, **smb.conf** in the /etc/samba/ directory. That configuration file is split into two sections, "Global Settings" and "Share Definitions." This chapter is focused on the shared filesystem; directives from the first section are discussed in Chapter 8.

As with NFS, the configured options in the Samba configuration file supersede any regular local permissions for the shared files and directories.

The standard share in Samba is of user home directories. It's associated with the [homes] stanza. In general, default options in this stanza allow an authenticated user to access his or her home directory on the local system. However, that directory is not shared—and should not even be visible to other users, courtesy of the following directive:

> **NOTE**
>
> Some Samba directives may appear to be misspelled. Sometimes, multiple spellings are allowed; for example, browsable and browseable have the same meaning in a Samba configuration file.

```
browseable = no
```

Some directives are functionally identical. For example, you may see one of the following default directives in the [homes] stanza:

```
read only = yes
writeable = no
```

Of course, if you want to allow users write access to their home directories, these directives can be changed. If you've set up write access in your Samba configuration file, the following directives apply to the creation of files and directories, respectively:

```
create mask = 0700
directory mask = 0700
```

The `create mask` value sets up read and write permissions for the user owner of new files. The `directory mask` value sets up read, write, and execute permissions for the user owner of new directories.

While the [homes] share is visible only to the owner of a home directory, anyone can still connect to that home directory by default. You can prohibit such access with the following directive:

```
valid users = %S
```

Other directives associated with shared directories that you might consider or watch out for include those listed in Table 5-5.

Several Samba directives can be configured to point to users. Those directives can also point to groups. For example, the following directive limits write access to the users who are members of the `admin` group:

```
write list = @admin
```

TABLE 5-5 Samba directives related to shared directories.

SAMBA DIRECTIVE	DESCRIPTION
acl check permissions	Checks ACL-based permissions from a Microsoft client
acl group control	Allows users of a group owner to change permissions and ACLs
admin users	Lists users with full administrative privileges
guest ok	Configures the share so no password is required; synonymous with `public`
hosts allow	Sets hostnames or IP addresses of allowed systems; opposite of `hosts deny`
locking	Supports a lock file to prevent simultaneous access to the same file
path	Sets a directory path for the share
printer admin	Lists users allowed to administer printers
write list	Lists users allowed read-write access to a share

Alternatively, the following directive would prohibit access from a group that is often given administrative access on some systems:

```
invalid users = @wheel
```

Network Permissions for the vsFTP Daemon

Several FTP services are commonly used on many Linux systems. However, the very secure FTP daemon is acknowledged as a secure option. In fact, it is the only option for an FTP server on current installations of Red Hat Enterprise Linux 5. So to keep things simple, this section focuses on file-sharing security options associated with that service. Although this section focuses on vsFTP, many of the same principles apply to other FTP services.

The main vsFTP configuration file is **vsftpd.conf**. Depending on the distribution, it may be found in the /etc/ or the /etc/vsftpd/ directories. Most of the standard directives in this file have a direct bearing on how files are shared. While most FTP servers allow anonymous access, the following directive suggests that it is disabled by default:

```
anonymous_enable=NO
```

If you do enable anonymous access to an FTP server, it becomes especially important to isolate the directories associated with that server. As described earlier, it's an excellent idea to isolate the directory with the FTP server in a separate partition or volume. One advantage is that it configures a chroot jail by default for anonymous users. The chroot jail directory is configured as the home directory of the ftp user, as defined in the /etc/passwd file.

You can also set up the FTP server to allow users access to their home directories. This directive enables user access to their home directories:

```
local_enable = YES
```

If you enable local access, it's important to set up a chroot jail for those users. That's made possible with the following directive:

```
chroot_local_user = YES
```

Other relevant directives from standard versions of the vsftpd.conf file are shown in Table 5-6.

FYI

The chroot jail can help prevent black-hat hackers from getting to the key files on your systems. However, it isn't perfect. Some FTP developers believe that any sort of chroot jail presents its own kinds of risks. The directory used for the chroot jail could conceivably be used as the root for configuration files, commands, and libraries, enabling that user to create his or her own commands that may be able to escape from the chroot jail. Disabling executable access within a chroot jail can help prevent the use of such commands.

TABLE 5-6   vsFTP security-related service directives.

DIRECTIVE	DESCRIPTION
anon_upload_enable	Allows uploads by anonymous users; can be set to NO
anon_mkdir_write_enable	Allows anonymous users to create directories; can be set to NO
chroot_list_file	Sets up a list of users who are limited to their home directories
local_umask	Configures permissions for created files and directories
pam_service_name	Specifies the PAM configuration file in the /etc/pam.d/ directory
rsa_cert_file	Specifies the RSA certificate file
rsa_private_key_file	Specifies the file with the RSA private key
secure_chroot_dir	Configures a directory that should not be writable by the ftp user
userlist_enable	Configures a list to allow or deny users
write_enable	Allows users to write to a server; can also apply to anonymous users

Filesystems and Quotas

Quotas can limit the resources taken by a user or by a group of users. When appropriate, quotas are enabled. Limits are configured on the amount of space (based on blocks) and on the number of files (based on **inodes**). Quotas can protect the space available on critical directories. Quotas can give you time if there's a legitimate reason to expand the space allocated to a directory such as /home/. Quotas can help limit the damage if a black-hat hacker has compromised an account on one of your systems.

Poorly configured logs or message systems can create huge numbers of files. For example, systems configured in debug mode create logs for every event. Systems configured to create, say, pictures every second can create tens of thousands of files every day. Such systems could easily affect the life of hard-drive media.

While quotas may not directly enhance system security, they can certainly help limit damage should there be a security breach. In the following sections, you'll see how to configure quotas on a selected filesystem, the commands used to manage quotas, and how to get quota reports on your users.

The Quota Configuration Process

To set up a quota on a filesystem, you'll need to mount it appropriately. User and group quota options for the `mount` command are **usrquota** and **grpquota**. Mount options are configured in the `/etc/fstab` configuration file. Any filesystem that may be written to by users is a good candidate for quotas. In that respect, the prime user filesystem is associated with the `/home/` directory.

If you haven't configured a separate filesystem for the `/home/` directory, the following steps apply to the top-level root directory (`/`). In the `/etc/fstab` file, you'd add the `usrquota` and `grpquota` options to the fourth column. As an example, assume that you have a system where `/home/` is mounted on the `/dev/sda2` partition. The appropriate line in `/etc/fstab` would look similar to the following:

```
/dev/sda2  /home  ext4  defaults,usrquota,grpquota 1 2
```

If you've just made this change and don't want to reboot the system, run the following command, which refers to `/etc/fstab` for required options to the `mount` command.

```
# mount -o remount /home
```

If successful, you'll see it in the output from the `mount` command. For this particular configuration, you'd see the following output:

```
/dev/sda2 on /home type ext4 (rw,usrquota,grpquota)
```

Next, you'll need to create the actual quota configuration files with the **quotacheck** `-cugm /home/` command. That command combines four switches that (`-c`) create new quota files, (`-u`) apply the quota files to users, and (`-g`) apply the quota files to groups, (`-m`) without remouting the filesystem. If successful, it'll add **aquota.user** and **aquota.group** files to the `/home/` directory. The quotas that you create will be stored in these files.

Quota Management

Linux quotas are based on the concept of soft and hard limits. While the soft limit is a permanent limit, users and groups are allowed to exceed that limit for a grace period. In contrast, users are not allowed to exceed a configured hard limit.

Once you've configured the basic quota files, you're ready to edit the quota of a specific user. As an administrative user, run the **edquota** `-u` *username* command. The `-u` stands for user and is the default for the `edquota` command. If you want to edit the quota for a group, run the `edquota -g` *groupname* command.

The command as shown opens a quota configuration file in the default editor for the distribution. If this is the first time you've configured quotas, the screen may appear confusing, as the columns are wrapped. Figure 5-2 displays quotas in a slightly expanded screen.

In the case shown, user `michael` has files of nearly 700,000 blocks. As each block is 1k, that user currently has about 700MB of files on 305 inodes on the `/dev/sda2` partition.

```
Disk quotas for user michael (uid 500):
  Filesystem         blocks       soft       hard     inodes       soft       hard
  /dev/sda2          698172          0          0        305          0          0
~
~
```

Editing a user quota.

If you wanted to limit user michael to 1 GB of space and 10,000 files, you could set up the following quotas:

```
Disk quotas for user michael (uid 500):
  Filesystem       blocks       soft       hard     inodes       soft       hard
  /dev/sda2        698172    1000000          0        305      10000          0
```

In this case, the soft limit becomes the implicit hard limit. But that's something you may want to do unless the rules are crystal clear. After all, people make mistakes. So you may want to set hard limits as well, with a number a bit higher than the soft limit. One example is shown here, where the hard limit is 10 percent above the soft limit:

```
  Filesystem       blocks       soft       hard     inodes       soft       hard
  /dev/sda2        698172    1000000    1100000        305      10000      11000
```

A user is allowed to exceed the soft limit for a grace period. Once the changes are saved, you can review the current grace period with the edquota -t command. The result is shown in Figure 5-3, and is almost self-explanatory. The default grace period is seven days. A user is allowed to exceed the soft limit, but not the hard limit, for those seven days. After the grace period has passed, the user has to be back under the soft limit or that user will no longer be able to write to disk. You can change the grace period as shown, in days, hours, minutes, or seconds.

If you're satisfied with the limits set on the first user, you can copy those quotas to other users. The following command uses the quota configured for user michael as a (-p) prototype for the users that follow in the list:

```
# edquota -up michael kim mike larry kate
```

If you've set up quotas for one group and want to transfer those same quotas to more groups, the command would be similar. The following command uses the quotas set for group1 and copies them for the groups named group2 and group3:

```
# edquota -gp group1 group2 group3
```

```
 GNU nano 2.0.7          File: /tmp//EdP.aZ2Kq3z              Modified

Grace period before enforcing soft limits for users:
Time units may be: days, hours, minutes, or seconds
  Filesystem              Block grace period    Inode grace period
  /dev/sda11                   7days                 7days




^G Get Help   ^O WriteOut   ^R Read File  ^Y Prev Page  ^K Cut Text   ^C Cur Pos
^X Exit       ^J Justify    ^W Where Is   ^V Next Page  ^U UnCut Text ^T To Spell
```

Quota grace periods.

Quota Reports

Once quotas have been put into place, administrators will want to get periodic reports. You may want to warn any users who are near their quotas. Alternatively, if lots of users are near their quotas, you may consider getting more storage and raising the limits. To review the current status for all users, run the following command, which leads to output similar to that shown here:

```
# repquota -a
*** Report for user quotas on device /dev/sda2
Block grace time: 24:00; Inode grace time: 24:00
                Block limits                File limits
User        used  soft  hard  grace   used  soft  hard    grace
dickens  +-  124   100   110  1days    15     0     0    1days
```

As shown, user dickens has exceeded her soft and hard limit. The grace shown period is 24 hours. If you receive a call from that user asking why she can't save files, this information tells you why.

Filesystems and Access Control Lists

One area where Linux did not initially include the same level of security as some other operating systems was in ACLs, which allow you to set different permissions for specific users and groups. Linux developers started to address this flaw back in 2002. So ACL support in Linux is mature. It's available for the standard Linux filesystems, including ext2, ext3, ext4, reiserfs, and XFS. As suggested earlier, it's also available for directories shared through NFS. The ACLs available for Samba are somewhat different, as they are based on the functionality developed for Microsoft operating systems.

ACLs provide a second level of discretionary access control. The ACL options you set can override the basic discretionary access control options described earlier in this chapter. In other words, ACL settings can supersede basic read, write, and execute permissions for the user and group owners of files and directories.

In this section, you'll see how filesystems can be configured with ACLs, review available ACL commands, and learn how to use these commands to set ACLs on files and directories.

Configure a Filesystem for ACLs

The process to configure a filesystem for ACLs is similar to the process for configuring a filesystem for quotas. The appropriate mount option to configure ACLs is acl. To implement ACLs permanently, configure it on appropriate filesystems in the /etc/fstab configuration file. Any filesystem that requires custom access by certain users is a good candidate for ACLs. The prime candidate for such customization is the /home/ directory.

If you haven't configured a separate filesystem for the /home/ directory, the following steps apply to the top-level root directory (/). In the /etc/fstab file, add the acl option to the fourth column. As an example, assume that you have a system where `/home/` is mounted on the `/dev/sda2` partition. The appropriate line in `/etc/fstab` would look similar to the following:

```
/dev/sda2  /home  ext4  defaults,acl 1 2
```

If you've just made this change and don't want to reboot the system, run the following command, which refers to `/etc/fstab` for required options for the `mount` command:

```
# mount -o remount /home
```

If successful, you'll see it in the output from the `mount` command. For this particular configuration, you'd see the following output:

```
/dev/sda2 on /home type ext4 (rw,acl)
```

ACL Commands

The two standard ACL commands are **getfacl** and **setfacl**. These commands are almost self explanatory, as they get and set the ACL settings for the current file. These commands work only in filesystems mounted with the `acl` option.

> **TIP**
>
> If you need to collect files from an ACL-enabled filesystem in an archive, consider the `star` command. It is sort of an enhanced `tar` command that can collect and restore ACL information to and from an archive.

If you've configured the /home/ directory filesystem with ACL support, you should be able to run the `getfacl` command on the file or subdirectory of your choice in that filesystem. If you want to go farther, the following applies the `getfacl` command recursively on the home directory of user `michael`:

```
$ getfacl -R /home/michael
```

Next, there's the `setfacl` command. It includes two basic options: `-m` to set or modify ACL rules and `-x` to remove ACL rules. ACL rules can be configured in four categories:

- **u:user:permissions filename**—Sets ACL permissions for the specified user, by username or UID number
- **g:group:permissions filename**—Sets ACL permissions for the specified group, by groupname or GID number
- **m:permissions filename**—Sets the standard effective rights mask for ACL permissions for users and groups
- **o:permissions filename**—Sets ACL permissions for users who are not members of the group that owns the file

Configure Files and Directories with ACLs

In this section, you'll see how ACLs can be configured, and how they can make a difference. You'll use the `setfacl` command to override standard discretionary access control permissions and ownership. Before running the steps in this section, make sure that:

- The `acl` package is installed. The package has the same name on both Red Hat and Ubuntu systems.
- The partition, volume, or RAID array with the `/home/` directory is mounted with ACLs, as described in the previous section.
- At least two regular users are configured, with files owned by each user in their own home directories.

First, run the `ls -l` and `getfacl` commands on the file or directory of your choice. Unless you've already set an ACL, the output from both commands should confirm the same information.

Now select a different user—someone who does not own the file or directory just reviewed. Make sure that user is not a member of the group that owns the file. For example, the following command provides read, write, and execute permissions on the `ITTIS418/` subdirectory:

```
$ setfacl -m u:donna:rwx ITTIS418/
```

Now you'll have to give user `donna` ACL execute permissions on the underlying directory—in this case, `/home/michael/`:

```
$ setfacl -m u:donna:x /home/michael/
```

These commands can be run by the user owner of the `ITTIS418/` subdirectory. No system-administrative privileges are required. You can confirm these ACL rules with the `getfacl` command, applied to the noted directories. Now you can further protect the `ITTIS418/` subdirectory. The following command limits access to the user who owns that directory:

```
$ chmod 700 ITTIS418/
```

Despite the limitation in standard user privileges, the configured ACLs mean that Donna has full read, write, and execute access to the files in the `/home/michael/ITTIS418/` directory. If you want to remove those ACL rules, run the following commands:

```
$ setfacl -x u:donna ITTIS418/
$ setfacl -x u:donna /home/michael/
```

Best Practices: Filesystems, Volumes, and Encryption

If you understand the FHS, you'll know which directories can be mounted on different filesystems. More importantly, you'll know which directories should be mounted on different filesystems to help protect the system in case a black-hat hacker manages to break in. Candidate directories for separate filesystems include `/boot/`, `/home/`, `/opt/`, `/srv/`, `/tmp/`, and `/var/`. Appropriate subdirectories can also be considered for separate filesystems.

The right filesystem format can also help protect the system in case of a break-in. Journaling filesystems such as `ext3`, `ext4`, `xfs`, and `reiserfs` can speed recovery in case of problems. However, journaling takes extra space and may therefore be unnecssary for smaller filesystems.

In Linux, you can encrypt individual files, directories, and entire filesystems. Encryption tools can be split into user-space and kernel-space tools. Three of many available Linux encryption tools are `gpg`, `ecryptfs`, and `cryptsetup`. In this chapter, you saw how to use these tools to encrypt files, directories, and filesystems, respectively.

Local file and folder permissions provide one level of discretionary access control. The associated read, write, and execute permissions apply to the file's user owner, the file's group owner, and all other users. You can change ownership with the `chown` and `chgrp` commands. You can change permissions with the `chmod` command.

File and folder permissions differ when shared over a network. In fact, the file and folder permissions that you see may not work as they may be overridden by the configuration of the network sharing service. NFS sharing has other security issues, unless you use NFSv4 with Kerberos-based authentication. Samba shared directories include a number of options for configuring how files are shared. Directories shared with the vsFTP daemon service can be further protected with a chroot jail.

If a black-hat hacker does compromise one of your systems, quotas can limit damage. Once configured on a filesystem, quotas can be configured by user or group. Quotas can limit the amount of space or number of inodes taken by a user or group. You can configure hard and soft limits in each category, buffered by a grace period. You can review what users and groups do with regular quota reports.

With ACLs, you can take discretionary access controls to another level. ACLs can be configured using the same files and commands as quotas. Once configured, you can review current ACLs with the `getfacl` command. If you configure ACL rules for a specific user, you can further limit access to key files and directories to other users.

CHAPTER SUMMARY

In this chapter, you examined the FHS with a focus on what directories to configure on separate filesystems. You should now know more about Linux options for filesystem formats, especially in the context of journaling. You've skimmed the surface on available Linux encryption tools for files, directories, and filesystems.

Discretionary access controls on Linux start with regular file and folder ownership and permissions. The file and folder permissions for networked directories can be customized on NFS, Samba/CIFS, and vsFTP services. Any damage to a system can be limited by user and group quotas on space and inodes. Discretionary access controls can be taken a step further with ACLs.

KEY CONCEPTS AND TERMS

`aquota.group`	`gpg`	Advanced Encryption Standard (AES)
`aquota.user`	`grpquota`	Disk encryption subsystem
`chgrp`	`mkfs`	DSA
`chmod`	`nfsnobody`	enterprise cryptographic filesystem (eCryptfs)
`chown`	`nobody`	Elgamal
`cryptsetup`	`quotacheck`	Filesystem
`ecryptfs`	`reiserfs`	Filesystem hierarchy standard (FHS)
`edquota`	`root`	Inode
`ext2`	`setfacl`	Journaled filesystem
`ext3`	`smb.conf`	Kernel-space
`ext4`	`usrquota`	Linux unified key setup (LUKS)
`fdisk`	`vsftpd.conf`	RSA
`getfacl`	`xfs`	Secure hash algorithm (SHA)
		Software RAID
		User-space

CHAPTER 5 ASSESSMENT

1. Which of the following directories are suitable for separate filesystems? (Select two.)

A. `/etc/`
B. `/home/`
C. `/lib/`
D. `/var/`

2. Which of the following directories typically includes files associated with third-party applications?

A. `/etc/`
B. `/home/`
C. `/opt/`
D. `/usr/`

3. Which of the following directories is most well suited as a read-only filesystem?

A. `/boot/`
B. `/home/`
C. `/mnt/`
D. `/srv/`

4. Which of the following filesystem formats is best suited for a smaller filesystem?

A. `ext2`
B. `ext3`
C. `ext4`
D. `reiserfs`

5. The command that lists currently loaded GPG keys is _____.

6. Which of the following directories contain GPG private and public keys?

    A. .gpg
    B. .gpgkeys
    C. .gnupg
    D. .keys

7. Which of the following commands is associated with the Linux unified key setup disk encryption specification?

    A. dcrypt
    B. ecryptfs
    C. gpg
    D. cryptsetup

8. Which of the following commands prohibits access from all users except the user owner and members of the group that owns the file named filename?

    A. chmod 770 filename
    B. chmod 707 filename
    C. chmod 077 filename
    D. chmod 007 filename

9. Which of the following commands sets the SUID bit on the file named filename?

    A. chmod 1770 filename
    B. chmod 2750 filename
    C. chmod 4555 filename
    D. chmod 3777 filename

10. If you try to change files remotely on a shared NFS directory as the root administrative user, what happens?

    A. The change fails, because the root user on one system is the nobody user on another system.
    B. The change is successful.
    C. The change is successful even if the NFS directory is shared in read-only mode.
    D. The change fails unless you log in with the root administrative password from the remote system.

11. Which of the following Samba directives specify permissions of files created on a shared network directory?

    A. create_octal
    B. create_mask
    C. create_options
    D. create_write

12. Which of the following directories is appropriate for quotas?

    A. /etc/
    B. /home/
    C. /opt/
    D. /usr/

13. Which of the following commands lists quota usage by user?

    A. quota
    B. repquota
    C. quotacheck
    D. quotarep

14. What configuration file is used to configure ACLs for a filesystem?

    A. /etc/fstab
    B. /etc/acl
    C. /etc/pam.d/acl
    D. /etc/filesystems

15. The command that lists the current ACL rules on the local file named test1 is _____. Assume your user account is the owner of file test1.

Every Service Is a Potential Risk

I N AN IDEAL WORLD, every system would be self-contained, with everything a user needs, isolated from the network. But that's not realistic. You can minimize risks, however. To that end, every service is a potential risk.

If you're running a service such as an Apache Web server, you realize that service is subject to risks. You're probably watching for news on Apache, ready to pounce on updates that address security issues.

But what if a print server is already running on the same server? Is it okay if a different file server is installed, but just not running? While there are services with their own control scripts, you also need to remember those services controlled by the **internet super server**. What happens when a compiler is left on a system after a new kernel has been built? In some cases, you can isolate services with a chroot jail. When you consider the services on a system, X servers and clients are a risk as well. In addition, the productivity tools found on X servers are also subject to attacks.

Chapter 6 Topics

This chapter covers the following topics and concepts:

- How basic systems can be hardened into bastions
- How to configure bastions in a virtualized environment
- What the risks of source code and development tools are
- Which default services to uninstall
- How to manage internet super server services and deactivate service scripts
- Which services can be isolated in chroot jails
- Why to avoid X servers and X clients
- What the risks of GUI-based productivity tools are
- What best practices in service deployment are

Chapter 6 Goals

When you complete this chapter, you will be able to:

- Configure a bastion server from a minimal Linux installation
- Set up a system with just the needed functionality
- Minimize the use of development tools
- Deactivate services in testing

Basic Bastion Hardening

A **bastion server** is configured to minimize the risk that a black-hat hacker can compromise any systems configured on that server. The ideal bastion server is used for a single purpose. Generally, it'll have two open ports—one for the service, one for the remote administrative connection. When properly configured, a bastion server has a number of advantages:

- **Minimal additional software**—The server has just the software required for the service, and nothing else that could present a security risk.
- **Closed ports**—The only open ports are for the service and a remote administrative tool.

In fact, when you build a bastion, you can start with a minimal installation. It may be an excellent baseline from which you can build single-use bastion servers. All you need on the baseline is the remote service required to administer the bastion, typically a Secure Shell (SSH) server. While serial port connections are also frequently available, such an option is more difficult even if you have physical access to the server room.

While Ubuntu Server Edition provides an option for a minimal installation, it may not be what you want. If you want to create a minimal installation of Red Hat Enterprise Linux server, some work is required during the installation process. When installation is complete, some default services aren't really necessary. You may want to uninstall some packages that could also otherwise compromise the secure nature of the baseline system.

Generally, bastions are designed for a network area known as a **demilitarized zone (DMZ)**, an area protected from the Internet by one level of firewalls. The main network is further protected from this area with a second router. As shown in Figure 6-1, bastions are typically configured in the DMZ area of a network.

Figure 6-1 depicts three distinct networks: the wide area network (WAN), the DMZ, and the protected internal network. The WAN may be a corporate network or the Internet. The DMZ is an internal network with one private IP network address. The protected internal network has a distinct and separate private IP network address.

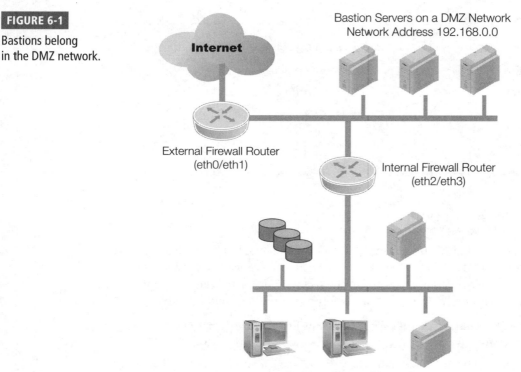

FIGURE 6-1

Bastions belong
in the DMZ network.

The network addresses shown are just two possible examples. Traffic between the WAN (Internet) and the protected internal network is filtered through two different firewall routers.

Each firewall router has two network devices. In Figure 6-1, the first Ethernet device (eth0) on the external firewall router is connected to the WAN (Internet) and has a public IP address. The second Ethernet device (eth1) on that same router is connected to the DMZ network. All traffic directed to and from the DMZ and the protected internal network is filtered through a firewall on this router.

Each bastion server on the DMZ network is used to serve data to users on the Internet. Each bastion server has a single function, such as serving Web pages, sharing files via the File Transfer Protocol (FTP) service, or sharing authoritative name service information via a caching Domain Name System (DNS) name server. The external firewall router should stop network traffic that would otherwise harm internal systems, such as denial of service (DoS) packets. In addition, that external firewall router should filter requests for each service, and redirect appropriate requests to the right bastion server.

Now look at the internal firewall router. The first Ethernet device (eth2) on that router is connected to the DMZ network. The second Ethernet device (eth3) on that router is connected to the protected internal network. The internal firewall router should also stop the same network traffic that would otherwise harm internal systems. It should be designed as if a black-hat hacker has broken into and taken control of a system on the DMZ network.

The only network traffic that should be directed from the external firewall router to the internal network is information requested form those internal network clients. That traffic should be filtered to stop inappropriate traffic such as DoS, rapid attempts at repeated logins, and so on.

In many cases, the functionality of both routers is incorporated into one system with three network cards. That system would include the functionality of both firewalls. If configured on a Linux system, that system should be configured with packet forwarding for one or both of Internet Protocol version 4 (IPv4) and Internet Protocol version 6 (IPv6) traffic in the /etc/sysctl.conf file and /proc/ settings as described in Chapter 7.

A Minimal Ubuntu Installation

A minimal installation is a straightforward process for Ubuntu Server Edition. Since release 8.04, Ubuntu has included a minimal installation option from its initial boot menu. The installation is compact; excluding swap space, it requires less than 400 MB of space on a hard drive and a minimum of just 128 MB of RAM. A minimal installation does not include a GUI, any service that you may configure on a bastion, or even the SSH service. Before you set up such a minimal Ubuntu baseline installation, you'll want to install an administrative service like SSH. Of course, you'll also want to set up at least basic IPv4 networking. If your Dynamic Host Configuration Protocol (DHCP) server supports hostname assignments, great. Otherwise, when you copy the partitions from the baseline system, you'll want to make sure to configure a unique hostname for that system. Once configured, you'll be able to copy the partitions or even the virtual disk files to create additional Ubuntu installations.

Once the baseline installation is copied, you can verify the new installation, assign a new hostname, and install the necessary software packages based on the desired functionality of the bastion host. Then you'll want to review the current list of services and packages to see what can be uninstalled. Finally, you'll want to install the service that fits the function of the specific host. While that function may be any of the services associated with Linux, you shouldn't install more than one such service on any single bastion.

A Minimal Red Hat Installation

A minimal installation is a straightforward process for Red Hat. If you accept the defaults, however, Red Hat Enterprise Linux 5 (RHEL 5) includes extra software such as a GUI, the OpenOffice.org suite, and even games. None of these software packages are required for a Red Hat bastion. As long as you avoid these GUI-based packages, it's possible to set up RHEL 5 with a relatively small amount of RAM. While 192 MB is frequently adequate, some trial and error may be required to find an optimal amount of RAM for your bastion system.

When creating a Red Hat prototype for a bastion, you'll need to deselect these options during the installation process. But even when these options are deselected, the minimal Red Hat installation includes a number of services that aren't needed on most bastion servers.

If you're maintaining such installations on the Red Hat network, you'll have to register each copy of that system separately. All you need to register the system is to run the `rhn_register` command. It's not a problem if you run this command from a remote system.

Once the Red Hat installation is complete, the real work begins.

Service Reviews

Once you've configured the selected distribution, you should check currently active and installed services. Active services can typically be found in one of two locations: the scripts in the `/etc/init.d/` directory or the files in the `/etc/xinetd.d/` directory. Figure 6-2 shows the list of `/etc/init.d/` services for a minimal installation of Red Hat Enterprise Linux 5.

> **NOTE**
>
> Through Red Hat Enterprise Linux 5, the default runlevel and associated parts of the boot process were configured in the `/etc/inittab` configuration file. While that file is based on the originally cloned configuration of UNIX System V, or SysV for short, it is in the process of changing. Starting with the Ubuntu 8.04 release, Ubuntu is moving toward a system known as **Upstart**, where the same information is contained in the files of the `/etc/event.d/` directory. The companies behind other major Linux distributions, including Red Hat and Novell, have indicated that they will move future releases toward the Upstart system.

The services that are actually activated during the boot process are listed in the related directory associated with the default runlevel for the distribution. The default runlevel for Debian-style systems including Ubuntu is runlevel 2. The default runlevel for Red Hat–style distributions generally depends on whether a GUI was included in the installation process. If so, the default Red Hat runlevel is 5. Otherwise, the default boot runlevel for such systems is 3.

Now take a look at Figure 6-3 for the services that are active in a Red Hat runlevel 3. The figure displays the contents of the `/etc/rc3.d/` directory. Briefly, the services that start with an S are started in this runlevel, followed by those services that start with K, which are shut down when entering this runlevel. Even though this is a minimal installation, you should already sense that some work is required to pare this down. You'll see how in more detail later in this chapter.

FIGURE 6-2

Available service scripts in the `/etc/init.d/` directory.

```
[root@RHEL5-Bastion ~]# \ls /etc/init.d/
acpid            dnsmasq         killall         NetworkManager   rpcgssd
anacron          dund            krb524          nfs              rpcidmapd
apmd             firstboot       kudzu           nfslock          rpcsvcgssd
atd              functions       lvm2-monitor    nscd             saslauthd
auditd           gpm             mcstrans        pand             sendmail
autofs           haldaemon       mdmonitor       pcscd            single
avahi-daemon     halt            mdmpd           portmap          smartd
avahi-dnsconfd   hidd            messagebus      psacct           sshd
bluetooth        ip6tables       microcode_ctl   rawdevices       syslog
capi             ipmi            multipathd      rdisc            wpa_supplicant
conman           iptables        netconsole      readahead_early  xinetd
cpuspeed         irda            netfs           readahead_later  ypbind
crond            irqbalance      netplugd        restorecond      yum-updatesd
cups             isdn            network         rhnsd
[root@RHEL5-Bastion ~]# ■
```

```
[root@RHEL5-Bastion ~]# \ls /etc/rc3.d/
K01dnsmasq            K89dund              S12restorecond    S28autofs
K02avahi-dnsconfd     K89netplugd          S12syslog         S55sshd
K02NetworkManager     K89pand              S13irqbalance     S56cups
K05conman             K89rdisc             S13portmap        S56rawdevices
K05saslauthd          K91capi              S14nfslock        S56xinetd
K10psacct             K99readahead_later   S15mdmonitor      S80sendmail
K20nfs                S02lvm2-monitor      S18rpcidmapd      S85gpm
K24irda               S04readahead_early   S19rpcgssd        S90crond
K50netconsole         S05kudzu             S22messagebus     S95anacron
K69rpcsvcgssd         S06cpuspeed          S25bluetooth      S95atd
K73ypbind             S08ip6tables         S25netfs          S97rhnsd
K74ipmi               S08iptables          S25pcscd          S97yum-updatesd
K74nscd               S08mcstrans          S26acpid          S98avahi-daemon
K85mdmpd              S09isdn              S26apmd           S99firstboot
K87multipathd         S10network           S26haldaemon      S99local
K88wpa_supplicant     S11auditd            S26hidd           S99smartd
[root@RHEL5-Bastion ~]#
```

FIGURE 6-3

Active services in runlevel 3 start with S.

Package Reviews

Sometimes, you just need to take inventory. But even the minimal installations for Red Hat and Ubuntu systems include hundreds of different packages. One way to review the current list of packages on a system is with the applicable package-management tool. On Ubuntu systems, the following command lists all currently installed packages:

```
# dpkg -l
```

On Red Hat systems, the following command lists all currently installed packages:

```
# rpm -qa
```

Of course, the list of packages from these commands can be redirected to text files for further analysis. But it would help, if these packages were classified in different categories. And if you don't want a GUI on the local system, such tools are fairly rare. Ubuntu includes a useful tool that works at the command line, Aptitude, which you can start with the `aptitude` command. As shown in Figure 6-4, it includes information on upgradable and installed packages. As shown in the Installed Packages categories, such packages are listed by functionality.

Red Hat doesn't provide a similar command-line based package management tool. However, if you've registered the system on the Red Hat Network, it's easy to find a similar list of packages. Different options allow you to see what's installed, what's upgradable (along with associated security alerts), and more. Perhaps most useful, the Red Hat Network allows you to verify the integrity of installed packages, to make sure they haven't been modified by unauthorized users.

Ubuntu includes similar tools in its Landscape system management and monitoring service.

The installation and removal of packages is a fundamental skill, so the discussion of the `rpm` and `dpkg` commands in the following sections should be a review for you.

> **NOTE**
>
> The `aptitude` command is also a front-end to the `apt-get` and `apt-cache` commands. As such, it can be used to directly install, remove, and search any available package.

> **NOTE**
>
> For more information on the Red Hat Network and Canonical's Landscape remote system-management tools, see Chapter 11.

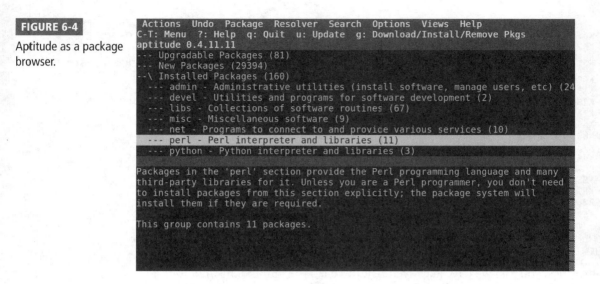

FIGURE 6-4

Aptitude as a package browser.

The Dynamic Host Configuration Protocol Server Issue

The U.S. National Security Agency (NSA) recommends that you avoid the use of DHCP services if possible. While not included in a minimal installation, DHCP and many other services are included in typical installations of most Linux distributions. Unfortunately, with the use of virtual machines, it's difficult to live without DHCP servers.

Most systems are configured to receive networking information and more from DHCP servers. If a DHCP server is used, the NSA suggests that you minimize the information configured from that server. Specifically, the NSA suggests the following points on any configured DHCP servers:

- **Avoid dynamic DNS**—Use the `ddns-update-style none;` directive in the DHCP configuration file.
- **Deny client decline messages**—The `deny declines;` directive can resist attempts by black-hat hackers to exhaust a pool of IP addresses.
- **Avoid serving remote networks**—If you can avoid the use of the Bootstrap Protocol (BOOTP) with the `deny bootp;` directive, you'll remove one more possible attack mode.
- **Minimize provided information**—Don't let the DHCP server provide domain names, DNS servers, NIS servers, NTP servers, or gateway information unless necessary. Such information can make life easier for a black-hat hacker.

Installation and Removal on Red Hat Systems

The Red Hat package-management command is `rpm`. If you want to install a package that's already downloaded to the local directory, just run the `rpm -i` *packagename* command. But users who have experience with Red Hat packages understand that command rarely works by itself. Packages have dependencies. For example, you can't install the Red Hat Samba Server Configuration tool unless the Samba server package is already installed. That relationship is known as a dependency. You could download the Samba package and try to install both packages together, but what if the Samba package also has unmet dependencies?

Conversely, if both packages are already installed, you can't uninstall the Samba server unless you also uninstall the Samba Server Configuration tool. If you know the names of both packages, the following command could work:

```
# rpm -e samba system-config-samba
```

But what if other packages also depend on the Samba server? You'd see an error message. For both installations and removals, the list of dependencies can go on and on. That situation is known colloquially as **dependency hell**, which is the reason for the development of the **yum** command.

Originally developed for the Yellowdog Linux distribution, the command is now known as the Yellowdog Updater, Modified (yum). It automatically finds dependencies when you as an administrator want to install and remove packages from a system.

So in the effort to create a bastion server, you may run a command such as the following to uninstall the open source sendmail e-mail server:

```
# yum remove sendmail
```

If you're knowledgeable about Red Hat systems, however, the messages shown in Figure 6-5 should make you stop and think.

If you uninstall sendmail, you may also need to uninstall the package associated with software RAID and the Linux Standards Base. If the local system does not require RAID and does not need to comply with such Linux standards, such changes may be acceptable.

Otherwise, you may need to take other measures to secure your system, such as deactivating the sendmail service, making sure it can't be activated, and blocking the TCP/IP ports associated with that service.

```
--> Processing Dependency: smtpdaemon for package: mdadm
--> Running transaction check
---> Package mdadm.i386 0:2.6.9-2.el5 set to be erased
---> Package redhat-lsb.i386 0:3.1-12.3.EL set to be erased
--> Finished Dependency Resolution

Dependencies Resolved

================================================================================
 Package           Arch          Version          Repository         Size
================================================================================
Removing:
 sendmail          i386          8.13.8-2.el5     installed          1.3 M
Removing for dependencies:
 mdadm             i386          2.6.9-2.el5      installed          1.7 M
 redhat-lsb        i386          3.1-12.3.EL      installed          22 k

Transaction Summary
================================================================================
Install     0 Package(s)
Update      0 Package(s)
Remove      3 Package(s)

Is this ok [y/N]:
```

FIGURE 6-5

Do you really want to uninstall packages for software RAID and the Linux Standards Base?

Installation and Removal on Ubuntu Systems

Ubuntu uses the Debian package-management command, `dpkg`. If you want
to install a package that's already downloaded to the local directory, just run the
`dpkg -i` *packagename* command. Like Red Hat packages (described in the previous
section), few Ubuntu packages work alone and most have dependencies. For example,
you can't install the Samba Web Administration tool unless the Samba server package
is already installed.

For similar reasons, if both packages are already installed,
you can't uninstall the Samba server unless you also uninstall
the Samba Web Administration tool (SWAT). If you know the
names of both packages, the following command will work:

```
# dpkg -r samba swat
```

If other packages also depend on the Samba server, you'd see
an error message regarding dependencies. While you could try
again with the dependent packages, those packages could also
have dependencies. You can use the **apt-get** and **apt-cache**
commands to work around that situation known as dependency
hell.

These commands automatically find dependencies when you as an administrator
want to install and remove packages from a system. So in the effort to create a bastion
server, for example, you might run a command like the following to uninstall filesystem
infrastructure associated with the X Window system:

```
# apt-get remove x11-common
```

But if you have a need to use GUI tools to administer remote systems, the filesystem
infrastructure may be useful sometime in the future.

Bastions in a Virtualized Environment

One of the advantages of a virtual machine is the ease with which
new systems can be created. Another advantage is that virtual
systems can be configured with just the hardware that's required.
Virtual machine systems are commonly configured as large files
in a single directory. Once you're satisfied with the configuration
of one virtual machine, it's easy to create more. Just copy the files
from one directory to a new directory.

Virtual machines use large "virtual disk" files to simulate hard
drives. Because Linux doesn't require a lot of space, such files
don't have to be all that large. The files associated with a minimal
installation of RHEL 5 require less than a gigabyte of space. The
files associated with a minimal installation of Ubuntu Server
Edition require even less space.

Systems Customized for a Virtual Machine

When configuring a virtual machine, it's best to include as little virtual hardware as possible. For example, if the virtual machine is to be used as a server, chances are good that it won't require a sound card. If you don't need to simulate USB devices, you don't need to include them in the system. Before creating a virtual machine, you need to consider the amount of space required for the hard drive. To that end, you need to consider the following:

- **Virtual RAM requirements**—While the minimum RAM for most Linux systems is 128 to 192 MB, more would be required for the service(s) to be run in the system.
- **Operating-system space**—For a minimal installation, typically 1 GB is a reasonable amount of space. This does not include the space required for the service(s) to be installed, any log files, data files, user files, and so on.
- **Service space**—The space required for a service is highly variable. It may also depend on the data to be included along with the log files that may be created and stored on the virtual system.
- **Swap space**—Most default Linux installations configure swap space in a separate partition or logical volume. The normal size of that partition or logical volume is twice the amount of RAM.

These factors assume that you have a host system with the capacity to handle the needs of all virtual machines in terms of RAM and hard drive space. If for some reason you actually want a GUI on the virtual system, the space required will grow significantly.

Of course, it is fairly easy to add hard disk space as a system grows. If you believe that space requirements may grow significantly, you might choose to set up a logical volume. Of course, because it is relatively easy to set up new virtual machines, you could always copy needed data to that new larger virtual machine.

Virtual Machine Networks

Generally, there are three options for networks with respect to a virtual machine. Virtual machines can share bandwidth of the network card of the host system. The choice you make determines the degree of protection afforded to such machines. The three options are:

- **Bridged network**—Typically, a bridged network card directly accesses the same network services as the host system. It gets its IP address information from the same DHCP servers. It connects to the network as if it were just another client.
- **Network address translation (NAT)**—When configured with NAT, virtual clients on a system are configured on their own private network. The host system functions as a gateway between the NAT private network and outside networks. The normal way for external systems to connect to virtual clients on the NAT is with port forwarding.
- **Host-only network**—Similar to a NAT, except communication through the host is disabled. Virtual machines on a host-only network can communicate with the virtual host and with other virtual guests on the same private network.

The configuration of a virtual machine as a bastion depends on the role of the virtual machine host. If that host serves as a gateway between the LAN and an external network such as the Internet, virtual machines configured in a NAT may themselves be in a DMZ.

The Risks of Source Code and Development Tools

> **NOTE**
>
> **Tarball** is a colloquial term for a package that is archived (and normally compressed) with the tar command. It is a common format for compressed archives of source code, such as the Linux kernel.

Linux users with a little skill can download and compile source code. Frequently, the development tools are prepackaged with a download. For example, if you download the latest packages for VMware server in tarball format, these packages include the development tools required to compile the source code and install the binary files that are built on your system.

Perhaps the most extensive range of development tools is associated with the Linux kernel. If you compile a custom kernel, you may want to do so on a different and isolated system, and then install the new kernel on the production system.

Development Tools

Whenever you install the source code of a package, you'll probably also need development tools. Development tools are in some ways open invitations to black-hat hackers. Certain development tools can be used to create more problematic malware. If a black-hat hacker breaks into one system on your network—and that system has development tools installed—that black-hat hacker can build malware from inside your network.

Development tools fall into a number of categories. In brief, these categories include programming languages, compilers, and build tools. One way to review a list of development tools on Red Hat and Ubuntu systems is with GUI tools such as Pirut and Synaptic. Although these tools probably should not be installed on bastion systems, a review of these tools can help you learn what to look for with respect to development tools.

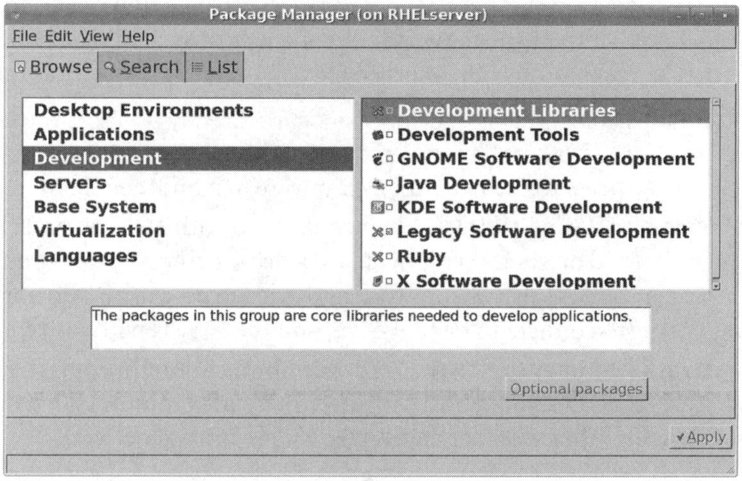

FIGURE 6-6

Categories of Red Hat development tools.

TABLE 6-1 Linux development tools.

PACKAGE	DESCRIPTION
automake*	A series of packages for creating a Makefile, which can be used to configure how a system is compiled
gcc*	A series of tools associated with the **GNU Compiler Collection (GCC)**
java-1.6.0-openjdk	Open Java development kit runtime environment
perl*	Packages associated with the Perl programming language
python*	Packages associated with the Python programming language
ruby*	Packages associated with the Ruby programming language

The Red Hat GUI package manager is also known as Pirut. You can start it from a Red Hat GUI with the `pirut` command. As shown in Figure 6-6, development tools are available in a number of categories.

Several important development tools are highlighted in Table 6-1. Unless you're actively developing source code on a system, these tools should not be installed. There are a few cases where some of these tools are required to run certain packages. You'll see these packages as dependencies when you try to remove certain services.

To review a similar listing of development tools for Ubuntu, open the Synaptic package manager. One way to do so is with the `synaptic` command in a GUI. Figure 6-7 illustrates one list of development tools, along with descriptions of a single package.

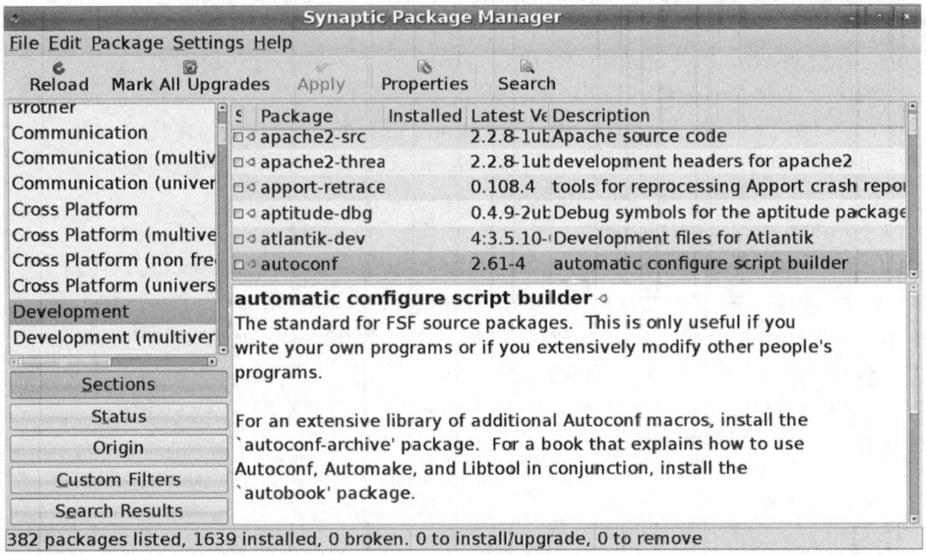

FIGURE 6-7

Categories of Ubuntu development tools.

Of course, you can review information about the package of your choice from the command-line interface. For example, the following commands display information about the `make` package on a Red Hat and an Ubuntu system, respectively. (The Red Hat command won't work unless the `make` package is actually installed.)

```
# rpm -qi make
# apt-cache show make
```

Build Packages

The source code associated with many tarballs may include compilers. For example, if you've installed a VMware virtual machine from a tarball, you may have a subdirectory such as `vmware-server-distrib/` somewhere on your system. Fortunately, the files unpacked to that directory depend on the availability of an appropriate GNU C Compiler to process the source code into something useful.

In general, once you've downloaded and installed a package from a tarball, you should delete the directory (and files) to where the tarball was unpacked (and not the directory with the tarball itself). In many cases, the files in this directory take up a lot of space. In some cases, it may include build tools that may be useful for any black-hat hacker who breaks into this system.

The `make` command has a special place in this picture. It's frequently used to compile the source code and then build a kernel. It should also be removed from systems unless you're actively working on customizing a new kernel. For detailed information on how a kernel is customized and built, see Chapter 10.

The minimal Ubuntu installation does not include `man` commands. If you install the `man` package, the C language preprocessor (`cpp`) package is installed as a dependency.

Uninstalling Default Services

Earlier in this chapter, you read about how to find the services that are activated by default on a system. The developers behind a Linux distribution try to make their systems work for as wide a range of users as possible. But that flexibility is not consistent with the need for security. While extra services provide additional functionality, they also provide extra ways for a black-hat hacker to break into your systems.

The best way to prevent a service from compromising your security is to uninstall that service. But that's not always possible. You may be working on the configuration of a service. Some services are required for other reasons, as described earlier in the description of the sendmail service. In this section, you'll review how services can be uninstalled and deactivated. You'll also review some of the major services included on default minimal installations to better understand whether those services are necessary parts of your systems.

Uninstall When Possible

If you don't need a service, uninstall it. The process is straightforward, especially if you're familiar with the yum and apt-get commands. For example, if you want to uninstall the Samba file server on a RHEL 5 system, you'd run the following command:

```
# yum remove samba
```

Just watch for dependencies. Before accepting what yum will do, watch the messages. If there are dependencies, the command will prompt for confirmation to make sure you actually want those dependent packages to be uninstalled. If there's a problem, you can always deactivate the Samba service as described in the next section.

In addition, commands that uninstall packages on Red Hat systems will often leave existing configuration files with an extension such as .rpmsave. You may want to remove such files, especially if the server has just been moved to another system. That configuration could provide important clues to a black-hat hacker on weaknesses in that service.

Alternatively, to uninstall the Samba server on an Ubuntu system, you have two basic options with the apt-get command:

```
# apt-get remove samba
# apt-get purge samba
```

The purge option uninstalls the target package—and deletes associated configuration files. Especially because most configuration files are readable by any user, you don't want to leave any hints for black-hat hackers who break into your systems.

> ▶ **TIP**
>
> On Ubuntu systems, some services are started in all runlevels. For a list of these services, review the files in the /etc/rcS.d/ directory.

Deactivate if Still in Work

If you want to keep an extra service on a system, it's best to deactivate it—in other words, turn it off, and make sure it stays off if the system has to be rebooted. For example, you may be working on some special configuration for Samba. If you're not ready to put it into production, that service should be deactivated. If the Samba service is not active, the associated TCP/IP ports are not shown. (Yes, if a service is inactive, there's still a risk that a black-hat hacker who gets into a system could turn on the service.)

Stop a Service

As reboots of Linux systems are fairly rare, the first step is to directly deactivate the service. In most cases, services are controlled by a script in the /etc/init.d/ directory. Depending on the distribution, script names may vary slightly. For example, the script for the Samba server in Red Hat is smb and samba in Ubuntu. To stop the noted script, just run it with the stop option. For RHEL, the command would be as follows:

```
# /etc/init.d/smb stop
```

NOTE

The internet and extended internet super server services specify "internet" in lower case, as both services relate to an interconnection of networks, not to the Internet.

Some services are part of the extended internet super server. Management commands for such services are described later in this chapter.

A few services may not have scripts in the `/etc/init.d/` directory or configuration files associated with the extended internet super server. In that case, you'll just have to apply the `kill` or `killall` commands to the service daemon. For example, if a hypothetical `abcd` daemon is running on your system, you can run the `killall abcd` command.

Alternatively, you could find the **process identifier (PID)** associated with the `abcd` daemon and apply the `kill` command to that PID number. The `kill` command is more flexible, as it can send a number of different signals to daemons that are currently running.

Change the Service Defaults

Generally, it's fastest to change most Linux configuration options at the command-line interface. Two similar commands to that end are **update-rc.d** and **chkconfig**. While the commands are different, they both work with different scripts in the standard runlevels of 0, 1, 2, 3, 4, 5, and 6. The standard for most Linux distributions is to activate services in runlevels 2, 3, 4, and 5. In the same way, Linux distributions should be set to deactivate most services in runlevels 0, 1, and 6.

Many major Linux distributions are converting their service and runlevel system to Upstart, configured in the `/etc/event.d/` directory. Once a script is converted, you'll be able to use the daemon more directly, with a command like *service* start. As Upstart development is still in progress, details are subject to change. For more information, see *http://upstart.ubuntu.com/*.

The `update-rc.d` Command

If you're on an Ubuntu system, the `update-rc.d` command controls the configuration of service scripts in the standard runlevels. If you want to remove a service script from runlevel management—say, the Samba service—run the following command:

```
# update-rc.d -f samba remove
```

If you prefer to make sure the service is stopped in all runlevels, the following command deactivates the Samba service in standard runlevels:

```
# update-rc.d samba stop 20 2 3 4 5 .
```

In this case, the `20` specifies the priority. For example, if you see `K20abc` and `K21def` in the `/etc/rc2.d/` directory, the `abc` service is stopped before the `def` service. The command doesn't work without the dot after the list of runlevels.

Of course, the process can be reversed; the following command sets the Samba service to start in runlevels 2, 3, 4, and 5:

```
# update-rc.d samba start 20 2 3 4 5 .
```

The chkconfig Command

If you're on a Red Hat system, the chkconfig command can help. First, the chkconfig --list command lists all current SysV-configured services and indicates whether they are active. If such services are configured in different runlevels, they're set to either stop or start when the system moves to that runlevel. Here is one excerpt:

```
smb 0:off 1:off 2:off 3:on 4:off 5:on 6:off
```

In this case, the Samba service is set to start in runlevels 3 and 5. You can use the chkconfig command to set the service to start or stop in the runlevel of your choice. For example, the following command sets the Samba service to start in runlevels 2, 3, 4, and 5:

```
chkconfig smb --level 2345 on
```

That command is equivalent to chkconfig smb on. You can reverse the process; the following command deactivates Samba in runlevels 2, 3, and 4:

```
chkconfig smb --level 234 off
```

Alternatively, the chkconfig smb off command deactivates Samba in all runlevels.

Services in Question

A minimal installation of RHEL 5 includes more services than a minimal installation of Ubuntu Server Edition. But to set up a bastion server for either distribution, you need to know at least a bit more about each service. So this section examines the /etc/init.d/ directory of a minimal installation of each distribution. On a typical installation, you'll see more services in this directory.

Table 6-2 includes active services from a minimal installation of both RHEL 5 and Ubuntu Server Edition. Look at each of these services on your systems. Most of these services appear only in one distribution. If you keep any of these services active, be sure that you understand why. That knowledge can help you if a related security issue arises in the future. Two services that should be retained are the halt and single services. These services are associated specifically with runlevels 0 and 1, respectively.

The Action column includes the option that generally applies to most current servers. As you can see from the table, most of these services should be disabled on most systems. For certain services, your system may be an exception. If unsure, read the options carefully. Yes, Table 6-2 is a long list, but so is the work required to create a secure system. Once you create a secure bastion using this information, you can use it as a template for other secure bastion systems.

TABLE 6-2 Service scripts in Red Hat's `/etc/init.d/` directory.

SERVICE SCRIPT	DESCRIPTION	ACTION
acpid	Advanced configuration and power interface (ACPI) daemon; should remain enabled unless you don't care about power management.	Enable
anacron	Service that runs `cron` scripts if the system is down when jobs are scheduled; disable if the server is powered up 24/7.	Disable
apmd	Advanced power-management (APM) daemon; if ACPI is enabled, APM isn't necessary and can be disabled.	Disable
atd	The AT daemon runs one-time jobs that are queued, and can be regulated by user as described in Chapter 7.	Maybe
auditd	The audit daemon is important for security-related events, including those highlighted by SELinux.	Enable
autofs	The automounter mounts removable and network directories on demand.	Disable
avahi-daemon	The Avahi daemon is the Linux implementation of the Microsoft zeroconf technology and the Apple Bonjour service discovery protocol. It uses port 5353 to discover printers and shared directories on a local network. Sometimes used for sharing music via Rhythmbox.	Disable
avahi-dnsconfd	For discovery of local Domain Name Service (DNS) servers.	Disable
bluetooth	For Bluetooth hardware support.	Disable
bootlogd	For logging boot messages.	Enable
capi	For Integrated Services Digital Network (ISDN) cards.	Disable
conman	Service for console management, including SSH and Telnet connections.	Enable
console-setup	For text console configuration.	Enable
cpuspeed	Service for CPU power management. On later Ubuntu systems, controlled by the ondemand script.	Enable
crond	Cron daemon for regular administrative jobs; can be regulated by user, as described in Chapter 7.	Enable
cryptdisks-*	Encryption service for disks.	Enable
cups	Common UNIX Printing System; can disable unless a printer is installed locally or if you need to print from the local system.	Disable
dnsmasq	For small-scale DNS and DHCP servers.	Disable

TABLE 6-2 *continued*		
SERVICE SCRIPT	**DESCRIPTION**	**ACTION**
dund	For Bluetooth-based dial-up networking.	Disable
firstboot	A service that is run once after the operating system is installed.	Disable
functions	For functions used by other /etc/init.d/ scripts.	Enable
gpm	For the console-based mouse pointer; can be useful to copy text.	Depends
grub-common	For GRUB 2.0 boot logging.	Enable
haldaemon	Red Hat suggests you keep this active for the applications that depend on it; the NSA suggests that this daemon is vulnerable in multiple ways.	Depends
hidd	For Bluetooth input devices.	Disable
ip6tables	Firewall for IPv6 networking.	Disable
ipmi	A service for the Intelligent Platform Management Interface (IPMI) to monitor system health.	Enable
iptables	Firewall for IPv4 networking.	Enable
irda	For communication with infrared devices.	Disable
irqbalance	To balance hardware interrupts over multiple processors; disable if only one CPU is on the local system.	Enable
isdn	For support of an ISDN modem.	Disable
keyboard-setup	Initiates keyboard detection during the boot process.	Enable
krb524	For converting Kerberos 5 credentials to Kerberos 4.	Disable
kudzu	Red Hat suggests enabling kudzu for hardware probing; the NSA suggests that it should be disabled.	Depends
lvm2-monitor	For monitoring logical volumes; not necessary unless logical volumes are configured locally.	Depends
mcstrans	For translating category labels in SELinux; required by a few services.	Depends
mdmonitor	For watching over software RAID arrays.	Depends
mdmpd	For watching software RAID multiple path devices.	Depends
messagebus	To listen for real-time changes in hardware.	Depends
microcode_ctl	Standard for Intel 32-bit CPUs.	Depends
multipathd	For configuring multiple devices to storage.	Depends

TABLE 6-2 *continued*

SERVICE SCRIPT	DESCRIPTION	ACTION
netconsole	For remote recording of kernel panic messages; may disable until kernel panic issue becomes difficult.	Disable
netfs	For system mounting of remotely shared directories from NFS and Samba servers.	Depends
netplugd	A daemon that monitors connections to LANs.	Depends
network	For basic networking.	Enable
NetworkManager	Automates switching between network connections; useful for systems with wired and wireless connections.	Disable
nfs	Required for shared Network File System (NFS) connections.	Disable
nfslock	For the NFS file-locking service.	Disable
nscd	Name service caching daemon (NCSD) for networked authentication services.	Enable
pand	For Bluetooth connections to Ethernet networks.	Disable
pcscd	Smartcard support.	Depends
portmap	To convert remote procedure call (RPC) numbers to TCP/IP ports; used by NFS and the Network Information Service (NIS).	Disable
psacct	For kernel process accounting log files.	Enable
rawdevices	For connections to Oracle databases.	Disable
rc.local	Runs commands in /etc/rc.local; avoid if possible.	Depends
rdisc	For router discovery.	Depends
readahead_early	Loads programs during the boot process; the NSA recommends disabling.	Disable
readahead_late	Loads programs during the boot process; the NSA recommends disabling.	Disable
restorecond	SELinux monitor for files.	Enable
rhnsd	Red Hat Network (RHN) action monitor, needed if you administer this system from RHN.	Enable
rpcgssd	Supports credential searches for NFS.	Disable
rpcidmapd	The NFS name-mapping daemon.	Disable
rpcsvcgssd	Server-side credential searches for NFS.	Disable

TABLE 6-2 *continued*

SERVICE SCRIPT	DESCRIPTION	ACTION
saslauthd	Simple authentication and security layer service, used for some services such as sendmail.	Depends
sendmail	An open source Simple Mail Transfer Protocol (SMTP) e-mail service.	Depends
smartd	Monitor for modern hard drives.	Enable
sshd	SSH server.	Enable
syslog	Log service.	Enable
wpa_supplicant	Wireless network access.	Disable
x11-common	Filesystem infrastructure for additional GUI software.	Disable
xinetd	Extended internet super server.	Disable
ypbind	Binding for NIS clients and servers.	Disable
yum-updatesd	Automatic updates.	Depends

If the service noted in Table 6-2 is to be disabled, look at the description. You may actually need the service; if so, be aware of the risks. If the rationale applies to your system, try to uninstall the service first. Unless the process also uninstalls something important, proceed with uninstalling the service. Otherwise, stop the service with the script in the /etc/init.d/ directory. Disable the service in all runlevels with the chkconfig or update-rc.d commands described earlier.

If you're having trouble identifying the name of the service, the rpm -qf command can help. For example, on Red Hat systems, the following command identifies the bluez-utils package as the owner of the bluetooth service script in the /etc/init.d/ directory.

```
# rpm -qf /etc/init.d/bluetooth
```

The best-practice status of a few services is in dispute. For example, while the NSA suggests that the Hardware Abstraction Layer daemon should be disabled, documentation from the *Red Hat Magazine* suggests otherwise. While many distributions are aggressively moving toward IPv6, the NSA suggests that most administrators should avoid that network standard. In a similar fashion, while Red Hat recommends that you keep the Kudzu hardware-probing service active, the NSA disagrees.

Several services are related to NFS. If you do not have a reason to use NFS for sharing directories, you should disable NFS and related services, including nfs, netfs, nfslock, rpcgssd, rpcsvcgssd, and rpcidmapd.

> **NOTE**
>
> As of this writing, Red Hat Enterprise Linux 6 just entered its beta release phase. Indications so far suggest that fewer services will be enabled by default on this distribution release.

Managing Super Servers and Deactivating Service Scripts

Two different Linux daemons are associated with the term "super server." While the first super server was configured in the /etc/inetd.conf file, it is still used on occasion on Ubuntu systems. But for most Linux services on most Linux distributions, the regular super server is obsolete. The current version is known as the extended internet super server, configured in the /etc/xinetd.conf configuration file. Both super servers are designed as a single daemon that watches for connections on multiple ports, on behalf of multiple services. Both super servers are controlled by scripts in the /etc/init.d/ directory.

In most cases, the services in both super servers communicate using Transmission Control Protocol (TCP) packets. As such, they can be protected in part with TCP Wrappers control files, as discussed in Chapter 7.

The /etc/init.d/ directory is important because it includes services that are started in various runlevels. Take a look at this directory on a standard (not minimal) Red Hat or Ubuntu system. With a very few exceptions, it includes scripts that control not only the super servers, but also most regular services. Many Linux developers have been migrating services from super servers to stand-alone scripts in the noted directory.

The Original Super Server

The original internet super server is configured in the /etc/inetd.conf file. One of the few services that uses this super server on Ubuntu systems is SWAT, which also suggests that the original internet super server is not truly secure. When SWAT is installed, you may find the following configuration directive in /etc/inetd.conf:

```
swat stream tcp    nowait.400    root
⮡ /usr/sbin/tcpd /usr/sbin/swat
```

This directive suggests that SWAT communicates with a stream of TCP packets, is owned by the root administrative user, and no more than 400 instances of SWAT should be available. But wait: 400 instances? That many instances of an insecure service should make you stop and think. In fact, when installing SWAT (and some other regular super server services), you'll see a message suggesting that you convert to xinetd, the daemon associated with the extended internet super server.

If there is still some reason to use the regular internet super server, it'll be controlled by either an inetutils-inetd or a openbsd-inetd script in the /etc/init.d/ directory.

The Extended Internet Super Server

The **extended internet super server** is sometimes known by its daemon, xinetd. It's configured in the /etc/xinetd.conf file, which points to individual configuration files in the /etc/xinetd.d/ directory. The standard version of the /etc/xinetd.conf file includes a defaults directive for about 20 standards listed in the associated man page.

TABLE 6-3   Directives from `/etc/xinetd.d/vmware-authd`.

DIRECTIVE	EXPLANATION
`disable=no`	The service is enabled, as long as the `xinetd` service is also running.
`port=902`	Communication is on TCP/IP port 902.
`socket_type=stream`	For stream communication.
`protocol=tcp`	Communication is with TCP packets.
`wait=no`	For a multi-threaded service.
`user=root`	Owned by the root administrative user, which may be a risk.
`server=/usr/sbin/vmware-authd`	The location of the actual daemon.
`type=unlisted`	Required when the TCP/IP port is not listed in `/etc/services`.

The `xinetd.conf` file frequently includes logging information and access restrictions. Directives such as the following can limit attacks. This directive makes a client wait 10 seconds after 50 attempts:

```
cps = 50 10
```

This `instances` directive limits the number of total simultaneous connections:

```
instances = 50
```

The `per_source` directive limits the number of simultaneous connections by source:

```
per_source = 10
```

The main configuration work is done in files in the `/etc/xinetd.d/` directory. Of particular interest to those who use virtual machines is the `vmware-authd` file, which enables network access to VMware virtual machines. The directives from that file are explained in Table 6-3.

Regular Service Scripts

Regular service scripts are located in the `/etc/init.d/` directory. With rare exceptions, these scripts can be used to at least start, stop, and restart a service. As these scripts are all text files, you should take a look. At the end of each of these scripts, you'll see a full list of available control commands. Most are self-explanatory, such as `start`, `stop`, `restart`, and `status`. For example, the following command stops and restarts the Samba service on a Red Hat system whether or not Samba is already running:

```
# /etc/init.d/smb restart
```

Two options require a little more explanation. The `reload` option does not stop or start a service. It just reloads the configuration file. If you've just changed a configuration file, it's a quick way to put it into effect without restarting a system. A restart would kick off any connected users.

The **condrestart** option restarts a system only if the system was already running. Many /etc/init.d/ scripts include a number of other options; perhaps the most important include the word `force` in the script, which can be helpful if a service is not otherwise responding to commands.

While developers are working on replacing regular service scripts in the Upstart system, it is unlikely that the scripts in the /etc/init.d/ directory will be completely replaced in stable Linux distributions. And if they are, developers will have to make the change appear seamless to the administrator.

Isolate with chroot Jails

Conceptually, a **chroot jail** is sort of like a virtual machine. In fact, it's considered by some as one type of operating-system-level virtualization. In most cases, a chroot jail includes all of the binaries, libraries, configuration files, and executables required to run a service that is so contained. A properly configured chroot jail does not allow privilege escalation of any sort, whether through SUID- or SGID-bit modified executable files or other means of gaining administrative access.

If a black-hat hacker is able to break into a service, his actions should be confined to the files and subdirectories in the chroot jail. With administrative access, that hacker may be able to break out of the chroot jail into the main directory tree for the local system.

Significant services that have been configured with chroot jails include the Berkeley Internet Name Daemon (BIND) software for DNS, the very secure FTP daemon (vsFTPd), and the Postfix e-mail service. As described in Chapter 5, the vsFTPd chroot jail could be configured to limit both anonymous and regular users to appropriate directories.

One interesting implementation of a chroot jail is based on the Red Hat `bind-chroot` package, which configures the files needed for the BIND DNS service in the /var/named/chroot/ directory. For more information on BIND and Postfix, see Chapter 9.

Avoid X Servers and X Clients Where Possible

Regular users demand the GUI. So it's impossible to avoid the GUI in most situations. But the GUI isn't required for most systems with Linux servers. It isn't even required for servers that share graphical images such as the Apache Web server. Since the GUI presents a number of security risks, you should avoid installing the GUI on Linux servers when possible.

In Linux, X is a common reference to the GUI. The main GUI server for Linux is based on the work of developers sponsored by the X.org foundation. The X server uses hardware on the local system to display graphical images. These images come from X clients, which may be started either locally or remotely.

Most of the latest Linux distributions, including Ubuntu and Red Hat, have disabled the X systems that present the most challenging security risks. Options such as `xhost` and `xauth` have been disabled. Of course, you can install them, but data sent using such commands, including passwords, is sent in clear text.

If You Must Have a GUI

Linux systems that must be configured with a GUI should be protected carefully. First, you should disable any sort of access through the **X Display Manager Control Protocol (XDMCP)**. If active, users who browse your networks can see that system as a login option. As you can see from the `/etc/services` file, XDMCP works through port 177. Of course, if you're setting up access to GUI-based terminal servers, you should look at the work of the Linux Terminal Server Project (LTSP). For more information, see *http://www.ltsp.org/*.

X clients can still be run remotely even if port 177 is closed. The primary means is through an SSH server. When a user runs the `ssh -X remotehost` command, that user is given access to remote GUI clients unless the following directive is added to the SSH server configuration file (`sshd_config` in the `/etc/ssh/` directory):

```
X11forwarding no
```

The Surprising Generic Text Tool

Telnet. That name should evoke fear in the mind of any security professional, as it transmits data such as usernames and passwords in clear text. (For more information, see Chapter 8.) However, the `telnet` command is an excellent way to verify the accessibility of a service over a network. Based on standard port numbers listed in `/etc/services`, try the `telnet` command online. For example, the following command can verify access to an SMTP e-mail service using the standard port number. Of course, you'll need to substitute an actual SMTP URL or IP address for *email.example.org*.

```
$ telnet email.example.org 25
```

To find the URL of an SMTP service, run the `host example.org` command, substituting your favorite URL for *example.org*. In most cases, you'll be able to run the `telnet` command to connect to that e-mail server using the command model shown above.

You can use the `telnet` command to verify connectivity to other services. As long as the applicable TCP/IP port is open on the target server and the service is running, you should see the following response message:

```
Trying 192.168.0.1
Connected to some.example.org (192.168.0.1).

Escape character is '^]'.
```

If you choose to block all connections, the `telnet` command is still useful locally. If you're configuring a system, the `telnet` command with the appropriate port number can help verify that a service can communicate.

FIGURE 6-8

The `elinks` Web
browser.

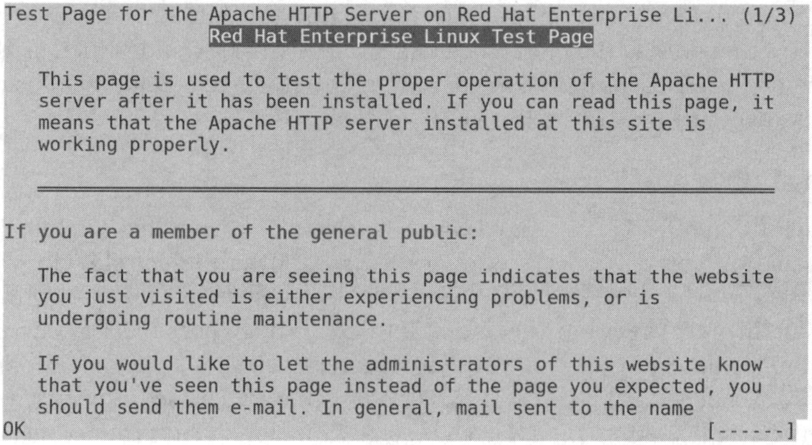

```
Test Page for the Apache HTTP Server on Red Hat Enterprise Li... (1/3)
                     Red Hat Enterprise Linux Test Page

      This page is used to test the proper operation of the Apache HTTP
      server after it has been installed. If you can read this page, it
      means that the Apache HTTP server installed at this site is
      working properly.
      _____
      _____

   If you are a member of the general public:

      The fact that you are seeing this page indicates that the website
      you just visited is either experiencing problems, or is
      undergoing routine maintenance.

      If you would like to let the administrators of this website know
      that you've seen this page instead of the page you expected, you
      should send them e-mail. In general, mail sent to the name
   OK                                                              [------]
```

Test with Text Tools

Many excellent text- and console-based tools are available for Linux. These tools can be used to check data from a number of different "graphical" services. For example, `elinks` is a console browser that you can use to review data from Web servers. On a Red Hat system with a running Apache Web server, the `elinks 127.0.0.1` command returns the page shown in Figure 6-8.

Try `elinks` on the Web sites of your choice. You might be surprised with what you can do with this console browser. It should give you some confidence in Linux text tools.

If you're testing an e-mail service, several excellent text-based tools are available, including `mutt`, `pine`, and `mail`. As with any standard e-mail client, these text-based tools can be used to connect to the e-mail services of your choice.

There's even a console-based client for testing audio, `cmus`. If you're looking for other text-based tools, just search the shared online repositories for a distribution. Commands such as `apt-cache search` *term* and `yum search` *term* can provide surprising results.

The Risks of Productivity Tools

As a Linux guru, you can avoid GUIs on local servers. Your systems will be more secure as a result. However, regular users need productivity tools. To meet the standard requirements of a publisher, this book is being written in one of those productivity tools in a GUI. So while you can minimize the use of GUIs in servers, you can't avoid them completely.

When you install and administer desktop systems, you need to stay up to speed on security issues related to those productivity tools. One of the issues you may have to deal with is choice. The choice available to Linux users in productivity tools can make it more difficult to keep their systems secure. Chapter 11 describes in basic terms how you can create a custom repository for a local network. When properly configured, that repository can limit the choices available to your users, thereby limiting the risks associated with productivity tools.

TABLE 6-4	Linux GUI Web browsers.	
GUI BROWSER	**DEVELOPER**	**URL**
Amaya	World Wide Web Consortium (W3C)	*http://www.w3.org/Amaya/*
Epiphany	GNOME Foundation	*http://projects.gnome.org/epiphany/*
Firefox	The Mozilla Foundation	*http://www.mozilla.com/firefox/*
Konqueror	KDE e.V. (Registered in Germany)	*http://www.konqueror.org/features/ browser.php*
Opera	Opera Software, ASA	*http://www.opera.com/support/*

Browsers

Yes, the standard Web browser for Linux workstations is Firefox, developed by the Mozilla Foundation. If you administer Linux workstations, you should monitor Mozilla's list of security advisories at *http://www.mozilla.org/security/announce/*. Those security advisories are classified in four categories: critical, high, moderate, and low, depending on the level of risk.

The major graphical Web browsers for Linux are listed in Table 6-4, along with their URL. If you compare these browsers, you may note a lot of similarities. When Netscape released its browser under an open source license, the Mozilla foundation and others started using and improving their source code.

The list of browsers shown in Table 6-4 just includes those browsers that are supported. Several other options are available from other open source development groups. Each of them may have their own security issues, and may be less well supported. It would be difficult to monitor security alerts for all of these Web browsers. So even though it may go against the principles of open source, it would reduce your workload to limit the Web browsers available on the local network.

Office Suites

Now that you've seen the variety of Web browsers available, it should not be necessary to cite a similar list of office suites. If you want interoperability with Microsoft Office, the OpenOffice.org suite is the best choice. In fact, this book was drafted using OpenOffice. org Writer, version 3.1, which reads from and writes to the Word 2007 .doc and .docx formats. Other applications from the OpenOffice.org suite are also interoperable with other Office 2007 (and earlier) applications. But as such, the OpenOffice.org suite may be subject to security risks associated with its own macros as well as macros that were designed for Microsoft Office.

One issue related to the OpenOffice.org suite is updates. When updates are required, they can be substantial, easily involving the transfer of hundreds of megabytes of data to each Linux desktop system. For some networks, the cost of an Internet connection depends on the bandwidth. A local repository as described in Chapter 11 can help minimize the bandwidth required from OpenOffice.org downloads. It can also help you retain configuration control. For example, if your data has not yet been tested with OpenOffice.org version 3.*x*, a local repository can help you limit the choice available to your users.

E-mail

Linux includes as many options for e-mail clients as it does for browsers. Some just do e-mail, others are more fully featured personal information managers (PIMs). For example, with the right plug-in, the Evolution groupware suite can work as a client to Microsoft Exchange servers. (Of course, Linux includes its own PIM server equivalent, known as Novell Groupwise. But that's a server application.)

Other more straightforward e-mail clients include the following:

- **Mozilla Thunderbird**—A secure e-mail client and Really Simple Syndication (RSS) feed reader. Thunderbird is Mozilla's companion to the Firefox Web browser.

- **Balsa**—An e-mail client for the GNOME desktop environment, without the groupware features (or overhead) associated with Evolution.

- **Kmail**—An e-mail client for the KDE desktop environment.

- **Sylpheed**—A lightweight GUI e-mail client with excellent Japanese language support.

Best Practices: Service Deployment

Every service is a potential risk. For this reason, it's best to configure as few services as possible on any system.

The ideal bastion server is configured with a single purpose in mind. It'll have two open ports: one for the purpose of the server, one for the SSH connection to administer that server. Bastions are more practical to configure today, given the availability of virtual machines. Fortunately, Linux in a virtual machine does not require a lot of resources. In addition, you do not need to include all standard physical hardware in a virtual machine.

Generally, bastions should be configured in the DMZ portion of a network. While the DMZ is protected in part from an outside network such as the Internet, it is not as well protected as the remainder of the private network. Bastions are typically configured from a minimal installation of Linux. This chapter examined how you can create such a minimal installation for both RHEL 5 and Ubuntu Server Edition.

The minimal installations of many distributions, including RHEL 5, include many more services than is desirable on a bastion host. Ideally, you should uninstall unneeded services. But that is not always realistic, as some critical software may not work unless some services that may appear to be unnecessary are also installed. But you can at least make sure unnecessary software is not active. Opinions vary on some software; for example, Red Hat and the NSA have come to varying conclusions on some services.

When bastions are configured on a virtual machine, generally you should set up something other than a bridged network. A combination of NAT and port forwarding can be used to direct desired traffic to bastion servers.

In general, administrators will take care to remove development tools from every active system. If a black-hat hacker breaks into a system with development tools, that black-hat hacker could use those tools to build more dangerous malware.

Other services are controlled through the regular and extended internet super servers. Some services may be made more secure with the use of a chroot jail.

You should avoid the installation of a GUI where possible. Many users will require a GUI, however. Most Linux distributions have disabled the `xauth` and `xhost` commands because of security risks. If possible, you should also disable access via the XDMCP protocol.

Most Linux administrators work without a GUI. That's made possible courtesy of some important and sometimes even surprising tools. The SSH service enables secure remote administration. Surprisingly, the `telnet` command with the right port number can be used to verify activity in a number of services. Other text tools such as `elinks`, `mutt`, and `mail` can be used to test various services.

When you do need to configure a GUI, it's best to limit available choices of productivity tools. Because Linux is all about choice, many options are available for browsers, office suites, and e-mail clients. To reduce the risks to a network and to reduce the load on a network connection to the Internet, you may want to limit those choices.

CHAPTER SUMMARY

This chapter is all about risk management. Bastions minimize the risk that a black-hat hacker can compromise those systems. Uninstalled source code tools reduce the tools available to such black-hat hackers. While it's useful to start with a minimal installation, additional work needs to be done to reduce that installation to a system that qualifies as a bastion, especially for RHEL 5. Some services can be further protected with the help of chroot jails.

When you do need to set up a GUI system on a desktop, it's safest to limit available choices. If you allow users access to the full range of options available on Linux, your workload will increase—and that increases the risk that you might miss a security update that really affects local users.

KEY CONCEPTS AND TERMS

`apt-cache`	Bastion server	Internet super server
`apt-get`	Chroot jail	Process Identifier (PID)
`chkconfig`	Demilitarized zone (DMZ)	Tarball
`condrestart`	Dependency hell	Upstart
`update-rc.d`	Extended internet super server	X Display Manager Control
`yum`	GNU Compiler Collection (GCC)	Protocol (XDMCP)

CHAPTER 6 ASSESSMENT

1. What part of a network is best for bastion servers?

   A. A DMZ
   B. The protected network
   C. Virtual hosts in a bridged network
   D. A bastionized network

2. Which of the following directories contains scripts that control services?

   A. `/etc/default/`
   B. `/etc/sysconfig/`
   C. `/etc/xinetd.d/`
   D. `/etc/init.d/`

3. Which of the following commands lists currently installed packages on a Linux system?

   A. `rpm -qi`
   B. `rpm -qa`
   C. `rpm -qf`
   D. `rpm -ql`

4. Your LAN is on the `192.168.0.0/24` network. Which of the following virtual machine network options gives local virtual machines addresses on that network?

   A. Host-only
   B. NAT
   C. Bridged
   D. DHCP

5. Which of the following options is a development tool that compiles source code?

   A. `configure`
   B. `make`
   C. `gcc`
   D. `cpp`

6. Scripts in which of the following directories can be used to deactivate a currently running service?

   A. `/etc/rc5.d/`
   B. `/etc/rcS.d/`
   C. `/etc/event.d/`
   D. `/etc/init.d/`

7. Enter the command on Red Hat distributions that includes the default status of services with `/etc/init.d/` scripts at each runlevel:

   _____.

8. Which service script in the `/etc/init.d/` directory is *not* related to SELinux?

   A. `auditd`
   B. `dund`
   C. `mctrans`
   D. `restorecond`

9. Which service script in the `/etc/init.d/` directory is *not* related to NFS?

   A. `netfs`
   B. `nfslock`
   C. `rpcsvcgssd`
   D. `ncsd`

10. Enter the full path to the main configuration file associated with the extended internet super server: _____.

11. Which of the following options for scripts in the `/etc/init.d/` directory does not kick off users who are currently connected to a service?

   A. `restart`
   B. `reload`
   C. `condreload`
   D. HUP

12. Which of the following directories contain the standard chroot jail location for Red Hat BIND DNS servers?

   A. `netfs`
   B. `nfslock`
   C. `rpcsvcgssd`
   D. `ncsd`

13. Which of the following is a protocol that supports remote login access to a GUI system?

   A. Telnet
   B. SSH
   C. XDMCP
   D. LTSP

14. Which of the following clients can connect to a Microsoft Exchange server?

   A. Balsa
   B. Evolution
   C. Kmail
   D. Thunderbird

15. Which of the following commands starts a console-based Web browser?

   A. `konqueror`
   B. `opera`
   C. `firefox`
   D. `elinks`

Networks, Firewalls, and More

THIS CHAPTER FOCUSES ON SECURING THE SYSTEM. If your systems use the Transmission Control Protocol/Internet Protocol (TCP/IP) protocol suite for networking, network packets may travel along one or more of 65,000 virtual ports. On a network as diverse as the Internet, standard port numbers facilitate communication. Services you provide online may even advertise their information in some ways. Obscurity in port numbers and other advertised information may make take your system out of the line of fire of some black-hat hackers.

System security requires regulation of packets transmitted over the network. Some services that use TCP packets can be regulated with networking access control lists (ACLs) in a system known as **TCP Wrappers**. You can configure more fine-grained control of network communication with network filtering commands; the key Linux network filter command is `iptables`.

System security sometimes requires a network inventory. Older enterprises may still support remote access by means such as **telephone modems**, serial ports, and more. Newer systems are frequently configured with wireless hardware that is active and vulnerable by default. Related services can often be related by ACL configuration files.

You can do more to enhance system security with mandatory access controls. Two major Linux options in this area are **Security Enhanced Linux (SELinux)** and **Application Armor (AppArmor)**. Unfortunately, these access control options can't both be used on the same system.

Chapter 7 Topics

This chapter covers the following topics and concepts:

- How to identify different services and their TCP/IP ports
- How to configure obscurity of open ports
- How to protect some services with TCP Wrappers
- What some appropriate packet filtering firewall commands are
- What alternate attack vectors are
- Which issues relate to wireless networks
- How to configure Security Enhanced Linux (SELinux) for a system
- How to set up AppArmor profiles
- What best practices are for networks, firewalls, and TCP/IP communications

Chapter 7 Goals

When you complete this chapter, you will be able to:

- Manage services on different TCP/IP ports
- Protect different services with TCP Wrappers and firewalls
- Understand the risks associated with alternative network connections
- Use SELinux and AppArmor to enhance security

Services on Every TCP/IP Port

As there are over more than 65,000 port numbers associated with TCP/IP services, the accounting for different network services can get confusing. To reduce confusion, the **Internet Assigned Numbers Authority (IANA)** specifies default port numbers and protocols for literally thousands of services.

The association between port numbers and services is documented in the /etc/services file. Other Linux configuration options refer to this file. For example, when the iptables command is used to configure a firewall on a Red Hat system, the associated rules are stored in the /etc/sysconfig/iptables file. When the iptables service is made active, however, and translated to a list of rules, configured iptables rules use the information in /etc/services to substitute protocol acronyms for port numbers. For example, since that file specifies ssh for port 22, the iptables rules would show ssh in place of port 22.

Protocols and Numbers in /etc/services

Take a few moments to browse through the /etc/services file. If you have some experience with networks, you should recognize some of these port numbers. In fact, if you've passed the exams associated with certain Linux certifications, you've had to memorize more than a few "well known" port numbers. If you know standard port numbers, you can create appropriate firewalls that accommodate active services more quickly.

IANA classifies port numbers in three categories: well known, registered, and dynamic or private ports. They are described as follows:

- **Well known**—The well-known TCP/IP port numbers range from 0 to 1023. As specified by IANA, these port numbers are limited for use by system (or root) processes or by programs executed by privileged users.

- **Registered**—Registered ports have been assigned to various services. While it is best to limit the use of these ports to privileged users, it's not always required, such as for various chat services.

- **Dynamic or private**—IANA does not register services in this range of ports, leaving them free for clients who choose their ports dynamically or for privately configured protocols.

If you're using a protocol analyzer to detect the port numbers associated with network packets, be careful. IANA ports are associated with servers. The port numbers associated with clients frequently vary. Client port numbers for TCP services typically range from 1024 to 4096. Some well-known ports are listed in Table 7-1.

TABLE 7-1 A sample of well-known port-numbers.

PORT NUMBER	DESCRIPTION
21	File Transfer Protocol (FTP) connections (port 20 is the standard for FTP data transfer)
22	Secure Shell (SSH)
23	Telnet
25	Simple Mail Transfer Protocol (SMTP)
80	Hypertext Transfer Protocol (HTTP)
110	Post Office Protocol version 3 (POP3)
143	Internet Message Access Protocol (works for versions 2 and 4)
443	Secure HTTP (HTTPS)

Protection by the Protocol and Number

If you're creating a firewall, pay attention to the standard ports and protocols listed in `/etc/services`. Some services work with both TCP and User Datagram Protocol (UDP) packets. To allow access to such services, you need to know how to create firewall rules that support access to both types of packets on the target port number(s).

Of course, if you're one of those administrators who uses nonstandard port numbers, document everything carefully. Administrators who work with your networks need that information to know how to make authorized connections.

Obscurity and the Open Port Problem

It isn't as easy as it looks to configure nonstandard ports. With the available Linux tools, black-hat hackers can easily identify the use of a nonstandard port. However, not all black-hat hackers use Linux tools, so obscurity can promote security. Obscurity goes beyond ports into the information that is made publicly available about your networks.

Obscure Ports

The great majority of Web sites use the standard TCP/IP port 80 for serving nonsecure Web pages. A few webmasters configure nonstandard port numbers. Alternative ports that are frequently used for Web sites include 81, 82, 8080, and 8090. For most services, to configure a nonstandard port, you need to explicitly cite the desired port in the configuration file. User clients also need to know how to access those obscure ports. The connection from a client could be simple; for example, the `elinks www.example.org:81` command uses the noted console Web browser to connect to the noted uniform resource locator (URL) on port 81.

> **NOTE**
>
> If you set up an obscure port for a Web site, provide instructions on how to access that Web site, as described in this section.

The connection to a client may require a switch; for example, the following command connects to an SSH server on port 2424:

```
# ssh -p 2424 michael@host.example.org
```

Opening Obscure Open Ports

The work required to set up obscure open ports may be for naught without corresponding changes to the firewall. As shown later in this chapter, an appropriately configured firewall accepts packets that are directed at specific ports (and more). Packets with other destinations and characteristics are rejected.

In other words, when configuring obscure ports for a service, configuring different ports for clients and servers is not enough. You also need to configure an open port in the firewall. If associated traffic uses both TCP and UDP packets, you'll need to configure that obscure port for both types of packets. In Chapter 13, you'll look at the `nmap` command to identify open ports on a remote system. If that command does not identify properly configured obscure open ports, the associated service probably hasn't been restarted or reloaded.

But that's also a weakness, since the nmap command can detect the services running even on obscure ports.

Obscurity by Other Means

The use of nonstandard open ports is just one way to obscure local systems and networks. Services can be obscured by their login messages. Services can also be obscured by their error messages. While Chapter 8 covers the Secure Shell (SSH), the following directive in the main configuration file (/etc/ssh/sshd_config) points to the /etc/issue.net file as the login message for users:

```
Banner /etc/issue.net
```

Once configured, you can add appropriate legal warnings or other messages that may mislead any black-hat hackers. The same file is associated with login messages to Telnet, should you choose to take the risks associated with that protocol, which transmits sensitive information in clear text. (For that reason and others, the use of Telnet is not recommended.)

As for error messages, the information shown when a user navigates to a non-existent Web page can also be important. If you're using the Apache Web server, that information depends on the ServerTokens directive in the associated configuration file. Full information leads to the following message when a user tries to navigate to a nonexistent Web page:

```
Apache/2.0.63 (Unix) mod_ssl/2.0.63 OpenSSL/0.9.8e-fips-rhel5
➥ JRun/4.0 mod_auth_passthrough/2.1 mod_bwlimited/1.4
➥FrontPage/5.0.2.2635 Server at example.com Port 80
```

That's a lot of information that a black-hat hacker may be able to use. Assuming the noted Web server actually includes the noted versions of the listed software, a black-hat hacker should be able to check for known flaws in each of those systems.

If Apache were configured with a less informative setting, the user would see the following information instead:

```
Apache Server at example.com Port 80
```

That's a lot less information for a black-hat hacker. In other words, obscurity can make it more difficult for a black-hat hacker to break into your systems.

Protect with TCP Wrappers

The TCP Wrappers system was originally developed to protect the services controlled through the internet super server and extended internet super server services described in Chapter 6. It's been extended statically and dynamically to additional services as will be described shortly. You'll see how such services can be protected through the /etc/hosts.allow and /etc/hosts.deny configuration files.

What Services Are TCP Wrapped?

As mentioned, there are several groups of services that may be protected by TCP Wrappers. If you're looking for candidate services, examine the following configuration files and commands:

- **Regular internet super server**—Any services configured in the /etc/inetd.conf file can be protected by TCP Wrappers, as long as the TCP daemon (/usr/sbin/tcpd) is included in the server column of the associated configuration directive.

- **Extended internet super server**—Any services configured in the /etc/xinetd.conf file can be protected by TCP Wrappers. Normally, the /etc/xinetd.conf file points to individual services in the /etc/xinetd.d/ directory.

- **Services dynamically linked to libwrap.so.0**—Run the ldd command on the full path to a target daemon, such as the SSH service at /usr/sbin/sshd. If you see a libwrap file in the output, there's a dynamic link between the noted service and TCP Wrappers.

- **Services statically linked to libwrap.so.0**—Run the strings command on the full path to a target daemon, such as the Portmap service at /sbin/portmap. If you see a libwrap or /etc/hosts.allow file in the output, there's a static link between the noted service and TCP Wrappers.

All such services can be protected with appropriate directives in the /etc/hosts.allow and /etc/hosts.deny configuration files.

Configure TCP Wrapper Protection

Any services that have the protection of TCP Wrappers are filtered through rules configured in the /etc/hosts.allow and /etc/hosts.deny files. Rules in these files may be configured by Internet Protocol (IP) address, domain, or user. Because rules in these files may conflict, they are considered in the following order:

- **/etc/hosts.allow**—Rules in this file are checked first. If the service is explicitly allowed, control is returned to the service. Any rules in /etc/hosts.deny are ignored.

- **/etc/hosts.deny**—Any service that makes it beyond /etc/hosts.allow looks at rules in this file. Any rule in this file that explicitly denies access to a service is considered. These rules may send a message to the client.

- If no rule applies—If no rule is configured in either file, access is granted.

Directives in both configuration files may be set up with the following format:

```
daemons : clients [ : command  ]
```

One way to set up maximum protection with TCP Wrappers is to include the following rule in the /etc/hosts.deny file. It denies access to all daemons from all clients:

```
ALL : ALL
```

You can then configure other rules in /etc/hosts.allow to explicitly allow access to desired services. First, confirm that the SSH service is associated with TCP Wrappers with the following command:

```
$ ldd /usr/sbin/sshd | grep libwrap
```

Once the status of SSH and TCP Wrappers is confirmed, you can allow access to SSH with an appropriate rule in the /etc/hosts.allow file. The following rule would allow access to all hosts in the noted IP address network to the Secure Shell service:

```
sshd : 10.22.33.
```

Exceptions can be made with the help of the EXCEPT directive, as illustrated here:

```
sshd : 10.22.33. EXCEPT 10.22.33.44
```

Similar rules can be made by domain names:

```
sshd : .example.org EXCEPT temp1.example.org
```

Alternatively, access can be limited by username:

```
sshd : michael@10.22.33.44
```

Access can also be limited by groupname, where the @ symbol labels admin as a group and serves as an identifier of an associated host:

```
sshd : @admin@10.22.33.44
```

You can go farther with the /etc/hosts.deny file, as it can be used to send messages to users or administrators. For example, Stanford University recommends the use of the following directive, which should be entered all on one line:

```
ALL:ALL  : spawn echo "%d\: %u@%h" |
➥/bin/mailx -s "TCPalert for %H"
➥as-admin@some.example.com : banners /etc/banners
```

The noted directive specifies the daemon (%d), the client username (%u), and the client hostname (%h), and sends it as an e-mail message to the noted admin@some.example.com e-mail address. The noted banner file (/etc/banners) can be used to send appropriate welcome or warning messages based on the service being controlled. Stanford University, in its documentation (ref: *https://www.stanford.edu/dept/as/ia/security/policies_standards/ AS_standards/libwrap_access_control_standard_1.0.html*), suggests that its administrators configure the following appropriate welcome message for their users:

> Access to this system is limited to authorized users for University business purposes only. Unauthorized access to or use of this system is prohibited and may subject you to civil and criminal prosecution. Use of this system may be monitored for the purpose of maintaining system security and unauthorized access or usage.

Stanford University also suggests that its administrators set up the following message for users who are denied access to TCP Wrappers services. The hostname of the server is substituted for %h in the message.

You have attempted to connect to a restricted access server which you have not been authorized to connect to. Unauthorized access to this system is an actionable offense and will be prosecuted to the fullest extent of the law.

It appears that you have attempted to connect from host %h and that host does not have permission/authorization to access this server. Your actions have been recorded and are being reported to the system administrators of this system.

You will now be disconnected!

Of course, the wording should be revised per the policies and characteristics of your organization.

Packet Filtering Firewalls

When Linux is protected with a packet filtering firewall, it is protected with a set of rules defined by the iptables command. This command can be used to check various parts of a network packet using patterns. If the pattern is matched, you can configure that iptables command to accept, reject, deny, or even forward that packet. Different sets of rules can be created for bastion hosts in a demilitarized zone (DMZ) as well as private networks behind that DMZ.

Before exploring the iptables commands that filter packets, be aware that the iptables command is frequently used to masquerade the addresses of a private IP network as a second IP address, typically a public IP address on the Internet.

In addition, any iptables rules that forward a packet won't work unless forwarding options in the /proc/ directory, typically in the /proc/sys/net/ipv4/ip_forward file. Such options can be configured on a more permanent basis in the /etc/sysctl.conf configuration file.

While the options described here apply to Internet Protocol version 4 (IPv4) networking, similar commands and options apply to Internet Protocol version 6 (IPv6) networking. In most cases, the only differences are the addresses along with the applicable command (ip6tables instead of iptables).

Packet filtering relies on information embedded in the header of each packet. Based on that information, you can create iptables-based rules that can redirect the packet. That information can include network cards, IP addresses, port numbers, and more.

This section serves as a brief introduction to the iptables command. A good firewall can include dozens of commands, which can identify different packets and/or source/destination addresses. The iptables command can also be configured to specify desired actions to take on those packets. Several excellent books are available that can help you customize iptables firewalls in quite a bit of detail; some references are listed in the back of this book.

Basic Firewall Commands

In a typical firewall configuration file, you'll find chains of `iptables` commands. The rules defined by each `iptables` command in a chain are considered one by one, in order. The basic format of the command is as follows:

```
iptables -t table option direction packet_pattern -j action
```

Now let's examine each of these options in turn.

The `iptables` Table Option

The first option associated with `iptables` is the `-t` option, also known as the table switch. Two basic options for this switch are available (the default is `filter`):

- **filter**—Specifies rules for filtering packets.
- **nat**—Short for network address translation, the `iptables -t nat` command can be used to configure masquerading.

For example, the following command configures masquerading on the first Ethernet device, `eth0`. This presumes some other network device such as `eth1` is connected to and configured on some internal private IP address network:

```
iptables -t nat -A POSTROUTING -o eth0 -j MASQUERADE
```

Normally, this is followed by two other commands that allow forwarding between the noted Ethernet network cards:

```
iptables -A FORWARD -i eth0 -o eth1 -m state
↪--state RELATED,ESTABLISHED -j ACCEPT
iptables -A FORWARD -i eth1 -o eth0 -j ACCEPT
```

These two commands provide an introduction to the other `-t` switch, for packet filtering. As the `-t filter` option is the default, it does not need to be included in the command. The first command takes packets from the external interface (`eth0`) and checks the state of their modules (`-m state`). For those packets where connections have been ESTABLISHED or are RELATED to an existing connection, the `iptables` rule jumps (`-j`) to ACCEPT the packet. The second command accepts and forwards all packets from network card `eth1` destined for outside networks through network card `eth0`.

Of course, `iptables` rules can be more complex.

Options and Directions for the `iptables` Command

In this section, you'll examine six basic options for the `iptables` command. In most cases, `iptables` options can be specified as letters or more expressive word switches, as follows:

- **-A (--append)**—Appends a rule to the end of a chain
- **-I (--insert)** *n*—Inserts a rule in a chain of rules, as rule number *n*
- **-R (--replace)** *n*—Replaces a rule in a chain of rules, as rule number *n*
- **-D (--delete)** *n*—Deletes a rule in a chain of rules, as rule number *n*

- **-L (--list)**—Lists existing iptables rules
- **-F (--flush)**—Deletes (flushes) all configured rules in the specified chain

The last two commands are frequently executed on their own. For example, the iptables -L command lists all currently active rules defined in associated configuration files. If there is a problem, you may choose to temporarily disable the current firewall with the iptables -F command. As long as any firewall configuration files still exist, you should be able to reactivate the current firewall with the following command:

```
# iptables-restore /path/to/iptables_configuration_file
```

When appropriate, these options should be coupled with a direction based on the source and destination of the packet. The three available directions are as follows:

- **INPUT**—Applies the iptables rule to incoming packets.
- **OUTPUT**—Applies the iptables rule to outgoing packets.
- **FORWARD**—Applies the iptables rule to incoming packets that are being sent (forwarded) to other systems.

Packets and Patterns for the iptables Command

Once the option and direction for the iptables command is determined, the next step is the pattern match for the packet. In other words, the iptables command can be used to check the packet for characteristics such as the IP address. For example, the following options are based on source and destination IP addresses:

- **-s *ip_address***—The rule is applied to packets that come from the noted source address.
- **-d *ip_address***—The rule is applied to packets that are directed to the noted destination address.

Other characteristics may be associated with the protocol and TCP/IP port defined in the packet. For example, the -p switch can specify the packet type at the application layer of the TCP/IP protocol suite. The three packet-type options at this level are TCP, UDP, and the Internet Control Message Protocol (ICMP). The TCP and UDP protocols are usually associated with a port number.

Actions for the iptables Command

The previous parts of the iptables command help define a packet. Once defined, you need to tell the iptables command what to do with the packet. The four options that follow are associated with the -j switch:

- **-j DROP**—The packet is dropped; no response is sent to the source of the network packet.
- **-j REJECT**—Despite the name of the option, the packet is dropped; however, an error message is sent to the system that is the source of the network packet.

- **-j LOG**—The packet is logged; other -j switches may specify actions that may follow.
- **-j ACCEPT**—The packet is accepted, and is sent to the destination specified in the header of the packet.

Sample iptables Commands

With the iptables options shown, you should be able to understand several different kinds of commands. As an example, Figure 7-1 shows an excerpt of a Red Hat /etc/sysconfig/iptables configuration file. These options are added to the iptables command during the boot process. If you're administering Red Hat systems, pay careful attention. Some of these rules may not be necessary for your configuration. In fact, many firewalls include hundreds of iptables commands. Such complexity can lead to errors. In many cases, fewer iptables rules leads to a more secure system.

> **FYI**
>
> While this discussion is based on a Red Hat iptables configuration file, similar guidelines apply to Ubuntu-based configuration files. One example, based on Ubuntu's uncomplicated firewall (ufw) package, stores comparable configuration files in the /etc/ufw/ directory.
>
> While the iptables chain used for Red Hat systems is normally named RH-Firewall-1-INPUT, that's just a label. If you use the ufw package, you'll end up with several different chains. For that reason, this section is focused on the Red Hat-based firewalls.

```
:RH-Firewall-1-INPUT - [0:0]
-A INPUT -j RH-Firewall-1-INPUT
-A FORWARD -j RH-Firewall-1-INPUT
-A RH-Firewall-1-INPUT -i lo -j ACCEPT
-A RH-Firewall-1-INPUT -p icmp --icmp-type any -j ACCEPT
-A RH-Firewall-1-INPUT -p 50 -j ACCEPT
-A RH-Firewall-1-INPUT -p 51 -j ACCEPT
-A RH-Firewall-1-INPUT -p udp --dport 5353 -d 224.0.0.251 -j ACCEPT
-A RH-Firewall-1-INPUT -p udp -m udp --dport 631 -j ACCEPT
-A RH-Firewall-1-INPUT -p tcp -m tcp --dport 631 -j ACCEPT
-A RH-Firewall-1-INPUT -m state --state ESTABLISHED,RELATED -j ACCEPT
-A RH-Firewall-1-INPUT -m state --state NEW -m tcp -p tcp --dport 21 -j ACCEPT
-A RH-Firewall-1-INPUT -m state --state NEW -m tcp -p tcp --dport 2049 -j ACCEPT
-A RH-Firewall-1-INPUT -m state --state NEW -m tcp -p tcp --dport 22 -j ACCEPT
-A RH-Firewall-1-INPUT -m state --state NEW -m udp -p udp --dport 137 -j ACCEPT
-A RH-Firewall-1-INPUT -m state --state NEW -m udp -p udp --dport 138 -j ACCEPT
-A RH-Firewall-1-INPUT -m state --state NEW -m tcp -p tcp --dport 139 -j ACCEPT
-A RH-Firewall-1-INPUT -m state --state NEW -m tcp -p tcp --dport 445 -j ACCEPT
-A RH-Firewall-1-INPUT -m state --state NEW -m tcp -p tcp --dport 80 -j ACCEPT
-A RH-Firewall-1-INPUT -m state --state NEW -m tcp -p tcp --dport 81 -j ACCEPT
-A RH-Firewall-1-INPUT -m state --state NEW -m udp -p udp --dport 81 -j ACCEPT
-A RH-Firewall-1-INPUT -m state --state NEW -m tcp -p tcp --dport 902 -j ACCEPT
-A RH-Firewall-1-INPUT -j REJECT --reject-with icmp-host-prohibited
COMMIT
```

FIGURE 7-1

Firewall rules from /etc/sysconfig/iptables.

The first two commands specify that `INPUT` and `FORWARD` packets are to be accepted and read by the next rule, `RH-Firewall-1-INPUT`.

Next, the following command accepts all input from the loopback adapter, as specified by the standard loopback device, `lo`:

```
iptables -A RH-Firewall-1-INPUT -i lo -j ACCEPT
```

The command that follows accepts all ICMP messages; the most common ICMP message is from a `ping` command:

```
iptables -A RH-Firewall-1-INPUT -p icmp --icmp-type any -j ACCEPT
```

The following directives are associated with ports 50 and 51. They relate to the packets that support Internet Protocol Security (IPSec) communication for authenticating and encrypting each network packet. If you don't plan to set up a virtual private network (VPN) or a similar encapsulated connection, consider omitting these directives:

```
iptables -A RH-Firewall-1-INPUT -p 50 -j ACCEPT
iptables -A RH-Firewall-1-INPUT -p 51 -j ACCEPT
```

The next directive cites port 5353, which is associated with the **multicast Domain Name Service (mDNS) protocol**. That protocol provides DNS functionality for systems configured with zero configuration networking. That is also known as automatic private IP addressing (APIPA) on Microsoft systems and Bonjour on Apple systems. If you don't need mDNS, consider omitting this directive.

```
iptables -A RH-Firewall-1-INPUT -p udp
↪--dport 5353 -d 224.0.0.251 -j ACCEPT
```

The directives that follow are based on a local Common UNIX Printing System (CUPS) server. The standard CUPS server communicates with TCP and UDP packets on port 631. If you don't need to set up printers on or printing from this system, consider omitting these directives.

```
iptables -A RH-Firewall-1-INPUT -p udp
↪-m udp --dport 631 -j ACCEPT
iptables -A RH-Firewall-1-INPUT -p tcp
↪-m tcp --dport 631 -j ACCEPT
```

The directive that follows continues established connections:

```
iptables -A RH-Firewall-1-INPUT -m state
↪--state ESTABLISHED,RELATED -j ACCEPT
```

In most firewall configurations, the next set of directives apply only if services on the noted ports are active. To see the associated ports, review the `/etc/services` file. The final directive sends a `REJECT` message in response to communication attempts on all other ports.

Many bastion hosts require relatively few `iptables` commands. For example, a bastion host with a Web server that also supports SSH-based remote administration could work with just the following rules:

```
iptables -A INPUT -j RH-Firewall-1-INPUT
iptables -A FORWARD -j RH-Firewall-1-INPUT
iptables -A RH-Firewall-1-INPUT -i lo -j ACCEPT
iptables -A RH-Firewall-1-INPUT -p icmp --icmp-type any -j ACCEPT
iptables -A RH-Firewall-1-INPUT -m state
↪--state ESTABLISHED,RELATED -j ACCEPT
iptables -A RH-Firewall-1-INPUT -m state
↪--state NEW -m tcp -p tcp --dport 22 -j ACCEPT
iptables -A RH-Firewall-1-INPUT -m state
↪--state NEW -m tcp -p tcp --dport 80 -j ACCEPT
iptables -A RH-Firewall-1-INPUT -j REJECT
↪--reject-with icmp-host-prohibited
```

If your systems support Internet Protocol version 6 (IPv6) networking, be sure to make similar changes to the associated configuration file. On Red Hat systems, that file is `/etc/sysconfig/ip6tables`.

From this point, the firewall becomes much more complex. Additional changes, discussed next, regulate different kinds of network packets in detail.

Additional `iptables` Rules

The `iptables` rules listed at the end of the previous section might be too simple. Several additional rules of interest may prevent **denial of service (DoS) attacks**, prevent attempts to connect from private IP address blocks, and slow attempts to attack SSH services. From the literature in the "References" section at the end of this chapter, you should come up with additional rules for the local configuration.

Denial of Service Rules.   Three rules that can prevent or at least slow down DoS attacks are described in the "Linux Packet Filtering HOWTO," available from *http://www.iptables.org/documentation/HOWTO/packet-filtering-HOWTO.html*. While the references there are to the older Linux 2.4 kernel, the description associated with the `iptables` command still applies today.

The following command limits accepted TCP packets to one per second:

```
# iptables -A RH-Firewall-1-INPUT -p tcp
↪--syn -m limit --limit 1/s -j ACCEPT
```

Incidentally, this command is no longer necessary. You can get equivalent protection from a kernel setting. Just activate the boolean option in the `/proc/sys/net/ipv4/tcp_syncookies` file. (In other words, change the value of the file from 0 to 1.)

Next, the following command limits connection attempts from port scanners:

```
# iptables -A RH-Firewall-1-INPUT -p tcp
↪--tcp-flags SYN,ACK,FIN,RST RST -m limit --limit 1/s -j ACCEPT
```

Note how access is limited. In other words, this `iptables` rule accepts one packet
with TCP flags per second.

Change Default Rules.   The noted changes to default `iptables` commands may be
for naught unless the default rules for packets that are input and forwarded are changed.
On a Red Hat system, examine the `/etc/sysconfig/iptables` file. The default as shown
here for those packets is permissive:

```
:INPUT ACCEPT [0:0]
:FORWARD ACCEPT [0:0]
```

These options should be changed to the following:

```
:INPUT DROP [0:0]
:FORWARD DROP [0:0]
```

Restrict the `ping` and Related Messages.   The U.S. National Security Agency has some
specific recommendations on how to manage packets associated with the `ping` command,
along with related packets associated with the ICMP protocol. Their first recommendation
is to remove the following rule from the minimal firewall configuration shown earlier:

```
iptables -A RH-Firewall-1-INPUT -p icmp
↪--icmp-type any -j ACCEPT
```

This rule accepts all ICMP packets, exposing the local system to so called "ping storms"
of packets that deny service to others. The following alternatives accept legitimate
responses when local users run the `ping` command:

```
iptables -A RH-Firewall-1-INPUT -p icmp
↪--icmp-type echo-reply -j ACCEPT

iptables -A RH-Firewall-1-INPUT -p icmp
↪--icmp-type destination-unreachable -j ACCEPT

iptables -A RH-Firewall-1-INPUT -p icmp
↪--icmp-type time-exceeded -j ACCEPT
```

The responses are as implied by the options attached to the `--icmp-type` switch:
for example, `echo-reply` accepts ICMP messages that respond to a `ping` command.
If you want to allow others to `ping` your system, with limits, the following command
rule limits responses to `ping` commands to one per second.

```
iptables -A RH-Firewall-1-INPUT -p icmp
↪--icmp-type echo-request -m limit --limit 1/s -j ACCEPT
```

If you don't want local systems to respond to `ping` command requests, substitute the following command rule:

```
iptables -A RH-Firewall-1-INPUT -p icmp
↪--icmp-type echo-request -j DROP
```

Block Information from Suspicious IP Addresses.   When communicating on the Internet, if you identify a packet with a source IP address that should be on a private network, be suspicious. Such addresses may be an attempt by a black-hat hacker to hide the identity of his system. To that end, secure firewalls will DROP packets with a source IP address associated with private network, or any other address that should not be assigned to a regular system. For IPv4 addresses, such rules should include the following:

```
iptables -A RH-Firewall-1-INPUT -i eth0
↪-s 10.0.0.0/8 -j LOG --log-prefix "Dropped private class A address"

iptables -A RH-Firewall-1-INPUT -i eth0
↪-s 172.16.0.0/12 -j LOG --log-prefix "Dropped private
↪class B address"

iptables -A RH-Firewall-1-INPUT -i eth0
↪-s 192.168.0.0/16 -j LOG --log-prefix "Dropped private
↪class C address"

iptables -A RH-Firewall-1-INPUT -i eth0 -s
↪224.0.0.0/4 -j LOG --log-prefix "Dropped multicast address"

iptables -A RH-Firewall-1-INPUT -i eth0 -s
↪-s 240.0.0.0/5 -j LOG --log-prefix "Dropped class E address"

iptables -A RH-Firewall-1-INPUT -i eth0
↪-d 127.0.0.0/8 -j LOG --log-prefix
↪"Dropped attempt to connect to the loopback address"
```

If you've set up IPv6 addresses, corresponding rules should be added to the corresponding firewall configuration file.

Slow Attacks on SSH Services.   With port scanners and a little work, a black-hat hacker should find it easy to identify not only open ports, but also the traffic expected on those ports. Once that's done, the black-hat hacker can try some typical hostnames and dictionaries of standard passwords. But dictionaries are large. A black-hat hacker who tries to break into a system with a dictionary attack can be slowed down with two `iptables` command rules similar to the following:

```
iptables -A RH-Firewall-1-INPUT -i eth0 -p tcp -m tcp
↪ --dport 22 -m state --state NEW -j SSH_RULE

iptables -A SSH_RULE -i eth0 -p tcp -m tcp --dport 22
↪-m state --state NEW -m recent --update --seconds 60
↪--hitcount 3 --rttl --name SSH -j DROP
```

The first command specifies that the firewall jumps (-j) to the SSH_RULE firewall rule. The second command limits the number of login attempts to three; after three failures, the external user has to wait 60 seconds to try again. That should discourage even users who are just trying a few thousand dictionary words with a typical username.

The iptables Service

On Red Hat systems, there is an iptables service in the /etc/init.d/ directory normally started during the boot process. It reads options from the /etc/sysconfig/iptables configuration file. On Ubuntu systems, when an iptables firewall is configured, additional configuration may be required to make sure the firewall starts during the boot process. But the results may be similar. For example, the aforementioned ufw package also installs a ufw script in the /etc/init.d/ directory.

If you prefer to create a custom firewall, you can use the iptables-save and iptables-restore commands. When applied to a specific file, these commands can save current rules to and restore them from a given file. Such commands can then be added to appropriate network configuration scripts to make sure the firewall is started during the boot process.

Examples of Firewall-Management Tools

If all this seems confusing, GUI-based tools can be helpful. The basic firewall described earlier was created with the Red Hat Security Level Configuration tool, which is shown in Figure 7-2. It allows easy configuration of a firewall. The standard options shown in the Trusted Services window are based on external access to the noted local servers. The port numbers shown in the Other Ports area at the bottom of the screen are the port numbers of additional traffic allowed into the system.

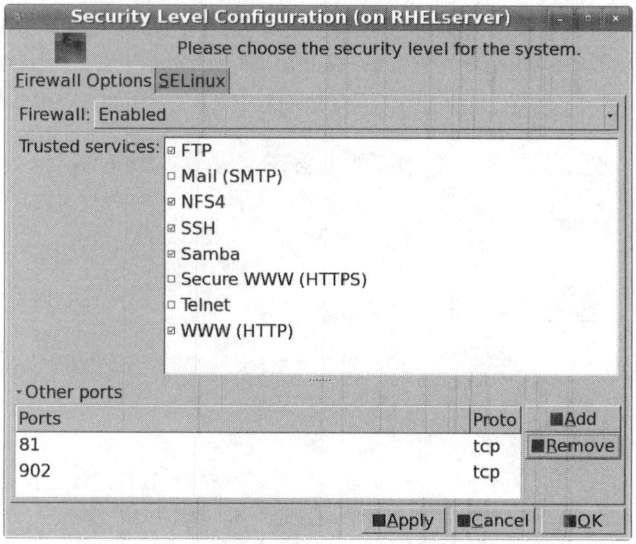

FIGURE 7-2

The GUI Security Level Configuration tool.

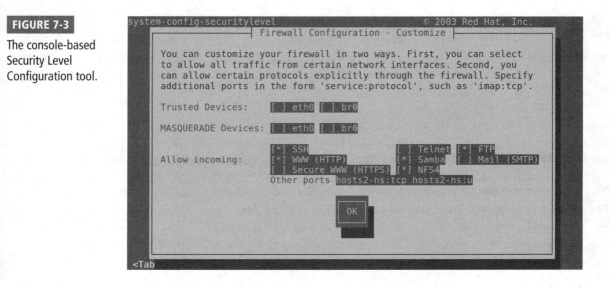

```
system-config-securitylevel                    © 2003 Red Hat, Inc.
              ┌─ Firewall Configuration - Customize ─┐

    You can customize your firewall in two ways. First, you can select
    to allow all traffic from certain network interfaces. Second, you
    can allow certain protocols explicitly through the firewall. Specify
    additional ports in the form 'service:protocol', such as 'imap:tcp'.

    Trusted Devices:     [ ] eth0  [ ] br0

    MASQUERADE Devices:  [ ] eth0  [ ] br0

                         [*] SSH               [ ] Telnet [*] FTP
    Allow incoming:      [*] WWW (HTTP)        [*] Samba  [ ] Mail (SMTP)
                         [ ] Secure WWW (HTTPS) [*] NFS4
                         Other ports hosts2-ns:tcp hosts2-ns:u

                              ┌────┐
                              │ OK │
                              └────┘


 <Tab
```

Differences between GUI tools can be instructive. For example, Figure 7-3 shows
the console-based version of the same tool. This low-level graphical tool includes more
features than its GUI cousin, as it supports masquerading as well as the ability to exempt
traffic from a specific network card. And yes, it can be run on a terminal, without a GUI.

Now for some contrast, examine the GNOME uncomplicated firewall (Gufw) firewall
configuration tool, which you can start in an Ubuntu GUI with the gufw command.
As shown in Figure 7-4, it includes options similar to those available for the Red Hat
Security Level Configuration tool.

If you believe firewall commands are confusing, try some of these tools. More
important, examine the effect of a change through these tools on the associated iptables
configuration files. Save an iptables configuration file. Make a change with a configuration tool. Review the changes in the iptables configuration file. The changes should
help you understand which iptables command can help secure different systems.

Gufw

File Edit Help

Current Configuration   **Enabled**
● Deny incoming traffic
○ Allow incoming traffic   ☑ Firewall enabled

Add a new rule
Simple Preconfigured Advanced

[Allow ┊] [Service ┊] [ftp   ┊] [✛Add]

Rules
To   Action From
21:tcp   ALLOW Anywhere

[⇥Remove] [☑ Select all]   [☒Close]
Operation done

A Firewall for the Demilitarized Zone (DMZ)

If you have bastion servers that provide services such as Web sites and FTP-based file sharing, consider configuring them in a DMZ. A DMZ network is separate from but fits between the Internet and an otherwise wholly private network, as shown in Figure 7-5.

The networks described in Figure 7-5 require additional explanation. Figure 7-5 depicts three distinct networks. The wide area network (WAN) may be a corporate network or the Internet. The DMZ is an internal network with one private IP network address. The protected internal network has a distinct and separate private IP network address. To translate between networks, both routers are configured to masquerade IP addresses. The network addresses shown are just two possible examples. Traffic between the WAN (Internet) and the protected internal network is filtered through two different firewall routers.

Each firewall router has two network devices. In Figure 7-5, the first Ethernet device (eth0) on the external firewall router is connected to the WAN (Internet). The second Ethernet device (eth1) on that same router is connected to the DMZ network. All traffic directed to and from the DMZ and the protected internal network is filtered through a firewall on this router.

7

Networks, Firewalls, and More

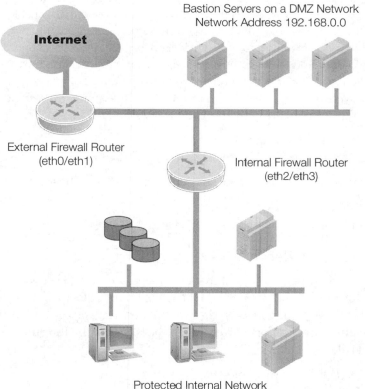

Bastion Servers on a DMZ Network
Network Address 192.168.0.0

Internet

External Firewall Router
(eth0/eth1)

Internal Firewall Router
(eth2/eth3)

Protected Internal Network
Network Address 10.100.0.0

FIGURE 7-5

A DMZ belongs between the Internet and an internal network.

Each bastion server on the DMZ network is used to serve data to users on the Internet. Each bastion server has a single function, such as serving Web pages, sharing files via the FTP service, or sharing authoritative name service information via a caching Domain Name System (DNS) name server. The external firewall router should stop network traffic that would otherwise harm internal systems, such as DoS packets. In addition, that external firewall router should filter requests for each service and redirect appropriate requests to the right bastion server.

Now look at the internal firewall router. The first Ethernet device (eth2) on that router is connected to the DMZ network. The second Ethernet device (eth3) on that router is connected to the protected internal network. The internal firewall router should also stop the same network traffic that would otherwise harm internal systems. It should be designed as if a black-hat hacker has broken into and taken control of a system on the DMZ network.

The only network traffic that should be directed from the external firewall router to the internal network is information requested by those internal network clients. That traffic should be filtered to stop inappropriate traffic such as DoS, rapid attempts at repeated logins, and so on.

In many cases, the functionality of both routers is incorporated into one system with three network cards. That system would include the functionality of both firewalls. If configured on a Linux system, that system should be configured with packet forwarding for both Internet Protocol version 4 (IPv4) and Internet Protocol version 6 (IPv6) traffic in the /etc/sysctl.conf file and /proc/ settings described earlier in this chapter.

Two examples of commands that would enable forwarding to a bastion host Web server on the DMZ are as follows. The first command routes all incoming TCP packets associated with port 80 to the system on IP address 192.168.100.50. It assumes the second Ethernet card (eth1) is the network card between the DMZ and the Internet.

```
iptables -A PREROUTING -t nat -i eth1
↳-p tcp --dport 80 -j DNAT --to 192.168.100.50:80
```

The second rule specifically accepts TCP packets sent to port 80 into the DMZ network.

```
iptables -A RH-Firewall-INPUT -p tcp
↳-m state --state NEW --dport 80 -i eth1 -j ACCEPT
```

A Firewall for the Internal Network

Assuming a DMZ is configured, you'll want to set up a separate firewall between the DMZ network and the internal network. The first two command rules for such a firewall are shown here. The network card between the internal network and the DMZ is the first Ethernet card (eth0); the network card between the DMZ and the Internet is eth1. The first command rule is as follows:

```
iptables -A FORWARD -i eth1 -o eth0 -m state
↳--state ESTABLISHED,RELATED -j ACCEPT
```

It's followed by the following rule, which allows all traffic from the protected internal network out to the Internet. Of course, if organizational policies dictate, you may want to limit such traffic.

```
iptables -A FORWARD -i eth0 -o eth1 -j ACCEPT
```

To allow systems on the internal network to communicate with the Internet, you need a rule that masquerades the IP addresses of the internal network directly to the network card connected to the Internet:

```
iptables -t nat -A POSTROUTING -o eth1
➥-j SNAT --to public_IP_address
```

The `public_IP_address` is the IPv4 address between the DMZ and the Internet.

Alternate Attack Vectors—Modems and More

Today, most attention is focused on regular Internet connections, as if high-speed network connections are the only way to get onto the Internet. Older networks may still have legacy connections such as telephone modems and even serial ports.

Security extends beyond regular network connections. For example, the electro-magnetic emissions of a computer monitor can be used by black-hat hackers to identify critical information. Wireless networks involve a special type of electromagnetic emission, as discussed later in this chapter.

In addition, any black-hat hacker who breaks into a local system may have access to nonstandard services. Some services can be run with administrative permissions and should be regulated carefully.

Attacks Through Nonstandard Connections

Most home users connect through cable modems, Digital Subscriber Line (DSL) adapters, and similar network connections over the public Internet. But not all users have access to such high-speed lines. Many servers still support connections over serial ports. Some systems can even track the electromagnetic output of devices such as monitors to decipher user input.

The Telephone Modem and Related Devices

This section covers those devices that communicate over the older system known as the **public switched telephone network (PSTN)**. A telephone modem is a device that modulates data to the sine waves associated with voice transmission. A second telephone modem on the target network demodulates the sine waves back to digital data. Those features make up the terms modulator-demodulator, or modem for short.

Many users still have access to telephone modems. Because there are still many areas in the Unites States without affordable high-speed Internet access, telephone modems are still, in many cases, the only way a user can get onto the Internet. Nevertheless, telephone modems are a frequently forgotten part of the network infrastructure.

Because Linux is fairly easy to administer from the command-line interface, the 56Kbps transmission speed associated with a telephone modem is sufficient for administrative connections. It's also fast enough for older users, who are accustomed to text-based tools for e-mail, Web browsing, and more.

But as the title of this section implies, connections over the PSTN go beyond telephone modems. Related connections include **Integrated Services Digital Network (ISDN)** devices and other devices that communicate directly on the **public switched data network (PSDN)**.

While the connections for such devices vary on older networks, logins from such devices to Linux systems are generally governed by **Remote Authentication Dial In User Service (RADIUS)**. Authentication via RADIUS can be configured through a local shadow password suite, LDAP servers, or even a preconfigured group of RADIUS usernames and passwords.

RADIUS supports both the **Password Authentication Protocol (PAP)** and the **Challenge-Handshake Authentication Protocol (CHAP)**. CHAP is a bit more secure, as it can send a challenge to a client system at any time.

Serial Ports

Serial ports are included in this section because communication can be enabled over such ports with a so-called "null modem." Such a connection is commonly used to enable a connection to a text console, which is sufficient to administer Linux systems. If a serial port is available on a server, it can be configured as a console with all the regular Linux authentication schemes described in Chapter 4. In other words, a black-hat hacker can connect a laptop terminal to that serial port and log in directly to that system, bypassing security measures such as firewalls that may be present on that system or network.

At the very least, that user can then identify the operating system, potentially force a reboot, and possibly break into an unprotected account on the target machine.

To that end, you need to consider different ways to lock out the serial port. You could add a physical lock, or perhaps seal the port with clay. If it's connected to a removable internal card, you could remove that card. If the port is controlled within the Basic Input/Output System (BIOS) or Unified Extensible Firmware Interface (UEFI) menus, you could disable that port.

Tracking Other Electromagnetic Output

Electrical signals, when unshielded, send information over more than just wires. Just as electricity is produced by turning a magnet inside a coil of electrical wires, magnetic force can be produced by electricity running through a wire. This phenomenon is an effect of electromagnetic radiation.

One method used by black-hat hackers to take advantage of electromagnetic output is known as **Van Eck phreaking**, first proven by Dutch researcher Wim van Eck. He showed it's possible to take the radiation from modern computer displays and recover the associated

The North Atlantic Treaty Organization (NATO) has conducted a series of studies of electro-magnetic output from computers. The study is code-named TEMPEST. The results were documented in National Security Telecommunications and Information Systems Security Advisory Memoranda (NSTISSAM), which have been partially declassified. The associated standards may be cost-prohibitive for most organizations.

image. Van Eck phreaking works with both cathode ray tube (CRT) and liquid crystal display (LCD) monitors. Similar attacks have proven successful against the electromagnetic radiation generated by keyboards, printers, and other devices.

Attacks on Nonstandard Services

It's also important to protect services on Linux. These services go beyond the standard services associated with service-based accounts in the shadow password suite. A couple of services are of particular importance, as they can be used to configure administrative commands on a schedule. These services are the job schedulers, known as **cron** and **at**. These services can be protected with configuration files in the /etc/ directory.

It is not the purpose of this book to describe the workings of these two services. However, the following sections will cover those configuration files that regulate access to these services.

The cron Service

The cron service is a scheduler for jobs to be run on a regular basis. In general, cron jobs can be configured to run hourly, daily, weekly, or monthly. Administrative cron jobs are configured in the /etc/crontab configuration file. Users can run their own cron jobs if their accounts are allowed or not denied in the /etc/cron.allow and /etc/cron.deny files. The contents of these files are simple: They contain a list of users, one user per line.

If neither of these files exists, access to the cron service varies by distribution. If you're working on a Red Hat system, access is limited to users with administrative privileges. If you're working on an Ubuntu system, all users are able to access the cron service.

If only the /etc/cron.deny file exists, all users not listed in that file are allowed to create their own cron jobs. If both files exist, then only those users listed in /etc/cron.allow are permitted to set up their own cron jobs, and the contents of the /etc/cron.deny file are ignored. In other words, if /etc/cron.allow exists, it doesn't matter whether the /etc/cron.deny file exists.

To limit the damage associated with a compromised account, it can be helpful to add the usernames of at least service user accounts to /etc/cron.deny. If a black-hat hacker compromises one of those accounts, he at least won't be able to set up administrative jobs with those accounts. Of course, such accounts should never be included in the /etc/cron.allow file.

The at Service

The at service is a scheduler for jobs to be run on a one-time basis. Such jobs can be configured to run at any time in the future. Access to the at service depends on the status of the /etc/at.allow and /etc/at.deny files. Normally, the /etc/at.deny file exists when the at package is installed.

If an /etc/at.allow file exists, only users listed in it may submit jobs using the at service. If the /etc/at.allow file does not exist, the service will allow access to any user who is not listed in the /etc/at.deny file. If neither file exists, access is limited to the root administrative user.

To limit the damage associated with a compromised account, it can be helpful to add the usernames of at least service user accounts to /etc/at.deny. If a black-hat hacker compromises one of those accounts, that person at least won't be able to set up administrative jobs with those accounts. Of course, such accounts should never be included in the /etc/at.allow file.

While it would be safest to limit access to the root administrative account, that's not always practical. It's a terrific convenience for users to be able to run jobs on systems at night, during periods when the computer is not heavily used.

Wireless-Network Issues

Wireless networking is nearly ubiquitous in public areas. It's not difficult to find free wireless access points. Many of these access points are not secure. In fact, many do not even require passwords. The security issues associated with wireless hardware is the basis for the OSSTMM Wireless Security Expert (OWSE) certification.

The risks of wireless hardware extend to most off-the-shelf systems. Most systems include active wireless network cards by default. When analyzing the state of your wireless security, don't forget any Bluetooth devices that might be installed.

When configuring a wireless network, *Hacking Linux Exposed* recommends the use of the practical wireless deployment methodology (PWDM). For the latest version, see *http://pwdm.org/*. It's a complete view of the wireless network configuration process, from facilities through procurement through security.

While there are problems with wireless security, it's important to have at least an acceptable use policy for the variety of available wireless hardware. Whether a user is connecting to a network from a laptop, a mobile phone, a netbook, or some other networkable device, an acceptable use policy can help users understand the risks. *Hacking Linux Exposed* recommends that the acceptable use policy cover the following areas:

- Access policy
- Authentication policy
- Accountability policy
- Availability

- System and network maintenance policy
- Acquisition guidelines
- Violations reporting
- Audit policy

The OSSTMM Wireless Security Expert

Linux professionals who achieve the OSSTMM Wireless Security Expert (OWSE) certification are qualified in a number of ways. Their education starts with the basics of
radio-frequency spectrum analysis and continues with the fundamentals of the 802.11
protocols of the **Institute of Electrical and Electronics Engineers (IEEE)**. More important,
the OWSE qualifies an administrator as knowledgeable in wireless packet analysis as well
as in the techniques available to penetrate supposedly secure wireless networks.

Default Wireless Hardware

A lot of hardware, especially laptops and other mobile devices, is unsecured and active
out of the box. Tools are available that can "trick" these systems into connecting to the
networks of a black-hat hacker. If these systems are also connected to a local wired
network, that wireless connection can serve as an entrée between the black-hat hacker
and the wired network.

Linux and Wireless Hardware

Many open source security experts suggest that you use wireless access points (WAPs)
with customizable firmware. Two major Linux-based firmware solutions are **wireless
receiver-transmitter (WRT) software**, known as DD-WRT and OpenWrt. Both firmware
solutions are available on a number of commercial off-the-shelf wireless routers.

Finding native Linux support for wireless hardware can be a challenge. The availability
of a Linux wireless driver often depends on the chipset. Some manufacturers change
chipsets while retaining the same part number for their wireless devices.

While there are ways to use Microsoft drivers on Linux systems based on software
wrappers, such options don't enable the full capability of the devices and may even
subject such devices to black-hat hacker break-ins based on troubled Microsoft libraries.
When fully featured, Linux wireless cards can be configured in several different modes.
The details are not directly related to security.

Cracks in Wireless Security

Three basic security algorithms are available to secure WAP-based routers. While no
solution is perfect, you can at least configure **wireless intrusion detection systems (WIDSes)**
to see if a black-hat hacker is making progress against your networks. The three security
algorithms are as follows:

technical TIP

Most security administrators believe that WEP is completely insecure. With Linux tools, the cracking of WEP is so easy, it should never be used on a production network.

WIDSes such as WPA and WPA2 may be cracked if they use weak pre-shared keys based upon dictionary words. For this reason, you should always use a long, strong pre-shared key constructed in a manner similar to a password. More information on this process is available from *http://www.aircrack-ng.org/* and *http://www.airtightnetworks.com/home/resources/knowledge-center/wpa-wpa2-tkip-attack.html/*. Even with secure wireless protocols, networks are still susceptible to other attacks such as the spoofing of hardware addresses and honeypots.

- **Wired equivalent privacy (WEP)**—Uses stream ciphers and checksums for confidentiality and integrity. Works with open-system and shared-key authentication. While it works with keys of up to 256 bits, WEP packets can be intercepted and decrypted. Standard 40-bit WEP keys can be decrypted with tools available from normal Linux repositories in a matter of minutes.
- **Wi-Fi Protected Access (WPA)**—Uses the Temporal Key Integrity Protocol (TKIP), which uses a unique encryption key on every packet.
- **Wi-Fi Protected Access, version 2 (WPA2)**—Uses the Counter Mode with Cipher Block Chaining Message Authentication Code Protocol (CCMP), with the Advanced Encryption Standard (AES) algorithm.

In addition, you can add a little obscurity by hiding the name of the WAP, also known as the extended service set identifier (ESSID), as well as by changing the password frequently.

In addition, you can use a wireless intrusion detection system (WIDS). While the aforementioned `aircrack-ng` package can be used to "recover" lost WEP and WPA keys, it can also monitor wireless networks for intrusions. When combined with the `kismet` package, it can be used to detect a range of attacks from floods to packet injections.

Bluetooth Connections

When considering wireless connections, don't forget Bluetooth devices. Not all such devices support encryption. Bluetooth devices are configured in files in the `/etc/bluetooth/` directory. Individual devices may be configured in the `hcid.conf` file in that directory. If the Bluetooth device can support encryption, you can enable it in the `hcid.conf` file. Add the following directive to the stanza associated with your Bluetooth device:

```
encrypt enable;
```

Security-Enhanced Linux (SELinux)

SELinux was developed by the U.S. National Security Agency (NSA) as a mandatory access control system. It provides an additional layer of protection using Linux security modules included in the kernel. The NSA helped Red Hat integrate SELinux into Red Hat Enterprise Linux. Because the NSA released the source code for SELinux under open source licenses, the same software is available for other Linux distributions.

While there are a number of detailed SELinux configuration files, the basic configuration is stored in the `/etc/sysconfig/` directory, in the `selinux` file. It's actually linked to the `/etc/selinux/config` file. The two directives in this file are simple:

> **NOTE**
>
> Because SELinux is primarily used on Red Hat systems, the focus of this section is on Red Hat-based configuration files. Nevertheless, it's possible to configure SELinux on other AppArmor-focused distributions, including Ubuntu and SUSE Linux. Just remember: SELinux and AppArmor can't be used on the same system.

- **SELINUX**—May be set to `enforcing`, `permissive`, or `disabled`. The `enforcing` and `disabled` modes are self-explanatory. In contrast, `permissive` mode logs all policy violations in the `messages` and `audit/audit.log` files in the `/var/log/` directory.
- **SELINUXTYPE**—May be set to `targeted` or `strict`. The default targeted daemons include the following services: Dynamic Host Configuration Protocol (DHCP), Apache, the Berkeley Internet Name Domain (BIND) version of the Domain Name Service (DNS), the Name Service Cache Daemon (NCSD), the Network Time Protocol (NTP) service, the Portmap service, the Simple Network Management Protocol (SNMP) service, the Squid Web Proxy server, and the system logging service.

Detailed configuration options are listed in the `/selinux/` directory. If you've changed `SELINUX` to or from `disabled`, you may need to reboot the system to make sure all related files are properly labeled. Especially if `SELINUX` is being enabled, this process can add a number of minutes to the boot process.

SELinux access permissions are represented by bitmaps known as **access vectors**. The way they're stored is known as an **access vector cache (AVC)**.

FYI

SELinux is an intimidating subject for many users. The complexity associated with SELinux configuration is one reason why many administrators use AppArmor. One of the problems is that it's time consuming to configure SELinux to work with custom configurations. If you're having problems with SELinux and a specific service, you may want to temporarily disable SELinux protection for that service. This is not ideal, but at least SELinux protection will still be available for other targeted services, as defined by the SELINUXTYPE directive in the `/etc/sysconfig/selinux` configuration file.

On the other hand, Novell no longer directly employs AppArmor developers. Nevertheless, AppArmor development continues, courtesy of developers associated with the openSUSE project (*http://en.opensuse.org/AppArmor*).

The Power of SELinux

On one level, SELinux is conceptually like a good firewall. All actions are first denied. SELinux contexts are then created for users, applications, and services to work normally. These contexts are associated with just the configuration files and program libraries needed by authorized users to make desired applications and services work.

SELinux can be used to assign access and transition rights to every user, application, process, and file. Interactions between these entities are governed by SELinux policies. If any of these entities don't belong, then neither access nor transition rights are granted. For example, if the service user named apache somehow gets full root administrative access, that user still won't be allowed to modify a different service such as an FTP server.

Basic SELinux Configuration

The simplest way to find the current status of SELinux on the local system is with the **sestatus** command. It confirms the configuration shown in the /etc/sysconfig/selinux file. If you want to find the current SELinux status of files in the local directory, try the ls -Z command. As an example, look at the SELinux characteristics of the default FTP server configuration directory:

```
$ ls -Z /var/ftp/
drwxr-xr-x  root root system_u:object_r:public_content_t pub
```

The output shows the SELinux characteristics of the pub/ subdirectory in the /var/ftp/ directory. If you'd rather configure a different directory for the FTP server, SELinux contexts on that directory must be the same. In other words, that directory must be associated with the system user (system_u), system objects (object_r), on a directory type associated with public information (public_content_t).

One way to change another directory to conform is by running some **chcon** commands. Specifically, you would want to change the SELinux context associated with that user, system, and directory. For example, to change the user and type contexts on a /srv/ftp/ directory, you'd run the following command:

```
# chcon -u system_u -t public_content_t /srv/ftp/
```

A number of other commands can help you configure SELinux from the command-line interface. As you customize SELinux for your systems, there will be many cases where you modify SELinux policies to enable normal operation of regular services on the target system.

Configuration from the Command Line

On Red Hat systems, most of the important command-line SELinux tools are part of the policycoreutils, setools, and libselinux-utils packages. That package includes a couple of configuration files: sestatus.conf and selinux/restorecond.conf in the /etc/ directory. These files include lists of critical files and services to be watched for changes. You may want to add more files and services to these lists. The commands from the three aforementioned packages are described briefly in Table 7-2.

TABLE 7-2 Basic SELinux control commands.

COMMAND	DESCRIPTION
audit2allow	Reviews cited logs and returns options that would allow actions that violate current SELinux policies. To see how it works, run the `audit2allow < /var/log/audit/audit.log` command.
audit2why	Translates SELinux audit messages into more understandable reasons for an SELinux violation. To see how it works, run the `audit2why < /var/log/audit/audit.log` command.
avcstat	Displays AVC statistics related to SELinux activity.
chcat	Specifies categories for SELinux security. Configured in `/etc/selinux/targeted/setrans.conf`; to see current categories, run the `chcat -L` command.
fixfiles	Relabels specified files; do not apply to a whole system except by rebooting to avoid instability; for example, the `fixfiles -R packagename restore` command restores the original contexts of files from the noted *packagename*.
genhomedircon	Generates contexts from home directories of valid regular users. For example, the `genhomedircon` command by itself uses the `file_contexts` configuration to create a `file_contexts.homedir` configuration in the `/etc/selinux/targeted/contexts/files/` directory.
getenforce	Returns the current mode of SELinux: `enforcing`, `permissive`, or `disabled`.
getsebool	Finds the value of the noted SELinux boolean. For the complete list, run the `getsebool -a` command; values are stored in the `/selinux/booleans/` directory.
load_policy	Loads the currently configured policy into the kernel; activates configured changes.
matchpathcon	Identifies the default SELinux security context for a specified directory.
open_init_pty	Opens and runs a program in a pseudo-terminal.
restorecon	Restores the original SELinux file security contexts. When used with `-r`, the command, works recursively.
restorecond	Specifies the daemon associated with the original SELinux contexts on a file. When run by itself, it focuses on files listed in the `/etc/selinux/restorecond.conf` file.
run_init	Runs an `init` script in SELinux contexts, based on the `/etc/selinux/targeted/contexts/initrc_context` file.

TABLE 7-2 *continued*	
COMMAND	**DESCRIPTION**
secon	Reviews the SELinux contexts of a file, program, or user input.
sechecker	Checks SELinux policies of profiles and modules. For a current list, run the sechecker -l command.
sediff	Analyzes the difference between two SELinux text policy files.
seinfo	Returns statistics from SELinux policy files. For examples, look for the policy.kern and policy.21 files in an /selinux/ subdirectory.
sesearch	Queries policies by type, including audit, type, role, and more.
semanage	Manages SELinux policies for logins, users, ports, interfaces, contexts, and translations.
semodule	Loads and manages SELinux policy modules; lists of binary modules are stored in the /etc/selinux/targeted/modules/previous/modules/ directory.
semodule_deps	Shows dependencies between the base module package. /usr/share/selinux/targeted/base.pp and an individual policy package in the /etc/selinux/targeted/modules/active/modules/ directory.
semodule_expand	Expands a base module package to a binary policy file; used internally by the SELinux manage library.
semodule_link	Links modules together; primarily used by developers.
semodule_package	Creates an SELinux policy package file.
sestatus	Returns the current top-level SELinux run status.
setenforce	Modifies the current mode of SELinux to enforcing or permissive.
setsebool	Sets a boolean value for an SELinux option.
togglesebool	Changes the value of an SELinux boolean, as listed in the /selinux/booleans/ directory.

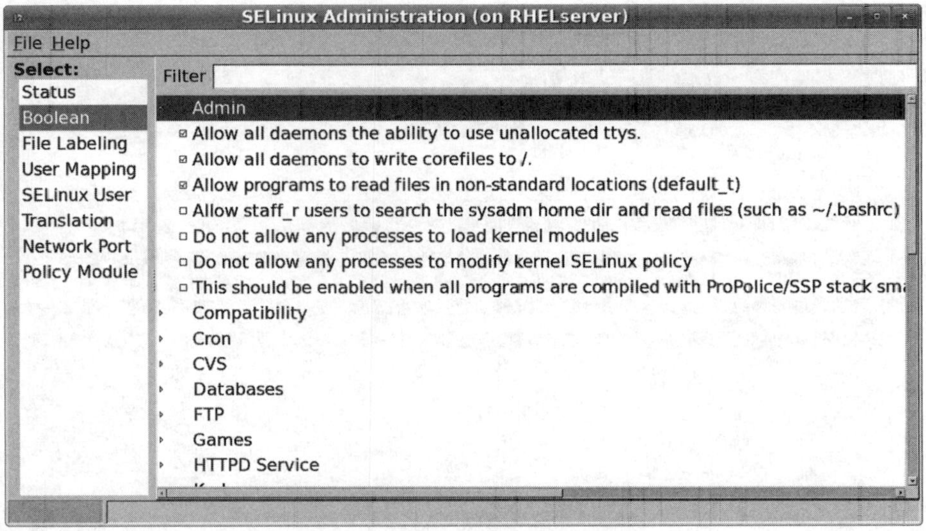

FIGURE 7-6

The SELinux
Administration tool.

The SELinux Administration Tool

If you're relatively new to SELinux, the GUI-based SELinux Administration tool
can be helpful. Take a look at Figure 7-6. It illustrates the boolean nature of SELinux
settings, along with options for administrative users. It's also an excellent way
to illustrate the configuration options available. To start this tool in a GUI, run
the `system-config-selinux` command.

You'll come back to this tool shortly as an organized way to review what can
be configured with SELinux.

The SELinux Troubleshooter

In a graphical desktop environment, SELinux, when active, provides information when
something violates configured SELinux rules. You could review the associated log files
(`/var/log/messages` and `/var/log/audit/audit.log`), but many of these files
include messages that are cryptic to the casual Linux administrator. To start the SELinux
Troubleshooter, you'll need to run the following command from a GUI console:

```
# sealert -b
```

If you're just learning SELinux, the SELinux Troubleshooter is one of the few excellent
reasons to use the GUI. While it's a front-end to the `audit2allow` and `audit2why`
commands, it can help you isolate individual SELinux problems, along with their
solutions. As shown in Figure 7-7, it even suggests the actions to take if you do not
believe the error is a security breach.

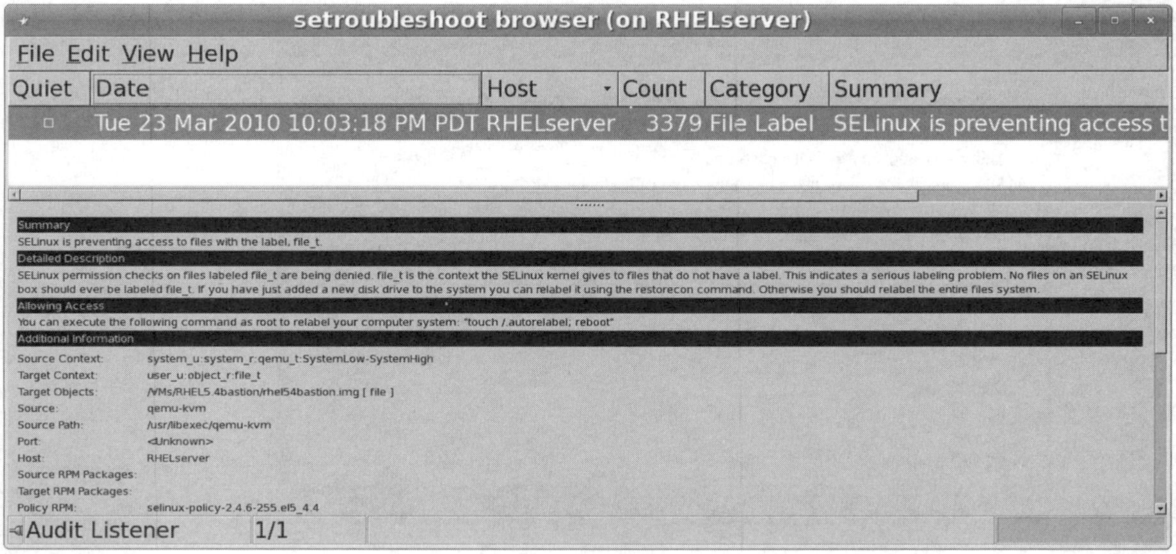

FIGURE 7-7

The SELinux Troubleshooter.

SELinux Boolean Settings

Detailed configuration of SELinux is made possible by the boolean files in the /selinux/booleans/ directory. As suggested by the name, the directory is full of files with just one binary number. In other words, the setting associated with the file name is either on or off (1 or 0). The /selinux/booleans/ directory, unfortunately, is not a complete list for what's available, as default booleans aren't included in that directory. The following sections are based on the boolean options in the SELinux Administration tool shown back in Figure 7-6.

Be aware, the following sections do not list every individual boolean. They also do not explain the details behind a boolean, as those details would require another book. Because some of the detailed booleans also address features not covered in this book, they may require additional research on your part. Many of those details are not included in the glossary, as they are not by themselves central to the security features of Linux. Fortunately, most of the descriptions of individual booleans in the SELinux Administration tool are excellent.

Where the categories are associated with specific daemons, there is usually a boolean option to disable SELinux protection of that daemon. If you're having trouble getting a service to work with SELinux, you may consider activating that option temporarily until you can create the features and policies to get SELinux working with that daemon.

For more information, see the latest Red Hat Enterprise Linux Deployment Guide, available online from *http://www.redhat.com/docs/manuals/enterprise/*. The titles in the following sections correspond to the boolean subcategories in the SELinux Administration tool. These titles are subject to change and expansion as SELinux development continues.

Admin

SELinux administrative booleans can allow system users to use unallocated terminals, write to the top-level root directory, read files from directories not specially configured, support administrative user access to the home directories of other administrative users, prevent the loading of kernel modules, prevent processes from modifying SELinux policy, and enable buffer-overflow protection from the ProPolice protector.

Compatibility

SELinux compatibility booleans are related to administrative privileges with respect to tracing or debugging problems. You may consider keeping this ability disabled on bastion hosts, as this ability would also help a black-hat hacker develop a more dangerous Trojan on your systems.

Cron

SELinux `cron` daemon booleans can help regulate what `cron` jobs can do, with respect to relabeling SELinux file contexts. It also affects the extra rules associated with the `fcron` service, which is sort of like the regular `cron` daemon with extra features.

CVS

If you use the concurrent versions system (CVS) for development, you may consider allowing it to read shadow passwords. On the other hand, such a capability could lead to a security breach if a black-hat hacker gains access to the CVS daemon.

Databases

This section supports SELinux features associated with the MySQL and PostgreSQL database daemons.

FTP

SELinux FTP daemon booleans can help regulate features of installed FTP services. As this is based on a Red Hat configuration, it has been tested with the very secure File Transfer Protocol (vsFTP) service. Different settings in this section support uploads to directories configured with the `public_content_rw_t` security context, along with access to the Common Internet File System (CIFS) and Network File System (NFS) servers for file transfers.

Games

This section supports SELinux features associated with game services.

HTTPD Service

There are nearly 20 SELinux booleans available to help regulate access to the hypertext transfer protocol daemon (HTTPD). These booleans assume that you're working with the Apache Web server. These booleans are associated with several features from pluggable authentication modules (PAMs) to scripts to interactivity with CIFS, NFS, and FTP services.

Kerberos

The SELinux Kerberos booleans are simple. One allows access to Kerberos authentication from other services. It's something to consider if you want to enable the more secure features of NFS version 4. Other Kerberos booleans are associated with the Kerberos administrative and key control daemons.

Memory Protection

The memory protection booleans are related to executable files. This is one area where maximum protection is appropriate, as unconfined executable files can easily lead to attacks that overload a system.

Mount

The booleans in this section relate to the automounter service. For most secure systems, the automounter is not required. As suggested in Chapter 6, automounter features can be configured on other services.

Name Service

The name service is a reference to DNS and the related NCSD daemon for cached network searches. SELinux protection for the master zone file could help prevent attacks on master DNS servers.

NFS

NFS is a reference to the network file service. SELinux boolean features can enable or prevent Kerberos-based authentication through the general security services daemon (GSSD).

NIS

NIS is a reference to the insecure Network Information Service (NIS). Default SELinux booleans disable access to NIS.

Polyinstatiation

Polyinstatiation supports different views for different users.

pppd

Short for the point-to-point-protocol daemon, pppd supports communication primarily over telephone modems.

Printing

Printer-related SELinux booleans are focused on CUPS. Options allow you to disable SELinux protection for various CUPS-related daemons. Alternatively, it allows you to substitute the Line Print Daemon (LPD) for CUPS.

rsync

The `rsync` service is frequently used for backups, as it can synchronize the data on two systems. The power of `rsync` comes from how it only transfers changed data over a network connection. Data transferred over `rsync` can be encrypted with the help of the SSH service.

Samba

Samba is the Linux implementation of Microsoft file and printer sharing. SELinux booleans in this area allow you to enable major Samba features. These features include the ability to act as a domain controller, to read and write to shared directories, to use NFS directories, to share user home directories, and more.

SASL Authentication Server

The Simple Authentication and Security Layer (SASL) server is another method to support network authentication through the files of the shadow password suite. SELinux disables such access by default.

SELinux Service Protection

The SELinux service protection category allows you to disable SELinux protection for a wide variety of applications and services, from the Amanda backup service to Xen for virtual machines.

SpamAssassin

If you want SpamAssassin software to have access to the latest databases of unwanted e-mail, you'll want to allow the associated daemon to have network access.

Squid

Squid is the standard Linux Web proxy server. As with SpamAssassin, you'll want to allow the associated daemon to have network access.

SSH

SELinux policies related to SSH can enable administrative and host-based access. While administrative access via SSH is often the only practical secure way to administer remote systems, host-based access is inherently insecure.

Universal SSL Tunnel

The Secure Sockets Layer (SSL) is one way to create a secure tunnel for communication over a public network such as the Internet. While it's frequently run as part of the extended internet super server, a SELinux boolean allows it to be run more securely as a separate daemon.

User Privs

Short for user privileges, the SELinux booleans in this section can support access by regular users to commands needed by some power users. These booleans support access from the `cdrecord` command to shared network directories, access to the `ping` command, and more.

Web Applications

The SELinux booleans in this section relate to privileges for standard user network applications, including the Evolution Personal Information Manager, the Thunderbird e-mail reader, and the Mozilla Firefox Web browser.

X Server

The SELinux booleans in this category support multiple users on the same X Server. That's possible as users can log into the same X Server remotely using the X Display Manager control protocol (XDMCP).

Zebra

Finally, SELinux supports the ability of the `zebra` daemon to write to routing tables.

Setting Up AppArmor Profiles

AppArmor is the major open source alternative to SELinux. Both provide mandatory access control for files, directories, and users. Some administrators believe that AppArmor policies are easier to create and configure. However, the protection afforded by AppArmor depends on the policies you create for the services and critical files on the local system.

If you've installed AppArmor and SELinux packages on the same system, be aware that these mandatory access control systems are not compatible. Because AppArmor drivers are integrated into current Linux kernels, you can disable AppArmor with the following entry on the kernel command line in the bootloader:

```
apparmor=0
```

Basic AppArmor Configuration

AppArmor has four basic modes: `enforce`, `complain`, `audit`, and `unconfined`. These modes are roughly parallel to the SELinux `enforcing`, `permissive`, and `disabled` modes. In other words, if you're just learning AppArmor, you could set up `complain` or `audit` mode and learn how AppArmor works from the log messages. In fact, AppArmor normally uses the same log files as SELinux: `messages` and `audit/audit.log` in the `/var/log/` directory.

Because AppArmor is the primary mandatory access control option on the Ubuntu distribution, the configuration described in this chapter reflects what is seen on that distribution. Nevertheless, the primary developers for AppArmor are sponsored by Novell, the company behind SUSE Linux. Because Ubuntu does not currently have a GUI tool to administer AppArmor, you'll take a brief look at SUSE's AppArmor administrative tool, which is part of its yet another setup tool (YaST) package.

For now, run the **`apparmor_status`** command from an administrative account. If the AppArmor module is loaded, you'll see that confirmed in the output. You'll also see a list of loaded AppArmor profiles. This list will include the full path to executable files and processes with AppArmor profiles. These profiles are further subdivided by those set to `enforce` and `complain` modes.

AppArmor Configuration Files

The standard configuration files for AppArmor are stored in the `/etc/apparmor/` directory. If you don't see several configuration files in this directory, you'll need to install the `apparmor`, `apparmor-utils`, and `apparmor-notify` packages. AppArmor profiles for specific commands and services are stored in the `/etc/apparmor.d/` directory. Those profiles will be described shortly.

Despite the name, the primary AppArmor configuration file is `logprof.conf`, in the `/etc/apparmor/` directory.

logprof.conf

The `logprof.conf` file includes a number of basic AppArmor settings. Not all of them are active; for example, the file on the Ubuntu 10.04 release refers to a release that's a more than a year older (Intrepid Ibex). But with that in mind, a couple of the stanzas in this file include valuable information.

The [settings] Stanza.   Directives in the [settings] stanza include the directories with AppArmor configuration files. If you're looking for additional preconfigured AppArmor profiles, it points to the `/usr/share/doc/apparmor-profiles/extras/` directory. It configures logs in standard locations: `/var/log/messages`, `/var/log/syslog`, and files in the `/var/log/audit/` directory.

The [qualifiers] Stanza.   Directives in the [qualifiers] stanza include shells, which should not have AppArmor profiles. This stanza includes basic commands such as `mount` that don't work if confined with AppArmor rules. It lists basic shell commands that should not be profiled, such as `awk`, `ls`, and `chmod`.

notify.conf

The standard directive in this file limits access to the `aa-notify` command to members of the `admin` group. While the configuration file specifies `apparmor-notify`, the actual command is `aa-notify`, which is linked to the `apparmor_notify` command.

severity.db

The `severity.db` file includes a substantial number of key files, with severity levels between 0 and 10. For example, look at this excerpt for severity levels related to files in the `/etc/init.d/` directory:

```
/etc/init.d/*      1 10 0
```

The numbers relate to read, write, and execute access. As the scripts in this directory are well known, it's not a big deal if they're read or executed. However, if someone overwrites one of these scripts, you as a security administrator need to know about it.

subdomain.conf

The code in the `subdomain.conf` file is information only for now. However, it provides insight into possible future directions for AppArmor.

AppArmor Profiles

Most AppArmor profiles can be found in the /etc/apparmor.d/ directory. The default profiles in this directory cover a number of standard services and servers, including the Apache Web server, the ping command, the Samba file server, and more.

Take a look at the sbin.dhclient3 file. It's the AppArmor profile for the /sbin/dhclient3 command. Most AppArmor profiles have include directives to incorporate the contents of other files. For example, the following directive, if it were active (the # is a comment character), would include the contents of the abstractions/base configuration profile:

```
#include <abstractions/base>
```

The capability options that follow relate to the functionality of the command. Take a look at the following four capability options:

```
capability net_bind_service,
capability net_raw,
capability sys_module,
capability dac_override,
```

These options associate the sbin.dhclient3 profile with the noted capabilities: to acquire DNS information from a Berkeley Internet Name Domain (BIND) server; to access raw network packets; to work with system modules; and to override discretionary access controls.

The following options relate to network information, to be expected in packets in raw form. Most of the files that follow are associated with different access modes.

AppArmor Access Modes

Access modes are features associated not only with the executable file, but with related configuration, logging, lock files, and whatever else may be related to the command profile itself. The access modes that you'll see in a configuration profile are described in Table 7-3. Be aware: You can configure only one mode from ux, Ux, px, Px, and ix on a single executable file.

Sample AppArmor Profiles

AppArmor is a work in progress. You may be interested in profiles beyond the standards shown in the /etc/apparmor.d/ directory. An extensive list is available in the /usr/share/doc/apparmor-profiles/extras/ directory. If you want to install one of the services associated with these profiles, you may choose to copy one of these "extra" profiles into the /etc/apparmor.d/ directory. Once copied, you can activate the profile with the /etc/init.d/apparmor reload command.

TABLE 7-3	AppArmor access modes.
MODE	**DESCRIPTION**
r	Read
w	Write (cannot use with append)
a	Append (cannot use with write)
ux	Execute, in unconfined mode
Ux	Execute, in unconfined mode, supports unconfined child processes
px	Profile execute mode, works only if related files/commands also have AppArmor profiles
Px	Profile execute mode, works only if related files/commands also have AppArmor profiles, supports unconfined child processes
ix	Inherit execute mode; inherits the current profile
m	Maps to an executable file
l	Allows links to other files
k	Supports file locks

AppArmor Configuration and Management Commands

There are several AppArmor commands. The `apparmor_status` command, as described earlier, lists configured profiles of commands and services, along with their `enforce` or `complain` modes. Additional AppArmor commands start with `aa-` and reside mostly in the `/usr/sbin/` directory. The purpose of each command is described in Table 7-4.

An AppArmor Configuration Tool

If you feel the need for a graphical tool to configure AppArmor, it's available on SUSE Linux. While it's not one of the distributions covered in this book, SUSE Linux is an excellent distribution with enterprise-quality support, courtesy of Novell. Figure 7-8 illustrates a step in SUSE's AppArmor configuration wizard, available through its YaST package. Those of you familiar with SUSE will recognize the console version of the tool, which is a low-level graphics version of that can be used remotely without a GUI.

TABLE 7-4 AppArmor commands.

COMMAND	DESCRIPTION
aa-audit	Requires an existing security profile for a command or service. If that profile exists, the aa-audit command changes the profile to audit mode.
aa-autodep	Creates a sample security profile for a command or service.
aa-complain	Requires an existing security profile for a command or service. If that profile exists, the aa-complain command changes the profile to complain mode.
aa-enforce	Requires an existing security profile for a command or service. If that profile exists, the aa-enforce command changes the profile to enforce mode.
aa-genprof	Reviews the /etc/apparmor.d/ directory for an existing profile for a command or service. If the profile does not exist, it's created using the aa-autodep command.
aa-logprof	Reviews existing logs for suggested profile updates.
aa-notify	Lists denial log messages.
aa-status	Reviews current profiles and processes.
aa-unconfined	Lists networked processes not controlled by AppArmor.

FIGURE 7-8

An AppArmor configuration tool.

```
YaST2 - GenProf @ susevm

 Ini
     This wizard will help you create a new AppArmor security
     profile for an application, or you can use it to enhance
     an existing profile by allowing AppArmor to learn new
     application behavior.

     Please enter the application name for which you would like
     to create a profile, or select Browse to find the
     application on your system.

     Application to Profile
     _____

                              [Browse]
                 [Create]              [Abort]
 [Hel                                              t]
```

Best Practices: Networks, Firewalls, and TCP/IP Communications

When securing a system, you need to know about various TCP/IP ports and how services communicate over these ports, as defined in `/etc/services`.

Obscurity may be one option to help secure a network. If you configure an obscure nonstandard port for a service, you need to make sure that both clients and servers work with that port. Furthermore, you need to make sure any firewalls allow communication through the nonstandard port. Obscurity works in other ways. In login messages, you can throw off a black-hat hacker with the right kind of message. In error messages, you can configure some services to provide as little information as possible.

While the TCP Wrappers system was originally designed to protect services associated with the internet super servers, it can also protect services statically and dynamically linked to the `libwrap.so.0` libraries. Access to such services can be regulated with options in the `/etc/hosts.allow` and `/etc/hosts.deny` files. Access can be regulated by host, by IP address, and even by username.

The Linux packet filtering firewall command is `iptables`. Different `iptables` rules can be created to protect a DMZ, to forward communications to bastion hosts, and to protect an internal network. The `iptables` command can also be used to masquerade IP addresses, supporting communications between different IP address networks. While the default rules associated with a bastion host are simple, you should do more to block communication from suspicious IP addresses, slow or prevent potential attacks, and more.

When considering network security, don't forget the alternate attack vectors. Many networks still support connections through telephone modems and serial ports. Black-hat hackers can even find what's on your screen by tracking electromagnetic emissions. While these services aren't directly related to networks, don't forget to protect administrative services such as `cron` and `at`.

Wireless communications are another problem. Even if corporate policies prohibit wireless communication, a lot of new hardware comes with vulnerable active wireless network devices. In any case, a prohibition on wireless communications is not realistic in the current world. So you should have some sort of organizational policy. The OSSTMM addresses this with the OWSE certification. A WIDS can test the integrity of wireless security algorithms, including WEP, WPA, and WPA2. When addressing wireless security, don't forget the Bluetooth connection.

Security beyond the network includes mandatory access control systems such as SELinux and AppArmor. SELinux was developed by the NSA and integrated into Red Hat Enterprise Linux to help secure that distribution. Because it is open source, SELinux can be installed on other distributions. SELinux enables access control of a wide variety of services. It's primarily configured in boolean settings in the `/selinux/booleans/` directory. If you're just learning SELinux, examine the SELinux Administration tool to see what can be done with this system. In addition, the SELinux Troubleshooter may suggest solutions when you run into errors.

For mandatory access control systems, AppArmor is the major open source alternative to SELinux. Standard AppArmor profiles are stored in the `/etc/apparmor.d/` directory. AppArmor profiles include a variety of access modes for the service or command in question. Such profiles also regulate how related commands and services are used.

CHAPTER SUMMARY

Network security starts with an understanding of available TCP/IP ports. Obscurity in TCP/IP communication may discourage some black-hat hackers. Access to services controlled by the internet super servers along with those services related to TCP Wrappers libraries may be regulated by the `/etc/hosts.allow` and `/etc/hosts.deny` files. Access through various TCP/IP ports can be regulated by `iptables` as a packet filtering firewall.

When planning network security, it is important to consider all means of communications with a network, including telephone modems, wireless devices, Bluetooth adapters, and more. When working with security in general, consider implementing a mandatory access control system. The two major Linux options in this area are SELinux and AppArmor. Both systems can help confine compromised parts of a system; the mandatory access control can help prevent one compromised system from affecting another system.

KEY CONCEPTS AND TERMS

`apparmor_status`

`at`

`chcon`

`cron`

`secon`

`sestatus`

Access vector

Access vector cache (AVC)

Application Armor (AppArmor)

Challenge-Handshake
   Authentication Protocol
   (CHAP)

Denial of service (DoS) attack

Institute of Electrical and
   Electronics Engineers (IEEE)

Integrated Services Digital
   Network (ISDN)

Internet Assigned Numbers
   Authority (IANA)

Multicast Domain Name Service
   (mDNS) protocol

Password Authentication
   Protocol (PAP)

Public switched data network
   (PSDN)

Public switched telephone
   network (PSTN)

Remote Authentication Dial
   In User Service (RADIUS)

Security Enhanced Linux
   (SELinux)

TCP Wrappers

Telephone modem

Van Eck phreaking

Wireless intrusion detection
   system (WIDS)

Wireless receiver-transmitter
   (WRT) software

CHAPTER 7 ASSESSMENT

1. Well-known TCP/IP ports range from _____ to _____.

2. The nmap command checks for open ports on a remote system.

   A. True
   B. False

3. Which of the following configuration files is considered first with respect to TCP Wrapper security?

   A. /etc/inetd.conf
   B. /etc/xinetd.conf
   C. /etc/hosts.allow
   D. /etc/hosts.deny

4. Which of the following library files is associated with TCP Wrappers?

   A. /etc/libwrap.so.0
   B. /lib/libwrap.so.0
   C. /usr/lib/libwrap.so.0
   D. /var/lib/libwrap.so.0

5. Which of the following iptables command switches adds a rule to the middle of a chain?

   A. -A
   B. -I
   C. -L
   D. -C

6. Which of the following actions is not used with the -j switch for the iptables command?

   A. DROP
   B. REJECT
   C. LOG
   D. FORWARD

7. The iptables command switch associated with a destination port is _____.

8. The PSDN network is associated with regular telephone modems.

   A. True
   B. False

9. Which of these files must exist for regular users to access the at daemon?

   A. /etc/at
   B. /etc/at.deny
   C. /etc/at.conf
   D. /etc/at/at.deny

10. Which of the following IEEE protocols is most closely associated with wireless networking?

    A. 802.3
    B. 802.5
    C. 802.11
    D. 802.15

11. Which of the following commands lists the SELinux characteristics of a file?

    A. ls *filename*
    B. ls -SE *filename*
    C. ls -l *filename*
    D. ls -Z *filename*

12. Which of the following commands can be used to customize the SELinux characteristics of a file?

    A. fixfiles
    B. chcon
    C. restorecon
    D. secon

13. To start the SELinux Troubleshooter in a GUI, run the following command: _____.

14. Which of the following directories include active AppArmor profiles?

    A. /etc/apparmor/
    B. /etc/apparmor.d/
    C. /usr/share/doc/apparmor-profiles/
       ↪extras/
    D. /usr/share/doc/apparmor-profiles/

Networked Filesystems and Remote Access

THIS CHAPTER IS FOCUSED ON FILE-SHARING SYSTEMS. Because file-sharing servers are typically administered remotely, you also need to understand the ins and outs of remote access systems.

The Network File System (NFS) service can be mounted as if it were a local system. The latest version of NFS can be secured with more than just host-level restrictions. Careful configuration can help keep the very secure File Transfer Protocol (vsFTP) server living up to its name. Samba can be used to securely manage domain-based networks. Even though Microsoft no longer supports some of the networks it has developed, Samba does.

In general, you should configure as few services as possible on any single system. In the context of this chapter, that means you might configure NFS and the Secure Shell (SSH) on system A, the vsFTP and SSH on system B, Samba and SSH on system C, and so on. SSH on these systems facilitates remote administration.

Because SSH is a common element, you need to know how to configure that service securely. But there will be users who prefer Telnet. For those users, there are options. Furthermore, there are options for those users who still work with other clear-text protocols. With respect to remote access, don't forget the lowly telephone modem. Even today, one-third of U.S. home users do not have high-speed connections.

Chapter 8 Topics

This chapter covers the following topics and concepts:

- What basic principles for systems with shared networking services are
- How to secure NFS as if it were local
- How to keep vsFTP very secure
- How Linux can be configured as a more secure Windows server
- How SSH can be kept secure
- What basic principles of encryption on networks are
- How to help users who "must" use Telnet
- How to secure modem connections
- How to move away from clear-text access
- What best practices are for networked filesystems and remote access

Chapter 8 Goals

When you complete this chapter, you will be able to:

- Secure shared networked filesystems
- Maximize the security associated with SSH
- Encrypt communications
- Provide secure alternatives to clear-text systems

One System, One Shared Network Service

In previous chapters, you read about some of the reasons to set up bastion hosts. In essence, running fewer services on a system requires a reduced amount of resources. Fewer running services also means there are not as many ways for black-hat hackers to break in. Finally, fewer running services means a reduced number of temptations for black-hat hackers.

The most secure systems start from a baseline bastion host with an absolute minimum of services. If you administer services remotely, it might be wise to install and configure SSH on that baseline system. Only when you're ready to set up a system with a shared network service should that service be installed.

There are exceptions to the concept of one system, one shared network service. For example, to take advantage of **Kerberos** for network authentication, you need to install that authentication service as well as the Network Time Protocol (NTP) service to keep those systems in sync. Unless NTP is running on a server, it's not possible to get Kerberos running on that server.

FYI

Kerberos was developed at the Massachusetts Institute of Technology (MIT) as part of Project Athena, a distributed computing environment still in use at MIT. Other important software components that are now part of Linux began as part of Project Athena, including the X Window System and the Lightweight Directory Access Protocol (LDAP). Kerberos is named after the Greek mythological guard dog, sometimes known as Cerberus.

Once NTP and Kerberos are set up, the next step is to set up services that work with the **generic security services application program interface (GSSAPI)**. The details depend on the service. For example, NFS requires special Kerberos configuration options; Telnet requires additional packages. Details are discussed later in this chapter.

Configure an NTP Server

This section summarizes those steps required to get an NTP server up and running on a system. For more information on securing the NTP service, see Chapter 9. The installation process should be easy for experienced Linux users like yourself. For both Red Hat and Ubuntu systems, the relevant package name is `ntp`.

Once installed, NTP services are easy to configure. The default versions of NTP installed for both Red Hat and Ubuntu systems include a `server` directive with the URL of an associated NTP server. Examples include the following:

```
server 0.rhel.pool.ntp.org
server ntp.ubuntu.com
```

If the objective is to keep systems on a local area network (LAN) in sync with each other, it may be best to configure an NTP server on a local network. If the objective is to keep systems on remote networks in sync, it may make more sense to configure connections to the same remote NTP servers, or perhaps two NTP servers equally distant from the target networks.

Some "Stratum Two" servers listed on *http://psp2.ntp.org/bin/view/Servers/WebHome* may be available for public use. The rules are created by the owners of each of these servers. Administrators of public NTP servers frequently limit access to their systems, as overloaded NTP servers are less accurate.

NTP servers should be excluded from proxy services such as Squid, as they can also introduce variable time delays. For more information on Squid, see Chapter 9.

Install and Configure a Kerberos Server

In this section, you'll review basic information required to install a Kerberos server. As the actual steps, configuration files, and package names vary by distribution, this section provides only general information. Beware: Often, there are multiple ways to perform the same actions with various Kerberos commands.

Kerberos goes beyond basic authentication, using a concept known as a key distribution center (KDC) to verify the credentials of a user before allowing access to various network services. When verified, the KDC issues a ticket-granting ticket (TGT), a sort of time-limited super-ticket that supports access to other systems without additional authentication.

The Kerberos server that grants TGTs is known as a ticket-granting server (TGS), which works hand in hand with the KDC. The configuration that follows sets up both functions on a single system.

Basic Kerberos Configuration

If you use Kerberos for network authentication, it requires the installation of Kerberos software on both the client and the server. Otherwise, services such as Telnet that normally send usernames and passwords in clear text will not be protected. This section assumes that separate systems have been set up as Kerberos servers and clients. With that in mind, once proper packages are installed on the server, you'll need to first modify the /etc/krb5.conf file.

When reviewing this file, note the subtle differences between the **Kerberos realm** and the associated Uniform Resource Identifiers (URIs). For example, if the Kerberos realm on the local network is EXAMPLE.ORG, the domain is example.org.

> **NOTE**
>
> The actual domains and Kerberos realms will vary. The Internet Assigned Numbers Authority (IANA) has assigned the example.com, example.net, and example.org domains for documentation purposes such as this book. However, these names are not to be assigned or used on the Internet. This system extends to the Kerberos realms EXAMPLE.COM, EXAMPLE.NET, and EXAMPLE.ORG.

Any changes made to /etc/krb5.conf should be matched with changes either to the Domain Name System (DNS) database or the /etc/hosts files for each applicable system. Critical directives in /etc/krb5.conf include the following. For the purpose of this section, the local network is configured on the example.org domain. Note the port numbers associated with the Kerberos key distribution center (kdc) and the administrative server (admin_server), as associated with the noted directives.

```
[libdefaults]
    default_realm = EXAMPLE.ORG
[realms]
    EXAMPLE.ORG = {
        kdc = RHELserver.example.org:88
        admin_server = RHELserver.example.org:749
        default_domain = example.org }
[domain_realm]
    .example.org = EXAMPLE.ORG
    example.org = EXAMPLE.ORG
```

Once these changes are made, run the following command to create the Kerberos database. The directory with the command varies; if it is not in your PATH, look in directories such as `/usr/sbin/` and `/usr/kerberos/sbin/`.

```
# kdb5_util create
```

You'll be prompted with information that should match the default realm, along with the master password for the Kerberos database. If you forget that database password, you'll have to delete the files in the `/var/lib/krb5kdc/` or `/var/kerberos/krb5kdc/` directories (depending on distribution) before re-creating the database by rerunning this command.

Once the basic database is available in the appropriate directory, it's time to set up keytab files, which are pairs of Kerberos principals and clients. Once created, Kerberos authentication between the two systems works without a password. To start the process, run the `ktutil` command, which starts a `ktutil:` prompt. Most commands that you can run at that prompt are shown in the `ktutil man` page.

At that prompt, you can enter user-account information along with encryption keys. For example, the following `addent` commands at the `ktutil` prompt adds `michael@EXAMPLE.ORG` as a **Kerberos principal** with the `-p` switch, a unique identity to which a Kerberos server can assign tickets. The `-k 1` specifies key version number 1. The `-e rc4-hmac` specifies an encryption scheme, created by Ron Rivest. The `rc4` stands for Ron's code, version 4. (The "Ron" is a reference to Ron Rivest, one of the developers behind the RSA algorithm for public key cryptography.) It's associated with the hash-based message authentication code (`hmac`).

```
ktutil:  addent -password -p admin@EXAMPLE.ORG -k 1 -e rc4-hmac
ktutil:  addent -password -p michael@EXAMPLE.ORG -k 1 -e rc4-hmac
```

In a similar fashion, you can set up different forms of encryption. The following commands set up key version 1 for the Advanced Encryption Standard with 256 bits (`aes256`), with message processing using ciphertext stealing.

```
ktutil:  addent -password -p admin@EXAMPLE.ORG
➥ -k 1 -e aes256-cts
ktutil:  addent -password -p michael@EXAMPLE.ORG
➥ -k 1 -e aes256-cts
```

The keys can then be written to a local keytab file. The following commands write it to the `michael.keytab` file in the local directory.

```
ktutil:  wkt michael keytab
```

Once `keytab` files have been created for all desired users, the next step is to merge `keytab` files into the `/etc/krb5.keytab` file. First, the following commands read in `keytab` files for users `michael` and `donna` into local memory:

```
ktutil: read_kt michael.keytab
ktutil: read_kt donna.keytab
```

Then the following command writes those keytab files to the krb5.keytab file in the local directory.

```
ktutil: write_kt krb5.keytab
```

To implement it for use with Kerberos, you need to copy it to the /etc/ directory. Now that users have been set up, the next step is to set up keys to connect the local Kerberos server system with desired clients. You can create such keys with the kadmin.local command, which opens a kadmin.local: prompt. The following command sets a random key, of a host with the noted fully qualified domain name (FQDN).

```
kadmin.local:  addprinc -randkey host/ubuntuserver.example.org
```

Do not be concerned about any warning message. Just beware: Policies can be created as defined in the man page for the kadmin command. If the command is successful, you'll see the following message:

```
Principal "host/ubuntuserver.example.org@EXAMPLE.ORG" created.
```

Now you're just about ready to set up the system with the Kerberos key server to authenticate users for other systems described throughout the rest of this chapter. All you need to do is start or reload the applicable service scripts in the /etc/init.d/ directory with names like krb5kdc, kadmin, and krb5-admin-server. The actual script names will vary by distribution.

Additional Kerberos Configuration Options

The previous section covered just the basic configuration options required to get Kerberos working. But to make it work for desired services, more is required in key configuration files, namely /etc/krb5.conf. As discussed previously, the [libdefaults] stanza includes the default_realm, which is set to the capitalized version of the local domain name—in that case, EXAMPLE.ORG. Additional options of interest in that stanza include the following:

```
kdc_timesync = 1
forwardable = true
proxiable = true
```

The kdc_timesync option keeps the Kerberos server running if there's a temporary problem with the connection to the NTP server. The next two options can help cache and forward Kerberos keys if there's a problem with one of multiple Kerberos servers.

One more problem: Kerberos version 4 is known to have security issues. Nevertheless, older releases of Kerberos version 5 software enable access using version 4 tickets, courtesy of the krb524init command. That command is no longer included in the Kerberos servers released with Ubuntu Lucid Lynx and RHEL 6. On older systems, to avoid this potential security issue, you should make sure the following directives are set to false:

```
krb4_convert = false
krb4_get_tickets = false
```

Secure NFS as if It Were Local

As suggested in Chapter 6, older versions of NFS weren't fully secure. Before NFS version 4 (NFSv4), there was no user-based authentication. As such, a black-hat hacker with a system on the local network could connect to NFS directories shared with that network. If that NFS share included a user home directory, all the black-hat hacker needed to do was to set up a client system with the appropriate username and ID number on the local client system. He could then get full access to that user's home directory files through the remote share.

That has changed with the help of Kerberos, which can at least authenticate client systems. So a black-hat hacker with a portable system won't be able to connect to your NFS shares. Of course, this assumes that black-hat hacker hasn't found another way to break into a client that already has an NFS-based Kerberos ticket.

The NFSv4 and Kerberos combination won't work unless it's run on a Linux distribution loaded with kernel 2.6.18 or above. Red Hat Enterprise Linux 5 and most distributions released since 2008 meet that requirement.

Configure NFS Kerberos Tickets

Proceed to the Kerberos server. At the `kadmin.local:` prompt, you'll create **Kerberos tickets** for NFS clients. If coupled with appropriate configuration options in the `/etc/exports` file, Kerberos tickets can be used to limit access to authorized clients.

NFS is frequently used to share the `/home/` directory from a central server. Because that directory contains files for all regular users, each user needs to be able to access that directory from any connected and authorized client system. On some distributions, only the `kadmin.local` command works in place of the `kadmin` command in the following steps. To that end, you can create a Kerberos ticket for a system using the following steps:

1. Access the `kadmin:` prompt with administrative privileges with the `kadmin` command. You'll need administrative privileges; for the Kerberos administrative key created earlier, you'd access the `kadmin:` prompt with the following command:

    `# kadmin michael/admin@EXAMPLE.ORG`

2. Add a random NFS key for the client system with the following command. If your domain and realms are different, change the command accordingly.

    `kadmin: addprinc -randkey nfs/ubuntuhh.example.org@EXAMPLE.ORG`

3. Enter the next command to add this ticket to the keytab for the local server:

    `kadmin:  xst nfs/ubuntuhh.example.org@EXAMPLE.ORG`

You'll need to repeat steps 1 and 3 on the client system. Once this is complete, you can configure a shared directory on the NFS server with Kerberos options.

Configure NFS Shares for Kerberos

Shared NFS directories are configured in the `/etc/exports` file. For regular NFS shares, the standard configuration includes domain names or IP addresses along with mount options. For example, the following directive is a typical regular NFS share directive:

```
/backups    192.168.0.0/255.255.255.0(rw,sync)
```

This is a straightforward share of the `/backups/` directory with the systems on the noted IP network address and subnet mask. The `rw` and `sync` mean that the share is read-write and reads and writes are done synchronously. Other options are shown in the `man` pages for the `mount` command and `/etc/exports` file.

Generally, NFS directories should rarely if ever be exported with the `no_root_squash` option, as that would allow root administrative access to the shared directory. That `root` user could even be just a local user on a system that has an IP address in the address range associated with the network address and subnet mask.

In contrast, if the packages for NFSv4 are installed, you can set up a share similar to the following, which authenticates shares to clients specifically assigned by the Kerberos server:

```
/backups    gss/krb5i(sync,rw)
```

Once configured on the NFSv4 server, users on Kerberos-authorized client systems will be able to connect to the share. Such users would either need root administrative privileges or require appropriate configuration changes to the `/etc/fstab` file. These changes should include the `krb5i` option.

Keeping vsFTP Very Secure

This section is an extension of Chapter 5, which addresses basic network permissions for the very secure File Transfer Protocol (vsFTP) service. While many FTP server options are available, vsFTP is the server used by Red Hat, SUSE, Debian, and even the developers of the Linux kernel.

To review, the standard vsFTP configuration file is `vsftpd.conf`. The directory varies by distribution. For example, it's in the `/etc/` directory for Ubuntu and the `/etc/vsftpd/` directory for Red Hat. If an option is not described in this section, review Chapter 5. For a full list of available vsFTP directives, see the Web site associated with vsFTP developers: *http://vsftpd.beasts.org/*.

Configuration Options for vsFTP

For many users, a vsFTP server can be a terrific convenience. The FTP protocol is still perhaps the most efficient way to upload and download large files. But such a service comes with risks. To that end, you may want to regulate and even isolate the directories where vsFTP stores files for anonymous uploads and downloads. The developers behind different Linux distributions configure that anonymous directory in different locations, such as `/var/ftp/`, `/srv/ftp/`, and `/home/ftp/`. The following directive sets up a specific directory for anonymous access to the vsFTP server:

```
anon_root = /secure
```

Unless otherwise configured, vsFTP is actually run as one of the internet super server services described in Chapter 7. It's safer to run vsFTP as its own service, with its own control script in the /etc/init.d/ directory. Both Ubuntu and Red Hat versions of vsFTP make this possible with the following directive:

```
listen = yes
```

However, if the vsFTP server is to work on an Internet Protocol version 6 (IPv6) network, you could configure the following alternative directive. Just be aware that vsFTP won't work with both versions of the listen directive:

```
listen_ipv6 = yes
```

Frequently, administrators like you are responsible for transmitting corporate or organizational policies regarding the use of services like vsFTP. If the following directive is enabled, vsFTP looks for a hidden .message file in each accessible directory unless overridden by a message_file directive.

```
dirmessage_enable = yes
```

Given the popularity of many anonymous FTP services, logging information about uploads and downloads may be useful. It's activated with the xferlog_enable directive shown next. While the default log file is /var/log/vsftpd.log, it can be changed with the xferlog_file directive. If you do change that file, be sure to change the corresponding file in the /etc/logrotate.d/ directory; otherwise, the size of this file could easily overwhelm many systems.

```
xferlog_enable = yes
```

One option for uploads is to change the ownership of such files to a specific user, such as nobody or another user configured with minimal privileges. That can reduce the risk of an uploaded script or binary file that otherwise affects the security of the FTP server. Of course, this assumes user nobody is properly configured in the shadow password suite (or other user database) with appropriate minimal privileges.

```
chown_uploads = yes
chown_username = nobody
```

If you want to specifically set a **nonprivileged user**, the following directive can help:

```
nopriv_user = nobody
```

A couple of additional options can work sort of like screensavers; the following options end the connection if no commands or additional file transfer bits are detected in the given number of seconds. Some administrators may prefer to reduce the value of the idle_session_timeout directive.

```
idle_session_timeout = 600
data_connection_timeout = 120
```

Generally, secure FTP servers do not allow connections based on the American standard code for information interchange (ASCII), as that can lead to denial-of-service (DoS) attacks.

Additional vsFTP Configuration Files

Two other configuration files are directly used for the vsFTP service: `ftpusers` and `user_list`. The list of users in these files is based on the default set of service users. In other words, it includes users with user IDs (UIDs) below 100, 500, or 1000, depending on the distribution. If a black-hat hacker breaks into one of these accounts, he or she may be able to obtain limited administrative privileges (or more) through these accounts. These files can help prevent black-hat hackers from using these privileges at least on the vsFTP server.

If more services are installed on the local system, you may see additional service users in the files of the shadow password suite. In that case, you should add those users to the appropriate files. Red Hat systems specifically cite `/etc/vsftpd/ftpusers` in the associated pluggable authentication module (PAM) configuration file, `/etc/pam.d/vsftpd`.

> **TIP**
>
> Security Enhanced Linux (SELinux) provides additional protection for vsFTP. Directories shared using FTP servers should be labeled with the `public_content_t` type. If you want to configure a directory for uploads, you'll need to configure that directory with the `public_content_rw_t` type. The same options work for directories associated with `rsync` servers.

Linux as a More Secure Windows Server

In Chapter 5, you read about how Linux can share specific directories using Samba. This section focuses on the global settings associated with Samba, including how it can be set up as a **Primary Domain Controller (PDC)**, or its cousin, the **Backup Domain Controller (BDC)**. With the right options, the PDC database of usernames and passwords can be maintained on a Linux server.

Samba is the Linux implementation of Microsoft's Server Message Block protocol. As this evolved into the Common Internet File System (CIFS), Samba has kept pace. As case generally does not matter at the Microsoft command line, the value given to most Samba directives can be upper or lower case. For example, `security = USER` works as well as `security = user`.

Not all Samba directives are described in this book. For a more complete list, see the Samba documentation at *http://www.samba.org/samba/docs/man/manpages-3/smb .conf.5.html*. When Samba 4 is officially released, there will likely be some major added options.

Administrators who believe in Linux are likely to accept the notion that a Linux system, when substituted for a Windows system, is more secure. Some security professionals may disagree with that assessment. However, Linux systems maintained as PDCs are currently more secure, as Samba developers monitor and maintain such services while Windows developers no longer do so.

> **NOTE**
>
> Because PDCs are based on the Microsoft Windows NT 4 Server operating system, Microsoft hasn't supported PDCs on networks in years. However, PDCs on Linux servers configured with the Samba file server are still supported. As long as Windows XP clients are supported, Microsoft should support those systems as PDC clients. However, since this is a book on Linux security, no claims are made with respect to Microsoft security support.

NOTE

Samba directives include many synonyms. For example, `hosts allow` is the same as `allow hosts`. Samba directives also accommodate common alternative spellings, such as `browsable` and `browseable`. If you see one directive in documentation and a similar directive in a configuration file, look a little deeper. The directives might actually mean the same thing.

Samba Global Options

This section focuses on directives in the main Samba configuration file, `smb.conf`, in the `/etc/samba/` directory. The directives associated with sharing directories were discussed in Chapter 5; this section focuses primarily on the directives in the `[global]` section of this file. When reading this file, be aware there are two different comment characters; any line that starts with a pound sign (#) or a semicolon (;) is a comment in this file.

Any Linux system configured with Samba can be set up as a server on a Microsoft network. While this section is based on the Samba configuration file from Red Hat Enterprise Linux version 5.4, the same directives can be used on any Linux system where the same (or later) version of Samba is installed. The following subsections are based on the sections from the sample version of that file.

One thing that may appear different about many Samba directives is that they're multiple words. Don't be fooled. Multiple-word directives such as `server string` and `add user script` are a single directive.

Network-Related Options

Microsoft networks began with workgroups of computers where directories were shared solely based on passwords. As such, Samba used the `workgroup` directive to specify the name of the network of the noted group of computers. When the latest Microsoft networks evolved into domains, Samba retained the same `workgroup` directive to specify the name of the domain. So depending on the type of network being configured, the value assigned to `workgroup` can be the name of either a workgroup or a domain.

As shown here, the `workgroup` directive is normally coupled with the `server string` and `netbios name` directives. The example shown returns "Samba Server Version" followed by the version number of the Samba server, as specified by the `%v`. It's shown as a comment in a Microsoft My Network Places window or in the output of a Microsoft `net view` or a Samba `smbclient -L` command.

```
workgroup = bigdomain
server string = Samba Server Version %v
netbios name = trivialinfo
```

If obscurity is part of your security strategy, consider changing the values of `server string` and `netbios name`. The values shown there can throw off the casual black-hat hacker. The `netbios name` directive is associated with the **Network Basic Input/Output System (NetBIOS)** name of a system, which is associated with the session layer of the **Open Systems Interconnection (OSI)** model of networking. If the `netbios name` is not assigned, the system hostname is used.

The `interfaces` and `hosts allow` directives can limit access to the Samba server in two ways. The examples shown here limit the interfaces and addresses to which Samba listens. The `hosts allow` directive can be revised to limit access to a domain or even individual host names.

```
interfaces = lo eth0 192.168.12.2/24 192.168.13.2/24
hosts allow = 127. 192.168.12. 192.168.13.
```

Logging Options

It may be helpful to set up logs by different machines. The following directives would set up log files by NetBIOS name or IP address. The `max log size` directive sets a limit on log files, in kilobytes.

```
log file = /var/log/samba/%m.log
max log size = 50
```

Standalone Server Options

This section is closely related to the next section. Some of the options and directives are mutually exclusive. For example, while you should activate only one `security` directive in this configuration file, examples of `security` directives are listed in both sections. The two `security` options described in this section are `user` and `share`.

Security-conscious professionals should almost never set `security = share`, as that allows access to shared directories to users without accounts. All they'd need is the password for the shared directory. So for a standalone server, a PDC, or a BDC, you'd want to set up the following directives:

```
security = user
passdb backend = smbpasswd
```

The `smbpasswd` or `tdbsam` options allow administrators to set up or change user passwords with the `smbpasswd` command. Be aware: The Samba user password database is separate from the Linux password database, and is stored in files in the `/etc/samba/` directory. In the configuration shown, it's stored in the `smbpasswd` file. If set to `tdbsam`, user-account information is stored in the `passdb.tdb` file.

Alternatively, if you want to use an LDAP database, set `passdb backend = ldapsam`. You may consider including a number of other related directives shown in Table 8-1. The table just lists some of the most important LDAP directives; for example, options associated with logging are not included in the list and may be found in the Samba documentation described earlier. Some of the listed directives may be used to map Linux UIDs and group IDs (GIDs) to other authentication databases.

If the local system is configured as the one Microsoft server on the local network, the authentication database will be stored on the local system. Depending on how `smb.conf` is configured, that will be in files either in the `/etc/samba/` or the `/etc/samba/private/` directory.

TABLE 8-1 LDAP-related Samba directives.

LDAP DIRECTIVE	DESCRIPTION

`client ldap sasl wrapping`	Allows LDAP traffic to be encrypted using the simple authentication and security layer (SASL); associated the following Microsoft registry key:
	`HKLM\System\CurrentControlSet\Services\`
	`➥NTDS\Parameters\LDAPServerIntegrity`

`idmap backend`	Supports a database association between Microsoft security identifiers (SIDs) and Linux UIDs and GIDs
`idmap gid`	Specifies a range of GIDs to be mapped to Microsoft SIDs; not limited to LDAP authentication databases
`idmap uid`	Specifies a range of UIDs to be mapped to Microsoft SIDs; not limited to LDAP authentication databases
`ldap admin dn`	Specifies the distinguished name to contact the LDAP server
`ldap group suffix`	Sets the suffix to be used for LDAP groups, such as `ou=Groups`
`ldap machine suffix`	Defines the suffix to be used for LDAP systems, such as `ou=Computers`
`ldap password sync`	Defines whether the Microsoft LDAP database is to be updated when a Samba password is updated
`ldap suffix`	Sets the base entry for the object, such as `dc=example,dc=org`
`ldap user suffix`	Sets the suffix to be used for LDAP users, such as `ou=People`

FYI

One trivial bit is the terms associated with user authentication on Linux and Microsoft systems. Users on Linux systems log in to a computer. Users on Microsoft systems log on to a computer. Because Samba is the Linux implementation of Microsoft networking, the Samba configuration file configures Microsoft-style user logons.

Thus, the comments in the Samba server configuration file specify "login" and the associated directives use `logon`.

If you are configuring a PDC, pay attention to the [`netlogon`] and [`profiles`] stanzas in the "Shares Definitions" section of the `smb.conf` configuration file. These stanzas determine how logon information is shared by user.

Domain Members Options

This section includes many of the same directives as the previous "Standalone Server Options" section. In this [global] part of the file, directives should be used only once. Three options are noted in this section for the security directive:

- **domain**—Assumes the local system has been added to an NT domain; refers authentication requests to another server.
- **server**—Works if the local system has not been added to an NT domain, if a local smbpasswd database is available. Vulnerable to man-in-the-middle attacks.
- **ads**—Sets the local system as a domain member in an Active Directory domain.

Because these options require access to some other system for authentication, they won't work without the password server directive to point to the FQDN or IP address of that server. If you've set up a Kerberos server with an active directory, use the realm directive to specify the name of the Kerberos realm.

Domain Controller Options

Local Samba servers can be configured to send and receive login information from Microsoft systems. To that end a Samba-enabled Linux system can be configured as if it were a Microsoft client. Login scripts can be configured for machines and users with the logon script directive:

```
logon script = %m.bat
logon script = %u.bat
```

Profiles can be enabled with the logon path directive. For example, the following directive specifies a shared profile/ directory on some server named authentication; the %U means user profile information is stored in a subdirectory named for the user.

```
logon path = \\authentication\profile\%U
```

Browser Control Options

On a Microsoft network, the browser collects the domain or workgroup name of every system on the network. But only one system can be a browser at a time on a LAN. The browser control options section includes directives that drive which system is assigned as the **master browser** on a Microsoft network. The terms assume that different systems put themselves up for "election" as the master browser. The relevant directives are as follows:

- **domain master**—Determines whether the local system forces an election for the domain.
- **local master**—Determines whether the system puts itself up for election.
- **os level**—Sets the advertising level for browsing elections; may be set between 0 and 255.
- **preferred master**—Determines whether the local system forces an election for the local network.

Name Resolution

Name resolution on Microsoft networks is based on the status of **Windows Internet Name Service (WINS)** and DNS servers. A WINS server contains a database of NetBIOS names and IP addresses. If the NetBIOS name does not exist, the WINS server defaults to the hostname of the system. The basic directives in this section are straightforward:

- `wins support`—Enables a WINS server on the local system.
- `wins server`—Configures a pointer to a running WINS server.
- `wins proxy`—Redirects WINS requests to a system specified by `wins server`.
- `dns proxy`—Supports NetBIOS name resolution via DNS.

Printing Options

By default, a Samba server shares printers configured using the Common UNIX Printing System (CUPS) over the Windows network. The following options load CUPS printers and configure raw data for processing by Microsoft printer drivers:

```
load printers = yes
cups options = raw
```

Samba as a Primary Domain Controller (PDC)

If you want to configure a Windows NT–style PDC, pay attention to the `security` directive described earlier. It works with the `[netlogon]` and `[profiles]` stanzas in the "Share Definitions" section of the `smb.conf` configuration file. The `[netlogon]` stanza is for storage of user-specific Microsoft logon scripts. The `path` determines the directory where those scripts are stored. It's associated with the username, based on the `logon script` directive described earlier.

```
path = /var/lib/samba/netlogon
```

The `guest ok` access can be set to no to prevent users from changing scripts of others. The `writable` and `share modes` options shown also limit access to the administrative user.

```
guest ok = no
writable = no
share modes = no
```

The `[profiles]` stanza is used to allow users to log on from different workstations. The profiles in the noted `path` directory allow users with Microsoft clients to have the same look and feel on each workstation. Profiles may be stored in username-specific subdirectories as defined by the `path`.

```
path = /home/samba/profiles/%U
```

The next three directives allow users to change profiles and write those changes. To set up standard profiles, you may choose to set `read only = yes`.

```
read only = no
create mask = 0600
directory mask = 0700
```

The last two directives limit access to authorized users:

```
guest ok = no
browseable = no
```

Make Sure SSH Stays Secure

Previous chapters included a number of references to SSH. In this section, you'll see how to best secure SSH clients and servers. One of the benefits of SSH is encryption. However, until an SSH connection is made, transmissions are still sent in clear text. So a black-hat hacker may be able to determine that an SSH connection is being established and eavesdrop on any communications that take place before the user initiates the SSH connection.

In addition to using SSH to configure interactive username/password connections, you may also automate the SSH connection process through the use of public/private key pairs.

The Secure Shell Server

The standard SSH server configuration file is `sshd_config`, in the `/etc/ssh/` directory. It works very well on its own. On most distributions, all you need to do is install the server with a package name like `openssh-server` and make sure it's running. You should be able to connect from a remote system with commands described in the next section on the SSH client.

It's important to modify the default SSH server configuration file to promote security, however. Directives listed here are based on the default versions of `sshd_config` installed for Red Hat and Ubuntu systems. First, the standard SSH port number is 22, as confirmed here:

```
Port 22
```

Because SSH version 1 has known security weaknesses, most administrators encourage the use of SSH version 2. However, the default SSH server accepts both versions of SSH. Therefore, most `sshd_config` files limit access to SSH version 2 with the following directive:

```
Protocol 2
```

Assuming you accept the use of SSH version 2, other directives associated with SSH version 1 are ignored (and as such will not be covered here). The `ListenAddress` directive can limit the networks configured for SSH. For example, the following directive looks for and listens to network cards with the noted IP address:

```
ListenAddress 192.168.10.1
```

The following HostKey directives specify Digital Signature Algorithm (DSA) and Rivest Shamir Adelman (RSA) host key files that can be used to help verify the integrity of the host server. SSH won't work unless permissions on these files are limited to the root administrative user:

```
HostKey /etc/ssh/ssh_host_dsa_key
HostKey /etc/ssh/ssh_host_rsa_key
```

However, there are companion public key files, ssh_host_dsa_key.pub and ssh_host_rsa_key.pub, that can and should be readable by all users. The next important directive, SyslogFacility, determines where logging information is stored. It's normally set to AUTH or AUTHPRIV. The log file for AUTH or AUTHPRIV messages is normally defined in the /etc/syslog.conf file. For more information on logging, see Chapter 12.

The authentication directives that follow are mostly self-explanatory. The LoginGraceTime disconnects if a login hasn't happened in the noted time. While the default is yes, PermitRootLogin should almost always be set to no to minimize the risk of a black-hat hacker decrypting an administrative password sent over a network. StrictModes keep users from setting world-writable files over an SSH connection. MaxAuthTries limits the number of login attempts per connection.

```
LoginGraceTime 2m
PermitRootLogin no
StrictModes yes
MaxAuthTries 6
```

The additional authentication options shown here support the use of private/public key authentication with passphrases as described later in this chapter. The AuthorizedKeysFile specifies the location of authorized SSH keys in each user's home directory:

```
PubkeyAuthentication yes
AuthorizedKeysFile .ssh/authorized_keys
```

Generally, you want to retain user-based authentication. To that end, the following host-based authentication option is disabled by default and should remain that way:

```
HostbasedAuthentication no
IgnoreRhosts yes
```

However, you need to retain the following default option to avoid black-hat hackers who substitute their systems for known systems:

```
IgnoreUserKnownHosts no
```

Once you've set up passphrases, you can revise this to no to disable clear-text tunneled passwords:

```
PasswordAuthentication yes
```

Of course, when passwords are used, they should not be empty:

```
PermitEmptyPasswords no
```

If you need SSH connections over a telephone modem, you may consider activating this option. However, there are interaction problems with PAMs.

```
ChallengeResponseAuthentication no
```

If you've set up a Kerberos server, you can change some of these default Kerberos options for Kerberos or regular passwords. Methods to do so include Kerberos tickets or **Andrew Filesystem (AFS)** tokens:

```
KerberosAuthentication no
KerberosOrLocalPasswd yes
KerberosTicketCleanup yes
KerberosGetAFSToken no
```

Related to Kerberos tickets is the generic security services application programming interface (GSSAPI), as described earlier in the section on NFSv4:

```
GSSAPIAuthentication no
GSSAPIAuthentication yes
GSSAPICleanupCredentials yes
GSSAPICleanupCredentials yes
```

If you need GUI-based tools, the next directive can be especially valuable. **X11** is the name of a protocol associated with the Linux X Window system. It allows you to start and use GUI tools remotely:

```
X11Forwarding yes
```

If login banners are used to transmit corporate or organizational policies for remote users, you'll want to activate the following directive and enter those policies in the /etc/issue.net file:

```
Banner /etc/issue.net
```

One of the values of the SSH server configuration file is its ability to encrypt FTP connections. The following directive supports connections to user home directories with the sftp command:

```
Subsystem    sftp    /usr/libexec/openssh/sftp-server
```

> **TIP**
>
> Black-hat hackers frequently try to break into SSH servers. One open source effort to block known black-hat hackers is available from *http://denyhosts. sourceforge.net/*, developed by Phil Schwartz. SSH is a TCP Wrappers service, as discussed in Chapter 7. The DenyHosts software takes advantage of this by adding address information from repeat offenders to the local /etc/hosts.deny file.

8

Networked Filesystems and Remote Access

The Secure Shell Client

Several SSH client commands are made available when the SSH client package is installed. These commands include `ssh` for client connections, `scp` for secure copying, and `sftp` for encrypted connections to FTP servers.

Anonymous FTP connections are not allowed with the `sftp` command.

SSH Logins

The most straightforward way to log into a remote system is with the `ssh user@hostname` command. If no username is specified, the `ssh` command assumes the current user account on the local system also applies on the remote system. You can substitute the FQDN or IP address for the `hostname`.

If you want to log in remotely with X11 forwarding, use `ssh`'s `-X` switch.

Secure SSH Copying

The `scp` command can copy a file over a secure shell connection. If you run a command like the following, expect to be prompted for the noted user's password or passphrase on the remote system. Once those are verified, the `copy` command is processed, copying the noted `localfile` to the `/backups/` directory on the remote system.

```
scp localfile michael@remote.example.com:/backups/
```

Create a Secure Shell Passphrase

Passphrases are more secure than passwords. They use private/public key pairs with some large number of bits, typically 1,024 and above. The key pairs are associated with a passphrase. The example in this section sets up a secure shell passphrase for logins from a client to a remote server. It starts with the `ssh-keygen` command, which leads to the messages that follow. Unless you're creating a key for the root administrative user (which is not recommended), these commands should be run from a regular user account:

```
$ ssh-keygen
Generating public/private rsa key pair.
Enter file in which to save the key (/home/michael/.ssh/id_rsa):
```

The noted file is the location of the RSA private key. Most users will accept the default location, at which point the next message prompts them for a passphrase. The best passphrases are complete sentences, with upper- and lower-case characters, numbers, and punctuation. The following messages omit the actual key fingerprint. The passphrase isn't shown on the screen to minimize the risk posed by "shoulder surfers."

```
Enter passphrase (empty for no passphrase):
Enter same passphrase again:
Your identification has been saved in /home/michael/.ssh/id_rsa.
Your public key has been saved in /home/michael/.ssh/id_rsa.pub.
The key fingerprint is:
```

By default, the encryption key is based on the RSA algorithm, which can be configured at 768 bits and above. Keys with large numbers of bits, such as 4,096, may take some time to create. While the same command can create DSA keys with the -t dsa switch, only 1,024-bit DSA keys are available. You should now see the noted id_rsa and id_rsa.pub files in your home directory, in the .ssh/ subdirectory.

The next step is to copy the id_rsa.pub public key to the remote server. While you could use a USB key for this purpose, you can also use the ssh-copy-id command to transmit the public key:

```
$ ssh-copy-id -i .ssh/id_rsa.pub LucidServer.example.org
```

If this is the first time a SSH connection is being made to the noted LucidServer system, you'll see messages similar to those shown here:

```
The authenticity of host 'lucidservermin.example.org
(192.168.100.27)' can't be established. RSA key fingerprint
is [some deleted hexadecimal number]
```

Assuming the IP address is what you expect, proceed with the connection by typing in yes at the displayed prompt:

```
Are you sure you want to continue connecting (yes/no)? yes
Warning: Permanently added 'lucidserver.example.org'
(RSA) to the list of known hosts.
```

If you never want to transmit even an encrypted password over a network, the following message should give you pause. If you prefer, stop here and get out that USB key.

```
michael@lucidservermin.example.org's password:
```

If you proceed with a working password, the contents of the noted id_rsa.pub file are appended to the end of the .ssh/authorized_keys file on the remote system. In other words, if you're truly paranoid, copy the id_rsa.pub file to a USB key, connect the USB key to the remote system, and run the following command on the remote system (in this case, the lucidserver.exmaple.org system):

```
$ cat id_rsa.pub >> .ssh/authorized_keys
```

If successful, you should now be able to use the passphrase to connect to the remote system. You should be prompted with the following prompt:

```
Enter passphrase for key '/home/michael/.ssh/id_rsa':
```

Alternatively, if X11 communication is enabled over the network, you may be prompted with a window similar to that shown in Figure 8-1.

Unlock private key

**Enter password to
unlock the private key**

An application wants access to
the private key 'id_rsa', but it is
locked

Password: [   ]

▫Automatically unlock this private key when I log in.

Deny   ⏎OK

Networks and Encryption

You've just read about one method of encrypted communication, using SSH. Other methods are available. One that is commonly used is Internet Protocol Security, known in Linux as IPSec. It works at both ends of a connection, tunneling communications through protocols 50 and 51. In tunneling mode, it is a form of virtual private networking.

Another method is based on the Secure Sockets Layer (SSL) protocol. For most systems, it's been superseded by Transport Layer Security (TLS). In most cases, it uses a different port to enable encrypted communication for common services. Uses of SSL and TLS will be discussed in more detail, starting with the discussion of e-mail clients later in this chapter. For more information, look for discussions on secure versions of networked applications in Chapter 9.

The focus of this section is IPSec connections. An IPSec connection a method for connecting remote hosts and networks using a secure tunnel. IPSec can connect different private networks over the Internet. It relies on encapsulation to hide communications over public networks.

Different port and protocol numbers are used for IPSec connections. Assuming a firewall is configured on each network, you'll have to make sure these ports and protocols are open on the respective networks:

- **Encapsulating Security Payload (ESP) protocol**—Uses protocol number 50. ESP traffic can be allowed through an `iptables` firewall with a `-p 50 -j ACCEPT` switch.

- **Authentication Header (AH) protocol**—Uses protocol number 51. AH traffic can be allowed through an `iptables` firewall with a `-p 51 -j ACCEPT` switch.

- **Internet Key Exchange (IKE) protocol**—Uses the User Datagram Protocol (UDP) over port 500. IKE traffic can be allowed through an `iptables` firewall with a `-p udp --dport 500 -j ACCEPT` switch.

- **Network Address Translation (NAT) traversal protocol**—Uses the Transmission Control Protocol (TCP) and UDP over port 4500. NAT traffic can be allowed through an `iptables` firewall with `-p tcp --dport 4500 -j ACCEPT` and `-p tcp --dport 4500 -j ACCEPT` switches.

IPSec encryption depends on the IKE service, sometimes known as *racoon*. The IKE service is configured in files in the `/etc/racoon/` directory. On Ubuntu systems, IPSec is configured in the `/etc/ipsec-tools.conf` file. Alternatively, if you use Red Hat's

Network Configuration tool, you'll see appropriate configuration directives in dedicated files in the /etc/sysconfig/network-scripts/ directory.

The Red Hat configuration is described first in each of the following subsections, as it includes just those parameters that need to be configured. In either case, if the connection is successful, you should be able to run a command like tcpdump on both ends to detect traffic traveling with the noted port numbers.

Host-to-Host IPSec on Red Hat

On Red Hat systems, IPSec host-to-host connections are configured in two files in the /etc/sysconfig/network-scripts/ directory. One is ifcfg-*host*, where *host* is the name of the host-to-host device. The configuration is simple, including just four directives:

```
DST=192.168.122.127
TYPE=IPSEC
ONBOOT=yes
IKE_METHOD=PSK
```

The local host is assumed as one end of the connection. the DST is the destination. It's an IPSec connection activated during the boot process, and the IKE method uses a pre-shared key (PSK). There should be a matching file on the remote system. The difference is in the IP address associated with the DST directive.

Both systems also require authentication keys. The file will be stored in the same /etc/sysconfig/network-scripts/ directory, with a name of keys-*host*. The file should be set with read and write permissions for just the root administrative user.

Host-to-Host IPSec on Ubuntu

On Ubuntu systems, an IPSec host-to-host connection begins in the /etc/ipsec-tools.conf file. The script shown here is based on the setkey -f command, on a host with IP address 192.168.0.100. This file creates a security policy database (SPD) for a host connection from IP address 192.168.0.100 to 10.0.0.100. It flushes any previous regular and SPD policies:

```
#!/usr/sbin/setkey -f
flush;
spdflush;
```

Then it adds SPD policies for traffic to and from the noted IP addresses. The esp and ah directives enable traffic over protocol numbers 50 and 51 as described near the beginning of the "Networks and Encryption" section.

```
spdadd 192.168.0.100 10.0.0.100 any -P out ipsec
    esp/transport//require
    ah/transport//require;
spdadd 10.0.0.100 192.168.0.100 any -P in ipsec
    esp/transport//require
    ah/transport//require;
```

```
path pre_shared_key "/etc/racoon/psk.txt";
path certificate "/etc/racoon/certs";

remote 10.0.0.100 {
        exchange_mode main,aggressive;
        proposal {
                encryption_algorithm 3des;
                hash_algorithm sha1;
                authentication_method pre_shared_key;
                dh_group modp1024;
        }
        generate_policy off;
}

sainfo anonymous {
        pfs_group 2;
        lifetime time 1 hour
        encryption_algorithm 3des;
        authentication_algorithm hmac_md5;
        compression_algorithm deflate;
}
```

FIGURE 8-2

An `/etc/racoon/racoon.conf` file for host-to-host IPSec connections.

A matching `/etc/ipsec-tools.conf` file should be created on the remote system, with IP address 10.0.0.100. The IP address should be reversed in the remote version of this file. Both files should be set as read-write only by the root administrative user.

Now you'll create two files on the local system—in this case, the one with an IP address of 192.168.0.100. Both files will be in the `/etc/racoon/` directory. The first file is `racoon.conf`; one sample customized for this connection is shown in Figure 8-2.

Now you'll create a `psk.txt` file in the `/etc/racoon/` directory. The default version includes some options; you'll need to include the IP address of the remote system:

```
10.0.0.100  0ab35slj349gas
```

You'll want the same files on the remote 10.0.0.100 system, with the IP addresses switched in each file. Once these changes are made to both systems, you should be able to run the following command on both systems:

```
# setkey -f /etc/ipsec-tools.conf
```

> **TIP**
>
> A slightly different method for host-to-host IPSec connections is available from the Ubuntu community documentation at *https://help.ubuntu.com/ community/IPSecHowTo*.

If successful, you should be able to apply the `tcpdump` command on both systems. Specifically, the following `tcpdump` command should list all traffic going to the remote 10.0.0.100 system over the network device `eth0`. The `-n` specifies numeric addresses and the `-i` specifies the network device:

```
# tcpdump -n  -i eth0 host 10.0.0.100
```

Network-to-Network IPSec on Red Hat

The basic configuration for network-to-network IPSec connections on Red Hat systems is similar to the previously described IPSec host-to-host connections. The two applicable files are configured in the `/etc/sysconfig/network-scripts/` directory. One is `ifcfg-net`, where *net* is the name of the network-to-network device. The configuration is a bit more complex, as it includes a few more directives. But several should already be familiar:

```
ONBOOT=yes
IKE_METHOD=PSK
DSTGW=192.168.122.1
SRCGW=192.168.0.1
DSTNET=192.168.122.0/24
SRCNET=192.168.0.0/24
DST=192.168.122.27
TYPE=IPSEC
```

The "new" directives include the destination network gateway address (`DSTGW`), the source network gateway address (`SRCGW`), the destination network address (`DSTNET`), and the source network address (`SRCNET`). The network address format is in Classless Inter-Domain Routing (CIDR) notation, which should already be familiar to anyone who has previous Linux command-line experience.

The second applicable file is for the authentication keys. While the name of the file should be something like `keys-net`, the format should be identical to the previously described `keys-host` file for host-to-host connections. Of course, the actual key should be different.

Network-to-Network IPSec on Ubuntu

A similar configuration for Ubuntu-based network-to-network IPSec connections is available from the default version of the `racoon-tool.conf` file in the `/etc/racoon/` directory.

When You "Must" Use Telnet

Just as the customer is always right, the user is always right. One might think that all users with more computer experience would be more understanding of security concerns. But old habits die hard. Users who have used Telnet for remote connections may always want to use Telnet for remote connections.

Unfortunately, it's far too easy to read usernames and passwords sent using clear-text protocols such as Telnet. You'll read more about clear-text access later in this chapter. For now, it's important to consider the more secure alternatives for remote connections to regular Telnet.

A comparison of Telnet
and SSH remote access
methods.

Logging In Via Telnet

```
[michael@RHELserver ~]$ telnet 192.168.122.27
Trying 192.168.122.27...
Connected to LucidServerMin (192.168.122.27).
Escape character is '^]'.
Ubuntu lucid (development branch)
LucidServerMin login: michael
Password:
Last login: Thu Apr  1 09:40:13 PDT 2010 from rhelserver.example.org on
  pts/0
Linux LucidServerMin 2.6.32-14-generic-pae #20-Ubuntu SMP Sat Feb 20 07
:07:46 UTC 2010 i686

For official documentation, please visit:
 * http://help.ubuntu.com/
michael@LucidServerMin:~$ Connection closed by foreign host.
```

Logging In Via SSH

```
[michael@RHELserver ~]$ ssh 192.168.122.27
Enter passphrase for key '/home/michael/.ssh/id_rsa':
Linux LucidServerMin 2.6.32-14-generic-pae #20-Ubuntu SMP Sat Feb 20 07
:07:46 UTC 2010 i686

For official documentation, please visit:
 * http://help.ubuntu.com/
Last login: Thu Apr  1 09:41:33 2010 from RHELserver.example.org
michael@LucidServerMin:~$
```

Persuade Users to Convert to SSH

Ideally, you'll be able to persuade local users to connect to the SSH service described earlier
in this chapter using passphrases. You might even turn off Telnet servers and present SSH
as the only available alternative. SSH is the most secure option available for remote access.
One possibility is to present the steps associated with the two different remote access
options, side by side. One example is shown in Figure 8-3, where a login to a regular
Telnet server is compared to a login to an SSH server using a passphrase. If you can
convince appropriate users that the SSH connection is no more difficult than the Telnet
connection—and is more secure—you will have done an excellent job selling the most
secure remote access option available.

Install More Secure Telnet Servers and Clients

Unfortunately, not all users are easily convinced. You may need to consider alternatives—
specifically, more secure versions of Telnet. Packages associated with SSL and Kerberos
are available. Unfortunately, if the client is not using SSL or Kerberos-based Telnet clients,
the default configuration of either Telnet server accepts regular clear-text Telnet clients.

You can address this issue on both the client and server. On the client, you can delete or
move the commands associated with regular Telnet clients. You could create links between

the expected client commands in their expected directory locations and the actual SSL or Kerberos-enabled client commands. For example, the following commands create soft links between the standard Telnet client command and the more secure options described in this section:

```
# ln -s /usr/bin/telnet-ssl /usr/bin/telnet
# ln -s /usr/kerberos/bin/telnet /usr/bin/telnet
```

You can also make sure the Telnet server accepts only those connections for which it was designed. The SSL version of Telnet is configured in the internet super server configuration file, /etc/inetd.conf. In that file, you can add the -z secure switch, which accepts only secure connections. If a remote user tries to connect with a regular Telnet client, that person will see the following message before he or she can enter a username or password:

```
telnetd: [SSL required - connection rejected].
Connection closed by foreign host.
```

In a similar fashion, a Telnet client attempt to connect to a Kerberos-enabled Telnet server works only when appropriate Kerberos server and client options are configured as described earlier in this chapter. Without those settings, a user who attempts to connect to a Kerberos-enabled Telnet server will get the following message before he or she can enter a username or password:

```
Unencrypted connection refused. Goodbye.
Connection closed by foreign host.
```

Remember the Modem

If you have to administer connections from telephone modems, the standard is known as the Remote Authentication Dial In User Service (RADIUS). The open source implementation of this software is based on the work of the FreeRADIUS project, available from *http://freeradius.org/*. The implementation of RADIUS is beyond the scope of this book. However, it can be downloaded from the noted Web site, and is also available from standard Ubuntu software repositories.

The Basics of RADIUS

RADIUS is designed to provide authentication, authorization, and accounting for remote users who want to connect to a network service. In RADIUS documentation, these functions are known as AAA. First, with respect to authentication, different modules allow you to link its authentication directives with the username and password databases of your choice. Those databases are used to authenticate users, as well as to set up what such remote users are authorized to do. You can set up accounting for the actions of users in various RADIUS configuration files.

TABLE 8-2 Basic FreeRADIUS configuration files.

FILE	DESCRIPTION
aacct_users	Specifies the accounting method for active users
attrs	Includes security and configuration information for RADIUS realms; related to the `rlm_attr_filter` module
attrs.access_reject attrs.accounting_response	Enforces minimal information attributes when access to a RADIUS server is rejected or for accounting; related to the `rlm_attr_filter` module
attrs.pre-proxy	Specifies authentication information to be sent through a proxy to another RADIUS server; may be coupled with `post-proxy` information
certs/	Sets the directory with SSL certificates, when applicable
clients.conf	Defines client configuration
dictionary	Refers to mostly hardware-specific dictionary files in the `/usr/share/freeradius/dictionary/` directory for different attributes
eap.conf	When EAP authentication is used, defines different certificates and responses
experimental.conf	Defines experimental modules
hints	Specifies hints to be added or stripped; commonly used with Point-to-Point Protocol (PPP) and related requests
huntgroups	Defines IP address ranges with restricted access
ldap.attrmap	Matches RADIUS and LDAP directory items
modules/	Sets the directory with RADIUS modules
otp.conf	Supports "one-time password" authentication
policy.conf, policy.txt	Describes sample policies
preproxy_users	Specifies user information for a remote RADIUS server
proxy.conf	Defines a proxy server configuration
radiusd.conf	Defines the main RADIUS configuration file
sites-available, sites-enabled	Sets directories with enabled and available virtual servers
sql.conf	Includes Structured Query Language (SQL) modules
sqlippool.conf	Defines an interface to a pool of IP addresses
templates.conf	Preconfigures multiple options
Users	Defines how users are handled

In other words, it uses authentication systems such as the Password Authentication Protocol (PAP), Challenge-Handshake Authentication Protocol (CHAP), and the Extensible Authentication Protocol (EAP). The first two options are commonly associated with connections over telephone modems. EAP is an authentication system often used on wireless networks.

Such authentication systems require access to a username and password database. RADIUS can work with a variety of such databases, including the LDAP, the Network Information Service (NIS), Microsoft's Active Directory, Novell's eDirectory, and even the old standby, the local shadow password suite.

RADIUS Configuration Files

When installed on an Ubuntu system, configuration options are commented into a number of files in the `/etc/freeradius/` directory. On some other systems, you'll find these files in the `/etc/raddb/` directory. Table 8-2 describes the function of each of these files and subdirectories.

Moving Away from Clear-Text Access

To understand the risks associated with clear-text access, take a look at Figure 8-4. It's an excerpt from the Wireshark network analyzer. It can read the contents of every packet sent over the local network. Every system on an Ethernet network can listen in on all network communications, even those between two remote systems on the LAN. That's just the way Ethernet works. Figure 8-3 illustrates the contents of one packet, which happens to be one letter of a password.

Wireshark is readily available for most Linux distributions, including Red Hat and Ubuntu. Earlier in this chapter, you saw alternatives to regular Telnet that are better at hiding usernames and passwords in network communication.

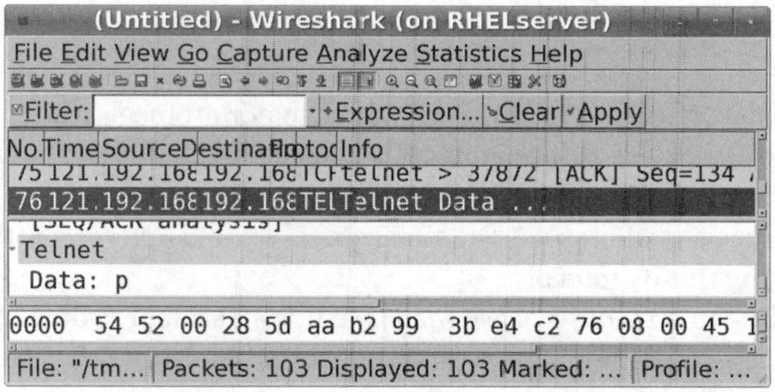

FIGURE 8-4

The Wireshark network analyzer looks at the contents of packets.

The Simple `rsync` Solution

The `rsync` command is frequently used for backups. You'll see how backups work in Chapter 14. For now, this section examines the basic features of the `rsync` command. The first time you back up a system with the `rsync` command, everything might seem slow. With its archive features, the `rsync` command can back up more than just the information in regular files. It can preserve more, including the following:

- Ownership by users and groups
- Last file-access times
- Permissions
- Symbolic links between files

An archive `rsync`-based backup with all such original information can form the basis for a "gold baseline." The dates associated with files on the backup provides assurance that such files have not been changed after a certain date. Such a date can be important in case of a security breach, especially if your managers suddenly refuse to trust files created after that date.

One of the risks associated with the `rsync` command is that it normally transmits data in clear text. If SSH clients are installed on the local system, `rsync` doesn't have to take such risks. For example, the following command takes the contents of user `michael`'s home directory recursively (with all subdirectories) and sends it to the remote system named `backup.example.org` in the `/backups/` subdirectory:

```
$ rsync -e ssh -aHz /home/michael backup.example.org:/backups/
```

The `-e ssh` tunnels the backup packets over an SSH connection. If you haven't yet connected to the noted remote system, the remote SSH server prompts for a password or sends a message to verify the passphrase described earlier in this chapter. The `-a` transmits the files in archive mode. The `-H` includes hard-linked files in the archive. The `-z` compresses the data being transmitted, speeding the backup.

E-mail Clients

Standard e-mail clients connect to servers using three major protocols: the **Simple Mail Transfer Protocol (SMTP)**, the **Post Office Protocol version 3 (POP3)**, and the **Internet Message Access Protocol version 4 (IMAP4)**. Most users configure e-mail clients such as Evolution, Thunderbird, and especially Microsoft's Outlook Express to send and receive their e-mail communications using those protocols.

Every time a request to send or receive e-mail is sent from a client to an e-mail server, the username and password is also sent over the network. With those clear-text protocols, it's easy for a black-hat hacker to identify those usernames and passwords with tools such as Wireshark.

TABLE 8-3 Clear-text e-mail protocols and secure alternatives.	
CLEAR TEXT E-MAIL PROTOCOL/PORT	**SECURE ALTERNATIVE/PORT**
IMAP4/143	IMAPS/993
POP3/110	POP3S/995
SMTP/25	SMTPS/465

Fortunately, there are secure alternatives to each of those protocols, briefly described in Table 8-3. In these cases, the alternative includes an "S" in the name, which is short for secure. In all cases, such protocols communicate over different port numbers. In general, the IMAP4 and POP3 protocols serve e-mail to clients, and the SMTP protocol transmits e-mail from clients.

These are just standard ports. Some e-mail administrators have been known to use nonstandard port numbers in the hope that obscurity will minimize attempts by spammers to use their e-mail servers.

Such secure alternatives won't work unless they're configured in appropriate e-mail server configuration files. To review how these configuration files work and can be changed, see Chapter 9. Just as a preview, some e-mail administrators use port 587 for e-mail transmission using the submission protocol, which is for practical purposes interchangeable with port 465 for the secure SMTP (SMTPS) protocol. Some open source SMTP e-mail services can be modified to use either port 465 or 587.

Best Practices: Networked Filesystems and Remote Access

While it's best to minimize the number of networked services on any one system, that may not be enough for a secure system. Ideally, all you need on a server is one networked service and an SSH server to administer that service remotely. But if you want Kerberos authentication, you'll need a Kerberos server as well. And keeping Kerberos servers in sync requires access to NTP servers. If you do use Kerberos servers, stick with version 5. Once these are configured, you'll note that those clients that connect to your servers have been previously authenticated with genuine Kerberos tickets.

One benefit of Kerberos is with services such as NFS. While NFSv4 doesn't directly authenticate by user, it can help to authenticate NFSv4 clients with Kerberos. Shared NFS directories that look for Kerberos tickets are less likely to fall into the hands of black-hat hackers.

The vsFTP service can be secured in a number of ways with respect to special directories, privilege management, timeouts, user lists, and more. While most vsFTP options are configured in the vsftpd.conf file, users can be limited in the ftpusers and user_list files. When enabled, PAM can further enhance vsFTP security.

With Samba, a Linux system can take a role as a more secure Windows server. It can be configured as a PDC, as a stand-alone server, and as a member of an Active Directory domain. Various Samba options can enhance obscurity, limit access by network interface and IP address, set up WINS name resolution, and more.

Samba can be configured with local databases for domains or can refer to other systems to verify usernames and passwords. Samba can be configured as a master browser for the LAN or even the Microsoft domain. Samba can be configured to serve Microsoft logon scripts and profiles to support a consistent level of access on different remote systems.

The SSH server can be configured in detail in the `sshd_config` file. Options can help regulate how users log in, the use of public keys, authentication with Kerberos tickets, and more. SSH commands even support secure encrypted connections to FTP servers, along with secure copying to and from remote SSH servers. SSH passphrases can be configured to enhance security even further; with a private/public key pair, the passphrase isn't even seen on the network.

Many users have to communicate over the Internet. Enterprise networks are connected over the Internet. Without encryption, such communications would be especially vulnerable. You can reduce the risks with IPSec connections. Such connections can be configured on a host-to-host or network-to-network basis. To support IPSec, the key protocol numbers are 50 and 51; the key port numbers are 50, 51, 500, and 4500. Red Hat and Ubuntu configure IPSec connections in different file locations, in the `/etc/sysconfig/network-scripts/` and `/etc/racoon/` directories, respectively.

Telnet is still a popular option for remote connections. Because it's a clear-text protocol, it's easy to find usernames and passwords sent over Telnet with tools such as Wireshark. If you can't convince users to convert to SSH, you can at least set up Telnet services associated with SSL or Kerberos.

If you need to set up remote connections by telephone modem, the most popular standard is RADIUS. It can be configured to authenticate using protocols such as PAP, CHAP, and EAP. It can be configured to authorize users via a variety of username/password databases. RADIUS includes a number of complex configuration files stored either in the `/etc/freeradius/` or the `/etc/raddb/` directory.

As you pay attention to clear-text protocols like Telnet, you should also remember the clear-text methods used for backups and e-mail. Fortunately, the advantages of SSH can be incorporated directly into rsync commands. In addition, there are secure versions of major e-mail protocols available that can be configured on client systems. Of course, that still requires a matching configuration on e-mail server systems, one of the topics covered in Chapter 9.

CHAPTER SUMMARY

While it's best to minimize the number of services on any one system, that's not always consistent with the best options for security. In this chapter, you examined Kerberos, along with how it can be used to enhance NFS security with the help of NTP services. Beyond Kerberos, the vsFTP service includes a wide variety of options that have made it the preferred FTP service for Red Hat, SUSE, and the developers of the Linux kernel.

This chapter also described how Samba can be configured in a number of different roles on Microsoft-based networks. It described how you can maximize the security features of SSH, including the use of passphrase-secured private/public key pairs. It showed you basic configuration options associated with IPSec. It described more secure options to regular clear-text Telnet for remote access. Also in the area of remote access, RADIUS is the major Linux package for connections from telephone modems. In addition, you need to know about secure options for the `rsync` commands and various e-mail protocols, as they normally also send data in clear text.

KEY CONCEPTS AND TERMS

Andrew Filesystem (AFS)

Authentication Header (AH) protocol

Backup Domain Controller (BDC)

Encapsulating Security Payload (ESP) protocol

Generic security services application program interface (GSSAPI)

Internet Key Exchange (IKE) protocol

Internet Message Access Protocol version 4 (IMAP4)

Kerberos

Kerberos principal

Kerberos realm

Kerberos ticket

Master browser

Network Address Translation (NAT) traversal protocol

Network Basic Input/Output System (NetBIOS)

Nonprivileged user

Open Systems Interconnection (OSI)

Post Office Protocol version 3 (POP3)

Primary Domain Controller (PDC)

Simple Mail Transfer Protocol (SMTP)

Windows Internet Name Service (WINS)

X11

CHAPTER 8 ASSESSMENT

1. Which of the following services are required with Kerberos?

   A. Telnet
   B. NFS
   C. NTP
   D. Samba

2. Which of the following files would you expect to contain Kerberos keys?

   A. `krb5.keys`
   B. `users.krb`
   C. `michael.key`
   D. `user.keytab`

3. The protocol that allows Kerberos to work with different file-sharing services is _____.

4. The vsFTP `directory` directive changes the default directory for anonymous access.

   A. True
   B. False

5. Which of the following Samba directives sets the name for the local server?

   A. `hostname`
   B. `netbios name`
   C. `server_name`
   D. `domain name`

6. If you want to set up a PDC, what should be the value of the `security` directive?

   A. `user`
   B. `domain`
   C. `server`
   D. `ads`

7. Which of the following bits of information is contained in a WINS server?

   A. Usernames
   B. Permissions
   C. NetBIOS names
   D. Hostnames

8. Name the full path to the directory with SSH keys for user `donna`.

9. Which of the following directives specify that SSH listens on a network card with a network address of 192.168.0.0?

   A. `ListenAddress 192.168.0.1`
   B. `ListenAddress 192.168.0.0/24`
   C. `ListenAddress 192.168.0.0/255.255.255.0`
   D. `ListenAddress 192.168.0.255`

10. In what file on a remote system would you copy an SSH public key?

   A. `.ssh/authorized_keys`
   B. `.ssh/id_rsa.pub`
   C. `.ssh/id_dsa.pub`
   D. `.ssh/id_authorized.pub`

11. TCP/IP port 443 is associated with IPSec connections.

   A. True
   B. False

12. Which of the following directories may contain configuration files for IPSec connections? (Select two.)

   A. `/etc/sysconfig/network-scripts/`
   B. `/etc/ipsec/`
   C. `/etc/network/`
   D. `/etc/racoon/`

13. Which of the following services or protocols can be used to add security to Telnet?

   A. SSL
   B. NTP
   C. SSH
   D. PAP

14. Which of the following authentication systems is not normally configured with RADIUS?

   A. CHAP
   B. PAP
   C. PPP
   D. EAP

15. Which of the following ports is a secure alternative for SMTP?

   A. 25
   B. 110
   C. 993
   D. 465

Networked Application Security

I N THIS CHAPTER, you'll examine the security features and options associated with a number of networked applications and services, including Apache; Squid; the Berkeley Internet Name Domain (BIND); mail transfer agents (MTAs) such as sendmail, Sendmail, and Postfix; Voice over IP (VoIP) services such as Asterisk; the Common UNIX Printing System (CUPS); and the Network Time Protocol (NTP). Options for obscurity are also addressed. Because Apache and BIND are especially popular options on the Internet, both application services are prime targets for black-hat hackers.

An extensive array of applications can be included with Apache. These applications include different databases and scripting languages. Squid is a Web proxy server; as such, it can cache and filter Web content. Attacks on Domain Name Service (DNS) software such as BIND can keep customers away from corporate Web sites; even worse, problems in the DNS database can redirect customers to malicious Web sites.

As e-mail and spam have become ubiquitous, black-hat hackers have looked for ways to break into e-mail services. Security on systems like sendmail and Postfix is especially important. As Asterisk has developed into the Linux open source Voice over IP (VoIP) application, black-hat hackers have looked at it as a different way to tap into corporate communications. Properly configured, CUPS security can apply to appropriate hosts and users. While a break into an NTP server may not have many direct consequences, the unsynchronized systems that may result can affect everything from Kerberos tickets to inventory databases.

Chapter 9 Topics

This chapter covers the following topics and concepts:

- Which options you have for secure Web sites with Apache
- How to work with Squid
- How to protect DNS services
- What the various e-mail transfer agents are
- How to use Asterisk
- How to limit printers
- How to protect time services
- How to obscure local and network services
- What best practices are for networked application security

Chapter 9 Goals

When you complete this chapter, you will be able to:

- Regulate Web sites, Web access, and name services
- Modify MTAs to focus on secure services
- Protect miscellaneous networked applications, including Asterisk and NTP
- Customize how printers are managed.

Web Services: Apache and Friends

Apache is the most popular Web server on the Internet. For years, Netcraft data on Web servers has listed Apache with more than 50 percent market share. It's easy to configure multiple Web sites on a single Apache server, all connected on a single IP address. It's almost as easy to configure these Web sites with Secure Sockets Layer (SSL) certificates to encrypt communications between the Web server and user client browsers. While Transport Layer Security (TLS) has superseded SSL in many cases, TLS is effectively just the next version of SSL. And most documentation still refers to SSL.

One reason Apache is so popular is that it does not work alone. It can be integrated with a variety of database and scripting languages. One popular combination is known as the Linux/Apache/MySQL/P (LAMP) stack, where the "P" can stand for **Perl**, **Python**, or **PHP: Hypertext Preprocessor (PHP)**.

The sections that follow describe the components of the **LAMP stack** and highlight some of the modules that are most frequently integrated with Apache. In following sections, you'll see some of the methods that can be used to limit access to a Web site and how you can configure Apache to serve secure Web sites.

Note that this book does not address the details on how to configure or create a regular or a secure Web site. For an excellent primer on the subject, see Rich Bowen and Ken Coar's *Apache Cookbook: Solutions and Examples for Apache Administrators*, published in 2008 by O'Reilly Media.

The LAMP Stack

As suggested earlier, the components of the LAMP stack vary depending on the preferred scripting language. Because this is a book on Linux, and because secure options for Apache are described later in this chapter, the focus of this section is on basic MySQL configuration (SQL is short for structured query language) and the associated scripting languages. This section is just an overview; there are many excellent books on both MySQL and each of the noted scripting languages.

> **TIP**
>
> On Ubuntu server systems, a quick way to install the packages of the LAMP stack is with the console-based `tasksel` browser. Run the `tasksel` command with administrative privileges. It'll install all the packages required for the LAMP stack.

The focus of this section is the Apache configuration files. The names and directories with these files vary by distribution. For example, on Red Hat systems, the main Apache configuration file is `httpd.conf` in the `/etc/httpd/conf/` directory. On Ubuntu systems, the main Apache configuration file is `apache2.conf` in the `/etc/apache2/` directory.

MySQL and Apache

Many Web sites require access to databases. Those databases may help with authentication, logs, inventory, and more. Appropriate packages may include software that links to the desired scripting language, such as Perl, Python, or PHP. Many excellent books on MySQL are available, including Paul Dubois's *MySQL (4th Edition)*, published in 2008 by Addison-Wesley. This section just describes security-related directives in the default version of the main MySQL configuration file.

The main MySQL configuration file is `my.cnf`. Depending on the distribution, you may find that file in the `/etc/` or `/etc/mysql/` directory. Security-related directives from that file are described in Table 9-1.

TABLE 9-1 Default security-related MySQL directives in `my.cnf`.

DIRECTIVE	DESCRIPTION
`bind-address`	IP address of associated network card to which MySQL listens
`datadir`	Directory with MySQL data; may require special protection
`port`	Port number
`ssl-ca`	SSL certificate authority file
`ssl-cert`	SSL certificate file
`ssl-key`	SSL certificate key file

9

Networked
Application Security

If you use MySQL, be sure to open port 3306 on any applicable firewall between the Web server and MySQL database server. Don't open that port on an external firewall (unless required for other reasons). If you prefer a different port, that's easy to configure in the main MySQL configuration file with the `port` directive.

NOTE

Now that Oracle has become the corporate sponsor of MySQL, the future of this open source database system is unknown. Oracle has its own excellent database systems. Fortunately, excellent open source database alternatives are available, including PostgreSQL. In fact, Red Hat Enterprise Linux includes PostgreSQL and not MySQL packages in its repositories. For more information, see *http://www.postgresql.org/*.

The first time you install MySQL on Debian-style systems, including Ubuntu, the installation process prompts you for a MySQL `root` password. This user is different from the standard Linux `root` administrative user, and should be configured with a different password. To set that password differently, use the `mysqladmin` command, similar to the following. In this command, the quotes are required around the new password.

```
# mysqladmin -u root password "newpassword"
```

Unless a MySQL `root` account is configured, any user on the local system has access to the MySQL database. That could be a significant security issue.

Apache and Scripting Languages

The installation of any scripting language should be a red flag for any security professional. If a black-hat hacker breaks into a system, that person could use that language to build more powerful malware within your network. However, a scripting language of some sort is normally required for an enterprise-level Web site. So when installing a group of packages such as the LAMP stack, it helps to choose one scripting language.

It's easier to monitor news for one scripting language for security updates. If multiple languages are installed, uninstall all but one if possible.

Apache Modules

One of the strengths of the Apache Web server is its modularity. If you have access to both Red Hat and Ubuntu systems, examine the differences. You'll learn more about how Apache can be configured. One list of modules is shown in Figure 9-1.

The process for disabling a module depends on how the Apache configuration files are set up. Current Ubuntu systems include `mods-available/` and `mods-enabled/` subdirectories in the `/etc/apache2/` directory. As the names suggest, those subdirectories list available and enabled modules. Obviously, it's best if the package associated with the module is uninstalled. But you can also use the `a2dismod` command. For example, the following command removes the PHP version 5 (`php5.conf`, `php5.load`) configuration files from the `mods-enabled/` subdirectory:

```
# a2dismod php5
```

```
michael@UbuntuHH:~$ \ls /etc/apache2/mods-enabled/
alias.conf            autoindex.conf  mime.load
alias.load            autoindex.load  negotiation.conf
auth_basic.load       cgi.load        negotiation.load
authn_file.load       dir.conf        setenvif.conf
authz_default.load    dir.load        setenvif.load
authz_groupfile.load  env.load        status.conf
authz_host.load       headers.load    status.load
authz_user.load       mime.conf
michael@UbuntuHH:~$
```

FIGURE 9-1

Apache modules
on Ubuntu.

You can reverse the process with the corresponding a2enmod command. Once loaded, you'll need to reload or restart the standard Apache script with a command like the following:

```
# /etc/init.d/apache2 force-reload
# /usr/sbin/apachectl -k restart
```

Current Red Hat systems don't include an equivalent command to disable or enable a module. So to disable a module, you'll need to remove or comment out the directive in the Apache configuration file. For example, the following directive enables common gateway interface (CGI) scripts:

```
LoadModule cgi_module modules/mod_cgi.so
```

On both systems, you can review currently loaded modules with the apachectl (Red Hat) or apache2ctl (Ubuntu) command, with the -t -D DUMP_MODULES option.

On Red Hat systems, some modules are loaded with configuration files in the /etc/httpd/conf.d/ directory. For example, if PHP is installed, you'll see the php.conf file on that directory. Such modules are loaded courtesy of the following directive in the main Apache configuration file:

```
Include conf.d/*.conf
```

So if you were to change the extension of the php.conf file, Apache would not load that module the next time it is reloaded or restarted.

The modules that should remain loaded depend on the desired functionality of the Apache server. For a list of available modules, refer to the relevant section of Apache documentation at *http://httpd.apache.org/docs/2.2/mod/*. The developers of the Apache project have been consistent with their documentation; in other words, if you're working with Apache version 2.0, modules are documented at *http://httpd.apache.org/docs/2.0/mod/*.

Security-Related Apache Directives

In this section, you'll look at the main Apache configuration file and focus on security-related directives not otherwise covered in the sections that follow. This section is focused on the default Red Hat version of the Apache configuration file.

A couple of security-related Apache directives are `Listen` and `ServerTokens`. The `Listen` directive can specify an alternative port for Web pages. For example, the following directive can be found in the configuration for an SSL-enabled Web site. Port 443 is the standard for the secure Hypertext Transfer Protocol (HTTPS).

```
Listen 443
```

The `Listen` directive can also specify the IP address of a network card, which is useful if there are multiple network cards on the local system. For example, the following directive would listen for requests through port 443 on the noted IP address:

```
Listen 192.168.100.10:443
```

The `ServerTokens` directive can be of special interest. It determines what's seen if a user navigates to a nonexistent Web page. While it's nominally an "error message," that message can provide far too much information to a black-hat hacker. In the default configuration `ServerTokens Full` is set, which leads to the following error message sent in response to a nonexistent Web page request:

```
Apache/2.2.3 (Red Hat) DAV/2 PHP/5.1.6 mod_ssl/2.2.3
OpenSSL/0.9.8e-fips-rhel5 Server at 192.168.100.1 Port 80
```

If a black-hat hacker recognizes a version of one of these applications that happens to be vulnerable, he's in business, and your systems will be at risk. So ideally, this information should be kept as minimal as possible. For example, the `ServerTokens Prod` directive leads to the following error message:

```
Apache Server at 192.168.100.1 Port 80
```

Perhaps an even better way to deny information to a black-hat hacker is a custom error page. Look for the `DocumentRoot` and `ErrorDocument` directives in the Apache configuration file. It'll help you identify an appropriate location for a custom error file. In other words, black-hat hackers don't even have to know that this is an Apache Web server.

KeepAlive Directives

The next important security-related directive in the Apache configuration file is `KeepAlive`, which supports persistent connections from remote systems.

In a more secure system, the values of `KeepAlive` directives are kept to a minimum. But such a configuration is not consistent with the availability of Web pages served by Apache. Good values for `KeepAlive` directives do improve client performance.

Related directives (`MaxKeepAliveRequests`, `KeepAliveTimeout`) are almost self-explanatory and are well explained by the comments in the Red Hat version of the configuration file. In brief, while `MaxKeepAliveRequests` specifies the maximum number of allowed keep-alive requests on each connection, the `KeepAliveTimeout` directive specifies the wait period for the next request, in seconds.

TABLE 9-2 Standard Multi-Processing Module directives.

DIRECTIVE	DESCRIPTION
StartServers	Child server processes created during the Apache start process
MinSpareServers	Minimum idle child server processes
MaxSpareServers	Maximum idle child server processes
ServerLimit	Maximum number of clients; also see ThreadLimit in the Apache documentation
MaxClients	Maximum number of client connections processed simultaneously
MaxRequestsPerChild	Maximum number of requests per child server process
MinSpareThreads	Minimum number of idle threads to handle additional requests
MaxSpareThreads	Maximum number of idle threads to handle additional requests
ThreadsPerChild	Number of threads created per child process
MaxRequestsPerChild	Maximum number of requests in the life of a child process

Multi-Processing Modules (MPMs)

Closely related to the KeepAlive directives are the **Multi-Processing Modules (MPMs)** directives. Both the default Red Hat and Ubuntu versions of the Apache configuration file use nearly all the same directives, which are described in Table 9-2. These directives relate most closely to the availability of the Apache system. While you could maximize each of the directives shown, they're limited by the hardware of the local system, other processes that may be running, and the space available to the system. Some trial and error may be required to find optimal settings for these directives. These directives are not in alphabetical order, so they more closely match how they're configured in the Apache configuration file.

An Apache User and Group

Apache processes should be configured and owned by a single unprivileged user, typically apache or www-data. Such ownership can be configured with the User and Group directives:

```
User apache
Group apache
```

To ensure such users are unprivileged, make sure anyone who logs into that account doesn't get a shell. That can be configured in the /etc/passwd file. If a distribution configures such users with a regular shell like /bin/sh, that is not as secure as a fake shell such as /bin/false or /sbin/nologin. With a fake shell, a user who is actually able to log into such accounts does not get a command-line shell.

Do Not Allow Overrides with `.htaccess`

An `.htaccess` file can be a handy way to add Apache directives for specific directories or virtual hosts. But the `.htaccess` file can be dangerous. With the dot in front, it's a hidden file, outside the view of a normal search.

If a black-hat hacker is able to add an `.htaccess` file to a Web server directory, that user can override anything you've configured with directives in that file. To disable the use of the `.htaccess` file, add the following directive in any stanza with the `Directory` tag:

```
AllowOverride None
```

Do Not Allow Access to User Directories

It's probably far too easy to configure access to user home directories on the system with the Apache server. With the `mod_userdir` module and the `UserDir enable` directive, user directories can be shared over the Apache Web server. Unless you want files in user home directories exposed to the world, it's something to disable.

To disable Apache-based access to user home directories, disable the `mod_userdir` module. If you're not prepared to do that, at least avoid the `UserDir enable` directive unless the system includes only guest accounts with files that can be shared publicly.

Minimize Available Options

The `Options` directive is important. It allows you to configure extra features within a `Directory` stanza. The default setting is `Options All`, which includes a number of features shown in Table 9-3 that are inconsistent with a secure system. It includes all features except `MultiViews`.

Each of these `Options` directives may be a potential security risk. Because the default includes all but one of the directives, any black-hat hacker who is able to insert a file

TABLE 9-3 Apache `Options` and associated features.

DIRECTIVE	DESCRIPTION
ExecCGI	Allows the execution of CGI scripts if the `mod_cgi` module is enabled
FollowSymLinks	Supports the following of symbolically linked files in the directory
Includes	Allows the use of server-side includes if the `mod_include` module is enabled
IncludesNOEXEC	Allows the use of server-side includes except for executable files
Indexes	Lists files in directories where no `DirectoryIndex` file, typically `index.html`, is included if the `mod_autoindex` module is enabled
MultiViews	Supports error-tolerant reads of filenames
SymLinksIfOwnerMatch	Supports the following of symbolically linked files in the directory if the link and the file are owned by the same user

into one of the listed directories may cause problems. Alternatively, if that user is able to delete an `index.html` file, it may expose that directory to all who browse that system.

The way to avoid the security risks associated with Table 9-3 is to disable all `Options` with the following directive:

```
Options None
```

Configure Protection on a Web Site

Typically, multiple Web sites are configured on individual Apache Web servers. That's made possible with an appropriate configuration of virtual hosts. Web site accessibility can be limited to a certain IP address network with the following directives, which deny access from all systems except those that send requests from addresses with the noted IP network address and network mask:

```
Order deny,allow
Deny from all
Allow from 192.168.0.0/255.255.255.0
```

The same group of directives can be used in a stanza for a specific directory. If desired, you can substitute a partial or complete domain name such as `example.org` or `.com` f or the noted IP address.

One other protection system is based on users created with the `htpasswd` or `htdigest` commands. If the file with users and passwords is `/etc/httpd/conf.d/apacheusers`, you could take advantage with the following directives restricting access to a specific Web site or directory:

```
AuthName "Authorized users only"
AuthType Digest
AuthUsersFile /etc/httpd/conf.d/apacheusers
Require valid-user
```

Users who are allowed to access the resource can be limited by username or groupname.

Configure a Secure Web site

By default, Web sites that use the HTTPS protocol use port 443. But enabling the appropriate SSL module requires different commands on different systems. On Red Hat systems, when the `mod_ssl` package is installed, an `ssl.conf` file with sample directives for a secure Web site can be found in the `/etc/httpd/conf.d/` directory. On Ubuntu systems, when the `a2enmod` command described earlier is applied to the `ssl` module, similar sample directives can also be found in an `ssl.conf` file, this time in the `/etc/apache2/mods-enabled/` directory.

Because the contents of these files are normally included in the main Apache configuration file with an appropriate `Include` directive, all you need to do is customize the `ssl.conf` file for the desired secure Web site. But a secure Web site requires a certificate authority.

TABLE 9-4 Certificate authority (CA) file extensions.	
FILE EXTENSION	**DESCRIPTION**
.crt	Configured for the server certificate
.csr	Created with the certificate signing request
.key	Associated with the CA key

Configure a Certificate Authority

A **certificate authority (CA)** is an entity that issues digital certificates. The actual certificates are based on a private/public key pair. While such key pairs can be generated locally, they would not be official CAs associated with major online enterprises. Such key pairs can be expensive. However, "official" CAs are required if you want a Web site that doesn't lead to an "invalid security certificate" error. If you're interested, such official CAs are available from companies such as VeriSign and GoDaddy.

The standard filenames associated with CAs are arbitrary. However, there are standard file extensions for CAs, as listed in Table 9-4.

To create a self-signed certificate, you can use the openssl command. For example, the following command creates a CA key file named server.key, generated with Rivest, Shamir, Adelman (RSA) parameters, using a 256-bit Advanced Encryption Standard (aes256) cipher of 1,024 bytes.

```
# openssl genrsa -aes256 -out server.key 1024
```

This command prompts for a passphrase. Once the server.key file is created, you can create a certificate-signing request file. The following command uses that server.key file to create that server.csr file.

```
# openssl req -new -key server.key -out server.csr
```

You're prompted for the following information. If you're setting up an official certificate-signing request, the answers must be true and verifiable.

- The passphrase used to create the server.key file.
- A country name, based on a standard two-letter country code. Official two-letter country codes can be found in the ISO standard 3166.
- The full name of the state or province associated with the Web server.
- The full name of the locality associated with the Web server.
- The full name of the company or organization behind the Web server.
- An appropriate organizational unit name.
- The name of the responsible administrator.
- The e-mail address of the responsible administrator.
- A challenge password and alternative company name that can be used to verify the request.

The `server.csr` file that's created by the given command can be used as part of an official CA request. If you want to purchase an official CA, that file is part of what you'd send to a CA such as VeriSign or GoDaddy.

If you choose to create your own self-signed certificate for secure Web sites, the following command creates the actual server certificate file-in this case, `server.crt`.

```
# openssl x509 -req -days 30 -in server.csr
↪-signkey server.key -out server.crt
```

The private/public key infrastructure is based on the `x.509` standard of the International Telecommunications Union (ITU). Based on the command, the newly created `server.crt` certificate is good for 30 days.

The `server.crt` and `server.key` files (the filenames can vary) can then be used in conjunction with the `SSLCertificateFile` and `SSLCertificateKeyFile` directives. But those two directives just scratch the surface of what can be done with SSL and Apache. For a more complete list of Apache SSL directives, see *http://httpd.apache.org/docs/2.2/mod/mod_ssl.html/*.

Working with Squid

Any Web proxy server can be configured for two basic purposes. It can cache frequently accessed information, and it can regulate user access to remote Web sites.

As for caching, the proxy server for an enterprise where hundreds of users access the same online dictionary Web site can store that information locally. The definitions on that dictionary would be accessed from the Internet only once. Further requests for the same definitions would be returned in this case from the Squid proxy server. A time limit is associated with cached data, to make sure that data isn't stale. Because access to locally cached data is faster, perceived Internet performance is improved for local users.

Squid uses the **Inter-Cache Protocol (ICP)** for transfers between peer and parent/child caching servers. It can be used in two directions. As a traditional proxy server, it caches data on behalf of other systems on the local network. As a front-end accelerator, it caches on behalf of clients on remote networks.

Of course, Squid can be configured to avoid caching Internet information that may change in real-time, such as information related to scores of sports events. And obviously, it should also be configured to avoid caching otherwise private information such as user logins to remote financial Web sites.

As for regulation, Squid can block access to certain domains. If you want to keep users from navigating to certain domains, Squid can access lists of such domains. Of course, the reliability of such limits depends on restrictions. In other words, if a client can bypass a Squid proxy server, users can bypass Squid limits on those domains.

> **technical TIP**
>
> With a few firewall rules, you can channel all Web requests from inside your network through a proxy server. On the gateway between the internal network and the Internet, you'll need to regulate outgoing traffic. Specifically, with the following `iptables` rule, all traffic destined for port 80 for regular outgoing Web connections is redirected to port 3128, the standard for proxy server connections:
>
> ```
> iptables -t nat -A PREROUTING -p tcp --dport 80
> ↪-j REDIRECT --to-port 3128
> ```
>
> For more information on firewall rules and the `iptables` command, see Chapter 7.

Basic Squid Configuration

Squid is perhaps the leading open source proxy server. It is a caching proxy that supports Hypertext Transfer Protocol (HTTP), HTTPS, and FTP communications. The basic Squid configuration file is `squid.conf`, in the `/etc/squid/` directory. Although the file includes more than 4,000 lines, it is simple to configure. First, the standard port number associated with Squid communication is 3128, which is documented in the following directive:

```
http_port 3128
```

Generally, access is limited based on access control lists (ACLs). Although they share the same acronym as access control lists for Linux files, they are different within Squid. ACLs on Squid can limit access by IP address, hardware address, source domain name, destination domain name, time, Universal Resource Locator (URL), port number, protocol, browser, referrer, username, and more.

The simplest use of Squid ACLs limits access by IP address. For example, the following directive specifies an ACL rule for a local source private IP address network along with the localhost system:

```
acl localhost src 127.0.0.1/32
acl some_net src 192.168.0.0/24
```

Be aware, this second command replaces the following default, which allows access from all systems:

```
acl all src 0.0.0.0/0.0.0.0
```

Then, the following commands allow access from the localhost system, along with systems on the noted private IP address network, before denying access to all other systems:

```
http_access allow localhost
http_access allow some_net
http_access deny all
```

This is the minimum configuration required to set up Squid on a local area network (LAN). The next step is to create basic cache directories in the /var/spool/squid/ directory with the following command:

```
# squid -z
```

Once the Squid service is running, you should be able to set up client browsers on the local network to connect through the Squid service on port 3128. Of course, you'll also have to make sure that port is open in any applicable firewalls.

If you want to configure access to additional ports, examine the acl SSL_ports and acl Safe_ports directives. In the default squid.conf file, these directives are used to specify ports for secure and other connections. These directives are often coupled with the following directives:

```
http_access deny !Safe_ports
http_access deny !SSL_ports
```

The exclamation point (!) is also known as a bang. In code, it's a reference to "anything but." In other words, the directives shown here deny access to all but configured Safe_ports and SSL_ports.

Of course, with more than 4,000 lines, Squid can do a lot more. The sections that follow just scratch the surface of what Squid can do.

 TIP

If you've activated SELinux, be sure to activate the squid_connect_any boolean in the /selinux/booleans/ directory.

Security-Related Squid Directives

Squid can do a lot more. This section just scratches the surface of security-related squid directives. This section is based on the default squid.conf configuration file for version 2.6. These directives include the following:

- **auth_param**—A directive that can be configured with a basic, a digest, or an NT LAN Manager (NTLM) authentication scheme.
- **authenticate_***—A series of directives that provides a timeout for connections from clients.
- **acl**—Basic Squid-related access control list directives were described earlier in this chapter.
- **http_access**—Basic Squid-related http_access directives were described earlier in this chapter.
- **http_reply_access**—Specifies systems allowed to answer replies. While the default is http_reply_access allow all, limits can regulate what your users can access online.
- **icp_access**—Access should be limited to other Squid caching servers.
- **htcp_access**—Based on the Hypertext Caching Protocol (HTCP), it sets ACLs to discover other caching servers.

Limit Remote Access with Squid

You can configure limits on remote client access to undesirable domains with the `http_access` and `acl` directives. The simplest way to put this into effect is with a text file of undesirable domain names. For this section, call it `baddomains.txt` in the `/etc/squid/` directory.

In the Squid configuration file, the following line creates an ACL associated with destination domains:

```
acl baddomains dstdomain "/etc/squid/baddomains.txt"
```

Once the ACL is created, the following `http_access` command can deny access to that list of undesirable domains:

```
http_access deny baddomains
```

For detailed information on the latest developments in Squid, see *http://www.squid-cache.org/* along with *Squid: The Definitive Guide* by Duane Wessels, published in 2004 by O'Reilly Media.

DNS: BIND and More

This book does not address the detailed configuration of a DNS server. However, it does address security issues related to such configuration. The focus of this section is the Berkeley Internet Name Domain (BIND) software. With that in mind, you should be aware of the four different types of DNS servers available:

- **Master**—A master DNS server is the authoritative server for a domain.
- **Slave**—A slave DNS server relies on a master DNS server for data.
- **Caching-only**—A caching-only DNS server refers requests to other DNS servers. It also stores recent requests in a local cache.
- **Forwarding-only**—A forwarding-only DNS server refers all requests to other DNS servers.

The Basics of DNS on the Internet

DNS is a distributed database of domain names and IP addresses. Domain names like `www.example.com.` are properly shown with a period at the end. That period is the root domain. That top-level database of DNS servers is known as a root nameserver. If you've installed DNS software on a local system, you can review the list of root nameservers in a file like `named.root` or `db.root`.

Each of these root nameservers can refer to authoritative nameservers at the next level, for domain names such as `com.`, `net.`, or `org.`. Those authoritative nameservers can go one level deeper to identify the authoritative nameservers for domains such as `jblearning.com.`.

When a client computer searches for the IP address associated with a domain name, it first looks in the database associated with the local DNS server. If that domain name is not found locally, that DNS server may be configured to send the request to another DNS server. If the domain name is still not found, that request may be sent to one of the root nameservers. That search process is known as a **recursive query**.

A substantial number of DNS servers may be involved in a search for a domain name. That provides plenty of opportunity for a black-hat hacker to jump into the search to redirect unsuspecting users to fake domains. To that end, DNS is a frequent target of attacks. One way to redirect unsuspecting users to fake domains is based on an attack known as cache poisoning.

DNS Network Configuration

With such potential vulnerabilities in mind, you may consider configuring different kinds of DNS servers on different parts of a network. To that end, it's important to protect the master authoritative DNS server for your network. Review the network configuration shown in Figure 9-2. It is the same configuration shown in Chapters 6 and 7, with DNS servers added.

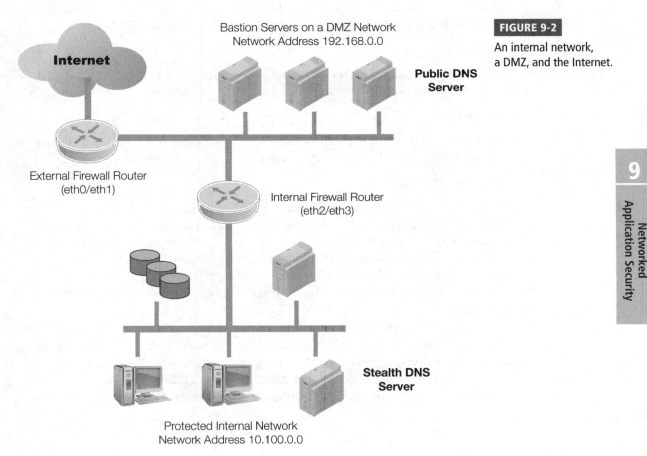

FIGURE 9-2

An internal network, a DMZ, and the Internet.

Bastion Servers on a DMZ Network
Network Address 192.168.0.0

Public DNS Server

Internet

External Firewall Router
(eth0/eth1)

Internal Firewall Router
(eth2/eth3)

Stealth DNS Server

Protected Internal Network
Network Address 10.100.0.0

9

Networked
Application Security

The best place to protect the master authoritative DNS server for a domain is on an internal network, protected by multiple firewalls. You can then configure a second master server with stronger limits that acquires information directly and only from the master DNS server on the internal network.

One method to put this into effect, suggested by Ron Aitchison in his book *Pro DNS and BIND*, published in 2005 by Apress, is the concept of the stealth nameserver. As noted in Chapter 4 of that book, such a DNS server "does not appear in any publicly visible NS records for the domain."

Under that configuration, the DNS server functionality for the domain is split between a public DNS server (possibly within a demilitarized zone [DMZ]) and a stealth DNS behind a firewall.

The public DNS server would provide authoritative-only responses. It would not cache any information. It would not accept any recursive queries. For more information on the related risks, see the previous section.

Secure BIND Configuration

A typical secure BIND configuration file would include a number of directives to minimize its vulnerabilities to black-hat hackers. For example, the following directive does not provide any information on the current version number of BIND software:

```
version "not listed";
```

An `authoritative-only` name server should not search other DNS servers for additional information. The following directive disables such recursive searches:

```
recursion no;
```

Any secure DNS server should not allow transfers of zone databases to minimize the risk of cache poisoning. The following directive allows transfers to no other DNS servers:

```
allow-transfer{none;};
```

A second element of a secure BIND configuration involves a chroot jail. It's automatically configured on Red Hat systems based on the `bind-chroot` package. It can be configured on Ubuntu systems as well; one set of instructions is available online in the Community Ubuntu Documentation, at *https://help.ubuntu.com/community/BIND9ServerHowto/*. In either case, a black-hat hacker who breaks into the BIND directory system does not have administrative privileges and cannot get to the directories of other services on that system.

If you have to allow transfers between DNS servers, take advantage of the **Transition SIGnature (TSIG)** key, normally stored in the `rndc.key` file. It can be coupled with a `keys` directive in the DNS configuration file. An `allow-update` directive can be coupled with configured TSIG keys. Because it is standard practice to create new TSIG keys on a regular basis, you should become familiar with the `dnssec-keygen` command.

Security may include limits on access. That's made possible with the `acl` directive. Properly configured, it can help define a group of IP addresses. One example is shown here:

```
acl "ipgroup1" { 192.168.0.1; 10.20.30.0/24; };
```

The `ipgroup1` term can then be used in other directives.

A BIND Database

A standard authoritative BIND database should include records for all IP addresses on a domain. Such records are stored in what are known as zone files.

If the functionality of a DNS server is split as described earlier in a stealth configuration, you'd see two different zone file databases. One database, for the DNS server within the internal network, would include IP addresses for all systems on the network. The second database, for the `authoritative-only` DNS server in the DMZ, would include just the information required for communications from outside systems. Specifically, that database would include the IP address any other DMZ DNS servers, any other public servers such as Web servers, and any e-mail servers for delivery.

DNS Targets to Protect

To summarize, when configuring an authoritative DNS server for a public system, you'll want to protect **zone files** and **zone updates**, as well as prevent **cache poisoning**. Yes, these are three different concepts explained in previous sections.

- **Zone files**—A complete zone file would include hostname and IP-address data on all systems on the local domain, a database of systems from which a black-hat hacker can pick and choose for attacks. Public zone files should be limited to that information required for Internet communications, including Web servers and e-mail servers.

- **Zone updates**—A slave DNS server relies on a master DNS server for data. A black-hat hacker who is able to configure a slave DNS server could get the network DNS data.

- **Cache poisoning**—Data forwarded from DNS servers maintained by black-hat hackers could redirect your customers to malicious Web sites.

Mail Transfer Agents: sendmail, Sendmail, Postfix, and More

The alphabet soup associated with many Linux services continues with various e-mail services. E-mail client applications such as Evolution and Thunderbird are known as **mail user agents (MUAs)**. Services such as fetchmail that collect e-mail from networks are known as **mail retrieval agents (MRAs)**. E-mail services that send such mail along to client applications are known as **mail delivery agents (MDAs)**. When e-mail client applications send messages for delivery, they use **mail transfer agents (MTAs)** such as sendmail, Sendmail, and Postfix.

Yes, there is a difference between sendmail and Sendmail. The lower-case sendmail application is the standard open source MTA that is installed by default on Red Hat systems. It is an open source project sponsored the Sendmail consortium. The upper-case Sendmail application is a commercial product used by enterprises; for example, it's the MTA engine behind Google's Gmail.

Sometimes, **mail submission agents (MSAs)** are integrated with MTAs in services such as sendmail and Postfix. When MSAs and MTAs work together, the MSA can focus on authenticating users and the MTA can prevent relaying from users who don't have local e-mail addresses.

In any case, MTAs such as sendmail and Postfix are configured primarily for the Simple Mail Transfer Protocol (SMTP) and the submission protocol on ports 25 and 587, respectively. MDAs such as Dovecot can be configured to manage traffic using the Post Office Protocol version 3 (POP3) and the Internet Message Access Protocol (IMAP), along with the related protocols with security in their names: POP3S and IMAPS.

Open Source sendmail

The open source sendmail MTA is the default outbound e-mail engine for many Linux distributions. When installed, configuration files can be found in the /etc/mail/ directory. Because the main configuration file (sendmail.cf) includes nearly 2,000 lines, it's a highly customizable system. But because the main configuration file is so large, it has intimidated many Linux administrators. Complexity can be a drawback with respect to security. If you don't understand a security update, the changes you make to the sendmail software may not address the security issue.

That complexity led to the development of the sendmail macro configuration file, sendmail.mc. It's written in a format that is easier to explain. The dnl directives in that file are comment characters. All information after the dnl on a line is ignored. Some important security-related directives from the default version of the configuration file are described here. First, any include directives include the contents of the filename described.

Next, the VERSIONID directive provides a comment on the file. In some cases, it may be based on the actual version number of the released sendmail software, which is something that you want to avoid providing a black-hat hacker. To that end, the following directive may be safer:

```
VERSIONID(`setup for linux')dnl
```

One odd format in sendmail configuration files is the quotes. Such quoted directives have a back quote (`) at the start and a regular single quote (') at the end of the quote. Any define options that follow specify parameters such as files or limits. For example, the following directive specifies the name of the file with user aliases:

```
define(`ALIAS_FILE', `/etc/aliases')dnl
```

More important, they may include authentication methods. For example, the following TRUST_AUTH_MECH directive specifies a list of trusted authentication mechanisms. The confAUTH_MECHANISMS directive lists options offered for authentication. So if these directives from the default Red Hat version of the sendmail.mc file are activated, users who connect to these systems from an MUA client such as Evolution or even Microsoft Outlook can choose from external Message Digest 5 (MD5) associated with the **Java Cryptography Extension (JCE)**, MD5 associated with a **challenge-response authentication mechanism (CRAM)**, regular, or plain-text logins.

```
dnl TRUST_AUTH_MECH(`EXTERNAL DIGEST-MD5 CRAM-MD5 LOGIN PLAIN')dnl

dnl define(`confAUTH_MECHANISMS', `EXTERNAL GSSAPI DIGEST-MD5
↪CRAM-MD5 LOGIN PLAIN')dnl
```

Generally, regular or plain-text logins should not be used without some encryption. But that may not always be possible with some older MUA clients, such as an older version of mutt. Fortunately, several authentication mechanisms are available and configured, including the generic security service application programming interface (GSSAPI) as well as the MD5 options just described.

You may want to create SSL certificates using the private and public key pair techniques described earlier in this chapter for secure Web sites. The following directives, if active, search for needed certificates and keys in the noted files:

```
dnl define(`confCACERT_PATH', `/etc/pki/tls/certs')dnl

dnl define(`confCACERT', `/etc/pki/tls/certs/ca-bundle.crt')dnl

dnl define(`confSERVER_CERT',
↪`/etc/pki/tls/certs/sendmail.pem')dnl

dnl define(`confSERVER_KEY',
↪`/etc/pki/tls/certs/sendmail.pem')dnl
```

The FEATURE directive includes an extensive array of options. Some important options for this directive are listed in Table 9-5.

---

technical TIP

With the FEATURE directive, avoid specifying the relay_local_from, relay_mail_from, and accept_unresolvable_domains options, because that can open your system to use by spammers. Networks served by the sendmail service can be configured in /etc/mail/access.

In addition, you can take advantage of the /etc/mail/access file to reject e-mails from the domains of known spammers and black-hat hackers. For more information on anti-spam features in sendmail, see *http://www.sendmail.org/m4/anti_spam.html/*.

TABLE 9-5 Open source sendmail FEATURE options.

OPTION	DESCRIPTION
accept_unresolvable_domains	Supports access from domains; *avoid this option* if possible
always_add_domain	Adds the domain name even on e-mail to local users
blacklist_recipients	Allows you to specify users in /etc/mail/access that should not receive e-mail
domaintable	Maps addresses from one domain to another
mailertable	Overrides routing to specific domains
redirect	Rejects mail sent to redirected e-mail addresses
relay_local_from	Supports access from all e-mails that specify a local e-mail address; *avoid this option* if possible
relay_mail_from	Supports access from all e-mails that specify an e-mail address in /etc/mail/access; *avoid this option* if possible
smrsh	Uses a shell more restricted than the regular bash shell
use_ct_file	Reads /etc/mail/trusted-users for a list of users who are trusted
use_cw_file	Reads /etc/mail/local-host-names for a list of alternative hostnames

The DAEMON_OPTIONS directive in default files limits access to the local system. If you want to allow the server to listen to all systems, comment out the line. If you want to allow the server to listen to the network card with an IP address of 192.168.0.10, change the directive as shown for Internet Protocol version 4 (IPv4) addresses.

```
DAEMON_OPTIONS(`Family=inet,  Name=MTA-v4, Port=smtp,
➥ Addr=192.168.0.10')dnl
DAEMON_OPTIONS(`Family=inet,  Name=MSP-v4, Port=submission,
➥ Addr=192.168.0.10')dnl
```

The port numbers, as listed in /etc/services, are 25 and 587. If you're configuring e-mail services for remote systems, be sure appropriate firewalls allow access through those ports. Unfortunately, if you use a specific IP address in that directive, that can lead to problems. Some firewalls block messages from certain IP addresses, such as those from private IP address networks. In that case, you could comment out these directives.

As suggested in the opening comments to the sendmail.mc file, once configuration changes are made to this file and other files in the /etc/mail/ directory, the following command processes those changes to the sendmail.cf and .db files in that directory:

```
make -C /etc/mail
```

Commercial Sendmail

Eric Allman, the creator of the open source sendmail server, founded Sendmail, Inc. to extend the product into the enterprise. Sendmail, Inc. sponsors developers who work on open source sendmail. In addition, Sendmail, Inc. has created a number of commercial products with commercial code. Much of this code is eventually released as open source software and incorporated into open source sendmail. Nevertheless, commercial Sendmail is a different product.

As suggested at *http://www.sendmail.com/sm/solutions/*, commercial Sendmail products are available in four areas:

- **Gateway protection**—Includes options to filter, process, and control messages before they are accepted on the network.

- **Inbound protection**—Specifies requirements for clean and authenticated e-mail messages.

- **Outbound protection**—Supports compliance of outgoing e-mail messages to organizational policies.

- **Internal protection**—Addresses multiple domains on the same network.

As you can see, the functionality of commercial Sendmail products in many ways goes beyond that of the open source sendmail software.

The Postfix Alternative

Because of the complexity of open source sendmail software, many administrators prefer alternatives. One relatively popular open source alternative is Postfix. It's the default MTA for the Ubuntu and SUSE Linux distributions. Methods for configuring Postfix vary. For example, on Ubuntu systems, the following command provides a number of prompts for configuring this MTA:

```
# dpkg-reconfigure postfix
```

Basic options include the following:

- **Internet site**—Configures Postfix to send and receive e-mail using SMTP.
- **Internet with smarthost**—Integrates the procmail MRA with Postfix.
- **Satellite system**—Sets up Postfix to transmit e-mail to a different system.
- **Local only**—Limits the Postfix configuration to users on the local system.

This section assumes you've selected Internet with smarthost, the most capable of the Postfix options. Once selected, you're prompted for the following information:

1. The domain name covered by this Postfix server, such as `example.org`
2. The relay host for outgoing e-mail, such as an SMTP server for an ISP (if this e-mail server is not a satellite system, you may choose to leave this blank)
3. An e-mail address of the actual mail system administrator

4. A list of domains and hostnames governed by this server

5. Whether to force synchronous updates, which is unnecessary unless the Internet connection is not reliable

6. A list of IP address networks governed by this server; a sample list would look like the following line:

   127.0.0.0/8 192.168.0.0/24 10.100.0.0/16

7. Whether to configure procmail for local delivery, to appropriate directories for local user accounts

8. A limit of mailbox sizes, in bytes

9. A local address extension (rarely changed)

10. Whether to use IPv4, Internet Protocol version 6 (IPv6), or both for addressing

The choices made in these steps are written to the `main.cf` file in the `/etc/postfix/` directory. Take a look at this file. You may want to change a few more things. For example, the following directive would deny information about the server to any black-hat hacker:

```
smtpd banner = "some email service"
```

If you want to secure this service with SSL or TLS certificates, the following directives provide a guide on the types of files to be created and their expected directory locations:

```
smtpd_tls_cert_file=/etc/ssl/certs/ssl-cert-snakeoil.pem
smtpd_tls_key_file=/etc/ssl/private/ssl-cert-snakeoil.key
```

As noted by the `alias_maps` directive, e-mail aliases are stored in the same `/etc/aliases` file configured for sendmail. Finally, some systems limit Postfix access to the localhost system with the `inet_interfaces` directive. While you could specify a certain IP address on the local system, that IP address is attached to the message. That could cause problems for the message at a firewall that filters out messages from private IP addresses. In that case, you'd want to leave the default value for that directive:

```
inet_interfaces = all
```

Dovecot for POP and IMAP

As suggested earlier, Dovecot is an MDA that receives e-mail messages from SMTP services and collects them for delivery to MUAs such as Evolution, Outlook, and Thunderbird. The configuration file is `dovecot.conf`, which may be located in the `/etc/` or `/etc/dovecot/` directory, depending on the distribution.

While the default Dovecot configuration file is long, the steps needed to configure this file are pretty simple. First, the `protocols` directive lets you define which protocols are covered by this server:

```
protocols = imap imaps pop3 pop3s
```

If you've included secure protocols, be sure to retain the following directive:

```
ssl_disable = no
```

Of course, secure protocols require SSL support, made possible in Dovecot with the following directives:

```
#ssl_cert_file = /etc/ssl/certs/ssl-cert-snakeoil.pem
#ssl_key_file = /etc/ssl/private/ssl-cert-snakeoil.key
```

The protocol directive can help define the IP address of the network card to which Dovecot listens, along with any nonstandard port numbers. The following examples use nonstandard port numbers for the four addressed protocols on the noted IP address:

```
protocol imap
↪{ listen = 192.168.0.10:10143 ssl_listen = *:10993  }
protocol pop3
↪{ listen = 192.168.0.10:10110 ssl_listen = *:10995 }
```

More E-mail Services

These are just a few of the excellent e-mail services available. Other important SMTP services include Exim and Qmail. Related to security on e-mail services is spam. To that end, SpamAssassin is covered in Chapter 11.

If You Asterisk

Asterisk is the open source software implementation of a private branch exchange (PBX) program for telephone networks. As such, it is a VoIP solution for telephone communications. While much of Asterisk is released under an open source license, some Asterisk software is proprietary. The software available from *http://www.asterisk.org/* is developed by a group known as the Open Source Telephony Project. The project is sponsored by Digium, known as the Asterisk Company. The software available from Digium includes proprietary components. For more information on proprietary options, see *http://www. digium.com/en/*.

This section is focused on security issues related to the open source Asterisk software available from *http://www.asterisk.org/* or already loaded on Linux repositories for major distributions including Ubuntu and Fedora. With more than 60 configuration files, detailed configuration options for Asterisk are beyond what can be covered in this book. See the References section for a couple of excellent books on Asterisk.

When considering Asterisk, be aware that while an occasional dropped packet may not be a big deal, reliably speedy packet flow is important to keep conversations from becoming jumpy. Based on the characteristics of various protocols in the Transmission Control Protocol/Internet Protocol (TCP/IP) suite, the best fit for such communications is the User Datagram Protocol (UDP). Asterisk communications, like other VoIP communications, use the **Session Initiation Protocol (SIP)** and the **Real-time Transport Protocol (RTP)** to send data through UDP packets. If this seems like a bunch of alphabet soup, read the noted books in the References section.

Basic Asterisk Configuration

Asterisk configuration files are typically installed in the `/etc/asterisk/` directory. Most of the configuration filenames relate to different features. Asterisk configuration is centered around the dialplan, which can be a directory, a set of menu options, or even a group of channels. These are known as contexts, and can be used to implement features such as the following:

- **Access limits**—Limit access to long-distance calls to certain telephones.
- **Routing**—Route calls based on their extensions.
- **Autoattendant**—Set up automated greeting with message prompts.
- **Menus**—Set up automated menus for different departments.
- **Authentication**—Require passwords to access certain extensions.
- **Callback**—Return calls to route through the presumably cheaper Asterisk system.
- **Privacy**—Create blacklists for unwanted calls.
- **PBX multihosting**—Configure multiple PBXs on the same Asterisk server.
- **Daytime/nighttime**—Set up different actions at different hours
- **Macros**—Create scripts for different functions.

These features are described at *http://www.voip-info.org/*.

While there are too many configuration files in the `/etc/asterisk/` directory to detail in this section, they do include features that range from A to Z. For example, the `adsi.conf` file specifies the analog display services interface (ADSI) associated with messages on the small screens included with many common business telephones. The `zaptel.conf` file configures a telephony hardware driver application programming interface (API), now known as the Digium Asterisk Hardware Device Interface (DAHDI).

Security Risks with Asterisk

When configuring Asterisk, you need to be aware of the legal responsibility associated with telephone systems. While such laws vary by jurisdiction, in general, you should not configure spoofing of other telephone numbers, you should not overload or otherwise disrupt service on other telephone networks, and you should not use Asterisk to intercept calls from other users.

Naturally, as a security professional, you need to make sure that these situations don't arise on your systems.

Denial of Service on Asterisk

Asterisk is different from other services in that it can support multiple connections between the same two IP addresses. And you want such connections, to enable multiple users from one company to talk with multiple users on another company simultaneously. So the rules that you create to prevent denial of service (DoS) attacks on Linux are somewhat different from those associated with the standard service.

- **Virtual LANs (VLANs)**—The network partitions enabled by **virtual LANs (VLANs)** can keep traffic separate.
- **Appropriate firewall rules**—Voice traffic requires some priority; firewall rules should be set with a type of service (TOS) that minimizes delay with a switch such as `-j TOS --set-tos Minimize-Delay`.
- **Limit packet floods**—Firewall rules should allow connections over the SIP and RTP protocols but should stop SYN flood attacks.

Asterisk Authentication

Without authentication, black-hat hackers may be able to hijack a call on either end of the connection. Asterisk authentication is possible by a number of methods, including the Lightweight Directory Access Protocol (LDAP), the Remote Authentication Dial In User Service (RADIUS), and host-based authentication.

More Asterisk Security Options

Additional Asterisk security options use information at the data link layer of the TCP/IP protocol suite. These security options include the following:

- **Dynamic Host Configuration Protocol (DHCP) snooping**—DHCP snooping limits network access to systems with known IP and hardware addresses.
- **Dynamic address resolution protocol (ARP) inspection**—This checks the binding between the IP address and Media Access Control (MAC) hardware addresses, minimizing the risk of spoofed hardware addresses.
- **IP Source Guard**—Checks IP addresses against associated hardware addresses based on information stored in a DHCP lease file.
- **VLAN access control lists (ACLs)**—Reviews ACLs created for a VLAN to minimize the risk of spoofing.

Limit Those Printers

The standard service for Linux printer configuration and management is the Common UNIX Printing System (CUPS). It's a versatile system. While the default version of CUPS communicates using the Internet Printing Protocol (IPP) on port 631, it can be used to manage printers from a variety of other services, including Samba, the older Line Printer next generation (LPRng) service, HP JetDirect printers, and more. Microsoft operating systems support IPP. Apple, Inc. owns CUPS software and has maintained it under open source licenses. Because the Macintosh operating system is based on a relative of Linux, the Berkeley Standard Distribution, Apple has made CUPS the default print server for its operating systems.

CUPS is configured in files in the `/etc/cups/` directory. The main CUPS configuration file is `cupsd.conf`, the focus of the rest of this section.

Printer Administrators

One directive typically located early in the `cupsd.conf` file is `SystemGroup`. Groups that are listed after this directive are groups authorized to administer printers on this CUPS system. You can add users to the specified group in the `/etc/group` and `/etc/gshadow` configuration files. The groups may vary. On Red Hat systems, members of the `sys` group are default print administrators; on Ubuntu systems, members of the `lpadmin` group are default print administrators.

Shared Printers

CUPS printers are local, unless remote access is allowed. Remote access starts with the `Listen` directive, which by default enables access through port 631 on all IP addresses. If you want to limit access to one of multiple network cards on a system, you could set up a directive like the following, where 192.168.0.10 is the IP address of the local network card that is allowed to receive CUPS communications:

```
Listen 192.168.0.10:631
```

If printers are shared through other systems such as Samba, ports for that service must also be open.

Shared printers can be shown on the local network with the following default directives, which are almost self explanatory. They activate browsing of local printers, and determine whether the `BrowseAllow` or the `BrowseDeny` directive is considered first. Either or both of these directives could be included with an IP address or domain name for a single host or a network. The final line, the `BrowseLocalProtocols` directive, specifies the use of printer browsing using CUPS and the DNS-based Service Discovery (DNSSD) protocol for CUPS print browsing.

```
Browsing On
BrowseOrder allow,deny
BrowseAllow all
BrowseLocalProtocols CUPS dnssd
```

Remote Administration

Remote administration of CUPS servers is based on the three `Location` stanzas that follow in the `cupsd.conf` file. The format of the three stanzas is quite similar. They are all confined by `Location` directives. They all specify host- or possibly user-based access. The difference is based on the label associated with each `Location` stanza.

The `Location` stanza supports access to locally configured printers. The default version of this stanza limits such access to the local system:

```
<Location />
    Order allow,deny
</Location>
```

You can extend that access to the local network with the following directive:

```
Allow @LOCAL
```

If desired, you can substitute an IP address and network mask for the target network, such as `from 192.168.0.0/255.255.255.0`. Systems on the noted network might also have access to administrative tools and configuration files, depending on the stanzas that follow. Alternatively, you could limit access even further with a couple of directives such as the following:

```
Allow from 192.168.0.10
Deny from 192.168.0.0/255.255.255.0
```

The second stanza, with the `<Location /admin>` directive, allows access to administrative areas, to allow a review of current print settings.

The third stanza defines users and systems allowed to add and modify printers on the local CUPS service. The `AuthType Basic` directive refers to the regular user-authentication database. `Require user @System` points to the `SystemGroup` directive. Because the @ in this case specifies groups, it means user members of the groups listed with the `SystemGroup` directive are CUPS print administrators.

```
<Location /admin/conf>
    AuthType Basic
    Require user @SYSTEM
    Order allow,deny
    Allow @LOCAL
</Location>
```

Other stanzas in this file specify other administrative functions such as the ability to move or delete print jobs. The `@OWNER` option, when included, allows the user owner of such print jobs to perform the noted print functions.

The CUPS Administrative Tool

Of course, you can administer CUPS from a local system. In fact, CUPS is one rare service where the tool preferred by most open source administrators is a Web-based tool. On a local CUPS system, you can access the tool by navigating to `http://127.0.0.1:631`. Despite the `http://` in front of the URL, traffic to the CUPS administrative tool travels over port 631, which is the standard port for the IPP protocol.

Administrative actions within the CUPS Web-based tool lead to a prompt for a username and password. Authorized user accounts are members of the group defined in the `SystemGroup` directive in the `cupsd.conf` configuration file.

If remote administration is enabled, as described in the previous section, you can navigate to the domain name or IP address of the CUPS server, also using port 631.

Protect Your Time Services

Time services on Linux rely on the NTP protocol. Basic information on NTP server configuration was covered in Chapter 8. This section goes further, describing those directives in the /etc/ntp.conf file that can help secure a local NTP server. If an NTP server is overloaded in any way, it may not be a security issue per se. However, because it affects the reliability of the time seen from that server, it can have other consequences. For example, if the NTP server of an inventory system is not synchronized to the NTP server of a sales system, customers may try to order products that are out of stock.

The security-related directive in this file is restrict. First, take a look at the directive as configured in the default ntp.conf file. The -4 and -6 correspond to IPv4 and IPv6 networking.

```
restrict -4 default kod notrap nomodify nopeer noquery
restrict -6 default kod notrap nomodify nopeer noquery
```

The other options affect security of the NTP server in the following ways:

- **default**—Access to all NTP clients is allowed by default.
- **kod**—Prevents attacks from kiss of death (KOD) packets.
- **notrap**—Denies access to the message trap service for logging.
- **nomodify**—Prevents other NTP servers from modifying the status of this server.
- **nopeer**—Prevents attachments from other NTP servers.
- **noquery**—Disallows queries of the NTP service.

Assuming you don't want to open this up as a public NTP server, the default option should not be used. However, some address is required; one option is the IP address of the local network. In addition, you may want to allow time queries, and allow other NTP servers, perhaps from remote networks administered by colleagues, to communicate with your NTP server. So the IPv4 restrict directive would change to the following:

```
restrict -4 192.168.0.0 mask 255.255.255.0 kod notrap nomodify
```

In a similar fashion, you could set up similar restrictions on an IPv6 network:

```
restrict -6 0011:838:0:1:: mask ffff:ffff:ffff:ffff::
↪kod notrap nomodify
```

Options for Obscurity: Different Ports, Alternative Services

To some extent, when you installed Linux, you made a choice for obscurity. But as you've seen so far in this book, obscurity can mean different things when applied to different services. Obscurity goes beyond the use of nonstandard ports for network communications.

Obscurity can mean using less-popular services. For example, you might choose Postfix over sendmail for an e-mail service. You could choose Bernstein's djbdns DNS server over BIND. You could even choose a different bootloader such as the trusted Grand Unified Bootloader (TrustedGRUB) or the Linux Loader (LILO).

Obscurity can also mean using different labels. For example, you could use the Samba `server string` directive to label that Microsoft-style file server as if it were something else. You could use the Postfix `smtpd_banner` directive to apply a label from sendmail to make black-hat hackers think they're dealing with that alternative SMTP server. You could include incomplete information in a login banner for the Secure Shell (SSH) or secure Telnet services. You could keep version information to a minimum in Apache with the `ServerTokens` directive.

The methods you can use to obscure local and network services are almost as diverse as the number of services available on Linux. This section is just a reminder to look at or even audit the services on your networks to make sure they use obscurity in the best way to secure local systems.

Best Practices: Networked Application Security

As with services in general, it is best to keep installed and enabled features to a minimum. This maxim is especially important with a complex service like the Apache Web server. With Apache, it's important to keep included modules to a minimum.

Of course, with Apache, you can do more to improve security. With the LAMP stack, MySQL can include security certificates. It's best if you choose only one scripting language from those associated with LAMP (Perl, Python, PHP). SSL certificates can be configured for MySQL as well as for secure Apache Web sites. Overrides such as `.htaccess` should not be allowed, as they make it easy for a black-hat hacker to insert code into an Apache configuration.

The Squid Web proxy server can be used for two basic purposes. It can cache frequently accessed data, improving perceived Internet performance. It can also limit access to undesirable Web sites. Key Squid directives include `acl` and `http_access`.

Because DNS is a distributed database of domain names and IP addresses, there are many DNS servers that are potentially vulnerable. If a black-hat hacker penetrates or otherwise poisons the cache for your authoritative DNS server, that person can redirect your users to the Web sites of his or her choice. To minimize such risks, you should disable recursion on authoritative name servers. TSIG keys can authenticate DNS servers that do exchange data.

Linux supports a number of excellent MTAs, including open source sendmail, commercial Sendmail, Postfix, and more. MTAs can send data using the SMTP and submission protocols. Related to MTAs are MSAs such as Dovecot, which can receive e-mail using a number of regular and secure protocols. It's important to set up authentication for such services to prevent spammers from using them to distribute their malware.

Asterisk is the open source PBX solution. As such, it provides detailed VoIP configuration options for routing telephone calls through the Internet. But as a network solution, it may also be vulnerable to attacks such as DoS, DHCP snooping, and hardware address spoofing. To minimize risks such as unauthorized toll charges and spoofed phone calls, it's important to set up authentication with Asterisk.

CUPS is the open source print service sponsored by Apple. It can be configured with a special group of print administrators. With the `Location` stanzas, you can configure CUPS to share printers, to share administrative views of different systems, and to allow remote administration.

The Linux time service is based on the NTP protocol. The basic `restrict` directive in the `ntp.conf` file can limit access by IP address. That option is superior to the default, which allows access to all systems. It can also be used to stop KOD packets and prevent access, attachments, or queries from other NTP servers.

CHAPTER SUMMARY

In this chapter, you examined some of the security-related features of a number of servers. Because the Apache Web server is complex, it's important to minimize the modules loaded with that service. The Squid Web proxy server can be used to speed access via caching and prevent access to undesirable Web sites.

While mail services such as sendmail, Postfix, and Dovecot have their own security issues, options such as SSL keys and domain checks can minimize those issues. As an open source PBX service, Asterisk has its own set of security issues. CUPS printers can be regulated to share and permit administration from remote systems. It can configure print administrators in special groups. It's important to keep time services secure to ensure the reliability of the time seen from these NTP servers.

KEY CONCEPTS AND TERMS

Asterisk

Cache poisoning

Certificate authority (CA)

Challenge-response
  authentication mechanism
  (CRAM)

Inter-Cache Protocol (ICP)

Java Cryptography Extension
  (JCE)

LAMP stack

Mail delivery agent (MDA)

Mail retrieval agent (MRA)

Mail submission agent (MSA)

Mail transfer agent (MTA)

Mail user agent (MUA)

Multi-Processing Modules
  (MPMs)

Perl

PHP: Hypertext Preprocessor
  (PHP)

Python

Real-time Transport Protocol
  (RTP)

Recursive query

Session Initiation Protocol (SIP)

Transition SIGnature (TSIG)

Virtual LAN (VLAN)

Zone files

Zone updates

CHAPTER 9 ASSESSMENT

1. Which of the following services is *not* part
of the LAMP stack?

A. Linux

B. Apache

C. MySQL

D. Postfix

2. Which of the following commands sets a
password for the MySQL administrative user?

A. `mysqladmin -u admin password`
   `↳"newpassword"`

B. `mysqladmin -u root password`
   `↳"newpassword"`

C. `mysqladmin -u mysql password`
   `↳"newpassword"`

D. `mysqladmin -u user root`
   `↳"newpassword"`

3. Which of the following commands removes the
php5 module in Apache on an Ubuntu system?

A. `a2enmod php5`

B. `a2rmmod php5`

C. `a2dismod php5`

D. `a2modprobe php5`

4. What is the command that can create users
and passwords for access to a Web directory
in Apache?

5. The `server.csr` file includes identifying
information about your system.

A. True

B. False

6. Which of the following port numbers
is associated with Squid?

A. 80

B. 3128

C. 443

D. 8080

7. Which of the following should *not* be included
on a public DNS server?

A. Mail server IP addresses

B. DNS server IP addresses

C. Web server IP addresses

D. Squid server IP addresses

8. Which of the following commands reads
all changes made to files in the `/etc/mail/`
directory for open source sendmail?

A. `make -C /etc/mail`

B. `m4 /etc/mail`

C. `make /etc/mail/sendmail.mc`

D. `m4 /etc/mail/sendmail.mc`

9. Which of the following open source sendmail directives is used to specify e-mail protocols?

A. define
B. DAEMON_OPTIONS
C. FEATURE
D. MAILER

10. Which of the following configuration files is most important for Postfix?

A. main.cf
B. master.cf
C. maps.cf
D. submit.cf

11. In Dovecot, if you want to activate both regular and secure POP3 and IMAP services, what options would you add to the protocols directive?

12. Which of the following is *not* a protocol closely associated with Asterisk?

A. IPP
B. SIP
C. RTP
D. UDP

13. Which of the following directives in the main CUPS configuration file specifies groups of users who are allowed to administer CUPS?

A. Lpadmin
B. Admin
C. System
D. SystemGroup

14. Which of the following NTP restrict options relate to logging?

A. kod
B. notrap
C. nopeer
D. noquery

15. Which of the following directives specify and can limit the information given about an Apache system?

A. banner
B. System
C. ServerTokens
D. server string

Kernel Security Risk Mitigation

THIS CHAPTER IS ALL ABOUT THE KERNEL, the essence of the Linux operating system. Because the kernel is highly configurable, it represents an opportunity to better secure your systems. Unfortunately, it also a chance for black-hat hackers to take advantage of mistakes made by users who are less skilled at kernel configuration.

Because of the complexity of the kernel, most Linux professionals rely on kernels configured by reliable developers. Many such developers work for the corporate sponsors of a distribution such as Red Hat, Novell, or Canonical (Ubuntu). Corporate Linux kernel developers start with the work of the volunteer developers affiliated with the Linux Kernel Organization. The **stock kernel** incorporates the latest features requested by users. It incorporates many of the features developed for specialty Linux distributions. Such development is made possible by open source licenses.

When choosing a kernel, you can take one of two basic approaches. You can stick with the kernel customized for a distribution or you can start with the stock Linux kernel. The developers behind both the Red Hat and Ubuntu distributions do an excellent job customizing their Linux kernel for enterprise-ready systems. To keep their customers happy, they generally have updates that address security issues available on a timely basis.

Whichever approach you choose, you can further customize and compile the kernel. It's best if this work is done on a developmental system. Once the custom kernel and associated files are developed, compiled, and tested on the developmental system, you should be able to transfer those files to production systems.

Chapter 10 Topics

This chapter covers the following topics and concepts:

- Which options you have with distribution-specific functional kernels
- What the stock Linux kernel is
- How to manage upgrades to the stock Linux kernel
- What to look for in a security or kernel update
- What development software is available for a custom kernel
- Which Linux kernel development tools are available
- How to build your own secure kernel
- How to increase security using kernels and the /proc/ filesystem
- What best practices are for kernel security risk mitigation

Chapter 10 Goals

When you complete this chapter, you will be able to:

- Choose the kernel best suited to your systems
- Customize options within the Linux kernel
- Compile the source code for a kernel, with patches
- Configure how the kernel works in real-time

Functional Kernels for Your Distribution

The developers behind most Linux distributions want to make things as easy as possible for their users. They provide installation programs to load and configure their distributions on a wide variety of hardware. They release software in packages, compiled in binary format. All the user has to do is load and install the package.

The kernels released by Linux developers vary at least by **architecture**. Because the kernel includes interfaces between hardware and software, kernels vary with that most fundamental architectural hardware component, the CPU.

The developers behind some Linux distributions may also configure, customize, and release different binary kernels for different functional situations. For example, as administrators may not install a graphical user interface (GUI) on many servers, developers may choose to deactivate features associated with high-end graphics cards for a server kernel.

Kernels by Architecture

Linux kernels are available for a wide variety of architectures. Because the developers at the Linux Kernel Organization release only the source code for the kernel, it is left to the developers behind a distribution to customize, compile, and test a kernel for each specific architecture. Such testing takes time and effort. At last count, Debian Linux released production kernels for more than a dozen different architectures, including the following:

- **Standard 32-bit**—The normal 32-bit PC architecture; may be labeled with an i386, i586, or i686 in the package name.
- **Standard 64-bit**—The normal 64-bit PC architecture; frequently labeled with an amd64 or x86_64 in the package name.
- **Alpha**—The CPU developed by the original Digital Equipment Corporation, now owned by HP.
- **Advanced RISC Machine (ARM)**—The CPU originally developed by the former Acorn Computers, Ltd., now licensed by a number of companies.
- **Itanium**—A 64-bit CPU from Intel. Other Intel 64-bit CPUs are available.
- **Motorola 68000 (m68k)**—A 32-bit CPU developed by Motorola.
- **PowerPC**—A 32-bit CPU developed by Apple, IBM, and Motorola.
- **s390**—The IBM system 390 32-bit CPU.
- **Sparc**—A 64-bit CPU originally developed by Sun Microsystems.

In addition, Red Hat builds its Enterprise Linux distributions for the IBM **iSeries** and **pSeries** CPUs. However, it does not support any of the other CPUs except for standard 32-bit and 64-bit systems, along with 64-bit Intel **Itanium** systems on its older releases. Red Hat is not supporting the Itanium CPU on its newest releases.

One feature incorporated into different kernels on mostly older Linux distributions is symmetrical multiprocessing (SMP), used for systems with multiple CPUs. On most current Linux distributions, that feature has been incorporated into the main kernel.

On the other hand, Ubuntu limits its officially supported releases to two different architectures: the 32- and 64-bit Intel-compatible CPU. The package names of such binary kernels may be a bit misleading, as they commonly include i386 for the 32-bit kernel and amd64 or x86_64 for the 64-bit kernel. Such kernels work on systems with both Intel and Advanced Micro Devices (AMD) CPUs. That focus enables Ubuntu to customize kernels for different purposes.

> **NOTE**
>
> While Ubuntu developers build a kernel that emulates the ARM architecture, that kernel is not officially supported by Canonical, Ubuntu's corporate sponsor.

Kernels for Different Functions

The developers behind most Linux distributions create kernels for different functions. Those who use Xen for virtual machines should be familiar with the specialized kernel for that purpose. Among the most popular Linux distributions, Ubuntu builds kernels for a wide array of functions. One list of such Ubuntu kernels is shown in Figure 10-1. Some of the packages shown are **meta packages**; for example, the linux-image-generic package is automatically linked to the package built for the latest production Linux kernel release.

```
linux-image - Generic Linux kernel image.
linux-image-2.6.32-19-386 - Linux kernel image for version 2.6.32 on i386
linux-image-2.6.32-19-generic - Linux kernel image for version 2.6.32 on x86/x86_64
linux-image-2.6.32-19-generic-pae - Linux kernel image for version 2.6.32 on x86
linux-image-2.6.32-19-virtual - Linux kernel image for version 2.6.32 on x86/x86_64
linux-image-2.6.32-304-ec2 - Linux kernel image for version 2.6.32 on x86/x86_64
linux-image-386 - Generic Linux kernel image
linux-image-ec2 - Linux kernel image for ec2 machines
linux-image-generic - Generic Linux kernel image
linux-image-generic-pae - Generic Linux kernel image
linux-image-server - Linux kernel image on Server Equipment.
linux-image-virtual - Linux kernel image for virtual machines
linux-image-2.6.31-10-rt - Linux kernel image for version 2.6.31 on Ingo Molnar's fu
ll real time preemption patch
linux-image-rt - Realtime (RT) Linux kernel image
```

FIGURE 10-1

Ubuntu kernel package options.

The meta-packages shown in Figure 10-1 are described in Table 10-1. Figure 10-1 is based on selected output from the `apt-cache search linux-image` command. It does not include debug or development kernels. Such kernels are not suitable for production, in part because they have not been tested for security. It specifies the meta-package associated with the kernel, as the installation of a meta-package automatically installs the latest version of the kernel so described. Of course, if something other than the latest version of a kernel is best for a system, you should be able to choose that package by version number. A list of such earlier kernel version packages should be shown when you run that `apt-cache search linux-image` command.

TABLE 10-1 Typical Ubuntu Linux kernel packages.

PACKAGE	DESCRIPTION
linux-image	Installs latest available generic Linux kernel image
linux-image-386	Installs latest available Linux kernel for 32-bit systems
linux-image-ec2	Installs latest available Linux kernel for systems connected to Amazon's Elastic Compute Cloud
linux-image-generic	Installs latest available Linux kernel for 32-bit systems
linux-image-generic-pae	Installs latest available Linux kernel for 32-bit systems, preferring a kernel customized for at least 4 GB of RAM
linux-image-server	Installs latest available Linux kernel configured for servers
linux-image-virtual	Installs latest available Linux kernel optimized for guest systems inside virtual machines
linux-image-rt	Specifies the real-time kernel that uses features developed by Ingo Molnar of Red Hat

In general, these meta-packages are linked to kernels customized for 32-bit systems. Some of these meta-packages may not work for 64-bit systems, unless the associated kernel is also designed to work for such systems.

There are fewer functional kernel packages for Red Hat Enterprise Linux. Red Hat does build different kernels for regular and Xen-based systems.

The Stock Kernel

The stock kernel is the generic kernel released by the developers of the Linux Kernel Organization at *http://kernel.org/*. The overall leader of that organization is **Linus Torvalds**, who developed the first kernel in 1991. Linux kernel version 0.01 was released late that year. In 1992, Torvalds adapted the GNU General Public License (GPL) for all Linux kernel releases. Torvalds is still acknowledged as the overall lead developer of the Linux kernel, coordinating the efforts of thousands of other developers.

> **NOTE**
>
> Be aware that the package names associated with the Linux kernel may change from time to time, and may vary by distribution. For example, Ubuntu kernel packages used to have the word `kernel` in the package name. Red Hat kernel packages still include `kernel` in their package names. For the latest information, use a search command like `yum search kernel` or `apt-get search linux`. For more information on these search terms, see Chapter 11.

The stock kernel is sometimes known as the "mainline" or "vanilla" kernel. The many Linux kernel developers work on releases that may be stable or unstable. The current maintainer of the stable release tree is **Greg Kroah-Hartman**. Other key developers are responsible for different kernel subsystems.

To understand the sequence of Linux kernels, you need to understand the Linux kernel numbering system.

Kernel Numbering Systems

Production versions of most current Linux stock kernels include four numbers, such as 2.6.32.4, in a *majorversion.majorrevision.updateversion.patchnumber* format. The following is a brief explanation of these kernel numbers:

- *Majorversion*—Specifies a version with drastic changes from a previous kernel.
- *Majorrevision*—Associated with major changes to the kernel. Through version 2.6, even-numbered major revisions were stable. Odd-numbered kernel versions such as 2.5 were unstable. If and when version 2.7 is released, it may also be an unstable release.
- *Updateversion*—Released for important updates and new features to the kernel.
- *Patchnumber*—Associated with bug fixes and security updates to the kernel.

Kernels with new update versions are released approximately every three months. As of early 2010, there are no near-term plans for the next major revision (presumably kernel version 2.7).

The first release of an update version kernel has three numbers, such as 2.6.32. The first patch of that update version is release 2.6.32.1.

The developers behind some of the most important Linux distributions may release their enterprise-ready distributions with slightly older kernels. That supports a longer period of testing with a stable kernel. When new features are incorporated into later kernels, the developers behind many Linux distributions may **backport** those features. For example, Red Hat developers have backported many features associated with kernels 2.6.19–2.6.33 into its build of the 2.6.18 kernel for its Red Hat Enterprise Linux 5 releases.

Production Releases and More

The developers associated with the Linux Kernel Organization maintain production kernels associated with multiple update version numbers. When administrators build a kernel to a certain update version, they may choose to stick to that update version for a while so they do not have to test their systems for compatibility with the new features associated with later updates.

Linux kernel developers release security patches for a number of different kernel update versions. For example, as of this writing, stable security patches are available for Linux kernel version numbers 2.6.33, 2.6.32, 2.6.31, 2.6.27, and 2.4.37.

The Linux Kernel Organization releases more than just production kernels. Developers test kernels in work. Kernels associated with a development branch are frequently associated with chief developers; for example, a kernel with a `-ac` suffix is associated with Alan Cox. Kernels that are nearly ready for release may have a `-rc` suffix, indicating they are a release candidate.

Generally, if there's an important security issue, it's most efficient to wait for the latest production release. Security issues get special attention not only by the Linux Kernel Organization, but also by the developers behind major Linux distributions.

Download the Stock Kernel

To use a stock Linux kernel, start with the version available from the Linux Kernel Organization at *http://kernel.org*. You may choose to start with the latest stable kernel or some older kernel that is still maintained. The stock kernel is available as source code. Before it can be put into effect on a system, it must be compiled, as discussed later in this chapter.

Stock kernels are normally available in a compressed `tar` command archive, compressed either with the Lempel-Ziv Gzip or the Burrows-Wheeler block sorting text compression algorithm with Huffman coding. Kernels compressed in these formats have `.tar.gz` and `.tar.bz2` extensions, respectively.

You can download the compressed archive stock kernels from *http://www.kernel.org/ pub/* or *ftp://ftp.kernel.org/pub/*. Kernel packages should be downloaded to the /usr/src/ directory.

If you have doubts about the integrity of the source code, download the associated compressed archive file with the .sign extension. For example, if you've downloaded the linux-2.6.34.1.tar.gz file, you can also download the linux-2.6.34.1.tar.gz.sign file. Instructions associated with this signature are available at *http://www.kernel.org/ signature.html*.

Once downloaded, the source code can be unpacked into a subdirectory with something similar to one of the following commands. Substitute the version number of the downloaded Linux kernel for 2.6.34.1.

```
# tar xzf  linux-2.6.34.1.tar.gz
# tar xjf  linux-2.6.34.1.tar.bz2
```

The tar command is one of those rare Linux commands where there is no dash in front of command switches. The z switch uncompresses .tar.gz files; the j switch uncompresses and .tar.bz2 files.

If you need to know more about the changes made to a production kernel, download the ChangeLog file associated with the release version.

Stock Kernel Patches and Upgrades

If a downloaded, uncompressed, and unarchived stock Linux kernel is available in an appropriate directory, you don't need to repeat the process for the next release. All you need to do to update the source code is to download the appropriate patch. Two different types of patches are available. For example, to update source code from version 2.6.34.1 to 2.6.34.2, the appropriate patch is available in the package file named patch-2.6.34.2.gz or patch-2.6.34.2.bz2. Once copied to the /usr/src/ directory, you can apply the patch with one of the following commands:

```
# zcat patch-2.6.34.2.gz | patch -p0
# bzcat patch-2.6.34.2.bz2 | patch -p0
```

It's also possible to patch kernel source code between update versions. For example, the patch-2.6.35.gz file can be used to update Linux kernel source code from version 2.6.34 to 2.6.35. However, patches can be applied only consecutively. For example, to update source code from 2.6.33 to 2.6.35, you would need to apply both the patch-2.6.34.gz and patch-2.6.35.gz updates.

> **TIP**
>
> It's generally a bad idea to use a generic patch on kernel source code released for a specific distribution. For example, the source code for the latest Red Hat Enterprise Linux 5 kernels include backports from the latest Linux kernel releases. A patch applied to that source code may overwrite those backports, removing features that you may need.

Security and Kernel Update Issues

Kernel security can be divided into two interrelated areas. First, there are security issues that arise related to the stock Linux kernel. Second, there are security issues that arise related to the Linux kernel as built by the developers of a distribution.

When updating a kernel, it's best to make sure that any existing working kernel is retained on your systems. If there is a problem with the updated kernel, those systems will still be bootable and available with the older working kernel.

In general, that's easiest to put into effect with the binary kernels built by the developers of a distribution. Because such kernels are already in binary format, you do not need to compile them. You can install them directly on the distribution.

However, custom kernels work better for many systems. Custom kernels can be optimized to load more quickly. More importantly, custom kernels can exclude options such as modules that may be loaded by black-hat hackers to present security risks.

Stock Kernel Security Issues

The developers associated with the Linux kernel communicate primarily by messages on mailing lists. To keep up to date with the latest developments in the Linux kernel, navigate to `http://lkml.org/`, the Linux kernel mailing list. But it's time-consuming to monitor this list, as there are frequently hundreds of messages between developers on a daily basis.

One option more focused on generic security issues is available at *http://www .linuxsecurity.com/*. For a digest of information, see the latest Linux advisory watch available from that Web site. For many administrators, distribution-specific security monitors may be more appropriate, and are discussed in Chapter 11.

Linux kernel developers can't test updates against all configurations. Any updates they create may lead to problems. So it's important to test all updated kernels before installing them on production systems. This warning also applies to security updates.

In limited situations, you might choose not to install a new kernel for a security update. For example, if there's a security issue related to Bluetooth hardware, it's important only if there are Bluetooth components installed on your systems. If there aren't, you might choose to avoid installing that update. But be aware that a security issue that affects one system could easily affect a related system such as network hardware.

Distribution-Specific Kernel Security Issues

The Linux kernel as built for specific distributions such as Red Hat and Ubuntu includes a number of features that differ from the stock kernel. With thousands of options, the differences are too numerous to mention. So while distribution-specific kernels are built from the stock Linux kernel, the security issues related to distribution-specific kernels may vary.

But as with the stock kernel, you may not want to always update a distribution-specific kernel. Some updates don't relate to security issues. Other updates may include hardware that may not be installed on your systems. In all cases, it's a risk to update a Linux kernel.

As the developers behind Linux distributions can't possibly test all configurations, it's up to you to test distribution-specific kernel updates in production.

The standard command to update packages on Ubuntu systems is `apt-get update`. By default, it excludes later versions of the Linux kernel from an update.

On the other hand, the standard command to update packages on Red Hat systems is `yum update`. It does not exclude later versions of the Linux kernel unless the `--exclude=kernel-*` switch is included in the command:

```
# yum update --exclude=kernel-*
```

For more information on the `apt-get` and `yum` update commands, see Chapter 11.

Installing an Updated Kernel

When implementing a new kernel, be careful. Make sure to use appropriate install commands and switches with the package-management commands for your distribution. That ensures that the existing kernel remains in place, still available to boot local systems if the updated kernel does not work for whatever reason.

In contrast, if you upgrade a kernel, the process overwrites any existing kernel. If the new kernel doesn't work for any reason, you'll have to go through a rescue process to reinstall the older working kernel. And that is a time-intensive process.

There are two basic methods to install an updated kernel. The first method relates to update tools such as `yum` or `apt-get` to download and install kernels from existing repositories on remote systems.

On Ubuntu systems, you can run the `apt-get install` command with the name of the updated kernel. If you want to install the latest version of the kernel, you could specify the appropriate meta-package shown in Table 10-1. For example, the following command installs the latest version of the Ubuntu kernel customized for virtual machines:

```
# apt-get install linux-image-virtual
```

In the same fashion, you can use the name of the Red Hat kernel to install the latest version of that kernel; for example, the following command installs the latest version of the **Xen kernel**:

```
# yum install kernel-xen
```

> **NOTE**
> Starting with Red Hat Enterprise Linux 6, Red Hat will no longer support Xen, nor will it include a Xen kernel in that release.

Alternatively, if you've downloaded the actual updated kernel package, you can use the `rpm` or `dpkg` commands. You should already be familiar with the details of these commands; in both cases, the `-i` switch installs the target package.

Binary kernel packages built by the developers of Linux distributions should automatically update applicable bootloader files such as `/etc/lilo.conf` or `/boot/grub/menu.lst`. If properly updated, these files should include stanzas for both the current and the new kernel. If you've set up custom features for an existing kernel in the bootloader, you may need to modify the stanza for the new kernel to include those same messages.

Note that some distributions regulate the number of kernels that can be installed on a system. The kernel and initial RAM disk files associated with a kernel can be quite large. Many distributions, including Red Hat, configure the /boot directory on a fairly small separate partition. By default, Red Hat Enterprise Linux 5 specifies a size of 100MB for this partition.

If you've compiled a custom kernel, the initial RAM disk for that kernel can easily reach several dozen megabytes, which can limit the number of kernels that are practical to install on a system.

Kernel Development Software

To recompile a kernel, you'll need to install packages associated with C language libraries and compilers, kernel header files, preprocessors, and related development tools. If you want to use menu-based kernel customization tools, additional packages are required.

Required development software varies a bit by distribution. Some of the differences are based on the way Ubuntu and Red Hat systems are configured. The commands for Ubuntu systems have changed from the **Hardy Heron (8.04)** to the **Lucid Lynx (10.04)** releases. The packages required for Red Hat systems are also subject to change.

When installing such software, keep careful records of the packages that are installed. When installed on production systems, the software associated with compiling the kernel may present risks. It may also allow black-hat hackers to compile more dangerous malware from within your systems. If kernel development software is installed on a production system, be sure to remove that software after the new kernel is operational.

Red Hat Kernel Development Software

The packages listed in this section can be used to customize and build a kernel on Red Hat systems. While the same basic functionality is required to build kernels on other Linux systems, at least the package names will vary. The key packages are listed in Table 10-2.

TABLE 10-2 Red Hat kernel development packages.

PACKAGE	DESCRIPTION
binutils	Binary utilities
cpp	C language pre-processor
gcc	GNU's not UNIX (GNU) C language compiler
glibc-headers	Kernel header files
glibc-devel	Kernel development files associated with C language libraries
ncurses	New curses library for updating character screens; supports the make menuconfig command

The listed packages support the terminal menu-based configuration options associated with the `make config` and `make menuconfig` commands when run in the directory with the kernel source code. If you prefer graphical kernel customization tools, you'll need packages associated with the Tool command language (Tcl) and the associated cross-platform Tk toolkit. Depending on the type of graphical customization tool, you may also need development tools associated with the Qt toolkit, GLib headers, and the Glade interface designer.

A number of these packages work with the Perl programming language, so associated packages should also automatically be installed as dependencies if you use the `yum` command to install these packages.

Ubuntu Kernel Development Software

The packages required to customize and compile the Linux kernel on an Ubuntu system vary by release. For the Hardy Heron (8.04) release, you can install these tools with the following command:

```
# apt-get install fakeroot linux-kernel-devel ccache
➥ libncurses5 libncurses5-dev
```

For the Lucid Lynx (10.04) release, you can install these tools with the following command:

```
# apt-get install fakeroot kernel-package build-essential ccache
➥ libncurses5 libncurses5-dev
```

These commands install packages with equivalent functionality to those described in the previous section for Red Hat systems. As this is a general book on Linux security, it will not cover such details as the differences between the two Ubuntu releases.

As with the noted Red Hat packages, the installed packages support the terminal-menu–based configuration options associated with the `make config` and `make menuconfig` commands when run in the directory with the kernel source code. If you prefer to customize systems with graphical tools, you'll need tools and toolkits similar to those described for Red Hat systems.

Kernel Development Tools

This section is focused on the options available to customize a kernel. It's based on stock kernel source code described earlier, from the developers at the Linux Kernel Organization. To customize a kernel, you'll also need the kernel development tools just described. While this section focuses on the ncurses-based kernel customization console tool, the basic options described here would also apply to the available command-line or graphical tools.

You could also start with the source code released by the developers of a distribution. Instructions for downloading and preparing that distribution-specific source code are available later in this chapter.

Before Customizing a Kernel

Apply any patches. If you're starting from the source code of a stock kernel, download desired patches from the Linux Kernel Organization servers and apply them to the unpacked source code with the zcat or bzcat commands described earlier.

Navigate to the directory with the kernel source code. If it's the stock kernel, that directory will have a name like /usr/src/linux-source-2.6.32/. The version number may vary. If you're running these commands on an Ubuntu system, you can do so with sudo-based privileges. Alternatively, from a Red Hat system, these commands are most effectively run from the root administrative account. These first commands clean out any remaining object files and remove any existing kernel configuration in the local directory. If you've just installed the kernel source code, these commands are not necessary.

```
# make clean
# make mrproper
```

The next step is to select a baseline. You could accept the baseline inherent in the source code. You could select one of the configuration options available in the configs/ or arch/x86/configs/ subdirectory. If the system architecture is not a standard 32- or 64-bit Intel/AMD CPU, substitute for x86/ accordingly.

Alternatively, you could start with the configuration of the current system, available in the /boot/ directory, in the config-`uname -r` file, where `uname -r` substitutes the version number of the currently loaded kernel. This option is more appropriate if you're starting with distribution-specific kernel source code. If you use this option with the stock kernel, the results are less predictable.

If you start with an existing config-* file, make sure to copy that to the hidden .config file, in the directory with the source code for the kernel.

```
michael@ubuntuLucidSvr3:/usr/src/linux-source-2.6.32$ make config
scripts/kconfig/conf arch/x86/Kconfig
*
* Linux Kernel Configuration
*
*
* General setup
*
Prompt for development and/or incomplete code/drivers (EXPERIMENTAL) [Y/n/?]
Local version - append to kernel release (LOCALVERSION) []
Automatically append version information to the version string (LOCALVERSION_AUTO) [
N/y/?]
Kernel compression mode
> 1. Gzip (KERNEL_GZIP)
  2. Bzip2 (KERNEL_BZIP2)
  3. LZMA (KERNEL_LZMA)
choice[1-3?]:
Arbitrary version signature (VERSION_SIGNATURE) [Ubuntu 2.6.32-19.28-server 2.6.32.1
0+drm33.1]
Support for paging of anonymous memory (swap) (SWAP) [Y/n/?]
System V IPC (SYSVIPC) [Y/n/?]
POSIX Message Queues (POSIX_MQUEUE) [Y/n/?]
```

FIGURE 10-2

Customizing a kernel with make config.

```
.config - Linux Kernel v2.6.33 Configuration
                         Linux Kernel Configuration
     Arrow keys navigate the menu.  <Enter> selects submenus --->.  Highlighted
     letters are hotkeys.  Pressing <Y> includes, <N> excludes, <M> modularizes
     features.  Press <Esc><Esc> to exit, <?> for Help, </> for Search.
     Legend: [*] built-in  [ ] excluded  <M> module  < > module capable

             General setup  --->
         [*] Enable loadable module support  --->
         -*- Enable the block layer  --->
             Processor type and features  --->
             Power management and ACPI options  --->
             Bus options (PCI etc.)  --->
             Executable file formats / Emulations  --->
         [*] Networking support  --->
             Device Drivers  --->
             Firmware Drivers  --->
             File systems  --->

                   <Select>     < Exit >     < Help >
```

FIGURE 10-3

Customizing a kernel with
`make menuconfig`.

Start the Kernel Customization Process

Navigate to the directory with the kernel source code. From this directory, there are
several methods for customizing a Linux kernel before it's compiled. You could open
the aforementioned `.config` file in a text editor and change settings in that file directly.
That option is considered impractical for all but the most knowledgeable Linux developers,
however. Alternatively, you could run the `make config` command. It's a simple script.
As shown in Figure 10-2, it prompts you to make choices for each option associated
with the Linux kernel.

While the questions are straightforward, there are literally thousands of options
associated with the Linux kernel. If you miss an option to be changed, you'd have to
press Ctrl+C to abort and run the `make config` command again to start over. That makes
it impractical to customize the kernel with the `make config` command.

The practical method for customizing a kernel without a GUI uses `ncurses`-based configuration menus. In the directory with the kernel source code, run the `make menuconfig`
command. You should see a menu similar to that shown in Figure 10-3.

As the functionality of the Linux kernel evolves, some of the options in the kernel
configuration menus will vary. However, most of the options described in the sections
that follow are relatively stable.

Kernel Configuration Options

Even if you choose to never reconfigure a kernel, do explore the available options.
An understanding of these options can help you better understand the strengths and
weaknesses of the Linux kernel, including in the area of security.

The options described in the sections that follow are based on the kernel configuration
menu associated with the stock version of the Linux kernel, version 2.6.33, as released
by the Linux Kernel Organization. The wording associated with some menu options may

vary slightly. For example, newer kernels have replaced the Loadable Module Support submenu with the Enable Loadable Module Support submenu.

Many kernel configuration options interact with others. The wrong choices can lead to a kernel that fails to boot a system. If you're in doubt about an option, stick with the default. Some kernel configuration options are labeled as EXPERIMENTAL and should be treated as such. In other words, they are not proven in a production environment.

Help options are available for most Linux kernel configuration options. The Help menu will normally specify the actual descriptive kernel option, such as CONFIG_HOTPLUG_PCI for hot-pluggable Peripheral Component Interconnect (PCI) controllers.

On the other hand, if you configure a kernel with fewer features, that leads to a kernel with fewer opportunities for black-hat hackers to break into your systems. As long as you are careful to maintain system backups and existing kernels, some trial and error can help you configure a more secure kernel.

General Setup

General setup options run the gamut from kernel compression modes to the use of swap space to initial RAM disk support. In most cases, you should not change any options in this section.

Enable Loadable Module Support

The default options automatically load appropriate module devices for existing and newly installed hardware. As Linux distributions rely on a modular kernel, you shouldn't generally change that basic functionality. One new potentially interesting feature in the stock kernel is related to module verification, which uses GNU Privacy Guard (GPG) keys to verify modules. It's a common option for kernels built for Red Hat systems.

Enable the Block Layer

Block-layer kernel settings are associated with larger files in the terabyte range. Without such settings, fairly common Linux filesystems such as the third and fourth extended filesystems (ext3 and ext4) won't work.

Processor Type and Features

With the development of multi-core CPU processors with different features, this menu includes a number of relatively new options. The stock kernel does not enable paravirtualized guest support, which is essential if you want to configure virtual machines with **paravirtualized** shortcuts for hardware.

Power Management and ACPI Options

As the power management on current computers uses the Advanced Configuration and Power Interface (ACPI), the title of this section is somewhat redundant. It includes power management options associated with systems that may hibernate or be suspended to RAM. Some administrators believe that hibernation files may themselves present a security risk. To that end, you may consider disabling hibernation in the kernel. Just remember, there's no guarantee that any change to a kernel configuration will lead to a working kernel.

The source code associated with older kernels may include options associated with Advanced Power Management in this section.

Bus Options

Most computer systems include PCI cards. Support for such cards is typically enabled in this part of the kernel configuration. The Linux kernel normally includes support for a variety of PCI and similar devices. For example, if your systems can connect to PC card and PCI hot-pluggable hardware, consider disabling such options in the kernel—unless of course you're actually planning to use such hardware on these systems.

Executable File Formats/Emulations

Current Linux kernels normally include support for binary commands and scripts in executable linkable format (ELF). Options for such formats are listed in this section. Unfortunately, current kernels don't support fine-grained control of ELF options.

Networking Support

The networking-support menu in the Linux kernel is extensive. Besides those relating to standard and wireless networking, options in this section can allow or disable support for infrared, Bluetooth, Worldwide Interoperability for Microwave Access (WiMAX), and other networking hardware.

The Networking Options submenu shown in Figure 10-4 also provides extensive options related to the kinds of network packets that the kernel can work with. Packets associated with the Dynamic Host Configuration Protocol (DHCP), the Bootstrap Protocol (BOOTP), and the Reverse Address Resolution Protocol (RARP) are recognized in the default Linux stock kernel. That ability can be disabled in this menu.

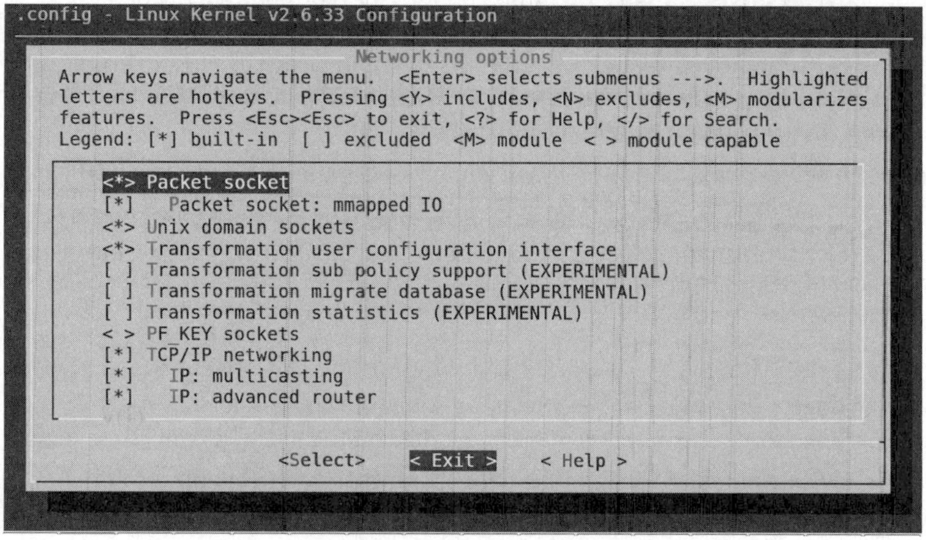

FIGURE 10-4

Kernel networking options.

Device Drivers

The device-driver section is extensive in the Linux kernel. It's worth spending some time in this area. If you want to disable access to certain devices, you can do so here. Any device that is disabled in the kernel is not available to a black-hat hacker. For example, if you disable parallel port devices, a black-hat hacker won't be able to copy files to parallel port drives.

This section is divided into a number of different areas. The following list (and yes, it is a long list) highlights primarily those sections that include options related to physical devices. These sections are presented in the order shown from the stock Linux kernel, version 2.6.33.

- **Memory technology devices**—Supports flash cards, RAM chips, and similar devices.
- **Parallel port support**—Associated with devices connected to parallel ports.
- **Plug and play support**—Enables Linux configuration of plug-and-play devices.
- **Block devices**—Works with nonstandard hard disks and network block devices.
- **ATA/IDE/MFM/RLL**—Associated with older hard drives based on Advanced Technology Attachment (ATA), Integrated Drive Electronics (IDE), modified frequency modulation (MFM), and run length limited (RLL) standards. The option is deprecated on newer kernels.
- **SCSI device support**—Includes drivers associated with Small Computer System Interface (SCSI) connections.
- **Serial ATA and parallel ATA drivers**—Specifies drivers associated with Serial Advanced Technology Attachment (SATA) and parallel advanced technology attachment (PATA) systems, mostly hard drives.
- **Multiple devices driver support**—Includes options for redundant array of independent disk (RAID) arrays and logical volume management (LVM) systems. Can be set to automatically detect RAID arrays or set linear RAID or RAID versions 0, 1, 4, 5, 6, and 10. Be aware, this is software RAID, so the acronym is misleading as it relates to independent partitions, not disks.
- **Fusion MPT device support**—Supports fusion message passing technology (MPT) devices; associated with higher-speed SCSI adapters.
- **IEEE 1394 (FireWire) support**—Specifies modules associated with FireWire hardware, associated with standard 1394 of the Institute of Electrical and Electronics Engineers (IEEE).
- **I2O device support**—Works with intelligent input/output (I2O) devices.
- **Macintosh device drivers**—Enables the use of Macintosh input devices such as a mouse; some Linux distributions may be installed on the latest Macintosh systems.
- **Network device support**—Specifies the network card drivers available for Linux.
- **ISDN support**—Enables support for Integrated Services Digital Network (ISDN) devices for digital connections to the public telephone network.

- **Telephony support**—Associated with network cards that convert voice calls to network data; such devices are not associated with the Asterisk Voice over IP (VoIP) software described in Chapter 9.

- **Input device support**—Configures support for basic input devices such as keyboards, mice, touchpads, and more.

- **Character devices**—Associated with byte-stream devices such a virtual terminals, serial ports, some video cards, and more.

- **I2C support**—Works with devices that use inter-integrated circuits (I2C), associated with low-speed peripherals.

- **SPI support**—Used by serial peripheral interface (SPI) systems that communicate with sensors and flash memory.

- **PPS support**—Related to pulse-per-second (PPS) signals associated with some antennas from global positioning system (GPS) devices.

- **GPIO support**—Enables connections to general-purpose input/output (GPIO) devices.

- **Dallas's 1-wire Bus**—Allows communication over single-pin devices.

- **Power supply class support**—Enables modules associated with monitoring of devices such as uninterruptable power supplies (UPSes) and batteries.

- **Hardware monitoring support**—Related to devices that monitor the status and health of the system, such as temperature monitors.

- **Generic thermal sysfs driver**—Supports an alternative hardware monitor for thermal management; may control cooling devices.

- **Watchdog timer support**—Enables monitoring devices that automatically reboot a nonresponsive system.

- **Sonics Silicon Backplane**—Supports connections to devices with the Sonics Silicon Backplane bus.

- **Multifunction device drivers**—Enables access to an array of different multifunction devices.

- **Voltage and current regulator support**—Allows dynamic support of voltage regulators; if the system supports it, such regulators may conserve power and battery life.

- **Multimedia support**—Configures support for multimedia devices such as video for Linux.

- **Graphics support**—Enables support for selected graphical devices.

- **Sound card support**—Configures hardware support for various Linux sound schemes.

- **HID devices**—Supports access to human interface devices (HIDs) such as keyboards and mice, if they're not already supported in other driver sections.

- **USB support**—Allows connections to a wide array of universal serial bus (USB) devices.
- **Ultra wideband devices**—Enables connections to ultra wideband devices, a low-power radio technology also associated with wireless USB and future wireless Bluetooth and IEEE 1394 hardware.
- **MMC/SD/SDIO card support**—Allows connections to various multimedia cards (MMCs), such as secure digital (SD) and secure digital input output (SDIO) cards.
- **Sony MemoryStick card support**—Includes cloned software that enables connections to Sony MemorySticks.
- **LED support**—Related to devices that control light-emitting diode (LED) lights other than those present on keyboards.
- **Accessibility support**—Enables access to selected devices that help people with disabilities access computers.
- **InfiniBand support**—Allows connections through high-performance InfiniBand data connections.
- **EDAC (Error Detection and Correction) reporting**—Enables logging of core system hardware errors.
- **Real time clock**—Supports a variety of clock hardware.
- **DMA engine support**—Enables support for direct memory access (DMA), which can bypass the CPU.
- **Auxiliary-Display support**—Sets up access for auxiliary displays.
- **Userspace I/O drivers**—Supports a small variety of hardware that supports I/O through userspace systems.
- **Staging drivers**—Includes drivers that do not meet normal standards of Linux kernel developers. Avoid this option if possible.
- **X86 platform specific device drivers**—Includes drivers primarily associated with brand-specific laptop functionality.

Firmware Drivers

The Linux kernel includes support for a few specialized firmware drivers, normally associated with boot systems such as the Basic Input/Output System (BIOS).

Filesystems

This section includes integrated and modular support for a wide variety of local and network-based filesystems. One way to disable access to certain filesystems such as the Network File System (NFS) and Samba is to disable it in the kernel as configured in this section.

Be aware that this section includes support for a number of filesystems at an experimental level. Such options should not be enabled on production systems.

Kernel Hacking

Most kernel hacking options are designed for kernel developers who want to see what happens with the kernel in detail in basic operation.

Security Options

As these kernel options are directly related to this book, you'll want to analyze these options in detail. Many of these options relate to features associated with Security Enhanced Linux (SELinux). These options are presented in the order shown from the stock Linux kernel, version 2.6.33. They include the applicable kernel setting, if you want to search further online.

- **Enable access key retention support**—Supports the retention of authentication tokens and access keys. According to IBM, such keys may also be used to cache authentication data. Related to the CONFIG_KEYS option.

- **Enable the /proc/keys file by which keys may be viewed**—Access keys are made visible in the /proc/keys file. Related to the CONFIG_KEYS_DEBUG_PROC_KEYS option.

- **Enable different security models**—Required to implement security models such as SELinux and Application Armor (AppArmor). Related to the CONFIG_SECURITY option.

- **Enable the securityfs filesystem**—Associated with trusted platform modules (TPMs) described in Chapter 3. Related to the CONFIG_SECURIITYFS option.

- **Socket and networking security hooks**—Supports the use of security modules to regulate the use of sockets and networks. Related to the CONFIG_SECURITY_NETWORK option.

- **XFRM (IPSec) networking security hooks**—Supports per-packet controls associated with policies for communications through Internet Protocol Security (IPSec) tunnels, associated with the transformer (XFRM) transformation framework. Related to the CONFIG_SECURITY_NETWORK_XFRM option.

- **Security hooks for pathname based access control**—Supports access controls based on pathnames. Related to the CONFIG_SECURITY_PATH option.

- **Enable Intel (R) trusted execution technology (Intel (R) TXT)**—Associated with the Intel trusted boot module. Related to the CONFIG_INTEL_TXT option.

- **(65536) Low address space for LSM to protect from user allocation**—Protects the first 64MB of RAM from allocation as userspace for **Linux security modules (LSMs)**. Related to the CONFIG_LSM_MMAP_MIN_ADDR option.

- **NSA SELinux support**—Supports the use of SELinux. Related to the CONFIG_SECURITY_SELINUX option.

- **NSA SELinux boot parameter**—Allows SELinux to be disabled during the boot process with the selinux=0 directive. Related to the CONFIG_SECURITY_SELINUX_BOOTPARAM option.

- **NSA SELinux runtime disable**—Supports disabling SELinux before related policies are loaded on the current system. Related to the CONFIG_SECURITY_SELINUX_DISABLE option.

- **NSA SELinux development support**—Supports the development of additional features on SELinux. Related to the CONFIG_SECURITY_SELINUX_DEVELOP option.

- **NSA SELinux avc statistics**—Collects the use of SELinux permissions, in access vector cache (AVC) format. Supports the use of SELinux. Related to the CONFIG_SECURITY_SELINUX_AVC_STATS option.

- **NSA SELinux checkreqprot**—Determines whether SELinux checks for the protection requested by a specific application. Related to the CONFIG_SECURITY_SELINUX_CHECKREQPROT_VALUE option.

- **NSA SELinux maximum supported policy format version**—Supports the use of SELinux. Related to the CONFIG_SECURITY_SELINUX_POLICYDB_VERSION_MAX option.

- **Simplified mandatory access control kernel support**—Enables the use of **simplified mandatory access control kernel (SMACK)** support, an alternative to SELinux and AppArmor. Related to the CONFIG_SECURITY_SMACK option.

- **TOMOYO Linux support**—Enables the use of **TOMOYO**, an alternative to SELinux and AppArmor. Related to the CONFIG_SECURITY_TOMOYO option.

- **Default security module (SELinux)**—Sets the default mandatory access control option as SELinux. Related to the DEFAULT_SECURITY_SELINUX option.

Cryptographic API

The options in this section provide kernel support for several dozen cryptographic options, associated with the cryptographic application programming interface (API). Such options are classified into a number of sections, including the following:

- **Crypto core or helper**—Includes cryptographic algorithms and related tools

- **Authenticated encryption with associated data**—Specifies options primarily related to IPSec

- **Block modes**—Supports a variety of block ciphers

- **Hash modes**—Includes options for hashing messages and more

- **Digest**—Specifies a variety of digest algorithms

- **Ciphers**—Includes a variety of cipher algorithms

- **Compression**—Specifies support for various compression algorithms

- **Random number generation**—Supports random-number-generation tools for cryptographic modules (this is beyond the support provided by the /dev/random device)

Virtualization

This section includes basic virtualization modules for the Kernel-based Virtual Machine (KVM) and the Virtio devices commonly used for KVM. Unless you're compiling the source code associated with a Xen-based kernel, you won't see Xen-related options in this or other kernel sections.

Library Routines

Options in the library routines section include compression options in the kernel.

Build Your Own Secure Kernel

The previous section included information on some of the many different ways to customize the Linux kernel. But that is not enough. You need to know how to compile that kernel. This section summarizes the steps required to build a custom kernel. Details frequently vary by distribution. If details are not described in this section, they were already covered earlier in this chapter. These steps include the following:

1. Install required development tools.
2. Download and unpack the source code.
3. Navigate to the directory with the source code. Determine a baseline configuration from a local `configs/` subdirectory or a `config-*` file in the `/boot/` directory.
4. Open a kernel configuration tool with a command like `make menuconfig` and make desired changes.
5. Compile the kernel based on the new custom configuration.
6. Install the new kernel; create and install a new initial RAM disk that matches the new kernel if required.
7. Make sure the bootloader is updated with stanzas for the existing and the new custom kernels, along with matching initial RAM disks.
8. Test the result. Try rebooting into the new kernel. If it doesn't work, boot into the previously working kernel.

> ⚠️ **WARNING**
>
> When configuring a custom kernel, take care to preserve the files associated with an existing kernel. If the custom kernel leads to an unbootable or otherwise troubled system, you'll be able to use the existing kernel to boot that system.

Download Kernel Source Code

There are two basic choices for kernel source code. You could start with the source code released by the developers at the Linux Kernel Organization. Alternatively, you could start with the source code released by the developers of your target distribution. Source code from the Linux Kernel Organization was discussed earlier in this chapter. In contrast, the process for downloading the source code for a distribution is a bit different.

Download Ubuntu Kernel Source Code

For Ubuntu systems, the easiest way to download the source code for the current kernel is to run the following command:

```
# apt-get install linux-source
```

When running this command, you'll notice that the source code has three numbers; for the Lucid Lynx 10.04 release in April of 2010, it's 2.6.32. In other words, Ubuntu starts with the noted update version, before any patches. It may add its own patches before releasing the associated source code.

Download Red Hat Kernel Source Code

While Red Hat doesn't release its binary packages under open source licenses, it does release its source code under those licenses. That source code is publicly available from *ftp://ftp.redhat.com*. On that server, source code packages are available in one of the two following directories, associated with Red Hat clients and servers:

```
/redhat/linux/enterprise/5Client/en/os/SRPMS/
/redhat/linux/enterprise/5Server/en/os/SRPMS/
```

A test of the kernel source code from these two directories with the diff command suggests that they are the same packages. While the kernel source code package on the two directories are the same, the general list of packages on these directories differ.

When you download the source code, make sure it's of the correct version number. To verify the version number of the currently loaded kernel, run the uname -r command.

Once the source code package is downloaded, it can be written to an appropriate subdirectory of /usr/src/ with the following command. The uname -r command in back quotes substitutes the version number of the currently loaded kernel.

```
# rpm -i kernel-`uname -r`.src.rpm
```

That installs the basic source code to /usr/src/redhat/ subdirectories. The next step is to build the source code. Navigate to the /usr/src/redhat/SPECS/ subdirectory. Now run the following rpmbuild command. The -bp switch unpacks the source code with applicable patches. The --target switch specifies the platform; the uname -m command with the back quotes substitutes the architecture, such as x86_64 or i386.

```
# rpmbuild -bp --target=`uname -m` kernel-2.6.spec
```

For Red Hat Enterprise Linux 5, the command unpacks the source code into the following directory:

```
/usr/src/redhat/BUILD/kernel-2.6.18/linux-2.6.18.`uname -m`/
```

As of this writing, the version number for Red Hat Enterprise Linux 6 is 2.6.32.

Install Required Development Tools

If you haven't already installed the development tools described earlier in this chapter, do so now. As described earlier in this chapter, you'll need development tools to compile and customize the kernel. The actual packages to be installed vary by distribution and release.

Navigate to the Directory with the Source Code

The directory with the source code varies by distribution. Details were described earlier in this chapter. That directory may have a name like `/usr/src/linux-2.6.32/`. On Red Hat systems, it may be named something like `/usr/src/redhat/BUILD/kernel-2.6.18/linux-2.6.18.x86_64/`. Once in that directory, you'll need a baseline configuration in the `.config` file in the local directory.

Standard architecture-specific configurations are available in a `configs/` subdirectory. Alternatively, you can copy the configuration of the currently loaded kernel from the `/boot/config-`uname -r`` file, or you can process the current configuration with the `make oldconfig` command.

If you've compiled the kernel before, it's best to make sure any files that remain from previous custom kernels are clean with the following command:

```
# make clean
```

Open a Kernel Configuration Tool

Now it's time to configure the kernel. Open a kernel configuration tool. For example, the `make menuconfig` command opens the console-based tool described earlier in this chapter. While other equivalent kernel configuration tools are available, they're functionally equivalent to this console-based tool.

When changes are made, you're prompted to save those changes. If those changes are successfully saved, you'll see it in the output to the `ls -l .config` command, which should reflect the current date and time.

Compile the Kernel with the New Custom Configuration

Before compiling the kernel, open the file named `Makefile` in the local directory. Look at the EXTRAVERSION directive. It specifies the suffix to be added to the newly compiled kernel. You may want to add an additional identifier to that directive; I've added my name here:

```
EXTRAVERSION = -prep.mike1
```

Be aware, it takes time to compile a kernel. On slower systems, the process may even take a couple of hours. Make sure there's at least a couple of gigabytes of free space on the volume where the kernel is being compiled. If the volume fills up before the process is complete, you'll have to delete unneeded files and start again.

> **TIP**
>
> The developers behind the Linux kernel are working to make it easier to compile the kernel. Options for the `make` command are described in the `Makefile` file in the directory with the kernel source code.

If the process stops with an error, pay attention to the last messages before the error. There may be an incompatible option in the custom configuration. The commands required to compile a kernel vary slightly, depending on the distribution and release.

Compile a Kernel on Ubuntu Systems

On Ubuntu systems, the following command should create the new kernel as a Debian-style package in the local directory.

```
# make-kpkg buildpackage --initrd kernel_image
```

Compile a Kernel on Red Hat Systems

On Red Hat systems, the command is even simpler. But this is one time when it's important to be in the root administrative account. Compiling a kernel on a Red Hat system even with `sudo` privileges can lead to errors. From the root administrative account, the following command creates a kernel and sets up a custom RPM in the `/usr/src/redhat/RPMS/`uname -m`/` directory:

```
# make rpm
```

Compile a Stock Kernel

When compiling a stock kernel, the distribution-specific commands may not always work. If they don't work, and you're confident that the problem is not related to some custom configuration error in the kernel, run the following command to compile that stock kernel:

```
# make
```

While not strictly necessary, you should also run the following command. Without it, Linux may not have access to modules that are compatible with the custom kernel:

```
# make modules_install
```

When the process associated with these commands is complete, the following command should set up the new kernel and initial RAM disk in the `/boot/` directory. It should make needed changes to the bootloader:

```
# make install
```

Install the New Kernel and More

The distribution-specific commands to compile a kernel should create appropriate binary packages in the directories just described. You should be able to run associated package-management commands such as `rpm` or `dpkg` to install the newly customized and compiled kernel. When you do, make sure to use the install switch with the package-management command to avoid overwriting any current and presumably working kernel.

If successful, you should find both the new custom kernel and existing working kernel in the /boot/ directory. Alternatively, if you've run the `make install` command with the stock kernel, the new kernel should be installed in the /boot/ directory.

If there is no initial RAM disk included with the new custom kernel, you can create one with the `mkinitrd` command. For example, the following command should create an appropriate Red Hat initial RAM disk in the /boot/ directory:

```
# mkinitrd /boot/initrd-2.6.18-6.mike1.img  2.6.18-6.mike1
```

The format for initial RAM disks varies by distribution.

Check the Bootloader

Finally, you need to make sure the new custom kernel has an appropriate and separate stanza in the bootloader configuration file. Assuming the system is configured to boot from a Linux bootloader, the difference between stanzas for the custom and existing kernel should be limited to the version number of the kernel and initial RAM disk files. For more information on Linux bootloaders, see Chapter 3.

Test the Result

Now it's time to test the result. For this, you may want to change the bootloader configuration file to make it easier to bring up the associated boot menu. You can then reboot the system, open the bootloader menu, and select the new custom kernel.

If the boot process is successful, make sure to test the new kernel with appropriate conditions associated with production systems. Once satisfied with the results, you can then change the bootloader configuration file to make it difficult to bring up the boot menu, and boot directly into the newly customized kernel using the guidelines discussed in Chapter 3.

If the boot process or any of the other tests are not successful, you should be able to reboot the system into the existing working kernel.

If the new kernel is as success, you should be able to use the same custom kernel on other systems. Once satisfied with the results, you can then transfer the kernel and associated files to production systems.

Kernels and the /proc/ Filesystem

Besides creating a custom kernel, you can do more with it to help secure Linux systems. One method uses the dynamic kernel options documented in the /proc/ directory filesystem. While the /proc/ directory includes information on detected hardware, currently running processes, memory, and more, actual kernel options are shown in /proc/sys/ subdirectories. For example, the status of the /proc/sys/net/ipv4/ip_forward file determines whether Internet Protocol version 4 (IPv4) packets are forwarded through the system.

Most kernel configurable files in the /proc/sys/ directory are boolean; in other words, they have a value of 0 or 1. If the file is active, its value is 1. So to activate IPv4 forwarding on a system, you'd write the number 1 to the /proc/sys/net/ipv4/ip_forward file. One way to do so is with the following command:

```
# echo "1" > /proc/sys/net/ipv4/ip_forward
```

But the /proc/ directory filesystem is dynamic. Changes to these files do not survive a reboot. To make such changes permanent, you'll need to add appropriate options to the /etc/sysctl.conf file. The corresponding directive in that file is as follows:

```
net.ipv4.ip_forward = 1
```

You may note that there is no reference to proc or sys in that directive, as all kernel configuration options reside in the /proc/sys/ directory.

The following sections are based on a presentation by Steve Grubb of Red Hat at the 2008 Red Hat Summit. In that presentation, Grubb recommended kernel configuration changes in the areas described in the sections that follow.

The focus of these sections is IPv4 networking. If you've also enabled Internet Protocol version 6 (IPv6) networking, don't forget to make parallel changes to matching directories in the /proc/ filesystem and matching directives in the /etc/sysctl.conf file.

Don't Reply to Broadcasts

Normally, a system will respond to a ping command addressed to the broadcast address of a network. For example, the following command should receive responses from all systems with IP addresses on the 192.168.0.0/24 network:

```
$ ping -b 192.168.0.255
```

A black-hat hacker who can identify the IP address of a system can start attacking that system. A black-hat hacker who can identify the IP addresses of all systems on a network can attack those systems simultaneously. To prevent that, you'd activate the following option:

```
/proc/sys/net/ipv4/icmp_echo_ignore_broadcasts
```

As suggested by the name, the option ignores broadcast messages using Internet Control Message Protocol (ICMP). It works because the ping command uses ICMP. The corresponding option in /etc/sysctl.conf is as follows:

```
net.ipv4.icmp_echo_ignore_broadcasts = 1
```

This option does not prevent responses to targeted ping commands, just broadcasts. One advantage is that it also prevents what is known as a smurf attack, where a broadcast is sent using a **spoofed** or faked source address of the intended target computer.

Protect from Bad ICMP Messages

ICMP messages can be **mangled** or spoofed, resulting in ICMP messages that do not conform to regular standards. In the spirit of denying black-hat hackers as much information as possible, you can activate the following option:

```
/proc/sys/net/ipv4/icmp_ignore_bogus_error_responses
```

As suggested by the name, the option ignores bogus ICMP messages. The corresponding option in /etc/sysctl.conf is as follows:

```
net.ipv4.icmp_ignore_bogus_error_responses = 1
```

Protect from SYN Floods

A SYN flood is another denial-of-service (DoS) attack based on a rapid succession of SYN packets requesting synchronization with a target system. A SYN cookie can help prevent dropped connections, which can lead to additional SYN messages. You can activate the SYN cookie option in the following file:

```
/proc/sys/net/ipv4/tcp_syncookies
```

As suggested by the name, the option activates SYN cookies on Transmission Control Protocol (TCP) connections. The corresponding option in /etc/sysctl.conf is as follows:

```
net.ipv4.tcp_syncookies = 1
```

Activate Reverse Path Filtering

Reverse path filtering can help regulate traffic through routers, limiting such traffic to packets destined for networks associated with that router. In other words, with reverse path filtering, a message destined for IP address 10.10.10.10 that is sent to a router associated with IP network addresses 192.168.0.0 and 192.168.1.0 is dropped. You can activate reverse path filtering on the following files:

```
/proc/sys/net/ipv4/conf/all/rp_filter
/proc/sys/net/ipv4/conf/default/rp_filter
```

As suggested by the directory path, it's a configuration option for default and all networks. The corresponding options in /etc/sysctl.conf are as follows:

```
net.ipv4.conf.all.rp_filter = 1
net.ipv4.conf.default.rp_filter = 1
```

Close Access to Routing Tables

If a black-hat hacker can change the routing tables on your systems, that person can redirect your users to his or her systems. If the black-hat hacker can spoof a gateway system, that person can change the routing tables on other systems on the network.

To that end, if that black-hat user could redirect traffic intended for an internal corporate page to a remote site that requests Social Security numbers, that could be trouble. You can prevent outsiders from changing your routing tables by deactivating the following files:

```
/proc/sys/net/ipv4/conf/all/accept_redirects
/proc/sys/net/ipv4/conf/all/secure_redirects
/proc/sys/net/ipv4/conf/default/accept_redirects
/proc/sys/net/ipv4/conf/default/secure_redirects
```

As suggested by the directory path, it's a configuration option for default and all networks. The corresponding options in /etc/sysctl.conf are as follows:

```
net.ipv4.conf.all.accept_redirects = 0
net.ipv4.conf.all.secure_redirects = 0
net.ipv4.conf.default.accept_redirects = 0
net.ipv4.conf.default.secure_redirects = 0
```

Avoid Source Routing

Source routing allows a user to specify the route a packet takes from a system to a destination. If you want to retain control over how packets are sent over a network, it's best to disable this option for network users. You can deactivate such options by deactivating the following files:

```
/proc/sys/net/ipv4/conf/all/accept_source_route
/proc/sys/net/ipv4/conf/default/accept_source_route
```

As suggested by the directory path, it's a configuration option for default and all networks. The corresponding options in /etc/sysctl.conf are as follows:

```
net.ipv4.conf.all.accept_source_route = 0
net.ipv4.conf.default.accept_source_route = 0
```

Don't Pass Traffic Between Networks

Yes, there are some systems that should be configured as routers, to pass information between networks such as a private local network and the Internet. But such options should be activated only on routers, and not on regular systems. To deactivate a system as a router, deactivate the following files:

```
/proc/sys/net/ipv4/ip_forward
/proc/sys/net/ipv4/conf/all/send_redirects
/proc/sys/net/ipv4/conf/default/send_redirects
```

As suggested by the directory path, it's a configuration option for default and all networks. The corresponding options in /etc/sysctl.conf are as follows:

```
net.ipv4.ip_forward = 0
net.ipv4.conf.all.send_redirects = 0
net.ipv4.conf.default.send_redirects = 0
```

Log Spoofed, Source-Routed, and Redirected Packets

In computer networking, packets normally have source and destination addresses. By definition, one of those addresses should be associated with the local network. But it's relatively easy to set up spoofed addresses. Packets with addresses that should not be possible are known as **Martian packets** (as in "packets from Mars"). To see if and how often black-hat hackers may be trying to spoof addresses, you'll want to check log files. The following files, if active, make sure information on Martian packets is logged:

```
/proc/sys/net/ipv4/conf/all/log_martians
/proc/sys/net/ipv4/conf/default/log_martians
```

As suggested by the directory path, it's a configuration option for default and all networks. The corresponding options in /etc/sysctl.conf are as follows:

```
net.ipv4.conf.all.log_martians = 1
net.ipv4.conf.default.log_martians = 1
```

Best Practices: Kernel Security Risk Mitigation

Perhaps the key tool in a battle to secure a Linux system is the kernel. That makes sense, because the kernel is the essence of the Linux operating system. The developers behind major Linux distributions do an excellent job creating and updating secure kernels in binary format, ready for quick installation. Different distributions may configure and test Linux kernels for one or over a dozen different architectures.

The developers behind different distributions may focus their efforts on other levels of functionality. For example, Ubuntu releases different distributions for servers, guest virtual machines, Xen hosts, and even the Amazon enterprise cloud. All Linux distributions start with the stock kernel released by the developers behind the Linux Kernel Organization, led by Linus Torvalds.

Releases of the stock kernel follow a *majorversion.majorrevision.updateversion .patchnumber* format. New update versions are released approximately every three months. Several stable versions are maintained simultaneously. Administrators who want to update their stock kernel can use patches released by the Linux Kernel Organization.

The Linux kernel mailing list at *http://lkml.org/* can help you monitor security issues related to the stock kernel. The developers behind Linux distributions maintain their own mailing lists that highlight security issues related to custom kernels built for their releases. Because not all kernel updates relate to security issues, you may not want to install all updates. If you do install a kernel update, it's important to preserve the currently installed kernel in case the update causes trouble for your systems.

If you want to customize the Linux kernel, you can start with the stock kernel or the source code released by the developers behind a Linux distribution. You'll also need development software to customize the kernel and compile the customized code.

Before customizing a kernel, take care to clean the directories associated with the source code with commands like `make clean`. Consider starting with a baseline configuration either in a `configs/` subdirectory or the `/boot/` directory. Even if you prefer to leave this work to the developers behind a Linux distribution, review the options available for the Linux kernel with something like the console-based tool accessible with the `make menuconfig` command.

Custom kernel configurations are saved to the hidden `.config` file in the directory with the kernel source code. Custom extensions can be configured in the `Makefile` file in that directory. The commands required to compile the custom kernel vary by distribution; other commands may be used for stock kernels. Once complete, make sure the custom kernel does not overwrite the currently running kernel in the `/boot/` directory and any associated bootloader configuration files.

Once you're satisfied with a kernel, you can do more to secure a system in the `/proc/` filesystem. Dynamic kernel configuration options are available in `/proc/sys/` subdirectories, in boolean files. Some of these options can protect a system from DoS attacks, spoofed source and destination addresses, remote reconfiguration of routing tables, and more. The same options can be configured in the `/etc/sysctl.conf` file to make sure desired changes survive a reboot.

CHAPTER SUMMARY

This chapter focused on the Linux kernel. As the center of the Linux operating system, it lies at the core of Linux security. While most users start with a kernel created by the developers behind a distribution, you can also start with the stock kernel created by the developers of the Linux Kernel Organization. Whichever one you choose, it's important to keep that kernel up to date with appropriate patches and updates. But not all updates relate to security. Because kernel updates can affect the functionality of your systems, care is required.

Kernels can be customized based on source code released either from the Linux Kernel Organization or by the developers behind a selected Linux distribution. With the right development tools, you can customize the options associated with a kernel and then compile them into a binary format. You need to take care to preserve any existing kernel, as problems with a newly customized kernel could otherwise leave a system unbootable.

KEY CONCEPTS AND TERMS

Architecture
Backport
Hardy Heron (8.04)
iSeries
Itanium
Kroah-Hartman, Greg

Linux security modules (LSMs)
Lucid Lynx (10.04)
Mangled
Martian packet
Meta package
Paravirtualized
pSeries

Simplified mandatory access
 control kernel (SMACK)
Spoofed
Stock kernel
TOMOYO
Torvalds, Linus
Xen kernel

10

Kernel Security
Risk Mitigation

CHAPTER 10 ASSESSMENT

1. Which of the following features is no longer associated with a separate kernel on many Linux distributions?

   A. Virtual machine hosts
   B. Xen
   C. SMP
   D. Servers

2. When an updated kernel is released with a security update, which of the following numbers in the kernel is changed?

   A. Major version
   B. Minor version
   C. Update version
   D. Patch number

3. Which of the following commands can be used to unpack and uncompress a stock kernel in `.tar.bz2` format?

   A. `tar xzf`
   B. `tar xjf`
   C. `tar xbf`
   D. `tar xuf`

4. The Web site associated with the Linux Kernel Organization is _____.

5. Which of the following actions should you *not* take when implementing a new kernel?

   A. Upgrade
   B. Install
   C. Patch
   D. Compile

6. Which of the following directories contain a file with the configuration of the kernel that is currently running on the local system?

   A. `/usr/src/redhat/BUILD/kernel`
      ↳ `-`uname -r`/linux-`uname -r`/`
   B. `/usr/src/linux-`uname -r`/configs/`
   C. `/usr/src/linux-`uname -r`/`
   D. `/boot/`

7. Which of the following commands starts a console-based menu-driven tool for customizing the kernel?

   A. `make config`
   B. `make menuconfig`
   C. `make xconfig`
   D. `make gconfig`

8. Which of the following kernel options is *not* related to mandatory access controls?

   A. SELinux
   B. TOMOYO
   C. Cryptographic API
   D. AppArmor

9. Name the section of the kernel configuration tool related to formats such as `ext2` and `ext3`.

10. In what configuration file can you customize the filename of the compiled kernel?

    A. `make`
    B. `config-`uname -r``
    C. `.config`
    D. `Makefile`

11. When a new kernel is compiled and installed, what file should contain different stanzas to two different kernels available during the boot process? (Select two.)

    A. `/boot/grub/menu.lst`
    B. `/etc/bootloader`
    C. `/etc/lilo.conf`
    D. `/usr/src/linux-`uname -r`/.config`

12. If you see the `net.ipv4.icmp_echo_ignore_broadcasts = 1` option in the `/etc/sysctl.conf` file, what file contains that boolean option?

    A. `/proc/net/ipv4/`
       ↳ `icmp_echo_ignore_broadcasts`
    B. `/proc/sys/net/ipv4/`
       ↳ `icmp_echo_ignore_broadcasts`
    C. `/proc/net/sys/ipv4/`
       ↳ `icmp_echo_ignore_broadcasts`
    D. `/proc/icmp_echo_ignore_broadcasts`

13. Which of the following directives in the `/etc/sysctl.conf` should be set to 0 to deactivate routing on the local system?

    A. `net.ipv4.ip_forward`
    B. `net.sys.ipv4.ip_route`
    C. `net.ipv4.ip_routing`
    D. `net.sys.ipv4.ip_source`

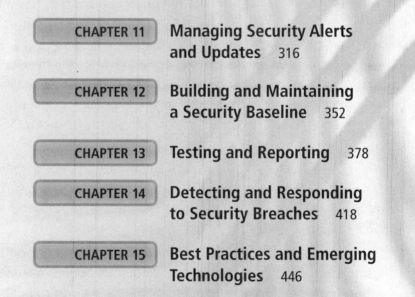

PART THREE

Building a Layered Linux Security Strategy

Managing Security Alerts and Updates

COMPUTER SECURITY is a constant battle. From the moment a security alert is released, there's a race between black-hat hackers who look for vulnerable systems and administrators who install updates for those systems. That's tempered by the risks associated with some updates, since developers can't test updates against every possible hardware and software configuration. You may need to make your own judgment on whether to install an update based on the associated bug report.

The battle starts with the distribution. The developers behind Linux distributions do an excellent job releasing security updates on a timely basis. Because these updates are released as binary packages in structured repositories, it's relatively easy to install such updates with any needed dependent packages. The developers behind a distribution also incorporate updates from the developers of applications such as the OpenOffice.org suite. Linux administrators have allies in this process, including organizations as powerful as the Institute for Security and Open Methodologies (ISECOM), the U.S. National Security Agency (NSA), and the open source community.

While fewer instances of malware directly affect Linux, some malware can be carried by Linux when served to other operating systems such as Microsoft Windows. Antivirus and anti-malware systems are important in a Linux security strategy.

The best way to keep a Linux system up to date depends on the number of systems being updated, as well as whether you need to create specialized updates. Some commercial update managers allow you to push updates to one or several systems simultaneously. Both open source and commercial updates are based on repositories maintained by the developers behind a distribution. If you want, you can create customized repositories for an enterprise or even just a local area network (LAN).

Chapter 11 Topics

This chapter covers the following topics and concepts:

- How to keep up to speed with distribution security
- How to keep up to speed with application security
- Which antivirus options are available
- What bug reports are
- How security works in the open source world
- How to decide whether to use automatic updates or analyzed alerts
- How to manage Linux patches
- What the options for update managers are
- What commercial update managers are
- What open source update managers are
- What best practices are for security operations management

Chapter 11 Goals

When you complete this chapter, you will be able to:

- Keep up to speed with Linux security issues
- Select an appropriate antivirus system
- Get help from the open source community
- Choose an update-management system

Keep Up to Speed with Distribution Security

While Linux is Linux, many security issues are distribution specific. In this section, you'll review various options to keep up to speed with the latest security issues for each distribution. Because this book is focused on the **Red Hat** and **Ubuntu** distributions, this section reviews security lists associated with those and allied distributions. Although Red Hat Enterprise Linux is the stable enterprise-ready distribution released by Red Hat, some enterprises choose other distributions based on Red Hat software. Two of the major options are Fedora, the open source developmental test bed for future Red Hat Enterprise releases; and CentOS, based on the Red Hat Enterprise Linux source code released under the GNU General Public License.

The challenges presented in this section should motivate you to standardize systems on one Linux distribution.

> **NOTE**
>
> This chapter includes references to a number of uniform resource locators (URLs), which were valid at the time of this writing, in April of 2010. All URLs, however, are subject to change.

Red Hat Alerts

Red Hat is more than just Red Hat Enterprise Linux (RHEL). While RHEL is the flagship Red Hat distribution, it's not the only option associated with Red Hat software. This book lists just two major alternatives to RHEL: Fedora and CentOS Linux. Unfortunately, that is patently unfair to the many other distributions that use Red Hat software and Red Hat–style packages.

Red Hat Enterprise Linux

For RHEL, two methods are available for monitoring security advisories. There's the public **Red Hat security advisories (RHSAs)** mailing list, and there's the list of errata on the **Red Hat Network (RHN)**. Anyone with an e-mail address can sign up on the RHSA mailing list at *https://www.redhat.com/mailman/listinfo/rhsa-announce/*. An equivalent Really Simple Syndication (RSS) feed is also available. Anyone with a subscription on the RHN can access the errata, with associated security advisories. The information on both lists is essentially the same.

However, anyone with a paid subscription can download the binary packages from the RHN that can address security issues. Any system that is connected to the RHN can be configured to automatically download and install such updates. More options for pulling and pushing such updates are described later in this chapter.

If you find a security issue with an RHEL system, Red Hat encourages you to contact its Security Response Team at *secalert@redhat.com.* Per *https://www.redhat.com/security/team/contact/*, e-mails sent to that address are kept confidential if you so desire.

In their efforts to provide enterprise-level support, Red Hat provides security updates for its RHEL releases for at least seven years.

CentOS Linux

The developers of CentOS Linux use the RHEL source code released by Red Hat under open source licenses. As such, the CentOS Linux distribution is known as a **rebuild** of RHEL. Most security issues with CentOS software also apply to Red Hat software. But there are differences. To avoid trademark issues, CentOS modifies some released RHEL source code to omit RHEL trademarks.

Many Linux adherents use CentOS, as there is no charge for access to that distribution in its binary format. Of course, CentOS cannot offer Red Hat support for its distribution. And there's commonly a time lag between the release of a Red Hat security update and a CentOS security update.

CentOS does update its distribution when updated RHEL source code is publicly released. But it takes a little while for the volunteers behind CentOS to compile the source code and test it on the CentOS rebuild distribution.

CentOS also has a mailing list for security advisories at *http://lists.centos.org/mailman/listinfo/centos-announce/*. Equivalent information is also made available on CentOS message boards. CentOS advisories and updated packages typically lag behind those associated with Red Hat by a few days. But of course, CentOS is more freely available than Red Hat.

So the choice is yours: Are the costs associated with a subscription to RHEL worth
the faster security updates?

Fedora Linux

Fedora Linux is in many ways the test bed for RHEL. New versions of RHEL are released
approximately every one to three years. RHEL does get enterprise-level support and
the benefits associated with the RHN. On the other hand, new versions of Fedora Linux
are released approximately every six months.

Fedora Linux is typically released with the latest stable version of the Linux kernel.
However, as the developers at the Linux Kernel Organization create security patches
for multiple Linux kernels, the latest stable kernel is not necessarily a security advantage.

As of this writing, Fedora security alerts are handled primarily through online wikis.
The prime Fedora security Wiki page can be found at *http://fedoraproject.org/wiki/Security*.

While Fedora Linux is primarily supported by the "community," Red Hat engineers
do develop software for that distribution. However, Fedora is officially released by a group
of volunteers. Security updates depend on the availability of the volunteer developers
and the time allocated by Red Hat to keep Fedora up to date. In addition, Fedora Linux
is supported for a total of 13 months.

Ubuntu Alerts

Strictly speaking, the Ubuntu distribution is the release that includes the GNU Network
Object Model Environment (GNOME) as the default graphical user interface (GUI) desktop
environment. In contrast, the **Kubuntu** distribution includes the K Desktop Environment
(KDE); and the **Xubuntu** distribution includes the **Xfce desktop environment**.

Security issues may arise that are unique to each of these desktop environments.
However, these distributions share the same basic core. Ubuntu, Kubuntu, and Xubuntu
all include the same software for command-line–based applications from Apache to Zebra.

Security issues for all Ubuntu-based distributions supported by Canonical are collected
in **Ubuntu security notices (USNs)**, available online at *http://www.ubuntu.com/usn/*.

The availability of a USN depends on the support given to a release. Ubuntu releases
a new version of each of its distributions every six months. These releases include
Ubuntu, Kubuntu, and Xubuntu on the desktop and Ubuntu Server Edition for the server.
Standard Ubuntu releases are supported for 18 months. Releases are given code names
and numbers. For example, Ubuntu's Karmic Koala distributions were released in October
of 2009 with a code number associated with the date (9.10).

Every two years, Ubuntu releases its distributions with long-term support (LTS).
Its first LTS release, made in June of 2006 and code-named Dapper Drake, was assigned
a code number of 6.06. Its latest LTS release, code-named Lucid Lynx, was made in April of
2010, with a code number of 10.04. Ubuntu LTS releases have extended levels of support:

- **Desktop releases**—Supported for three years
- **Server releases**—Supported for five years

Because many security notices affect multiple Ubuntu releases, there is no differentiation between the server and desktop in the USN list. A properly configured USN specifies the affected releases. If you prefer to monitor Ubuntu security notices via mailing lists, subscribe to the Ubuntu Security Announcements mailing list at *https://lists.ubuntu.com/mailman/listinfo/ubuntu-security-announce/*. And as Ubuntu is based on the Debian Linux distribution, you may also choose to monitor Debian security notices as well.

Keep Up to Speed with Application Security

The developers behind most Linux distributions incorporate solutions to application-related security issues in updated packages. Red Hat and Ubuntu incorporate announcements on security issues related to applications on their main security lists, including USN and RHSA.

Just as there's a lag between the release of a security update for RHEL and CentOS, there may also be a lag between the release of a security update for an application such as the OpenOffice.org suite on the application Web site and the repositories associated with the Red Hat and Ubuntu distributions. Because enterprises pay RHEL and Canonical for support on the RHEL and Ubuntu distributions, their developers may be more strongly motivated to keep that time lag to a minimum.

The following sections highlight how you might choose to keep up to speed with several important user applications and server services. Be aware, this is an option for an aggressive administrator who is allowed to take extra time to keep up to speed on security issues from a number of sources.

One major source of interest is maintained by the MITRE Corporation, a nonprofit research organization, on behalf of the National Cyber Security Division of the U.S. Department of Homeland Security. Their list of vulnerabilities is known as the **Common Vulnerabilities and Exposures (CVE) list**. For more information, see *http://cve.mitre.org/cve/*.

User Applications

This section is focused on user applications, primarily those found on GUI desktop environments. In fact, the three examples listed in this section are GUI applications. The OpenOffice.org suite is the open source alternative to Microsoft Office. In fact, this book was drafted using OpenOffice.org Writer, with the help of OpenOffice.org Impress. Files from these applications were then edited using Microsoft Word and PowerPoint.

If your users work with console-based applications such as `mutt` for e-mail or `elinks` for Web browsing, you may also consider monitoring the mailing lists or similar notification systems provided by the developers of those applications.

The OpenOffice.org Suite

Just as with standard Linux distributions, OpenOffice.org has its own security team. When problems are found, they're highlighted online in security bulletins. If you want, you can sign up for OpenOffice.org security alerts at *http://www.openoffice.org/security/alerts.html*.

The developers behind OpenOffice.org update their software on a regular basis. When available, OpenOffice.org may be highlighted in an alert associated with one of the OpenOffice.org applications.

Some security alerts may be an addressed by an update to the OpenOffice.org suite. Others may be addressed in policy. For example, if a **virus** is being transmitted through some image format, the bulletin may suggest that you (and your users) avoid loading files with that type of image—at least until the next version of the OpenOffice.org suite is made available.

When possible, it's easier to implement an update from the repositories associated with a distribution. But such updates aren't always available. For example, OpenOffice.org 3.*x* wasn't made available in the repositories for the Red Hat Desktop until a couple of years after OpenOffice.org version 3.0 was first released. But the OpenOffice.org 2.*x* series was still sufficiently capable for most users.

Users who need OpenOffice.org 3.*x* on Red Hat systems could download associated packages directly from *http://download.openoffice.org/*. Updates are available in both Red Hat Package Manager (RPM) and Debian package formats suited for both Red Hat and Ubuntu-type systems.

Web Browsers

Web browsers are one area where choice may make life more difficult for security professionals. Half a dozen different browsers are available just from regular Ubuntu repositories, easily accessible to users with direct online access. So it may be in your interest to limit what users can download and install. One method based on custom repositories is described later in this chapter.

This section describes just two Web browsers commonly used on Linux: Mozilla Firefox and Konqueror. Mozilla Firefox is the same open source browser commonly found on both Microsoft and Apple operating systems.

The Mozilla Foundation is the open source organization behind the Firefox Web browser and other open source tools such as the Thunderbird e-mail manager and the SeaMonkey Internet application suite. Mozilla maintains a list of security announcements at *http://www.mozilla.org/security/announce/*. Such announcements are classified by product at *http://www.mozilla.org/security/known-vulnerabilities/*.

In contrast, Konqueror is part of the KDE desktop environment. As such, security issues are maintained by the developers at the KDE Foundation. Fortunately for KDE, there have been very few security issues directly related to that desktop environment. As you can see at *http://www.kde.org/info/security/*, there have been just a few dozen advisories released in the past decade on KDE software, including Konqueror as a Web browser.

Adobe Applications

Given the popularity of Adobe formats such as the Portable Document Format (PDF) and Flash player, it's important for Linux administrators to monitor the status of such applications. Adobe security advisories can be found online at *http://www.adobe.com/support/security/*.

Updates can be problematic. Repositories for older Ubuntu releases may not have even the most up-to-date packages for the Adobe Reader. However, Adobe does provide packages in both Debian and Red Hat package-management formats, which makes it possible to incorporate those packages in a local repository, as described later in this chapter.

Alternatively, Linux has several native PDF readers, along with open source alternatives for Adobe technologies like the Flash player. Such packages are often more readily available through standard Ubuntu and Red Hat repositories. The standard GNOME and KDE alternatives are known as evince and KPDF. For more information, see *http://projects.gnome.org/evince/* and *http://kpdf.kde.org/*. Security issues do appear from time to time on these open source applications.

Service Applications

For those who do not have to administer Linux desktop environments, the challenge will be a bit more limited. All a Linux administrator needs to do is monitor the security alerts associated with the applications running on his or her servers.

The basic pattern for security with respect to open source service applications is pretty consistent. Just as open source development proceeds in the public eye, open source security alerts and updates are publicly available. To that end, this section describes how you can keep up to speed with security issues related to the Apache Web server, the Samba file server, and various File Transfer Protocol (FTP) servers.

The developers behind most Linux distributions, including Red Hat and Ubuntu, support the installation of these services by providing appropriate packages in binary format. Such packages include a number of preconfigured options. If you considered customizing the Linux kernel as described in Chapter 10, you might also consider customizing how service applications such as Apache and Samba are built from their source code trees.

The Apache Web Server

Administrators who run the Apache Web server can stay up to date with related security issues through the Apache Server Announcements list. To sign up, send an e-mail to *announce-subscribe@httpd.apache.org*. For a current list of vulnerabilities, navigate to *http://httpd.apache.org/security_report.html*.

The developers behind Apache maintain several versions of its Web server software in a manner similar to the developers behind the Linux kernel. As of this writing, they still maintain version 1.3 and 2.0. They release security updates to these versions of their Web server on a regular basis.

Apache has an excellent guide to keeping Web sites secure on its servers. For more information, see *http://httpd.apache.org/docs/2.2/misc/security_tips.html*. These tips are updated with each new version; if version 2.4 is active when you read this, replace 2.2 with 2.4 in the URL.

If you've discovered a security issue that has yet to be reported, the Apache security team encourages reports on their private mailing lists. For more information on the procedures, see *http://www.apache.org/security/*.

While Apache version 2.4 may not be officially released for some time, unstable versions of this software are available. Normally, production systems should not include beta versions of critical service applications such as Apache. However, Apache 2.4 includes several enhanced security features, including the ability to check an **Online Certificate Status Protocol (OCSP)** server for the current status of a digital certificate. If a black-hat hacker is able to get his or her own official certificate through nefarious means, OCSP access can protect users.

For your convenience, Apache does make its software available in binary packages suitable for Red Hat and Ubuntu systems (in formats suitable for the `rpm` and `dpkg` commands). However, such packages may not have been tested by the developers behind these distributions.

> ⚠️ **WARNING**
>
> Unstable versions of any software may cause unpredictable results. While security is important, developers of unstable distributions have to focus on adding features and removing bugs from that software, which might delay any changes that address security issues.

The Samba File Server

Administrators who run the Samba file server can stay up to date on the Samba Security Releases Web page at *http://samba.org/samba/history/security.html*. Updates are provided in patch format. To incorporate these updates, you'll need the Samba source code. You can then apply the noted patch in a manner similar to applying a patch to the Linux kernel source code as described in Chapter 10.

Alternatively, you can wait until the developers behind a distribution process the patch into their own binary files. Once updated, you can use the applicable package management tool to download and upgrade the new Samba software.

The patch release as described on the Samba security Web site is different from the release made by the developers of a distribution. Such developers may have to do additional work to incorporate the newly released patches in a manner compatible with other packages associated with the distribution.

The developers behind Samba maintain several versions of its file server software in a manner similar to the developers behind the Linux kernel. As of this writing, they still maintain versions 3.3 through 3.5. The developers behind Linux distributions may incorporate the code for those patches in earlier versions of Samba. For example, Ubuntu developers would take the patch associated with Samba version 3.5, and incorporate the associated code in its Samba 3.0.28a release. That practice is also known as a **backport**.

If you believe that you've discovered a significant security issue in a Samba release, the developers encourage e-mail reports to *security@samba.org*.

File Transfer Protocol Servers

The great majority of administrators stick with Apache for Web services and Samba for Microsoft-style file-sharing services on Linux. In contrast, Linux administrators make a variety of choices when installing a server for FTP files. While the very secure File Transfer Protocol (vsFTP) server is the default for Red Hat, **SUSE**, and even the Linux Kernel Organization, it is far from the only popular FTP server for Linux. Three other major options are as follows:

> ⚠️ **WARNING**
>
> Just because software can be downloaded and installed from the repositories associated with a distribution doesn't mean that it's supported or secure. For example, the noted WU-FTPD service is not maintained or secure as of this writing. Even though it has not been maintained since 2004, it is still available from the unsupported repositories of some major Linux distributions.

- **Pure File Transfer Protocol daemon (Pure-FTPd)—** An actively supported server that can run 100 percent with non-root accounts. For more information, see *http://www.pureftpd.org/*.

- **Pro File Transfer Protocol daemon (ProFTPd)—**An actively supported server with a basic configuration file similar to the Apache Web server, with respect to the configuration of multiple virtual FTP servers. For more information, see *http://www.proftdp.org/*.

- **Washington University File Transfer Protocol daemon (WU-FTPD)—**A commonly used FTP server through the early part of the 2000s. While it is not maintained, it is still available from the Ubuntu Universe repositories.

Linux Has Antivirus Systems Too

Antivirus systems, loosely defined, include systems that can detect all types of malware. While not all malware affects an operating system, it can be transmitted by e-mail and be carried by files with common formats. This section covers some of the available malware systems for Linux. On any computer system, malware falls into several categories, which include the following:

- **Rootkit**—A **rootkit** is malware that can help a black-hat hacker gain administrative control over a computer system.

- **Spyware**—**Spyware** is malware that collects user information; may include keystroke loggers.

- **Trojan horse**—A **Trojan horse** is a type of malware that hides as a desirable program that facilitates unauthorized access.

- **Virus**—Strictly speaking, a computer virus is a program that can copy itself and infect a computer. Loosely speaking, the term computer virus refers to all malware.

- **Worms**—Self-replicating malware that can send itself to other systems is known as a **worm**. A worm is different from a virus in that it does not require direct user involvement to spread.

Responsible Linux administrators include antivirus software on their systems. While there are fewer viruses targeted at Linux, they do exist. One problem associated with Windows operating systems is the number of users who run it with administrative privileges. While Linux is configured to discourage running most commands with administrative privileges, it is possible to configure Linux with only the root account. So Linux is not immune. While Linux may be a more difficult target for black-hat hackers, it is still a target. Some Linux applications such as the Apache Web server have a dominant market share.

Even though black-hat hackers create fewer malware components for Linux systems, Linux can still act as a carrier. In other words, Linux services such as e-mail servers, FTP servers, file servers, and more can carry malware that remains dormant until exposed to a Microsoft or an Apple operating system.

Perhaps the most common malware for Linux systems is based on the **rootkit**, software that allows a black-hat hacker to take over a system with root administrative privileges. Related to the rootkit is any malware that supports easier access for unauthorized users.

Be aware, only some of the tools described in this section are released under the GNU General Public License (GPL).

The Clam AntiVirus System

The **Clam AntiVirus (ClamAV)** system "is an open source (GPL) antivirus toolkit for UNIX, designed especially for e-mail scanning on mail gateways" (per *http://www.clamav.net/lang/en/*). In other words, it's designed to work with e-mail servers such as sendmail, Postfix, and Exim. It works on UNIX-type operating systems including **Solaris**, the **Berkeley Standard Distribution (BSD)**, and Linux.

It supports searches within archives, compressed files, and more. It's updated on a regular basis. If you use ClamAV, it may be in your best interest to subscribe to the associated mailing lists at *http://lurker.clamav.net/splash/*. As noted on that page, mailing lists are available in several languages.

Just be aware, ClamAV is not supported by Red Hat or Canonical. While it can be installed from Ubuntu Universe repositories, packages from such repositories are not officially supported by Canonical. Repositories for installing ClamAV are maintained by third parties. For more information, see *http://www.clamav.net/lang/en/download/packages/packages-linux/*.

Commercial support is available from Sourcefire, Inc., which also provides commercial intrusion-detection solutions at *http://www.sourcefire.com/*.

AVG Antivirus Option

While **AVG** is focused on the Microsoft antivirus market, the group does make anti-malware tools for Linux. The cost and degree of support varies. These tools are as follows:

- **AVG Anti-Virus for Linux**—AVG makes a freely downloadable antivirus tool targeted primarily for Linux clients. It makes that software available in a number of formats, including those based on Red Hat and Ubuntu (Debian) package-management systems. As noted by AVG, this software is made available for private and non-commercial use. While AVG does maintain message boards for this software, few messages on that board relate to Linux.

- **AVG Server Edition for Linux**—AVG makes a commercial antivirus tool as well; this edition includes antivirus, anti-spyware, and anti-spam tools.

The Kaspersky Antivirus Alternative

Kaspersky has a suite of anti-malware products available for Linux. These are all commercial products. The four products are cumulative; for example, Kaspersky Business Space Security includes all features of Work Space Security. Commercial Kaspersky services that provide protection for some individual open source products such as mail servers are also available.

- **Work Space Security**—Supports anti-malware systems for workstations and smartphones, with antivirus, anti-spam, and personal firewall protection.
- **Business Space Security**—Includes protection for Linux file sharing via Samba.
- **Enterprise Space Security**—Adds mail server support; can work with sendmail, Postfix, Exim, and Qmail.
- **Total Space Security**—Includes protection for proxy servers (Squid), mail gateways, and anti-spam features.

For more information, see *http://www.kaspersky.com/linux/*.

SpamAssassin

While there are a variety of commercial solutions to minimize the amount of spam present in e-mail messages, what is perhaps the open source standard in spam prevention is known as **SpamAssassin**. It's a common e-mail filter for many Internet service providers (ISPs).

It's actually part of the standard repositories for Red Hat Enterprise Linux 5 (RHEL 5), which means it is supported by Red Hat. In other words, if you have an appropriate subscription to the Red Hat Network, Red Hat engineers may actually support the work you do with SpamAssassin.

It is known more formally as the Apache SpamAssassin project, as its developers are sponsored by the same Apache project that is behind the Apache Web server. For more information, see *http://spamassassin.apache.org/*.

Detecting Other Malware

One system designed to check for rootkits is known as chkrootkit. It's designed to check a system for known rootkits along with typical symptoms of an unknown rootkit, such as deletions of and changes to key log files. For more information, see *http://www .chkrootkit.org/*.

Functionally similar to chrootkit is a tool known as Rootkit Hunter (*http://www .rootkit.nl/projects/rootkit_hunter.html*). It was originally developed by Michael Boelen in the Netherlands, but other open source developers have since taken the lead in Rootkit Hunter development. For the latest information, see *http://rkhunter.sourceforge.net/*.

As suggested in the README file for Rootkit Hunter, rootkit-detection tools (including chkrootkit) are just components in a layered security strategy.

If you want to use Google to search within the public archives of a mailing list, use the `site:` tag. For example, the following search in Google searches for all instances of the word Samba in the Red Hat Enterprise Linux 6 mailing list:

```
samba site:redhat.com/archives/rhelv6-list/
```

Similar searches are possible of public bug reports using the associated URL with the `site:` tag.

Get Into the Details with Bug Reports

All security reports are important to some people. But if you haven't installed a service such as WU-FTPD, security reports on that particular service may not matter to you. On the other hand, security reports on an Apache project could refer to any of the services developed through the Apache Software Foundation, as listed at *http://apache.org/*.

In many cases, you'll need to get into the details of the security advisories, which are often also included in bug reports. One place to start when reviewing the status of security on Linux is *http://www.linuxsecurity.org/*. Security updates have been collected on that Web site, currently sponsored by Guardian Digital, for well over a decade. It includes the latest advisories, divided by distribution.

In most cases, the developers behind distributions, applications, and services maintain mailing lists associated with their software. If you think there's a problem and have searched existing bug reports, most developers encourage you to discuss the issue on their mailing lists. Others may have already encountered a similar problem. If they don't already have a solution, they may be able to help you better determine the scope of the problem. Many mailing lists can be searched, either on their Web sites or through a regular search engine such as Google.

There are exceptions. If you believe you've identified an important security issue and have the experience to understand the issue, many projects provide an e-mail address to which the report can be sent privately.

Ubuntu's Launchpad

Launchpad is a Canonical contribution for open source software development. In some ways, it is similar to Source Forge. But it has many other functions. As noted at *https://launchpad.net/*, it is a software-development platform that provides the functionality described in Table 11-1.

Ubuntu gathers issues related to security in the USN described earlier in this chapter. The Ubuntu security team triages security-related bugs. Currently, triaged bugs can be found at *https://bugs.launchpad.net/~ubuntu-security/*.

TABLE 11-1 Security-related functions of Launchpad.	
FUNCTION	**DESCRIPTION**
Bug tracking	Goes beyond user reports to identify packages and distributions for later evaluation by Ubuntu developers. May include bugs associated with other projects and even other Linux distributions. Formerly known as Bugsy Malone. May include security issues.
Code	Provides a platform for developing source code on open source projects. Based on the bazaar version control system at *http:// bazaar.canonical.com/en/*. Closely related to the Code Review function at *https://help.launchpad.net/Code/Review/*. May be used to track the development of new security updates.
Ubuntu	Hosts development work on package updates and new distribution releases. May be used to track the development of new security updates.
Mailing lists	Sponsors mailing lists related to security and more.

If you believe there's a security issue with an Ubuntu release, navigate to the noted URL and search the active bugs. Some of the bugs include interchanges with other users. It takes some judgment to determine whether the bug is a security issue that affects you.

If you're not sure whether a problem is a security issue, report it on Launchpad. Sometimes, a user with more experience in the subject area can help you address the problem. If the issue is a bug, Ubuntu developers will classify it as such. If the issue is in fact a security problem, someone from the Ubuntu security team will classify it as such and triage it for attention.

Red Hat's Bugzilla

Bugzilla is derived from the bug-tracking system used for projects sponsored by the Mozilla Foundation. It's been adapted by Red Hat as the system for its bug reports at *https:// bugzilla.redhat.com/*. If you believe there's a problem with a Red Hat distribution, you could first discuss it on a Red Hat mailing list. Many excellent developers monitor these lists with a desire to help others. If the problem that you present is a security issue, many of these developers can help you highlight the issue with the Red Hat Security Response Team.

The next step would be to search the bug reports at the noted URL. If you have a subscription to the Red Hat Network, you'll have access to more bug reports. A few bug reports are limited to Red Hat employees and official beta testers.

If the problem you've found has not already been reported, the next step is to create a bug report. Red Hat developers will assess that report. If they don't believe it's a problem, they'll close it, with a reason. If it's similar to another bug report, they may close it, citing it as a duplicate. If it's a unique problem, they'll list an action and priority. If it's a security issue, it will be highlighted as such.

Application-Specific Bug Reports

A lot of software that's included with a distribution is developed by others. While distributions such as Red Hat and Ubuntu put it all together, some bugs are application specific. To make sure a problem is addressed by the right developers, you may want to report the problem on the bug systems provided by those developers.

If you report a problem in the bug system associated with a distribution and it is judged to be a problem, the responsible developers will report the issue upstream. In other words, they'll create an application-specific bug for you or otherwise notify the developers behind an application. But that takes time. If you've found an actual security issue, time may be of the essence.

The bug reports for many applications are based on the associated graphical desktop environment. Most Linux GUI applications are developed under the auspices of one of the two major desktop environments, GNOME and KDE. Other desktop environments frequently use applications built for these GUIs. For example, the Xfce desktop environment uses a number of GNOME applications. In addition, it's fairly common for users to include KDE applications in the GNOME desktop environment and vice versa.

Whichever bug-tracking system applies, remember to check for a previous report first. You may even find a solution to your problem. Otherwise, you may be able to create a better report for appropriate developers.

GNOME Project Bugs

Bugs associated with the GNOME project can be found at and reported to *https://bugzilla .gnome.org/*. That bugzilla is associated with a number of GNOME applications. A few examples include the Brasero disc burner, the Evolution personal information manager, the Nautilus file manager, the Totem media player, the Vino **virtual network computing (VNC)** server, and the GNU Image Manipulation Program (GIMP).

In other words, if you identify a problem with most applications in the GNOME desktop environment, the first step is to check the bug reports associated with the GNOME bugzilla. If they confirm that a bug is a security issue in released software, GNOME developers give it their highest priority.

A couple of major GNOME applications have their own bug-reporting systems, including the Firefox Web browser and the OpenOffice.org suite. While GNOME developers do contribute to these products, they are sponsored and developed by different organizations.

KDE Project Bugs

Bugs associated with the KDE project can be found at and reported to *https://bugs.kde.org/*. That bugzilla is associated with a number of KDE applications. A few examples include the K3b disc burner, the KMail e-mail client, the Konqueror file manager and Web browser, the Kaffeine media player, the DigiKam photo manager, and the KOffice suite.

The focus of the KDE project is somewhat different from GNOME in that it includes its own native office suite, Web browser, and e-mail manager.

Other Applications

The developers behind several major applications have their own bug-reporting tools. The following are just three examples:

- **OpenOffice.org Suite**—The reporting procedure is shown at *http://qa.openoffice.org/ issue_handling/pre_submission.html*.
- **Mozilla Project Applications**—Bug reports for Mozilla applications, including the Firefox Web browser and the Thunderbird e-mail manager, can be made at *https:// bugzilla.mozilla.org/*.
- **Adobe products**—Bug reports for Adobe products, including Acrobat Reader and Flash Player, can be made through *https://www.adobe.com/cfusion/mmform/ index.cfm?name=wishform*.

Service-Specific Bug Reports

Bug reports for a number of different open source services may also be security related. They may also just be your contribution to helping developers create better software. This section briefly describes the bug-reporting tools for a few major applications. Some services have fully featured bugzilla-style systems; others have so few bugs that any such reports can be made directly to mailing lists. These are just a few of the many available services, but should give you an idea of the process for other services.

If you've developed a patch to a bug that you've identified, most developers will gladly review your patch for inclusion in their service software.

Apache

The developers behind the Apache project explicitly request that reports of security issues be made per the instructions at *http://httpd.apache.org/security_report.html*. Nevertheless, there will be times that bug reports are escalated into security issues. Apache bug-report procedures are described at *https://httpd.apache.org/bug_report.html*.

Briefly, the Apache developers encourage users to discuss the possible problem first on their users' mailing list, based on the procedures listed at *https://httpd.apache.org/ userslist.html*.

Squid

While Squid maintains an invitation-only mailing list for bug reports, it also maintains a more publicly available bugzilla system at *http://bugs.squid-cache.org/*. As with the developers of other bug databases, they encourage users to first search their FAQ at *http:// wiki.squid-cache.org/SquidFaq/*. They have a number of guidelines for bug reports at *http:// wiki.squid-cache.org/SquidFaq/BugReporting/*. If you follow these guidelines closely, you may even find the solution to a problem before reporting a bug.

There are very few primary developers of Squid. They'll evaluate bug reports for any security implications. Incidentally, Squid has a variety of sponsors, from the U.S. National Science Foundation to Kaspersky Labs.

Samba

The developers behind Samba also maintain a bugzilla-based bug-tracking system. Their process is described at *http://www.samba.org/samba/bugreports.html*. Of course, you should search their documentation and bug reports first. They also maintain a series of mailing lists at *https://lists.samba.org/mailman/*.

Incidentally, the bug-reporting Web page includes procedures for proposed source code patches.

vsFTP

As of this writing, very few bugs are reported for the vsFTP server. At least, that's the report on the home page for vsFTP developers, *http://vsftpd.beasts.org/*. Because there is no bug-reporting option listed on the vsFTP Web page, this is one area where it may be more efficient to report the bug through a distribution. It is the default FTP service for Red Hat systems. It is in the main repository for Ubuntu systems. So the developers behind both distributions have committed to support this service.

Security in an Open Source World

The paradigms in an open source world are different. Most Linux users do not have support contracts from Red Hat, Canonical, or any other company that may support this operating system. Nevertheless, as you should already know, there is a substantial open source community available in mailing lists, blogs, Internet Relay Chat (IRC) channels, and more.

As noted by **Eric Raymond** in *The Cathedral and the Bazaar*, one of the secrets of the success of open source is the power of the community, which Raymond dubbed "Linus's Law," in reference to Linus Torvalds: "Given enough eyeballs, all bugs are shallow." In other words, open source relies on the power of the community. In fact, it would not be possible for the 2,000 employees at Red Hat or the 200 employees at Canonical to compete with Microsoft's nearly 100,000 employees without the help of the open source community.

With many thousands of developers, the open source community has organized itself into a number of areas, including security. Three key security-related open source organizations are the Institute for Security and Open Methodologies (ISECOM), the U.S. National Security Agency (NSA), and the Free Software Foundation (FSF).

The Institute for Security and Open Methodologies

As described in Chapter 1, ISECOM is perhaps the leading organization dedicated to the security of open source software. Many of the key players at ISECOM are the authors of *Hacking Linux Exposed*. ISECOM is the organization behind the Open Source Security Testing Methodology Manual (OSSTMM), currently undergoing its third revision.

ISECOM is also the sponsor of several different professional certifications, including the OSSTMM Professional Security Analyst (OPSA), the OSSTMM Professional Security Expert (OPSE), the OSSTMM Professional Security Tester (OPST), and the OSSTMM Wireless Security Expert (OWSE).

ISECOM has taken the lead in promoting the interests of open source software in security forums worldwide. They've pushed open source solutions through the Open Trusted Computing (OpenTC) consortium, sponsored by the European Union. This has been especially important in countering the issues raised by the Trusted Computing Group (TCG) and the associated Trusted Platform Module (TPM) described in Chapter 3.

Remember, in the Linux community, a hacker is a good person who just wants to create better software. In contrast, the security community and much of the general public believe that a hacker is a malicious person who wants to break into their computer systems. So this book uses the terms "black-hat hacker" to refer to malicious users and "white-hat hacker" to refer to good developers in the open source community.

The National Security Agency

One critical advance in security on the Linux operating system is the release of Security Enhanced Linux (SELinux). As described in Chapter 7, it was first developed by the NSA. Despite the nature of the NSA as a U.S. intelligence agency, the NSA has made it part of its "Information Assurance" mission to enhance the security of major operating systems.

To that end, the NSA took the lead in developing SELinux. It has released SELinux under the GPL. In other words, the source code for SELinux is publicly available. Anyone who does not trust the NSA can inspect the source code for themselves.

While the NSA has clearly done more work on securing Linux as an operating system, it has officially stated that it does not "promote any specific software or platform." As a part of its mission, the NSA has also created a configuration guide specifically designed to enhance the security of Red Hat Enterprise Linux 5.

The Free Software Foundation

> **NOTE**
>
> This explanation of the GPL is not intended as legal advice. If you need legal advice with respect to open source licenses, one option is the group of lawyers associated with the Software Freedom Law Center, accessible online at *http://www .softwarefreedom.org/*.

The FSF is the group behind the development of the commands and libraries cloned from UNIX. When coupled with the Linux kernel as originally developed by Linus Torvalds, these commands and libraries were used to create the original Linux operating system.

The FSF is the organization behind the GPL. As the developer of many commands and libraries cloned from UNIX, the FSF and allied developers have released the source code behind those commands and libraries under the GPL. Under that license, the FSF retains the copyrights to their work. Under the GPL, others may use and build upon that work, as long as they acknowledge the work originally done by the FSF. If the source code has been changed, that must also be released under the GPL.

User Procedures

If you're relatively new to open source software, be aware that the culture around open source software is different. If you use open source software, you're a part of the community. As such, you're welcome to join mailing lists and similar forums to ask for help. In return, it is hoped that you will provide help when possible on the same lists and forums.

Of course, if you have a support contract from a company such as Red Hat or Canonical, it's in your best interest to take full advantage of that resource. Most Linux users don't have that advantage, however, and work through the community instead.

In general, the gurus who populate many Linux and open source mailing lists appreciate users who have done their homework before asking a question. That means taking advantage of documentation available on Web sites for a distribution, for applications, and for services, and even the HOWTO documents provided through the Linux Documentation Project at *http://www.tldp.org/*.

If you don't find the answer to a problem in your research, the next step is to ask a question on a relevant mailing list. It may take some research to find the right mailing list; there are more than a hundred available just for Red Hat software. If and when you do ask a question, make it as easy as possible for those who will read your message. The following is an incomplete list of guidelines that can help:

- **If you have a new problem, start a new thread**—Make sure the subject line is short and descriptive. Stay focused on the topic at hand. Post in text mode; many Linux gurus use text-based e-mail readers.

- **Provide a brief description of the issue**—Include key parts of applicable configuration files and log messages. Note the versions of the software and services in question.

- **Document what you've done**—List the changes you've tried and note the documents you've read. This shows the community that you've done your homework before asking gurus to use their valuable time to help.

- **Add responses to the bottom of a message**—Most Linux gurus much prefer users who add their responses to the bottom of an e-mail message so they can follow the discussion from top to bottom.

A more detailed discussion of how to communicate a problem in the Linux community is available in this author's *Linux Annoyances for Geeks*, published by O'Reilly Media in 2006.

Automated Updates or Analyzed Alerts

It's certainly a viable option to set up a system to automatically download and install all updates, with the possible exception of new kernels. With the number of developers who work on Linux, the reliability of updates to Linux packages is high. But because there are no statistics available on the reliability of such updates, the choice boils down to a matter of trust.

The question of trust goes beyond a simple assessment of the integrity of open source developers. If you administer systems with special configurations or require high availability, you have reason to check every update on a non-production system first. It's not possible even for the open source community to test every update on every possible configuration of hardware and software.

Do You Trust Your Distribution?

The focus of this book on the Red Hat and Ubuntu distributions is patently unfair to the dozens of other excellent Linux distributions that are available. But some limits were necessary to keep this book focused on security rather than on comparing different Linux distributions. Many other distributions are backed by industry leaders, such as SUSE by Novell. Some distributions may be more appropriate for different nations or cultures, such as **Mandriva** for France and Brazil, **Turbolinux** for Japan, **Red Flag Linux** for China, and more. SUSE is an important Linux distribution in the European Community. If you're from one of these countries and can get support for a distribution more appropriate for your locale, these are excellent alternatives.

But the question of trust goes beyond national and cultural borders. If the updates provided for a distribution always work on the systems you administer, then the developers behind that distribution have earned some level of trust.

However, the developers of a distribution to some extent depend on the developers of open source applications and services. The developers of a distribution can test application and service updates for compatibility with the distribution. In some cases, they'll test such updates against certified hardware configurations.

Do You Trust Application Developers?

So the question continues. Linux is famous for the diversity of available applications. But with such diversity comes risk. Diversity in applications may lead to some combination of software that causes problems, or may otherwise fail.

The developers behind an application do their best, with available resources, to test their software on the major Linux distributions. They do their best to test their software at least with different architectures. But the resources available for many applications are severely limited.

With that in mind, you may want to limit the applications available for systems on any networks that you administer. To do so, you'll need to take control of updates, either with custom patch-management repositories or the update managers described later in this chapter.

If you run Linux primarily as a server, applications should be less important. A GUI isn't required to run major Linux services such as Apache, Samba, Squid, the Common UNIX Printing System (CUPS), and so on.

Do You Trust Service Developers?

If you use Linux as a server, the question beyond trusting the developers of an application is whether you trust the developers behind a service. The answer may vary by service, as most Linux services are developed and maintained by different groups.

Some major services such as Apache and Samba are developed and maintained by dozens, perhaps hundreds of developers, testers, and more. With such resources, they can respond fairly quickly to security issues and other problems. They can also test updates as applied to different distributions and even hardware configurations. But not all Linux services can call upon so many developers and testers.

With the choices available for services, a related question is whether you trust other administrators. Some enterprising administrators may substitute a different service, such as Postfix for sendmail to manage e-mail on a network. That may even be the right decision. But to retain configuration control over such decisions, you may want to create a custom repository for the systems on the local network. And that is the province of **Linux patch management**.

Linux Patch Management

Current versions of Linux distributions require Internet access to download updated software. That software is downloaded from a group of packages known as a repository. The repositories for a distribution are frequently mirrored on different servers worldwide.

But such connections depend on the speed of the repository or mirror, along with the geographical proximity of that system. Even if you find a repository mirror that's fast and relatively close, the packages that need to be downloaded from that system may be huge. For example, updated packages associated with the OpenOffice.org suite can easily exceed hundreds of megabytes. If that download is multiplied by a few dozen (or more) systems on the local network, the additional load on an Internet connection may be expensive.

A local repository can be a simple mirror of that remote system. A local repository is downloaded only once, minimizing the load on a corporate Internet connection. One additional reason to create a local repository is to limit what users and administrators can install on their systems. If you support access to all repositories, users may choose that second and third office suite. Users may choose that fifth Web browser. And then you'll be responsible for making sure all such systems are secure.

The methods for configuring repositories vary widely. Repositories for Red Hat Enterprise Linux and Ubuntu systems provide two diverse models that encompass the range of what's available for different Linux distributions.

Before exploring the differences between repositories and update systems, you need to know more about the commands and configuration files that work with different repositories. The yum command is most closely associated with Red Hat systems; the apt-* commands are most closely associated with Ubuntu systems through their heritage in the Debian distribution. However, these commands are not distribution specific. For example, some repositories associated with the apt-* commands have been configured for Red Hat–style distributions such as Fedora Linux.

The advantage of the yum and apt-* commands is that they can automatically identify dependent packages. For example, if you try to install the system-config-samba configuration tool on a Red Hat system, the yum command automatically determines that packages associated with the Samba file server are also required and includes the associated packages in the installation.

Standard yum Updates

The predecessor to the yum command was originally built for a Linux distribution known as Yellowdog Linux. When it was adapted by developers at Duke University for the Red Hat distribution, it became known as the Yellowdog updater, modified, or yum for short.

The yum command uses repositories configured through the /etc/yum.conf configuration file. Normally, that file includes repositories defined in the /etc/yum.repos.d/ directory. Yes, the formats of the yum configuration files differ slightly between Fedora and Red Hat Enterprise Linux systems.

> **NOTE**
>
> For an example of the list associated with the mirrorlist directive, navigate to *https://mirrors.fedoraproject.org/metalink?repo=updates-released-f13&arch=i386*. It should download a text file of mirrors in a file named metalink. The file will list available Fedora mirrors in eXtensible Markup Language (XML) format.

Updates on Fedora

For the Fedora distribution, the update repository is defined with the following stanza in the fedora-updates.repo file. In the first directive, the release version is substituted for $releasever, and the basic architecture is substituted for the $basearch variables.

```
[updates]
name=Fedora $releasever - $basearch - Updates
```

The directives that follow support a rotating search of repository mirrors, as defined by the text file associated with the noted mirrorlist directive. The failovermethod directive starts with the first URL in the noted text file.

```
failovermethod=priority
↪updates/$releasever/$basearch/
mirrorlist=https://mirrors.fedoraproject.org/metalink?repo=
↪updates-released-f$releasever&arch=$basearch
```

Alternatively, you could set up a single URL for updates. In fact, to set up a local update repository, you'd use the baseurl directive to point to a local Web or FTP server with update packages:

```
#baseurl=http://download.fedoraproject.org/pub/fedora/linux/
```

The final three directives in the stanza activate the repository, support checks of the packages with a GNU Privacy Guard (GPG) key, and identify the location of the GPG key on the local system:

```
enabled=1
gpgcheck=1
gpgkey=file:///etc/pki/rpm-gpg/RPM-GPG-KEY-fedora-$basearch
```

While the mirrors and packages differ, the basic format for updates on rebuild distributions such as the Community Enterprise Operating System version 5 (CentOS 5) is essentially the same as it is for Fedora Linux.

In other words, while CentOS 5 uses the same source code as Red Hat Enterprise Linux 5, it uses the Fedora Linux system for updated packages. This allows CentOS to avoid having to replicate the Red Hat Network, which until recently was not open source.

Updates on Red Hat Enterprise Linux

Updates on Red Hat Enterprise Linux systems are done through connections to the Red Hat Network. It's a powerful tool that enables an administrator to pull updates with the yum command or push them directly from a Web-based interface to one or many systems. The Red Hat Network is discussed later in this chapter. The connection to the Red Hat Network is based on configuration files in the /etc/sysconfig/rhn/ directory. Specifically, registration information is stored in systemid file.

Alternatively, you can convert Red Hat Enterprise Linux systems to pull updates from a local repository. However, that choice means that required updates will not be tracked on a Red Hat Network account and may invalidate any support contract you have with Red Hat. Alternatives for locally based updates through Red Hat are based on a Proxy and a Satellite server.

As of this writing, Red Hat is working on an open source product that can manage updates to Red Hat Enterprise Linux, CentOS, Fedora, and related systems, known as **Spacewalk**. For more information, see *http://www.redhat.com/spacewalk/*.

Standard apt-* Updates

The apt-* commands uses repositories configured through the /etc/apt/sources.list configuration file. The default version of that file includes connections to a number of repositories. First, the deb and deb-src directives in this file connect separately to repositories for binary and source code packages. So the following directives for the Ubuntu Lucid Lynx (10.04) release specify connections to the main and restricted repositories:

```
deb http://us.archive.ubuntu.com/ubuntu/ lucid main restricted
deb-src http://us.archive.ubuntu.com/ubuntu/ lucid main restricted
```

While these directives specify the default repository for U.S.-based systems, the associated IP address suggests that the server is actually located in the United Kingdom. So for faster updates, you may want to replace the *http://us.archive.ubuntu.com/ubuntu/* URL with one of the official mirror sites listed at *https://launchpad.net/ubuntu/+archivemirrors/*. As shown on that Web page, Ubuntu mirrors may use the Hypertext Transfer Protocol (HTTP), the FTP protocol, or the rsync protocol, with a bandwidth and location more suited to your network.

But as shown in the following directives, security updates come from a different URL. Because of the time-sensitive nature of security updates, it may be best to accept the default, even if your systems are not located in Europe. If desired, you can add universe and multiverse to the end of these directives.

```
deb http://security.ubuntu.com/ubuntu lucid-security main restricted
deb-src http://security.ubuntu.com/ubuntu lucid-security main restricted
```

For more information on the types of packages available from different Ubuntu repositories, see the sidebar.

Ubuntu Repositories

The Ubuntu distribution classifies repositories into four categories, with four different groups of functions. Repositories fall into the following categories:

- **Main**—Packages in the Ubuntu **main repository** are supported and released under open source licenses.
- **Restricted**—Packages in the Ubuntu **restricted repository** are supported and have restrictive licenses. Restricted packages are generally limited to those packages that help Ubuntu work out of the box with hardware associated with closed-source drivers.
- **Universe**—Packages in the Ubuntu **universe repository** are unsupported, but are released under open source licenses.
- **Multiverse**—Packages in the Ubuntu **multiverse repository** are unsupported, and are also released under restrictive licenses.

Repositories in these categories may be further subdivided by the way they are released. These divisions include the following:

- **Standard**—Standard packages are those released with the final release of a distribution, such as the Lucid Lynx release in April of 2010.
- **Updates**—Update packages are later versions of packages in the standard category.
- **Security**—Security updates are later versions of packages in the standard category, which address security issues.
- **Backports**—Backport packages incorporate new features from later releases. For example, a backport of a kernel package may include a new feature from a later version of a kernel.

In other words, packages may be organized in 16 different groupings. For example, in the main category, there's a standard, an updates, a backports, and a security repository.

In addition, Ubuntu provides packages from partners in separate `partner` repositories. Such repositories are also further subdivided into standard, updates, backports, and security repositories. Some third parties also sponsor their own repositories that can be configured like and integrated with Ubuntu repositories. Even if such software has been tested by Ubuntu developers, it may or may not be supported by Canonical. And remember, software in the universe and multiverse repositories is also not supported by Canonical.

Options for Update Managers

This is a general section that reviews basic alternatives for updating one or many systems on a network. If you're responsible for just a single system, it's most efficient to use the update tools at hand from the local system. If you want, you can configure automated updates. While the default is to pull updates from remote repositories, with the right tools, you can also push updates from systems such as the Red Hat Network. And with the appropriate changes to `yum` or `apt-*` command configuration files, you can configure access from local or remote repositories.

How to Configure Automated Updates

Automatic updates can be configured for Ubuntu and Red Hat distributions. Updates for both systems depend on the installation of a specialized package. The following sections describe the process for each distribution.

Automatic Ubuntu Updates

To set up automatic updates on Ubuntu systems, you'll need to install the `unattended-upgrades` package. This package includes the `50unattended-upgrades` configuration file in the `/etc/apt/apt.conf.d/` directory. Such upgrades are run on a daily basis, based on the `apt` configuration file in the `/etc/cron.daily/` directory. That file refers to settings in the `10periodic` file in the `/etc/apt/apt.conf.d/` directory.

Once the `unattended-upgrades` package is installed, you'll need to add the following directive to the `10periodic` file:

```
APT::Periodic::Unattended-Upgrade "1";
```

Examine the `50unattended-upgrades` file. The following directives suggest that while security upgrades are downloaded and installed by default, updates from the regular update repositories are not, as they are commented out with the double forward slash (`//`), a typical comment character in C++ scripts.

```
Unattended-Upgrade::Allowed-Origins {
    "Ubuntu lucid-security";
//   "Ubuntu lucid-updates";
};
```

The remaining directives, shown in Figure 11-1, are from the Hardy Heron (8.04) version of the file, essentially identical to the Lucid Lynx (10.04) version of the file. This file includes a stanza with names of packages to not update. One package you might include in that list is the Linux kernel, because automatic updates of that package are most likely to lead to problems on production systems.

```
// Automaticall upgrade packages from these (origin, archive) pairs
Unattended-Upgrade::Allowed-Origins {
        "Ubuntu hardy-security";
//      "Ubuntu hardy-updates";
};

// List of packages to not update
Unattended-Upgrade::Package-Blacklist {
//      "vim";
//      "libc6";
//      "libc6-dev";
//      "libc6-i686";
};

// Send email to this address for problems or packages upgrades
// If empty or unset then no email is sent, make sure that you
// have a working mail setup on your system. The package 'mailx'
// must be installed or anything that provides /usr/bin/mail.
//Unattended-Upgrade::Mail "root@localhost";
~
~
~
~
"/etc/apt/apt.conf.d/50unattended-upgrades" [readonly] 19 lines, 595 characters
```

FIGURE 11-1

Ubuntu 50unattended-upgrades configuration file.

The final directive, if the comment characters are removed, would send an e-mail to the root administrative user on the local system when an unattended upgrade is run.

If an appropriate e-mail service is available, you could change that e-mail address to an actual e-mail address.

Automatic Red Hat Updates

Automatic upgrades on Red Hat Enterprise Linux systems can be configured courtesy of the yum-updatesd.conf configuration file in the /etc/yum/ directory. By default, automatic updates are disabled with the following directives:

```
do_update = no

do_download = no

do_download_deps = no
```

To enable automatic updates, you'd change these directives to yes to perform updates and download updated packages and dependent packages.

Automatic upgrades on other Red Hat systems are possible with the help of the yum-cron package. While that package was created for Fedora systems, it is also available through the **Extra Packages for Enterprise Linux (EPEL)** project. Available packages for that project can be downloaded from *https://fedoraproject.org/wiki/EPEL*. Packages associated with EPEL 5 are designed for use on Red Hat Enterprise Linux 5 as well as on rebuild distributions such as CentOS 5.

Once the yum-cron package is installed, it includes a daily cron job, yum.cron, in the /etc/cron.daily/ directory. That job uses parameters configured in the /etc/sysconfig/yum-cron file to determine whether to just check for updates, just download updatable packages, or proceed with installation-based parameters set in the /etc/yum/yum-daily.yum file. That file is fairly simple, based on a yum command shell.

You can start a yum shell on a system with the yum shell command. The directives shown in the yum-daily.yum file are run in that shell:

```
update
ts run
exit
```

The first directive, update, collects a list of updatable packages. Those packages are collected in a transaction set, ts for short. The ts run directive takes that list of updatable packages, downloads, and installs them on the local system before exiting the yum command shell via the exit directive.

> **▶ TIP**
>
> If you're running Red Hat Enterprise Linux and want some feature from the Fedora project, take a look at the EPEL project at *https://fedoraproject.org/wiki/EPEL*. Backports based on Fedora packages have been developed as part of the EPEL project for use on Red Hat Enterprise Linux systems.

Pushing or Pulling Updates

Updates can be pushed or pulled. In other words, with the help of administrative tools like the Red Hat Network, **ZENworks**, **Landscape**, or Spacewalk, administrators can push the installation of updates on remote systems. While that may not be cost effective on a network with one or two systems, it becomes a time saver when administering a few dozen systems. Properly configured, administrative-update tools can push the same updates to dozens of systems simultaneously.

Of course, such simultaneous updates work only if they've been tested and are then applied on systems with identical hardware and software configurations.

Some update tools also support remote administration. With the right centralized administrative tool, you may not even have to configure a remote login service such as the Secure Shell (SSH).

Local or Remote Repositories

To go a step further, you could limit the number of packages available in local repositories. One way to do so is to limit those repositories available to local systems. On Ubuntu systems, you could configure clients and servers to avoid connections to the unsupported universe and multiverse repositories. On Red Hat systems, you could limit the channels. For example, one RHEL 5 system may be subscribed to additional channels named Network Tools, Virtualization, Supplementary, and Optional Productivity Apps. On the Red Hat Network, you may disable subscriptions from a system to all of these channels.

On all systems, you can avoid connections to third-party repositories. While many third-party repositories are reputable, they are designed to include popular software not specifically supported by the developers of distributions such as Red Hat and Ubuntu.

> **FYI**
>
> Third-party repositories designed for Ubuntu and even Red Hat Enterprise Linux are frequently located in countries where copyright laws hold less sway. For example, some third-party repositories include video players that may bypass certain legal requirements such as the Digital Millennium Copyright Act (DMCA).
>
> While such packages are popular among Linux users, the presence of such packages on systems that you administer may expose your organization to legal liability.

Configure a Local Repository

It's easiest to use the remote repositories already configured for most Linux distributions. The connections to such repositories have already been tested. If a problem arises with such systems, many administrators are likely to complain, and the problem is likely to get fixed quickly without any additional intervention.

However, there are advantages to maintaining a local repository. At minimum, a local repository reduces the load on a corporate Internet connection. If you want to keep it simple, you could use an rsync command to just mirror a remote repository or use a service made available for that purpose such as Red Hat's Proxy or Satellite Servers. The commercial options are described in the next section.

Just a few mirrors support rsync connections. Those that do should understand that the rsync command is used to synchronize local and remote systems. To review the repositories that are mirrored on the servers of the Linux Kernel Organization, run the following command:

```
$ rsync mirrors.kernel.org::
```

Be aware: Mirrors, especially if they involve multiple architectures, can occupy dozens of gigabytes of space. So you need available space, and you should run the command at a time when demand on the Internet connection is relatively low. To explore the Ubuntu-based mirrored repositories, run the following command:

```
$ rsync mirrors.kernel.org::ubuntu/dists/
```

You can then select a repository subdirectory, such as lucid-updates/ for update packages for the Ubuntu Lucid Lynx release. The following command includes all such update packages in the main, restricted, universe, and multiverse repositories and synchronizes them to the local /updates/ directory:

```
$ rsync -avz
↪ mirrors.kernel.org::ubuntu/dists/lucid-updates/. /updates/
```

The switches synchronize files in archive (-a) mode, with verbose (-v) output, using compression (-z) in the data-transfer stream. You can repeat the process for other repositories, such as backports in the lucid-backports/ subdirectory.

There's always some time delay between the packages on a mirror and the packages at the source. To minimize that delay, you could `rsync` a local mirror with that maintained by Ubuntu. For more information on what's available on Ubuntu's U.S. mirrors, run the following command:

```
$ rsync us.archive.ubuntu.com::ubuntu/
```

Once a mirror is available locally, you'll still need to share the directory using a server such as Apache or vsFTP. You can then point clients and servers on the local network to that repository in their `/etc/apt/sources.list` file.

> **TIP**
>
> One alternative for mirroring Ubuntu repositories is based on the `apt-mirror` command. For more information, see *http://apt-mirror.sourceforge.net/*.

Commercial Update Managers

If you administer a large number of Linux systems, it may be cost-effective to use a commercial update manager. These systems allow you to update a number of different systems simultaneously. For example, you could, with one command, update all regular 32-bit systems with one group of packages. You could update all regular 64-bit systems with a second group of packages. Alternatively, you could set up a group of Web servers, ready for updates to the Apache Web server and related database packages.

There are three major commercial update managers available for Linux. The Red Hat Network can help you administer subscribed systems from clients/servers or from a central Web-based interface.

The Red Hat Network

There are several reasons to subscribe to the Red Hat Network. It supports downloads of binary copies of the Red Hat Enterprise Linux distribution. It supports downloads of new and updated packages from the network, both from the local system and from a remote Web-based interface. The updates available from the Red Hat Network include security updates released on a timely basis.

Red Hat does release the source code of such packages under the GPL. However, it takes some time for third parties to reprocess those packages, remove trademarks, and collect them into a format suitable for installation CDs and DVDs. Perhaps more important, it takes some time for third parties to process the source code of security updates. And who knows what may happen to your systems during that period of time.

The Red Hat Network allows you to monitor the status of connected systems. It also allows you to control the channels of software available to subscribed systems. More important, it allows you to create scripts remotely to be run on those systems. Those scripts aren't limited to updates; scripts pushed from the Red Hat Network to subscribed systems can perform any administrative function. Red Hat scripts can be written even for **Kickstart**-based installations on bare metal hardware.

One problem associated with the Red Hat Network is that its servers are not mirrored. If many enterprises are downloading updates or DVD-sized ISO files, Red Hat Network servers can get overloaded. And many enterprises prefer a higher degree of control. For those purposes, Red Hat offers two add-on products with the Red Hat Network.

Client/server registration on the Red Hat Network may happen during the installation process. If you want to register a newly created clone—say, of a virtual machine on the Red Hat Network—run the `rhn_register` command and follow the prompts that appear. You'll need information from the governing Red Hat Network account.

For more information, navigate to *https://rhn.redhat.com*.

Red Hat Satellite

The **Red Hat Satellite Server** effectively provides a local version of the Red Hat Network, suitable for enterprises. With a local copy of all associated Red Hat software packages, especially security updates, a Red Hat Satellite Server is not limited by restrictions on an Internet connection. Perhaps just as important, it provides local control over those packages that are downloaded and installed to client/server systems.

This server includes an embedded Oracle database manager to monitor and maintain the packages on the systems managed through the server.

Red Hat Proxy

A **Red Hat Network Proxy Server** works like a caching server. Update requests first check for available packages from the proxy server on the local network. If requested packages are not available locally, the request is forwarded to the Red Hat Network. Those packages are then copied to the proxy server and downloaded to the requesting client/server. Update requests from a second client/server can then access those same packages on the local proxy server.

Canonical Landscape

Canonical is the privately held corporate sponsor behind the Ubuntu distribution. Like Red Hat, Canonical is trying to make money from its work on Linux. To that end, Canonical sells subscriptions to Landscape, its Web-based system management service.

Landscape provides many of the same features as the Red Hat Network. As noted at *https://landscape.canonical.com/*, Landscape includes the following features:

- **Alerts**—Canonical sends security alerts to the e-mail addresses of users with Landscape accounts.
- **Package management**—Landscape enables deployment of one or many packages from the Web-based management tool.
- **System monitoring**—Landscape allows you to monitor the health of connected systems.
- **Cloud management**—Because Ubuntu now includes a release for the Amazon enterprise cloud, the Landscape system provides management tools for systems connected to that environment.

A subscription to Landscape is not required for a binary copy of an Ubuntu distribution CD or DVD. Nevertheless, the features associated with Landscape can be a time saver for administrators who would otherwise have to create scripts to connect to and monitor remote clients/servers.

To connect an Ubuntu system to Landscape, run the following command to download appropriate packages with dependencies:

```
# apt-get install landscape-client
```

Once the appropriate packages are installed, run the `landscape-client` command, and follow the prompts that appear. You'll need information from the governing Landscape account.

Novell's ZENworks

Novell offers its ZENworks platform as a multi-distribution system management tool. It can be used to manage systems that run both the SUSE Linux Enterprise Server and Red Hat Enterprise Linux distributions.

Novell's ZENworks Linux Management platform is a different but related product to its ZENworks system management product for Microsoft operating systems. As with the Red Hat Network and Canonical's Landscape, ZENworks can be used to administer Linux systems in groups. ZENworks can be used to manage packages on one system or a group of systems.

While ZENworks has a Web-based interface, it also supports systems management from the command line. For more information, see *http://www.novell.com/documentation/zlm72/*. If you're interested in a version other than ZENworks Linux Management 7.2 (`zlm72`), substitute accordingly.

Open Source Update Managers

If your resources are limited or if you prefer open source solutions on principle, alternatives are available. As with other open source solutions, the additional cost is in time. Some of the tools are already available. Earlier in this chapter, you read about tools such as `yum-cron` and `unattended-upgrades` that can be configured to automatically download and install updated packages. With appropriate changes, such updates can be limited to security-related updates. Certain packages can be excluded from the update.

If additional system monitoring is required, you may be able to set up logging to a centralized server. Some techniques for that purpose are described in Chapter 12.

Of course, you can configure and distribute scripts from a central interface to remote clients and servers. Those scripts can be configured to run selected commands as needed. For systems where the SSH service is running, they can be copied directly to appropriate directories with the `scp` command.

In the big picture of update management, the key tools are the `apt-*` and `yum` commands. They can be used to update, install, remove, and otherwise manage the packages of your choice. For this reason, the following sections are focused on those commands. The last part of this section briefly describes the Red Hat Spacewalk open source system management solution.

TABLE 11-2 Standard apt-* commands.

COMMAND	DESCRIPTION
apt-cdrom	Includes CD/DVDs (or appropriately mounted ISO files) for updates
apt-file	Searches for files within uninstalled packages
apt-ftparchive	Generates a package archive from a list of packages in a directory; used for creating key files on a local repository
apt-get	Installs, updates, removes, and purges packages with dependencies

Various apt-* Commands

The apt-* commands are a series of commands developed for Debian Linux. These commands can be used to install, remove, or provide additional information about packages available from distribution-specific repositories. Standard apt-* commands are summarized in Table 11-2.

The aptitude command works as a front-end to many apt-* commands. In addition, the aptitude command, when run by itself, opens a console-based configuration tool for Debian-style packages, including those found on Ubuntu systems.

Various yum Commands

You can use the yum command to pull updates on Red Hat-style systems, including Red Hat Enterprise Linux, Fedora Linux, and CentOS Linux. The yum command is rich and diverse; this section addresses just a few basic options for the yum command. For a full list, run the yum command by itself. Figure 11-2 illustrates just the basic options available for yum.

Here are some basic examples of the yum command. To install a new package named samba, you'd run the following command:

```
# yum install samba
```

If the Samba server package is already installed and an upgraded version is available, the preceding command updates the package with any dependencies. Alternatively, the following command updates the Samba package if it is already installed:

```
# yum update samba
```

If you're interested in installing a new kernel package, avoid the update option. The install option preserves the installation of any existing kernel side by side with any updated kernel.

The update (and related) option is powerful when updating a series of packages for a system. For example, the following command checks connected repositories for available updates:

```
# yum check-update
```

If the list of available updates is satisfactory, you can download and install all those updates with the following command:

```
# yum update
```

If you want to exclude a package from the list of updates, the --exclude switch can help. For example, the following command excludes the noted packages from an update:

```
#  yum update --exclude=samba,samba-common,samba-client
```

Of course, the yum command can be used to uninstall a package, with dependencies. For example, the following command removes the Samba file server with any dependent packages:

```
# yum remove samba
```

You can also take advantage of how packages are organized on Red Hat distributions. For example, the following command lists available package groups:

```
# yum grouplist
```

```
List of Commands:

check-update   Check for available package updates
clean          Remove cached data
deplist        List a package's dependencies
downgrade      downgrade a package
erase          Remove a package or packages from your system
groupinfo      Display details about a package group
groupinstall   Install the packages in a group on your system
grouplist      List available package groups
groupremove    Remove the packages in a group from your system
help           Display a helpful usage message
info           Display details about a package or group of packages
info-security  Returns security data for the packages listed, that affects your system
install        Install a package or packages on your system
list           List a package or groups of packages
list-security  Returns security data for the packages listed, that affects your system
localinstall   Install a local RPM
makecache      Generate the metadata cache
provides       Find what package provides the given value
reinstall      reinstall a package
repolist       Display the configured software repositories
resolvedep     Determine which package provides the given dependency
search         Search package details for the given string
shell          Run an interactive yum shell
update         Update a package or packages on your system
update-minimal Works like update, but goes to the 'newest' package match which fixes a problem that af
fects your system
upgrade        Update packages taking obsoletes into account
```

FIGURE 11-2

The yum command is powerful.

If there's a group of packages to be installed, such as Server Configuration Tools, you can install all the mandatory and default packages in that group with the following command:

```
# yum groupinstall "Server Configuration Tools"
```

To identify the mandatory and default packages in any group, navigate to the /var/cache/yum/ directory. In a subdirectory associated with a repository, find the comps.xml file. The packages associated with each package group can be found in that file.

Red Hat Spacewalk

If you just need an open source system management solution but don't want the trouble of writing and maintaining scripts for groups of systems, one emerging alternative is based on the Spacewalk project. It's being developed from the Red Hat source code associated with the Red Hat Satellite Server described earlier in this chapter.

It is not yet a production system, but could be by the time you read this book. Spacewalk requires access to different packages associated with the EPEL project. Because the Red Hat Network includes Kickstart functionality for new installations, Spacewalk includes equivalent open source functionality from the **Cobbler project**. For more information, see *http://www.redhat.com/spacewalk/* and *https://fedorahosted .org/cobbler/*.

Best Practices: Security Operations Management

This chapter focused primarily on the management of security updates. Because many Linux security issues are distribution specific, the developers behind the major distributions maintain their own security-alert systems. Red Hat maintains a security announcements list and supports updates through its system management tool, the Red Hat Network. Canonical maintains a list of security notices, known as the USN, and supports updates through its system management tool, Landscape. Because Canonical includes software associated with many applications, their security notices incorporate input from the developers of those applications. If you trust these developers, you may want to take advantage of available automated update tools.

If certain applications are mission-critical for your organization, you may want to monitor appropriate security lists maintained by their sponsoring groups. Just be aware, there are user applications such as the OpenOffice.org suite and Web browsers, along with service applications such as Apache, Samba, and vsFTP.

Linux has antivirus and anti-malware systems. Some of these systems are designed to minimize the risk of Linux as a malware carrier between Microsoft systems. But such systems also address malware written for Linux, such as rootkits, Trojan horses, worms, and more.

Sometimes, you'll need to get into the details of associated bug reports. To that end, Ubuntu maintains its Launchpad system and Red Hat has a Bugzilla system for classifying and tracking bugs. Different user and service applications maintain their own systems. If you know how to navigate through these systems, you'll have a better idea whether key developers are taking the problems that you see seriously. If you've done the research, don't hesitate to report a bug. If it is a security issue, some developers ask for private reports.

In the open source world, organizations such as ISECOM, the NSA, and even the FSF are working toward improving security on open source software. If you believe you've identified a problem, be aware of the open source culture before reporting it. If you do a little research first, you may get the attention of prominent Linux developers and a faster solution.

There are several reasons to create a local update repository. The simplest reason is to reduce the load on the network's Internet connection. Other reasons relate to limiting software available to local systems. In addition, a local update repository allows you to test updates before they're installed on local systems.

If you just need to reduce the load on an Internet connection, solutions such as the Red Hat Satellite Server and the Red Hat Proxy Server are available. If you need to administer a substantial number of systems, centralized system management tools such as the Red Hat Network, Canonical's Landscape, and Novell's ZENworks Linux Management tools can be helpful. Alternatively, if you prefer open source centralized management solutions, monitor the work of Red Hat's Spacewalk project.

CHAPTER SUMMARY

This chapter describes what you can do with security alerts and updates. Security alerts are provided not only by the developers behind Linux distributions but also by the developers behind major Linux applications from the OpenOffice.org suite to the Apache Web server. The `apt-*` and `yum` commands are two ways to install such updates; packages that automatically download and install updated packages are also available.

Alternatively, if you administer a variety of Linux computers, system management solutions such as the Red Hat Network and Canonical's Landscape can help you manage groups of systems. They can help you monitor the status of such systems, pushing different sets of updates to these systems as desired.

KEY CONCEPTS AND TERMS

AVG	Multiverse repository	SpamAssassin
Backport	Online Certificate Status	Spyware
Berkeley Standard Distribution (BSD)	Protocol (OCSP)	SUSE
Bugzilla	Pro File Transfer Protocol daemon (ProFTPd)	Trojan horse
Clam AntiVirus (ClamAV)	Pure File Transfer Protocol daemon (Pure-FTPd)	Turbolinux
Cobbler project	Raymond, Eric	Ubuntu
Common Vulnerabilities and Exposures (CVE) list	Rebuild	Ubuntu security notices (USNs)
Extra Packages for Enterprise Linux (EPEL)	Red Flag Linux	Universe repository
Fedora Linux	Red Hat	Virtual network computing (VNC)
Kaspersky	Red Hat Network (RHN)	Virus
Kickstart	Red Hat Network Proxy Server	Washington University File Transfer Protocol daemon (WU-FTPD)
Kubuntu	Red Hat Satellite Server	Worm
Landscape	Red Hat security advisories (RHSAs)	Xfce desktop environment
Launchpad	Restricted repository	Xubuntu
Linux patch management	Rootkit	ZENworks
Main repository	Solaris	
Mandriva	Spacewalk	

CHAPTER 11 ASSESSMENT

1. For at least how long does Red Hat provide security updates for its Enterprise Linux distributions?

   A. Two years
   B. Five years
   C. Seven years
   D. Ten years

2. For Ubuntu's LTS releases, Canonical will provide security updates for its server distribution releases for at least five years.

   A. True
   B. False

3. Why would you read a security alert and not just download and install a security update to a key system such as the Linux kernel? (Select three.)

   A. The update may affect interactions between the operating system and local hardware.
   B. The update does not affect any systems that you use personally.
   C. The update may not be bootable.
   D. The update relates to Xen, which is a special kernel not used on the local system.

4. Which command is commonly used to install and update packages from the command line on Red Hat systems?

5. Even though Apache 2.4 is currently not production software, which of the following is a new feature of that version of Apache that may enhance security?

  A. Password protection for Web sites
  B. Access to secure certificates
  C. The ability to host multiple secure Web sites
  D. Access to OCSP servers

6. Which of the following FTP servers is *not* maintained but may still be readily available on the repositories for a distribution?

  A. WU-FTPD
  B. Pure-FTPd
  C. vsFTP
  D. ProFTPd

7. Which of the following types of malware is *not* found on Linux?

  A. Rootkits
  B. Microsoft viruses
  C. Trojan horses
  D. None of the above

8. Which of the following includes a system for tracking bugs in software?

  A. ZENworks
  B. Red Hat Network
  C. Landscape
  D. Launchpad

9. Before creating a bug report, which of the following actions should you take?

  A. Copy all log files to the report.
  B. Research any FAQs.
  C. Reinstall the software.
  D. Reboot the system.

10. What is the full path to the `yum` configuration file on a Red Hat Enterprise Linux 5 system?

11. Which of the following files contain the addresses of remote repositories?

  A. `/etc/apt/sources.list`
  B. `/etc/apt/apt.conf`
  C. `/etc/apt.conf`
  D. `/etc/apt/apt.conf.d/10periodic`

12. The multiverse repository includes packages that are *not* supported and do *not* include open source software?

  A. True
  B. False

13. Which of the following files in the `/etc/apt/apt.conf.d/` directory determine whether unattended upgrades are run?

  A. `apt.conf`
  B. `10periodic`
  C. `50unattend-upgrades`
  D. `99update-notifier`

14. Which of the following configuration files is associated with unattended upgrades on Red Hat Enterprise Linux systems?

  A. `/etc/yum.conf`
  B. `/etc/yum/yum-daily.yum`
  C. `/etc/yum/yum-updatesd.conf`
  D. `/etc/yum.repos.d/yum-updatesd.conf`

15. Which of the following system management services is open source?

  A. Red Hat Network
  B. Landscape
  C. Spacewalk
  D. All of the above

Building and Maintaining a Security Baseline

I N THIS CHAPTER, YOU'LL REVIEW basic steps required to create an appropriate baseline system for both the Ubuntu and Red Hat distributions. As noted in previous chapters, a good baseline keeps installed software to a minimum. A good baseline is secure, with firewalls and other security controls that block unauthorized access from both external and internal sources.

Some secure baseline configurations include read-only filesystems. That's one reason for the popularity of live CD distributions. Such media can be booted on most systems, with a fully functional version of Linux loaded into system Random Access Memory (RAM). You'll examine several options for live CDs with security-management tools. Once these are loaded onto a system, you'll be able to use such tools on local filesystems. Such filesystems don't even have to be mounted.

The performance of a system baseline, along with production systems created from that baseline, can be monitored through appropriate log files. If you administer a group of systems, you'll want to collect logs from those systems. But log files are just a static snapshot of the performance of a system.

System performance also depends on more dynamic measures, such as system load, network status, currently running services, and more. The integrity of a baseline and systems derived from that baseline can be checked with integrity scanners.

Chapter 12 Topics

This chapter covers the following topics and concepts:

- How to configure a simple baseline
- What read-only and bootable operating systems are
- How to keep a baseline system up to date
- How to monitor local logs
- How to consolidate and secure remote logs
- How to identify a baseline system state
- How to check for changes with integrity scanners
- What best practices are for building and maintaining a secure baseline

Chapter 12 Goals

When you complete this chapter, you will be able to:

- Create and maintain a secure baseline Linux system
- Use bootable operating systems to your advantage
- Configure logs locally and remotely
- Scan a system for integrity against black-hat hackers

Configure a Simple Baseline

In this section, you'll review appropriate parts of the installation programs for the Red Hat and Ubuntu distributions. When configuring a simple baseline, you'll need to start with these programs. To that end, it's important to have a basic understanding of how best to take advantage of these programs.

The Red Hat installation program is known as **Anaconda**, which has been used to install Red Hat systems for more than a decade. The Ubuntu installation program was developed from that used for Debian Linux, which has an even older heritage.

In general, the text-mode installation options for each program are more flexible. Normally, the installation program can be booted from a CD, DVD, or a USB drive. Alternatively, the installation program can also be installed over a network using a Basic Input/Output System (BIOS) or Unified Extensible Firmware Interface (UEFI) connection to a network card configured with a Pre-boot eXecution Environment (PXE).

A Minimal Red Hat Baseline

The Red Hat installation programs have evolved. As released for Red Hat Enterprise Linux 5 (RHEL 5), the minimal Red Hat installation included a number of services not needed in a standard bastion server. But RHEL 5 was released in 2007. Red Hat has been working on its installation since then through its Fedora Linux releases. As of this writing, it has just released the first beta of Red Hat Enterprise Linux 6 (RHEL 6), which includes fewer packages in its minimal installation.

Two versions of Red Hat Enterprise Linux are currently fully supported. As of this writing, RHEL 5 will be fully supported through at least the first quarter of 2011 and be supported with at least security updates through at least the first quarter of 2014. As such, it will remain a viable option for baseline configurations for some time to come.

When RHEL 6 is released in the second half of 2010, it will get full support for at least three years, and security updates for at least seven years. It's based in part on the Fedora 12 release, with a slightly different kernel, version 2.6.32. As built by Red Hat, that kernel includes features from later releases.

When booting from the installation program of RHEL 5, you're taken to a `boot:` prompt. At that prompt, you can start the graphical user interface (GUI) installation process automatically or start the text-mode installation process by typing in the following command:

```
boot: linux text
```

When you reach the screen shown in Figure 12-1, select Customize Software Selection and then select OK to continue. You can then deselect all package groups. Otherwise, the default RHEL 5 installation includes the GNU Network Object Model Environment (GNOME) desktop and much more that isn't appropriate for a baseline configuration.

Customizing an
RHEL 5 installation.

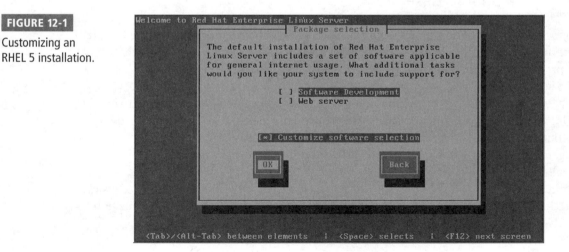

FIGURE 12-2

Starting an RHEL 6 text-mode installation.

When booting from the installation program of RHEL 6, you're taken to the screen shown in Figure 12-2. Highlight the first option and press the Tab key. You'll see the following line in the middle of the screen.

```
vmlinuz initrd=initrd.img stage2=hd:LABEL=
↪"Red Hat Enterprise Linux 6" askmethod
```

To start installation in text mode, add the word text at the end of the line and press Enter. With text-mode installation, RHEL 6 assumes you're looking for a fairly minimal installation. While text mode doesn't support customization options, RHEL 6 text installation leads to about 25 percent fewer packages in about half the space.

Next, you'll have to use the techniques described in Chapter 6 to minimize the software and services installed on the system.

A Minimal Ubuntu Baseline

This section assumes you're using a fairly recent release of Ubuntu Server Edition. Fortunately, the details of the text-mode installation program haven't changed significantly during recent releases. Yes, you can install Ubuntu Server Edition from the DVD. However, if you instead boot from the Server Edition CD, it automatically starts text mode of the Ubuntu installation program. But as incremental changes still happen, this description is subject to change.

Once you've configured standard options like the language and keyboard, a base Ubuntu installation is installed. After that process is complete, you'll have the following options with respect to how upgrades are managed:

FIGURE 12-3

Ubuntu software
selection options.

```
┌────────────────┤ [!] Software selection ├────────────────┐
│                                                            │
│  At the moment, only the core of the system is installed. To tune the │
│  system to your needs, you can choose to install one or more of the │
│  following predefined collections of software.            │
│                                                            │
│  Choose software to install:                              │
│       ┌──────────────────────────────────┐                │
│       │ [ ] DNS server                    │                │
│       │ [ ] LAMP server                   │                │
│       │ [ ] Mail server                   │                │
│       │ [*] OpenSSH server                │                │
│       │ [ ] PostgreSQL database           │                │
│       │ [ ] Print server                  │                │
│       │ [ ] Samba file server             │                │
│       │ [ ] Tomcat Java server            │                │
│       │ [ ] Virtual Machine host          │                │
│       │ [ ] Manual package selection      │                │
│       └──────────────────────────────────┘                │
│                                                            │
│                     <Continue>                            │
│                                                            │
└────────────────────────────────────────────────────────────┘

<Tab> moves; <Space> selects; <Enter> activates buttons
```

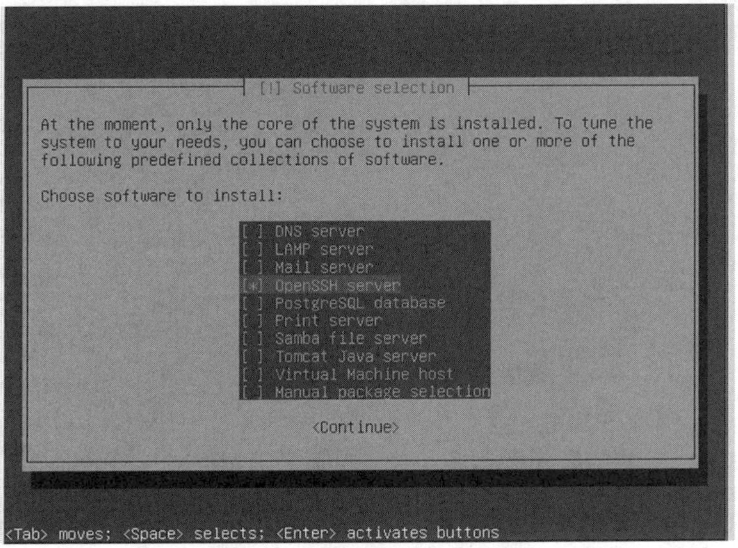

- **No automatic updates**—The default; additional configuration may be required.
- **Install security updates automatically**—Configures security as described in Chapter 11 using the 50unattend-upgrades file in the /etc/apt/apt.conf.d/ directory. If you're concerned that updates may adversely affect systems so configured, this option may not be suitable for you.
- **Manage system with Landscape**—Installs the Landscape client package on the local system; assumes a subscription to Landscape with a sufficient number of entitlements.

During the installation process, you're given a series of software selection options as shown in Figure 12-3. For a bastion system, you might only need to select the OpenSSH server option for the Secure Shell (SSH) server described in Chapter 8. If you've chosen the Manage System with Landscape option just described, you may not even need to install the OpenSSH option, as Landscape supports remote configuration and commands on connected clients.

Next, you'll have to use the techniques described in Chapter 6 to minimize the software and services installed on the system.

Read-Only or a Live Bootable Operating System

One of the risks from black-hat hackers is that they'll write something you don't want to one of the filesystems on your network. Perhaps the most straightforward way to prevent such writes is to mount as many filesystems as possible in read-only mode.

The other way to preserve an operating system is to store it on read-only media such as a DVD drive. Linux includes a wide variety of distributions that can be booted directly from CD and DVD drives.

Appropriate Read-Only Filesystems

As discussed in Chapter 5, several filesystems need to be writable for a working operating system, including `/home/` for user home directories, `/var/` for log files and spools, and `/tmp/` for systems where the GUI is in operation. In many cases, you may also set up the `/usr/` directory as a read-only filesystem until updates are required.

This list omits those directories that are generally included as part of the top-level root directory (`/`) filesystem, including `/bin/`, `/dev/`, `/etc/`, `/lib/`, `/root/`, `/sbin/`, and `/sys/`. While some of these directories can work in read-only mode, they all need to be part of the top-level root directory filesystem for a Linux system to be bootable. And directories like `/dev/` and `/sys/` are dynamic; in other words, files are written to these directories during the boot process and while certain types of "hot-swap" hardware are attached to the system.

But even for a directory such as `/usr/`, it can be a pain to make that filesystem read-only. One alternative is to mount the noted directory with as many limits as possible. For example, it can be helpful to add the following mount options to certain filesystems:

- **nosuid**—Disables super user ID (SUID) and super group ID (SGID) permissions on files in the local filesystem.

- **noexec**—Disables executable binaries on files in the local filesystem.

- **nodev**—Does not allow block or special character files such as partition devices and terminals in the local filesystem.

To that end, one recommendation made at the Red Hat Summit in 2008 included one or more of these mount options in the `/etc/fstab` configuration file for several different directories, as described in Table 12-1.

TABLE 12-1 Special mount options to apply to certain directories.

DIRECTORY	MOUNT OPTION AND DESCRIPTION
`/boot`	Include noexec and nodev to avoid executable files and partitions with inappropriate mount options.
`/home`	Include nosuid and nodev to avoid files that can be executed by others and partitions that can be opened with inappropriate mount options.
`/tmp`	Include noexec and nodev to avoid executable files and partitions with inappropriate mount options; this directory is accessible by all users.
`/var`	Include nosuid to avoid uploaded files owned by one user that can be executed by others.

Live CDs and DVDs

A Linux live CD/DVD is a fully functional version of a Linux distribution. When booted from media such as a CD or DVD, it loads a fully functional version of Linux into the RAM of a local system. As it is independent of any local hard-drive media, it is especially well-suited to diagnosing problems with other connected physical media.

A number of groups of Linux developers create live CDs and DVDs. They're available for a number of standard distributions, including Ubuntu, Fedora, SUSE, CentOS, and many more. A more complete list is available at *http://www.livecdlist.com/*. Perhaps the first and still most prominent live CD–based distribution is Knoppix. That distribution has gained prominence as one with a variety of rescue and recovery tools. In Chapter 13, you'll see how Knoppix and related distributions include tools well suited for penetration testing and security response.

With the diversity of live CD/DVDs that are available, one surprise is the lack of a live CD option at least for RHEL 5. But the process for creating a live CD of a distribution is not that hard. The Community Enterprise operating system version 5 (CentOS 5) has built a live CD from RHEL 5 source code. For a fairly complete list of the major options for live CD distributions, see *http://www.livecdlist.com/*.

These fully functional Linux operating systems can be booted from a CD/DVD drive. The BIOS/UEFI of a system can be set to automatically boot from that drive. With a couple of small changes, log file information can be written to a portable storage device such as a remote server or a USB key. With a couple more changes, such systems can be configured as bastions of a sort, as black-hat hackers can't write to read-only media.

The weakness of such systems is that they include too many active services, typically with a GUI desktop environment. The strength of such systems is that they frequently include administrative and security-related tools that can help identify and diagnose problems on a troubled system.

Update the Baseline

Once you have a baseline Linux system, it's something worth protecting. It's a secure system, ready to copy to different machines, real and virtual. All that's needed to make the baseline into a fully functional bastion server or a desktop environment is to just add the programs required for the desired functionality. As you've seen in earlier chapters, while the `tasksel` command makes the process easy on Ubuntu systems, the `yum grouplist` command makes the process almost as easy on Red Hat systems.

But there's a learning process with respect to the baseline. Experience with production systems will teach you about things that should be added—or left out of the baseline.

A Gold Baseline

A gold baseline configuration is a place to start. With a good gold baseline, you won't need to run through the installation process again and again. If the gold baseline is configured as a virtual machine, all you'll need to do is copy the virtual machine files from one directory to another. If it's a physical system, the process is a little more involved; but a command like dd can be used to copy everything from the partition(s) of one drive to the partition(s) of a second physical hard drive.

A gold baseline should have the following characteristics:

- **Simplicity**—No package is installed on the system unless necessary for smooth operation and monitoring.

- **Network security**—Traffic is blocked to all ports on the system except those necessary to maintain basic network connections. If you administer a system with SSH, the associated port (TCP port 22) should be open as well.

- **Mandatory access controls**—A system such as SELinux or AppArmor should be enabled to minimize risks if one or more account is compromised.

It's possible that you'll want multiple baseline configurations to reflect separation in different filesystems, such as a separate /home/, /var/, or /tmp/ directory.

To make that baseline work on a server, you'll need to make sure that system is up to date with the latest changes related to security and functionality. But every change involves risk. In general, once a change is known to work on your systems, the original packages should be deleted. Such packages are normally stored locally in subdirectories of /var/cache/yum/ and /var/cache/apt/. If a black-hat hacker can see what updates are installed, that person can start to identify weaknesses on those systems.

Of course, if you've created bastion servers from that baseline, those servers should also be updated based on the guidelines for security and functional updates that follow.

In addition, if users are currently connected to bastion servers created from a baseline, take care. With many services controlled by scripts in the /etc/init.d/ directory, it is possible to apply the reload option to reread any configuration files that may have been changed by an update.

For example, if a recent security update to the Samba server has just been installed, you should make sure such changes have not affected custom settings in the associated smb.conf configuration file in the /etc/samba/ directory. If you do make subsequent changes to the smb.conf configuration file, you can minimize the inconvenience to users with the following command:

```
# /etc/init.d/samba reload
```

Depending on the distribution, you may need to substitute smb for samba in the command shown.

There may be good reasons to avoid the installation of an update. In fact, every update may be a risk, as described in the sections that follow. Of course, the developers behind major distributions such as Red Hat and Ubuntu do their best to minimize such risks. If that risk is too large, you may need to revise options associated with local or remote repositories, as discussed in Chapter 11. Such changes can prevent such updates from being installed on local systems.

Security Updates

It's easy to say "Just install all security updates." But some updates may cause problems with some hardware, software, or other installed components. For that reason, all updates, even security updates, should be tested before they're implemented on production systems.

Security updates related to the Linux kernel may be especially troublesome. Some third-party software such as database managers may be certified only to certain versions of the kernel. The installation of a new version of the Linux kernel, even if it addresses a security issue, may affect any support agreement associated with that software. In that case, you may need to address the issue with the third-party software vendor.

Other issues relate to software that is compiled against the source code for one version of a kernel. For example, if you've done the work to install some virtual machine software, a new version of a kernel may require that you recompile that software with the revised source code.

If a security update causes problems, then additional work is required. First, you need to know the reason for the update. For example, if the update is based on Samba interaction with shortwave radio hardware, and local systems do not have such hardware, an update *might* not be required. On the other hand, if the update is based on something that is done on a regular basis on local systems, you'll need to make a choice. Ask yourself the following:

- Is it acceptable to disable the service with the security issue? Is it a mission-critical service for your organization?

- Does the security issue relate to any of the issues associated with the confidentiality, integrity, and availability (CIA) triad or Parkerian hexad discussed in Chapter 1? Does the security issue put at risk any commitments to customers? Does the security issue put you or your organization at risk of violating a legal, regulatory, or industry standard?

If you can say no to all of these questions, then it may be possible to continue running the service in question. But such cases are rare.

If a security update passes your tests, it should be included in gold baseline systems. So when such systems are used to create bastion servers, the security updates are already included.

FYI

Some systems security professionals refer to the CIA triad as the "A-I-C" triad (availability, integrity, and confidentiality) to avoid confusion with the U.S. Central Intelligence Agency, which is commonly referred to as the CIA. Either abbreviation is acceptable. However, if you use CIA, make sure people understand you're referring to "confidentiality, integrity, and availability."

Functional Updates

Functional updates do not themselves respond to security issues. To determine whether a functional update enhances or hurts security, you can refer to the concepts associated with the CIA triad and the Parkerian hexad back in Chapter 1. Updates such as those that change the default wallpaper on a desktop environment do not enhance security. However, such updates may be encouraged for other reasons such as corporate policies (such as when that wallpaper includes a corporate logo).

It may be instinctive to install a functional update. But functional updates can lead to other problems. Reasons to avoid the installation of such an update include the following:

- **Kernel updates**—Some kernel updates only enhance the functionality of a system. However, the same issues relating to third-party software certification and compiled software as described earlier may also apply.

- **Interactions with other software**—The developers behind the update may have tested their revisions. But the developers behind related software may not have a chance to do their testing. If you depend on that other software, updates could cause problems.

- **No need**—If you don't need the additional functionality, why take the risk?

Baseline Backups

It's important to preserve a baseline configuration as if it were gold. A baseline configuration is the starting point for other services. A baseline configuration can save time when compared to a new installation.

Before installing an update to a gold baseline, make sure that baseline is backed up. While methods are available to uninstall backups, such methods can be time consuming.

Monitor Local Logs

When properly configured, log files are stored in the /var/log/ directory or subdirectories. There are two services associated with Linux operating system logs: the system and kernel log services. Slightly older systems such as RHEL 5 and Ubuntu Hardy Heron use the older system and kernel log services, as configured in the /etc/syslog.conf file. Newer systems such as RHEL 6 and Ubuntu Lucid Lynx (10.04) by default use the newer **RSyslog** service, which supports secure tunneled connections and database management.

Because many services have their own logging systems, the next section explores some of these services. The next major section explores the RSyslog service.

The System and Kernel Log Services

The system and kernel log services originated as two different services. However, their functionality has been combined in a single package on most systems. On both Red Hat and Ubuntu systems, the package is named syslogd and is configured in the /etc/syslog.conf file. Red Hat and Ubuntu have two different takes on this file.

TABLE 12-2 Linux log facility subsystems.

FACILITY	DESCRIPTION
auth, authpriv	Includes login authentication messages
cron	Adds messages from the cron daemon, typically from /etc/crontab
daemon	Lists messages associated with the status of services
kern	Includes messages associated with the Linux kernel
mail	Adds messages associated with running e-mail services
syslog	Lists internal syslog service messages
user	Relates messages from user-mode programs

When taken together, these services classify log messages in two areas: the facility, which is the logging subsystem; and the priority, which is the importance of the log message. Log facilities are described in Table 12-2.

Not all log facilities are included in Table 12-2. For example, the lpr facility is associated with the now rarely used Line Printer next-generation service. The Common UNIX Printing System (CUPS) has its own logging configuration. The news facility is related to systems that maintained older newsgroups through the Network News Transfer Protocol (NNTP). The uucp facility was based on remote commands; its functionality has been taken by the Secure Shell.

Log message priorities are classified in the following order of importance:

- **debug**—Provides the greatest detail, used for troubleshooting.
- **info**—Adds logging notes at the information level.
- **notice**—Includes messages that might require attention.
- **warn**—Provides warning messages; may also be shown as warning.
- **err**—Adds error messages; **err** may also be shown as error.
- **alert**—Specifies problems that justify an **alert** and require immediate attention.
- **emerg**—Very important messages; **emerg** may also be shown as panic or crit.

There's also an implicit priority of none, which negates log messages from the associated facility. System log files organize log messages in a *facility.priority log_file* format. For example, the following directive sends all messages of an **info** priority (or higher) but excludes mail log messages. The directive also sends emergency kernel messages to the /var/log/messages file:

```
*.info;mail.none;kern.emerg     /var/log/messages
```

Log messages are commonly rotated on a weekly basis, as configured in the /etc/logrotate.conf file. When rotated, older log files are given a numeric filename extension such as .1 as defined in /etc/logrotate.conf.

Messages from these older services can be sent to remote systems. For example, the following line would send all previously noted messages to the system with a hostname of `logserver`. That logserver system should be configured with a matching `/etc/syslog.conf` file to receive such messages.

```
*.info;mail.none;kern.emerg        @logserver
```

The weakness of this directive is that log messages are sent over the network in clear text. This problem can be addressed with the RSyslog service, described shortly.

The Ubuntu Log Configuration

The default `/etc/syslog.conf` file for Ubuntu systems is fairly well organized. As suggested earlier, not all of the facilities configured in this file are still significant. This section ignores such directives. The first default directive is pretty straightforward, as it sends all authentication messages to the `/var/log/auth.log` file:

```
auth,authpriv.*     /var/log/auth.log
```

The next directive sends all messages from all facilities of all priorities except authentication messages to the `/var/log/syslog` file. The dash (-) in front of the file means that logging messages aren't synchronized every time. In other words, while some log messages may be lost in the event of a system crash, system performance is not affected by the frequency of logging messages.

```
*.*;auth,authpriv.none    -/var/log/syslog
```

Additional directives in the file are relatively self-explanatory. For example, the next active line sends all messages related to the starting and stopping of a daemon to the `/var/log/daemon.log` file.

```
daemon.*    -/var/log/daemon.log
```

The remaining directives in this file are straightforward. For example, the following directives send kernel log messages to the `kern.log` file; log messages from e-mail servers are sent to the `mail.log` file; and user-mode log messages are sent to the `user.log` file, all in the `/var/log/` directory:

```
kern.*      -/var/log/kern.log
mail.*      -/var/log/mail.log
user.*      -/var/log/user.log
```

The following messages divide logging messages from e-mail servers into three categories. By default, log messages of the given priority and higher are sent to the given log file. So the final directive would contain the least amount of logging information:

```
mail.info   -/var/log/mail.info
mail.warn   -/var/log/mail.warn
mail.err    /var/log/mail.err
```

The two directives that follow demonstrate the backslash (\), which escapes the meaning of the carriage return. In other words, with the backslashes, the following three lines are combined into a single directive, which sends all **debug**-level messages but nothing related to the auth, authpriv, news, and mail facilities to the /var/log/debug file. The =debug refers to messages at only the debug level and nothing of a higher priority.

```
*.=debug;\
    auth,authpriv.none;\
    news.none;mail.none;\        -/var/log/debug
```

The next four lines are also a single directive, which sends all messages of the info, **notice**, and **warn** priorities to the /var/log/messages file. Messages from the facilities with the .none extension are not included in the list:

```
*.=info;.=notice;.=warn;\
    auth,authpriv.none;\
    cron,daemon.none;\
    mail,news.none;\       -/var/log/messages
```

The Red Hat Log Configuration

Although the default Red Hat log configuration file may appear to be less well organized, it simply reflects a different set of priorities with respect to logging information. First, the following line sends all info-level messages to the /var/log/messages file:

```
*.info;mail.none;authpriv.none;cron.none/var/log/messages
```

Messages related to all login attempts through the authpriv facility are sent to the /var/log/secure file:

```
authpriv.*    /var/log/secure
```

All messages related to e-mail servers are sent to the /var/log/maillog file:

```
mail.*     -/var/log/maillog
```

Information related to the execution of cron jobs are sent to the /var/log/cron file:

```
cron.*    /var/log/cron
```

All users get emergency log messages, which frequently indicate that a system is about to shut down. The asterisk (*) indicates that messages are sent to all consoles.

```
*.emerg      *
```

Logs from Individual Services

A number of services have their own individual logging systems. While the /var/log/ directory includes individual files that collect logs from standard logging services, pay attention to the subdirectories. Many of those /var/log/ subdirectories include log files from certain services.

In the following sections, you'll explore just three services with custom log files configured in their own subdirectories. While the formats of these log files are consistent with what is defined in /etc/syslog.conf or /etc/rsyslog.conf, they are different logging services. The three services selected are just examples; other services with /var/log/ subdirectories may have their own log files defined in their main configuration files.

CUPS Logs

Three log files are defined by default on CUPS systems: access_log, error_log, and page_log. Generally, log information is set to either the info or warning level with the following directive:

    LogLevel warning

Available levels of log information fit within the standard hierarchy described earlier. The names of the log files may be slightly misleading:

- **access.log**—Provides information on CUPS access of printers over the network
- **error.log**—Includes information on configuration messages with and without errors
- **page.log**—Specifies successful access to printers from local or remote systems

Apache Logs

Depending on the distribution, Apache log files may be found either in the /var/log/httpd/ or the /var/log/apache2/ directory. The actual names of the log files are subject to custom configuration in the appropriate configuration files associated with regular and secure Web sites. Key directives in these files include the following:

- **ErrorLog**—Specifies the log file to receive error messages
- **CustomLog**—Used to log requests, usually coupled with a LogFormat directive to specify the information to be recorded
- **TransferLog**—Specifies a log file based on the previously defined CustomLog format or a standard common log format

Perhaps the most valued part of an Apache log file is based on the LogFormat directive, which can collect all sorts of information on users who connect to Web sites configured on the target Apache server. Some significant LogFormat options are described in Table 12-3.

This is just a fraction of the information that can be logged from each user click on a Web site. The information from all of user clicks collected on your Web sites can easily grow quite large. But that information may be quite useful in deciphering the behavior of your users.

TABLE 12-3 Apache `LogFormat` options.

OPTION	DESCRIPTION
%a	Remote IP address
%D	Time to serve the request, in microseconds
%f	Filename served
%h	Hostname of the remote system
%l	Login name of the remote user
%t	Time of the request
%u	Remote username
%U	Requested uniform resource locator (URL)
%v	The name given to the Web site serving the request, normally of the virtual host

Samba Logs

As you already have read, Samba is the name of the Linux service for connecting to Microsoft-based networks. For more information, refer to Chapter 8. Most log files associated with Samba are driven from the following directive in the main Samba configuration file, `/etc/samba/smb.conf`:

```
log file = /var/log/samba/log.%m
```

The %m is translated to the hostname or, if a Network Basic Input/Output System (NetBIOS) server isn't available, the Internet Protocol (IP) address of the machine that connects to the local Samba server. For example, if the Samba server is on the 192.168.0.0/24 network, you might see a log file such as `log.192.168.0.10` in the `/var/log/samba/` directory. Regular and error messages are sent to that log file; you might see messages related to successful and failed connections in that file. Some machine-specific log files in that directory might be empty, indicating simply that the given system was detected as a browseable server on the local network.

Consolidate and Secure Remote Logs

RSyslog builds on the original system and kernel log services, including its basic configuration file, `/etc/syslog.conf`. The weakness of that older service is that it sends logging information to remote or central servers in clear text. In other words, a black-hat hacker who wants to collect information on the current state of your systems could have a field day if that person can identify the system that is configured as a central logging server—that is, unless that service is configured with the RSyslog service.

While the RSyslog service is configured primarily in the `/etc/rsyslog.conf` file, the way the service is started by default is rather important.

Default RSyslog Configuration

While the strength of RSyslog comes as a remote server, remote transmission of logging information is disabled by default. Generally, you should install at least the `rsyslog` and `stunnel` packages on client and server systems. If you want encryption, two basic choices are available in separate packages, based on Transport Layer Security (TLS) and the Generic Security Services Application Programming Interface (GSSAPI). On Red Hat and Ubuntu systems, these options are available in the `rsyslog-gnuutils` and `rsyslog-gssapi` packages, respectively.

The way the RSyslog service starts is driven by a central configuration file, `rsyslog`. The location of that file varies a bit by distribution. On Red Hat systems, it's in the `/etc/sysconfig/` directory. On Ubuntu systems, it's in the `/etc/default/` directory.

Depending on the release, the applicable variable in the `rsyslog` file is either `RSYSLOGD_OPTIONS` or `SYSLOGD_OPTIONS`. To some extent, the name of the variable doesn't matter, as both are given as options to the RSyslog daemon when it starts. If you want to use compatibility-mode options, substitute the `-c 2` option on Red Hat systems or `-c 0` on Ubuntu systems for the value of the aforementioned variable.

The Standard RSyslog Configuration File

The RSyslog configuration file is normally divided into three sections: modules, global directives, and rules, which normally incorporates the basic rules described earlier for the `/etc/syslog.conf` file. As described at *http://www.rsyslog.com/doc-rsyslog_conf_modules .html*, modules fall into a number of categories. Global directives set parameters such as timestamps and permissions.

RSyslog Modules

Modules with the RSyslog service can be configured in a number of areas. First, the default modules are straightforward, as they enable local system and kernel logging:

```
$ModLoad imuxsock
$ModLoad imklog
```

Two additional modules are available in comments, based on communication through either the User Datagram Protocol (UDP) or the Transport Control Protocol (TCP). Port 514 is the default for the system logging service. If you've replaced it with RSyslog, that port would be available:

```
#$ModLoad imudp
#$UDPServerRun 514
```

If you want to set up the local system as an RSyslog-based logging server, you'd want to enable these two directives, as TCP communication is required for encrypted transmission of log files:

```
#$ModLoad imtcp
#$InputTCPServerRun 514
```

Some documentation suggests the use of port 61514 (in place of 514) to avoid conflicts with any remaining older system-logging daemons. Whatever port is selected should be considered in any firewall between RSyslog clients and servers.

Other RSyslog modules can be defined in the following categories:

- **Input**—Other input modules of interest relate to TCP communication, GSSAPI communications, and more.
- **Output**—Output modules process messages especially for databases.
- **Parser**—Parser modules process received messages.
- **Message modification**—Message modification modules are still in development.
- **Library**—Library modules can be configured by users.

RSyslog Global Directives

Because RSyslog is relatively new, the global directives are more complete in the versions released for Ubuntu Hardy Heron and RHEL 6. The following standard `$Action` directive uses the traditional format for log message timestamps:

```
$ActionFileDefaultTemplate RSYSLOG_TraditionalFileFormat
```

Be aware, there are nearly 50 different `$Action` directives available; these can configure everything from log file size to timeouts to frequencies. One handy option is to filter duplicate messages, which can reduce the load when a system makes the same mistake every few seconds.

The default setting shown here sends all log messages to the local system over a TCP connection using the suggested port of 61514. In these directives, while the double @@ symbol is associated with TCP packets, the single @ is associated with UDP packets.

```
*.*   @@127.0.0.1:61514
```

Of course, if this is a client system sending logging information to a remote server, you'd change the 127.0.0.1 IP address to that of the logging server.

RSyslog Configuration Rules

Some configuration rules set basic parameters for log files. For example, the following directives from the Ubuntu Lucid Lynx version of the `/etc/rsyslog.conf` file should be conceptually familiar from other services, as they set ownership and permissions on related files. The rules from that version of the configuration file are described in Table 12-4.

The RSyslog developers recommend that administrators use the `$PrivDropToUserID` and the `$PrivDropToGroupID` directives rather than the `$PrivDropToUser` and `$PrivDropToGroup` directives. If the `syslog` user does not exist, the `$PrivDropToUser` syslog and `$PrivDropToGroup` syslog directives would mean that RSyslog is run with root administrative privileges.

In that situation, if a black-hat hacker were able to break into the `syslog` account, that person would get full root administrative privileges on the local system. Alternatively, you could just be careful to make sure the `syslog` user and group are properly configured in the password-authentication database.

TABLE 12-4 · Configuration rules from /etc/rsyslog.conf.

RULE	DESCRIPTION
$FileOwner syslog	Sets the user owner of associated files to the syslog user
$FileGroup adm	Sets the group owner of associated files to the syslog user
$FileCreateMode 0640	Assigns 640 privileges to files created through the RSyslog service
$DirCreateMode 0755	Assigns 755 privileges to directories created through the RSyslog service
$Umask 0022	Sets the noted value for umask; may supersede the $FileCreateMode and $DirCreateMode variables
$PrivDropToUser syslog	Assigns a user associated with the RSyslog service
$PrivDropToGroup syslog	Assigns a group associated with the RSyslog service

RSyslog Incorporates Syslog Configuration Rules

There are two ways to incorporate configuration rules from the /etc/syslog.conf file. Those rules could be included directly into the /etc/rsyslog.conf file. Alternatively, those rules could be included from smaller files with a directive such as the following:

```
$IncludeConfig /etc/rsyslog.d/*.conf
```

This directive includes the contents of any *.conf files in the /etc/rsyslog.d/ directory. On an Ubuntu Lucid Lynx system, the 50-default.conf file in that directory is essentially identical to the /etc/syslog.conf file from the older system and kernel log services described earlier.

Identify a Baseline System State

A baseline is a default system configuration. In an ideal world, you could take the gold baseline described earlier and use it as the starting point for production systems. To that end, any new system should differ from the baseline only with respect to the new packages that may be installed for functionality, for updates, and for security issues. But that does not reflect reality.

Systems deviate from a baseline in a number of ways. Log files are added. Users add personal and work files to their home directories. Fortunately, such changes affect only a limited number of directories. You should be able to limit additional changes.

Some users may install a new service. But wait: If you have configuration control of the systems on the local area network (LAN), no new services would be installed— at least not without your knowledge.

But a baseline configuration includes more. It includes the current network state of the system, the interfaces that are used, the firewalls that are configured, the ports that may be open, and so on. Of course, one exception is based on key network settings—specifically the IP address and hostnames of each system.

Finally, a baseline configuration includes information on how the system runs. Information here is more subjective. But based on a given hardware configuration, a baseline system could be expected to run within certain parameters. The following sections will help you define a baseline system state in all of these areas.

Collect a List of Packages

Perhaps the simplest tool for a baseline system state is based on the governing package-management command. For example, the following command includes all packages currently installed on a Red Hat system:

```
# rpm -qa
```

Look at the output. It includes version numbers for each package. If saved to a file, you could use it in the future to identify changes in the list of installed packages over time.

A similar list of packages is available in Ubuntu systems, using the following command:

```
# dpkg -l
```

While the output of the noted dpkg command include a bit more information, that output can also serve as a database. If saved to a file, you could also use that database to derive the differences in lists of installed packages at different dates.

Of course, if you've started with a gold baseline and installed a service such as the Samba Web server, you'd expect the differences to include related packages. But any additional packages that are not the result of a dependency, an update, or a security issue are and should be suspect.

Compare Files, Permissions, and Ownership

One thing done by integrity scanners is to check the status of files compared to a baseline. On any Linux system, some files are expected to change. Some change all the time. That is normal. But changes to key files such as the Linux kernel, modules, configuration files, and service scripts may be a problem. Generally, files in these categories can be divided into stable and unstable directories.

Even so, some changes to files in stable directories can be explained. Administrators may change configuration files. Security updates can change the kernel. The installation of new services can add files to stable directories.

TABLE 12-5 Tripwire configuration variables.

VARIABLE	DESCRIPTION
SEC_CRIT	Critical files that can't change, primarily in the `/boot/`, `/lib/modules/`, and `/root/` directories.
SEC_BIN	Files that generally should not change, except when a system is updated. Applies mostly to binary files, but includes configuration files in the `/etc/` directory.
SEC_CONFIG	Configuration files that are accessed frequently. While such files change infrequently, access times are also recorded.
SEC_LOG	Log files may grow, but a change of ownership may indicate a black-hat hacker who is substituting false information.
SEC_INVARIANT	Directories that should always have the same user and group owner.
SIG_LOW	Label for files that are not critical, such as those in most user home directories.
SIG_MED	Label for files with some security impact, such as the user authentication database, configuration files, some binary files, and some library files.
SIG_HI	Label for files of high security importance, such as those in the `/boot/`, `/bin/`, `/sbin/`, and `/lib/` directories.

Integrity scanners such as **Tripwire** compare the state of stable directories. If there are changes, Tripwire can help detect them. If Tripwire isn't already installed on a local system, you'll see how to do so later in this chapter. One measure of stable and unstable directories is the standard Tripwire policy file, `twpol.txt`, in the `/etc/tripwire/` directory. That file includes several useful directives for different kinds of files and directories, as described in Table 12-5.

The categories and labels shown in Table 12-5 provide one measure for files that should be tracked, relative to a baseline configuration. The files and directories in each of these categories may vary depending on the type of system that is tracked.

Define the Baseline Network Configuration

One element that changes with each system is the baseline network configuration. By definition, different systems have to have different IP addresses, hostnames, and network card hardware addresses.

But if you've configured a baseline system, there should be common elements in the network configuration such as the network device filename. One example is `/dev/eth0`. If all these systems are on the same network, they should generally have the same routing table.

As discussed in Chapter 6, the U.S. National Security Agency (NSA) discourages the use of the Dynamic Host Configuration Protocol (DHCP) on client systems. That recommendation effectively requires a different network configuration file for each system.

Additional network configuration relates to open ports. There are three ways to measure open network ports, based on the following commands:

- `netstat -atun`—Listens to all (`-a`) network sockets for connections associated with the TCP (`-t`) and UDP (`-u`) protocols, with output in numeric (`-n`) format, to avoid load on Domain Name Server (DNS) services.
- `nmap ip_address`—Scans for open ports on the given `ip_address`. Run this command using the same IP address on the local system and on a remote system. Any differences may reveal the effectiveness of a firewall.
- `iptables -L`—Lists current firewall rules based on the `iptables` command.

This is not a complete view of the current network configuration, as individual services frequently have their own firewalls. But it is a starting point.

Collect Runtime Information

One more element of a baseline configuration is how well it runs on a local system. A good baseline configuration will have some room to spare with regard to disk space, RAM, Central Processing Unit (CPU) usage, and so on. A system that has been taken over by a black-hat hacker may no longer have that room to spare. It may also have unexpected processes running, such as the `ping` command on a system being used in a denial of service (DoS) attack.

But runtime information varies, so be flexible with the information you collect. A slight variance should not be important. Excessive use of swap space may be evidence of a memory leak as opposed to evidence of a Trojan horse.

With that in mind, runtime information can be collected with the following commands:

- `top`—Displays currently running Linux processes along with runtime, CPU load, RAM, and swap-space usage.
- `free`—Notes the current amount of free and used memory with respect to RAM and swap space.
- `vmstat`—Lists free RAM, memory allocated to buffers, memory swapped in and out, system interrupts, and CPU usage.
- `sar`—Collects custom system activity reports. May be configured as a `cron` job.

Perhaps the most useful of these commands is `sar`, because system activity reports can be collected like log files. System activity that exceeds certain levels can be reviewed for further issues. It's available on both the Red Hat and Ubuntu distributions from the `sysstat` package.

Check for Changes with Integrity Scanners

An integrity scanner is a system that can detect unwanted software on a computer. For the purposes of this section, it is essentially the same thing as an intrusion detection system (IDS). Software such as Tripwire and the **Advanced Intrusion Detection Environment (AIDE)** provide a number of options that can help you check the integrity of local Linux systems.

The right time to install an integrity scanner is just after you've set up a baseline configuration, before any such systems are made operational on a network. Unless a black-hat hacker has penetrated the repositories for your selected Linux distribution, that integrity scanner should be able to establish baseline settings for your standard configuration.

The noted IDSes are just two of those available from the Ubuntu universe repositories. While Tripwire has been included in older Red Hat releases, the only IDS available from Red Hat repositories is AIDE.

Tripwire

Perhaps the most well known of the Linux IDS systems is Tripwire. Developed originally in 1992 by Gene Kim, Tripwire pioneered many of the techniques now associated with intrusion detection.

Similar to the sendmail and Sendmail e-mail services discussed in Chapter 9, there are open source and commercial versions of the Tripwire software. Although both were originally based on open source code, the development path of the open source and commercial versions of this software began to diverge in 1999.

This section focuses on the open source version of Tripwire, documented at *http://sourceforge.net/projects/tripwire/*. If you need a commercial solution, there are several excellent Tripwire options described at *http://www.tripwire.com/*.

Because it is included in the Ubuntu universe repositories, Tripwire is fairly easy to install on such systems. If you're installing Tripwire on a Red Hat system, you'll first have to download the source code from the SourceForge Web site. You'll also need the GNU C Language compiler along with C++ language support.

Tripwire requires a site and local passphrase, which supports extra levels of security. Once this is configured, you can run the following command on a regular basis to detect deviations from the baseline:

```
# tripwire --check
```

Figure 12-4 illustrates a small section of a Tripwire report, using the `twpol.txt file` policies in the `/etc/tripwire/` directory as described earlier in this chapter.

The output is more alarming than is required, as the default `twpol.txt` settings set a high severity level to changes to files in the `/proc/` directory. As any experienced Linux user should know, files in this directory are dynamic. They change frequently, with the load on a system.

The report includes more than 1,000 lines of information, with data on changes detected to files on configured directories. You can analyze the file to review files that have been added or otherwise modified to see if there is a real problem.

```
 ------------------------------------------------------------------------

  Rule Name                       Severity Level   Added   Removed  Modified
  ---------                       --------------   -----   -------  --------
    Invariant Directories            66              0       0         0
  * Tripwire Data Files             100              1       0         0
  * Other binaries                   66              3       0         1
    Tripwire Binaries               100              0       0         0
  * Other libraries                  66              4       0         1
    Root file-system executables    100              0       0         0
  * System boot changes             100              1       0         1
    Root file-system libraries      100              0       0         0
    (/lib)
    Critical system boot files      100              0       0         0
  * Other configuration files        66              1       0         4
    (/etc)
    Boot Scripts                    100              0       0         0
    Security Control                 66              0       0         0
    Root config files               100              0       0         0
  * Devices & Kernel information    100            522     348         0

  Total objects scanned:  30575
  Total violations found:   887
                                                       56,1          3%
```

Advanced Intrusion Detection Environment (AIDE)

One feature enabled with AIDE is flexibility with respect to the default configuration database. Depending on the distribution, AIDE may be configured in the `aide.conf` file in the `/etc/` or `/etc/aide/` directory. The Ubuntu release includes a `cron` job in the `aide` file in the `/etc/cron.daily/` directory. To configure AIDE, open the `aide.conf` file.

As shown with the following `database` directives, the AIDE configuration database is normally set up in the `/var/lib/aide/` directory. You can configure that on any location, even a remote networked directory. When properly configured, AIDE can send intrusion detection reports to a central server, perhaps a central logging server.

Once the `aide.conf` file is configured, be sure to modify the `aide` `cron` job file in the `/etc/aide/` directory to conform to the location for the baseline database. To test it out, you'll need to run the following command to configure that first database. The `--config /etc/aide/aide.conf` switch is not required on the Red Hat version of AIDE.

```
# aide --init --config /etc/aide/aide.conf
```

Once configured, the noted Ubuntu cron job should re-run the AIDE IDS on a daily basis. On Red Hat systems, you should be able to create a `cron` job based on the `aide --check` command. That command uses the files identified in the `database` and `database_out` variables. You'll then be able to inspect those reports for possible intrusions.

For more information and the latest releases for AIDE, navigate to *http://sourceforge.net/projects/aide/*.

Best Practices: Build and Maintain a Secure Baseline

This chapter focused on baseline Linux systems, building on the information provided especially in Chapters 6 and 7 with respect to creating a minimal configuration and firewalls. When installing Red Hat Enterprise Linux, minimal installations are easiest to achieve through the text-mode version of the Anaconda installation program. RHEL 6 makes that process even more efficient.

In contrast, Ubuntu Server Edition already provides a relatively minimal installation in its default text-mode operation. Whichever distribution you select, additional work has to be done to minimize the number of installed services and to further secure the system.

Additional options include read-only or live bootable versions of Linux. Several directories may be suited to configuration as a read-only filesystem, subject to the changes required from functional and security-related updates. Alternatively, specialized mount options such as `nosuid`, `nodev`, and `noexec` can minimize risks to files in key directories. A number of excellent Linux distributions are available in live CD format.

Once you have a gold baseline, it is something worth protecting. A gold baseline is simple, is secure on a network, and is further protected by mandatory access control systems such as SELinux and AppArmor. With a gold baseline, you need to be aware of circumstances where it may be counterproductive to install security and other updates. Some updates may cause hardware to stop working, may lead to configurations where key third-party software such as databases are no longer supported, and may lead to the need to recompile some software, especially when new kernels are installed.

The performance of a system can be monitored through its logs. Local logs in Linux are in transition from the system and kernel logging services to the RSyslog service. The services in question share the same basic log facilities and message priorities. While the standard log files for Ubuntu and Red Hat systems vary, they use the same basic log facilities and priorities. Both distributions give way when a service has its own log configuration in a subdirectory of `/var/log/`. The benefit of RSyslog is the ability to configure centralized log servers, with log files transmitted over secure connections.

A baseline system state starts with a list of installed packages. It continues with IDSes such as Tripwire, which can classify current files in different categories of importance. It includes information on the baseline network configuration and standard runtime values, based on commands like `sar`.

Linux includes a number of options for IDSes, including Tripwire and AIDE. The time to install and set up an IDS is when a gold baseline is configured, before that baseline is configured with a specific service and connected to a network. Once a database of current files and directories with ownership and permissions is configured, an IDS can be run on a regular basis to make sure that no significant changes have been made to that gold baseline.

CHAPTER SUMMARY

A secure baseline is fundamental to a secure network. With a secure baseline, it's easier to configure bastion servers with confidence. You can start with the basic Red Hat and Ubuntu Server installation programs. Coupled with the techniques from Chapters 6 and 7, that can give you an excellent foundation. When coupled with the right mount options, that baseline can be as good as gold.

The quality of the baseline can be measured with logs, configured locally, or configured to send information to a central logging server. With that and related runtime information, you can identify a baseline system state. In addition, IDS tools such as Tripwire and AIDE can help you protect the integrity of that baseline system.

KEY CONCEPTS AND TERMS

alert
debug
emerg
err
info
notice
warn

Advanced Intrusion Detection Environment (AIDE)
Anaconda
RSyslog
Tripwire

CHAPTER 12 ASSESSMENT

1. Which of the following options support remote updates from a Web-based interface?

   A. Minimal installation
   B. No automatic updates
   C. Install security updates automatically
   D. Manage system with Landscape

2. Which of the following package groups are included in a default RHEL 5 installation?

   A. Automatic updates
   B. KDE
   C. GNOME
   D. Secure Shell server

3. What is the mount option that disables executable binaries in an /etc/fstab configuration file?

4. Which of the following directories is normally *not* appropriate as a read-only filesystem?

   A. /boot/
   B. /home/
   C. /root/
   D. /sbin/

5. Which of the following directories is a standard location for packages downloaded from an Ubuntu repository?

A. /var/cache/apt/

B. /var/cache/yum/

C. /tmp/

D. /root/

6. Which of the following is *not* a reason to test updates before installing them on a gold baseline?

A. Potential effects on compiled software

B. Support issues with third-party software

C. Source code is unverified

D. Potential interactions with other software

7. Which of the following log priorities provides the most important messages?

A. debug

B. err

C. info

D. notice

8. In a Samba log file, which of the following is associated with the %m variable?

A. Username

B. Hostname

C. Service version

D. User profile

9. What option in the /etc/syslog.conf configuration file includes mail messages of only the info priority? Use the *facility.priority* format.

10. Which of the following modules is associated with system logging in an RSyslog configuration file?

A. imuxsock

B. imklog

C. imudp

D. imtcp

11. Which of the following symbols in an RSyslog configuration file is associated with UDP connections?

A. !

B. @

C. @@

D. =

12. What is the simplest command that includes all packages on an Ubuntu system?

13. Which of the following commands can best collect information on the activity on a system?

A. top

B. sar

C. vmstat

D. free

14. Which of the following configuration files includes Tripwire configuration policies in a human-readable format?

A. twcfg.txt

B. tw.cfg

C. twpol.txt

D. twpol.enc

15. What command switch inspects the current configuration, comparing it with a previously derived baseline configuration? This switch works with both the tripwire and aide commands.

A. --inspect

B. --check

C. --compare

D. --review

Testing and Reporting

WHILE YOU MAY TAKE every conceivable step to secure local systems and networks, that is not enough. Tests come in real time when black-hat hackers try to break through those security measures. So before a black-hat hacker can break in, you should test systems and networks for known security issues and measures.

Any test should apply to all parts of a layered defense, from an external firewall to the passwords selected by local users. You can monitor those ports that have to be open to enable network communication. But if other ports are also open, black-hat hackers can use those ports to penetrate local systems without your knowledge. In this chapter, you'll see what ports are open and what can be done to keep unnecessary ports closed. The challenges have increased with the proliferation of virtual systems.

If such defenses prevent legitimate users from connecting, that would defeat the purpose of security. If a black-hat hacker does break in without your knowledge, however, that person may change files on local systems. Standard commands and integrity checkers can detect such changes. Excellent open source and commercial tools can be used to detect changes, potential security flaws, black-hat intrusions, and more.

Chapter 13 Topics

This chapter covers the following topics and concepts:

- Why you should test every layer of protection
- How to find open network ports
- How to run integrity checks of installed files and executables
- How to make sure security does not prevent legitimate access
- How to monitor virtual hardware

- What some options are for open source penetration testing tools
- What some options are for commercial penetration testing tools
- Where to install security testing tools
- What best practices are for testing and reporting

Chapter 13 Goals

When you complete this chapter, you will be able to:

- Use open source testing tools to identify potential flaws in a security configuration
- Take advantage of tools on bootable read-only Linux distributions
- Manage security issues on physical and virtual systems
- Review systems for changes in key files

Test Every Component of a Layered Defense

As you've explored different types of security throughout the book, you should realize that many of these security tools can be used together. When combined, the resulting layered defense can stop any number of attacks. But no security system is perfect. If there are weaknesses, you need to know what they are. While some security issues may not be avoidable in a functional system, consequent risks can be limited.

The layers of security on a network could include a series of firewalls. Firewalls based on the `iptables` command can be configured on external routers, internal routers, and individual systems. Firewalls can also be configured on many individual services. If a black-hat hacker breaks through these defenses, there is still the matter of protecting user accounts. Even if a user account is compromised, mandatory access control systems can further protect internal systems.

This section provides an overview of the sections that follow, so you have a "big picture" feel for what's required to test every component of a layered defense.

FYI

When some defenses have to be disabled, tests should not be run on current production systems. For example, if you disable a firewall to enable tests of other systems, even that temporary exposure could lead to trouble from black-hat hackers. Before disabling such systems, they should be withdrawn from production. Of course, if the network is still protected by external firewalls, that risk would be limited to those black-hat hackers with access inside your network.

Test a Firewall

Implicit in these tests is the issue of open network ports. As suggested in the opening comments of the /etc/services file, there are 65,536 ports available. Network communication normally proceeds through one of these three protocols: the Transport Control Protocol (TCP), the User Datagram Protocol (UDP), or the Internet Control Message Protocol (ICMP).

Any communication, legitimate or otherwise, has to proceed through these ports using one of the noted protocols. Tools that check for open network ports, such as the **nmap** and **nc** commands, are discussed later in this chapter. Because firewall commands may be difficult to decipher, output like the following excerpt from the nmap command may be easier to read:

```
Interesting ports on 192.168.1.23:
Not shown: 1679 closed ports
PORT STATE SERVICE
22/tcp open  ssh
Nmap finished: 1 IP address (1 host up) scanned in 1.383 seconds
```

Just be sure to apply the command from inside and outside the firewall, as the results may differ depending on active services and ports addressed by firewall rules.

For the purpose of testing defenses, once you've applied tools such as nmap and nc, temporarily turn off any firewall on a local system. One quick way to do so is with the iptables -F command. You'll review how to reactivate firewalls at the end of the next section.

Test Various Services

It's possible that an administrator will make a mistake with a firewall. It's also possible that a black-hat hacker will use a command like nc to redirect traffic through an open port in a firewall. If you want systems to be able to communicate on the Internet, it's not possible to close all network ports on the firewall.

The easiest way to test the protection afforded various services, however, is with a disabled iptables firewall. Only then can you test the effectiveness of internal protections on various services. Such services can be further protected with TCP Wrappers, along with configuration rules unique to certain services.

As you read through the tests for various services, you'll note the reliance on IP address–based restrictions. Yes, black-hat hackers can spoof IP addresses, including those normally found on private IP address networks. But that is one item that iptables rules such as the following can address, a benefit of a layered defense:

```
iptables -A RH-Firewall-1-INPUT -i eth0 -s 10.0.0.0/8
↪-j LOG --log-prefix "Dropped private class A address"
```

Specifically, this command appends (-A), a rule to the chain named RH-Firewall-1-INPUT. The rule is applied to network packets coming in through the network interface (-i) on device eth0. The rule is applied to packets with a source (-s) address in the 10.0.0.0/8 network. If an incoming packet meets these conditions, the incidence of the packet is logged with the noted prefix in the log file. But that just gives you an idea of the kinds of addresses being used by attackers. You should go one step farther with the following rule:

```
iptables -A RH-Firewall-1-INPUT -i eth0 -s 10.0.0.0/8 -j DROP
```

If you'd rather have an error message sent to such users, substitute REJECT for DROP.

Test TCP Wrappers Services

One general test can apply to any services otherwise protected by TCP Wrappers in the /etc/hosts.allow and /etc/hosts.deny configuration files described in Chapter 7.

For example, the following entry in the /etc/hosts.allow file limits access to the Secure Shell (SSH) service by username and IP address. This directive limits access to user michael on the noted IP address.

```
sshd : michael@10.22.33.44
```

You should be able to test this rule by trying to log in as user michael from a different IP address, as well as by trying to log in as a different user from the specified IP address.

Test Apache

Several services feature their own configuration checkers. For example, the Apache Web server includes a syntax checker in its basic control command. Depending on the distribution, the control command may be httpd or apache2ctl. The switches for these commands are the same. For example, the following command checks the syntax of Apache configuration files on an Ubuntu system:

```
# apache2ctl -t
```

In contrast, if virtual hosts are configured on an Apache Web server on a Red Hat system, the following command checks the syntax on each individually configured virtual host:

```
# httpd -S
```

While syntax checks are a basic part of the configuration of any service, a syntax check can help you identify services that may have been modified without your knowledge.

Of course, security checks on Apache go beyond syntax. If you've configured a secure Web site, you should check the status of secure certificates—especially if they've been purchased from a certificate authority. For that purpose, you can look for an Online Certificate Status Protocol (OCSP) server, as discussed in Chapter 11.

If you've configured password security on an Apache-based Web site, it'll normally be based on usernames and passwords configured with the htpasswd command. Unless such databases have been handed off to a Lightweight Directory Access Protocol (LDAP) server, an Apache authentication database is typically kept in or near the same directory as Apache configuration files.

Of course, you'll want to test such password-protected directories. Can users without entries in the Apache authentication database access such directories? If you navigate directly to the protected directory in question, the Apache server should automatically prompt for a username and password.

One strong recommendation from Chapter 9 is to disable the use of `.htaccess` files. As hidden files, they don't appear in the output to a casual search. So if a black-hat hacker were to include an `.htaccess` file in an Apache configured directory, he or she could include directives that override any configuration you've set up. Such problems can be avoided with the following directive in any `Directory` container:

```
AllowOverride none
```

Test Samba

As with Apache, one issue with respect to Samba is the syntax. If there is a problem, Samba may not be available to your users, violating that tenet of the CIA triad of confidentiality, integrity, and availability. The `testparm` command provides an excellent syntax check for a Samba configuration file. The output, as shown in Figure 13-1, is pretty straightforward.

If there's a problem with basic Samba security options, it should be revealed in this output. For example, the following option in the [`homes`] stanza would reveal the existence of user home directories to any user who connects to that service:

```
browsable = yes
```

With a list of usernames, a black-hat hacker can get to work, especially if those users work primarily on Microsoft Windows machines.

FIGURE 13-1

Testing Samba syntax with `testparm`.

```
Load smb config files from /etc/samba/smb.conf
Processing section "[homes]"
Processing section "[printers]"
Loaded services file OK.
Server role: ROLE_DOMAIN_MEMBER
Press enter to see a dump of your service definitions

[global]
        workgroup = MYGROUP
        server string = Samba Server Version %v
        security = ADS
        cups options = raw

[homes]
        comment = Home Directories
        read only = No
        browseable = No

[printers]
        comment = All Printers
        path = /var/spool/samba
        printable = Yes
        browseable = No
[root@RHELserver ~]#
```

Some Samba directories may be further limited with configuration options such as `hosts allow`, which limits access to the local Samba server to systems on the localhost and the noted private IP address networks:

```
hosts allow = 127. 192.168.12. 192.168.13.
```

Of course, Samba security extends to connected user-authentication databases. If it's a Windows NT-style database stored locally, the Samba server can be configured as a Primary Domain Controller (PDC). Security options are associated with that database. That database may be stored locally in a file in the `/etc/samba/` directory. Related options such as user and machine profiles are in essence Linux directories that hold Microsoft configuration files.

Testing Other Services

Apache and Samba are just two of the many Linux-based services available. The steps taken to test the security of those services should provide a model for testing the security of other network services that you may have configured on a Linux system. Basic details for such tests were described in previous chapters.

After Service Tests Are Complete

When you're finished testing various services, you should be able to restore the firewall with an appropriate script. Because the `iptables` command includes its own service on Red Hat systems, that command is pretty straightforward:

```
# /etc/init.d/iptables restart
```

Of course, that applies only to Internet Protocol version 4 (IPv4) networking. For Internet Protocol version 6 (IPv6) networking, the corresponding command and script is `ip6tables`. While the same scripts are not available on Ubuntu systems, tools such as the Uncomplicated Firewall front-end described in Chapter 7 provide a script that can activate and deactivate `iptables` and `ip6tables` firewall rules.

Test Passwords

As for passwords, a variety of open source testing tools are available. Of the top 10 password crackers at *http://sectools.org/crackers.html*, tools like **John the Ripper**, **Hydra**, and **RainbowCrack** can fairly quickly decrypt and identify simple passwords from files like `/etc/shadow` and `/etc/samba/smbpasswd`.

In general, you should be able to take the files with local authentication databases and test them with the noted tools. Given enough time, processing power, and direct access to such files, all such passwords can be cracked.

However, the process can take days, months, or even years, depending on the tool, the hardware, and the strength of the password. So if a black-hat hacker did break into a local system and could get access to local authentication databases, how long would it take for that person to crack such passwords? That and related questions will be explored later in this chapter.

Test Mandatory Access Control Systems

If a black-hat hacker is able to break into a user or a service account, the next line of defense is the mandatory access control system such as Security Enhanced Linux (SELinux) and Application Armor (AppArmor). If network services are properly protected, even a compromise in a service account would not lead to a compromise in a service.

For example, what happens if there's a compromise of the service account associated with the Apache Web server? Would a black-hat hacker, masquerading as that user, be able to write to key files? Generally, if SELinux is set to enforcing mode with an `httpd_sys_content_rw_t` context, the answer would be yes. But is that context necessary for the files in question? Could the service still function appropriately with a context of `httpd_sys_content_t`? Those are the tests and questions associated with mandatory access control systems such as SELinux or AppArmor.

Check for Open Network Ports

This section focuses on basic open source commands related to network ports, specifically nmap, `lsof`, `telnet`, and **netstat**. Many of the tools discussed in this chapter and book take advantage of these commands and are in effect front-ends, which frequently include some graphical face illustrating the output to these commands. Related to these commands is netcat, the `nc` command, which is discussed later in this chapter.

More extensive tools such as **System Administrators Integrated Network Tool (SAINT)** and **Nessus** are covered later in this chapter.

The `telnet` Command

One reason the `telnet` command still exists on the systems of many security administrators is its utility. It's an easy way to check for open ports over a network. For example, suppose a colleague has set up a Web site, but nobody can connect to it. She says it's up and running on her system. It's easy to test a connection to such a Web site with the following command, substituting the actual domain name for *domain.com*:

```
$ telnet domain.com 80
```

If ports between your systems are open and unblocked, you should see the following output:

```
Trying some_ip_address...
Connected to example.com (some_ip_address).
Escape character is '^]'
```

At that point, you should be able to press Ctrl+] to get the ^] character and press Enter to get to a `telnet>` prompt. From there, type the `quit` command to return to the command-line interface.

Similar commands should work with the port number for most standard services online. For example, if you run the telnet *your_mail_server.com* 25 command (substitute the name of the target e-mail server for *your_mail_server.com*) and get a Connection refused message, there may be a bad port number or perhaps a firewall rule that's blocking the connection to that outgoing e-mail server. If there's no response at all, the telnet command is likely getting through to the target server, but just not getting a response. That suggests nothing is listening on port 25. One of the limitations of telnet is that it can connect only to systems that use TCP ports. Later in this chapter, you'll look at the nc command, which can connect to systems that use TCP and UDP ports.

If some server is listening on port 25, you'll see it in the output of a netstat command with appropriate switches. It can also work with systems that communicate on both TCP and UDP ports.

The netstat Command

The netstat command is a powerful tool. With a variety of different switches, it can help you get into and better understand the networking subsystem. Knowledgeable Linux users should already know that the netstat -r command displays the routing table that applies to the current system. With the -n switch, the netstat command works in numeric format; in other words, it does not require access to Domain Name Service (DNS) or the /etc/services file.

The netstat command can tell you more. The -t switch specifies TCP ports. The -u switch specifies UDP ports. With the help of the -a switch, netstat can tell you about all connections on the local system. So put those switches together. Figure 13-2 displays the start of the output to the netstat -atun command.

```
Active Internet connections (servers and established)
Proto Recv-Q Send-Q Local Address           Foreign Address         State

tcp       0      0 127.0.0.1:2208          0.0.0.0:*               LISTEN

tcp       0      0 0.0.0.0:902             0.0.0.0:*               LISTEN

tcp       0      0 0.0.0.0:742             0.0.0.0:*               LISTEN

tcp       0      0 0.0.0.0:139             0.0.0.0:*               LISTEN

tcp       0      0 127.0.0.1:5900          0.0.0.0:*               LISTEN

tcp       0      0 127.0.0.1:5901          0.0.0.0:*               LISTEN

tcp       0      0 127.0.0.1:5902          0.0.0.0:*               LISTEN

tcp       0      0 0.0.0.0:111             0.0.0.0:*               LISTEN

tcp       0      0 127.0.0.1:30003         0.0.0.0:*               LISTEN

tcp       0      0 192.168.122.1:53        0.0.0.0:*               LISTEN
:
```

FIGURE 13-2

Identify what your system listens to with netstat -atun.

TABLE 13-1 Output from `netstat -atun`.

COLUMN	DESCRIPTION
Proto	Protocol, typically TCP or UDP. On some systems, protocols associated with IPv6 communication may be shown as TCP6 and UDP6.
Recv-Q	Received communication in the queue, in bytes, usually 0.
Send-Q	Transmitted communication in the queue that is not yet acknowledged, in bytes, usually 0.
Local Address	Local IP address and port number. See explanation that follows for more information.
Foreign Address	Remote IP address and port number. Unless there's an established connection, it's normally set to IPv4 address and port number 0.0.0.0:*, which is listening for connections from any IPv4 address. It may also be set to IPv6 address and port number :::*. See explanation that follows for more information.
State	Connection state, normally LISTEN or ESTABLISHED. A network service that is in the LISTEN state has not yet made a connection.

> **TIP**
>
> IPv4 address 0.0.0.0 is known as the default address, a placeholder for any address.

This is a lot of output, indicative of a system that's probably listening for too many connections. The output is described in Table 13-1, with columns listed from left to right. To see the actual column headers, you'll have to pipe the output to the `less` command pager, and then the views of the output would be limited. Alternatively, if a bastion host is configured on the local system, a view of all such listen connections can be seen in a normal output, and you'll see an example of such later in this section.

With Table 13-1 in mind, take another look at the output from the `netstat -atun` command shown in Figure 13-2. Take the first couple of lines of output, one at a time:

```
tcp  0  0 127.0.0.1:2208  0.0.0.0:*  LISTEN
```

The first line is a TCP connection associated with port 2208, just listening for requests from systems with any IP address (0.0.0.0). An Internet search might send you into a panic, as there are entries that suggest that port is a common backdoor for black-hat hackers. But it is also used by the Hewlett-Packard Linux Imaging and Printing Project, and may be necessary for communication with such printers. In addition, since the local address is set to the loopback address of 127.0.0.1, the system might be listening just to the local loopback adapter.

To confirm, you can run the variation on the `telnet` command described earlier, as it would apply to port 2208:

```
$ telnet localhost 2208
```

As the localhost address is normally associated with 127.0.0.1 in the `/etc/hosts` file, that connection should work. Try it again with the IP address of the local adapter. If the `netstat` status is true, the connection should be refused. The same command, when run from a remote system, may lead to a message that suggests that the connection was refused, typical of a block by an `iptables`-based firewall.

Now take the second line of output, which listens for TCP traffic from any address on port 902:

```
tcp  0  0 0.0.0.0:902  0.0.0.0:*  LISTEN
```

In this case, the `/etc/services` file is a bit misleading, because port 902 is the standard for **VMware** systems that are controlled over a network. That's confirmed by the output to the `telnet` *remote_ip_address* 902 command, as shown here:

```
220 VMware Authentication Daemon Version 1.10:
↪SSL Required, MKSDisplayProtocol:VNC
```

In this case, the port is open, even when the associated VMware service is stopped. The number of lines in Figure 13-2 goes on for some time. As suggested by that quantity of output, the associated system is potentially not very secure. In contrast, take a look at Figure 13-3, where the `netstat -atun` command is applied to a more secure system.

The displayed output is easier to explain. The first line, which specifies port 22, is associated with an SSH server. The second line, associated with the localhost address and port 25, illustrates a Simple Mail Transfer Protocol (SMTP) server such as Postfix or sendmail that is not yet listening to anything from a regular network address.

Take a closer look at the third line, associated with an `ESTABLISHED` connection:

```
tcp  0   0 192.168.122.19:22   192.168.122.1:56112   ESTABLISHED
```

It's a TCP connection on port 22, from the noted 192.168.122.1 IP address. Communication is being received back on that client on port 56112. The next two lines are associated with TCP networking over an IPv6 connection, as symbolized by the `tcp6` label. They're the IPv6 settings that correspond to the first two lines.

```
michael@ubuntulucidsvr2:~$ netstat -atun
Active Internet connections (servers and established)
Proto Recv-Q Send-Q Local Address          Foreign Address        State
tcp        0      0 0.0.0.0:22             0.0.0.0:*              LISTEN
tcp        0      0 127.0.0.1:25           0.0.0.0:*              LISTEN
tcp        0      0 192.168.122.19:22      192.168.122.1:56112    ESTABLISHED
tcp6       0      0 :::22                  :::*                   LISTEN
tcp6       0      0 ::1:25                 :::*                   LISTEN
udp        0      0 0.0.0.0:68             0.0.0.0:*
michael@ubuntulucidsvr2:~$
```

FIGURE 13-3

The `netstat -atun` command on a bastion server.

The final line specifies an open UDP port 68, normally associated with the **Bootstrap Protocol (BOOTP)**. If this system can get IP address information from the local system or does not need to use the Dynamic Host Configuration Protocol (DHCP), you may want to disable or even uninstall associated software.

Now take the command a step farther with the -p switch to identify the process in question. For the UDP BOOTP port just described, that specifies the dhclient process, which confirms the association between that port and the DHCP client.

The lsof Command

While the lsof command lists open files, it can be focused on network-related processes with the -i switch. Add the -n to keep IP addresses in numeric format, and you can quickly get a view of network-related processes on the local system:

```
# lsof -ni
```

If you've got a lot of active network services, the output could be substantial. One example is shown in Figure 13-4. Compare the output to the netstat -atunp command described earlier. Not only does that lsof -ni command organize connections by service, but it also includes user and process identifier (PID) information.

```
COMMAND    PID     USER   FD   TYPE   DEVICE SIZE NODE NAME
ssh        3037  michael   3u   IPv4 11425157      TCP 10.168.0.8:36277->10.168.0.60:ssh (ESTABLISHED)
racoon     5144     root   6u   IPv4    17509      UDP 127.0.0.1:isakmp
racoon     5144     root   8u   IPv4    17510      UDP 10.168.0.8:isakmp
racoon     5144     root  11u   IPv6    17513      UDP [::1]:isakmp
racoon     5144     root  12u   IPv6    17514      UDP [fe80::2ff:17ff:fe6b:c680]:isakmp
portmap    5163   daemon   3u   IPv4    13293      UDP *:sunrpc
portmap    5163   daemon   4u   IPv4    13294      TCP *:sunrpc (LISTEN)
rpc.statd  5182    statd   5u   IPv4    13324      UDP *:694
rpc.statd  5182    statd   7u   IPv4    13332      UDP *:56646
rpc.statd  5182    statd   8u   IPv4    13335      TCP *:42673 (LISTEN)
avahi-dae  5896    avahi  14u   IPv4    14154      UDP *:mdns
avahi-dae  5896    avahi  15u   IPv4    14155      UDP *:41511
mysqld     6007    mysql  10u   IPv4    14265      TCP 127.0.0.1:mysql (LISTEN)
cupsd      6204     root   2u   IPv6    14532      TCP *:ipp (LISTEN)
cupsd      6204     root   3u   IPv4    14533      TCP *:ipp (LISTEN)
cupsd      6204     root   5u   IPv4    14536      UDP *:ipp
sshd       6234     root   3u   IPv6 10064987      TCP *:ssh (LISTEN)
hddtemp    6254     root   0u   IPv4    14572      TCP 127.0.0.1:7634 (LISTEN)
master     6440     root  11u   IPv4    14952      TCP *:smtp (LISTEN)
nmbd       6472     root   6u   IPv4    15109      UDP *:netbios-ns
nmbd       6472     root   7u   IPv4    15110      UDP *:netbios-dgm
nmbd       6472     root   8u   IPv4    15112      UDP 10.168.0.8:netbios-ns
nmbd       6472     root   9u   IPv4    15113      UDP 10.168.0.8:netbios-dgm
nmbd       6472     root  15u   IPv4    61862      UDP 172.16.105.1:netbios-ns
nmbd       6472     root  16u   IPv4    61863      UDP 172.16.105.1:netbios-dgm
smbd       6474     root  19u   IPv4    15139      TCP *:microsoft-ds (LISTEN)
smbd       6474     root  20u   IPv4    15140      TCP *:netbios-ssn (LISTEN)
vsftpd     6598     root   3u   IPv4    15230      TCP *:ftp (LISTEN)
xinetd     6655     root   5u   IPv4    15340      TCP *:vmware-authd (LISTEN)
xinetd     6655     root   6u   IPv4    15341      TCP *:swat (LISTEN)
xinetd     6655     root   8u   IPv4    15342      TCP *:kshell (LISTEN)
xinetd     6655     root   9u   IPv4    15343      TCP *:eklogin (LISTEN)
xinetd     6655     root  10u   IPv4    15344      TCP *:telnet (LISTEN)
asterisk   6737 asterisk   7u   IPv4    15443      TCP 127.0.0.1:5038 (LISTEN)
```

FIGURE 13-4

The lsof -ni command on a multipurpose system.

The nmap Command

The nmap command is an incredible tool. Several books have been written about this network exploration tool and port scanner. To get a taste of what it can do, run the nmap command by itself. Now run it on the system of your choice, using an IP address or hostname. If a firewall has been configured on a system, it's interesting to note the differences from inside and outside the firewall.

The following sections address some of the options described in the nmap output. Those commands that require root administrative privileges are preceded by the standard root prompt, #.

Be aware, the nmap command can take several minutes to run over a network. If you're just learning the nmap command, it may be faster to run the commands described in the following subsections against an IP address on your local network. Of course, if you're testing a system behind a firewall, you can't measure the effectiveness of that firewall unless the nmap command is run on a system on the other side of that firewall.

In general, if you want more information in the output, the verbose (-v) switch can help. If you need still more information, the -vv switch adds even more verbosity. The description in this chapter is far from complete; there are several books written solely on the intricacies of the nmap command.

> **⚠ WARNING**
>
> As noted by the developers of the nmap command at *http://nmap.org/book/legal-issues.html*, improper use of the command "can (in rare cases) get you sued, fired, expelled, jailed, or banned by your ISP." So don't use the nmap command on a system unless you're specifically allowed to do so.

Target Specification

The nmap command can be targeted at a group of systems, an IP address, hostname, or fully qualified domain name formats. For example, the following command reviews the systems with IP addresses 192.168.0.1 through 192.168.0.3:

```
$ nmap 192.168.0.1-3
```

The following command reviews all systems on the noted network, in Classless Inter-Domain Routing (CIDR) notation:

```
$ nmap 192.168.0.0/24
```

Host Discovery

A black-hat hacker with access to a private network might start with a ping scan. In the following command, the -s switch scans and the -P switch applies the ping command to the systems on the target addresses:

```
$ nmap -sP 10.0.0.0/8
```

It just takes a few seconds to display a list of active systems on that network. One other useful switch from this section is the -n, which avoids the use of DNS servers for name resolution. If there is an excessive delay when running other nmap commands, the -n may help.

While such a command saves time, not all hosts respond to requests made with the ping command. The following command scans all hosts in the noted network:

```
$ nmap -PN 192.168.0.0/24
```

The command is time-consuming; it could easily take several hours to scan all the ports on all the IP addresses on the noted network. That's just for the 254 allowable IP addresses on that network. That process would take a lot longer for the 16,000,000 IP addresses on the class A private network, 10.0.0.0/8.

Scan Techniques

While the nmap command focuses on TCP packets, network communication also uses UDP packets. To scan a system for open UDP ports on a given IP address, run the following command:

```
# nmap -sU ip_address
```

Of course, network communication can proceed through more than just the TCP and UDP protocols. To find the full list of protocols enabled for an IP address, run the following command:

```
# nmap -sO ip_address
```

Port Specification and Scan Order

One of the idiosyncrasies of nmap is that it scans only most commonly used ports. The number of ports checked varies depending on the version of nmap used; for example, version 5.00 checks 1,000 ports by default. But for some, that's an incomplete scan. The -p switch can help; the following scan checks all 65,536 TCP/IP ports:

```
$ nmap -p 0-65535 ip_address
```

Of course, as that scan just applies to TCP ports, you may also be interested in the following command, which builds upon the switches described in a previous section to check UDP ports:

```
$ nmap -sU -p 0-65535 ip_address
```

Service Version Detection

With the -sV switch, the nmap command searches for the version number of all services communicating over open ports. Take a look at Figure 13-5, the output to the nmap -sV -p 0-65535 10.168.0.1 command. Note how it lists all open services and their version numbers. A black-hat hacker who looks at this output and is aware of weaknesses of older versions of certain servers may pounce on this information.

Of course, as a security professional, you can use this information to make sure that the given services are up to date, with the latest security updates. This information may also reveal ports that you may close, perhaps by uninstalling or disabling a service. Alternatively, you could close these ports with appropriate firewall commands.

```
PORT        STATE SERVICE          VERSION
21/tcp      open  ftp              vsftpd 2.0.6
22/tcp      open  ssh              OpenSSH 4.7p1 Debian 8ubuntu1.2 (protocol 2.0)
23/tcp      open  tcpwrapped
25/tcp      open  smtp             Postfix smtpd
80/tcp      open  http             Apache httpd
111/tcp     open  rpcbind           2 (rpc #100000)
139/tcp     open  netbios-ssn      Samba smbd 3.X (workgroup: WORKGROUP)
443/tcp     open  http             Apache httpd
445/tcp     open  netbios-ssn      Samba smbd 3.X (workgroup: WORKGROUP)
544/tcp     open  kshell           Solaris kerberised rsh
631/tcp     open  ipp              CUPS 1.2
877/tcp     open  ypbind            1-2 (rpc #100007)
901/tcp     open  http             Samba SWAT administration server
902/tcp     open  ssl/vmware-auth  VMware GSX Authentication Daemon 1.10 (Uses VNC)
1021/tcp    open  rquotad           1-2 (rpc #100011)
2000/tcp    open  callbook?
2105/tcp    open  klogin           Kerberized rlogin
3306/tcp    open  mysql            MySQL 5.0.51a-3ubuntu5.5
5038/tcp    open  asterisk         Asterisk Call Manager 1.0
7634/tcp    open  hddtemp          hddtemp hard drive info server
8834/tcp    open  unknown
37737/tcp   open  unknown
57817/tcp   open  status            1 (rpc #100024)
```

FIGURE 13-5

A list of open services with version information.

Operating System Detection

The operating system detection option, -O, may reveal the operating system associated with the target machine. As of this writing, it's not very precise; for example, it provides this output for the operating system along with a list of open TCP ports. Fortunately or otherwise, the noted operating system includes a Linux kernel version 2.6.24.

```
Device type: general purpose
Running: Linux 2.6.X
OS details: Linux 2.6.17 - 2.6.18
```

The scripts as listed fall into several categories. Some scripts may fall under multiple categories. Because new scripts and even new switches are under development, assume this is just a partial list. There may be a dozen or more scripts available in several of these areas. Scripts can be bundled together; for example, a command like the following applies all scripts associated with a scan of the Hypertext Transfer Protocol (HTTP) service:

```
# nmap --script=http-* 192.168.100.1
```

If the given script is misspelled or is not otherwise available, the nmap command should return an error with the following message related to the script:

```
did not match a category, filename, or directory
```

Some of the scripts described appear only in beta versions of nmap. While the use of beta software is normally discouraged in production software, it is a way to give you more tools to detect security issues as they're created by black-hat hackers. For more information on how to get such beta tools from the associated nmap Subversion repository, see Chapter 15.

Authentication (auth). The nmap authentication scripts may test usernames, passwords, and more on target systems, possibly through a brute-force attack. The authentication scripts can be used for networked services associated with a number of protocols. These protocols range from the Apple Filing Protocol (AFP) to Telnet. For example, the following command attempts a brute-force attack to guess usernames and passwords on the FTP server on the noted IP address:

```
# nmap --script=ftp-brute 192.168.100.1
```

Default. The default scripts associated with the nmap command can find default information for a wide variety of services, from DHCP to DNS to shared directories on Microsoft networks. For example, the following command checks the target system for the Conficker.C worm:

```
# nmap --script=p2p-conficker 192.168.100.1
```

Discovery. Discovery scripts for the nmap command can find information associated with a variety of network services, from banners to shared Samba and NFS directories. Discovery scripts include WHOIS information, Secure Sockets Layer (SSL) certificates, and more. For example, the following command checks the target system for a list of directories shared over the Samba file service:

```
# nmap --script=smb-enum-shares 192.168.100.1
```

The nmap command as shown provides more than just share information. It includes the version number of the Samba release, the path to the shared directory, anonymous access if allowed, connected users, and more.

Denial of Service and Exploit. As of this writing, there is one script for both the denial of service (DoS) and exploit categories. The script as shown reviews a target Samba server for a number of vulnerabilities beyond DoS:

```
# nmap --script=smb-check-vulns 192.168.100.1
```

External. The scripts in the external category are associated with the way servers look to external systems. Many of the scripts in this category can expose risks. For example, the following command determines whether an e-mail server on a remote system is an open relay that can be used by spammers to send messages through your systems:

```
# nmap --script=smtp-open-relay 192.168.100.1
```

For example, the following output is associated with a SMTP server on port 25:

```
25/tcp  open  smtp
|_smtp-open-relay: Server is an open relay (16/16 tests)
```

Fuzzer. Fuzz attacks on various servers test responses to problems like buffer overflows. So far, nmap includes only one script in this area, on DNS. For example, the following command uses a script to launch a DNS fuzzing attack against an associated server:

```
# nmap --script=dns-fuzz 192.168.100.1
```

Intrusive. There are many nmap command scripts that qualify in both the intrusive and authentication categories. Any attempt to guess usernames and passwords by brute force is an attempt to intrude and a test of authentication. The following command goes farther to see whether the network card associated with the IP address is running in promiscuous mode. If so, a black-hat hacker will be able to use a protocol analyzer on the local network:

```
# nmap --script=sniffer-detect 192.168.100.1
```

If so, you may see the following output:

```
Host script results:
|_sniffer-detect: Likely in promiscuous mode
```

Malware. Perhaps this should be a growing category of scripts. For the moment, three have been written for this topic: one each for authentication, Web servers, and SMTP servers. The following command checks a Web server for known compromises:

```
# nmap --script=http-malware-host 192.168.100.1
```

Safe. Scripts in the safe category named test the relative safety of named services. As befits this category, it includes several dozen scripts testing the safety of services from the Internet Mail Access Protocol (IMAP) to the LDAP. While a script that tests the capabilities of a Post Office Protocol version 3 (POP3) server such as Dovecot may not seem to fit the bill, it can reveal features that are unneeded or unused. Such features are frequently ripe for the picking by black-hat hackers. The noted script is shown here:

```
# nmap --script=pop3-capabilities 192.168.100.1
```

The following output excerpt suggests a lot of POP3 features that should be carefully reviewed.

```
110/tcp   open      pop3

|_pop3-capabilities: USER CAPA UIDL TOP OK(K)
➥ RESP-CODES PIPELINING STLS SASL(PLAIN)
```

Version. The scripts in this category detect more than just the version number of specific services. Not many scripts exist in this category yet, as the nmap -sV *ip_address* command does an excellent job detecting the version number and service associated with open ports. However, the following command does provide more information about existing Point-to-Point Tunneling Protocol (PPTP) services:

```
# nmap --script=pptp-version 192.168.100.1
```

In Linux, this is also known as Internet Protocol Security (IPSec), covered in Chapter 8.

Vulnerability (vuln). The scripts in the vulnerability category are all about testing for known vulnerabilities. Expect the number of scripts in this category to grow on a regular basis. In fact, the scripts in this category might be the most important reason to use beta versions of nmap software. The following example tries a known SQL injection on a target HTTP server:

```
# nmap --script=sql-injection 192.168.100.1
```

The scripts as listed fall into several categories. Some scripts may fall under multiple categories. Because new scripts and even new switches are under development, assume this is just a partial list. There may be a dozen or more scripts available in several of these areas. Scripts can be bundled together; for example, a command like the following applies all scripts associated with a scan of the HTTP service:

```
# nmap --script=http-* 192.168.100.1
```

If the given script is misspelled or is not otherwise available, the nmap command should return an error with the following message related to the script:

```
did not match a category, filename, or directory
```

Run Integrity Checks of Installed Files and Executables

Once you have a production system, it's important to monitor that system for changes. Of course, you should not be alarmed every time a new log is added to the /var/log/ directory. However, changes to critical files such as those in the /boot/ and /sbin/ directories may indicate a more serious problem. To detect such changes, you need to know how to check the integrity of target systems.

Sure, you could just set up a checksum on potentially vulnerable partitions or volumes, but that would be imprecise. If there's a problem, that checksum won't specify the files that have been changed.

The first method to check the integrity of a system is based on the integrity of installed packages. To that end, commands based on package management systems such as the Red Hat Package Manager (rpm) and the Debian package management program (dpkg) can help.

But the default configuration based on a package installation is not precise. It highlights problems with normal changes to standard configuration files. Sure, you could keep a list of those changes, but if a black-hat hacker were to get into a system and change those files further, there would be no way to tell just using package management commands.

That is the reason behind integrity checkers such as Tripwire and the Advanced Intrusion Detection Environment (AIDE). In general, you'll want to use such integrity checkers to log the configuration associated with a gold baseline before putting such systems online. Then, such integrity checkers can be run on a regular basis. When properly configured, they can highlight any unintended changes to the baseline configuration.

Verify a Package

The first method for verifying the integrity of a system is relative to its installed state. With the right command, you can compare the current list of installed packages and to an associated list of installed files. As you should already know, the basic commands vary depending on whether the distribution is built on packages associated with Red Hat or Debian systems.

Be aware, the use of package management commands may not even provide a complete measure of what is installed. Many enterprising users and administrators install packages more directly from source code, typically collected in a compressed tarball archive.

Verifying Ubuntu/Debian Packages

Because Ubuntu is built on Debian Linux, Ubuntu packages are built on the Debian package system. As such, it relies on commands like dpkg and **debsums**. To get a list of currently installed packages on these systems, run the dpkg -l command. Prepare to be overwhelmed as the list of hundreds or even thousands of packages whiz by. Of course, the value of such a list is as a database, which can be piped to a text file or searched through with the grep command.

One variation on dpkg -l that provides a more straightforward list of installed packages is as follows:

```
$ dpkg --get-selections
```

That's just a list of installed packages. When such packages are installed, they include a list of checksums, classified by package, separated by each installed file, in the /var/lib/dpkg/info/ directory. To take advantage of that list, run the debsums command. The output from that command is impressive; it's not uncommon for some desktop systems to include a couple of hundred thousand packages or more.

But not all packages include checksum information. In addition, some files are configured from a combination of packages, such as the initial RAM disk file in the /boot/ directory.

For those files associated with checksums, the only indication of a problem is a FAILED message after the filename.

Verifying Red Hat Packages

The Red Hat Package Management system is more precise when it checks the integrity of installed packages. It's a straightforward command, given the name of a target package. For example, the following command and output is typical for the Postfix e-mail server:

```
$ rpm -V postfix
..5....T  c /etc/postfix/main.cf
```

If there were no changes to the files relative to the original package, there would be no output. Eight tests are performed on each file, as described in Table 13-2. The codes would appear from left to right; a dot in place of the code means that the associated test has passed.

TABLE 13-2 Failure codes for `rpm -V`.

CODE	DESCRIPTION
5	Checksum associated with the Message Digest 5 (MD5) algorithm
S	File size
L	Symbolic link
T	File modification time
D	Device file
U	User owner
G	Group owner
M	File mode

In addition, if a c appears at the end of the failure-code list, the noted file is a configuration file. The output from the `rpm -V packagename` command can tell you more about the change to the file.

Of course, with hundreds and sometimes thousands of packages on a system, it's not enough to verify the files associated with one package. Fortunately, the `-a` switch helps the `rpm -qa` command check all installed packages. While changed files are not directly associated with the package, it's easy to identify the package that owns a file. For example, the following command identifies the package that owns the noted Samba configuration file:

```
$ rpm -qf /etc/samba/smb.conf
```

Be aware, as with the `debsums` command, such checks apply only to packages installed in the `rpm` package manager format.

Perform a Tripwire Check

Tripwire is an intrusion detection system described in detail in Chapter 12, with configuration files in the `/etc/tripwire/` directory. Briefly, Tripwire can collect information on key files on a computer based on how Tripwire is configured in the `twcfg.txt` and the reporting policies documented in the `twpol.txt` files. Once the configuration and policy are set, the following command creates a database of digital checksums for such files in the `/var/lib/tripwire/` directory:

```
# tripwire --init
```

Then you should run the following command to review associated policies. Standard policies for the Tripwire package that you've installed may check on files that don't exist on local systems. So you should run the following command right away, to modify configuration options and policies to minimize the number of false positives:

```
# tripwire --check
```

For example, the standard Tripwire configuration reports changes in files in the `/proc/` and `/dev/` directories. Current Linux systems change the contents or access time of numerous files in these directories every time a system is rebooted. Current Linux systems may also change files in the `/etc/` directory if the system acquires network address information using DHCP. Tripwire policies can be updated with the following command:

```
# tripwire --update
```

Then the standard Tripwire package is configured to check the local system on a daily basis, courtesy of the `tripwire` script in the `/etc/cron.daily/` directory.

Test with the Advanced Intrusion Detection Environment (AIDE)

As with Tripwire, AIDE supports periodic checks of installed and configured files. AIDE was first discussed in Chapter 12. This section goes into a bit more depth on how AIDE works, based on information in the `aide.conf` configuration file. The configuration for Ubuntu and Red Hat systems can vary somewhat. Of course, the details are subject to change, especially if the developers behind one distribution decide that the approach of the other distribution is better.

In either case, AIDE rules are defined with attributes as described in Table 13-3.

Some developers consider AIDE to be superior to Tripwire. In fact, AIDE packages are available from the main Ubuntu repository and supported Red Hat Enterprise Linux (RHEL) repositories. So the installation of AIDE is supported at least in some ways by developers for both distributions.

Ubuntu AIDE

When installed on Ubuntu systems, AIDE is configured in files in the `/etc/aide/` directory. In addition, per the `/etc/default/aide` file, configuration options for individual services are defined in files in the `/etc/aide/aide.conf.d/` directory. While the basic database files are similar, Ubuntu's version includes directives with combinations of default codes in the main `/etc/aide/aide.conf` file.

For example, the following directive suggests that AIDE can use a variety of checksums for every file. Each of the options listed is described in Table 13-3.

```
Checksums = md5+sha1+rmd160+haval+gost+crc32+
↪tiger+whirlpool
```

The `OwnerMode` directive that follows calculates the permissions, user owner, and group owner for all files so configured:

```
OwnerMode = p+u+g
```

The `Size` directive is applied to files where a constant size can help determine whether there has been a change with respect to the size and block count of a file:

```
Size = s+b
```

Additional directives in the `aide.conf` file describe additional directives that are applied in files in the `/etc/aide/aide.conf.d/` directory.

TABLE 13-3 AIDE rule codes.

CODE	DESCRIPTION
p	Permissions: read, write, execute
i	Inode: labeled location on a volume or partition
n	Number of links
u	User
g	Group
s	Size
b	Block count
m	Modification time; the last time ownership or permissions were changed
a	Access time; the last time the file was read or otherwise accessed
c	Change time; the last time the file was changed
S	Label for files expected to change in size, such as log files
acl	Access control list (ACL) labels
selinux	Security Enhanced Linux context
xattr	Extended file attributes
md5	Message Digest 5 (MD5) checksum
sha1	Secure Hash Algorithm (SHA) version 1 hash function; may also refer to sha256 for a 256-bit hash function
rmd160	A hash function based on a Java checksum algorithm based on a Message Digest 4 (MD4) hash; the rmd acronym is a shortened form that refers to the RACE Integrity Primitives Evaluation Message Digest
haval	A cryptographic hash function with variable length output
gost	A cryptographic hash function originally developed in the former Soviet Union
crc32	A cryptographic hash function based on a cyclic redundancy check (CRC)
whirlpool	Another cryptographic hash function

Red Hat AIDE

In contrast, the Red Hat AIDE configuration is somewhat more self-contained in the /etc/aide.conf file. The directives defined are somewhat different and are in some ways cumulative. For example, the R directive shown here defines a group of codes, as defined in Table 13-3.

```
R:   p+i+n+u+g+s+m+c+acl+selinux+xattrs+md5
```

This group is inserted in the value of the NORMAL directive shown here, which incorporates a couple of checksum hash functions.

```
NORMAL = R+rmd160+sha256
```

The directive that follows essentially creates a DIR directive equivalent to the R group of codes:

```
DIR = p+i+n+u+g+acl+selinux+xattrs
```

Some files should just be checked for access controls, as associated with the PERMS directive defined here. This directive essentially is a check of regular discretionary access permissions, ownership, ACLs, and SELinux contexts:

```
PERMS = p+i+u+g+acl+selinux
```

The excerpt of /etc/aide.conf shown in Figure 13-6 illustrates default checks on key directories. Several files have the ! character in front, described as the "bang," which means anything but. In other words, in this default configuration, files in the /usr/src/ and /usr/tmp/ directories, along with certain files in the /etc/ directory, are not checked by AIDE.

```
# Next decide what directories/files you want in the database.

/boot    NORMAL
/bin     NORMAL
/sbin    NORMAL
/lib     NORMAL
/lib64   NORMAL
/opt     NORMAL
/usr     NORMAL
/root    NORMAL
# These are too volatile
!/usr/src
!/usr/tmp

# Check only permissions, inode, user and group for /etc, but
# cover some important files closely.
/etc     PERMS
!/etc/mtab
# Ignore backup files
!/etc/.*~
/etc/exports  NORMAL
/etc/fstab    NORMAL
/etc/passwd   NORMAL
```

FIGURE 13-6

Excerpt from the default Red Hat version of aide.conf.

Make Sure Security Does Not Prevent Legitimate Access

It is possible to configure too much security on a system. In the area of passwords, if the requirements are too strict, users are more likely to forget their passwords. Users will then either overload administrators with password-reset requests or they'll write their passwords next to their workstations. Neither situation promotes true computer security. In the following sections, you'll look at reasonable password policies, how they can be implemented in the shadow password suite with the `chage` command, and how access can be regulated with pluggable authentication modules.

Reasonable Password Policies

In an ideal world, users will change their passwords frequently. If the lifetime of a password is less than the time it takes for a black-hat hacker to decipher the password using tools like those described earlier in this chapter, then it doesn't matter if password-authentication databases are even out in the open.

Of course, you never want to publicize a password-authentication database. Black-hat hackers can get access to some pretty powerful systems. Some companies sell rainbow tables, which can speed the process of decrypting a password.

To that end, the best passwords are passphrases, which can be complete sentences. But many authentication systems do not support options such as spaces in a password. Other than a passphrase, the best password is a combination of upper- and lowercase characters, along with numbers and punctuation.

With such passwords, the next question is how frequently you make users change their passwords. You want users to remember their passwords without having to write them down. One U.S. governmental guideline is based on the Federal Desktop Core Configuration (FDCC), as mandated by the U.S. Office of Management and Budget (OMB). While the password guidelines apply only to Microsoft Windows systems, the listed policy suggests that passwords:

- Have a minimum of 12 characters
- Be changed every 60 days

> **TIP**
>
> One way to help users remember such passwords is based on a sentence. For example, a password such as OT,Is3ba1e! could stand for "On Tuesday, I shot 3 birdies and 1 eagle!".

While these policies do not apply to users on Linux systems, these are reasonable minimum requirements. On the other hand, in organizations where security is important, such as intelligence agencies, users generally have a greater understanding of the need for password security. You should be able to set more rigorous limits in such cases.

The standard for configuring password policies is based on options in the `/etc/shadow` file. It can be configured with the `chage` command first described in Chapter 4. The current settings are defined in the output to the `chage -l` *username* command. The output and associated `chage` command options are shown in Table 13-4.

TABLE 13-4 Command options for chage.	
OUTPUT	**COMMAND OPTION**
Last password change	`-d YYYY-MM-DD`
Password expires	`n/a`
Password inactive	`-I YYYY-MM-DD`
Account expires	`-E YYYY-MM-DD`
Minimum number of days between password change	`-m days`
Maximum number of days between password change	`-M days`
Number of days of warning before password expires	`-W days`

When applicable, the date can be set in YYYY-MM-DD format. The password expiration date is based on the value of the "maximum number of days between password change" setting associated with the -M days switch shown in Table 13-4.

In addition, it's possible to set requirements for password complexity with the help of pluggable authentication modules (PAMs). The key file is /etc/pam.d/passwd. Password complexity requires the use of the pam_cracklib and pam_unix modules.

On Red Hat systems, the key directive can be found either in the system-auth or passwd-auth files in the /etc/pam.d/ directory. As suggested by the last directive on the line, three login attempts are allowed.

```
password     requisite     pam_cracklib.so try_first_pass retry=3
```

On Ubuntu systems, the key directive can be found in the common-password file in the /etc/pam.d/ directory:

```
password required pam_cracklib.so retry=3 minlen=6 difok=3
```

As suggested by the directives in the line, the minimum password length is six alphanumeric characters. The difok=3 option means that new passwords must have at least three characters different from the current password. Options that support password complexity are listed in Table 13-5.

Allow Access from Legitimate Systems

Access can be regulated if you add an appropriate module to the /etc/pam.d/login configuration file. Specifically, the following account module supports access limits through the /etc/security/access.conf file:

```
account     required     pam_access.so
```

The /etc/security/access.conf file includes examples of access limits by the root administrative user, by group, and by regular user. Such limits can be configured by console, by domain name, and by IP address.

13

Testing and Reporting

TABLE 13-5 Password complexity options for `pam_cracklib.so` and `pam_unix.so`.

OPTION	DESCRIPTION
`minlen`	Minimum password length, in alphanumeric characters
`dcredit`	Minimum number of digits in a password, in negative numbers
`lcredit`	Minimum number of lower-case letters in a password, in negative numbers
`ocredit`	Minimum number of other characters in a new password, in negative numbers
`retry`	Number of tries allowed to confirm when changing a password
`nullok`	Blank password allowed
`remember=n`	n previous passwords are remembered; a repeat of from that list of passwords is not allowed
`obscure`	A given password is compared to a previous password to make sure it isn't a palindrome, different only with respect to case, or otherwise too similar

Monitor That Virtualized Hardware

Virtual hardware is sort of a contradiction in terms. By definition, it is some sort of software configured to emulate hardware. It may in fact be configured to connect to physical hardware. For example, virtual universal serial bus (USB) ports are frequently configured to connect to actual USB hardware. Virtual machine hardware can represent everything that you might see in real hardware. There are a number of solutions for virtual machines that can simulate everything required for a computer within a software framework.

While there are many commercial options for virtual machines, there are also open source options.

Virtual Machine Hardware

Of course, the hardware in a virtual machine can represent just about everything that might be seen on a physical system. The hardware doesn't even have to exist on the local system; for example, many virtual machine systems can simulate Small Computer Systems Interface (SCSI) hard drives on regular PCs. In some cases, it's even possible to set up 64-bit virtual systems on 32-bit hosts.

In most cases, simulated hardware for virtual machines isn't as fast as the real underlying host hardware. That's understandable, as host hardware is also loaded by the host operating system. That is one reason for the push toward bare-metal virtualization, to take the host operating system out of the equation.

Some virtual machine hardware may be more efficient. For example, it's possible to mount the ISO files that may otherwise be burned onto CD and DVD discs directly onto virtual machine hardware. Because such connections are not limited by the physical speed of a CD/DVD drive, the connection between an ISO file and virtual machine hardware is typically faster than the connection between a physical CD/DVD disc and the associated drive.

As suggested in Chapter 2, virtual machines benefit from specialized CPUs. In fact, such CPUs are now quite common on many of the latest systems. Even some of the Atom-based CPUs found on netbooks include hardware-assisted virtualization.

Virtual Machine Options

Options for virtual machines are wide and varied. Software-assisted virtualization solutions can be installed on just about any modern PC, even many netbooks. For administrator convenience, several of these options can be used to create and administer virtual machines remotely. A few of the major options for virtual machines include the following:

- **Kernel-based Virtual Machine (KVM)**—A Linux kernel module with a virtual machine monitor; the default open source solution for both Ubuntu and RHEL 6.
- **Xen**—A virtual machine monitor for Linux systems that often requires a specialized kernel. Red Hat support for Xen ended with RHEL 5. Owned by Citrix.
- **VMware**—VMware includes a range of virtual machine options, from VMware Player for software-based virtual machines to vSphere as a bare-metal solution.
- **Virtualbox, open source edition**—A software-based virtualization package now part of the Oracle family of virtualization products.
- **Microsoft Virtual Server**—A solution that can run Linux systems only as guests.

This is just a sampling of the virtual machine options that are available. Many options not included in this list are also excellent. However, because KVM is the preferred open source virtualization solution for both Ubuntu and RHEL 6, it is the primary virtualization solution covered here. Be aware that because KVM and Xen require different kinds of changes to the kernel, they cannot be used simultaneously on the same system.

Monitoring the Kernel-Based Virtual Machine (KVM)

The standard solution developed by Red Hat for managing virtual machines is the Virtual Machine Manager. The graphical interface available through the `virt-manager` command is fairly trivial and straightforward, as shown in Figure 13-7. Note the status, CPU, and memory-usage columns. It's an easy way to monitor the status of a group of virtual machine systems. If one system suddenly acts up, it may be a symptom of legitimate heavy use—or it may be a symptom of a system that's under attack.

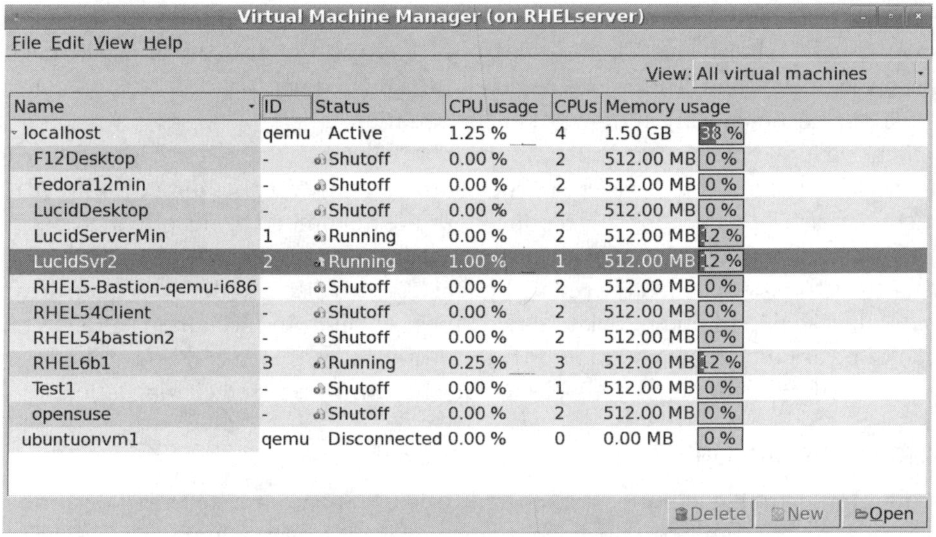

FIGURE 13-7

The Virtual Machine Manager.

The Virtual Machine Manager.

Creating a new virtual machine is also a straightforward process. Just right-click on the name of a virtual host and click New. A Virtual Machine Creation window appears. Of course, if you're working from the command-line interface, you may prefer to use a command-line tool. The following command prompts for basic information associated with the virtual machine:

```
# virt-install --prompt
```

As with most virtual machine systems, the data of the simulated hard disks is stored as large files in dedicated directories. The contents of such disks change frequently, even if only to reflect log file changes for standard cron jobs. So any monitoring of a gold baseline virtual machine has to be done with intrusion detection tools such as Tripwire and AIDE within that machine.

But with the proliferation of virtual machines, it's important to have a tool to monitor what's happening on each machine on a virtual host. To that end, this section focuses on the command-line monitoring tool, the virsh command. Unless opened with administrative privileges, you won't see the full capabilities of that tool. You'll see a virtualization interactive terminal with a virsh # prompt. Some important commands at this prompt are listed in Table 13-6. The help command provides a complete list.

Standard Open Source Security Testing Tools

There are many excellent open source security testing tools. This book can only cover a few of those tools. This section addresses Snort and the nc command. One reputable list of the top 100 network security tools is maintained by **Gordon "Fyodor" Lyon**, the creator of nmap and author of *Nmap Network Scanning: The Official Nmap Project Guide to Network Discovery and Security Scanning*. That list can be found at *http://sectools.org/index.html*.

TABLE 13-6 Virtual machine management commands at the `virsh #` prompt.

COMMAND	DESCRIPTION
`list`	Lists active domains
`attach-disk`	Supports the inclusion of physical devices, virtual images as drives, and ISO files as CDs/DVDs
`attach-interface`	Connects a virtual machine to network interfaces
`dominfo`	Provides status information on a domain
`domblkstat`	Notes read and write information of a hard-drive device on a domain
`migrate`	Moves a domain to a different host
`reboot`	Reboots a currently running domain
`shutdown`	Shuts down a currently running domain
`start`	Starts a currently inactive domain
`vcpuinfo`	Lists current CPU information for a domain, including numbers of CPUs
`vncdisplay`	Uses the Virtual Network Computing (VNC) system to open a display

As of this writing, nine of the top 10 network security tools can be configured on Linux. Many are covered elsewhere in this chapter and this book. Wireshark was already covered in Chapter 8. The top open security tools that can be configured on Linux include the following:

- **Wireshark**—Supports analysis of network packets
- **Snort**—An intrusion detection system (IDS) with modes for packet analysis, logging, and interaction with `iptables` firewall rules; associated rules are updated on a regular basis
- **Netcat**—A utility that can read both TCP and UDP packets
- **Metasploit Framework**—A platform for testing for code designed to take advantage of known vulnerabilities
- **Hping2**—A command-line packet analyzer that sends TCP and UDP packets based on the features of the `ping` command

Take care if you use any use of these tools on remote systems. Make sure you have the permission of responsible administrators before applying any of these tools. The warnings associated with the `nmap` command described earlier may apply.

Snort

Snort is a flexible IDS. It is actively maintained. With a set of rules that is regularly updated, Snort can help you keep local systems secure. It's readily available from the Ubuntu universe repository. RPM packages customized for Fedora and RHEL systems are available from the main Snort Web site at *http://www.snort.org/*.

When installing Snort on Ubuntu systems, the standard installation prompts you to configure a value for the HOME_NET directive, normally an IP address network in CIDR notation such as 192.168.0.0/24. That and related startup information is stored in the snort.debian.conf file, which is configured with the snort.conf file. Similar information for Red Hat systems can be configured in the /etc/sysconfig/snort file.

As noted in the *Snort Users Manual*, Snort can be configured to run in four different modes:

- **Sniffer mode**—Reads the contents of each packet, similar to Wireshark
- **Packet-logger mode**—Stores the contents of packets
- **Network IDS mode**—Supports packet analysis against a set of rules, typically downloaded from the Snort Web site
- **Inline mode**—Works with iptables-based firewall rules to configure additional actions on certain network packets

The modes described are cumulative; for example, the lessons learned from running Snort in sniffer mode apply to all other modes.

Sniffer Mode

Sniffer is a commonly used colloquial term for a protocol analyzer. As such, Snort can look inside the contents of packets as they're sent across a network. Sniffer mode may seem overwhelming, especially if you run Snort in verbose mode, with the snort -v command. If you do so and are overwhelmed by the packets that appear, you can stop the reading by pressing Ctrl+C.

One interesting warning that appears is that the command is slow. While the information speeds by on a screen, the data is being processed slowly relative to the packets that are actually being transmitted over a network. Because of the speed, some packets may be dropped, and data that may be associated with an intrusion may be lost.

However, the snort -d and snort -e commands go further. The -d dumps application layer data. The -e includes headers at the data-link layer, associated with communication at the hardware level. Try these commands on their own. Review the rules as they apply to different services.

If there's an error message related to missing rules, you may have to download them; the latest version is available from the Snort Web site.

Packet Logger Mode

If you've tried any of the commands in sniffer mode, you should realize the importance of being able to send the data to a log file. To avoid transmission problems associated with verbose mode, Snort can send information to a log file in compressed binary format.

As suggested in the *Snort Users Guide*, the following command sends information to a log file in a local `log/` subdirectory:

```
# snort -vde -l ./log
```

The command works only if a local `log/` subdirectory exists; you can create it as needed. Of course, the command can be modified to send logging information to a more standard directory:

```
# snort -vde -l /var/log/
```

But the `snort` command by itself may not know what network to listen to. That can be addressed with the `-h` switch; for example, the following command listens for packets on the noted IP address network:

```
# snort -vde -l /var/log/ -h 192.168.0.0/24
```

Once logging information is collected, it can be analyzed with another protocol analyzer such as Wireshark.

Network IDS Mode

Network IDS mode depends on an appropriate Snort configuration file, starting with `snort.conf` in the `/etc/snort/` directory. That file should take information from rules as defined in the `/etc/snort/rules/` directory. For example, the following command uses the noted `snort.conf` file as a configuration file:

```
# snort -vde -l /var/log/ -h 192.168.0.0/24
↪ -c /etc/snort/snort.conf
```

The `-c` switch can be used on the configuration file of your choice. In other words, you can test network IDS mode with different Snort configurations.

Inline Mode

Snort inline mode requires the installation of the `libipq` development library to enable packet queuing. In brief, it enables a QUEUE mode for the `-j` switch associated with the `iptables` command. In other words, with the `libipq` development library, `iptables` can be configured to ACCEPT, REJECT, DROP, or QUEUE a packet. Queued packets can be linked to Snort.

Because neither Ubuntu nor RHEL include the `libipq` development library in their repositories, such software should be considered carefully before being installed.

Netcat and the `nc` Command

The `nc` command is short for **netcat**, a service that reads and writes over network connections. It is versatile. It can act like a `telnet` command to check for access over an available port. It can act like an `nmap` command to scan a range of ports.

First, to demonstrate one simple capability, run the `nc` command on a target port on a supposedly secure Apache-based Web site on the Hypertext Transfer Protocol, Secure (HTTPS) port of 443:

```
$ nc -v 192.168.0.1 443
```

When the following message appears, type `GET / HTTP` at the next line:

```
Connection to 192.168.0.1 443 port [tcp/https] succeeded!
```

You may see too much information about the Apache server on the noted IP address. You'll want to deny black-hat hackers as much information as possible in this area. In Chapter 9, one method was based on the `ServerTokens` directive in the main Apache configuration file. To do more, perform an Internet search for the `Header unset Etag` command to see how that option reduces client reliance on cached information.

Sometimes, connections with a simple response provide a black-hat hacker with a bit too much information for comfort. For example, the following command confirms the availability of port 111, typically used for the Sun Remote Procedure Call (RPC) protocol:

```
$ nc -v 192.168.0.1 111
Connection to 192.168.0.1 111 port [tcp/sunrpc] succeeded!
```

That's an important hint to a black-hat hacker; port 111 and the Sun RPC protocol are frequently associated with relatively insecure services such as the Network File System (NFS) and the Network Information Service (NIS). If a black-hat hacker receives such a message, that person is likely wondering if he or she has hit the jackpot and will want to go further with respect to checking a group of port numbers.

For example, the following command would fairly quickly scan every port between 1 and 1024 on the noted IP address, randomly (`-r`), in verbose mode (`-v`), and just scanning for daemons that are listening on the noted ports (`-z`):

```
$ nc -rvz 192.168.0.1 1-1024
```

Try it out on a system, and watch how quickly the information is actually scanned. Given the value of the `nc` command, it's worth some trouble to analyze the switches described in Table 13-7.

---

technical TIP

Some versions of the `nc` command are compiled with an ominous-sounding option known as `GAPING_SECURITY_HOLE`. It's a method commonly used with the `-e` switch to execute a binary command when a remote user connects to a configured port.

If you feel the need to test this option on a standard distribution, you may need to compile it directly from netcat source code. While such source code is available from *http://nc110.sourceforge.net/*, additional work may be required to compile in the noted option. An easier alternative is to use the `nc` command from a source like a Knoppix live CD, which already includes the `nc` command with the ability to use the `GAPING_SECURITY_HOLE` option.

TABLE 13-7 Command switches for nc.

SWITCH	DESCRIPTION
-e	Executes a given command or script from a server; on a client, it pipes requests to the noted server
-g	Specifies a source route, effectively substituting a false source IP address in the packet when received by the destination
-l	Binds to a given port if and when it is coupled with -p, to await incoming connections
-n	Avoids hostname lookups; faster because it does not wait for responses from DNS servers
-p	Associates with a local port number for a connection to a remote system; may be used to spoof a port number or route connections through an unexpected and therefore possibly more secure route
-r	Allows the nc command to use random ports
-s	Allows the use of an IP address other than that of a network card
-u	Specifies the use of UDP communication
-v	Configures verbose mode
-z	Scans for daemons that are listening

Commercial Security Test Tools for Linux

Given the importance of security, you may be willing to pay to keep Linux systems secure. Yes, open source tools are excellent. The companies behind open source developers want to make money. Companies like Red Hat make money from subscriptions, from the support they can provide.

Different companies with open source security software have reacted differently. The developers behind Nessus closed their source code when version 3.0 was released in 2005. The developers behind Snort still release their code under open source licenses, but their latest configuration changes are released right away only to users who pay. In a similar fashion, SAINT began its journey as an open source version of the **Security Administrator Tool for Analyzing Networks (SATAN)**.

The following sections provide a brief overview of Nessus and SAINT. One advantage of these tools is a Web-based interface that for some would support easier management of IDSs for a network.

Nessus

Even though the code for Nessus is no longer released under open source licenses, it is number one on the *http://sectools.org/* list of top-100 security tools. The company behind the Nessus user interface (UI) is Tenable Security, which calls Nessus "the Network Vulnerability Scanner." As with other IDSs such as Snort, the value comes with the professional feed, which includes information on all current security issues.

When installed, Nessus configuration and command files can be found in the /opt/nessus/ directory. To set up secure communication to the Nessus UI via a Web browser, you'll need to set up a certificate authority. The simplest method is with the nessus-mkcert script in the /opt/nessus/sbin/ directory. You'll be prompted for basic information associated with a self-signed certificate.

Once this is configured, you can access the Nessus UI through a Web browser. Just navigate to the hostname or IP address of the machine with Nessus installed using HTTPS and port 8834. For example, on a system with IP address 10.192.168.10, you'd navigate to the following:

```
https://10.192.168.10:8834/
```

But logins require an appropriate username and password. The Nessus database is different from any standard Linux authentication database. To create a Nessus user,

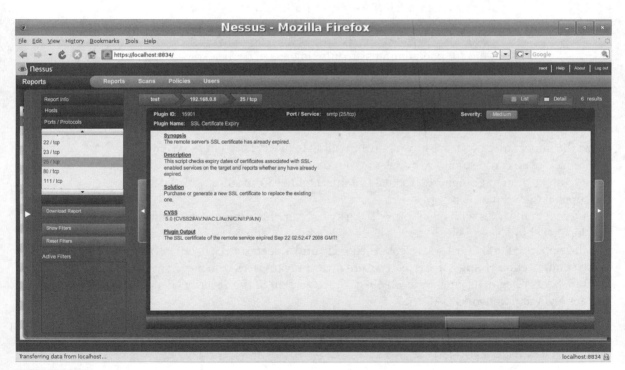

FIGURE 13-8

An excerpt from a Nessus report.

run the `nessus-adduser` command in the `/opt/nessus/sbin/` directory. You can choose to assign administrative privileges to that user, which allows him or her to add appropriate plug-ins. Access by such users can even be limited by IP address.

Once filters are set, a system is analyzed, and a report is created through the Web-based interface, the report can be analyzed by hostname or IP address along with analyzed protocol. For example, the Web-browser view shown in Figure 13-8 lists an issue of medium severity for port 25, using TCP communication. You should already know that port and protocol are associated with SMTP services such as sendmail and Postfix.

For more information on Nessus, navigate to *http://www.nessus.org/*.

System Administrator's Integrated Network Tool (SAINT)

Like Nessus, SAINT has an open source heritage. The SAINT Corporation does not release this tool under open source licenses. However, trial versions are readily available from *http://www.saintcorporation.com/*.

SAINT works hand in hand with open source tools such as Nmap, Samba, and SSH. Once installed, executable and configuration files can be found in the `/usr/share/saint/` directory. The `saint` script in this directory starts the process automatically, downloading any configuration updates.

One of the advantages of SAINT is in its interfaces. It's available as a virtual machine, configured for use as a VMware guest system. It's also available as a bootable USB key, configured from a live DVD of the Ubuntu distribution. Assuming the VMware guest or the bootable USB key has not been changed, you'll know that the tool itself has not been modified by black-hat hackers. Configuration on such media is a terrific convenience, as it means administrators do not have to work any special installation options. In fact, SAINT includes an icon on the noted desktops that starts the tool automatically.

An excerpt from a SAINT report as shown in Figure 13-9 provides good information about the problem along with a suggested solution.

Reports from SAINT specify issues at four levels of severity:

- **Critical problems**—Issues that allow unauthorized access or denials of service. Related issues include simplistic passwords, buffer overflows, and unrestricted file sharing.

- **Areas of concern**—Problems related to too much information for black-hat hackers, such as user information and service configuration. May provide sufficient information for other attacks.

- **Potential problems**—Issues where further investigation is justified, as there is insufficient information to judge the severity of the problem.

- **Services**—List of services currently running; generally, you should not have too many services running on any single system.

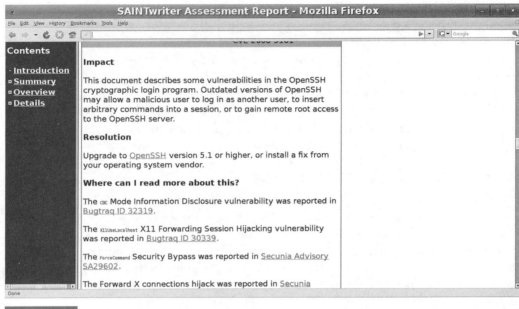

FIGURE 13-9

An excerpt from a SAINT report.

The Right Place to Install Security Testing Tools

If a system has been compromised, it's too late to install security testing tools on that machine. Issues such as backdoors or Trojan horses could provide opportunities for black-hat hackers who might want to mislead you about what they are doing. On the other hand, if you know a gold baseline system is secure, it's a candidate for the installation of security testing tools such as those described in this chapter.

The number of security testing tools that are available on live media such as CDs, DVDs, and USB keys suggests the excellence of such media as a secure location for security testing tools.

Hint: Not Where Crackers Can Use Them Against You

Ideally, security testing tools should be installed only on secure systems. But that leads to a bit of a loop. How do you know if a system is secure until security tools have been used to check a system? As strange as it sounds, there is a small element of faith involved. You can start with a reputable Linux distribution as released by a company like Red Hat or Canonical. You can work from standard installation programs as discussed in earlier chapters. Once those systems are up to date, you should have a reasonable baseline system.

There is risk involved. Black-hat hackers could have somehow included their code in the packages released for a distribution. They may have penetrated the mirror servers from where so many Linux distributions are downloaded and updated. They may take advantage of security issues before you're able to update a default system with fixes.

But there are safeguards. Open source developers test their software in the public eye. The source code is publicly available. If there are security issues, a great majority are revealed in the public testing process. Any issues that get by this process are publicized as soon as they are known by the community.

There are safeguards on the mirror servers that carry Linux distributions. Downloads with commands like yum and apt-get check GNU Privacy Guard (GPG) keys to ensure the integrity of a downloaded package. If you trust certain groups of developers, one option is to use security tools already included with live boot media.

Some Tools Already Available on Live CDs

One excellent option for security tools is live boot media, such as CDs, DVDs, and USB keys. Perhaps the model for live media for Linux systems is the Knoppix distribution. The live operating system that can be booted directly from a CD/DVD drive or even a downloaded ISO file is impressive. With the tools on the Knoppix distribution, you can back up or recover troubled media. You can reconfigure partitions and volumes. Even Nessus is included on the live Knoppix DVD as of version 6.2.

One impressive option for live DVD media is Ubuntu Pentest Edition. It includes about 300 tools for penetration testing. Some of the tools available for testing DNS servers are shown in Figure 13-10. While it is based on the Ubuntu distribution, the developers behind Ubuntu Pentest Edition are not affiliated with Ubuntu or Canonical. It includes tools for port scanning, virtual private network probing, database testing, and lots more.

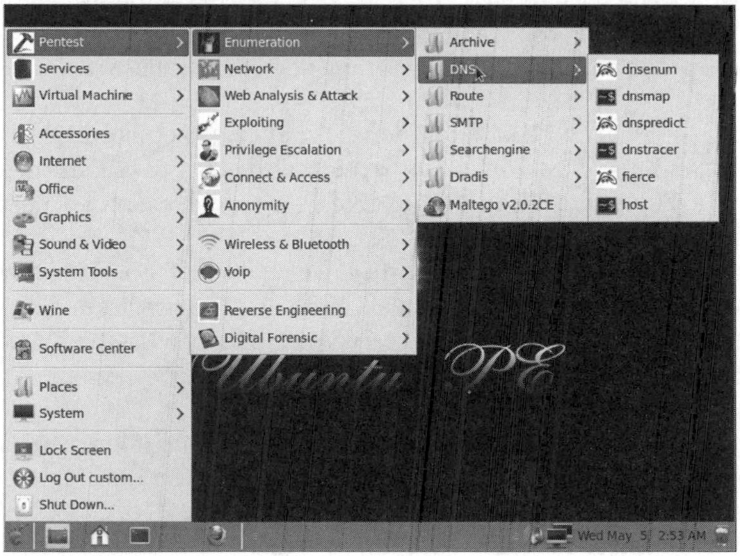

FIGURE 13-10

Ubuntu Pentest Edition.

A sampling of live media with penetration testing tools includes the following:

- **BackTrack**—Per the **BackTrack** Web site, "BackTrack has been customized down to every package, kernel configuration, script and patch solely for the purpose of the penetration tester." While it was originally built on the Slackware Linux distribution, it's now built on Ubuntu. For more information, see *http://www.backtrack-linux.org/*.

- **Knoppix Security Tools Distribution (STD)**—The **Knoppix STD** distribution is based on but not affiliated with Knoppix. It includes tools for forensics, IDSs, password checkers, protocol analyzers, and a variety of vulnerability-assessment tools. For more information, see *http://s-t-d.org/*.

- **Network Security Toolkit (NST)**—Based on but not affiliated with Fedora, the **Network Security Toolkit** includes a majority of the top 100 security tools listed at *http://sectools.org/*. For more information, see *http://networksecuritytoolkit.org/*.

Best Practices: Testing and Reporting

When testing a Linux system, it's important to test every part of a layered defense. Because some tests may require temporarily disabling some defenses, it's appropriate to withdraw a system from production before running some tests. Open ports on a system should appear different inside a firewall from outside a firewall. Tests of TCP Wrappers depend on the rules configured in the `/etc/hosts.allow` and `/etc/hosts.deny` files. Tests of some services may be specific to the limitations configured within the configuration files for that service. Tools such as John the Ripper can help identify passwords that are too simple. Be sure to re-enable any disabled services after tests are complete.

Services aren't accessible without open network ports. It's important to know what network ports are open on local systems to make sure that the only ports that are open are those ports required for local services. Tools that can help check for open network ports include `telnet`, `netstat`, `lsof`, and `nmap`. The `nmap` command is especially versatile, as it can scan different ports, protocols, and operating systems on a variety of target machines.

Several tools can help you check for unauthorized changes to key files. The `rpm -Va` and `debsums` commands use checksums to inspect installed files. But because even normal changes to configuration files are highlighted, more precise tools are needed. Two options to that end are Tripwire and AIDE.

Some systems have so many security rules, they're too difficult for people to use. That can lead to security problems. For example, when password policies are too strict, users who have trouble remembering their exotic passwords may write them down at their workstations. Password policies can be managed with the `chage` command; access can be regulated with the help of PAM files.

Several options are available for virtual machine hardware, from VMware to Virtualbox. The emerging standard for an open source virtual machine manager is KVM. While such virtual machines use large files that simulate hard disks, the contents of those files change frequently. So intrusion detection tools are important to monitor the integrity of such systems.

A variety of open source tools are available for security testing. Some of the major open source tools include Wireshark, Snort, and netcat. Snort includes modes for packet sniffing, packet logging, IDS, and inline interaction with the `iptables` command. The netcat command, `nc`, can identify a lot of information about open ports and the servers behind them, which highlights configuration issues with different services.

A variety of commercial security testing tools are also available. Two options originally based on open source software are Nessus and SAINT. Both tools include Web-based interfaces, with reports that can identify security issues by service, port, and more. SAINT can also be run from live media such as a DVD or from a dedicated virtual machine.

Speaking of live media, it's an excellent option for security testing tools. As such, a number of different developer groups have created dedicated live CDs/DVDs based on popular Linux distributions. If you trust these developers, you know that such systems won't be changed by black-hat hackers once burned to physical media. Of course, custom groups of security tools can also be configured on gold baseline systems customized for local networks.

CHAPTER SUMMARY

In this chapter, you examined different tools for checking firewalls, inspecting network ports, and testing the integrity of files on local systems. Various methods for testing layered defenses are more likely to identify flaws and better ensure the integrity of a system. Be aware, security policies that are too severe can lead to other problems. While it's important to test the strength of passwords with tools like John the Ripper, it's also important to make sure passwords don't have to be too complex to ensure user cooperation.

In this chapter, you also looked at a variety of options for open source and commercial penetration testing tools. They vary from regular commands such as nc to open source options such as Snort. A number of open source tools have been collected together in live media such as Ubuntu Pentest Edition and BackTrack.

KEY CONCEPTS AND TERMS

debsums	BackTrack	RainbowCrack
lsof	Bootstrap Protocol (BOOTP)	Security Administrator Tool
nc	Hydra	for Analyzing Networks
netstat	John the Ripper	(SATAN)
nmap	Knoppix STD	System Administrators
	Lyon, Gordon "Fyodor"	Integrated Network Tool
	Nessus	(SAINT)
	netcat	Snort
	Network Security Toolkit	VMware

CHAPTER 13 ASSESSMENT

1. Which of the following commands, when used inside and outside of a firewall, can best test the effectiveness of that firewall?

   A. `iptables`
   B. `telnet`
   C. `nmap`
   D. `lsof`

2. Which of the following is *not* a password-cracking tool?

   A. nmap
   B. John the Ripper
   C. Hydra
   D. RainbowCrack

3. What is the `telnet` command that would connect to an open port 25 and active server on a system with an IP address of 10.12.14.16?

4. Which of the following commands includes port information for TCP and UDP communication in numeric format?

   A. `netstat -aunp`
   B. `netstat -atnp`
   C. `netstat -aund`
   D. `netstat -atunp`

5. Which of the following commands can help you discover the active hosts on the 192.168.0.0/24 network?

   A. `nmap -sP 192.168.0.0/24`
   B. `nmap -sH 192.168.0.0/24`
   C. `nmap -sh 192.168.0.0/24`
   D. `nmap -sO 192.168.0.0/24`

6. Which of the following commands verifies installed files for all of the Debian-style packages installed on a system?

   A. `rpm -Va`
   B. `dpkg -Va`
   C. `debsums`
   D. `dpkg -qa`

7. You can install AIDE from supported repositories for both Red Hat Enterprise Linux and Ubuntu.

   A. True
   B. False

8. Which of the following commands sets a last password change date of April 1, 2010, for user `michael`?

   A. `chage -c 2010-04-01`
   B. `chage -d 2010-04-01`
   C. `chage -E 2010-04-01`
   D. `chage -I 2010-04-01`

9. What is the full path to the PAM configuration file that regulates logins on a Linux system?

10. Which of the following virtual machine options is the default open source solution for the latest Red Hat and Ubuntu distributions?

   A. KVM

   B. Xen

   C. Virtualbox, open source edition

   D. Hyper-V

11. Which of the following commands opens a graphical tool that depicts the current CPU and memory load for virtual machines on the target host system?

   A. `virt-viewer`

   B. `virsh`

   C. `virt-manager`

   D. `virt-top`

12. Nessus is still released under an open source license.

   A. True

   B. False

13. Which of the following modes does not apply to Snort as an intrusion detection system?

   A. Sniffer mode

   B. Inline mode

   C. Password mode

   D. Network mode

14. What is the `nc` command that would connect to and get verbose information on an open port 25 and active server on a system with an IP address of 10.12.14.16?

15. Which of the following is *not* an option for bootable Linux systems with security testing tools?

   A. BackTrack

   B. Knoppix STD

   C. Netcat

   D. Network Security Toolkit

13

Testing and Reporting

Detecting and Responding to Security Breaches

S O FAR, THIS BOOK HAS COVERED myriad security issues. You've looked at a variety of access controls, from standard read, write, and execute permissions through detailed options associated with Security Enhanced Linux (SELinux). Previous chapters have described how to keep services to a minimum, along with the dangers associated with a variety of services.

With that information in mind, you should know how to audit a system to identify baseline performance parameters; deviations may be causes for concern. You'll be able to identify user access through commands and log files. In addition, sensible policies can keep users within secure limits. But not all users are highly knowledgeable about computers, so you should monitor Linux user accounts for potentially risky behavior.

You need to be ready if there is a problem. With appropriate forensic analysis tools, you may need to recover data from RAM while a compromised system is still running. To that end, different kinds of portable media such as live CDs are available. Some are suitable for compromised systems, others for test systems. Care is required, especially if such data may be used as evidence in official investigations.

Once dynamic data is recovered and a system is powered down, then you should handle static data. There are appropriate ways to copy hard drives without changing any data on those hard drives. Investigations can then proceed with the copied drives. Once investigations are complete, you should consider sharing the results with the open source community. In general, corporate secrets can be preserved and you can get the credit for finding a security flaw if you do share appropriate results from any investigation.

Chapter 14 Topics

This chapter covers the following topics and concepts:

- How to do regular performance audits
- How to make sure users stay within secure limits
- How to log access into the network
- How to monitor account behavior for security issues
- How to create an incident response plan
- What kind of live CDs to have ready for forensics purposes
- When to put your response plan into action
- What tools are appropriate for secure backups and recovery
- How to save compromised data as evidence
- How to recover from a security breach
- How and when to share what happened with the open source community
- What best practices are for security breach detection and response

Chapter 14 Goals

When you complete this chapter, you will be able to:

- Understand typical system performance with appropriate user behavior
- Monitor user behavior through logins
- Know what to do when there's a security breach
- Understand when you should share information on a problem

Regular Performance Audits

To determine whether there's a problem, you need to have a baseline for a system not only in terms of files but also in terms of behavior while the system is running. In Chapters 12 and 13, you looked at tools like Tripwire and the Advanced Intrusion Detection Environment (AIDE). But the abilities of those tools are by and large limited to the static characteristics of a system. You also need to know what happens dynamically. To that end, Linux provides some basic tools such as the ps and top commands. Linux also allows tracking of system status with the **sysstat** package. If a problem is suspected or detected, additional commands are available, such as **strace**, **ldd**, and lsof.

The Basic Tools: `ps` and `top`

The fundamental audit command for a running system is the `ps` command. As suggested by its man page, it provides a snapshot of currently running processes. When run by itself, the `ps` command identifies just the processes associated with the current login shell. But that's not of much use.

Users can audit the processes running under their own accounts. For example, the following command lists all processes associated with user (`-u`) `michael`:

```
$ ps -u michael
```

As an administrator, you need to take a bigger-picture view of a system. To that end, the following command lists all processes (`a`) associated with users (`-u`), including those not associated with a terminal (`x`). The `ps` command is one of those rare Linux commands where not all switches require or even use a dash. Even though the `-u` switch normally includes a dash, the following `ps` command is the correct syntax of a command that lists all currently running processes.

```
$ ps aux
```

The output is an excellent database that can be saved as a file. It's sorted by user and process ID (PID) number. Perhaps just as important is the load on the Central Processing Unit (CPU) and Random Access Memory (RAM). Just be aware, occasional `cron` jobs as scheduled in `/etc/crontab`, and potentially by individual users, may skew the results. Because of such factors, you may want to run the `ps aux` command to determine a dynamic process baseline at a specific time. In addition, the load on certain processes, such as those related to the Apache Web server, may vary with the number of users who request information from that server.

As long as you're aware of the limits, it may be helpful to compare the output of the `ps aux` command at different times. Because the output is already sorted by PID number, an appropriate comparison of process names could help reveal suspicious processes. However, that's subject to processes that are constantly changing, such as hardware detection and `cron` jobs.

The `top` command provides a different kind of sorting of active processes. Take a look at the output in Figure 14-1. By default, it organizes processes first by their load on the CPU and then on RAM.

If you want to change the sort field, the directional keys (<, >) above the comma and period on a standard U.S. keyboard can help. As `top` is a dynamic command, it's difficult to store the associated information in a file. That can be addressed in three ways. First, you can always set up a screenshot of `top` command output from a GUI desktop. Second, general memory information related to RAM and swap space can be listed stored with the `free` command. Third, the load on the CPU and RAM can be listed and stored with the system status package, `sysstat`.

```
top - 17:33:44 up 3 days, 22:35,  5 users,  load average: 1.20, 0.98, 0.78
Tasks: 173 total,   2 running, 171 sleeping,   0 stopped,   0 zombie
Cpu(s): 27.5%us,   3.7%sy,  0.0%ni, 67.6%id,  0.0%wa,  1.0%hi,  0.3%si,  0.0%st
Mem:   3366868k total,  2771344k used,   595524k free,    92972k buffers
Swap:  1959888k total,    40188k used,  1919700k free,  1031672k cached

  PID USER      PR  NI  VIRT  RES  SHR S %CPU %MEM    TIME+  COMMAND
30621 michael   20   0  633m 375m  36m R   32 11.4 316:59.01 firefox
 7136 root      20   0  415m  74m  13m S   10  2.3 152:17.59 Xorg
 7927 michael   20   0 90748  45m  15m S    6  1.4   9:42.12 gnome-panel
 6763 asterisk -11   0 29744 9724 5848 S    3  0.3   0:46.18 asterisk
 7880 michael   20   0 13816 5032 3796 S    3  0.1  27:16.02 at-spi-registry
27340 michael   20   0 48864  16m 9564 S    3  0.5   0:00.74 screenshot
 7926 michael   20   0 27364  18m 9016 S    2  0.6  13:13.02 metacity
 7913 michael   20   0 17000 6036 4452 S    1  0.2   3:08.45 gnome-screensav
 8077 michael   20   0  689m 387m  94m S    1 11.8 128:50.33 soffice.bin
15521 michael   20   0  337m 205m  36m S    1  6.2  63:26.20 acroread
 2494 michael   20   0 45936  15m 8964 S    1  0.5   0:07.52 notification-da
 8098 michael   20   0  138m 105m 8384 S    1  3.2  11:36.88 gnome-netstatus
 7042 root      20   0  3304 1036  908 S    0  0.0   1:01.11 hald-addon-stor
 7933 michael   20   0 83628  28m  11m S    0  0.9   1:40.52 gnome-terminal
28897 michael   20   0  6324 3812 1952 S    0  0.1   1:35.80 ssh
    1 root      20   0  2844 1688  544 S    0  0.1   0:01.40 init
    2 root      15  -5     0    0    0 S    0  0.0   0:00.00 kthreadd
```

FIGURE 14-1

The top command provides a view of active processes.

The System Status Package

The system status package, known as `sysstat`, includes a number of commands that can report system status in a regular log. It includes the basic information associated with the `top` command, reported on a regular basis. Once the `sysstat` package is loaded and started, you can list the system status for the current day with the following command:

```
# sar -A
```

Unfortunately, the Ubuntu version of the system status package can collect only one month's worth of daily load reports. But if you're paying attention, that should be enough. If you want to pull a report, say, from the 13th of the month, run the following command:

```
# sar -f /var/log/sa/sa13
```

While the system status package configured for Red Hat Enterprise Linux (RHEL) 6 collects data for only seven days, it can be configured for as many days as needed in the `/etc/sysconfig/sysstat` configuration file.

For Additional Analysis

If you see a suspicious file or process, further investigation may be warranted. The following commands can help in that investigation: `lsof`, `ldd`, and `strace`.

Analyze Processes with `lsof`

The `lsof` command lists all files opened by currently running processes. The use of the `lsof -ni` command to identify network-related processes was described in Chapter 13. A variation of that command is used later in this chapter to help diagnose problems on a possibly compromised system.

When the `lsof` command is run with the full path to a daemon, it can tell you more about the processes associated with that daemon. For example, the following command should tell you about the multiple Samba server processes running on the local system. Note how `lsof` requires administrative privileges and the full path to the daemon.

```
# lsof /usr/sbin/smbd
```

Identify Associated Libraries with `ldd`

The `ldd` command lists the libraries associated with another command. It's useful with regular commands such as `ls` as well as daemons such as Samba. On your own systems, take a look at the output to these commands:

```
$ ldd /usr/sbin/smbd
$ ldd /bin/ls
```

Trace System Calls with `strace`

The `strace` command goes further, tracing the system calls associated with a command. Many of those calls should go through the libraries just listed from the `ldd` command. If a target command such as `ls` is not performing its intended function, the `strace` command can tell you more. For example, if you suspect that the `ls` command has been replaced by malware, the following command traces the system calls associated with that command:

```
$ strace ls
```

The last few calls before the `write` commands in the output are normally the key. If the suspect command is not running appropriate system calls when compared to what's seen from a gold baseline system, you should investigate further. Because there's a lot of output from the `strace` command, the `-o` option to write the output to a text file can be especially helpful:

```
$ strace -o analysis.txt ls
```

Make Sure Users Stay Within Secure Limits

User security starts with the password. As reported on ZDNet, a survey by the organizers of Infosecurity Europe 2004 offered a group of commuters a chocolate bar in exchange for their network-access password. Over two-thirds of the commuters eventually agreed to the request. Far too many users are not aware of the importance of account security.

One lesson learned from the study is that education is key. Fortunately, Linux users are likely to be more knowledgeable about computers, and therefore may be more amenable to rigorous security requirements. Nevertheless, Linux distributions do include drivers that can connect to smart-card readers and biometric-verification tools.

Of course, the inquisitiveness of Linux users can lead to different kinds of security risks. But their level of knowledge can only help in the effort to educate them on the need for security.

Appropriate Policies

While Linux users are generally more knowledgeable, it's still best to keep policies as simple as possible. Generally, the policies that apply to regular users can be divided into five areas:

- **Physical access**—Security starts with access limits on computers. For regular workstations, it can be consistent with access to other sensitive company documents.

- **Internet access**—Be clear with your users. Help them understand limits on access. If you monitor where users go online, tell them. Make sure users understand what is considered unauthorized Internet access and what penalties may be associated with such access.

- **E-mail access**—Users need to know what is or is not allowed in e-mail communications. If you monitor their e-mail communications, tell them. Have a clear policy on the storage of old e-mails.

- **Remote access**—Anyone who is allowed to access systems remotely has special responsibilities. Limits on access times may be appropriate, depending on the availability of connections. If remote access is available only by telephone modem, limits can increase availability to more users.

- **Passwords**—Password policies may be a challenge. Apart from the complexity requirements described in Chapter 13, users need to know policies with respect to sharing passwords or posting them in plain sight.

Additional policies may be required for other communication systems, such as for instant messaging inside and outside the company.

These are just policies for regular users. Policies for administrators should go further. Physical access policies for administrators extend to any facility with servers or other secure systems. Remote access policies should support rigorous access via the Secure Shell (SSH), such as the use of passphrases. Backup policies should also ensure the security of your sensitive information stored on backup media, an often-overlooked concern.

Education

If security were the only concern, nobody would be allowed to use computers. But just like the idea of disconnecting all computers from networks, that's not realistic. There will be users, and they will go online. With that in mind, it's important that users know the risks. You've read about basic policies. Unfortunately, to many employees, policy statements sound as incomprehensible as the teachers in Charlie Brown cartoons. That's where education comes in.

Even if there's no money for formal classes, it's helpful to make educational materials available. Many Linux users believe that their systems are invincible. They may be less concerned about Linux as a malware carrier. While most malware from Internet attack sites or black-hat e-mails may not affect a Linux system, some malware may still use Linux as a carrier, infecting other operating systems through shared folders and more.

User Installation of Problematic Services

Linux users may experiment with their home systems. Such experiments may be
as simple as the installation of a package from the Ubuntu Universe repository. These
experiments may go further when users download and compile a third-party package.
Such experiments are an excellent way to learn more about Linux. However, such
experiments may also pose risks to your corporate networks.

If users have a need for applications not currently in your gold baselines, they should
be able to request them. And if such applications are supported by an organization such
as Red Hat or Canonical, you should be able to provide those applications for your users.
Of course, such requests should be subject to security reviews. If a user is asking for the
installation of a Telnet server, you should be ready to educate that user on the benefits
of using the SSH service instead.

Log Access into the Network

There are two basic ways to see who has logged into a system and a network. Commands
are available to review users who are currently logged in and log files are available to review
logins, along with direct and indirect access to the root administrative account. System
authentication logs can do more, depending on how logging services have been configured.

Identify Users Who Have Logged In

Two commands identify users who are currently logged into a system: **w** and **who**.
As shown here, the **who** command displays currently logged in users along with remote
login locations, if applicable:

```
$ who
michael   tty1      2010-05-07 08:26
michael   pts/10    2010-05-06 22:46 (192.168.122.177)
michael   pts/11    2010-05-07 07:25 (10.168.0.1)
```

The output shows three logins for user michael. The first one is on the first local console,
tty1. The second login is from a known virtual machine with an Internet Protocol (IP)
address on the associated private network. The third login is from the IP address of
a router, which suggests a remote external login, forwarded to the local system. Unless
user michael is in two places at once, that external login may be a cause for concern.
For more information, try the **w** command, as shown:

```
$ w
michael   tty1      -            08:26  39:01  0.01s  0.01s -bash
michael   pts/10    192.168.122.177  22:46         10:19m
↪0.02s  0.02s -bash
michael   pts/11    192.168.0.1  07:25  0.00s  0.05s
↪0.01s trojan_horse
```

The w command includes information on the process currently being executed by the logged-in user. You may note that the output related to the terminal associated with the remote external login suggests that user is currently running a program called trojan_horse. While it seems unlikely that a true black-hat hacker would run a program with such an obviously suspicious name, that output would warrant further investigation.

The last command provides a more complete history of logins to the local system. That history can help in an investigation to look for other suspicious logins. Just keep in mind that command has provided misleading output in the past. If you're running the last command on an older system, that may lead to false positives for remote access. For details, search for bug 82540 in the **Red Hat Bugzilla** database at *https://bugzilla.redhat .com/*. In any case, the last command accesses a login database in the */var/log/wtmp* file.

On Red Hat systems, the utmpdump /var/log/wtmp command includes the last process run by the logged-in user, by PID number. If you need to investigate the actions associated with a login session, that PID number, when coupled with system status log information described earlier in the chapter, can help you determine what that user was running.

System Authentication Logs

Suspicious logins as regular users should cause concern. One thing that should cause more concern is suspicious use of the root administrative account along with related commands such as su and sudo. As described in Chapter 12, authentication logs are associated with the auth and authpriv facilities as configured in the system logging or the RSyslog services. The log files specified in the associated system logging or RSyslog service configuration should contain information on all login attempts, including the following:

- **Remote access**—Remote access from any system is logged by IP address, service, and port number.
- **Administrative access**—Local access with the su or sudo commands is logged either with the root administrative user ID of 0 or the associated USER = root environment variable.
- **Administrative jobs**—Access by services that require administrative privileges, such as a cron job or an e-mail transmission from Postfix, may also be logged.

Monitor Account Behavior for Security Issues

One reason the average Linux user is more knowledgeable is that Linux users are more likely to experiment with their systems. On a corporate network, it may be appropriate to look for the signs of such behavior in user home directories. If a user has downloaded source code on his or her system, that user may have already compiled that code into a binary program of some sort. In that case, there will be files somewhere in the tree of the user's home directory with executable privileges.

Of course, such checks are subject to organizational policies. In general, it's best if users know about such checks before they're performed so they are aware of the expectations with respect to their behavior. And such checks may not be reasonable if users are in fact Linux developers or testers.

Downloaded Packages and Source Code

A simple method to monitor a system for source code is to look for tarballs, which are normally provided in one or two compressed file archives, normally with `.tar.gz` or `.tar.bz2` extensions. They can be found in user home directories with the `find` command. Specifically, the following command starts with the `/home/` directory and looks in all subdirectories for files with the `.tar.gz` extension:

```
# find /home/ -name *.tar.gz
```

As desired, such commands can be run on a regular basis as a `cron` job. For example, to set up a daily `cron` job with such searches, add a command like that shown to a file i n the `/etc/cron.daily/` directory. Make sure the output of these commands is redirected to an appropriate file, perhaps in the `/var/log/` directory, suitable for later analysis.

Of course, Linux software comes in other formats. Software suitable for Red Hat distributions are downloaded as package files with `.rpm` extensions. In contrast, software packages for Debian-based distributions such as Ubuntu are available as package files with `.deb` extensions.

Executable Files

Naturally, users may set up their own executable files in their home directories. It's allowed with the `chmod` command. While a few executable files are necessary for certain applications, however, such files should be kept to a minimum. The `find` command can also be helpful in this area. For example, the following command searches for all files (`-type f`) with user, group, and other executable permissions, starting with the `/home/` directory:

```
# find /home/ -type f -perm /u=x,g=x,o=x
```

Unfortunately, the abilities of this command are limited, especially with respect to applications such as the Evolution Personal Information Manager. Many Evolution data files have to have executable permissions.

Perhaps as dangerous as executable files are those with Set User ID (SUID), Set Group ID (SGID), and sticky-bit permissions. Once created by a user, a black-hat hacker may arrange to have them run by a user associated with a service, potentially infecting that service with malware of some sort. The `find` command can be used to search for such files with the following command:

```
# find /home/ -type f -perm /u=s,g=s,o=t
```

While changes in file-executable permissions are tracked by tools such as Tripwire and AIDE in most of a system, they might not be tracked in user home directories. There are legitimate uses for executable scripts. For example, engineers might have big database jobs that they want to run at night through the `cron` daemon. So the tracking of executable files in user directories is often left to customized searches with the `find` command.

Create an Incident Response Plan

Not all security issues relate directly to computers. Don't forget the human element. The files on a computer are only as secure as the people responsible for them. Nevertheless, when a security issue appears, it is appropriate to be more vigilant. It is possible to increase the levels of security in a number of areas. Users can temporarily accept increased security if they understand the issues at hand.

Sometimes a security issue is obvious. Someone might identify a file or some other information that should be confidential but is in an insecure location. Sometimes, you might realize that a specific computer has not been updated with some security patch. If you're able to isolate a security issue to a specific computer, there are several things you can do.

With an appropriate incident response plan, you'll do what is required to collect information. Correct procedures can help you determine what went wrong and what should be done next. In addition, such procedures can help you preserve information as evidence in case the organization decides to seek legal remedies.

> **NOTE**
>
> This chapter does not directly address actual legal requirements with respect to a response to a security breach. In general, it is best to document everything that you may do.

Increased Vigilance

Every organization with valuable data should have computer security policies in place. As suggested earlier, such policies can be classified in several areas. If there is a reason to suspect black-hat hacker activity from a local user, you may not be able to share the information with other users.

If you want to pay more attention to user activity, start with the log files. Look at the history of commands run by a specific user. If a user has stuck with the bash shell, that history is normally stored in that user's home directory, in the .bash_history file. Of course, a careful black-hat hacker may substitute a file with benign commands, but not all black-hat hackers are so careful. Any access to administrative accounts should be documented in files discussed earlier such as secure and auth.log in the /var/log/ directory.

Any changes to systems accessible to suspected users can be checked with intrusion detection systems (IDSes) such as Tripwire and AIDE.

If you're able to share concerns with users, it's more likely they'll accept reasonable increased security measures in the areas discussed earlier. To recap, when appropriate, security can be increased in the following areas:

- **Physical access**—Limits on users who are allowed to operate certain workstations
- **Internet access**—Additional limits on access outside any corporate intranets
- **E-mail access**—Restrictions on communications outside the company
- **Remote access**—Reduced access to organizational networks
- **Passwords**—Immediate changes to all passwords

These are just examples of what can be done to increase security, based on less-rigorous policies. Actual policies in standard and higher-alert situations will vary.

Keep the System On (At Least for Now)

If you identify a system that has been compromised, be careful. The actions you take may determine how much can be learned from the situation, whether other systems may be at risk, and how data from a compromised system may be used with respect to potential legal action.

If you're new to computer forensics, read this section just as a guide. Any actions with respect to compromised systems should follow a prearranged plan. That plan should be endorsed by appropriate legal personnel to make sure any actions preserve evidence in a useful manner. This book is not intended to substitute for a real forensic action plan.

If it is safe, disconnect the system from a public network, but connect the system to an isolated network, as that allows you to use a protocol analyzer to read the network traffic going to and coming from the compromised system. On an Ethernet network, it's possible to use commands like tcpdump and tools like Wireshark to analyze that traffic. Don't forget to run appropriate nmap commands to see what ports are exposed on the subject system. You might get lucky if the black-hat hacker did not change the IP address of packets sent to the targeted system. In that case, you could block access from that IP address.

At some point, you may want to disconnect the compromised system from the network. Ideally, if it provides a mission-critical service, you'll have a backup in place with appropriate security updates, ready to substitute for the compromised system. If that is not possible, your users may have live without the service for a period of time.

If you power down a compromised system too soon, you may lose critical information. Linux stores dynamic information in RAM. That information is accessible through the **/proc/kcore** file. If you power down a system, that data may be lost.

To get a picture of data currently in RAM, you'll need a forensics kit. One popular option that has recently been commercialized is the tool formerly known as Helix Knoppix. Alternatively, the References section in the back of this book lists some articles on the Symantec Web site by Mariusz Burdach on how to create your own forensics kit. Briefly, that kit can be mounted on a compromised system, with direct access to important commands.

For example, if a forensic system is mounted on the /media/cdrom/ directory, you should be able to run commands from that directory. As suggested by Symantec, you should take the following steps while a system is still running:

1. Take a digital picture of the active monitor of the compromised system.

2. Mount the forensic CD or DVD on the troubled system with the following command (the -n switch avoids writing the mount to the /etc/mtab file):

   (troubled system) # mount -n /dev/cdrom /media/cdrom

   Be warned: There is certainly risk associated with using the mount command from a troubled system, especially if that command has been compromised by a black-hat hacker.

3. Use the netcat command, nc, to open communications from a remote system listening (-l 11111) on a specific port such as 11111:

   (diagnostic system) # nc -l 11111 > date_on_troubled_host

4. Use the `date` command from the forensic CD/DVD on the troubled system to record the date; the pipe with the `nc` command can then transmit that information to the remote listening system, with a timeout of 2 seconds (`-w 2`).

   (troubled system) # /media/cdrom/date |
   ↳ /media/cdrom/nc *diagnostic_ip_address* 11111 -w 2

5. Set up a checksum file with a command like `md5sum` or `sha1sum` so others can verify the integrity of the file.

6. Repeat the process with the current hardware and kernel routing tables, using the `arp -n` and `route -Cn` commands from the mounted forensic CD/DVD. It should document all connections from the troubled system.

7. Get the same information for network connections and associated processes with the `netstat -atunp` command.

8. Now you'll review the process again in detail, with the current contents of the RAM, as connected to the `/proc/kcore` file. So once again, use the netcat command, `nc`, to open communications from a remote system listening (`-l`) on a specific port such as 11111:

   (diagnostic system) # nc -l 11111 > kernel_core

9. Use the **dd** command from the forensic CD/DVD on the troubled system to dump the contents of the kernel core; when coupled with the `nc` command, that information can be forwarded to the remote listening system, with a timeout of 3 seconds (`-w 3`).

   (troubled system) # /media/cdrom/dd < /proc/kcore |
   ↳ /media/cdrom/nc *diagnostic_ip_address* 11111 -w 3

10. Set up a checksum file with a command like `md5sum` or `sha1sum` so others can verify the integrity of the file.

11. Repeat the process with key files in the `/proc/` directory, especially `modules`. Other important dynamic files from the `/proc/` directory are listed in Table 14-1.

12. Get a list of current processes and associated files with the output of the `lsof -nPl` command. The switches keep IP addresses, port numbers, and UID numbers in numeric format. In other words, they're not converted to hostnames, protocol names, and usernames, respectively. Of course, get the standard perspective of currently running processes with the `ps aux` and `ps axl` commands.

13. Get a copy of currently mounted filesystems from the `/etc/mtab` file, along with the filesystems that should be mounted from the `/etc/fstab` file. If there's a difference between the list of mounted filesystems and the list of filesystems that should be mounted during the boot process, that may be worth investigating.

In some cases, you may want to set up a full copy of the `/proc/` directory on separate media such as a USB key. Linux `/proc/` directories normally include subdirectories full of information associated with each running process. If there are any discrepancies between

TABLE 14-1 Important files in the `/proc/` directory for forensic analysis.

FILE	DESCRIPTION
`puinfo`	Hardware information focused on the CPU
`domainname`	Name of the domain for the local area network (LAN); in the `/proc/sys/kernel/` directory
`hostname`	Name of the local computer; in the `/proc/sys/kernel/` directory
`kallsyms`	Debugging information for the kernel
`modules`	Loaded kernel modules
`mounts`	Mounted filesystems; in the `/proc/self/` directory
`partitions`	Configured partitions
`swaps`	Configured swap volumes
`uptime`	Length of time the current system has been in operation
`version`	Currently loaded kernel, with version number and associated compiler

these subdirectories, the output of various `ps` commands may provide important clues, such as to processes that have been hidden by a black-hat hacker.

If you've configured a specialized service on a compromised system, don't forget any dynamic settings associated with that service. In general, such dynamic settings should be available in RAM and saved with the `/proc/kcore` file. However, you may choose to run a command like `sync` to make sure information currently in RAM is written to appropriate files.

Once the recovery of dynamic data is complete, you should be able to power off the system. The next step will be to remove and replicate hard drive media on the compromised systems.

▷ **TIP**

Some live Linux CDs may also be used to monitor and obtain data from suspect systems over a network. Basic techniques depend on the `tcpdump` command and Wireshark network protocol analyzer described in earlier chapters.

Have Live Linux CDs Ready for Forensics Purposes

As suggested in the previous section, you should have two different types of CDs (or other similar media) available for forensics purposes. Some are suitable for mounting on a compromised system, to help the investigator download and otherwise save dynamic data from areas like RAM. Others are suitable as forensic live media. As such, they can be used for booting diagnostic systems. Once booted, such media can be used to save a copy of the partitions and volumes configured on compromised systems.

Media to Recover Dynamic Data from Compromised Systems

Perhaps the most common option for recovering dynamic data from compromised systems is known as the Sleuth Kit. Another option that is no longer freely available is the distribution formerly known as Helix, now owned by Access Data. Which is the right option depends on cost and the amount of effort you're willing to put into the process. One option that incorporates the commands associated with the Sleuth Kit is the Master Key Linux, developed at Coventry University in the United Kingdom.

While there is a substantial number of organizations that offer "forensic" software for Linux, very few options support the recovery of dynamic data, especially from specific files in the /proc/ directory. For similar tools, search for Linux Memory Analysis tools. Other related tools under development include Second Look from *http://pikewerks.com/* and the Forensic Analysis Toolkit from *http://4tphi.net/fatkit/*. Neither of these tools is currently quite as advanced as the others.

If none of the previous options are suitable, you could create your own tool. Because Linux is open source, uncompiled tools are readily available online. With a little effort, you can compile the latest version of these tools into a custom system, ready to recover dynamic data from compromised systems. After reviewing the options, you may want to use two or more of the given tools on a compromised system.

Helix Live Response

Perhaps the most popular suggestion online for compromised Linux systems is Helix Knoppix. This option no longer exists in the open source sphere, however. Perhaps the popularity of Helix Knoppix has encouraged its developers to commercialize this Linux distribution. As suggested by the name, it was formerly created from the Knoppix live CD. While it could be booted like the Knoppix live CD, it could also be mounted directly on a suspect system. Key commands were available directly from the mount point.

Since Helix was acquired by Access Data, the developers have moved to a different model. It is now built on Ubuntu Linux. The forensic acquisition tools do not directly access files from the /proc/ directory. Helix products are no longer available under any sort of GNU General Public License (GPL). Support and purchasing is available from e-fense, with more information at *http://www.accessdata.com/* and *http://www.e-fense.com/*.

TABLE 14-2 Commands in the Sleuth Kit.	
COMMAND	**DESCRIPTION**
blkcalc	Maps output of the blkls command to filesystem data units, also known as a group of sectors
blkcat	Reads the contents of a data unit
blkls	Lists details of data units
blkstat	Specifies the allocation status of a data unit
ffind	Maps metadata to filenames
fls	Lists files and directories in a given filesystem
fsstat	Displays details of a filesystem, with a range of inodes
hfind	Finds hash values in a database
icat	Reads the contents of a file from its metadata address
ifind	Maps between metadata and data units
ils	Lists details on a range of metadata structures
img_cat	Shows the contents of an image file
img_stat	Displays details of an image file
istat	Lists details of a specified metadata structure
jcat	Displays the contents of a journal, for a filesystem like ext3
jls	Lists records in a filesystem journal
mactime	Creates a timeline of file activity
mmcat	Lists contents of a partition in a logical volume
mmls	Lists partitions and volumes on a drive
mmstat	Displays the disk label of a system
sigfind	Identifies binary signatures
sorter	Sorts files based on type

The Sleuth Kit

The **Sleuth Kit** is one open source collection of tools designed for use on compromised systems. Available online from *http://www.sleuthkit.org/*, it allows you to compile important commands for working with compromised systems. The basic download is available in tarball format. Once downloaded, you can build and install key executable files in the /usr/local/bin/ directory by doing the following:

1. Download and unpack the tarball with the Sleuth Kit files. It's normally available in `.tar.gz` format. Verify the download with the GNU Privacy Guard (GPG) key available from *http://www.sleuthkit.org/*.

2. Unpack the `sleuthkit-*.tar.gz` package with the following command. The version number is represented by *; the * character works in the command. The files from the archive should appear in the `sleuthkit-*` subdirectory.

   ```
   $ tar xzf sleuthkit-*.tar.gz
   ```

3. Navigate to the `sleuthkit-*/` directory. As noted in the `INSTALL.txt` file, three additional steps are required to compile and build the required commands.

4. Run the `./configure` script to configure the packages with locally available program libraries.

5. Run the `make` command to build the packages.

6. Run the `make install` command to compile the packages; by default, the commands are written to the `/usr/local/bin/` directory.

Of course, you'll want to write the executable files from the `/usr/local/bin/` directory to read-only media like CDs or DVDs. Once appropriate commands and libraries are written, you can then mount that media on a compromised system and use the commands built by this process. Some of the commands available from the Sleuth Kit are described in Table 14-2. As you can see from the commands, many of them are also well suited to analysis after a system is powered down.

Master Key Linux

One of the issues with the Sleuth Kit is that it is currently distributed as a tarball. It's still up to you to configure, compile, and copy the commands from the package to appropriate media. If that seems like a lot of trouble, one option is **Master Key Linux**. It's a live CD with the commands described earlier (and a few more) already set up. All you need to do is mount the CD and run the desired commands from the appropriate subdirectory. Currently, because development is led by students at Coventry University (UK), no commercial support is available. But if this option is of interest, the software is available from *http://www.masterkeylinux.com/*.

Build Your Own Media

It may be best to build your own media. When compiled from source code, you can set up commands on read-only media such as CDs or DVDs with all the libraries required to run those commands reliably. As noted in an article by Mariusz Burdach on the Symantec Web site at *http://www.symantec.com/connect/articles/forensic-analysis-live-linux-system-pt-1*, you may want to include the commands listed in Table 14-3 in that media. Just be aware that when downloading packages, many of the associated servers do not organize packages by date. So the latest version of a package may be somewhere in the middle of the listing.

TABLE 14-3 Commands to include in a forensic toolkit.

COMMAND	DESCRIPTION
cat	The cat command is available from the coreutils package. For more information, see *http://www.gnu.org/software/coreutils/*.
date	The date command is available from the coreutils package.
dd	The dd command is available from the coreutils package.
dmesg	The dmesg command is available from the util-linux-ng package, which can be downloaded from the Linux kernel servers at *ftp://ftp.kernel.org/pub/linux/utils/util-linux-ng/*.
nc	While the nc command is available from a variety of sources, one option is coupled with the nmap command, available online from *http://nmap.org/download.html*.

The steps required to install such packages are similar to those described for the Sleuth Kit. Detailed instructions should be available in a file named INSTALL in the directory of unpacked source code. Some customization may be required; for example, it's helpful to configure the source code to redirect tools to a specific directory with a command similar to the following:

```
# ./configure --prefix=/tools
```

Once the given tools are written to a CD or DVD, you'll then be able to mount such media on suspect systems, secure in the knowledge that the commands written to such media will not be changed.

Forensic Live Media

Many groups have created their own live media for forensic data recovery. While very few of these options support recovery of volatile data such as files in the /proc/ directory, most of these options provide excellent support for the investigator who wants to create a copy of suspect hard drives and analyze the data on those drives in detail. Several options for forensic live media are listed in Table 14-4. Some of these options include commands for recovering volatile data from a Microsoft operating system. Most of these options can boot into a customized version of Linux, loaded in RAM, with tools that can diagnose and otherwise examine files associated with a Linux or Microsoft system on a local drive. In general, that drive is not mounted when the live CD or DVD is loaded.

This list does not include the many live CD/DVD distributions that include additional forensic tools. In fact, most live CD/DVD distributions include command-line tools that can help with forensic analysis. But be careful. Standard live CD/DVD distributions may use or otherwise overwrite information on a swap partition. When booting some forensic

TABLE 14-4 Options for forensic live media.	
NAME	**DESCRIPTION**
BackTrack	A bootable live DVD distribution, which can be started without disturbing a swap partition, available from *http://www.backtrack-linux.org/*.
CAINE	Computer Aided Investigative Environment, available from *http://www.caine-live.net/*.
Chaox	Based on Arch Linux, Chaox focuses on penetration testing and forensic tools. For more information, see *http://blag.chaox.net/*.
Damn Vulnerable Linux (DVL)	Based on Slackware Linux, DVL is a teaching tool used by the International Institute Training Assessment Certification, sponsored by Cognitive Core in Germany. It includes BackTrack and additional security training tools. For more information, see *http://www.damnvulnerablelinux.org/*.
DEFT Linux	Built on Ubuntu Linux, it includes a number of live tools for recovering data from live Microsoft operating systems, available from *http://www.deftlinux.net/*.
FCCU Linux	A distribution built in Belgium, built on Debian Linux, available from *http://www.lnx4n6.be/*.
Network Security Toolkit (NST)	Built on Fedora Linux, NST provides a number of standard network security applications on its live media; it also includes an Internet Protocol Security (IPSec) mode for secure communications.
Securix NSM	A Debian-based distribution designed to introduce the user to network security monitoring (NSM).

live CD/DVD distributions, you may have to explicitly choose an option to avoid using the swap partition.

Many of these distributions include installation options that support a dedicated forensic workstation.

When You Put Your Plan into Action

Not all security issues are computer related. However, you may be able to identify security issues associated with a system, such as an uninstalled update, an unplanned open port, or perhaps even malware of some sort. Of course, if there are files that should be found only on secure systems, there may be a different sort of security breach. In any of these cases, you should have gold baseline systems ready to put into place as replacements. If you've avoided a previous update for other reasons, that may take some additional work.

Confirm the Breach

To confirm a breach, you need to know something about what happened. Has sensitive data been lost? If so, that by itself does not confirm a configuration issue, as it may be due to lax physical security. Has a user account been compromised? You can get a good sense of that from the commands that account for logins, as described earlier in this chapter. Can you identify malware on a system? You may be able to use some of the tools described in Chapter 11 for that purpose.

Until you can identify the specific breach and understand what needs to change on a system, it may be sufficient to simply temporarily implement higher levels of security, as discussed earlier in the chapter. But once a breach is confirmed, the next step is to identify any compromised systems.

Identify Compromised Systems

Sometimes, it's easy to identify a compromised system. You run an antivirus scanner on a system and it identifies malware. You see log files where someone has logged into a service account. You see activity on an e-mail server that far exceeds the demands placed on it by local users. Such events are symptoms of a compromised system.

Sometimes, the reason behind a compromised system is straightforward. You've identified a problem, and it matches the problem addressed by a security update. You originally thought the security update was not necessary.

But administrators don't always install every security update. Sometimes, such installations are avoided for excellent reasons. For example, kernel updates may affect support associated with third-party software. Related updates may require additional work on software that may be compiled during the installation process. The documentation behind some security updates may suggest that the security issue doesn't apply to systems on your network.

So while there are good reasons to avoid a security update, you need to be aware of the risks. If the subject system is compromised, the reason may be the uninstalled security update.

Have Gold Replacement Systems in Place

Unless the problem is with the associated service, you should be able to have a gold replacement system in place. If you've determined that the problem is an uninstalled security update, have a system in place with that update. Make sure that system has been documented with a tool such as Tripwire or AIDE.

Of course, if the problem with a service has not been determined, the users on the network may need to live without the service for awhile. If it's a mission-critical service, few people will be happy with you. Users will be more willing to wait if you're able to set up the service in question with reduced functionality to help address the security issues.

Backup and Recovery Tools

In the context of this chapter, backup and recovery tools are used to make copies or images of suspect media, normally hard drives. Perhaps the standard Linux tool to that end is the disk dump command, dd. It takes every bit of a storage volume, in a format that can be copied to an image. The alternative is the **rsync** command, which is well suited to copying files, preserving all relevant data such as links and last access times.

Disk Images for Later Investigation

While the dd command is still the standard, other excellent commands are available for disk imaging. One of the benefits of the dd command is that it copies everything, even the Universally Unique Identifier (UUID) number associated with the drive or volume. To that end, the simplest invocation of dd copies the contents of one hard drive to a second hard drive, as follows:

```
# dd if=/dev/sda of=/dev/sdb
```

Breaking down this command, it takes the hard drive represented by the /dev/sda device as the input file (if), and copies the content, block by block, to the output file (of), represented by the /dev/sdb device file.

The dd command can also be used to create disk images. For example, the following command saves the contents of that first hard drive, represented by /dev/sda, to the noted file, in a directory named /remote, which could be mounted from a remote, portable, or shared network directory.

```
# dd if=/dev/sda of=/remote/troubleddisk1.img
```

Sometimes, disks on compromised systems may be troubled. In fact, a black-hat hacker may have caused such problems to make copying and investigation more difficult. To that end, the options added to the command as shown here continue the backup process in case of errors (noerror); does not allow truncating (notrunc), which could lose important data; and supports the noted block size (bs=16384) in bytes, which is more likely to complete the duplication process.

If you see errors during the disk-duplication process, the **dd_rescue** command may be helpful. At the command line, it works essentially as a drop-in replacement for dd. But it is more likely to save data from a crashed filesystem, possibly even from an overused or otherwise damaged hard drive. If a regular dd_rescue command does not work, a dd_rescue -r command copies data from the end of the specified if volume first. One drawback is that dd_rescue can take several hours on a typical multi-gigabyte hard drive.

One drawback of the dd command is that it copies everything on a drive or partition, including free space. So if you're using the dd command to make a disk image of a 100 GB drive, it'll require a 100 GB file.

> **▷ TIP**
>
> The dd_rescue command can be especially useful if recovering data from a drive that has not been backed up, such as from a portable system.

TABLE 14-5 Options for the `rsync` command.

OPTION	DESCRIPTION
-a	Archive mode, equivalent to `-rlptgoD`
-D	Device files
-e	Transfer over a remote shell option such as RSH or SSH
-g	Group ownership
-H	Hard-linked files
-l	Soft-linked files
-o	User ownership
-p	Permissions
-r	Recursive mode
-z	Compressed data transfer

The `rsync` Command

For pure backups, the `rsync` command may make more sense. Unlike the `dd` command, it does not include the free space in a disk or partition in the backup. It just copies the actual files to the remote system. In addition, the `rsync` command is efficient; the second time it's used to copy a filesystem, all it transmits is anything that changed. That makes the `rsync` command well suited to backing up data over a network.

One of the problems originally associated with the `rsync` command is that it transmits data in clear text, using the Remote Shell (RSH) protocol. With the help of the `-e ssh` switch, `rsync` data is encrypted and transmitted over an SSH connection in encrypted format. In fact, one version of the `rsync` command does more. For example, the following command backs up user home directories to the `/backup/` directory on the noted remote system:

```
# rsync -aHz -e ssh /home/ bkadmin@bkserver:/backup/
```

The command prompts for either the password or the passphrase for the `bkadmin` user, in archive (`-a`) mode, copying hard-linked (`-H`) files, in compressed (`-z`) format. Since archive mode incorporates a number of options, you may want to refer to Table 14-5 for a list of `rsync` command options.

Mount Encrypted Filesystems

To work with encrypted filesystems, you'll need live CD/DVD media that can handle such filesystems. Perhaps the most complex case is encryption on a logical volume. If you're working with an Ubuntu system, you'll have to add a couple of packages to the live CD operating system, after it is booted. For Ubuntu systems, the key packages are `lvm2` and `cryptsetup`.

For RHEL systems, you can work with a Fedora system loaded from a live CD. While you'll also need to load a couple of packages, the package names are essentially the same: `lvm2` and `cryptsetup-luks`.

You can then load the cryptographic module, which is part of the `cryptsetup*` package. You should then be able to run a `cryptsetup` command similar to the following:

```
# cryptsetup luksOpen /dev/device path
```

If you've selected the right device, the command should prompt for the password or passphrase required to decrypt the volume.

The Right Way to Save Compromised Data as Evidence

Earlier in this chapter, you saw how to save dynamic data from a compromised system. You'll review that data. Once appropriate dynamic data is saved, you'll want to make a copy of the compromised hard disks. You can then analyze the copied volumes, secure in the knowledge that if there's a mistake, you can repeat the process. Of course, you'll want to make sure to document everything, including checksums of any copies that have been created.

Basic Principles for Evidence

This section and this book are not intended to be used as legal guidance. This is not a comprehensive list of requirements when computer data has to be saved and analyzed as evidence. In any case, actual requirements vary by jurisdiction. But in general, when saving compromised data as evidence, you must have excellent records. You need to document where the evidence came from, how that evidence was duplicated, and the methods used to analyze that evidence, and prove that the duplicate is identical to the original. That is all part of the chain of custody.

With a good chain of custody, evidence is secure. A black-hat hacker won't have a chance to tamper with or perhaps erase that incriminating data. A corrupt official won't have a chance to substitute data that falsely points the finger at others. To that end, an appropriate chain of custody meets the following requirements:

- Tamper-proof storage
- Documented location
- Receipts when the responsibility for data is transferred from one person to another
- A list of all known passwords and checksums

Remember the Dynamic Data

With the chain of custody in mind, you're ready to use the techniques described earlier in this chapter to save any dynamic data on a suspect system. To recap, you'll want to save any data that might otherwise disappear when a computer is powered down. At minimum, that means all data in volatile memory, which is generally limited to RAM. If you have forensic tools that can also save data from the swap partition, by all means do so. Otherwise, many of the live CD forensic tools described earlier can be started without using the swap partition, and can therefore save that data after the computer and/or hard drive media are powered down.

And in the spirit of the chain of custody, you'll want to document every step taken to save that data.

> **TIP**
>
> Do not use the original hard disk of the compromised system in any analysis. Commands like dd and dd_rescue are designed to create a bit-by-bit duplicate of an original disk. Physical write blockers can protect the integrity of the hard disk as evidence. One source for a forensic toolkit is the SysAdmin Audit Network Security (SANS) Institute.

Preserve the Hard Disks

One approach is to boot the compromised system and a diagnostic system in a simple network. You should then be able to use the network connection to copy the volumes of the troubled system. Alternatively, you could use a live CD to copy the data from a hard disk directly to an image file. Techniques described earlier were based on the use of the dd and dd_rescue commands.

Once the image file is saved, it can be mounted with the loopback device. For example, if the image of the hard disk is saved as the evidence.img file, you can mount that file on an empty /test/ directory with the following command:

```
# mount -o loop evidence.img /test/
```

Alternatively, there are methods available to set up such image files in virtual machines. When such a machine is configured without an external network connection, it's another way to record and/or test the data on such systems in isolation.

Disaster Recovery from a Security Breach

The response to a security breach depends on what happened. In general, you'll want to have gold baseline systems ready to go in case of a security issue. When appropriately configured, they can be put in place of compromised systems. Ideally, before you put that into place, you should determine whether there's a flaw in that gold baseline system.

When data is needed from compromised systems, that can be another matter. In that case, you need to know what has been compromised. During forensic analysis of a compromised system, you should be able to review the differences with the original configuration with tools such as AIDE or Tripwire. Reviewing the differences should help you identify what went wrong. It should identify files that have been changed or added by a black-hat hacker.

Determine What Happened

Use the information available from an integrity checker such as AIDE or Tripwire. That should give you a list of files that have changed. It should also tell you about files with different owners. Any suspect files should be investigated further with tools such as rootkits and malware checkers described in Chapter 11.

In addition, use the logs associated with mandatory access control systems, specifically SELinux and Application Armor (AppArmor). If the black-hat hacker has made a mistake, perhaps by trying to change a file in a protected directory, it should show up in related log files.

If you've created a gold baseline of processes, any suspect process may stick out like a sore thumb. A dynamic list of processes shown with the `top` command should include those systems that are taking up an unexpected amount of CPU or RAM memory. That process can then be further investigated with the `lsof`, `strace`, and `ldd` commands, which track such processes to other files. You may also be able to identify compromised services from the output. If that process leads to a suspicious script, you may have hit pay dirt. Look at that script. It may identify the way the black-hat hacker is affecting your system.

Once you've identified suspect files, you can try removing them. But that's not enough.

Prevention

Once you've determined the problem, the next step is prevention. What do you do to keep the black-hat hacker from doing the same thing to the next system? You should investigate how the black-hat hacker got access to your systems. If it was through the network, check the services associated with open ports. If it was through a compromised user account, make sure passwords are appropriate. If it was through a compromised service, make sure all security updates are installed. If that's not enough, you may need to find an alternative service. In the world of open source, there are alternatives for almost everything.

But it is also possible that the black-hat hacker got direct access, perhaps by booting a live CD on a compromised system. The steps required to identify that breach are more in the realm of physical security professionals, who may need to review surveillance tapes.

Replacement

After preventative measures have been taken, you're ready to replace a compromised system on a permanent basis. If the problem is based on a physical security breach, a compromised password, or something else beyond the control of an administrator, your work has been validated. A replacement based on a current gold baseline ensures that any malware that has infected the system can no longer affect other systems.

But if a problem has been identified with the configuration, more work is required. The gold baseline may not be secure until the configuration is changed. You may need to update service software—or potentially even install a substitute service before putting the replacement into production.

Open Source Security Works Only If Everyone Shares

Security in the open source community depends on users who share. But if you're the victim of a black-hat hacker, it may be difficult to admit that there was a problem.

> ⚠️ **WARNING**
>
> Any release of organizational information on a public forum should be approved with appropriate management and legal counsel.

If you simply did not install a known security update, the situation might be embarrassing. In any case, managers may hesitate to share incident reports with the community.

Nevertheless, open source software is dependent on participation from the community. If nobody shared their problems in the open source community, open source developers would not know where their software needs improvement.

If the Security Issue Is Known

Sometimes, administrators avoid security updates for good reasons. If that reason relates to requirements for third-party software, the developers behind that third-party software need to know about the problem. If the third-party software is supported, then the developers of that third-party software should be interested in the problem, especially if there is a support contract involved.

But even without a support contract, there is an ethos in the open source community. If the software released by a group of open source developers is known to cause harm, those developers should get to work on a solution. In a great majority of cases, once the problem is confirmed, that's exactly what those open source developers will do.

If the Security Issue Has Not Been Reported

Many open source development teams provide confidential means to report security issues, as described in earlier chapters. In many cases, the developers behind even open source software want a chance to evaluate the report before the information becomes public. While that seems to work against the philosophy behind open source software, it is sometimes most appropriate. If the security issue is serious, a competition could erupt between white-hat developers who work to plug the security hole and black-hat hackers who want to take advantage.

But not all issues are security related. For example, the false positive given by older versions of the `last -i` command described earlier is just that: a false positive. Such issues have likely been reported through appropriate bug collection databases, such as Red Hat's Bugzilla at *https://bugzilla.redhat.com/* or Canonical's Launchpad at *https://bugs.launchpad.net/*. Search these databases first if there are reasonable doubts about the issue at hand.

Like you, Linux security professionals are quite busy. To report a security issue, developers need some information about your systems. While the details depend on the suspect service, it's important to provide sufficient information to allow developers to replicate the problem on their systems.

Best Practices: Security Breach Detection and Response

You need to plan in case of a security breach. It's best if you have a gold baseline system ready to go to take the place of at least any critical system on the local network. Of course, unless you know the cause of the breach, blindly replacing a compromised system could prove foolhardy. You need to know what happened. If there's a flaw with the configuration of the system, you should update that gold baseline first.

To understand when there might be a problem, regular performance audits are appropriate. Systems that deviate significantly from baseline performance with respect to CPU and RAM usage may be suspect. Because you can't spend all day on watch, the system status tool can help. If an issue arises, commands like `lsof`, `ldd`, and `strace` can help check suspect processes.

Good security requires the cooperation of users. It helps if security policies are kept as simple as possible. Appropriate policies with respect to users fall into the areas of physical access, Internet browsing, e-mail, and remote access. Even then, it helps to have educational materials available. While Linux users are generally more aware about computers, they may not realize that Linux systems can be infected and can be carriers of malware for other operating systems.

Good security means you know who is logging into systems on the local network. Such information is available currently with commands like `who` and `w`, and historically based on the `auth` and `authpriv` directives. In the associated log files, you can track access by administrative and remote users, along with administrative jobs.

As a security professional, you should monitor what is seen from user accounts. Downloaded packages and source code in user home directories may be signs of unauthorized changes from a regular user. Just as serious may be the existence of executable files in user home directories. However, you may not want to prevent some users from setting up their own scripts.

To plan for a security breach, you need an incident response plan. When there's a suspected breach and the cause is not obvious, you may need policies that support a temporary increased level of vigilance. Once a suspect system is identified, don't turn it off until you can copy volatile data such as the contents of RAM.

Part of the plan includes the right tools, including live Linux CDs with forensic commands. Options such as the Sleuth Kit and Master Key Linux support access to compromised systems from their CD/DVD drives. Once volatile data is recovered, various options are available to duplicate and diagnose issues on compromised hard drives.

When a Linux security issue arises, it's not always related to the configuration of a Linux system. It could be a physical security issue. If there is a confirmed problem, you'll want to identify compromised systems and if possible have gold substitutes in place. Backup and recovery tools such as `dd` and `rsync` can be used on compromised hard drives. And don't forget the tools and commands associated with reading encrypted filesystems.

Problems with computer security may lead to legal issues. In general, you should document every step taken to save dynamic and static data. All data that is saved should be stored in secure locations, with appropriate passwords and checksums. Once a problem is identified, it's time to replace compromised systems. If the cause is unrelated to the system configuration, you can address the problem and set up a replacement from the current gold baseline. Otherwise, you'll need to update the baseline and possibly even set up a replacement service.

CHAPTER SUMMARY

In this chapter, you examined some of the tools and issues related to the detection of security breaches on a Linux system. If you've identified a compromised Linux system, it's important to recover any volatile memory before making an image of the hard disks, especially if it's being done for evidence. It's important to document everything as you go through this process. Live CDs can help in several ways.

Security also depends on users. They're more likely to follow simple, sensible policies in the areas of physical, Internet, e-mail, and remote access security. With such policies and appropriate log files, you'll be able to track user logins to help track suspicious activity. With an appropriate response plan, you'll have the tools to identify a troubled system in a way that allows you to replace it with a more secure system.

KEY CONCEPTS AND TERMS

`dd`	CAINE
`dd_rescue`	DEFT
`ldd`	Master Key Linux
`/proc/kcore`	Red Hat Bugzilla
`rsync`	Sleuth Kit
`strace`	
`sysstat`	
`w`	
`who`	

CHAPTER 14 ASSESSMENT

1. Which of the following commands can display the free memory in RAM and in a swap partition? (Select two.)

   A. free
   B. mem
   C. top
   D. swapon

2. It is important to have a security policy that applies to users for how they do their backups.

   A. True
   B. False

3. What command reads log files created through the system status tool?

4. Which of the following commands is used to identify users who have since logged out?

   A. who
   B. w
   C. last
   D. sar

5. Which of the following file extensions is *not* associated with software packages?

   A. .odt
   B. .tar.gz
   C. .rpm
   D. .deb

6. Which of the following is most important to recover from a compromised system before powering it down?

   A. /home/
   B. /etc/fstab
   C. /proc/kcore
   D. None of the above

7. Which of the following files is most likely to change when a system is powered down?

   A. /etc/mtab
   B. /etc/fstab
   C. /boot/grub/menu.lst
   D. /etc/crontab

8. Which of the following commands is least useful for recovering data from a live system?

   A. nc
   B. vi
   C. dmesg
   D. cat

9. What command can be used to duplicate the contents of a partition by its device file?

10. Which of the following commands is not associated with compiling the source code associated with other commands?

    A. config
    B. configure
    C. make install
    D. make

11. Which of the following actions is normally done from a forensic operating system booted from live media, when connected to a compromised hard drive?

    A. Recovering information from RAM
    B. Making a copy of the /proc/kcore file
    C. Recovering information from a swap partition
    D. Copying the contents of /etc/mtab

12. Which of the following commands does *not* include free space in the duplication process?

    A. rsync
    B. dd
    C. dd_rescue
    D. icat

13. Which of the following steps is *not* appropriate when saving compromised data from a hard drive?

    A. Keeping a compromised system connected to a network during an investigation
    B. Taking special care to avoid overwriting data in a swap partition
    C. Booting a live Knoppix CD distribution
    D. Powering down a compromised system after saving dynamic data

14. Which of the following steps should you take if you've identified a new security problem with open source software?

    A. Share the concern on a standard mailing list for the distribution.
    B. Share the concern on a standard mailing list for the compromised software.
    C. Communicate privately with the developers of the compromised software.
    D. Nothing, as it is important to protect proprietary information in the open source community.

Best Practices and Emerging Technologies

THIS CHAPTER IS IN MANY WAYS A RECAP. It incorporates many of the lessons of the previous 14 chapters to help you put best practices in place for various Linux systems and networks.

Security can be seen as a battle between black-hat hackers who want to break into computers and security professionals like you. As black-hat hackers find new ways to break through, open source developers will respond and find ways to block such attacks. It is then up to you to keep systems up to date to block such attacks.

Updates may not always work. In some cases, black-hat hackers may break into your systems before updates are available. In other cases, updates may cause problems for hardware. Some updates may even violate service agreements for third-party software. Updates can be especially problematic when they require tools that can also be used by black-hat hackers. It is important to test updates before putting them into effect on production systems.

Security also depends on users and administrators. This requires good policies for both groups, as well as compliance to such policies. Audits may be needed, not only to verify compliance to such policies but also to satisfy legal and regulatory requirements.

Security requires the help of everyone in the Linux community. It relies on the developers behind various Linux distributions. It depends on the developers behind major applications. It relies on the developers behind those proprietary applications designed for use on Linux. It's even helped by the quality of communication within the Linux community. When you know how to take full advantage of these resources, you'll have the best information available on how to secure Linux systems.

Some of the discussion in this chapter repeats lessons learned in previous chapters. That is appropriate, as this chapter focuses on best practices based on information described throughout the book.

Chapter 15 Topics

This chapter covers the following topics and concepts:

- How to maintain a gold baseline
- How redundancy can help ensure availability
- Which varieties of open source corporate support are available
- Why you should check compliance with security policies
- How to keep Linux up to date
- How to keep distribution-related applications up to date
- How best to manage third-party applications
- Why you should share solutions with the community
- Why you should test new components before using them
- What some future trends in Linux security are

Chapter 15 Goals

When you complete this chapter, you will be able to:

- Understand best practices for keeping Linux software up to date
- Take advantage of corporate and community support
- Plan for future changes in Linux security

Maintain a Gold Baseline

A gold baseline is secure. It's kept secure because only copies of that baseline are used in production. But just like any other system, it has to be kept up to date. By its very nature, the software in a gold baseline is focused on the core commands and libraries associated with a distribution, along with the Linux kernel. It may include critical services associated with all systems, such as the Secure Shell (SSH) and system log services. A black-hat hacker who breaks into any of these systems could more easily gain access to all systems associated with every Linux distribution.

While the diversity of available Linux distributions does help promote overall security, that diversity does not extend to the core bits associated with the kernel or those basic commands and libraries used on every Linux system.

To maintain that gold baseline, you need to monitor security news associated with selected distributions. When updates are made available, it is up to you to make sure those updates work on local systems, conform to any requirements associated with other software, and process that update on other systems. In addition, you'll need to make sure the database associated with intrusion detection tools such as the Advanced Intrusion Detection Environment (AIDE) and Tripwire is up to date.

Monitor Security Reports

Information associated with security reports on Linux was covered in Chapter 11. The developers behind various Linux distributions maintain security reports for all supported packages on their distributions. In general, when a security report is released, an updated package should be available for installation through standard repositories.

In principle, all security reports should be addressed. As discussed in Chapter 11, you might choose to avoid installing a security update if it affects a support contract, adversely affects a critical software application, or adversely affects important hardware. If you make that choice, the risks will continue until that update is installed. If that choice is related to the support level associated with third-party software, you could ask for help from the vendor firm. But it may say no.

If you choose to avoid the installation of an update, be sure to keep track of the security report. If an affected system is compromised, look at what happened. If the compromise matches the information listed in the security report, you are going to have to reconsider the installation. If the issue is related to third-party software, you can go back to its developers or find an alternative application.

Work Through Updates

Not all updates are security related. Some updates address bugs. Other updates may enhance features. Updates may affect individual software packages, or they may address the Linux kernel.

If you're responsible for a group of Linux systems, it may be appropriate to set up a dedicated repository. As discussed in Chapter 11, the techniques of Linux patch management support the development of independent repositories, which can be based on a mirror of existing libraries of packages released by the developers of your preferred distribution. Even Red Hat Enterprise Linux (RHEL) supports mirrors of their repositories on remote networks.

If you choose a custom group of updates—say, only for security and bug fixes— that group of packages can be organized into a unique repository.

Recalibrate System Integrity

Every time there's an update, you'll need to test the changes functionally. Once the changes have been verified on a test system, the next step is to update the gold baseline system. If the baseline works after the update, the next step is to recalibrate the current database created by the integrity-checking tool of your choice, such as AIDE or Tripwire.

That database documents the current state of any baseline system that has been configured. Deviations from that baseline can be found in reports from AIDE or Tripwire, which document unexpected changes to critical files.

Redundancy Can Help Ensure Availability

When problems arise with a system, it's helpful to have a replacement available and ready for use. The problem could be simple, such as a failing hard drive or an overloaded system.

If the system in question is running a service on which users depend, they'll be thankful when you have a replacement ready to go.

Having a redundant system available depends on the status of the gold baseline. How a gold baseline is maintained depends on its role. The steps required to configure redundant physical systems are different from those needed to maintain redundant virtual systems. For mission-critical services, it may also be helpful to have service-specific baseline systems available.

A Gold Physical Baseline

Virtualization has in some ways revolutionized the concept of a gold baseline. Before virtualization, gold baselines in computers meant stacks of hard drives, or at least hard drive images ready to be written to other physical devices. But not all systems should be virtualized. Gold physical baselines are important too.

For example, some administrators believe that the demands of database servers make them poor candidates for virtualization. Other administrators have similar beliefs with respect to collaboration suites such as Novell GroupWise and Microsoft Exchange. Multiple virtual guests on a single virtual host do have some latency with respect to Central Processing Unit (CPU) response; in other words, they're slower. The amount of latency, however, is highly debatable. So at least in the near future, some virtualization-friendly enterprises will continue to use physical systems for dedicated services.

To that end, a gold physical baseline system can still be stored as a virtual image. With the dd command, administrators can create image files from the hard drives of their choice. When new copies of the baseline are required, the dd command can also be used to duplicate that image to a new physical drive. For example, the following command writes the noted golden.img file to the second hard drive device on the system:

```
# dd if=golden.img of=/dev/sdb
```

A Gold Virtual Baseline Host

If you're taking advantage of virtual machines, gold baseline systems fall into two categories: virtual hosts and virtual guests. Virtual hosts are physical systems, typically configured with multiple and/or multi-core CPUs. Multiple virtual guests can run on each virtual host. Each virtual machine system is a guest. To understand the requirements for a gold baseline virtual host, you need to get into the hardware requirements for different virtual guests.

Hardware Requirements for a Gold Virtual Host

The following is a brief overview of how you can measure the hardware requirements for the virtual host and all virtual guests on that host. This section addresses the basic requirements. For details, refer to the documentation for the virtualization technology of your choice. Some of these options were briefly discussed in Chapter 2. As noted in previous chapters, despite the range of options, major Linux distributions are moving toward the Kernel-based Virtual Machine (KVM) system.

Conservatively, a gold virtual baseline includes sufficient RAM, CPU, and hard drive space for the maximum requirements of each component virtual machine. In practice, multiple virtual machines can share RAM and CPU. In other words, because properly configured systems don't normally use all their allocated RAM and CPU, you can effectively configure multiple virtual machines to overbook CPU and RAM.

However, KVM does have the following limits with respect to virtual hosts and guests:

- **Virtual host**—KVM can manage up to 256 CPU cores and 1 TB of physical RAM.
- **Virtual guest**—KVM can support virtual machines with up to 16 CPU cores and up to 256 GB of RAM.

In other words, gold baseline virtual hosts may require a large number of CPUs and a lot of RAM. But such requirements do not necessarily apply to local hard drive storage, as the space required for each virtual guest can be configured on remote storage systems including **network attached storage (NAS)**, **direct attached storage (DAS)**, and **storage area network (SAN)** systems.

To understand "overbooking," consider the following example. Assume you want to configure 10 virtual machine guests that require 512 MB of RAM each. Assume the virtual host requires 1 GB of RAM. In the most heavily loaded situation, that system would require about 6 GB of RAM.

If the virtual guests are properly configured, however, they'll require the maximum amount of RAM only rarely. So it is quite possible that the noted configuration would work on a virtual host with only 4 GB of physical RAM. The hypervisor—also referred to as the virtual machine monitor—supports sharing of available RAM and CPU resources by multiple operating systems. In the rare cases where every virtual machine is at maximum capacity, the virtual host would use configured swap space.

The actual allocation of RAM and other resources to different virtual hosts depends on the service. The behavior of such virtual hosts depends on the demands on that service. So the actual allocation of RAM and other resources to different virtual hosts varies widely.

Once configured, it may be helpful to have a redundant virtual host ready to go in case of hardware failure. After all, if that virtual host is running 10 or more virtual guests, it is a pretty important part of your network.

A Gold Baseline Virtual Guest

As just noted, virtual machines on KVM systems are not subject to severe limits. Once a gold baseline virtual machine is configured, it is relatively easy to use. The data in virtual guests are contained in just a few files in dedicated directories. To use a gold baseline virtual guest, all you need to do is make a copy of the applicable directory. If that virtual guest has been configured with static networking, you'll have to change the IP address, hostname, and other unique information so it doesn't conflict with other virtual guests. But that's it. All you need to do is install and configure the desired service, and it's ready to go.

One question is whether it's appropriate to keep several gold baseline virtual guests, such as for services that require extra disk space and for desktops. Fortunately, it is fairly easy to adjust the number of CPUs allocated to a virtual guest in major virtual machine systems, including KVM.

Service-Specific Gold Baseline Systems

Some services are more mission critical than others. For example, the Web sites associated with electronic commerce are more important than the File Transfer Protocol (FTP) server that may be used to share electronic copies of user manuals. So you may want to configure some service-specific gold baseline systems. That way, you'll be prepared in case a server goes down.

Some gold baseline systems should go beyond a basic operating system. Some services are mission critical to an organization. In such cases, it may be helpful to create a gold baseline, customized for that service. That would be similar to the bastion systems described in Chapter 6.

If there's a security issue that is unrelated to the subject service, some updates may be required, but that should not affect the service. Any associated configuration file should still perform the intended functions. However, the careful administrator will still test the resulting configuration.

If the service was brought down due to a direct security issue, however, additional analysis may be required. For example, Ubuntu Security Notice 612-2 highlighted an issue with the way encryption keys were created from passphrases. Because those encryption keys were vulnerable, administrators of SSH servers had to update their SSH servers and then arrange to regenerate encryption keys for all users.

Trust But Verify Corporate Support

The companies behind Linux distributions have found a way to make money. They sell their expertise. Organizations that purchase this type of expertise can expect some level of support with respect to updates, hardware certification, and certain core applications. Because these are the people who have put together and tested these distributions, they are qualified to help you put their software to work. Given the open source nature of this software, others may have similar levels of expertise. In fact, there are other companies that sell similar levels of support.

Some corporate officers are opposed to using software developed by volunteers. Many of these managers recognize that "free software" requires people with the skills to use such software. If they haven't hired such expertise, they can purchase it through corporate support.

Canonical and Red Hat are not the only companies that provide support for their Linux distributions. For example, not only does Oracle create its own rebuild of RHEL, but that company also sells its own support for its rebuild. Several hardware vendors such as Dell and HP sell servers with different Linux distributions and provide their own support for such. Of course, any number of consulting companies can also provide varying levels of support for your Linux systems.

Because support options are constantly evolving, this section simply summarizes the support options available from Red Hat and Canonical.

Red Hat Support Options

Red Hat support is based on subscriptions. Although reduced-price subscriptions are available—for example, for students and educators—they do not include official Red Hat support. Nevertheless, they do include direct access to downloadable Red Hat installation media along with product updates. All users with subscriptions have access to the Red Hat Network for Web-based administration of their systems, as described in Chapter 11. Other levels of support, which vary, include the following features:

- **Response times**—Red Hat support response times range from one hour to two business days.
- **Hardware certification**—RHEL has been tested and is certified to work with various hardware components and on certain complete systems.
- **Independent Software Vendor (ISV) support**—RHEL has been tested with a variety of applications.
- **Support for open source server applications**—RHEL supports Apache, Samba, the Network File System (NFS), and more.

Red Hat support may also vary with respect to physical and virtual systems. In response to the litigation that surrounds some open source software, Red Hat also includes an Open Source Assurance Program, which promotes the security of your Linux systems from potential lawsuits such as those described in Chapter 1. For more information, see *https://www.redhat.com/details/assurance/*.

Canonical Support Options

To repeat, Canonical is the corporate sponsor of the Ubuntu distribution. As such, it is an organization with an interest in selling support contracts. Canonical offers services for the desktop and the server, with a variety of support options. As discussed in Chapter 11, the company offers Landscape as a Web-based administrative tool. On the desktop, the services offered by Canonical include the following:

- **Windows network access**—Includes configuration of an Ubuntu system as a member of a Microsoft Active Directory
- **Remote desktop configuration**—Supports sharing of a desktop using remote desktop services
- **Desktop virtualization**—Helps the user configure Ubuntu and Microsoft operating systems as virtual machines on an Ubuntu host system

Canonical also offers professional services more directed at the server. Because the literature suggests that Canonical's support is more in the nature of consulting as opposed to a help desk, detailed investigation is left to the reader. For more information on Canonical support options, see *http://www.ubuntu.com/support/services/*.

Some Canonical support contracts are bundled with the sales of certain hardware, such as select systems sold by Dell Computers. For more information, see *http://www.ubuntu.com/dell/*.

Canonical encourages users to take advantage of the open source community. Such "support" is available to anyone who can present their issue and motivate regular users and developers to address that issue. Because this is not paid support, there is no guarantee or warranty associated with any answers that might be received.

Open Source Community Support

There are many excellent Linux users on message boards, mailing lists, chat rooms, and so on who seem to be always online, ready to help. Generally, they'll be more motivated if they know you're addressing a problem in the "real world." However, as Linux is a hobby to most of these users, their time is limited.

If you treat the users on the appropriate Linux forum with dignity and honor, there is no need to fear the occasional "flame war" that may arise. If you do your homework before posing a question, you're more likely to get a better and more complete response.

Before going to the open source community with a question, the following steps are appropriate:

- **Check available documentation**—Much excellent documentation is available online, including on the Web sites run by Ubuntu and Red Hat.
- **Review error messages**—Online sources are filled with tales of others who have encountered an encyclopedia of errors. It's quite possible that someone has already encountered the problems that you're having and has found a solution.
- **Include relevant hardware and software information**—The behavior of some applications may vary depending on whether they are run on a 32-bit or 64-bit system. Sometimes, the problem may be a simple as a missing software package.

If you've paid for corporate support, use it! But the same principles apply when working with consultants and help desk technicians. If you've done your homework as described, it'll show. And if support is paid for on an hourly basis, the time that is saved translates directly to money.

Check Conformance with Security Policies

While it's not necessary to run a full Open Source Security Testing Methodology Manual (OSSTMM) audit every day as discussed in Chapter 1, it can be helpful to audit various activities on a regular basis. For example, you might regularly run the password-cracking tools described in Chapter 13. If such tools discover user passwords in a few minutes, those passwords are most likely to be too simple, subject to easy access by black-hat hackers. The login tools described in Chapter 14 can be used to check the security practices of regular administrators. Of course, the other policies listed in Chapter 14 are important too.

User Security

As a basic audit of user security, refer to the policies described in Chapter 14. The following areas of user behavior should be monitored on a regular basis:

- **Physical access**—If users are limited by workstation, check appropriate logs. Are those users the only ones logging in through that workstation?
- **Internet access**—To regulate where users go online, you need software that checks such access. The open source solution to this issue is Squid, discussed in Chapter 9. This may be subject to privacy limits, depending on those governments and regulatory authorities that apply.
- **E-mail access**—As with Internet access, the inspection of user e-mails may be subject to privacy limits, per any laws and requirements of the jurisdiction of the employee and the server (which may differ).
- **Remote access**—Information on all access via logins should be collected on Linux systems and should be available through commands described in Chapter 14 and related log files.
- **Passwords**—As just suggested, password-cracking tools may be used to check the complexity of user passwords to highlight those users who may not be in compliance with organizational password complexity policies.

Administrator Security

As suggested in Chapter 14, security requirements for administrators should go farther than those for regular users. Because administrators set examples for other users, the basic requirements just described for regular users should be applied more rigorously to administrators. Password complexity is especially important, not only for the regular accounts owned by administrative users but also for the root administrative account.

Regular accounts used by administrators are frequently enhanced with the ability to run the sudo command, as described in Chapter 4. While the importance of the root administrative account password is straightforward, appropriate passwords for the regular account of each administrator is almost as important. If a black-hat hacker can decrypt that password, he or she can use it with the sudo command to run administrative commands.

Administrators generally have access to more systems than ordinary users, including server rooms. Even if that access is just through the SSH service, more rigorous access requirements should reflect the importance of data on those servers:

- **Remote access**—Administrator access over the SSH service and subsequent access to root administrative accounts are normally recorded in log files. Direct remote SSH logins to the root administrative account should also be tracked because such passwords could eventually be decrypted.
- **Physical access**—If physical administrator access to server rooms is also tracked, that can and should also be checked on a regular basis.

Keep the Linux Operating System Up to Date

It's important to keep the Linux operating system up to date, not only for security but also to address any bugs that might arise. The actions taken to address such updates can be classified into three categories, depending on whether they address baseline software, functional bugs, or add new features. Baseline updates relate to the Linux kernel, along with standard commands and libraries. Updates that address software bugs may or may not affect security. If you or your users want new features, it may be appropriate to install new releases of updated software.

But it is important to retain configuration control to make sure you know what is installed on Linux systems on the network. To that end, it's also important to keep related local software repositories up to date. If those repositories are not local, others may install software on their systems without your knowledge. So it is important to keep local repositories up to date with any new packages that you decide should be installed on local systems.

As few enterprises look forward to installing new versions of a Linux distribution, the support levels associated with a distribution release are important. That explains some of the appeal of Ubuntu Long Term Support (LTS) Server Edition and RHEL distribution releases. Canonical has committed to provide security updates for Ubuntu LTS server releases for at least five years. Red Hat has committed to provide similar updates for RHEL releases for at least seven years.

Baseline Updates

Updates of baseline packages are perhaps most important, as they apply to all Linux systems. Any change to baseline packages, especially those related to the Linux kernel, may have wider-ranging effects. It may affect communication between the operating system and local hardware.

If there are third-party packages installed, updates of baseline packages may affect their support status. If such packages were built to the libraries associated with one version of the kernel, such packages may have to be built again. That process may be more difficult to automate.

Functional Bugs

"Bug" is another word for software that doesn't work as it should. Sometimes the bug is purely functional, such as a command that doesn't work as advertised. Sometimes the bug is related to security. Ideally, all updates that address bugs should be installed. Nevertheless, it is possible to prioritize such updates if they can't all be installed.

Updates that address bugs in third-party packages may be another matter. When released by the developers of a service or application, they may not have been fully tested by the developers of a distribution. So the risks associated with such updates may sometimes be greater.

New Releases

Examples of the installation of a new release include the installation of Ubuntu Lucid Lynx on systems where Ubuntu Hardy Heron was previously installed. A more straightforward example is the installation of RHEL 6 on systems where RHEL 5 was previously installed.

New releases include updated software with new features in a number of areas, starting with a new kernel. While updates to the Ubuntu Hardy Heron and RHEL 5 kernels may include backports, they still start from the same kernel source code base. Some feature updates to the kernel and most other applications are not possible unless developers start from a more advanced stock kernel.

Remember, the kernel is the core of the operating system—the way applications communicate with system hardware. When the kernel goes through major changes, tests are always appropriate. While developers do their best to retain compatibility with previous versions, especially with respect to hardware, such compatibility is not always assured.

In addition, any update to the kernel normally means changes to any packages compiled against the previous version of the kernel. Required updates may include the tools used to compile such packages.

If You Choose to Upgrade a Distribution

Upgrades to a newer release of a distribution do not necessarily mean a fresh installation. On Ubuntu systems, once the /etc/apt/sources.list file has been modified to point to a new release, an upgrade is then possible with the apt-get dist-upgrade command. On Red Hat systems, the installation program associated with the installation CD/DVD detects previous existing versions of a distribution and offers to upgrade that existing system.

Distribution upgrades are not as nearly as rigorously tested as new releases. Most beta testers work with new releases on freshly formatted drives. So while a distribution upgrade may save some existing configuration files, administrators who take that route should apply the same rigor as if they were testing a new installation.

In general, upgrades of more than one major version, such as from RHEL 4 to RHEL 6, are not recommended. However, Ubuntu upgrades between LTS editions, such as from Hardy Heron to Lucid Lynx, are more common. Some users continue to upgrade between LTS editions despite the intervening major version releases (Intrepid Ibex, Jaunty Jackalope, Karmic Koala).

Keep Distribution-Related Applications Up to Date

Because the major Linux distributions include applications for both the server and the desktop environment, distribution-related applications fall into both categories. An administrator who is careful about configuration control will limit choice; this can limit risk because it limits the number of potentially compromised software packages that may be installed on a system.

The application releases associated with some distributions may incorporate only security updates and bug fixes. If you or your users need to move to a different version of an application with more functionality, a new release of a distribution may be required.

Server Applications

Linux has made its name as a server operating system. As such, there are excellent groups of developers working on maintaining and improving the whole range of server services.

For example, the highly anticipated release of Samba 4.0 should allow you to configure Linux as a domain controller on a Microsoft Active Directory network. Administrators who adapt such updates may save licensing costs and at the same time make it more difficult for black-hat hackers to penetrate such systems.

Linux administrators have come to expect similar advances on other major servers, from Apache through Squid, from the Secure Shell through Kerberos. When such advances add features or enhance security, you'll want to look at these new applications carefully.

Functional advances in server applications are typically tied to different releases of a Linux distribution. As such, if you want a new feature in a server, you'll have to make a choice: Install a new distribution release or install and compile a new release of a service from source code. Both options add complexity to your configurations. And complexity makes it more difficult for you to keep track of all the security issues that may arise.

Install a New Distribution Release

Hesitation is understandable when a new distribution is released. Such updates can take a lot of work. However, if the upgrade is of a bastion server with a single service, there's no requirement to install a new distribution release for other bastion servers.

Nevertheless, if you install multiple releases of a distribution, that means you'll have to monitor appropriate security lists for news on all installed releases. If you've set up a local set of repositories for one release of a distribution, that means you'd have to set up additional repositories. The effort associated with installing a new distribution release, even on a limited basis, is not trivial.

Install the New Release from Source Code

The developers behind open source services make their source code readily available, at least in tarball format. After all, that's a requirement of all basic open source licenses. Such source code can be compiled and installed on most Linux systems. If you're not ready to upgrade a distribution, that in fact may be the only way to install a new release of a service.

If you choose to compile and install such source code, you'll likely forfeit any support available from the companies that support a distribution. In fact, you'll have to take care to uninstall any older version of the subject service because normal updates could easily overwrite key files for the newer version compiled from source code.

If you get the source code directly from the developers of a service, it will be solely your responsibility to monitor the service for security issues. Every time an update is required, you may need to download and recompile the service again. Additional work may be required if the process is tied to a certain version of the kernel.

In some cases, the developers behind a service provide binary packages in formats suitable for Red Hat and Ubuntu systems. Such packages do not need to be compiled and are easy to install using standard `rpm` and `dpkg` commands. The packages do show up in databases of installed packages. They can even be incorporated into custom repositories. However, such packages face the same issues as compiled source code with respect to support from the companies behind a distribution along with security updates.

Desktop Applications

Sometimes you or users on the network just need that new feature. For example, the relatively recent version release of the OpenOffice.org suite included a number of new features that provided added compatibility with the latest features of the Microsoft Office suite. Likewise, new features in the upcoming release of the GNU Network Object Model Environment (GNOME) 3.*x* may make it a "must have" update for many desktop users.

The issues related to such updates are similar to those just described for server applications. To implement such updates, you'll need to either install a newer release of a Linux distribution or download, compile, and install the new desktop application in question.

A special case with desktop applications relates to the packages of the OpenOffice.org suite. While OpenOffice.org developers make their packages available in binary format, they're still huge. Installations and updates of such packages can easily run into the hundreds of megabytes for every desktop system.

Manage Third-Party Applications Carefully

Third-party applications are not part of a distribution, for various reasons. Sometimes those issues are related to licensing; sometimes they're related to support. While many developers behind third-party applications test their work with major distributions, there are rarely any warranties with respect to truly open source software.

Licensing Issues

There are two sets of issues associated with licensing. First, not all Linux software is open source. Anyone who does not release source code or does not allow others to modify his or her source code cannot use open source licenses. Second, some controversial software packages may pose different sorts of licensing issues.

Non–Open Source Licenses

Open source software is frequently not the same as freeware. In other words, while freeware can be freely provided to the public without cost, the code behind such software can still be proprietary. In contrast, the code behind open source software must be made freely available. Access to the source code via a public Web site or FTP server is an acceptable means to that end.

Open source licenses allow others to modify the source code and release it, as long as they give credit to the original developers. While the DNS software released by Daniel J. Bernstein (djbdns) is a common alternative on Linux systems, it is not open source because Bernstein's license does not allow for its modification.

Sometimes, the distributions associated with open source software may include proprietary components. In its April 2010 Lucid Lynx release, Canonical has chosen to license related coder-decoders (codecs), specifically **H.264** and Moving Pictures Experts Group Phase 1 Audio Layer 3 (MP3). Because neither codec is open source, that decision has led to disappointment in the open source community. Per a May 2010 ZDNet article, the viability of that license depends on how the Lucid Lynx distribution has been installed. Specifically, the Canonical licenses for H.264 and MP3 may not apply for those hardware manufacturers who install the Ubuntu Lucid Lynx release on hardware before putting them on sale.

Software with Different Legal Issues

One reason why the companies behind many Linux distributions do not license certain software components is legal. For example, there are many codecs that can be installed on Linux to read DVDs that are encrypted with the **Content Scramble System (CSS)**. While decryption libraries are commonly available for all Linux distributions, they are generally hosted by third parties on servers in nations where the enforcement of legal restrictions such as the **Digital Millennium Copyright Act (DMCA)** is not as rigorous. For such reasons, most companies that back Linux distributions do not include such packages on their repositories.

Support Issues

The support issues associated with a Linux distribution are best expressed as a function of the repositories associated with an Ubuntu release. As described in Chapter 11, Ubuntu includes universe and multiverse repositories for its releases. These repositories include packages that are not supported by Ubuntu. The difference between the two categories is based on licensing, with open source packages being grouped into the universe repository.

In other words, you may be able to find support for packages in the universe repository from its developers. If research is required, the apt-cache show command can help. For example, the following command provides basic information for the ABINIT scientific computing package:

```
$ apt-cache show abinit
```

In many cases, the output specifies the Web site for package developers along with an e-mail address for package maintainers. If such information is not readily available, it's reasonable to wonder whether the package is suitable for a secure environment.

RHEL supports all the packages in its repositories in one form or another. Many of the packages that may otherwise be found in Ubuntu universe and multiverse repositories can be found as part of the Fedora project, the Red Hat–based community Linux distribution, at *http://www.fedoraproject.org/*.

When Possible, Share Problems and Solutions with the Community

Users who share their issues with the open source community are more likely to get a quick response when they run into problems of their own. While there is no requirement to share any information with developers or other users, the open source community is in many ways like a small-town neighborhood. The users who lend a hand to their neighbors are more likely to get help in their times of need.

Three of the open source communities of interest are developers, users and developers on mailing lists, and users on more generic open source support sites. With so many options, the first question is, where do you turn?

Which Community?

One of the issues with open source software is the difficulties in identifying a responsible party. Be warned: Don't use developer mailing lists unless you are a developer, making a direct contribution to a project. Developers monitor the mailing lists and boards for regular users, so that is where you should direct questions and information. Interested groups of developers and users include the following:

- **The group behind the application**—One might believe that the developers of an application would take responsibility for all problems with that application. But as there are cases where application bugs are limited to one type of Linux distribution, application developers may not be the culprit.

- **The developers of the distribution**—When the companies behind a distribution offer support contracts, they frequently include applications in that contract. When such a contract is not available, users frequently rely on the communities associated with the major Linux distributions.

- **The group behind a graphical user interface (GUI) desktop environment**— More interested groups are the developers behind desktop environments such as the GNU Network Object Model Environment (GNOME) and the K Desktop Environment (KDE). Some applications are bundled with different GUIs.

It's certainly easiest if you can just discuss the issue with the developers of a distribution, especially through a support contract. But that's not affordable for all users.

Share with Developers

In general, the developers behind open source software want to hear about any problems and successes with their software. In many cases, however, they are overwhelmed with requests. In such cases, developers frequently review messages on mailing lists to get a sense of user response to their work.

In addition, the developers behind many applications maintain online bug reporting tools. For Red Hat distributions, the Web site is *https://bugzilla.redhat.com/*. For Ubuntu distributions, the Web site is *https://bugs.launchpad.net/*. The developers behind many applications and services have their own bug reporting tools

In general, developers suggest that you search their databases before reporting a bug. It's quite possible that someone else has encountered the same or a similar problem and has already reported it. If so, you'll get a chance to add an e-mail address to the reporting list to help you monitor the status of the bug.

While the reporting systems vary, you'll generally need the following information to report a bug:

- **Package name/version number**—To find the package name and version associated with a file, you can run the `rpm -qf` or `dpkg -S` commands with the full path to the file.

- **Applicable hardware**—The behavior of a package may vary with different CPUs.

- **A descriptive summary**—Developers behind many distributions have to deal with literally thousands of bug reports. An accurate, descriptive summary can help draw appropriate attention to your problem.

- **Steps to reproduce the bug**—To confirm the problem you're having, developers need to know what happened. If you can document the steps taken to reproduce the bug and you encounter the condition a second time, developers will know that you are serious.

- **Applicable log files**—Error messages frequently appear in log files. It is appropriate to include short excerpts in the main body of a log report. Huge log files should not be copied verbatim. If appropriate, they should be included as an uploaded attachment to the report.

Sometimes, the reported bug is just a misunderstanding. Do not be offended if a developer highlights your bug report as a duplicate of another. If it turns out you made a mistake by creating the bug report, it should be no big deal. However, repeated false bug reports from the same user are frequently noticed. In other words, developers—and other users—are less likely to respond to users who continuously "cry wolf."

Share on Mailing Lists

When sharing a problem on mailing lists, it's helpful to use the same principles as when reporting a bug. Make sure you've done appropriate research. Create a descriptive summary appropriate for a mailing list title. Cite the steps required to reproduce the bug. As applicable, cite the package, version number, and associated hardware.

However, mailing lists are generally not suited for very long log files. Some users may look at the inclusion of all but the most relevant excerpts of a log file as little better than spam.

Be aware, Linux mailing lists may still be a venue for flame wars. It is in some ways a tradition that goes back to the first debates between Linus Torvalds and **Andrew Tannebaum**, the founder of Minix, on the nature of an appropriate kernel for any operating system. However, not all users can manage a flame war as well as Torvalds and Tannebaum, so do not be afraid to walk away. Sometimes, that is the best way to preserve the goodwill of the Linux community.

Red Hat and Ubuntu themselves sponsor mailing lists on a substantial number of topics. For more information, see *https://www.redhat.com/mailman/listinfo/* and *https://lists.ubuntu.com/*. They also sponsor a wide variety of message boards. The basic principles that apply to sharing information on mailing lists also apply to message boards.

Test New Components Before Putting Them into Production

Open source software is excellent. For example, the Apache Web server would not have become dominant on the Internet unless it provided top-notch secure features. Open source developers do their best to test their software with every major combination of hardware and software, within reason. But they can't test every possible combination. And in rare cases, mistakes do happen.

So you should test every update before putting it into production. It can help others if you document the results. One way to jump ahead in the test cycle is to participate in the beta phase of software, before new features are officially released.

One axiom of testing is that you should always keep a version of the existing software configuration. If the testing fails or if a problem arises soon after you put the new or updated component into production, you'll be able to restore the older working configuration.

Test Updates

Especially in mission-critical applications and services, it's important to test new open source software before putting it into production. The same proviso applies even if you're just installing a new version of a software package.

With preproduction testing, it's important to make sure the service or application works as intended. It's important to test the system under simulated production conditions to confirm that the updated software can still handle the demands of your users.

If you've used the application or service before, you may have custom settings or configuration files from the previous version of the software. While developers normally strive to retain backward compatibility, that does not always happen. So if you have custom configuration files for older versions of recently updated software, it's appropriate to test those configuration files. If the new version of the software functions at least as well with the older configuration file, you can install that upgrade on a production system with some confidence. You can then incorporate the new features associated with the upgrade at your convenience.

If you need a new feature—say, an easier way to create a chroot jail for an important service—a beta test period may already be too late to get such a change implemented in the next version of an application or a distribution. If you're willing to contribute code to an important application, good developers will always consider such contributions carefully.

While public participation in open source projects is encouraged—even prized—it is a time-consuming endeavor. But if you have the time, your contributions will lead to benefits in terms of influencing the future direction of development of the prized service.

Document Results

Whatever happens with the update, document the results. That should help you improve the process associated with future updates. Perhaps more important, documentation of the update process can help future administrators work with systems on the local network.

Beta Testing

Beta tests are opportunities for important users like you to influence the development of important software applications. If new features proposed by developers aren't working, you'll get a chance to say so, while it's easier for developers to address the problem. If proposed new features make it less likely that you'll use their application, a beta test is an excellent time to say so.

In general, beta versions of software should never be put into production. By definition, the testing of such software is not complete. However, if a new feature is needed, that's the opportunity for users like you to provide feedback to developers, while they can still implement such changes in upcoming releases.

Future Trends in Linux Security

It is axiomatic that the best defense in Linux security is a layered defense. As such, developers are working toward improvements in every layer of that defense. Three areas in that regard are the development of a new firewall command, which is a successor to `iptables`; additional work on mandatory access control systems, both Security Enhanced Linux (SELinux) and Application Armor (AppArmor); and updates to penetration-testing tools, including the open source `nmap` command.

A New Firewall Command

The `iptables` command was introduced in 2001. While it will help protect Linux systems years into the future, the rules associated with `iptables` have become rather complex. As suggested in Chapter 7, complexity in firewalls can itself be a security flaw.

To address that issue, the original developer of the `iptables` command, Patrick McHardy, is working on a new command, **nftables**. Current plans suggest that it will have the following features:

- **Generic data representation**—Network packets can be classified with a wider array of characteristics.
- **Rules for multiple paths**—Network rules can be created for multiple network destinations.
- **Dictionary mappings**—There will be better support for different ranges of hosts and destinations.
- **Support for both Internet Protocol version 4 (IPv4) and Internet Protocol version 6 (IPv6) addresses**—The `nftables` command will replace both `iptables` and `ip6tables`.

More Mandatory Access Controls

The two relevant mandatory access control systems are SELinux and AppArmor. Development on both is still quite active. While both systems provide additional layers of security to a substantial number of services, they don't cover everything. As SELinux and AppArmor do not work together, they are natural rivals. It is possible that one of these systems will become dominant on future releases of Linux distributions.

Application Armor (AppArmor)

To paraphrase Mark Twain, rumors related to the demise of AppArmor are greatly exaggerated. AppArmor development did suffer when Novell laid off the developers working on that project. However, AppArmor is still the default mandatory access control system for Ubuntu, through the Lucid Lynx release. Current AppArmor development is still active in the Canonical system through Launchpad at *https://launchpad.net/ubuntu/+source/apparmor/*.

Security Enhanced Linux (SELinux)

As for SELinux, the U.S. National Security Agency (NSA) is still taking the lead in the development of this mandatory access control system. For the future, the NSA has a number of stated goals for SELinux, which include the following:

- **Support NFS version 4**—NFS is the one major file-sharing system not yet protected by SELinux.
- **Enhanced policy tools**—Improved policy tools will address the fears that many Linux administrators have with respect to SELinux.
- **Additional driver integration**—Additional tools will be added to support labeling of device drivers and related operations.

These are just a few of the stated goals. In essence, the NSA wants to see SELinux used to protect as much as possible within Linux.

Penetration Testing Tools

The developers behind penetration testing tools such as System Administrators Integrated Network Tool (SAINT) and Nessus, described in Chapter 13, constantly update their databases of security issues. If you subscribe to one of these services and keep up to date with their updates, it'll go a long way toward keeping your networks up to date with the latest security issues.

Of course, the open source command is nmap. "The History and Future of Nmap" at *http://nmap.org/book/history-future.html* suggests developments will center on related scripts, which are described Chapter 9 of Fyodor's book on the subject at *http://nmap.org/book/nse-usage.html*. That book is based on Nmap version 5.0 which is included in both the RHEL 6 and Ubuntu Lucid Lynx releases.

Scripts associated with the nmap command are stored in the /usr/share/nmap/scripts/ directory. Because new scripts are written frequently, you may want to download them from the associated **Subversion** repository, which is different from standard package repositories. One method, as described by one of the nmap developers, David Fifield, is based on the following commands, which download the latest nmap information in the local nmap/ subdirectory. The current list of scripts can be found in the nmap/scripts/ subdirectory.

```
$ svn co --username guest --password
➥ "" svn://svn.insecure.org/nmap
```

If the svn command is not recognized, you'll need to install the subversion package. If you prefer to use the latest nmap software instead of that made available for your distribution release, you can run the ./configure and make commands in the nmap/ subdirectory. The noted command builds its own version of the nmap command in the nmap/ subdirectory. The version available from the nmap Subversion repository may be a beta, so full testing of that release may not be complete.

This may be a case where it makes sense to install a later version of a software package, even a beta, before it's made available for a distribution to help discover security flaws as soon as possible. However, the cautions described earlier in this chapter about third-party software do apply.

Once installed, you can run one of the 100 scripts listed at *http://nmap.org/nsedoc/*, assuming those scripts are available in the aforementioned /usr/share/nmap/scripts/ directory. For example, the following command checks for recursion on the noted Domain Name Service (DNS) server:

```
# nmap --script=dns-recursion 192.168.100.1
```

For more information on various nmap scripts, see Chapter 13.

Single Sign-On

One more important area for development in Linux security is the single sign-on. It's hard enough for regular users to remember one username and password. When they're asked to remember multiple usernames and passwords and then change them frequently, users may revolt.

Linux developers are making progress toward the single sign-on in a number of areas. Most straightforward are the drivers that are available for biometric controls. But Linux also offers a variety of options to provide different levels of privileges.

For example, Red Hat continues to develop more configuration options associated with pluggable authentication modules (PAMs). Easier implementation of Kerberos can help administrators provide secure tickets to appropriate users.

In a heterogeneous environment of Linux and Microsoft operating systems, single sign-ons have required a common LDAP authentication database. When Samba 4.0 is released, that authentication database for both types of operating systems can be configured through a Linux server. Samba will enable Linux to work as an active directory domain controller.

CHAPTER SUMMARY

Best practices help you keep a network going, even through the disruptions associated with a security breach. Of course, it's helpful to keep such breaches to a minimum, and that's a topic for most of the other chapters. To keep a network going, redundancy with gold baselines can support easy replacement of troubled systems. Such baselines must be kept up to date. Specific problems can be addressed through corporate and open source support systems. If you share solutions with the community, they're more likely to respond when you have problems.

To make sure a network is secure, it's important to have regular security audits, including periodic checks of users and administrators between formal audits. Related challenges include updates of services and applications. More difficult challenges involve third-party software.

As for the future, with the `nftables` command, Linux firewalls will be simpler and more flexible. Mandatory access control systems such as SELinux and AppArmor will cover more services and devices. Penetration testing tools will include frequent updates to make sure the tools address the latest security issues. In the open source realm, the `nmap` command will add features through available scripts.

KEY CONCEPTS AND TERMS

nftables

Content Scramble System (CSS)

Direct attached storage (DAS)

Digital Millennium Copyright Act (DMCA)

H.264

Network attached storage (NAS)

Storage area network (SAN)

Subversion

Tannebaum, Andrew

CHAPTER 15 ASSESSMENT

1. Which of the following databases should be updated whenever a gold baseline system is updated with newer packages?

A. MySQL

B. PostgreSQL

C. AIDE

D. LDAP

2. The total RAM requirements of virtual guests can exceed what is available from the virtual host.

A. True

B. False

3. Which command can you use to duplicate a partition by its device file name?

4. Which of the following services is frequently cited as inappropriate for configuration in a virtual guest machine?

A. MySQL

B. Apache

C. Squid

D. DNS

5. Which of the following features of a virtual host supports resource sharing among virtual guests?

A. Multi-core CPUs

B. Virtual machine

C. Hypervisor

D. Networking

6. Which of the following companies provides specific support for the Linux desktop?

A. Canonical

B. Ubuntu

C. Red Hat

D. Apache

7. The OSSTMM methodology is customized for security audits on Linux networks.

A. True

B. False

8. What file must be modified on an Ubuntu system before running a distribution upgrade? Include the full path to the file.

9. Which of the following distributions normally provides security updates for the longest period of time?

A. RHEL

B. Fedora

C. Ubuntu LTS

D. Kubuntu

10. Which of the following software components is *not* open source?

A. GNOME

B. Apache

C. djbdns

D. OpenOffice.org

11. Which of the following commands can provide more information about a package named gimp?

A. apt-cache show gimp

B. apt-cache info gimp

C. apt-cache search gimp

D. apt-cache help gimp

12. Which of the following commands can be used to identify the package that owns the /bin/ls file?

A. dpkg-qf

B. dpkg-i

C. dpkg-S

D. dpkg-V

Answer Key

CHAPTER 1 Security Threats to Linux

1. B 2. C 3. D 4. B 5. A 6. B 7. C 8. D 9. A
10. A and B 11. C 12. D 13. Hacker 14. General Public License
(also acceptable: GPL, GNU GPL, GNU General Public License)

CHAPTER 2 Basic Components of Linux Security

1. D 2. *http://kernel.org* 3. C 4. B 5. A 6. C 7. B
8. D 9. B 10. A 11. B 12. D 13. A 14. C

CHAPTER 3 Basic Security: Facilities Through the Boot Process

1. D 2. C 3. D 4. A and C 5. B 6. A 7. `grub-md5-crypt`
8. B 9. A 10. B 11. C 12. B 13. B and D 14. C

CHAPTER 4 User Privileges and Permissions

1. B 2. B 3. D 4. `find / -group audio` 5. C 6. C and D
7. B 8. `visudo` 9. B 10. A 11. D 12. `/lib/security/`
13. B 14. A and B 15. C

CHAPTER 5 Filesystems, Volumes, and Encryption

1. B and D 2. C 3. A 4. A 5. `gpg --list-keys` 6. C
7. D 8. A 9. C 10. A 11. B 12. B 13. B 14. A
15. `getfacl test1`

CHAPTER 6 Every Service Is a Potential Risk

1. A 2. D 3. B 4. C 5. B 6. D 7. `chkconfig --list`
8. B 9. D 10. `/etc/xinetd.conf` 11. B 12. D 13. C
14. B 15. D

CHAPTER 7 Networks, Firewalls, and More

1. 0 to 1023 2. A 3. C 4. B 5. B 6. D 7. `--dport`
8. B 9. B 10. C 11. D 12. B 13. `sealert -b` 14. B

| CHAPTER 8 | Networked Filesystems and Remote Access |

1. C   2. D   3. GSSAPI (acceptable: generic security services application program interface)   4. B   5. B   6. A   7. C   8. /home/donna/.ssh/ (acceptable: /home/donna/.ssh)   9. A   10. A   11. B   12. A and D   13. A   14. C   15. D

| CHAPTER 9 | Networked Application Security |

1. D   2. B   3. C   4. htpasswd (acceptable: htdigest)   5. A   6. B   7. D   8. A   9. B   10. A   11. imap imaps pop3 pop3s   12. A   13. D   14. B   15. C

| CHAPTER 10 | Kernel Security Risk Mitigation |

1. C   2. D   3. B   4. *http://kernel.org/*   5. A   6. D   7. B   8. C   9. Filesystems   10. D   11. A and C   12. B   13. A

| CHAPTER 11 | Managing Security Alerts and Updates |

1. C   2. A   3. A, C, and D   4. yum   5. D   6. A   7. D   8. D   9. B   10. /etc/yum.conf   11. A   12. A   13. B   14. C   15. C

| CHAPTER 12 | Building and Maintaining a Security Baseline |

1. D   2. C   3. noexec   4. B   5. A   6. C   7. B   8. B   9. mail.=info   10. A   11. B   12. dpkg -l   13. B   14. C   15. B

| CHAPTER 13 | Testing and Reporting |

1. C   2. A   3. telnet 10.12.14.16 25   4. D   5. A   6. C   7. A   8. B   9. /etc/pam.d/login   10. A   11. C   12. B   13. C   14. nc -v 10.12.14.16 25   15. C

| CHAPTER 14 | Detecting and Responding to Security Breaches |

1. A and C   2. B   3. sar   4. C   5. A   6. C   7. A   8. B   9. dd   10. A   11. C   12. A   13. C   14. C

| CHAPTER 15 | Best Practices and Emerging Technologies |

1. C   2. A   3. dd   4. A   5. C   6. A   7. A   8. /etc/apt/sources.list   9. A   10. C   11. A   12. C

Standard Acronyms

3DES	triple data encryption standard	**DMZ**	demilitarized zone
ACD	automatic call distributor	**DoS**	denial of service
AES	Advanced Encryption Standard	**DPI**	deep packet inspection
ANSI	American National Standards Institute	**DRP**	disaster recovery plan
AP	access point	**DSL**	digital subscriber line
API	application programming interface	**DSS**	Digital Signature Standard
B2B	business to business	**DSU**	data service unit
B2C	business to consumer	**EDI**	Electronic Data Interchange
BBB	Better Business Bureau	**EIDE**	Enhanced IDE
BCP	business continuity planning	**FACTA**	Fair and Accurate Credit Transactions Act
C2C	consumer to consumer	**FAR**	false acceptance rate
CA	certificate authority	**FBI**	Federal Bureau of Investigation
CAP	Certification and Accreditation Professional	**FDIC**	Federal Deposit Insurance Corporation
CAUCE	Coalition Against Unsolicited Commercial Email	**FEP**	front-end processor
		FRCP	Federal Rules of Civil Procedure
CCC	CERT Coordination Center	**FRR**	false rejection rate
CCNA	Cisco Certified Network Associate	**FTC**	Federal Trade Commission
CERT	Computer Emergency Response Team	**FTP**	file transfer protocol
CFE	Certified Fraud Examiner	**GIAC**	Global Information Assurance Certification
CISA	Certified Information Systems Auditor	**GLBA**	Gramm-Leach-Bliley Act
CISM	Certified Information Security Manager	**HIDS**	host-based intrusion detection system
CISSP	Certified Information System Security Professional	**HIPAA**	Health Insurance Portability and Accountability Act
CMIP	common management information protocol	**HIPS**	host-based intrusion prevention system
COPPA	Children's Online Privacy Protection	**HTTP**	hypertext transfer protocol
CRC	cyclic redundancy check	**HTTPS**	HTTP over Secure Socket Layer
CSI	Computer Security Institute	**HTML**	hypertext markup language
CTI	Computer Telephony Integration	**IAB**	Internet Activities Board
DBMS	database management system	**IDEA**	International Data Encryption Algorithm
DDoS	distributed denial of service	**IDPS**	intrusion detection and prevention
DES	Data Encryption Standard	**IDS**	intrusion detection system

IEEE	Institute of Electrical and Electronics Engineers
IETF	Internet Engineering Task Force
InfoSec	information security
IPS	intrusion prevention system
IPSec	IP Security
IPv4	Internet protocol version 4
IPv6	Internet protocol version 6
IRS	Internal Revenue Service
(ISC)²	International Information System Security Certification Consortium
ISO	International Organization for Standardization
ISP	Internet service provider
ISS	Internet security systems
ITRC	Identity Theft Resource Center
IVR	interactive voice response
LAN	local area network
MAN	metropolitan area network
MD5	Message Digest 5
modem	modulator demodulator
NFIC	National Fraud Information Center
NIDS	network intrusion detection system
NIPS	network intrusion prevention system
NIST	National Institute of Standards and Technology
NMS	network management system
OS	operating system
OSI	open system interconnection
PBX	private branch exchange
PCI	Payment Card Industry
PGP	Pretty Good Privacy
PKI	public-key infrastructure
RAID	redundant array of independent disks
RFC	Request for Comments
RSA	Rivest, Shamir, and Adleman (algorithm)

SAN	storage area network
SANCP	Security Analyst Network Connection Profiler
SANS	SysAdmin, Audit, Network, Security
SAP	service access point
SCSI	small computer system interface
SET	Secure electronic transaction
SGC	server-gated cryptography
SHA	Secure Hash Algorithm
S-HTTP	secure HTTP
SLA	service level agreement
SMFA	specific management functional area
SNMP	simple network management protocol
SOX	Sarbanes-Oxley Act of 2002 (also Sarbox)
SSA	Social Security Administration
SSCP	Systems Security Certified Practitioner
SSL	Secure Socket Layer
SSO	single system sign-on
STP	shielded twisted cable
TCP/IP	Transmission Control Protocol/Internet Protocol
TCSEC	Trusted Computer System Evaluation Criteria
TFTP	Trivial File Transfer Protocol
TNI	Trusted Network Interpretation
UDP	User Datagram Protocol
UPS	uninterruptible power supply
UTP	unshielded twisted cable
VLAN	virtual local area network
VOIP	Voice over Internet Protocol
VPN	virtual private network
WAN	wide area network
WLAN	wireless local area network
WNIC	wireless network interface card
W3C	World Wide Web Consortium
WWW	World Wide Web

Glossary of Key Terms

COMMANDS

account | A PAM module that can verify account validity based on expiration dates, time limits, or configuration files with restricted users. Also known as account management.

alert | A log priority that specifies problems that require immediate attention.

apparmor_status | An AppArmor command that lists the configured profiles of various commands and services.

apt-cache | A command that searches the current cache of package information. Normally associated with the Ubuntu and Debian Linux distributions.

apt-get | A command normally used to install a package with all dependent packages. Normally associated with the Ubuntu and Debian Linux distributions.

aquota.group | The group quota management file.

aquota.user | The user quota management file.

at | A service for running administrative jobs on a one-time basis; protected by the /etc/at.allow and /etc/at.deny files.

auth | A PAM module that can verify passwords, group memberships, and even Kerberos tickets. Also known as authentication management.

/boot/grub/grub.conf | The main configuration file for GRUB version 1, also known as traditional GRUB.

chage | A command that can modify password-related information for a user, such as the password's expiration date.

chcon | A SELinux command that can be used to change the AVC contexts associated with a file.

chgrp | The command that assigns a new group owner to a file.

chkconfig | A command that manages the scripts that start and stop in different runlevels. Normally associated with the Red Hat and SUSE distributions.

chmod | The command that modifies permissions to a file.

chown | The command that assigns a new user owner to a file.

condrestart | An option frequently available on scripts in the /etc/init.d/ directory. When used, it restarts a service only if it is already running. This is in contrast to the restart option, which restarts a service even if it isn't already running.

cron | A service for running administrative jobs on a regular basis; protected by the /etc/cron.allow and /etc/cron.deny files.

cryptsetup | The command used to encrypt entire partitions using the device mapper.

dbus | A message bus system for interprocess communication between a variety of applications and devices.

dd_rescue | A variation on the dd command that reads data from back to front on a specified partition, volume, or drive. It is more error tolerant than dd.

dd | Known as the disk dump command, it supports a full copy of all data on a partition, volume, or drive.

debsums | A command on Ubuntu and Debian systems that uses the MD5 checksums to see if changes have been made to files relative to their original status as part of installed packages.

debug | The lowest log priority; also provides the greatest detail.

ecryptfs | The command associated with the enterprise cryptographic filesystem.

edquota | The command to check and edit user quotas.

emerg | A log priority that specifies very important messages; may also be shown as `panic` or `crit`.

err | A log priority that adds error messages; may also be shown as `error`.

/etc/fstab | The mount configuration file for Linux filesystems.

/etc/lilo.conf | The main configuration file for the Linux Loader (LILO).

/etc/services | The configuration file that associates Internet services with Transmission Control Protocol/Internet Protocol (TCP/IP) port numbers and protocols.

ext2 | The Linux second extended filesystem.

ext3 | The Linux third extended filesystem; includes journaling.

ext4 | The Linux fourth extended filesystem; includes journaling and support for larger files.

fdisk | One Linux partition configuration tool.

getfacl | The command to review ACL settings for a file.

gpg | The command that can encrypt and add digital signatures to a file.

groupadd | A command that can add a group.

groupdel | A command that can delete a group.

groupmod | A command that can modify the settings of a group in the files of the shadow password suite.

grpquota | The `mount` command option that sets user quotas; often found in `/etc/fstab`.

info | A log priority that adds logging notes at the information level.

iptables | The Linux packet filtering command for firewalls and masquerading. While it is the primary command used for packet filtering firewalls, it can also be used in network address translation.

ldd | A command that lists libraries used by a specified command; its use requires the full path to the target command.

lsof | A command to list open files; the `lsof -ni` lists open files related to networking, in numeric format.

mkfs | The Linux command to format and build a Linux filesystem. It's also a root for filesystem-specific commands such as `mkfs.ext3` and `mkfs.reiserfs`, which set up a filesystem to the given format.

nc | The implementation of the netcat command, which can test and communicate over TCP and UDP connections.

netstat | A command used to verify network connections by port, routing tables by Internet Protocol (IP) address, and more.

nfsnobody | The default account for unauthorized users who connect to the NFS file-sharing server.

nftables | A command being developed to replace `iptables` as a firewall configuration tool.

nmap | A flexible command that can be used to scan Transmission Control Protocol/Internet Protocol (TCP/IP) network communication by protocol and port.

nobody | The default account for users on certain configured file-sharing servers.

notice | A log priority that includes messages that might require attention.

optional | A PAM flag that labels a configuration line that is normally ignored unless there are no other PAM flags in the file.

password | A PAM module that can control changes to user passwords and limit the number of login attempts. Also known as password management.

portmap | The RPC port number mapper, commonly used for services such as NFS and NIS.

/proc/kcore | A file that dynamically represents the contents of RAM on the local system.

quotacheck | A command that creates, checks, and repairs quota management files such as `aquota.user` and `aquota.group`.

reiserfs | The Linux filesystem based on balanced trees, suited for groups of large and small files.

required | A PAM flag that labels a configuration line that must work for the authentication attempt to succeed. However, if the line fails, PAM continues to check the other lines in the file.

requisite | A PAM flag that labels a configuration line that must work for the authentication attempt to succeed. However, if the line fails, PAM immediately returns a failure in the authentication attempt.

root | By itself, root is the name of the standard Linux administrative user. The top-level root directory is symbolized by the forward slash (/). In contrast, the home directory of the root user is /root, which is a subdirectory of the top-level root directory (/).

rsync | A command that synchronizes files from one location to another; may be used in conjunction with SSH.

secon | A SELinux command that returns the context settings of a specified file or directory.

session | A PAM module that can control mounting and logging. Also known as session management.

sestatus | A SELinux command that returns the overall status of SELinux on the local system.

setfacl | The command to create or modify ACL settings for a file.

sg | A command that can connect with the privileges of another group. Requires a group password in /etc/gshadow.

smb.conf | The main configuration file for the Samba/CIFS file server.

sshd | The daemon for the SSH service.

strace | A command that traces the system calls used by another command; primarily used for troubleshooting.

su | A command that can connect with the privileges of another user. Requires the password of the target user. When no target user is specified, the root administrative user is assumed.

sudo | A command that can connect as the administrative user if authorization is configured in /etc/sudoers.

sufficient | A PAM flag that labels a configuration line. If the line works, PAM immediately returns a success message in the authentication attempt.

syslog | The system log message service, associated with the syslogd daemon. When combined with the kernel log daemon, known as klogd, it is sometimes shown as the sysklogd daemon.

sysstat | A package that tracks the RAM and CPU usage on a system, with the help of the cron service.

tpm-tools | The Linux package with management tools for the trousers package, associated with the Trusted Computing Software Stack and the TPM chip.

trousers | The Linux package associated with the Trusted Computing Software Stack, in support of the TPM chip.

update-rc.d | A command that manages the scripts that start and stop in different runlevels. Normally associated with the Ubuntu and Debian Linux distributions.

useradd | A command that can add a user.

userdel | A command that can delete a user.

usermod | A command that can modify the settings of a user in the files of the shadow password suite.

usrquota | The mount command option that sets user quotas; often found in /etc/fstab.

vsftpd.conf | The main configuration file for the very secure FTP daemon service.

w | A command that lists currently logged in users and the process currently being run by that user.

warn | A log priority that provides warning messages; may also be shown as warning.

who | A command that lists currently logged in users.

xfs | The Linux filesystem developed by Silicon Graphics suited to larger files.

yum | Short for Yellowdog Updater, Modified. A command that can install packages with all dependent packages.

A

Access vector cache (AVC) | An access permission associated with SELinux.

Access control lists (ACLs) | In Linux, access control lists allow authorized users to set the permissions associated with a file or directory. Those permissions can supersede standard discretionary access controls.

Access vector | In security, an access permission represented by a bitmap; commonly stored for SELinux security in an access vector cache.

Advanced Encryption Standard (AES) | An encryption standard configured by the National Institute of Standards and Technology (NIST).

Advanced Intrusion Detection Environment (AIDE) | An intrusion detection system; available in both Red Hat and Ubuntu repositories.

Anaconda | The Red Hat installation program.

Andrew Filesystem (AFS) | A distributed network filesystem, sometimes associated with Kerberos tokens.

Andrew Tannebaum | *See* Tannebaum, Andrew.

Apache | A Web server service used primarily on Linux. Apache is currently the most popular Web service on the Internet.

Application Armor (AppArmor) | A mandatory access control system used to create security profiles for different programs. Uses Linux security modules in the kernel. Not compatible with SELinux.

Architecture | In the context of computing, a reference to the type of CPU, such as i386 for 32-bit Intel and AMD systems.

Asterisk | The open source private branch exchange (PBX) VoIP service.

Authentication Header (AH) protocol | A protocol that guarantees integrity and data-origin authentication of network packets.

Authenticity | A Parkerian hexad concept related to the CIA triad concept of integrity. Authenticity can help users and administrators verify that important communications, such as messages, are genuine.

Availability | A CIA triad concept in which users have access to their data when they want it.

AVG | A company that creates anti-malware systems for Linux and other operating systems.

B

Backport | A feature from a future version of a software component that is incorporated into an update of an earlier release. Backports are commonly applied to kernels with a certain version number to incorporate additional features without overriding any sort of certification of third-party software related to that kernel.

Backport | In the context of the kernel, an incorporated feature from a later kernel.

BackTrack | A Linux distribution currently based on Ubuntu with penetration testing tools, released in live CD and live USB format. Available from *http://www.backtrack-linux.org/*.

Backup Domain Controller (BDC) | A backup for a PDC on a Microsoft Windows NT domain; Linux with Samba can be configured as a BDC.

Baseboard management controller (BMC) | An interface often embedded in the motherboard. In some cases, it may be configured to allow remote access to the system boot menus.

Basic Input/Output System (BIOS) | The first thing that's run when you power up an older computer. The BIOS identifies and tests connected hardware to a point where an operating system can be loaded from media such as a hard drive.

Bastion server | A secured host dedicated for a specific purpose. It is configured with a minimal number of services to limit its exposure to attacks.

Berkeley Internet Name Domain (BIND) | The most common DNS server on the Internet, originally created at the University of California at Berkeley, maintained by the Internet Systems Consortium.

Berkeley Standard Distribution (BSD) | A clone of UNIX, similar to Linux, released under different licenses.

Binary kernel | When the source code of a kernel is compiled in an installable package, it is changed from a human-readable format to a binary format readable only by a computer.

Biometric controls | Identification controls based on unique characteristics of authorized personnel. May be used for authentication to access a secure location such as a server room.

Black-hat hacker | A user who wants to break into computer systems and networks with malicious purposes in mind.

Bootstrap Protocol (BOOTP) | A protocol of the Transmission Control Protocol/Internet Protocol (TCP/IP) suite associated with automatic assignment of IP addresses; may also be used for the automatic acquisition of IP addresses from a Dynamic Host Configuration Protocol (DHCP) server on a remote network. Associated with UDP port 68.

Bugzilla | A Web-based bug-tracking and management tool commonly used on open source projects from Red Hat to the GNOME desktop environment.

C

Cache poisoning | A frequently malicious insertion of non-authoritative DNS data as if it were authoritative. May be used by black-hat hackers to redirect users to malicious Web sites.

CAINE | Short for Computer Aided Investigative Environment, a bootable live CD distribution available from *http://www.caine-live.net/*.

Canonical | The private company that is the corporate backer of the Ubuntu distribution.

CentOS | Short for the Community Enterprise Operating System, CentOS is sometimes known as a rebuild. This is because it is a distribution built by third parties, based on source code released for the Red Hat Enterprise Linux distribution.

Certificate authority (CA) | An entity such as VeriSign or GoDaddy that issues digital certificates for use by other parties. Secure Web sites without an official CA return an error message.

Certified Information Systems Security Professional (CISSP) | A vendor-neutral certification for information security created by (ISC)^2 that requires professional experience in multiple security domains.

Chain of trust | A sequence of programs that may be verified by the TPM. One Linux program in the chain of trust is TrustedGRUB.

Challenge-Handshake Authentication Protocol (CHAP) | A protocol for validating users before allowing access, which includes a challenge to verify the identity of a user.

Challenge-response authentication mechanism (CRAM) | A group of protocols where a service such as open source sendmail presents a challenge such as a request for a username and password.

Chroot jail | One type of operating-system–level virtualization. When a program or service routes clients to a directory, a chroot jail limits the risks to the system. In most cases, a chroot jail includes all of the binaries, libraries, configuration files, and executables required to run a service that is so contained.

CIA triad | The CIA triad specifies three goals of information security: confidentiality, integrity, and availability.

Clam AntiVirus (ClamAV) | A cross-platform antivirus software toolkit developed for and used on Linux, BSD, and derivatives of UNIX.

Cobbler project | An open source project for network-based installations of Linux distributions.

Common UNIX Printing System (CUPS) | The default print service for most modern Linux distributions. By default CUPS uses the Internet Print Protocol (IPP), but it can also administer with printers in a number of other protocols.

Common Vulnerabilities and Exposures (CVE) list | A list of operating-system security issues maintained by the MITRE corporation and sponsored by the National Cyber Security Division of the U.S. Department of Homeland Security.

Communications Security (COMSEC) | COMSEC is one of the ISECOM channels for security audits.

Confidentiality | A CIA triad concept associated with keeping private information private. It is often regulated by law.

Content Scramble System (CSS) | A Digital Rights Management (DRM) scheme used to encrypt commercial DVDs.

Cracker | In the open source community, a cracker is a malicious user who wants to break into a computer system.

Cyrus | An e-mail server developed at Carnegie-Mellon University, primarily for IMAP version 4 e-mail delivery.

D

Daniel J Bernstein's DNS (djbdns) | A relatively light-weight DNS server alternative to BIND. It is released under a public-domain license, which is not open source.

Default runlevel | The group of services and daemons started by default when Linux is booted. Other services and daemons are started in other runlevels. If Linux is already running, a move to the default runlevel may also stop other services and daemons.

DEFT | Built on Ubuntu Linux, DEFT includes a number of live tools for recovering data from live Microsoft operating systems, available from *http:// www.deftlinux.net/*.

Demilitarized zone (DMZ) | An area of a network that is protected from the Internet by one layer of firewalls. The main network is further protected from this area by a second layer of firewalls.

Denial of service (DoS) attack | An attack based on overloading a network service, denying access to regular users. Not all DoS attacks are malicious, as they can be accidental results of certain types of connection attempts. Nevertheless, they should be blocked or slowed down as if they were attacks.

Dependency hell | A colloquial description of one type of error message related to the attempted installation of a package with the `rpm` or `dpkg` command. The installation is not completed because the package depends on another. Dependency hell occurs when dependencies descend to another level.

Digital Millennium Copyright Act (DMCA) | A U.S. copyright law associated with digital intellectual property. Controversial in part because of fears of prosecution by researchers looking for better forms of encryption. One intent is to prevent the decryption of systems encoded with DRM schemes.

Direct attached storage (DAS) | A storage system connected directly to one or more computer systems using cables; unlike NAS, DAS systems do not use network protocols to share data.

Discretionary access control | A security control system that limits access to objects such as files and directories to specified users and groups. Discretionary access control may be modified by authorized users.

Disk encryption subsystem | The system used to encrypt partitions and disks. Part of the device mapper and associated with the loadable `dm_crypt` module.

Domain Name System (DNS) | A hierarchical database of domain names and Internet Protocol (IP) addresses. Two major DNS services on Linux are BIND and djbdns.

Dovecot | An open source e-mail service, designed for regular and secure versions of the POP and IMAP protocols.

DSA | Short for Digital Signature Algorithm, originally used by the U.S. government for digital signatures.

E

Electronic Frontier Foundation (EFF) | The Electronic Frontier Foundation (EFF) is a self-described "donor-funded nonprofit" created to protect the digital rights of consumers.

Elgamal | A probabilistic encryption scheme developed by Taher Elgamal (also spelled ElGamel).

Encapsulating Security Payload (ESP) protocol | An encryption protocol that normally provides authenticity, integrity, and confidentiality protection of network packets.

enterprise cryptographic filesystem (eCryptfs) | A system adapted by Ubuntu to encrypt directories; uses the `ecryptfs` command.

Eric Raymond | *See* Raymond, Eric.

Exim | The open source SMTP server developed by the University of Cambridge. The default MTA for Debian systems.

Extended internet super server | A server that listens for requests on multiple ports on behalf of multiple services. As a single daemon, it saves resources. The term "internet" is normally shown in lowercase, as it refers to an interconnected series of networks, not the Internet. Its configuration file is `/etc/xinetd.conf`. That file normally refers to service-specific files in the `/etc/xinetd.d/` directory.

Extra Packages for Enterprise Linux (EPEL) | An open source project to create packages over and above those available for Red Hat Enterprise Linux; may include functional backports from later versions of Fedora Linux.

F

Fedora Linux | The Linux operating system developed by the Fedora Project and sponsored by Red Hat.

File Transfer Protocol (FTP) | A standard protocol and service for exchanging files.

Filesystem | A protocol for organizing and storing files. Most filesystems require a format; typical filesystem formats include ext2, ext3, ext4, reiserfs, and xfs.

Filesystem Hierarchy Standard (FHS) | The way files and directories are organized in Linux. The FHS includes a list of standard directories and the types of files normally stored in those directories.

Free Software Foundation (FSF) | The organization behind the GNU project.

G

Generic security services application program interface (GSSAPI) | An application programming interface that accommodates communication primarily between Kerberos and services such as NFS.

GNOME Display Manager (GDM) | A graphical login manager built by the developers of the GNOME Desktop Environment. May be used to log into graphical desktop environments other than GNOME.

GNU Compiler Collection (GCC) | An open source compiler system that supports a variety of programming languages, including C, Java, and Fortran.

GNU General Public License (GPL) | One of several open source licenses used to share the source code for software.

GNU Privacy Guard (GPG) | The open source implementation of PGP, developed by the GNU Foundation.

GNU's Not Unix (GNU) | A recursive acronym for the work of the GNU Foundation, including the clones of UNIX tools and libraries found in current Linux distributions.

Gordon "Fyodor" Lyon | *See* Lyon, Gordon "Fyodor."

Gramm-Leach-Bliley Act (GLBA) | A U.S. law that specifies confidentiality requirements for personal financial data.

Grand Unified Bootloader (GRUB) | The default boot loader for Ubuntu, Red Hat, and many other Linux distributions. Two versions of GRUB are in common use, with different options for security.

Graphical desktop environment | In Linux, the graphical desktop environment is separate from but requires the use of an X Window System Server. It may also include a window manager to control the placement of windows within that GUI. Two common Linux graphical desktop environments are GNOME and KDE.

Graphical login manager | A service for graphical logins to a Linux GUI. Three standard Linux graphical login managers are GDM, KDM, and XDM.

Greg Kroah-Hartman | *See* Kroah-Hartman, Greg.

Group ID (GID) | The number associated with a group name in Linux, as defined in /etc/group and /etc/gshadow.

GRUB 2.0 | A newer version of the Grand Unified Bootloader (GRUB), not yet in use on many Linux distributions.

H

H.264 | A proprietary video-compression standard licensed by Canonical for use in the Lucid Lynx release of Ubuntu.

Hacker | In the open source community, a hacker just wants to create better software. The open source community definition of hacker is closer to white-hat hacker. Do not confuse this definition with the non–open source security community definition of hacker, which is closer to black-hat hacker.

Hardy Heron (8.04) | The name of the Ubuntu distribution released in April of 2008 with long-term support.

Hash function | A one-way function that converts a large amount of data to a single (long) number in an irreversible manner.

Health Insurance Portability and Accountability Act (HIPAA) | A U.S. law that specifies security requirements for personal health data.

Honeypot | A honeypot is a computer system designed to detect attempts by black-hat hackers to break into a network. It includes data that appears to be of value. It is carefully monitored, and isolated from other systems on the local network.

Hydra | A password tool designed to identify passwords that are too simple for a secure system.

I

Inode | A data structure associated with a file.

Institute for Security and Open Methodologies (ISECOM) | The organization associated with open source security certification and testing. ISECOM qualifies security professionals with four certifications: OSPA, OSPE, OSPT, and OWPE.

Institute of Electrical and Electronics Engineers (IEEE) | A professional organization of electrical and electronics engineers; also the group behind standards such as 802.11 for wireless communication.

Integrated Services Digital Network (ISDN) | A group of standards for digital transmission of voice and data over the public switched telephone network.

Integrity Measurement Architecture (IMA) | A Linux security module developed by IBM to check the integrity of executable files before they're loaded during the boot process.

Integrity | A CIA triad concept of trust, verified by means such as GPG keys.

Inter-Cache Protocol (ICP) | A protocol used for communications between Web proxy servers such as Squid.

International Information Systems Security Certification Consortium (ISC)² | An organization for security professionals. (ISC)² qualifies professionals through the SSCP and CISSP certifications.

Internet Assigned Numbers Authority (IANA) | The organization responsible for domain names, IP addresses, and Transmission Control Protocol/Internet Protocol (TCP/IP) protocols on the Internet.

Internet Control Message Protocol (ICMP) | Part of the Transmission Control Protocol/Internet Protocol (TCP/IP) suite of protocols, ICMP is a protocol normally used to send error and network status messages. The `ping` command also uses ICMP; it can be used to test a connection to a remote system.

Internet Key Exchange (IKE) protocol | A protocol for key exchange used to set up a security association between different systems.

Internet Message Access Protocol version 4 (IMAP4) | An application layer e-mail protocol that supports client access to remote servers.

Internet Protocol Security (IPSec) | A member of the Transmission Control Protocol/Internet Protocol (TCP/IP) protocol suite that supports encrypted IP connections.

Internet Protocol version 4 (IPv4) | A version of the Internet Protocol still in common use today. IPv4 addresses use 32 bits.

Internet Protocol version 6 (IPv6) | A more recent version of the Internet Protocol in common use today. IPv6 addresses use 128 bits.

Internet super server | A server that listens for requests on multiple ports on behalf of multiple services. As a single daemon, it saves resources. The term "internet" is normally shown in lower case, as it refers to an interconnected series of networks, not the Internet. Its configuration file is `/etc/inetd.conf`, and it's controlled by either the `openbsd-inetd` or `inetutils-inetd` service scripts in the `/etc/init.d/` directory. While it's obsolete on most distributions, it is still used by some third-party software.

iSeries | An IBM system that uses IBM Performance Optimization With Enhanced RISC (POWER) CPUs.

Itanium | A family of 64-bit CPUs developed by Intel. Red Hat has supported Itanium CPUs through Red Hat Enterprise Linux 5, but will not continue support in later releases.

J

Java Cryptography Extension (JCE) | A framework for encryption associated with the Java programming language; may also be used with open source sendmail.

John the Ripper | A password tool designed to identify passwords that are too simple for a secure system.

Journaled filesystem | Refers to a filesystem that keeps track of changes to be written. Recovery tools can then use the journal to quickly find data on files to be written.

K

Kaspersky | A company that creates anti-malware systems for Linux and other operating systems.

KDE Display Manager (KDM) | A graphical login manager built by the developers of KDE. May be used to log into graphical desktop environments other than KDE.

Kerberos | A computer network authentication protocol. Developed at MIT as part of project Athena, it allows clients to prove their identities to each other with secure tickets.

Kerberos principal | An identity associated with Kerberos tickets. It includes the user, the Kerberos administrator, and the realm.

Kerberos realm | Typically, the name of the domain for the LAN or enterprise network, in upper-case letters.

Kerberos Telnet | A version of the Telnet server that can use Kerberos tickets to enhance security.

Kerberos ticket | The "proof" on one system that verifies the identity of a second system.

Kernel | The core component of the operating system, which supports communication between applications and hardware.

Kernel-based Virtual Machine (KVM) | A virtual machine monitor. On Linux systems, it requires a specialized kernel module. Supports hardware virtualization and paravirtualization.

Kernel-space | Refers to tools that depend on drivers and modules loaded with the Linux kernel.

Kickstart | A network-based installation system first created for Red Hat distributions.

Knoppix | Knoppix is a Linux distribution most well known for its live CDs and DVDs.

Knoppix STD | A Linux distribution currently based on Knoppix with a variety of security testing tools, released in live CD format.

Kroah-Hartman, Greg | The Linux kernel developer responsible for the release of stable kernels.

Kubuntu | A release of the Ubuntu distribution that includes the KDE desktop environment as the default GUI.

L

LAMP stack | LAMP is an acronym associated with Web services. The first three letters stand for Linux, Apache, and MySQL. The last letter may stand for Perl, Python, or PHP. The LAMP stack is a system where these services are integrated.

Landscape | A system management tool available from Canonical for managing and updating clients associated with the Ubuntu distribution.

Launchpad | Developed by Canonical, Launchpad is a platform for bug tracking, open source software development, and more.

Lightweight Directory Access Protocol (LDAP) | A directory service for network-based authentication. LDAP communication can be encrypted.

Linus Torvalds | *See* Torvalds, Linux.

Linux distribution | A unified collection of applications, services, drivers, and libraries configured with a Linux kernel.

Linux kernel | The core of the Linux operating system. Different Linux kernels are in effect different operating systems. The Linux kernel includes a monolithic core and modular components.

Linux Kernel Organization | A nonprofit group established to distribute the Linux kernel and other open source software. Developers of Linux distributions start with this kernel. Linus Torvalds releases new versions of the Linux kernel through the Linux Kernel Organization at *http://kernel.org*.

Linux Loader (LILO) | An alternative Linux boot loader. It is a legacy boot loader for many Linux distributions.

Linux patch management | The system of package updates on the Linux operating system.

Linux Professional Institute (LPI) | A nonprofit organization that sponsors Linux certification exams.

Linux security modules (LSMs) | A framework for security support within the Linux kernel, associated with mandatory access control. Examples of LSMs include SELinux and AppArmor.

Linux unified key setup (LUKS) | A disk encryption specification that requires the `dm_crypt` module.

Live CD | May refer to a CD or DVD with a bootable operating system. That same data may also be loaded on a USB drive. Several Linux distributions are available in live CD format. When loaded, it provides password-free root administrative access to the system.

Lucid Lynx (10.04) | The name of the Ubuntu distribution released in April of 2010 with long-term support.

Lyon, Gordon "Fyodor" | A prominent white-hat hacker. Developer of the nmap command. Known in the open source security community by the single name "Fyodor."

M

Mail delivery agent (MDA) | Related to servers such as Dovecot that facilitate the delivery of e-mail to user clients.

Mail retrieval agent (MRA) | Associated with servers that collect e-mail from networks, such as fetchmail.

Mail submission agent (MSA) | Related to servers that authenticate user connections to e-mail services. Frequently integrated into MTAs such as sendmail and Postfix.

Mail transfer agent (MTA) | Associated with servers that transmit e-mail, such as sendmail and Postfix.

Mail user agent (MUA) | Associated with client e-mail applications such as Evolution and Thunderbird.

Main repository | A reference to the Ubuntu repositories of supported open source software.

Mandatory access control | A security control system that limits access to objects such as files and directories to specified users and groups. Mandatory access control may be modified only by authorized administrators. Examples of systems implementing mandatory access control include SELinux and AppArmor.

Mandriva | A Linux distribution based in France and Brazil.

Mangled | Describes a network packet with modified headers.

Martian packet | A packet with an impossible source or destination address. For example, a packet from the Internet with a source address of a private Internet Protocol (IP) address network would be a Martian packet.

Masquerading | A reference to network address translation where private Internet Protocol (IP) addresses on a network masquerade with a public IP address, normally of the gateway to the network.

Master browser | A system assigned to maintain a database of NetBIOS names and their services such as domain or workgroup membership.

Master Key Linux | A live CD distribution that incorporates the tools associated with the Sleuth Kit.

Message Digest 5 (MD5) | A cryptographic hash function with a 128-bit hash value. Also used to encrypt local Linux passwords in the /etc/shadow file.

Meta package | A Linux package that refers to other packages. For example, linux-image is a meta-package that refers to the latest version of the generic kernel built for Ubuntu.

Modular kernel | A kernel with components that are loaded during the boot process. Loaded components depend on detected hardware, configuration files, and more.

Monolithic kernel | A kernel with components that are loaded during the boot process. Loaded components depend on detected hardware, configuration files, and more.

Multicast Domain Name Service (mDNS) protocol | Supports automated Internet Protocol (IP) addressing without a Dynamic Host Configuration Protocol (DHCP) server. Related to Microsoft's automatic private IP addressing and Apple's Bonjour protocols. Communicates using both TCP and UDP over port 5353.

Multi-Processing Modules (MPMs) | Modules used to add functionality to the Apache Web server.

Multiverse repository | A reference to the Ubuntu repositories of unsupported software released under restricted licenses.

MySQL | The open source database program, currently owned by Oracle.

N

Nessus | A vulnerability scanning program with a Web-based interface, based on code that was previously released under open source licenses.

netcat | A utility that can read TCP and UDP packets, normally associated with the nc command.

Network Address Translation (NAT) traversal protocol | A method of enabling IPSec-protected IP datagrams to pass through network address translation.

Network attached storage (NAS) | A storage system connected to a network, normally using file-sharing protocols such as NFS and Samba.

Network Basic Input/Output System (NetBIOS) | A name for a computer system, commonly assigned on Microsoft-style networks; associated with the session layer of the OSI model.

Network File System (NFS) | A file-sharing service originally developed for UNIX.

Network Information Service (NIS) | A directory service for network-based authentication. Its database can be created from the files of the shadow password suite.

Network Security Toolkit | A Linux distribution currently based on Fedora with a variety of security testing tools, including many of those listed at *http://sectools.org/*. Released in live CD format.

Network Time Protocol (NTP) | A protocol and service for synchronizing clocks over a network.

Nonprivileged user | An account with standard end-user operating system permissions. This type of user does not have administrative permissions that would be found with a superuser, root., or administrative account.

O

Online Certificate Status Protocol (OCSP) | A protocol and server to search for revoked digital certificates.

Open Source Security Testing Methodology Manual (OSSTMM) | A manual for security audits, testing, and analysis, created through ISECOM.

Open source | A development practice in which source code is released publicly. Open source licenses allow others to use and even improve upon that same source code, as long as they give credit to the original developers. The GNU General Public License (GPL) is one open source license.

Open Systems Interconnection (OSI) | A model of networking similar to the Transmission Control Protocol/Internet Protocol (TCP/IP) protocol suite. While the OSI model has seven layers, the TCP/IP protocol suite has four layers.

Open Trusted Computing (OpenTC) | A consortium of security professionals and organizations sponsored by the European Union. ISECOM is working through OpenTC to modify standards for the TPM chip.

OSSTMM Professional Security Analyst (OSPA) | A certification sponsored by ISECOM for professionals who can assess legal requirements, design security tests, and measure controls in the context of the scientific method.

OSSTMM Professional Security Expert (OSPE) | A certification sponsored by ISECOM for entry-level security professionals.

OSSTMM Professional Security Tester (OSPT) | A certification sponsored by ISECOM for Linux professionals qualified to use various security programs.

OSSTMM Professional Wireless Security Expert (OWSE) | A certification sponsored by ISECOM for professionals who can audit a wireless network infrastructure.

Owner override | A feature requested by the EFF for inclusion in TPM chips that would enable fine-grained control over its use.

P

Paravirtualized | A reference to paravirtualization, a software interface that is similar to the underlying hardware. May require a special kernel.

Parkerian hexad | Supplements the CIA triad goals of confidentiality, integrity, and availability with three more goals: possession or control, authenticity, and utility.

Passphrase | A sequence of characters used to control access, frequently used to verify connections to encrypted services such as SSH. Unlike passwords, passphrases can include spaces. As such, the best passphrases consists of a sequence of words and numbers with upper and lower case characters along with punctuation.

Password Authentication Protocol (PAP) | A protocol for validating users before allowing access.

Patch | In the context of the Linux kernel, a patch is an incremental upgrade to the Linux kernel.

Perl | A dynamic scripting language developed by Larry Wall; frequently used with Apache for Web sites.

Phishing | An attempt to get users to reveal sensitive information such as usernames, credit-card numbers, and more, often through a spoofing attack.

PHP: Hypertext Preprocessor (PHP) | A scripting language associated with dynamic Web sites; frequently used with Apache.

Physical Security (PHYSSEC) | PHYSSEC is one of the ISECOM channels for security audits.

Ping of death | A malicious packet of ICMP data to a system that may be used to crash a target computer system.

Ping storm | A condition where a system sends a flood of ICMP packets to a server. May be created with the `ping -f` command.

Pluggable authentication modules (PAMs) | For Linux, PAM is a series of configuration files that provide dynamic authentication for administrative and other services.

PolicyKit | Supports fine-grained control administrative tools from regular accounts. The focus of the PolicyKit is on the GNOME desktop environment.

Possession or control | A Parkerian hexad concept for control of confidential information.

Post Office Protocol version 3 (POP3) | An application layer e-mail protocol that supports e-mail client downloads of incoming messages.

Postfix | An open source SMTP server originally developed at IBM. It's designed to be simpler than sendmail.

PostgreSQL | An open source database program, sponsored by a variety of open source and other IT companies.

Pre-boot eXecution Environment (PXE) | A feature of a network card and a BIOS/UEFI system that gives a system the ability to boot an operating system from a remote location.

Pretty Good Privacy (PGP) | A program that encrypts messages and more with digital signatures based on private and public encryption keys. First, the sender can use a private PGP key to encrypt a message; then the recipient(s) can use a public PGP key to decrypt that message.

Primary Domain Controller (PDC) | A master server on a Microsoft Windows NT domain that controls and can grant access to a number of computer resources based on the usernames and passwords in its database. Linux with Samba can be configured as a PDC.

Pro File Transfer Protocol daemon (ProFTPd) | A popular FTP server with a basic configuration file similar to the Apache Web server; supports multiple virtual FTP servers.

Process Identifier (PID) | A number associated with the process running on a Linux system. The PID of currently running processes can be found with the `ps` command.

Protocol analyzer | Colloquially known as a sniffer, a protocol analyzer can listen in on messages transmitted on a network. One Linux protocol analyzer is Wireshark.

pSeries | The IBM Reduced Instruction Set Computing (RISC) server and workstation product line designed for UNIX systems; some Red Hat Enterprise Linux releases are built for the pSeries.

Public switched data network (PSDN) | A reference to the current digital telephone network.

Public switched telephone network (PSTN) | A reference to the regular telephone network for voice communications.

Pure File Transfer Protocol daemon (Pure-FTPd) | An actively supported server that can run 100 percent with non-root accounts.

Python | A multi-paradigm programming language frequently used with Apache for Web sites.

Q

Qmail | The self-declared replacement for sendmail, developed by Daniel J. Bernstein, who also developed djbdns.

R

RainbowCrack | A password tool designed to identify passwords that are too simple for a secure system.

Raymond, Eric | A leader of the open source movement. Author of *The Cathedral and the Bazaar*. Also cofounder of the open source initiative at *http://www.opensource.org/*.

Real-time Transport Protocol (RTP) | A standard packet format for VoIP and video communications.

Rebuild | A Linux distribution built from the source code released by another distribution. For example, because CentOS uses Red Hat source code, CentOS Linux is a rebuild of Red Hat Enterprise Linux.

Recursive query | A search of a DNS database that is sent to other DNS servers if the information is not available locally.

Red Flag Linux | A Linux distribution developed in China.

Red Hat | The company behind the leading Linux distribution in the marketplace.

Red Hat Bugzilla | A system for bug reports on Red Hat distributions.

Red Hat Network (RHN) | A group of systems management services to manage packages, administer scripts, and more. Such services may be applied to subscribed clients and servers on a network.

Red Hat Network Proxy Server | A proxy server dedicated to caching downloaded packages from the Red Hat Network.

Red Hat Satellite Server | A version of the Red Hat Network designed for local use on an enterprise network; includes an embedded Oracle database.

Red Hat security advisories (RHSAs) | Announcements of security issues from the Red Hat Security Team.

Remote Authentication Dial In User Service (RADIUS) | A system for remote user authentication, frequently used to authenticate connections over telephone modems.

Restricted repository | A reference to the Ubuntu repositories of software released under restricted licenses.

Richard Stallman | *See* Stallman, Richard.

Root Trust for Measurement (RTM) | Part of a Trusted Computing concept, known as the roots of trust. The core RTM may reside in the first boot program, the BIOS or UEFI.

Root Trust for Reporting (RTR) | Part of a Trusted Computing concept, known as the roots of trust. The RTR reports on the integrity of a software component using SHA-1 keys.

Root Trust for Storage (RTS) | Part of a Trusted Computing concept, known as the roots of trust. The RTS uses an endorsement key created by the TPM to store data implicitly trusted by the operating system.

Rootkit | A specialized type of malware that enables a black-hat hacker to take root administrative access of a Linux system.

RSA | A public-key encryption algorithm, named for its developers, Rivest, Shamir, and Adleman.

RSyslog | The latest system for system and kernel logs; also supports secure transmission of log information to a central logging server.

Runlevel | A mode of operation in Linux associated with a group of services and daemons. Specified services and daemons are started or killed when starting a particular runlevel.

S

Samba | A file and printer sharing service compatible with Microsoft's Common Internet File System.

Sarbanes-Oxley (SOX) Act | A U.S. law that specifies financial-disclosure requirements for public companies.

Secure Hash Algorithm (SHA) | A set of cryptographic hash functions developed by the U.S. National Security Agency.

Secure Hash Algorithm 1 (SHA-1) | A set of cryptographic functions created by the U.S. National Security Agency (NSA). Because of a weakness in SHA-1, the National Institute of Science and Technology (NIST) has sponsored a competition for the development of SHA-3.

Secure Hash Algorithm 3 (SHA-3) | A set of cryptographic functions being developed through a competition sponsored by the National Institute of Science and Technology (NIST).

Security Administrator Tool for Analyzing Networks (SATAN) | An older open source network analyzer. Later versions were released under proprietary licenses as part of SAINT.

SELinux | A mandatory access control system that uses Linux security modules in the kernel. Developed by the U.S. National Security Agency. Not compatible with AppArmor.

sendmail | The open source SMTP server maintained by the Sendmail Consortium. Do not confuse this with the commercial SMTP server known as Sendmail.

Sendmail | A commercial SMTP server maintained by Sendmail, Inc. Do not confuse this with the open source SMTP server known as sendmail.

Session Initiation Protocol (SIP) | An Internet Protocol (IP) network protocol frequently used in VoIP communications.

Set Group ID (SGID) bit | A special permission commonly applied to a directory. With the SGID bit, users who are members of the group that owns the directory have permissions to read and write to all files in that directory. The SGID bit assigns the group owner of the directory as the group owner of all files copied to that directory.

Set User ID (SUID) bit | A special permission that allows others to execute the given file with the rights of the user owner of the file.

Shadow password suite | The files of the shadow password suite make up the local Linux password authentication database. The files are `/etc/passwd`, `/etc/shadow`, `/etc/group`, and `/etc/gshadow`. As originally developed, it also includes the Linux `login`, `su`, and `passwd` commands.

Simple Mail Transfer Protocol (SMTP) | An application-layer e-mail protocol primarily used for outgoing messages from clients.

Simplified mandatory access control kernel (SMACK) | A Linux security module for mandatory access control; functionally similar to SELinux and AppArmor.

Sleuth Kit | A package of tools that can be used to save volatile data; intended for use on read-only media as commands on compromised systems.

Snort | An intrusion detection system (IDS) with modes associated for packet analysis, logging, and interaction with `iptables` firewall rules; associated rules are updated on a regular basis.

Software RAID | A version of redundant array of independent disks (RAID) that uses partitions instead of disks as components of the array.

Solaris | A variant of UNIX originally developed by the former Sun Microsystems.

Source code | Human-readable computer language that can be collected and compiled into a computer program, library, or application.

SourceForge | A Web-based software development site, available at *http://sourceforge.net/*.

Spacewalk | An open source systems management server based on the source code of the Red Hat Network Satellite Server.

SpamAssassin | A program for filtering unwanted e-mail.

Spectrum Security (SPECSEC) | SPECSEC is one of the ISECOM channels for security audits, related to non-physical communications over the electromagnetic spectrum.

Spoofed | A reference to network transmissions with a false source address.

Spoofing | An attack where a malicious user assumes the identity of another user or organization.

Spyware | A type of malware that collects information on users without their knowledge.

Squid | A service that caches Internet data to speed response times that can also track the sites browsed by users.

Stallman, Richard | President of the Free Software Foundation (FSF), the organization behind the GNU project. Leading opponent of the TPM chip.

Sticky bit | A special permission commonly applied to a directory. With the sticky bit and full permissions, all users can write to the associated directory. However, ownership is retained, so users won't be able to overwrite files copied by other users.

Stock kernel | A reference to the kernel developed and released by the Linux Kernel Organization.

Storage area network (SAN) | A storage system that may consist of one or more NAS or DAS systems.

Storage Root Key (SRK) | An RTS key used to encrypt keys stored outside the TPM chip.

Subversion | A system for version control frequently used on many open source projects, including nmap.

SUSE | A Linux distribution originally developed in Germany, now owned by Novell.

System Administrators Integrated Network Tool (SAINT) | A vulnerability scanning program with a Web-based interface, based on code that was previously released as SATAN under open source licenses.

Systems Security Certified Practitioner (SSCP) | A vendor-neutral certification for information security created by (ISC)2. Suited to candidates working toward becoming security professionals.

T

Tannebaum, Andrew | The main developer behind the Minix distribution, one of the first clones of UNIX. Proponent of a micro kernel, in opposition to Torvalds' use of a modular kernel.

Tarball | A colloquial description of a (normally compressed) archive of files, managed with the `tar` command.

TCG Software Stack | An open source software stack of programs designed to work with the TPM chip. May be downloaded and installed as the `trousers` package.

TCP Wrappers | An access control list system for services associated with the internet super servers. It also can protect services linked to the `libwrap.so.0` library.

Telephone modem | A modulator-demodulator for translating data bits into the sine waves associated with the PSTN. Cable modems and DSL modems are not true modems, as they do not modulate or demodulate data.

Telnet | A protocol and service that uses clear-text authentication.

TOMOYO | A Linux security module for mandatory access control; functionally similar to SELinux and AppArmor.

Torvalds, Linus | The developer of the first Linux kernel. The current leader of Linux kernel developers.

Transition SIGnature (TSIG) | A protocol used to authenticate data exchanges between DNS servers.

Transmission Control Protocol (TCP) | A member of the Transmission Control Protocol/Internet Protocol (TCP/IP) protocol suite that supports reliable connections.

Tripwire | An intrusion detection system; open source and commercial versions are available.

Trivial File Transfer Protocol (TFTP) | A protocol and service that uses a simplified form of FTP.

Trojan horse | A kind of malware that disguises itself as a useful program or command.

Trusted Computing Group (TCG) | An industry consortium for security. The TCG defines standards in a number of areas, including networks, PC clients, servers, a software stack, storage, and trusted network connections. The TCG is the group behind standards for the TPM chip.

Trusted Platform Module (TPM) | A chip that may be installed on hardware such as a motherboard. May be used for password protection, software license protection, digital rights management, and disk encryption. Controversial with some in the open source community, including the Free Software Foundation (FSF) and the Electronic Frontier Foundation (EFF).

TrustedGRUB | A specialized version of GRUB that can work with the TPM chip in a chain of trust.

Turbolinux | A Linux distribution originally developed in Japan.

U

Ubuntu | A Linux distribution based on Debian Linux. The name is a word taken from the Zulu and Xhosa languages that roughly translates as "humanity toward others."

Ubuntu security notices (USNs) | Alerts based on security issues that affect different releases of the Ubuntu distribution.

Unified Extensible Firmware Interface (UEFI) | The UEFI is the first thing that's run when you power up a relatively new computer. It identifies and tests connected hardware to a point where an operating system can be loaded from media such as a hard drive.

Universe repository | A reference to the Ubuntu repositories of unsupported software released under open source licenses.

Upstart | A system designed to replace the /sbin/init command and the System V system of runlevels. Related configuration files can be found in the /etc/event.d/ directory.

User Datagram Protocol (UDP) | A member of the Transmission Control Protocol/Internet Protocol (TCP/IP) protocol suite that supports connectionless "best-effort" communications.

User ID (UID) | The number associated with a user name in Linux, as defined in /etc/passwd.

User private group scheme | The standard in Linux where a special group is created for every user. By default, the user and group names (along with the UID and GID numbers) are identical. The user is the only standard member of that group.

User-space | Refers to tools that do not depend on the Linux kernel.

Utility | A Parkerian hexad concept related to the CIA concept of availability. For example, encrypted data is not useful if the encryption key is lost.

V

Van Eck phreaking | A method for interpreting the emissions from computer displays to recover the associated image.

very secure File Transfer Protocol daemon (vsftpd) | The open source FTP server used by developers of Red Hat, SUSE, and Debian to share their distributions.

Virtio block device | A paravirtualized device in a hardware-virtualized machine, designed for faster virtual hard drives.

Virtual guest | The operating system installed inside a host's virtual machine software.

Virtual host | The operating system that hosts virtual machine software.

Virtual LAN (VLAN) | A LAN created on the same physical network as another LAN. Because both LANs are separate and distinct, they are virtual.

Virtual network computing (VNC) | A system for sharing views of graphical desktop environments over a network.

Virus | In computing, a program that can copy itself and infect a computer with malware.

VMware | A family of virtual machine software that works with everything from software-based virtualization with programs like VMware Player to bare-metal virtualization with programs like vSphere.

Voice over IP (VoIP) | A general term for voice-transmission protocols on Transmission Control Protocol/Internet Protocol (TCP/IP) networks.

W

Washington University File Transfer Protocol daemon (WU-FTPD) | A popular FTP server that is no longer supported and is reported to have security flaws.

White-hat hacker | In the Linux community, a hacker is a user who wants to create better software. In the non-Linux security community, a white-hat hacker is an authorized user who runs security diagnostic tools to test the security features of a system or network. In this book, a white-hat hacker serves both purposes.

Winbind | A component of the Samba file server that supports integration of Linux/UNIX and Microsoft authentication information.

Windows Internet Name Service (WINS) | A WINS server includes a database of NetBIOS names and Internet Protocol (IP) addresses.

Wireless intrusion detection system (WIDS) | Software that can help detect unauthorized attacks on a wireless network; one example is available from the aircrack-ng package.

Wireshark | A protocol analyzer. Previously known as Ethereal.

Worm | A self-replicating malware program; different from a Trojan horse, which is not self-replicating.

X

X Display Manager (XDM) | A graphical login manager built by the developers of the X.Org GUI server.

X Display Manager Control Protocol (XDMCP) | A protocol that enables remote logins to a GUI. It is normally associated with Transmission Control Protocol/Internet Protocol (TCP/IP) port 177.

X11 | One name for a protocol associated with the X Window system.

Xen | A virtual machine monitor developed at the University of Cambridge. On Linux systems, it requires a specialized kernel. Supports hardware virtualization and paravirtualization.

Xen kernel | A specialized kernel for virtual machine monitors that supports hardware-assisted virtualization on systems with suitably capable CPUs.

Xfce desktop environment | An alternative desktop environment to GNOME and KDE; the default desktop environment on the Xubuntu variant of Ubuntu Linux.

XFree86 | An older X Window System Server, commonly used in older Linux distributions.

Xubuntu | A release of the Ubuntu distribution that includes the Xfce desktop environment as the default GUI.

Z

ZENworks | A systems management server released by Novell. ZENworks Linux Management can be used to administer patches and more on both SUSE Linux Enterprise Server and Red Hat Enterprise Linux systems.

Zone files | When associated with DNS, a database of hostnames and Internet Protocol (IP) addresses for a specific authoritative domain.

Zone updates | A reference to data exchange between DNS servers with respect to hostnames and Internet Protocol (IP) addresses of a specific domain.

GLOSSARY

References

Aircrack-ng. http://www.aircrack-ng.org/ (accessed March 2010).

Aircrack-ng. Basic documentation (Aircrack-ng, September 9, 2009). http://www.aircrack-ng .org/doku.php?id=getting_started/ (accessed March 2010).

AirTight Networks. "WPA/WPA2 TKIP Attack" (AirTight Networks, 2010). http://www. airtightnetworks.com/home/resources/knowledge-center/wpa-wpa2-tkip-attack.html (accessed April 9, 2010).

Aitchison, Ron. *Pro DNS and BIND*. Berkeley, CA: Apress, 2005. http://www.zytrax.com/books/ dns/ (accessed April 6, 2010).

Amazon Elastic Compute Cloud (Amazon EC2). Amazon Web Services. http://aws.amazon.com/ ec2/ (accessed April 14, 2010).

Beale, Jay, and Russ Rogers. *Nessus Network Auditing*, 2nd ed. Burlington, MA: Syngress Publishing, 2008.

"BIND9 Server Howto" Ubuntu Community Documentation, April 2, 2010. https://help.ubuntu .com/community/BIND9ServerHowto/ (accessed April 8, 2010).

Bowen, Rich and Ken Coar. *Apache Cookbook: Solutions and Examples for Apache Administrators*. Sebastopol, CA: O'Reilly Media, 2008.

Briglia, Tom. "UNIX and Linux Access Control Standard" (Stanford University, 2007). https:// www.stanford.edu/dept/as/ia/security/policies_standards/AS_standards/libwrap_access_ control_standard_1.0.html (accessed March, 2010).

Burdach, Mariusz. "Forensic Analysis of a Live Linux System, Pt. I." (Symantec, March 22, 2004). http://www.symantec.com/connect/articles/forensic-analysis-live-linux-system-pt-1/ (accessed May 2010).

Burdach, Mariusz. "Forensic Analysis of a Live Linux System, Pt. II." (Symantec, April 11, 2004). http://www.symantec.com/connect/articles/forensic-analysis-live-linux-system-pt-2/ (accessed May 2010).

Carrier, Brian. *The Sleuth Kit Informer*, issue 1, February 15, 2003. http://www.sleuthkit.org/ informer/sleuthkit-informer-1.html (accessed May 2010).

Chapman, Ben, and Champ Clark III. *Asterisk Hacking*, Burlington, MA: Syngress Publishing, 2007.

Chapple, Mike. "Choosing the Right Firewall Topology: Bastion Host, Screened Subnet or Dual Firewalls" (SearchSecurity.com, October 17, 2005). http://searchsecurity.techtarget.com/ tip/1,289483,sid14_gci906407_mem1,00.html/ (accessed April 4, 2010).

———. "Nessus 3 Tutorial" (SearchSecurity.com, June 6, 2008). http://searchsecurity. techtarget.com/generic/0,295582,sid14_gci1159345_mem1,00.html (accessed May 2010).

Chapple, Michael J., John D'Arcy, and Aaron Striegel. "An Analysis of Firewall Rulebase (Mis) Management Practices." *The ISSA Journal* 7, no. 2, February 2009. https://dev.issa.org/Library/Journals/2009/February/ISSA%20Journal%20February%202009.pdf (accessed April 6, 2010).

Corbet, Jonathan. "Nftables: A New Packet Filtering Engine" (LWN.net, March 24, 2009). http://lwn.net/Articles/325196/ (accessed May 2010).

Curran, Christopher. "Red Hat Enterprise Linux 6 Virtualization Guide" Edition 1 beta (Red Hat, 2010). http://www.redhat.com/docs/en-US/Red_Hat_Enterprise_Linux/6-Beta/html-single/Virtualization/ (accessed May 2010).

"Department of Defense Trusted Computer System Evaluation Criteria," DoD 5200.28-STD, released December 1985. http://csrc.nist.gov/publications/secpubs/rainbow/std001.txt (accessed February 2010).

DiMaggio, Len. "Understanding Your (Red Hat Enterprise Linux) Daemons." *Red Hat Magazine*, March 9, 2007. http://magazine.redhat.com/2007/03/09/understanding-your-red-hat-enterprise-linux-daemons/ (accessed March 18, 2010).

DuBois, Paul. *MySQL*, 4th ed. Indianapolis: Addison-Wesley Professional, 2008.

"eCryptfs—Enterprise Cryptographic Filesystem" (Canonical, Ltd, 2010). https://launchpad.net/ecryptfs (accessed March 2010).

"English Country Names and Code Elements," ISO Standard 3166 (ISO, 2010). http://www.iso.org/iso/english_country_names_and_code_elements/ (accessed April 6, 2010).

Evans, Chris. Manpage of vsftpd.conf, the very secure File Transfer Protocol daemon (vsftpd, May 28, 2009). http://vsftpd.beasts.org/vsftpd_conf.html (accessed April 2010).

"Federal Desktop Core Configuration" (FDCC, April 16, 2010). http://nvd.nist.gov/fdcc/ (accessed May 2010).

Fenzi, Kevin. "Linux Security HOWTO" (Linux Documentation Project, January 2004). http://tldp.org/HOWTO/Security-HOWTO (accessed February 2010).

Fifield, David. "The NMAP Scripting Engine," presentation at the 2010 Free and Open Source Software Developers' European Meeting, February 6, 2010. http://www.bamsoftware.com/talks/fosdem-2010.pdf (accessed May 2010).

Fioretti, Marco. "How to Set Up and Use Tripwire." *Linux Journal*, April 28, 2006. http://www.linuxjournal.com/article/8758 (accessed April, 2010).

Free Software Foundation, The. "Gnu Privacy Guard (GnuPG) Mini Howto" (De Winter Information Solutions, August 10, 2004). http://www.dewinter.com/gnupg_howto/english/GPGMiniHowto.html (accessed March 2010).

Freestandards.org. "Filesystem Hierarchy Standard," developed in 2003; revised January 2004. Information available from http://www.pathname.com/fhs/ (accessed March 2010). The work of the Freestandards.org group is now being maintained by The Linux Foundation.

Fuller, Johnray, John Ha, David O'Brien, Scott Radvan, Eric Christensen, and Adam Ligas. "Fedora 12 Security Guide: A Guide to Securing Fedora Linux, Edition 12.1" (Red Hat, 2009). http://docs.fedoraproject.org/security-guide/f12/en-US/html/index.html (accessed February 2010).

Gerhards, Rainer. "HOWTO install rsyslog" (Rsyslog.com, 2008). http://www.rsyslog.com/doc-install.html (accessed April, 2010).

GNU Project, The. "GNU GRUB" (GNU.org, 2010). http://www.gnu.org/software/grub/ (accessed February 2010).

Grubb, Steve. "Hardening Red Hat Enterprise Linux 5." Presented at the Red Hat Summit, 2008. http://people.redhat.com/sgrubb/files/hardening-rhel5.pdf (accessed April 14, 2010).

Herzog, Peter. *OSSTMM 3.0 Lite: Introduction and Sample to the Open Source Security Testing Methodology Manual* (ISECOM, 2010). http://www.isecom.org/osstmm/ (accessed February 2010).

Herzog, Peter, et al. *Hacking Linux Exposed*, 3rd ed. New York, NY: McGraw-Hill, 2008.

Hoopes, John, ed. *Virtualization for Security: Including Sandboxing, Disaster Recovery, High Availability, Forensic Analysis, and Honeypotting.* Burlington, MA: Syngress Publishing. 2009.

Hornat, Charles, et al. "Interfacing with Law Enforcement FAQ: For Incident Handlers and Other Information Security Professionals," ver. 1.0 (The SANS Institute, January 15, 2004). https://www.sans.org/score/faq/law_enf_faq/ (accessed May 2010).

Horrigan, John. "Home Broadband Adoption 2009" (Pew Internet and American Life Project, June 2009). http://www.pewinternet.org/~/media//Files/Reports/2009/Home-Broadband-Adoption-2009.pdf (accessed April 2010).

IBM System X Virtualization Strategies. http://www-01.ibm.com/redbooks/community/pages/viewpage.action?pageId=2788036 (accessed February 2010).

Jang, Michael. *Linux Annoyances for Geeks*. Sebastapol, CA: O'Reilly Media, 2006.

———. *Linux Patch Management*. Upper Saddle River, NJ: Pearson Education, 2006.

———. *Linux Patch Management: Keeping Linux Systems Up To Date*. New York: McGraw-Hill, 2007.

———. *RHCE Red Hat Certified Engineer Study Guide*. New York: McGraw-Hill, 2007.

———. *Ubuntu Server Administration*. New York: McGraw-Hill, 2008.

Jones, Pamela. http://www.groklaw.net/ (accessed February 2010).

Kingsley-Hughes, Adrian. "Are Ubuntu Users Covered by H.264 License? It Depends" (ZDNet, May 5, 2010). http://www.zdnet.com/blog/hardware/are-ubuntu-users-covered-by-h264-license-it-depends/8228 (accessed May 2010).

Kismet. http://www.kismetwireless.net/ (accessed March 2010).

Kotadia, Munir. "New Hacking Tool: Chocolate" (ZDNet, April 20, 2004). http://www.zdnet.com/news/new-hacking-tool-chocolate/135565 (accessed May 2010).

Kroah-Hartman, Greg. *Linux Kernel in a Nutshell*. Sebastapol, CA: O'Reilly Media, 2007.

Kumar, Avinesh, and Sandesh Chopdekar. "Get Started with the Linux Key Retention Service" (IBM, April 11, 2007). http://www.ibm.com/developerworks/linux/library/l-key-retention.html/ (accessed April 14, 2010).

Linux Kernel Organization. "The Linux Kernel Archives" (Kernel.org, nd). http://kernel.org/ (accessed February 2010).

Lyon, Gordon "Fyodor." *Nmap Network Scanning: The Official Nmap Project Guide to Network Discovery and Security Scanning* (Insecure.com, 2009). http://nmap.org/book/toc.html (accessed May 2010).

Matulis, Peter. *Centralised Logging with rsyslog* (Canonical, September 2009). http://www.ubuntu.com/system/files/CentralLogging-v4-20090901-03.pdf (accessed April 2010).

MIT Kerberos Team. "Kerberos, the Network Authentication Protocol" (MIT.edu, April 8, 2010). http://web.mit.edu/Kerberos/ (accessed April, 2010).

National Security Agency, Central Security Service. "Security-Enhanced Linux" (NSA.gov, January 15, 2009). http://www.nsa.gov/research/selinux/ (accessed March and April, 2010).

National Security Agency, Operating Systems Division Unix Team of the Systems and Network Analysis Center. "Guide to the Secure Configuration of Red Hat Enterprise Linux 5, Revision 3" (NSA.gov, October 21, 2009). http://www.nsa.gov/ia/_files/os/redhat/rhel5-guide-i731 .pdf (accessed March 2010).

Olejniczak, Stephen P., and Brady Kirby. *Asterisk for Dummies*, Hoboken, NJ: Wiley Publishing, 2007.

Open Source TCG Software Stack, The. http://trousers.sourceforge.net (accessed February 2010).

Operating Systems Division Unix Team of the Systems and Network Analysis Center. "Guide to the Secure Configuration of Red Hat Enterprise Linux 5" revision 3. Released by the National Security Agency, October 21, 2009. http://www.nsa.gov/ia/guidance/security_ configuration_guides/operating_systems.shtml#linux2 (accessed March 18, 2010).

Orebaugh, Angela, and Becky Pinkard. *Nmap in the Enterprise: Your Guide to Network Scanning*. Burlington, MA: Syngress Publishing, 2008.

O'Sullivan, Jill, and Gene Ciaola. *Enterprise Resource Planning: A Transitional Approach from the Classroom to the Business World*. Hightstown, NJ: McGraw-Hill Primis Custom Publishing, 2008.

Pennington, Havoc, Anders Carlsson, and Alexander Larsson. "D-Bus Specification" version 0.12, 2007 (Freedesktop.org, nd). http://dbus.freedesktop.org/doc/dbus-specification.html (accessed February 2010).

Petullo, Mike. "Implementing Encrypted Home Directories." *Linux Journal*, August 1, 2003. http://www.linuxjournal.com/article/6481 (accessed March 2010).

Pogue, Chris, Cory Altheide, and Todd Haverkos. *UNIX and Linux Forensic Analysis DVD Toolkit*. Burlington, MA: Syngress Publishing. 2008.

Rash, Michael. *Linux Firewalls: Attack Detection and Response with iptables, psad, and fwsnort*. San Francisco, CA: No Starch Press, 2007.

Raymond, Eric. *The Cathedral and the Bazaar: Musings on Linux and Open Source by an Accidental Revolutionary*. Sebastapol, CA: O'Reilly Media, 2001.

Red Hat. "Red Hat Enterprise Linux 5 Deployment Guide, Edition 4" (Red Hat, October 2008). https://www.redhat.com/docs/en-US/Red_Hat_Enterprise_Linux/5.4/html/Deployment_ Guide/ (accessed March and April, 2010).

———. "Red Hat Enterprise Linux 5 Installation Guide, Edition 3" (Red Hat, 2008). http://www .redhat.com/docs/en-US/Red_Hat_Enterprise_Linux/5/html/Installation_Guide/index.html (accessed March 2010).

———. "Red Hat Enterprise Linux Documentation" (Red Hat, 2010). http://www.redhat.com/ docs/manuals/enterprise/ (accessed May 2010).

RFC 4340 Internet Assigned Numbers Authority. http://www.iana.org/assignments/ port-numbers/ (accessed March 11, 2010).

Russell, Rusty. "Linux Packet Filtering HOWTO" (The netfilter.org Project, January 24, 2002). http://www.iptables.org/documentation/HOWTO/packet-filtering-HOWTO.html (accessed March, 2010).

SAINT Corporation. "Running a Default Vulnerability Scan: A Step-by-Step Guide" (SAINT Corporation, 2009). http://www.saintcorporation.com/resources/SAINT_scan.pdf (accessed May 2010).

Samba Team. The configuration file for the Samba suite. (Samba.org, nd). http://samba.org/samba/docs/man/manpages-3/smb.conf.5.html (accessed April 2010).

"SELinux Future Work" (National Security Agency, Central Security Service, January 15, 2009). http://www.nsa.gov/research/selinux/todo.shtml/ (accessed May 2010).

"SettingUpNISHowTo." Community Ubuntu Documentation (Ubuntu Documentation, September 10, 2009). https://help.ubuntu.com/community/SettingUpNISHowTo (accessed February 2010).

Skoric, Miroslav. "LILO Mini-HOWTO" (The Linux Documentation Project, November 8, 2009). http://tldp.org/HOWTO/LILO.html (accessed February 2010).

Snort Project, The. *SNORT Users Manual 2.8.6* (Sourcefire, Inc., April 26, 2010). http://www.snort.org/assets/140/snort_manual_2_8_6.pdf (accessed April 16, 2010).

Stallman, Richard. "Can You Trust Your Computer?" (GNU.org, nd). http://www.gnu.org/philosophy/can-you-trust.html (accessed February 2010).

Suehring, Steve, and Robert Ziegler. *Linux Firewalls*. 3rd ed. Indianapolis, IN: Novell Press, 2006.

The MITRE Corporation. "Common Vulnerabilities and Exposures" (Mitre.org, March 16, 2009). http://cve.mitre.org/cve/ (accessed April 2010).

Verhelst, Wouter. "Securing NFS." *Free Software Magazine*, November 26, 2006. http://www.freesoftwaremagazine.com/columns/securing_nfs (accessed April 2010).

Virijevich, Paul. "Intrusion Detection with AIDE" (Linux.com, January 20, 2005). http://www.linux.com/archive/feature/113919/ (accessed April 2010).

Wessels, Duane. *Squid: The Definitive Guide*. Sebastopol, CA: O'Reilly Media, 2004.

Whitaker, Andrew, and Daniel P. Newman. *Penetration Testing and Network Defense*. Indianapolis: Cisco Press. 2006.

Zeuthen, David. "Desktop and Hardware Configuration." *Red Hat Magazine*, January 2005. http://www.redhat.com/magazine/003jan05/features/hal/ (accessed March 18, 2010).

———. "PolicyKit Library Reference Manual" (Freedesktop.org, 2007). http://hal.freedesktop.org/docs/PolicyKit/ (accessed February 2010).

Zhang, Wei. "Build a RADIUS server on Linux" (IBM, May 25, 2005). http://www.ibm.com/developerworks/library/l-radius/ (accessed April 2010).

Index